Freedom from Reality

CATHOLIC IDEAS FOR A SECULAR WORLD

O. Carter Snead, *series editor*

The purpose of this interdisciplinary series is to feature authors from around the world who will expand the influence of Catholic thought on the most important conversations in academia and the public square. The series is "Catholic" in the sense that the books will emphasize and engage the enduring themes of human dignity and flourishing, the common good, truth, beauty, justice, and freedom in ways that reflect and deepen principles affirmed by the Catholic Church for millennia. It is not limited to Catholic authors or even works that explicitly take Catholic principles as a point of departure. Its books are intended to demonstrate the diversity and enhance the relevance of these enduring themes and principles in numerous subjects, ranging from the arts and humanities to the sciences.

FREEDOM

from REALITY

---

*The Diabolical Character
of Modern Liberty*

D. C. SCHINDLER

University of Notre Dame Press
Notre Dame, Indiana

University of Notre Dame Press
Notre Dame, Indiana 46556
undpress.nd.edu

Published in the United States of America

Library of Congress Cataloging-in-Publication Data
Names: Schindler, D. C., author.
Title: Freedom from reality : the diabolical character of modern liberty /
D. C. Schindler.
Description: Notre Dame, Indiana : University of Notre Dame Press, [2017] |
Series: Catholic ideas for a secular world |
Includes bibliographical references and index. |
Identifiers: LCCN 2017030365 (print) | LCCN 2017042736 (ebook) |
ISBN 9780268102630 (pdf) | ISBN 9780268102647 (epub) |
ISBN 9780268102616 (hardcover : alk. paper) |
ISBN 9780268102623 (paperback ; alk. paper)
Subjects: LCSH: Liberty—Philosophy—History.
Classification: LCC B105. L45 (ebook) |
LCC B105.L45 S43   2017 (print) | DDC
123/.5—dc23
LC record available at https://lccn.loc.gov/2017030365

∞*This paper meets the requirements of ANSI/NISO Z39.48-1992
(Permanence of Paper).*

For Jeanne

CONTENTS

ACKNOWLEDGMENTS

The etymological connection between the words "symbolical" and "diabolical" was first made known to me nearly twenty years ago in the title of a section of the book *Leben in der Einheit von Leben und Tod*, by German philosopher Ferdinand Ulrich. That discovery opened up, among other things, what turned out to be a new way to think about the problem of freedom in modernity. The present book is the fruit of those reflections.

I wish to thank Mark Shiffman for reading the chapters on Locke and offering several helpful suggestions, and my father, David L. Schindler, who went through the entire manuscript and discussed it with me. Conversations with my colleagues at the John Paul II Institute in Washington, DC—Fr. Antonio Lopez, Michael Hanby, Nicholas Healy, Fr. Paolo Prosperi, David Crawford, Margie McCarthy, Joseph Atkinson, and, again, my father David L. Schindler—on the various cultural, metaphysical, and theological themes that are addressed in this book have been invaluable. There is nothing that can substitute for probing questions from those with whom one shares a basic vision of reality.

The staff at the University of Notre Dame Press has been delightful to work with; it is rare to meet with such a happy combination of courtesy and competence as I found in director Steven Wrinn, managing editor Rebecca DeBoer, production and design manager Wendy McMillen, and copy editor Scott Barker. I wish to offer special thanks to the series editor, Carter Snead, for his encouragement and support in this project.

Above all, I would like to express gratitude to my wife, Jeanne Heffernan Schindler, who introduced me to the unexpected joys of political philosophy, and of course to the deep reality of communal existence. This book is dedicated to her.

Introduction

What Is Good?

This book aims to dig as deeply as possible into the philosophical roots of the problematic modern conception of liberty and to propose an alternative way of thinking about freedom in the light of what is uncovered. The sense of what we take to be the problem is nicely captured in the following oft-quoted passage from G. K. Chesterton's *Heretics*:

> We are fond of talking about "liberty"; but the way we end up talking of it is an attempt to avoid discussing what is good. We are fond of talking about "progress"; that is a dodge to avoid discussing what is good. We are fond of talking about "education"; that is a dodge to avoid discussing what is good.
>
> The modern man says, "Let us leave all these arbitrary standards and embrace unadulterated liberty." This is, logically rendered, "Let us not decide what is good, but let it be considered good not to decide it."
>
> He says, "Away with all your old moral standards; I am for progress." This, logically stated, means, "Let us not settle what is good; but let us settle whether we are getting more of it."
>
> He says, "Neither in religion nor morality, my friend, lies the hopes of the race, but in education." This, clearly expressed, means, "We cannot decide what is good, but let us give it to our children."[1]

1

Now, it has become clear, since Chesterton's time, that his description of the "modern man" needs to be qualified in a number of ways: there is a sense in which modern man cares a great deal about morality and religion, and no longer advocates "unadulterated liberty" with the same naive enthusiasm Chesterton seems to ascribe to him. Indeed, there are just as many instances of summary and unapologetic restraints placed on liberty, in a manner that can be described as specifically modern. Nevertheless, Chesterton's observations hit on something essential, which has become if anything even more evident than it was when he first recorded them, namely, that we have separated what we mean by freedom from a substantial notion of the good, and we have in fact turned it thereby into a *substitute* for the good; that this substitution comes to expression not just in our explicit discussions of freedom, but more generally in our institutions and "values," and in a variety of other cultural phenomena; and, finally, that this substitution entails a fundamental logical incoherence, which is to say that it both expresses and gives rise to patterns of fragmentation and contradiction. At the same time, however, we will suggest in this book that an eclipse of the good from the horizon that defines the operation of the human will entails a radical shift in perspective that tends to hide the very problems this incoherence generates, or to cast them as irrelevant for all intents and purposes. To reflect on what this means, and what implications it has, is one of the primary goals of our exploration here.

To reflect properly on what is at issue and what is at stake requires, among other things, a resistance to this tendency, which may be characterized in this context as a reduction to pragmatic or political concerns as finally determinative. It is an oversimplification, but it is not altogether false, to say that the movement from the classical to the medieval and then to the modern period in the philosophical approaches to freedom is a movement from the ontological or metaphysical to the moral, and then to the political[2]—what it means to be free was asked initially as a question concerning a mode or state of being, then a question concerning the use and operation of the power of the will, and finally a question concerning the configuration of power (being—will—power). This description is certainly an oversimplification, because in a certain respect the question of freedom always at least implicitly includes all three dimensions at once, regardless of which particular dimension receives the primary focus, and also because a departure from metaphysical roots entails a distortion of both the moral and the political, isolated as separate realms. In the fragmentation that results, each comes to have both too much and too little significance; each encroaches on the others even as it surrenders its own proper meaning. However this may be, to the extent that the description hits the mark it means that we have tended increasingly to begin, so to speak, on the surface in our reflections on the question of freedom. But one cannot even understand the surface properly except from the perspective of the depths. It is accordingly our aim to trace the issues that arise in the question of the nature of freedom to their metaphysical roots. The extent to which the aim succeeds, and the value of the fruit the effort bears, is of course something that others will have to judge.

A basic presupposition of this book—which will have to justify itself over the course of the investigation—is that an adequate approach to the notion of freedom will have to include three features: (1) it must understand freedom primarily in *ontological* terms; (2) it must recognize *an essential connection between freedom and the good*; and (3) it must see *relation to the other* as an intrinsic part of the meaning of freedom. These three features, of course, are not the sole qualities of an adequate conception (there are certainly many more: a relation to intelligence and truth, a kind of self-possession, and so forth), but we single these out because they serve, as we hope to show over the course of our study, to bring what appears to be the essential nature of freedom particularly into focus.[3] Not all of these three aspects have always been thematic in the history of the discussions of freedom; indeed, in the classical view, the role of the "other" has tended to present certain problems, or at the very least tensions that mature into problems in the dawning of modernity. Nevertheless, we would like to propose, at the outset, that the three aspects we have mentioned are intrinsically related, to such an extent that each stands or falls with the others. To put the matter simply here—though we will eventually see a need to qualify aspects of this—the priority of the good is what makes freedom ontological, that is, a reality that is more than merely moral or voluntary insofar as it precedes the deliberate activity of the agent. By the same token, this priority entails a subordination of the will to what is other, so that a recognition of otherness of a particular sort as *intrinsic* to freedom is a condition for the continuing affirmation of the priority of the good.

As we hope to show, these three features converge, in terms of their metaphysical significance, in the notion of *actuality*. For classical thought, actuality is perfection or, in other words, it is what the good *is*. Moreover, being itself is understood in terms of actuality, though this interpretation recognizes an analogical diversity. Aristotle makes a distinction between first actuality, substance, which is defined by form, and second actuality, which is, as it were, the being's self-enactment through the achievement of its end. The end is precisely an *achievement*, and so represents more than what is simply given already in the form of the substance considered in itself. In this respect, man's full actuality, the free self-enactment of his nature, is necessarily also a self-transcendence—that is, it is an engagement with his other. Actuality thus brings together being, the good, and the other in a unified whole.

It is because of the centrality of this notion that Aristotle insisted on the absolute priority of actuality to potency (and thus to power and possibility),[4] which is what precisely makes potency intelligible and significant—indeed, in a basic sense *real*. As the will begins to emerge in the course of philosophical reflection, and move slowly into the center, it tends to be formulated as an increasingly autonomous "power" of the soul. Interpreted as an integral "part" of reality, that is, part of the meaning of actual goodness, the will "makes sense." But insofar as it is isolated in itself, over against the actuality of the real, it becomes disordered, chaotic, and destructive, but for the very same reason meaningless and unreal. One could characterize modernity, in fact, precisely as a detachment of potency from act, which entails a tendency to subordinate the latter to the former in a way that is perfectly *opposed* to the classical understanding.

All of this is stated in a condensed form, which will need to be unpacked and developed, but it may be helpful to the reader to see at the outset the "nutshell" version of the argument that will be offered in this book, which is divided into three parts. Part 1 is an exploration of the thought of John Locke, who is taken to offer a formulation of the concept of freedom, both at the anthropological and at the political level, that is representative of modernity generally. Part 2 explains the precise sense in which this concept is "diabolical" and endeavors to show the traces of this "diabolical" concept in the basic institutions and values of modern liberalism. Finally, part 3 seeks to retrieve an alternative conception of freedom by going back to original sources. It is hoped that this work of retrieval is the beginning of a project that will continue in future investigations.

In somewhat more detail, the argument of the present book unfolds as follows. Chapter 1, "Locke's (Re-)Conception of Freedom," presents Locke's substantial revision of the first edition of his *Essay Concerning Human Understanding*, which concerned above all a reworking of the chapter outlining his vision of freedom and the will, as a sort of symbol of the philosophical revolution in early modern thought. The driving question of the chapter is a basic one in the scholarly literature: Does Locke ultimately have a compatibilist or a libertarian theory of the will—or in other words, does Locke subordinate the will to a naturalistic determinism or does he present the will as a self-causing power that is finally responsible only to itself? The basic argument is that both of the interpretations can be justified, not because of any straightforward inconsistency in Locke's thinking, but most fundamentally because the notion of power, as Locke interprets it, is essentially dialectical or "self-subverting." In the first edition of the *Essay*, Locke had articulated the essence of the will as power, but he still retained features of more traditional views of the will as a kind of desire that is responsive to the good. Friends and critics therefore accused him of rendering the will a passive instrument of nature. In his revision, he cast off the traces of a classical vision of freedom and sought to strengthen the will's self-determining power by introducing concepts he seems to have acquired from a reading of Malebranche. This chapter concludes, however, that, because he leaves power in place as the essence of the will, he does not manage to resolve the basic problem. Instead, he injects the dialectic ever more profoundly into the logic of human agency.

It has become common for scholars to identify a tendency in Locke to make fundamental claims in his *Second Treatise on Government*, which he subsequently goes on to reverse (mostly by implication) as he unfolds the meaning of those claims. Chapter 2, "The Political Conquest of the Good in the *Second Treatise*," tries to show that these reversals are not (necessarily) deliberate attempts to deceive, but instead result from Locke's self-subverting notion of power that we describe in chapter 1: *pure* potency is effectively impotent in the face of actual conditions, and so what is affirmed as essential in one respect (as potential) can turn out to be effectively irrelevant in another (in actuality). Thus, through a reading of the *Second Treatise*, the chapter brings to light a number of the inconsistencies that lie at the foundation of Locke's political vision: the lawless state of war is in fact what the state of nature, apparently governed by the fundamental natural law of mutual respect, looks like when it is made *actual*. Along similar lines, because the equality of goods in the natural state is essentially a matter of potential, it can turn out to coincide in principle with the extreme inequality of possessions, especially once money is introduced. Political authority depends on consent, but that consent, by which one surrenders one's authority as an individual to the power of the state, ends up being imputed (i.e., imposed from above) as having been implicitly given. One thus has no actual control over one's consent. At the very same time, because, in Locke's view, individuals retain a "right to revolt" that is determinable according to their own criteria, the surrender they are taken to have made is never binding in fact, and so individuals arguably *never* consent to an authority greater than their own will. When power is made the principle of political organization, the result is a series of absolutes that get relentlessly displaced by their opposites, so that order can be established only in appearance, and as a mere instrument to be exploited for nonpolitical ends. The chapter ends with a summary consideration of Locke's notion of religious liberty in this light, as a transition to part 2.

In order to open up the investigation to the central theme of the book, chapter 3, "The Basic Shape of Modern Liberty," argues that what we have discovered in Locke is a pattern that can be seen in modern thought generally. The chapter makes this argument by presenting a succinct account of the anthropological and political notion of freedom in landmark modern thinkers who are conventionally taken to represent antipodes to Locke the supposed empiricist: namely, Spinoza (the supposed rationalist) and Kant (the supposed reconciler of rationalism and empiricism). We show that, in spite of genuine and significant differences in their theories, all of these thinkers share five features that we may take as characteristic of modern liberty: (1) a view of freedom as a kind of active power; (2) a belief that freedom of this sort is incompatible with heteronomy, paradigmatically in the form of another will; (3) a reduction of political order to the preservation of natural rights through the regulation of external behavior; (4) a rejection of any a priori religious tradition; (5) a tendency to allow freedom, in spite of its pure spontaneity, to collapse into various natural, ethical, and political determinisms.

Chapter 4, "Symbolical Order and Diabolical Subversion," proposes that the notion of the "diabolical" serves in a particular way to capture the essence of the modern conception of liberty. It first illuminates the meaning of the diabolical by contrasting it with its etymological opposite: the symbolical. The Greek verb *sym-ballō* means "to join together"; *symbols*, as Hans-Georg Gadamer has explained, were originally the *tesserae hospitales*, pieces of a bone or pottery broken apart and distributed to members of a bond formed in an act of hospitality, able to be rejoined by those members or their descendants in a future act, which is both a remembrance of the original generosity and a new event itself. The notion of the "symbolical" is borrowed from Paul Ricoeur in this context to describe the "premodern" cosmos, in which all things are tokens of the good that stands at the origin as first cause, and so all have a certain aptness for a fundamentally generous and generative unity. By contrast, *dia-ballō* means "to divide," "to set apart or at odds." A philosophical interpretation of the "diabolical," then, is offered in terms of six features, which are shown to bear a consistent inner logic: (1) the diabolical presents a deceptive image that substitutes for reality; (2) it is characterized by an essential negativity; (3) it renders appearance more decisive than reality, and indeed, *better* than reality according to the measure of convenience and efficiency; (4) it has a supra-individual dimension that is nevertheless impersonal: that is, it tends to take the form of an essentially self-referential system; (5) it is "soulless" in the sense of lacking an animating principle of unity; and (6) it is essentially self-destructive. Having characterized the diabolical, the chapter then returns to the basic pattern of modern liberty, elaborated in chapter 3, and shows how the notion serves to bring its various aspects to an intelligible unity. The chapter concludes by connecting modern liberty, on the one hand, with a contemporary expression (a definition of liberty offered by the U.S. Supreme Court), and, on the other, with an ancient pair of myths (the garden of Eden and Plato's cave).

Kant famously suggested that a proper political order ought not to depend on the virtue of its citizens but should be able to keep peace even in the case of a "society of devils." Thus, chapter 5, "A 'Society of Devils,'" argues that the reigning conception of freedom presupposed in modern thought has tended to give the form of the diabolical, outlined in chapter 4, to the various values, practices, and institutions on which freedom bears or in which it has a particular place. In a word, this chapter looks at the cultural and political manifestations of modern liberty in the light of the basic argument of the book. A preliminary section argues that a notion of liberty is embodied in the conceived structure of action and in the objective institutions that arise from and form action, especially in the particular configuration of means and ends. A "symbolical" configuration of the relation between means and ends is then presented as a foil to a "diabolical" configuration, which is taken to represent in a schematic way the general cultural form of modern liberty. The rest of the chapter shows how this form turns up in sometimes surprising ways in an array of phenomena, from the anthropological to the political and to the cultural more broadly. In each case, there turns out to be some form of a self-subversion, in which the only means permitted for the pursuit of the desired end contradict its attainment. The chapter explores this self-subversion under the following headings: choice, self-determination, autonomy, rights, privacy, equality, freedom of thought, freedom of the press, the power to vote, technology, free market, academic freedom, freedom of information, and, finally, power itself. It ends by showing how this form appears in a destructive way at the outermost and innermost spheres of human existence: God and the body.

We thus move to part 3. Within a brief compass, chapter 6, "Starting Over and Starting After: A First Foundation in Plato and Aristotle," begins by presenting an argument that a critique of culture made at the ontological level, though appearing *prima facie* to be more despairing, in fact opens up a real possibility of hope to the extent that it enters into the soil of reality, so to speak, beyond the roots of the problem; next, it points to an alternative understanding of freedom by recalling the original sense of the words for freedom and offering a philosophical interpretation of the etymology; and, third, it presents a brief apologia for the coming exposition of Plato and Aristotle as representatives of a common tradition that brings forth the original meaning. It is suggested that the reason intellectual histories of the notion of freedom and the will so often ignore Plato, or include him at best merely as a foil, is that they take the "diabolical" conception criticized in this book for granted as the norm.

Chapter 6 shows that freedom originally meant "belonging to an ethnic stock or family line." In chapter 7, "Plato: The Golden Thread of Freedom," Plato represents a specifically philosophical appropriation of this organic conception, giving it a properly metaphysical foundation and thus a metaphysical scope. For him, freedom most basically has the "symbolical" sense of the belonging together of all things in the good. This chapter, in one respect, concedes the general criticism of Plato for lacking a conception of free will as the spontaneous power to choose. On the other hand, however, it mounts a partial defense of Plato by arguing for the necessity of what such critiques often overlook, namely, the "effective" priority of goodness. This priority allows a unity between the intellect and, eventually, the will in our interpretation of human action, and it does not entail the elimination of creativity and spontaneity, as critics might fear, but in fact makes such things possible. The chapter culminates in a proposal that the primary model of freedom, in Plato, is "begetting/giving birth in the beautiful," a model that turns up analogously in all human action, no matter how trivial. It concludes by showing that this model of freedom is not disruptive or antagonistic by its own inner logic, as a diabolical conception cannot avoid being, but instead naturally generates further degrees of order. For the same reason, freedom turns out for Plato to have an essentially social, and so political, form.

Although Aristotle is typically taken to depart significantly from Plato on the issue in question, chapter 8, "Aristotle: Freedom as Liberality," proposes to read Aristotle principally as one who deepened the Platonic tradition and developed some of its indispensable components. Aristotle provides the classic formulation of the primacy of actuality, on the basis of which the present book mounts its critique of modernity. Focusing above all (but not exclusively) on the *De anima* and the *Nicomachean Ethics*, this chapter considers the implications of the primacy of actuality for Aristotle's understanding of motion in general, and then more specifically for the motions that characterize the human soul, namely, perception, thought, and action. It argues that such motions are to be understood most basically, not as mechanical events that effect some measurable change, but instead as analogous expressions of an unfolding of perfection. In the light of this interpretation, the neglected virtue of *liberality* (*eleutheriotēs*)—which, not incidentally, shares the root of freedom (*eleutheria*)—as the proper unity of giving and receiving wealth, turns out to present a paradigm of free action. In relation to this paradigm, the forms of human activity that Aristotle held to be highest, namely, contemplation and moral action, are shown to represent complementary expressions of the communication of goodness, the unity of giving and receiving the good. The chapter concludes by highlighting the essentially social dimension of freedom that we saw also in Plato: on the one hand, it argues that friendship presents a culminating synthesis of the contemplation and action that constitute human freedom, and, on the other, it interprets political authority as a unity of giving and receiving freedom in the concrete form of community.

The book ends with a brief conclusion that draws a basic contrast between the alternative ("symbolical") notion of freedom as a fruitful belonging together in the good and the ("diabolical") conception of freedom presented in parts 1 and 2. It ends by criticizing, once again, any response that would simply renounce the will and modern freedom (e.g., Heidegger) and proposes instead a recovery of the love of the good that the will cannot in any event evade.

PART ONE

John Locke and the Dialectic of Power

CHAPTER 1

Locke's (Re-)Conception
of Freedom

We enter into our reflection on the modern conception of freedom with a discussion of John Locke, not necessarily because he is the most influential or important of the early modern philosophers—though Lee Ward certainly has some justification for calling him "the canonical figure of Western liberalism"[1]—nor even because his interpretation of the nature of freedom is exceptionally clear. In fact, his writing on this topic is notoriously difficult to decipher, to such an extent that it has appeared to be not just confusing, but confused: as a contemporary critic observed regarding his attempt to explain the nature of freedom, "Here even Locke, that cautious philosopher, was lost."[2] The reason we choose Locke is *because* of the basic ambiguity in his thinking about freedom rather than in spite of it. The larger claim that we intend to make is that the modern conception of freedom has an inherent, indeed logical, tendency to subvert itself, and we aim to show in our first two chapters that this tendency comes to a certain perfection of expression in the thinking of Locke.

It is well known that conflicts in interpretation have attended the reception of Locke's idea of freedom from the first moment of the publication of his *Essay Concerning Human Understanding* in 1690,[3] and only intensified with his attempts to clarify his conception of freedom in the subsequent revised editions of the book.[4] Indeed, it was precisely the chapter that dealt with the question of free will, namely, the twenty-first chapter of the second book, already one of the longest in the *Essay*, that was subject to the most revision.[5] To put the controversy in modern terms: Is Locke a compatibilist, who believes (like Hobbes) that our *actions* are free but the volitions that produce those actions are not? Or is he a libertarian who thinks that, no matter how much one might be influenced by outside determinants, the will has the final say, so that we are justified in taking the will to be an absolute cause, and so to be accountable ultimately only to itself for its choices? Contemporary scholarship on Locke's notion of freedom has continued to struggle with resolving the problem of determining where Locke stands on the question of the will's freedom.

The difficulty can be set forth in a rather straightforward manner, though we will have to dwell on many of the details later in our discussion. In the initial edition of his *Essay*, Locke seems—though not without ambiguity even here, which is attested to by the immediate controversy—to incline toward a compatibilist perspective, that is, to hold that there is a freedom of action but a natural determinism of the will. This is something that concerned Locke when he finished, and, as he explains in a letter to William Molyneux—an admirer of Locke's, with whom Locke began to take up correspondence after the publication of his *Essay*—it was a tendency that emerged in the writing, contrary to his intentions as he began.[6] Locke says in the first edition that it is ultimately nonsensical to ask whether the will is free, since the category is intelligible only in relation to *agency*, and the will is not itself an agent but the faculty of an agent. The will is not self-determining, but it is determined in every situation by the greatest good that presents itself in that situation. "Upon a closer inspection into the working of men's minds, and a stricter examination of those motives and views they are turned by" ("Epistle to the Reader," 16), however, and prompted by questions friends and critics had raised, he felt a need to revisit the problem. In response to Locke's request for a critique, Molyneux admitted that Locke seemed to espouse a kind of intellectualism that failed to give due weight to the self-determining power of the will and was thus unable to explain the will's tendency to stray from reason—that is, the classic problem of *akrasia* ("incontinence" or "weakness of will"). In Molyneux's words, Locke appeared "to make all Sins to proceed from our Understandings, or to be against Conscience; and not at all from the Depravity of our Wills."[7] Moreover, Molyneux sent to Locke notes an acquaintance of his, Bishop William King, had made, which articulated in strong words a complaint that Locke failed to grasp the will's self-determining nature, rendering it a "passive power": whereas Locke had said that one can ask for no more freedom than to be able to act in accordance with one's will, King insisted this is true only if "that will not be crambed down his throat, but proceed meerly from the active power of the soul. [W]ithout any thing from without determining it to will or not to will."[8] In the second edition, Locke sought to mitigate the role of external determination by strengthening the agent's power, in a manner we will explore in detail below.

What is curious is that, although Locke makes what appear to be decisively new qualifications in the second edition (and also in the fifth), which fundamentally modify one's view of what freedom is, he *added* them to his original ideas as a supplement without in fact changing much of the substance of what he had previously written.[9] It may be true that, in the second edition's "Epistle to the Reader," he admits to having changed his mind about the question, but he also suggests in the text (and explains in a letter to Molyneux) that the change amounts to little more than the substitution of "one indifferent word" for another, "actions" for the word "things," which he had used in the first edition.[10] The change of understanding he confesses would thus appear to be rather slight. And so there seem to be several interpretive options available here, which we can boil down to the three most evident. *Either* (1) Locke was originally a compatibilist, but as a result of his closer consult of evidence and experience, and discussion with others, he altered his position and became a libertarian. *Or* (2) he was always a compatibilist, even in the later editions of his work, and what seem to be changes are in fact better interpreted as clarifications of his prior position or qualifications of his original position that would allow him to accommodate apparently contravening evidence without abandoning that position. *Or,* finally, (3) he was always a libertarian, and the ideas he introduced in subsequent editions merely enabled him to bring out more clearly and forcefully what was essentially a part of his thinking from the beginning. Serious scholars can be found defending each of these three interpretations.[11]

What we wish to propose is that the reason a serious defense of each of these three opposed interpretations of Locke can be found is that *they are all exactly correct*. Locke's view of freedom, in its final form, can be justifiably interpreted either as compatibilist or as libertarian, because the inherent logic points, as it were, in both directions at the same time. It is interesting in this context to note that, in the development of psychology in the centuries that followed, both the "associationists," who tended to be determinists, and the "faculty psychologists," who tended to be libertarians, pointed to Locke as the father of their school of thought.[12] Locke himself was evidently committed to preserving a full sense of human freedom, while at the same time he was resolute in his desire to avoid any tendency toward blind, arbitrary spontaneity. Because it is the *logic* of his conception that bifurcates simultaneously in these two directions, it becomes relatively unimportant for the purposes of our investigation what he himself intended to achieve. In what follows, therefore, our interest lies above all in the philosophical implications of his core ideas, rather than his own comments on them, or how his ideas were received by his contemporaries. To show these implications requires a much more precise presentation of those ideas, and so it is to this task that we turn first.

ON POWER

Let us first recall the context of Locke's presentation of his notion of freedom. The treatment comes in volume 2, chapter 21, of the *Essay*, which is entitled "Of Power." The general argument of the *Essay* is to show that the human mind is essentially a "white sheet," a blank piece of paper, which gets filled with content through the experience of the world: the *Essay* is thus a "natural history of the mind," in the sense that he follows an empirical, historical method in his interpreting the activity of the mind.[13] To make this argument, Locke attempts to show the genetic origin of our ideas in experience, first the simple ideas that we have, which cannot be reduced to anything more basic, and then the complex ideas, which are constructed upon those simple ideas and usually involve relations between several of them. The notion of *power* is a simple idea, according to Locke (2.7.8), which means that it is a univocal concept—"nothing but *one uniform appearance, or conception in the mind,*" which "is not distinguishable into different ideas" (2.2.1.145; all

emphasis we have throughout the book for Locke is in the original unless otherwise noted)—and thus is derived in an immediate way from
sensation and reflection.[14] In the context of this first mention, he notes
just that the simple idea of power arises from the experience of different forms of change (2.7.8.163). To say that it is a simple idea means that
"power" cannot be defined, though it can be known only by acquaintance with the experience of change.

But Locke returns to elaborate the notion of power as a "simple
mode" (as distinct from a "mixed mode"), which is a variation on a
simple idea that does not involve the introduction of another idea.
What Locke means by classifying power as a "simple mode" is apparently that it can be further differentiated within itself without the introduction of some other simple idea. The elaboration of the notion of
power occurs in chapter 21, just before Locke turns to the "mixed
modes," that is, combinations of simple ideas, the first of which is the
notion of substance.

Now, the reason Locke focuses this lengthy and complex chapter
on power almost exclusively on the experience of the human will is that
an exercise of the will, according to Locke, is the sole experience from
which we are able to derive the notion of power. The reason that it is exclusively our own exercise of will that affords a notion of power is that,
as Locke explains, it is only here that we see power in its most proper,
active sense as the ability to *bring about* a change, as distinct from
power in the passive sense as the ability to *undergo* a change. Clearly,
the active sense is primary, insofar as the changes that one thing undergoes have to be produced actively by something else.[15] Although it is
true that we witness the effecting of change constantly in the world
around us, it is nevertheless *also* true that every event can be causally
traced to the precedent conditions, and so on: as Locke says regarding
physical body in the natural world, "we observe it only to *transfer*, but
not *produce* any motion" (2.21.4.312). The activity of the will presents a
contrast to this: "The idea of the *beginning* of motion we have only
from reflection on what passes in ourselves" (2.21.4.313).

The crucial question that arises here is whether the exercise of the
will *is* in fact a beginning of motion—as we will see, it is just this question that Locke never definitively manages to answer. It is therefore no
surprise that the question of freedom would continue to occupy Locke

in later editions. We need to note the importance of this point. The notion of power is not just one of the various ideas that Locke reflects on in his account of the mind and its contents, but it represents, as Pierre Manent has suggested, the very center of the *Essay*, the reference point for all of the most significant notions he goes on to describe.[16] Indeed, once we consider the pragmatic turn of Locke's thought generally, we may say that the notion of power is the heart of his philosophy simply: it is the basis of his metaphysics, insofar as it presents the "principal ingredient" (2.21.3.311) of his notion of substance and of cause and effect; it is the basis of his epistemology, since all perceived qualities of the world are expressions of the power that things exert on the mind; it is the heart of his anthropology, since in rejecting all innate ideas he nevertheless founds his interpretation of human nature on the basis of innate *powers*;[17] and, needless to say, Locke conceives the goal of political philosophy to be the proper distribution of power:

> The Great Question which in all Ages has disturbed Mankind, and brought on the greatest part of those Mischiefs which have ruin'd Cities, depopulated Countries, and disordered the Peace of the World, has been, Not whether there be Power in the World, nor whence it came, but who should have it.[18]

If the notion of power, around which so much turns, can be derived from nowhere else but an insight into the will as a *beginning* of motion, then a proper interpretation of will is a matter of no small concern for the success of Locke's philosophy. His revision in this respect is not a matter of satisfying his critics, but of satisfying the demands of his own thinking.

VOLITION AND FREEDOM

Having considered the context in which Locke's discussion of human freedom occurs, and what is at stake for him in this discussion, let us now turn to the details of the discussion itself. Locke's definition of freedom appears quite straightforward, but it turns out to be rather complex when he attempts to elaborate and justify the elements of that definition. In the tightest nutshell, to be free, for Locke, is "to have the power to do what [one] will."[19] Locke explains that the power to do a particular thing is free only if it includes also the power *not* to do it. This aspect, which is one of the things that distinguishes his view from that of Hobbes, is so much a part of the essential meaning of freedom in his understanding as to require explicit mention in the more precise elaboration of the definition, which he thus gives as "a power in any agent to do or forbear any particular action, according to the determination of the mind" (2.21.8.316).[20] That this represents his definitive understanding of freedom, whatever qualifications he eventually adds, becomes evident when he refers to it again, towards the end of his life, as the settled definition. In letters to his Arminian friend Phillip van Limborch, in a debate they had concerning the indifference of the will, Locke affirms that freedom "consists solely in the power to act or not to act, consequent on, and according to, the determination of the will,"[21] and "Liberty for me is the power of a man to act or not to act, according to his will: that is to say, if a man is able to do this if he wills to do it, and on the other hand to abstain from doing this when he wills to abstain from doing it: in that case a man is free."[22]

As these formulations reveal, freedom for Locke concerns above all *action*. According to Locke, man has an active power to perform (or refrain from performing)—that is, *to begin* (or to forbear)—two different types of action, "thinking and motion" (2.21.8.315). One condition of freedom is that there be nothing that either prevents a man from exercising that power or coercively forces him to exercise it, in any given case. But this is only part of the matter. For Locke, in addition to this negative and external condition, there is a positive and internal one: the action must also be *voluntary*, which means that it must be an expression of the man's will. A free act, in other words, is one that is founded on a prior "act," what Locke calls "volition."[23] To understand Locke properly, it is crucial to grasp the distinction between volition and action proper. It is not the case, as one might initially think, that volition is internal (as an act of the mind), while action denotes an external movement of the body, an outward expression of what is in the mind, for as we just noted Locke classifies thinking as a type of action. Instead, volition is an internal activity that is distinct from thought; it is specifically the mind's *determining itself* to some action, whether that action be internal (thinking) or external (movement). Locke defines the will as the "power the mind has thus to order the consideration of any idea or the forebearing to consider it; or to prefer the motion of any part of the body to its rest, and vice versâ, in any particular instance" (2.21.5.313). There is thus first a power to think about actions and rank their desirability; volition, most properly speaking, is the "exercise of that power" (ibid.).

We can achieve some insight into what Locke precisely means by this somewhat obscure notion if we compare it to a similar sort of activity. Locke explains that the verb that comes closest to capturing the sense of "to will" is "*to prefer*," but he insists that these actions are nevertheless not the same insofar as I can say that I would prefer to fly than to walk, but I would never say that I *will* to fly (2.21.15.320). Behind Locke's judgment here seems to be an ambiguity in the phrase "to prefer," which on the one hand designates a kind of disposition (i.e., a state or way of being), while on the other hand, though this usage is now obsolete, it refers to the transitive *action* of placing one thing before another (which is indeed what its etymology implies).[24] In any event, the point is that for Locke volition strictly speaking is not a "wanting" in the sense of a positive disposition or condition of approval. (It is interesting to note already here that the distinction Locke seeks to draw between "willing" and "wanting" is an effort to rid the will, in its essence, of an appetitive dimension, insofar as that dimension implies its subordination to something outside of itself, as we will explain in the discussion of "unease" below.) Rather than being most basically a response to a prior reality, volition is an event, something that *happens*, the actualizing of a power, in relation to something over which we have some control. Locke thus specifies that volition "is an act of the mind knowingly exerting that dominion it takes itself to have over any part of the man" (2.21.15.320). Note that Locke very carefully says here "exerting" rather than "exercising": the *achievement* of dominion would be an action in the proper sense: the lifting of my arm, the turning of my head, and so forth. *Volition*, more specifically, is the directing of the mind to this action, whether or not the action is subsequently able to be achieved.[25] Since the will is a *power*, and power reveals itself in the effecting of some *change*, it follows that a volition is not a state, but an occurrence. On the other hand, Locke wishes to distinguish the act of will from the action of the man. He thus comes to characterize it as a kind of subaction, the act of intending a particular action, which can be described as a "directing" of the mind.[26]

Now, the fact that there is a distinction between volition and action proper, that volition in other words is the active *determination to* an action, but not yet the action itself at the level of the person's deliberate deed, allows Locke to make a distinction between an action's being voluntary and its being free. Volition is a necessary, but insufficient, condition for the freedom of an action. For it to be free in the full sense requires more than the agent's will—it requires, in addition, what we might call the cooperation of external circumstances. To show this, Locke presents his famous example of the man who is brought while asleep into a locked room with a close friend: he is there *willingly* or *voluntarily*, since conversing with his friend is what he desires to do, indeed, what he would actively *prefer* to do given other options, and yet he is not free, since his being in the room was not his action and he has no power to leave it. A similar distinction can be made with respect to the internal activity of thinking: certain thoughts might be put into my head, so to speak, without my so choosing—by virtue of some unconscious habit, for example—and yet I may enjoy them while they are there. In this case, I could be said to think something willingly, but not freely. Freedom presupposes voluntariness, but voluntariness does not necessarily entail freedom.[27]

Now, it is just this distinction between the voluntary and the free, and its implications, that has given rise to much of the controversy we alluded to earlier in the interpretation of Locke's views. On the one hand, the distinction separates Locke quite clearly from a more obviously compatibilist thinker like Hobbes. For the Hobbes of the *Leviathan*, freedom is exclusively a question of action and its external conditions, which is why we may speak equally of the freedom of a man to do x, y, and z, and of a river, which flows unimpeded along its course.[28] But Locke insists that unimpeded action is *not* free unless it is also the expression of a volition, an *act* of preference, which means that only what is rational can be considered free, since only that which *has* a mind can direct it to some action.[29] This is why Locke judges (contra Hobbes), for example, that a tennis ball cannot be free no matter how unimpeded its flight. On the other hand, however, Locke rejects what is typically taken to be a decisive question in the traditional debate concerning freedom, namely, whether the will itself is free—that is, whether the act of volition is a free action—as ultimately a meaningless question (though he modifies this judgment to a certain extent in the second edition, and most clearly in the posthumous edition, as we will see in the next section):

> I leave it to be considered, whether [the idea that freedom requires rational preference] may not help to put an end to that long agitated, and, I think, unreasonable, because unintelligible question, viz. *Whether man's will be free or no?* For if I mistake not, it follows from what I have said, that the question itself is altogether improper; and it is as insignificant to ask whether man's *will* be free, as to ask whether his sleep be swift, or his virtue square: liberty being as little applicable to the will, as swiftness of motion is to sleep, or squareness to virtue. (2.21.14.319)

The essential reason he offers for this rejection is that freedom concerns *action*, and the will is not itself an agent but only the faculty of an agent, that is, of an acting person. Moreover, freedom concerns action as the expression of a preference, and it does not make sense to say that the will has a preference: it is the agent who does. Finally, given that the will has been defined as a power, and freedom has been defined as a power, to ask whether the will is free, according to Locke, amounts to the patently absurd question whether a power has a power.[30]

But Locke does not simply rest his case with this *reductio ad absurdum*; he offers instead a more detailed account of the activity of the will in order to show—at least initially—why the question of freedom is not relevant at this level. He makes two arguments in this regard. The first argument, given in sections 23 and 24, draws essentially on his observation that we cannot help in any particular case preferring or not preferring something the very moment it is proposed to our understanding. There are two claims here. The first is that, when action that is *immediately to be done* is proposed to us, we cannot but take up some position in its regard; we necessarily will to do it or not to do it. This claim does not seem very controversial. The second claim is the bolder one: Locke is suggesting not only that necessity drives the fact of having to will one or the other, but also that it determines the content of the volition. He does not explain what he means by this, but what he seems to have in mind is that we cannot help but will a certain thing, that is, the mind cannot help but direct itself in a particular way, given who we are and the circumstances in which we find ourselves. To put it in other words— which are not Locke's but help to clarify his—the act of will, understood as preference, occurs immediately and automatically. We don't have control over what we like or dislike; we don't decide what we want. Instead, we make decisions with respect to wants that are simply given. To ask whether the act of will is free, as he puts it, thus amounts to the pointless question "whether a man can will what he wills, or be pleased with what he is pleased with" (2.21.25.328).[31] Do we have to determine whether we *want* to want what we want if we wish to say that we want it? Is it not sufficient simply to say, "This is what I want"?

The second argument is related to this last question, and in fact Locke articulates it briefly after making this point. In the first four editions, Locke had made essentially the same argument twice: at the end of section 23 and at the end of section 25. In the fifth edition, he eliminated the first instance and kept only the slightly briefer articulation, to which we refer here. Locke goes on to say, in this succinct formulation, that, if one of the requirements for an act of will to be free is that it itself be the result of an act of will, then we fall into an infinite regress: the act of will that makes this particular act of will free is either necessary or free. If it is free, it can only be by virtue of an antecedent act, which is in turn either necessary or free, and so on into infinity. There ultimately needs to be some determination external to the will, some preference that is not *chosen* but simply *given*, to set the series in motion, and therefore volition itself cannot ultimately be a free action.[32]

It becomes evident at this point that Locke has "backed into" a kind of compatibilism that is scarcely distinguishable in its general implications from that of Hobbes's, though it is certainly more sophisticated. To put the matter clearly: we may or may not be free, to the extent that we have the ability to do what we want to do, but this determination of the question of freedom is altogether separate from the question of the origin of our desire. Freedom is, in other words, perfectly compatible with the position that our preferences are themselves wholly the result of external causes, naturalistically conceived.[33] In this respect, at least,

Locke's view of freedom, just like Hobbes's, can be affirmed within the context of a universal mechanism, that is, without removing human action, no matter how lofty or idealistic it might *appear* to be, from the necessary chain of causal events governing nature as a whole.

In addition to all of the logical and moral problems that this position entails in the traditional objections, it also presents a fundamental difficulty in the context of Locke's *Essay* that is not often noticed:[34] the whole point of the discussion, as we indicated earlier, is to show the origin of the idea of power, which depends on our experience of the *production* of action *as opposed to* the mere *transfer* of activity that we witness everywhere else in the natural world. If the act of will, upon closer inspection, turns out to be itself nothing more than a transfer of power, then we have lost the basis for one of the fundamental building blocks, if not the very foundation, of Locke's philosophy. And so the entire building will collapse.

SECOND THOUGHTS

We have said that the positing of a "universal mechanism" is perfectly compatible with Locke's understanding of freedom, but that does not mean that Locke himself adopts it. It can be *harmonized* with Locke's position, as so far described, but *is* it in fact Locke's position? It is just on this point that Locke's work of revision in the second edition most decisively bears. The revising entailed the insertion of a few lines or the changing of a few words or phrases here and there in the first twenty-seven sections of chapter 21, but Locke added a great deal of new material to everything that comes after this in the chapter, apart from some concluding observations tying the discussion back to the general idea of power. What had been eleven sections of text he expanded into thirty-four sections, as Locke attempted to deal more adequately with the problem of free will, prompted in part, as we saw, by the problem of failing to do justice to what Locke originally affirmed to be the properly *active* quality of the will, which was set into relief by both Molyneux's and King's criticisms.

Locke believes generally that every event has a cause,[35] and this apparently excludes an event's being self-caused, which, given the normal sense of cause as something distinct from an effect, would amount to its "just happening," so to speak, without a cause that could be identified with some intelligible content. The principle means that the will's own act of determination, its volition, must itself be due in some respect at least to something *other* than itself. The cause of the will's determination appears in the first edition of Locke's *Essay* as the good, or more precisely, as the *greater good*: "*Good, then, the greater good, is that which determines the will*" (2.21.29.376).[36] In the revised edition, by contrast, he says, "to the question, What is it determines the will? the true and proper answer is, the mind" (2.21.29.330). There is thus a shift between what we might call a more *objective* account of human action in the first edition, to a more *subjective* account in subsequent editions, wherein it is the agent's mind that determines his will, though of course always in relation to objective options. Interestingly, Locke admits that the idea that the will is determined by the greater good is a maxim that has been "established and settled . . . by the general consent of all mankind" (2.21.35.335) to such an extent that he himself took it for granted in the first edition of his *Essay* and only subsequently came to his new view. There would thus appear to be something revolutionary in the alternative he is proposing—we will be suggesting that what is revolutionary is not in the first place the particular conclusions Locke comes to, but even more radically the empirical approach that brings him to view things as he does, an approach that gives all ideas, as it were, a new sense.[37] The terms of Locke's reconception—unease and the power to suspend— seem to have been inspired by his reading of Malebranche (who made "inquiétude" and the power to suspend judgment essential to freedom).[38] But as Jean-Michel Vienne points out, Malebranche conceived these notions within a classical, Platonic metaphysics of participation, in which the various acts of the will rested in and were ordered to participation in a "Supreme Good." What is most significant about Locke, we will be arguing here, is not these discrete notions themselves but *precisely* the novelty that Vienne indicates, namely, Locke's removal of these notions from any metaphysical participatory (and so intrinsic) relationship to the good.[39] If we wished to identify the birth of the modern conception of freedom, a reasonable candidate would be Locke's reconception of the notion in his revision of the *Essay*, which in his own judgment directly broke with the "established and settled" view.

What is behind Locke's shift in the second edition? What makes it possible, and what are its implications? The proximate motivation for the change, as we suggested, seems to be to account for the fact of *akrasia* and to give a more active power to the will by increasing the individual's responsibility for his actions beyond what his initial apparent "volitional determinism" would suggest.[40] There are two basic steps that Locke takes in his revision to place the will more fully in the power of the human agent, and thus—at least in appearance—to remove man from the mechanism of nature, that is, to interrupt, so to speak, the causal chain of events wherein each is simply a necessary result of the precedent conditions: first, he introduces "unease" as a motivating force, and second, he acknowledges the power man has to *suspend* his desires, a power that seems amply attested to in our immediate experience. What these changes have in common is that they both attenuate the power of attraction the good exerts on the will, conceived now as competing with the will's own power, and so they both serve to reinforce the will itself as the original source of the power it possesses. In other words, they both strengthen the will as a self-motivating force. As we will see, it is the second of these two additions that proves most decisive.

Unease

Locke had come to the conclusion in the revision of the *Essay* that the will is properly understood to be determined by the mind, but of course this only defers the question: What, then, determines the mind? Locke raises this question explicitly and offers an answer:

> What moves the mind, in every particular instance, to determine its general power of directing, to this or that particular motion or rest? And to this I answer,—The motive for continuing in the same state or action, is only the present satisfaction in it; the motive to change is always some uneasiness: nothing setting us upon the change of state, or upon any new action, but some uneasiness. (330–31)

Note here that there is some ambiguity whether Locke thinks of the continuance in the same state or action as an *act* of will. This ambiguity is due to his view of the will as a power—that is, an ability to produce a change—and it will turn out to be the cause of an unresolvable contradiction, as we shall see at the end of the chapter. The reason that Locke highlights the *unease*, here, that is felt in the absence of what is wanted—in contrast, for example, to the traditional notion of desire for the good—is above all the *immediacy* of its effective power.[41] This has three clear advantages over the original formulation, for Locke, given his intentions in undertaking the revision. In the first place, unease represents, one might say, precisely the physical manifestation of a perception or idea, which only thus has the force to set a person in motion. An idea in itself, for Locke, cannot *move* in the literal sense because it is not itself either physical or in motion, but it can move to the extent that it is translated, through a subject's perception and desire, into a physical force. The notion of unease therefore provides a more directly empirical and materialist account of human action. It is the immediacy of the force that makes it effective: one might say that just as unease is physical force precisely insofar as it is a translation of a motivating idea into the terms of immediacy, so too the pain it represents is the translation of the absence of a good into the terms of immediacy. As Locke puts it succinctly: "Another reason why it is uneasiness alone determines the will, is this: because that alone is present and, it is against the nature of things, that what is absent should operate where it is not" (2.21.37.336). Locke does not allow a *mediated* presence.

Second, unease individualizes motivation in a way that helps explain the widely divergent paths people follow in the face of similar goods.[42] Simply to perceive a good and understand it *as* good is not sufficient to provoke a person to pursue it. If this were sufficient, it would be difficult to make sense of what is an apparent fact of experience, namely, that people quite often make choices contrary to what they acknowledge to be good. According to Locke, it is not enough to *understand* a thing to be good; one must actually and actively want that thing, which means that one experiences its absence as a lack that causes uneasiness. An absent good can fail to move a person, but a present pain cannot:

> Thus, how much soever men are in earnest and constant in pursuit of happiness, yet they may have a clear view of good, great and confessed good, without being concerned for it, or moved by it, if they think they can make up their happiness without it. Though as to pain, *that* they are always concerned for; they can feel no uneasiness without being moved. (2.21.44.342)

This alternative interpretation of motivation individualizes insofar as it makes motivation depend on the particularity of the person in question, rather than, say, the objective morality or goodness of the option that presents itself: the person's history, previous choices, acquired habits, and everything else that makes him unique comes to bear on what in reality moves him. Even though good and evil might be said to have a universal meaning for Locke,[43] "and all good be the proper object of desire in general; yet all good, even seen and confessed to be so, does not necessarily move every particular man's desire; but only that part, or so much of it as is considered and taken to make a necessary part of *his* happiness" (2.21.44.341). If there is a variety of paths chosen in the world, it does not mean that human beings pursue something other than the good, but only "that the same thing is not good to every man alike. This variety of pursuits shows, that every one does not place his happiness in the same thing, or choose the same way to it" (2.21.55.350–51).

The third advantage is the implication of this reduction of motivation to an immanent immediacy: if unease is not yet, taken by itself, a transformation of the action of the good on the will into self-determination in the strict sense, it is at all events a very close approximation to it. To speak of desire for an absent good is to advert to something acting, so to speak, *upon* me from outside of myself; it is to acknowledge what we might call a "from above" sort of causality. If the good is what attracts "from above," unease is by contrast a force that propels, we might say, "from below." Now, it is evidently the case that, however we describe the matter, volition, the determination or the act of the will, is a relation between two terms: the subject's will, on the one hand, and the object (the good), on the other. But the nature of *both* terms changes depending on the side, as it were, from which we begin in our interpretation of the relation. If we begin "from above," then the will is measured by the good, which has a meaning in itself, and the will comes to appear most basically as receptive desire. But if we begin, by contrast, from below, then the will is primarily effective power, and the good is defined by this power: the significance it has as good is measured by the extent to which it is an ingredient in this power. In his discussion of the nature of freedom with Limborch, who relentlessly urged Locke to acknowledge some freedom in volition itself, Locke complains that Limborch improperly confuses desire (which is set on the good), and the will, which Locke insists is *not* directed to an end (i.e., a remote good), but instead terminates in action.[44] This insistence makes sense if one thinks of the will, as Locke does, specifically as an active, that is, productive, power.

Locke is very clear about the order of determination in the will's relation to its object and the implications of this order for the meaning of goodness. He defines the terms "good" and "evil" thus: "What has an aptness to produce pleasure in us is that we call *good*, and what is apt to produce pain in us we call *evil*" (2.21.43.340). Note the order: he does not say, "because a thing is good, it therefore produces pleasure," but rather, "because a thing produces pleasure, we therefore call it good"— and note, too, that in the former case it is natural to say that a thing *is* good, while in the latter case the thing is only *said* to be good, specifically *by us*, in whom it has proven to produce pleasure. Moreover, the good is not what pleases, but what is "*apt*" to "*produce*" pleasure—that is, the good is understood here, not as an actuality (as it is in classical philosophy), but as a particular form of *power*. Not only does Locke reduce the meaning of goodness to its empirical effects, but, so far as human action goes, he reduces it in fact to its *potential* empirical effects. We will return in our discussion of freedom and self-mastery, below, to reflect on the significance of the potentiality of the good that appears here in contrast to its actuality. For the moment, we will stick to the empirical reduction. What this reduction means is that, in Locke's reconception, goodness has been reduced to its immediate presence, which is another way of saying that it comes to have significance only inside of my perception. But this would imply that there is no difference between being and appearance in the meaning of the good; to reconceive the good in terms of its empirical effects, in other words, would be to reduce the reality of goodness to its mere appearance. And, indeed, Locke explicitly draws just this inference: "Things in their present enjoyment are what they seem: the apparent and real good are, in this case, always the same" (2.21.60.354).

Because the meaning of goodness thus becomes endlessly distributed—because, that is, its meaning depends in each case on its reception by individual perceivers—nothing definitive can be said about its content.[45] To put the point in more contemporary terms, Locke's represents a "relativistic" conception of the good, though it is very important to note, immediately, that this does not prevent him from affirming objective, universal, and permanent moral norms.[46] Thus, on the one hand, Locke is radical in his insistence that there is no such thing as a highest good for all mankind:

> Hence it was, I think, that the philosophers of old did in vain inquire, whether *summum bonum* consists in riches, or bodily delights, or virtue, or contemplation: and they might have as reasonably disputed, whether the best relish were to be found in apples, plums, or nuts, and have divided themselves into sects upon it. For, as pleasant tastes depend not on the things themselves, but on their agreeableness to this or that particular palate, wherein there is great variety; so the greatest happiness consists in the having those things which produce the greatest pleasure, and in the absence of those which cause any disturbance, any pain. (2.21.56.351)

As Ward has put it, one of Locke's most influential achievements is a "democratization of the mind,"[47] which necessarily coincides with, or follows from, the elimination of any notion of a natural or objective hierarchy of goods in the world. Pleasure is a function of taste, individual taste, and if pleasure presents the criterion of goodness, then what is good will vary as much as taste evidently does. Locke does not hesitate to put this claim in as extreme a way as he can:

> And therefore it was a right answer of the physician to his patient that had sore eyes: —If you have more pleasure in the taste of wine than in the use of your sight, wine is good for you; but if the pleasure of seeing be greater to you than that of drinking, wine is naught. (2.21.55.351)

On the other hand, however, it is clear that Locke would himself disapprove of the person who chose the pleasure of wine over the pleasure of eyesight; as he explained in his response to some of his immediate critics who worried that he was surrendering any objective foundation for morality, he intended to express in these passages not the way things *ought to be*, but only the way things in fact *are*.[48] His description is nothing more than a statement of fact. Though we cannot distinguish the apparent from the real good in any particular instance, a sensible person can see that certain goods chosen open up the possibility or even likelihood of greater pleasure *in the future*, and some will almost ensure future misery.

It is with this insight that what one might call a "normative" dimension enters into Locke's understanding of freedom in spite of what appears to be a relativistic conception of the good. The contemporary scholar who has no doubt laid the most stress on this dimension of Locke's thought is Gideon Yaffe. His principal presentation of the topic, the book *Liberty Worth the Name*,[49] draws its title from one of the few passages in chapter 21 of the *Essay* in which Locke discusses not the *nature* of freedom—what it *is*—but rather specifically how it *ought to be used*. The passage occurs in the context of Locke's mention (another decisive text for Yaffe) of the classical idea that God's freedom cannot be said to be limited by the fact that he *cannot* choose anything but what is good. Affirming this classical idea, Locke argues for it by raising and elaborating a rhetorical question:

> Would anyone be a changeling, because he is less determined by wise considerations than a wise man? Is it worth the name of freedom to be at liberty to play the fool, and draw shame and misery upon a man's self? If to break loose from the conduct of reason, and to want that restraint of examination and judgment which keeps us from choosing or doing the worse, be liberty, true liberty, madmen and fools are the only freemen: but yet, I think, nobody would choose to be mad for the sake of such liberty, but he that is mad already. The constant desire of happiness, and the constraint it puts upon us to act for it, nobody, I think, accounts an abridgment of liberty, or at least an abridgment of liberty to be complained of.[50] (2.21.51.347)

Yaffe, in light of this passage and others, argues that a normative view of freedom lay behind all of Locke's thinking on the subject, that he intended above all to present a view not so dissimilar in the end from the classical view of "ordered liberty." According to Yaffe, the most proper definition of freedom of will ("improperly so called"[51]) for Locke is "the capacity to adjust [the agent's] choices in accordance with the good."[52] Yaffe admits that, for Locke, the limits of our understanding prevent us from knowing what the good is without God's assistance.[53] Indeed, it is ultimately God's will that makes a particular choice good.[54] The foundation of freedom is therefore ultimately eschatological judgment: if our freedom is connected with the pursuit of happiness, and if one day all of our choices will either be rewarded by God with eternal happiness or punished with eternal misery, then freedom ought not to be understood as arbitrary, whimsical choice: instead, genuine freedom, a liberty "worth the name," is the choice of proper goods.

Whether Yaffe's interpretation of Locke is correct is not our primary concern here.[55] We will not attempt to decide the extent to which Locke's conception of freedom is in fact a normative one, nor will we take a position in the debate over the extent to which Locke's view of freedom, morality, and natural law *in fact* depends on the affirmation of a transcendent God as absolute judge, which would imply that his view cannot be translated into secular terms.[56] Our argument is that these questions, just like the question whether Locke is ultimately a compatibilist or libertarian, are secondary. What is most significant is Locke's interpretation of the essential meaning of the terms at stake: the will, freedom, and the good. The primary question for us is what Locke said these things *are* rather than how he says they *ought to be used*. What we wish to determine here, in other words, is not how important Locke thinks it is to use our freedom wisely, but rather what he says constitutes the nature or essence of freedom.

We note, in the long passage cited above, that Locke denies that a madman playing the fool manifests a freedom "worth the name." But, if he happens to abuse the freedom he has, is it nevertheless *freedom* that he abuses? In other words, would Locke say that the man who plays the fool is free in his so doing? According to Locke's definition of freedom, the only proper way to answer the question would be to ask whether there is anything that puts a restraint on his will or that prevents this behavior from being the expression of his decided volition. If there is nothing that so restrains him, then the man is free, even if he is doing something we might think ignoble, or even if we had some grounds for saying that it is behavior he himself will come to regret in the future. The key is the absence of an imposed restriction on the expression of his volition.[57]

In this regard, it is important to see a certain ambiguity in Locke's formulation in another part of this passage, which has to be recognized as a sort of sleight of hand. Locke says that the "constraint" that the desire for happiness—which, as we will show in part 3, is one of the foundational principles of the classical notion of freedom—puts upon the human agent is something that "nobody, I think, accounts an abridgment of liberty, or at least an abridgment of liberty to be complained of." He glides past this point, but we ought to recognize that there is a great deal at stake in whether it is the one or the other. To be sure, there is a great deal at stake only from the perspective of the *meaning* of freedom; practically speaking, that is, from a strictly empirical perspective, it makes little difference: if no one *in fact* complains, the problem is effectively irrelevant. How does this point bear on the meaning of freedom? If this desire, which evidently precedes the mind's determination of the will (the extent to which Locke actually accepts that it so precedes that determination is a question we will raise in the next section), is not an abridgment of liberty, it would mean that it is the good that first determines the will "from above," which means we remain within the framework of an essentially classical conception of freedom. But it is just this that Locke is clearly and decisively overturning in his articulation of the nature of freedom. If it is, by contrast, indeed an abridgment of liberty, but just one that no one would complain of, then we have Locke's "from below" account of the will running up against a limitation, which it accepts as such. Conceding the limitation has two advantages from the perspective of Locke's general project: it allows one in a sense to accommodate the normative, moral dimension of freedom that is a part of the classical view, while at the same time it allows one to do so without being compelled to alter in any fundamental sense one's essential conception of freedom as self-determination "from below." It becomes simply an external limit to what remains internally indifferent to what lies outside that limit.

This separation between the external and the internal is crucial; its importance will become especially important in the political order, as we will see in chapter 2. If the good determines the will in some sense "from above," there cannot be any facile separation between outside and inside, between the transcendent (or "absent") and the immanent (or "present"), or, what follows from this, between obligation and desire. We described the "action" of the classically conceived good on the will as attraction, and of course this is simply a description from the other side, as it were, of internal desire. But insofar as this action implies that the will is measured by the good, it is at the very same time a description of "obligation." It is interesting to note that classical discussions of the good are typically occupied with the question of how one ought to live—the question of moral obligation—and yet the good is *defined* in the classical tradition as "desirability."[58] We cannot explore in detail here how and why a split occurs between desirability and obligation in the evolution of the concept of freedom, but we see the result of this split in Locke's thinking. For Locke, the normative dimension is imposed in a wholly extrinsic manner through divine judgment; it is transcendent, not in the radical classical sense that coincides with constant immanent presence,[59] but in a purely extrinsic way: the moral significance comes through what is a historical event, namely, a divine judgment that *will* occur in a time *after* this life. As Locke puts it, "Were all the concerns of man terminated in this life" (2.21.55.351)—that is, if there were no afterlife, and so no divine judgment—then in fact all goods in this life would be in principle equal, distinguishable only on the basis of individual taste. The fact that some people choose to pursue one thing and others something else, as we saw in a passage we cited earlier, "would not be because every one of these did *not* aim at his own happiness, but because their happiness was placed in different things" (ibid.). The moral quality of the things makes no difference to their inherent desirability, but is "superadded" to them, we might say, by the divine law.[60]

Moreover, the reason to obey this law is ultimately in turn reducible to goodness interpreted once again entirely in terms of individual perception, that is, sensation: the reward or punishment of infinite happiness (pleasure) or infinite misery (pain) (2.21.72.364–65). To put the matter succinctly, what we have here is the replacement of the simultaneous unity of the transcendent and the immanent in the classical conception of the good by an isolation of these moments, which are nonetheless connected, perhaps even *inseparably*, but only as *successive* moments: the immanent is connected to the transcendent through law, and the transcendent is connected to the immanent through reward or punishment. As Yaffe explains it, *God creates* the connection between right action and pleasure.[61] Desirability and obligation are certainly brought together, for Locke, but without ever ceasing to be wholly extrinsic to each other, and his combining of the two aspects carries a certain persuasive power because it appears—at least *effectively*—to cover the same ground as the classical conception. This is the sleight of hand we mentioned, and the significance of this point will be seen to grow quite dramatically over the course of this book.

We have been discussing the first of the two steps Locke takes in his revision in the attempt to present freedom as a paradigm of active power, namely, his notion of *unease* as a motivating force, which takes the place of the "greater good." Before we turn to the second step, we will note two further aspects of Locke's notion that will become important for us later, and then show why the idea of unease is not yet sufficient to accomplish his aim of securing self-determination for the will. First, we note that Locke realizes, in his revision, that he needs to redefine the proper object of volition: instead of saying that volition terminates in *things*, he clarifies that, most properly speaking, it terminates in *actions*. As we mentioned at the beginning of this chapter, this is the point he said in a letter to Molyneux that was the essential change he made in his new view. He moreover insists on the importance of this point in his later discussion with Limborch. In that discussion, we recall, he is intent on *separating* the attraction to the good from the proper activity of the will, which consists of the capacity to bring about a change. The reason this separation is significant is that it serves to underscore the *immanence* of the act of will: the will is not directed to a *thing*—a good that is transcendent, that is, a good that lies "out there" in the world beyond the will; instead, it is directed only to the actions of the self. The will is not the capacity to be moved by the good, but rather a pulse of force from below. According to Aquinas, the activity of the will terminates specifically in the "bonum," which "in rebus est";[62] by contrast, for Locke, the will *never* reaches *things*: "For this we must carry along with us, that the proper and only object of the will is some action of ours, and nothing else. For we produce nothing by our willing it, but *some action in our power*, it is there the will terminates, and reaches no further" (2.21.41.340). The more immanent the act, the more it can be interpreted as a self-determination rather than as a determination by what is other.

Second, we note here, without yet developing its significance, that there is a particular connection between *unease* and *power*, a connection that comes to light when we recognize the classical distinction between power (potency) and actuality. In Locke's conception, pleasure does not motivate because it is actual; in the experience of pleasure, he says, one is not moved to effect a change, which is equivalent for Locke to the effort of volition.[63] Unease makes *reference* to pleasure, the actual state of being pleased, but precisely in a nonactual mode, that is, in the experience of its absence. It is something *to be achieved*, to be *worked for*. As Vienne has observed, contrasting Locke with Malebranche, Locke's notion of "unease" is "altogether negative," a "dissatisfaction without intentionality," since it lacks the ordering to the Supreme Good.[64] Absent pleasure does not motivate except insofar as it is actually felt as absent, that is, in the form of pain. In itself, pleasure is impotent. Moreover, pain is the proper measure for hedonism, which collapses into the isolated subject, because, as Hannah Arendt so insightfully observes, pain, unlike pleasure, is essentially self-referential: "Only pain is completely independent of any object, . . . only one who is in pain really senses nothing but himself; pleasure does not enjoy itself but something besides itself. Pain is the only inner sense found by introspection which can rival in independence from experienced objects the self-evident certainty of logical and arithmetical reasoning."[65] There is a connection between (pure) power and lack of transcendent reference. To put the matter in terms that will become crucial for us later, the unease that determines the mind is reality (actuality) *only in the form of unreality* (potency). We will return to dwell at length on this point, which represents a central theme of this book.

In his discussion of Locke, Manent notes that, when man flees evil—when he is moved to remedy the pain of unease—everything happens as if he were pursuing the good.[66] In other words, the classical view of desire for the good, desire for God, is replaced in Locke's reconception of freedom by a flight from evil. The exact same path may be traversed, but it is so now on fundamentally different terms and for a radically different reason. From a purely empirical or pragmatic perspective, however, the difference has no bearing. The two approaches are "effectively" the same, insofar as their outward results are indistinguishable. We have here an instance of what William Desmond calls a "counterfeit double": the flight from evil is a counterfeit double of the pursuit of the good.[67]

For all of its significance in Locke's reconception of freedom, "unease" remains only a first step, which is inadequate in itself. The reason for its inadequacy is that it does not yet overcome the decisive problem that Locke needed to resolve, namely, a conception of freedom as a proper *beginning* of action, and so as an instance of self-determination that would distinguish human agency from any other mechanistically determined event in nature, and thus yield insight into the meaning of that fundamental simple idea, power. So far, there is nothing in the notion of unease that would so distinguish human agency. Unease can quite evidently in principle be interpreted as a state in the mind that is produced by material conditions; everything we have said about "from below" causality is at the very least compatible with naturalism if not necessarily logically bound to it. The "immanentizing" of motivation in fact points precisely in the direction of mechanistic determinism. The very movement toward the self in itself in the interpretation of motivation somewhat ironically intensifies the danger of naturalism, of thinking of the will as just one of the moving parts of the great machine of nature, pulling on some parts only because it is itself being pushed by others.[68] And so Locke has to take a further step.

Suspense

What Locke finally identifies as "the source of all liberty" is the mind's "power to *suspend* the execution and satisfaction of any of its desires"; "in this," he goes on to say, "seems to consist that which is (as I think improperly) called *free-will*" (2.21.48.345). As we have already mentioned, there is, of course, controversy regarding the implication of Locke's parenthetical remark insofar as what is at stake is the extent to which this step represents a step *beyond* his original position, or merely a further clarification of that position. Our contention—which still needs to be explained and argued for—has been that either interpretation can justify itself in a more or less satisfactory way. The important thing is what this power of suspension is and means. At first blush, it seems to be relevant only occasionally: Locke continues to insist that, "for the most part," our wills are determined by the "greatest and most pressing" of the "great many uneasinesses" soliciting our will at any given moment (2.21.48.344).[69] In most cases, then, it would seem that Locke's position more or less aligns with that of Hobbes, or in any event that he allows in general a determinism with respect to volition. But the exceptional cases turn out, in a certain respect at least, to change everything. In any given instance, the mind has the capacity, in principle, to "veto," as it were, whatever solicitation proposes itself to the will. We say "in principle" because Locke seems to suggest that this native power can be strengthened or weakened according to the way one lives, that is, the choices one makes over the course of one's life, and this possibility introduces, as we shall explain, a responsibility that turns out to be ultimately limitless because it cannot be defined by any determinate reality. Originally, Locke had made *happiness* the reference point for all one's choices, and he suggested, furthermore, that what makes a particular person happy was simply given, just like one's personal taste. The apparently fixed character of what we take to constitute our ultimate fulfillment thus provides a sort of anchor that determines our choices. This fixity was the most basic reason, for Locke, that we cannot consider our volitions, but only our actions, as free. The introduction of the power of suspension, however, even if it is actualized only on rare occasions, transforms not only the character of our choices, but it also ineluctably penetrates into the very ground of those choices. This ground, too, now appears to fall under our control, and therefore becomes a matter of our responsibility. The one who has made bad choices habitually "has vitiated his own palate, and *must be answerable to himself* for the sickness and death that follows from it" (2.21.57.353; emphasis added).[70]

Let us explore this point more fully. Why, exactly, is the power to suspend desire so important? To say that we can suspend any given desire is to say that we can suspend "all, one after the other" (2.21.48.345). Indeed, this power is not only *potentially* universal in the sense that one *could*, if one wished, suspend each and every desire as it presented itself in succession, but in fact it is *actually* universal in a very precise sense: the very fact of having this power, *whether or not it is ever exercised*, changes the nature of every determination of the will, apparently without exception. If a particular "uneasiness" happens to determine my will, in light of this power I have to say that, even if I did nothing to cause this uneasiness myself and simply followed where it led, I nevertheless *allowed myself* to be so determined. In other words, even being the "most pressing" among the present options does not suffice on its own to make a choice finally determinative: the uneasiness must yet pass through the will's "executive fiat," so to speak. Nothing can determine me in the end without my consent; even the most passive reception of external stimulation thus becomes ultimately a form of self-determination. I was, perhaps, moved by an apparently irresistible desire in a particular case, but in principle *I could have* suspended this desire in spite of appearances, which means that even this acquiescence is ultimately a function of my will.[71] To put it in modern language, because any determination in principle could be rejected, every determination becomes in fact a choice. Even the failure to exercise the will is a choice: you choose in this case not to choose.[72] In Locke's own language, "If the neglect or abuse of the liberty he [who made an ill-ordered choice] had, to examine what would really and truly make for his happiness, misleads him, the miscarriages that follow on it must be imputed to his own election. *He had a power to suspend his determination*" (2.21.57.353).[73]

With this, the threat of naturalism seems to be definitively neutralized. If Locke had earlier qualified his affirmation of the mind as what determines the will by saying the mind in turn is determined by unease, he now clearly states that the mind retains sovereignty over this determination by virtue of what we have referred to as its "veto power." No natural cause is sufficient to account for volition . . . unless the will allows it to be. It follows that any volition, however extrinsically caused it may be, can be interpreted *retroactively* as a function of my will, my decision, my power. By virtue of this ability to suspend, the mind seems once and for all to transcend the causal mechanism of nature, and so Locke seems to have found an escape finally from the moral and spiritual problems that Hobbes's view is impotent to avoid.[74] Indeed, the apparently universal scope of the power of suspension would seem to make this transcendence *absolute*. There is ultimately nothing on earth, so it seems, to which the mind is subordinate in what we might call an ontological—as distinct from a moral or political—sense insofar as it has the power to trump any causal determination that happens to present itself. In this respect, the power of suspension makes us in a sense "like God," because it thus turns the mind into a sort of "unmoved mover."[75] If the mind is in fact the ultimately unmoved source of its determination, then the will does finally show itself capable of "beginning an action," which, we recall, is precisely what Locke was seeking in presenting the exercise of the will as the source of our conception of power. The notion of the "power to suspend" turns out to be indispensable to the larger project of the *Essay*.

Peter Schouls is the contemporary scholar who has no doubt laid the most stress on the "self-determining" aspect of the will in Locke's philosophy. He insightfully connects the conception of freedom as founded on the power to suspend with the general epistemological aim of the *Essay*, namely, to show that we are not born with innate ideas, things we, so to speak, always already take to be true, and to which we are always already committed. Instead, our mind for Locke is a blank slate at the start, and we subsequently work to fill it with content. According to Schouls, this "blank sheet" state is not just an initial condition that fades away through experience, as the sheet is, so to speak, filled up. Instead, the "blank sheet" represents the internal condition and so the abiding character of our experience: the ideal, for Locke, is a state of *continual revolution*;[76] we approach everything we encounter *de novo*, never taking it simply for granted, but judging it critically for ourselves in every instance. With Locke's philosophy, "we begin to feel that the whole world is new for everyone; we are absolutely free of what has gone before."[77] Thus, along these lines, education, for Locke, is not primarily an "imposition of biases," a communication of a culture or an introduction into a tradition, but rather a training of children to think for themselves. Teachers cannot help but write things upon the blank sheet of students' minds, but they ought to aim above all to provide children with the ability always first to erase what is given. Concretely, Schouls says, the form this teaching takes is the habitual reinforcement of the capacity to say "no."[78] The power of suspense is the expression of this spirit at the foundation of the particular acts of the will. It is just this original "no" that allows the individual "to start *de novo*,"[79] and the very point of Locke's discussion of the will, we recall, is to discover the paradigm of active power, which is the "*beginning*" of change.

THE FUNCTION OF REASON

It is crucial, however, to see that no matter how "absolute" this power may be, Locke does not at all intend to present it as "whimsical" or "arbitrary." To say that the mind determines itself does not have to mean its power is essentially indeterminate; self-determination can also be a means that allows the will to follow reason, and indeed for Locke this is its essential purpose. The point, for him, of suspending any particular desire that happens to be pressing upon us is precisely to give our minds the "liberty" to deliberate, to weigh it in comparison with other possibilities, and then to make a reasoned judgment about what is best. The emphasis on a self-determining deliberation sets Locke apart from Hobbes, at least in a certain respect.[80] Genuinely free action is action that follows upon specifically rational deliberation: "He that has a power to act or not to act, according as *such* determination directs [i.e., the mind's reasoned judgment], is a free agent: such determination abridges not that power wherein liberty consists" (2.21.51.348). The change in the nature of determination that the power of suspension brings about is therefore not so much from external to internal determination as it is from natural to rational determination.[81] Those that argue for continuity between the first and later editions of the *Essay* can point to the fact that Locke's insistence, from the beginning and all along the way, on the role of *reason* in freedom already distinguished him from Hobbes's naturalism, and they can interpret the later introduction of the power of suspension as nothing more than a working out of what this difference entails, namely, a further description of the conditions under which a choice is free.

The temporal dimension of this process is key: it allows me to take a certain distance from what is immediately present and to measure it against future pleasures and pains. Once I am, as it were, liberated from the pressures of time by the power of suspension, the only rational standard for my choices is eternity. In other words, proper choice will be made in light of eternity, that is, the pleasures and pains that await me in the life after this one as a result of the decisions I make now. It is here that God and the moral law become significant for Locke's understanding of freedom, as we saw in the earlier section, and it is what allows Locke to present an apparently "normative" interpretation, distinguishing

genuine from false freedom: "As therefore the highest perfection of intellectual nature lies in a careful and constant pursuit of true and solid
happiness; so the care of ourselves, that we mistake not imaginary for
real happiness, is the necessary foundation of our liberty" (2.21.52.348).
Thus, in line with his earlier arguments, Locke concedes that in most
immediate cases we always already prefer one thing to another, but he
points out that we are nevertheless free to direct our preferences with
respect to "remote" goods, and so change (over time) even our immediate desires: "The last inquiry, therefore, concerning the matter is,—
Whether it be in a man's power to change the pleasantness that accompanies any sort of action? And as to that, it is plain, in many cases he
can. Men may and should correct their palates, and give relish to what
either has, or they suppose has none. The relish of the mind is as various as that of the body, and like that too may be altered" (2.21.71.362).
The ideally free man, in sum, would be one who is able to allow his ultimate interests, rationally conceived, to determine his relation to any
and all immediate interests.[82]

Locke therefore clearly distinguishes his notion of freedom from
what is often called a "freedom of indifference," that is, "an indifferency
of the man; antecedent to the determination of his will" (2.21.73.367),
which means a detachment from what reason perceives as good. This is
a point on which he strongly insisted in his correspondence with Limborch, driven by a concern to avoid making freedom something
"blind," an avoidance he seems to take to be a nonnegotiable aspect of
a sound theory of liberty.[83] As Locke explains in the *Essay*, indifference
in the matter of physical capacity is *essential* to freedom: I am free to
raise my hand to my face only if I am indifferently capable of moving it
or not moving it, that is, only if there is no external or internal restraint
forcing it in a particular direction. But indifference with respect to reason is *inimical* to freedom: if there is an object moving to strike my
face, an indifference with respect to whether I lift my hand is a *want* of
freedom. To put the matter positively, freedom includes a ready capacity, and indeed a willingness, to do immediately what my reason judges
to be best. The more spontaneously I follow reason, according to
Locke, the freer I am.[84] In this respect, Locke's view of freedom is quite
close to that of Descartes.[85] It is because of the necessity of reason in
freedom that Locke can claim that there is no contradiction in saying

that God is absolutely free and saying that he is necessarily determined by what is best (2.21.50.347). Once again, it seems as if Locke's notion of freedom is essentially a classical one, which likewise affirms an indissoluble connection between freedom and reason.[86]

But there is a radical difference between Locke's view of reason and the classical conception, and this difference makes all the difference in the world in the two conceptions of freedom. We can bring this difference to light by asking whether Locke's (apparent) subordination of the power of suspension to reason in fact returns him to the danger of naturalism in the first edition's claim that the will is always determined by the highest good, a danger he had introduced that power precisely to avoid. Has Locke escaped a natural-mechanical determinism only to fall into a rational-logical determinism?[87] *If* we mean by "determinism" the idea that the will is determined *inevitably* by something *other* than itself, it seems that, even with the insistence on rational motivation, the answer remains no—though we will see shortly that this answer becomes quite paradoxical. To put the matter very simply, the ultimate reason that Locke's binding freedom to reason does not lift him beyond a view of freedom as pure self-determination "from below" is that he has an ultimately *functional* conception of reason.[88] This conception is, indeed, itself a function of the empirical method Locke is recognized as having introduced into his approach to this question.[89] Reason is no longer, as it is in the classical tradition,[90] that by which man transcends himself into the real—that is, knowledge as intimacy with the being of things (*intellectus = intus + legere*)—but rather that by which one discovers self-consistency. Locke conceives of reason as having an essentially self-referential structure. He famously defines knowledge not as a "grasp of what *is*," but as "the perception of the agreement or repugnancy of our ideas."[91] Reason is not able "to penetrate into the internal fabric and real essences of bodies" (4.12.11.350), which means that our "knowledge of our ideas terminate[s] in them and reach[es] no further" (4.4.2.227). The "essences" that people know, ultimately, are "of their own and not of nature's making" (3.6.31.82). Because reason cannot attain to an essence that lies outside of it, it does not have an intrinsic purpose—knowledge for its own sake—but only an external purpose. In other words, since knowing does not imply the achievement of intimacy with reality in any significant sense, it is "empty" in itself and can be justified only by what it *produces* beyond itself. Knowledge, for Locke, therefore has to prove its utility: "Men have reason to be well satisfied with what God hath thought fit for them, since he hath given them (as St. Peter says) πάντα πρὸς ζωὴν καὶ εὐσέβειαν, whatsoever is necessary for the conveniences of life and information of virtue; and has put within the reach of their discovery, the comfortable provision for this life, and the way that leads to a better" ("Introduction," 5.29). Man's end is not knowledge, therefore, but virtue, and "knowledge" is good insofar as it serves this end: "Our proper employment lies in those inquiries, and in that sort of knowledge which is most suited to our natural capacities, and carries in it our greatest interest, i.e., the condition of our eternal estate" (4.12.11.351). In short, reason is self-referential and therefore *essentially* a kind of tool.

To be sure, this is a very brief and broad-brushed account of the nature of reason in Locke's philosophy, which warrants a much more ample treatment in itself, but the point we wish to make in the present context is simply that, without a genuinely objective measure, such as the *truth* of reality, reason becomes identified with a process. As Vienne puts it, in Locke, the importance of the *exercise* of the understanding replaces that of its *content*.[92] This is not at all to say that reason in Locke's view is "arbitrary" or lacks a formal necessity (for example, the rules of logic); it is, rather, to point out that all of its necessity is only of the formal sort—that is, that it lacks a necessary reference to a *material* object. To put the matter concretely, even if oversimply: whereas for the classical tradition, a choice is rational to the extent that it is the knowing choice of a true good, for Locke, a choice is rational if it is the result of careful deliberation, irrespective in principle of its material content.[93] There may be an assumption that, if the process of reflection is carried out, a particular conclusion will, if not necessarily, at least likely follow, but it is above all the process, and not the conclusion, that makes the choice a rational one. A contemporary scholar justly describes the *Essay* as a sort of technology.[94] In other words, to put the point somewhat facetiously, for Locke, there is no reason *in principle* why a choice couldn't be at the very same time perfectly rational and perfectly immoral, or, for that matter, perfectly rational and perfectly stupid.[95] To be sure, as we saw earlier, Locke calls a person who acts stupidly and immorally "mad," which would seem to imply that his action does not deserve the attribute "rational." But we also need to recognize that such activity for Locke—namely, a rational choice of a bad object—is nevertheless *possible*, no matter how much it ought to be condemned.[96] We need only recall here Locke's own example of the man who prefers the taste of wine to the use of his eyes. As long as he settles on this preference after careful and dispassionate deliberation and weighing of the various alternatives, this is a choice we would have to call rational. To be sure, Locke may admit, in the *Second Treatise*, that anyone who deliberately harms others surrenders the claim to rationality, insofar as reason's natural law dictates mutual respect, but as we shall explore in chapter 2, this remains an essentially consequentialist argument concerning how a person ought to be treated; it has nothing to do with intrinsic intelligibility. An immoral or stupid choice is rational, that is, *precisely to the extent that* one sees clearly what one is choosing, with all the necessary and likely implications of one's choice, and accepts these—as we would say today, "taking full responsibility for one's actions."

Reason for Locke is thus not the classical notion of the reception of being in the soul or the conformity of the mind to reality (*adaequatio intellectus et rei*), which would imply that reason has a self-transcending form. Instead, reason is essentially self-referential: I am an intelligent and free agent to the extent that I act in full knowledge of what it is I am doing and I accept the consequences of my action.[97] *Because* of the essentially self-referential form of reason for Locke, there is no opposition in his understanding between the mind's being determined by reason and its total self-determination. This is why, in spite of this dependence of freedom on reason, we could not say that Locke falls into a rational-logical determinism in the sense that the will becomes inescapably bound to some particular object without alternatives. Locke does indeed speak of a "necessity" that the desire for happiness imposes on particular choices, namely, a necessity to suspend, discern, and weigh consequences,[98] but this is clearly a moral necessity rather than an ontological one: it represents an "ought." Even the apparent objectivity of God's judgment does not affect the mind's power of self-determination in Locke's understanding. In this context, we can see the continuity between Locke's conception of freedom and his attempt to show the inherent "reasonableness of Christianity," that is, to show how God's self-revelation *measures up*, as it were, to reason's self-determining standards.[99] It may be the case that I have no control over the content of the law or God's judgment of my actions, but I nevertheless remain perfectly free to defy these as long as I accept the consequences. Raymond Polin is in this respect at least right to say that "for Locke, . . . freedom represents a freedom for evil, the principle of *ein Urböses*, of a fundamental evil."[100]

FREEDOM AND SELF-MASTERY

We have suggested that Locke only "apparently" subordinates the power of suspension to reason, and we are now in a position to explain why. We should point out that, in this explanation, we are moving somewhat speculatively beyond the text and unfolding what are perhaps unintended implications of things Locke says. On the one hand, the point of the power of suspension is effectively to neutralize at one stroke the claim that any good may have over my mind in a given instance. It raises the mind above all goods, present and absent, transforming them, we might say, into options. This power lifts the mind above the causal chain of natural motion so that it can originate its own movement; it makes the mind an "unmoved mover," and thus allows it to move itself. To *what* does the mind move itself? The most direct and immediate answer would be to the attainment of pleasure, or more strictly speaking the elimination of a present uneasiness, which is what finally defines the good in any particular moment. But the consideration of the operation of reason opens this response up to a further dimension, insofar as it brings into view more than what is immediately present. In the broader view, the good is no longer simply what immediately gratifies; it is instead what *promises* to gratify even more greatly in the future. (Here we see the significance of Locke's characterizing the good's action on the will as a matter of potency rather than actuality, which we alluded to earlier.) But what promises to gratify most of all, beyond any possible comparison to any good enjoyed in this world, is the good of eternal reward in the "hereafter": "Since nothing of pleasure and pain in this life can bear any proportion to the endless happiness or exquisite misery of an immortal soul hereafter, actions in [a given person's] power will have their preference, not according to the transient pleasure or pain that accompanies or follows them here, but as they serve to secure that perfect durable happiness hereafter" (2.21.62.356). If the operation of reason is to deliberate, to compare options, then reason effectively functions as reason by suspending the relative claims of "this-worldly" goods. These goods, in other words, are relativized, and therefore just so far suspended in relation to, the one absolute good of eternal reward. If all goods, no matter how different in material content, share a common measure—pleasure—they can be compared to each other in quantitative terms.[101] In this case, the infinite pleasure of eternal reward *necessarily* eclipses the pleasure of any other good: "There is nothing in this World that is of any consideration in comparison with Eternity."[102] But this eschatological good is itself never realized precisely in this world, by definition, which means that, with respect to existence in history, this good is never actual as such. *It has actuality, instead, only as a possibility that always and necessarily trumps in every case any actual pleasure.* Note that it is the very same thing that makes this good absolute and makes it absent: its not being in any sense *immediately* gratifying is what makes it trump anything and everything that *would* be immediately gratifying.[103] But this means that it is present, not as an actuality itself, but only as a power—specifically, a power over other relative actualities. In short, the result of the full actuality of reason is the power that suspends every particular claim: reason, as the process of deliberation and so the measurement of particular actual goods against an absolute, *and therefore absent*, good, effectively serves the power of suspension. This statement can be interpreted as a claim that we reason precisely in order to be in control, which means we reason in order to neutralize the effective power that any particular thing might have over us. Thus, if the power to suspend is for the sake of reason, reason is in turn for the sake of the power of suspension. They both turn into each other at a basic level because they both in the end point to the same thing—*power*—which is for Locke the essence of freedom.

What we are proposing here bears a certain analogy to Max Weber's argument regarding the origin of capitalism.[104] This analogy, indeed, is not an accident: we will suggest in chapter 2 and elaborate in chapter 4 that there is an essential connection between money in the capitalist sense and the modern conception of freedom. According to Weber, the

Lutheran conception of work as vocation transforms its nature, that is, changes the precise way in which work is good. Work is no longer the cultivation of the world as something intrinsically good for the sake of an (actual) enjoyment of its fruits. Instead, it is now justified by something interpreted as *external* to it, namely, God's will. Weber suggests that, especially in Calvinism, which radicalizes the turn Luther introduces, this transcendent justification takes the immanent form of the accumulation of wealth. Accumulating wealth is a sign that one is doing God's will for two reasons simultaneously: first, since money is not in itself an actual good to be enjoyed, but rather a power for (endlessly deferred) future enjoyment, money can be a goal of activity without implying any sinful self-indulgence; second, insofar as one actually *accumulates* money, one shows that one is working diligently, responsibly, and virtuously, and at the same time that one is practicing self-denial by not squandering money on immediate desires. We are suggesting that the pursuit of eschatological happiness, that is, the putative doing of God's will, in Locke takes the immanent form of the accumulation of freedom—that is, of power, specifically, the power to suspend, which is an act of self-denial with respect to immediate gratification or, in other words, the virtuous enduring of present unease. Power is not the actual sharing in what is good, but rather the ability to detach from whatever goods happen to present themselves and to remain steadfast in one's seeking of true and lasting happiness. Self-control—that is, *freedom* of will—becomes the sign that one is doing God's will. Liberty and morality are, for Locke, virtually the same.

The power to determine oneself is most properly actualized, in other words, not in one gratification or another, but precisely *as* the power to keep oneself from being determined by any particular present good. This is what Locke means by the moral "use and exercise" of freedom. If what most basically orders the will is eschatological reward, which is precisely by definition inaccessible now and so essentially absent, the will can come to rest neither in this highest good nor in any particular present good, but *only in itself as self-determining power*. In the classical view, man's end lies essentially in knowledge.[105] In Locke, knowledge is no end, but simply a means, which is justified by its usefulness in this life, but most basically in the next: the purpose of knowledge, Locke writes in his journal, is comfort and virtue; but its "first and chiefest" purpose is how to get to heaven.[106] Virtue is most basically self-control, which means the power to determine oneself. In a nutshell, then, we are free only when we are rational, but to be rational means nothing more than to be in control of oneself (i.e., to be free). Now, we are not claiming that Locke intended this paradox or was conscious of it. Instead, we are suggesting that it is dialectically present in his conception; it appears only occasionally in a direct way, but seeing it allows one to explain the connection between the evidence of a normative aspect in his conception of freedom (i.e., his identifying of liberty and morality), on the one hand, and his equally evident emphasis on pure self-determining power, on the other. Revealingly, after explaining that the ability to suspend the determination of any particular desire (i.e., to neutralize the power that a particular desire might have over us) allows us to act with reasoned judgment, Locke says: "This is so far from being a restraint or diminution of freedom, that it is the very improvement and benefit of it; it is not an abridgment, *it is the end and use of our liberty*; and the further we are removed from such a determination, the nearer we are to misery and slavery" (2.21.49.345; emphasis added). We note here that the *end* of our liberty is described as the capacity to deliberate and make a rational decision. The end is not an actuality, in other words, but a potency, the ability to accomplish an as yet unrealized act. As we have seen, the realization is deferred until "after," which means that, in this life, the ersatz is power become an end in itself.

In his *Natural Right and History*, Leo Strauss concludes his study of Locke by describing Lockean life as the "joyless quest for joy."[107] This is in fact a paraphrase of Locke's explanation of the task of freedom given to men (at least he says as most experience it), which is "to make themselves unhappy in order to happiness" (2.21.70.362). The quest for joy is joyless because it is a pure means to an absent end, which, as pure, and so in the complete absence of the end it pursues, cannot but be made the thing itself. Denis de Rougement, in his *L'amour et l'Occident*, argues that an absolutely unrequited *eros*, set on the ever-absent transcendent God, invariably turns into the narcissism of desire, not *for* anything, but simply for desire itself.[108] We can see an analogy between this and Locke's notion of freedom: in this case, we have power instead of desire; lacking an actual end, it becomes power for the sake of power, a kind of detachment from the world so as to rise above it in mastery. According to Schouls, the "master passion," that is, the deliberate desire for happiness that governs human life, is essentially "the passion for being in control of our destiny."[109] For Locke, even our desires are meant to be under our control, as we discussed in the section on "suspense," above (see 2.21.70.362–63).

We will return to all of this, and sound out its many implications, over the course of this book, but before continuing it is important to point out one thing. Divine judgment, and thus the moral law, clearly plays a key role in Locke's thought, to such an extent that one might think Locke's doctrine of freedom is an essentially religious theory, which would thus have no appeal or influence in a secularized world. But in fact, the point is precisely that God *plays a role* in Locke's conception of freedom, that is, he serves a function: indeed, he plays a role specifically—*as absent*! As Robert Spaemann has argued, anything that is reduced to a functional significance can be replaced.[110] In the present case, we see that God has significance in Locke's theory most fundamentally *as absent*: it is the *after*-world that bears on this one, and it does so by detaching one from any and all particular things, that is, by giving to the mind the power to suspend. What is *actual*, then, is nothing but this very power to suspend *as* power; God's relevance "cashes out," so to speak, in this power. Because this power has no intrinsic relation to actuality, which it could have only if it is interpreted as participating in the transcendent good, it is intelligible already simply in relation to itself. (We recall that Locke presented power as one of the most basic *simple ideas*, ideas that do not require references to anything else in order to be intelligible.) In this case, it becomes, even in its pure instrumentality, an end in itself. When the power of freedom itself becomes the end, the question of God becomes more or less a matter of indifference.[111] It is not an accident, then, that Locke concedes that his theory of freedom is incompatible with a notion of God as omnipotent, and nevertheless is able to set this problem aside.[112] That problem, we could say, only becomes relevant for Locke in the eschaton; for now, we can simply treat the human mind as sovereign in itself: the will is the paradigm of active power, a real *beginning* of action, an unmoved mover, and so an immanent image of the omnipotent God. It is, perhaps, all we need of God in this world.

THE SELF-SUBVERSION OF POWER

It has become clear how fundamentally significant is the apparently slight change between the first and the second editions in the description of what motivates the mind to determine itself volitionally: from the highest good to the most pressing uneasiness. In classical language, a good is an actuality. To say that the will is determined by the good is to say that a *prior* actuality lies at the root of the will's potency, giving the will a primordially *receptive* structure and so giving it guidance precisely in the form of an encompassing order.[113] It is, moreover, to say that the good, even in its transcendence of the will as object of that will, is nevertheless *present* in some respect *in* the will, so that the will's potency has to be understood as a participation in the actuality of the good.[114] Locke rejects the determinative significance of the good by saying that the good is ineffectual *as absent*—or more specifically, it becomes effectual only in the will's *own* power. The positive meaning of goodness is thus deferred, and this deferral removes any traces of actuality in the will. This shift thus allows the will to be grasped as power in a relatively pure sense, and so not as receptive in any respect, but rather as a sort of "force" from below. Indeed, this is just what Locke was seeking as the sense-giving paradigm of "active power."

Now, this notion of freedom as power entails at least two fundamental problems, so fundamental as to make the notion radically self-subversive. We will end this chapter first by presenting the problems and then by showing how, from a "Lockean" perspective—that is, from the perspective of empirical positivism—the very depth of the problems is what allows them to be dismissed as irrelevant. The first one concerns the basic desire for happiness that, even for Locke, lies at the very root of the will. He states in many places that all human beings desire happiness, and even that this desire is the inclination of our nature. So far, he is reiterating the classical view. But, at the same time, as we have seen, for Locke, the will is essentially the capacity to direct itself, that is, it is a self-directing *power*. We recall that this notion of will lay behind his insistence to Limborch that the will be clearly distinguished from desire, the latter extending to things (even those over which we have no control), and the former extending only so far as our own actions. The question that arises in this context is the following:

What is the relationship between the natural desire for happiness and the activity of the will? To put the question another way: Do we choose to want to be happy? If so, do we desire to so choose? Which comes first, the desire or the volition? Locke seems to affirm both responses. On the one hand, he admits that the desire for happiness is a kind of necessity that is *imposed* on the will from without. To quote the decisive passage again here: "The constant desire of happiness, *and the constraint that it puts upon us to act for it*, nobody, I think, accounts an abridgment of liberty, or at least an abridgment of liberty to be complained of" (2.21.51.347; emphasis added). On the other hand, happiness is not given as actual, but it is something precisely *to be sought*, which in Locke's terms means it is specifically a *remote*, that is, an "absent," good. But according to Locke, a remote good does not move us as such; it "operates not on the will, nor sets us on work" (2.21.37.337). It does so only to the extent that it stirs an uneasiness in us, and *this* it does only to the extent that we deliberately recognize and *choose* it as something *we* in fact desire: "All good, ever seen and confessed to be so, does not necessarily move every particular man's desire; but only that part, or so much of it as is considered and taken to make a necessary part of *his* happiness" (2.21.44.341).[115] If the power to suspend is, indeed, universal, as we have interpreted it, it would seem to be a power even over this basic desire: it moves us *only if* we allow ourselves to be so moved, which means it is something ultimately determined by our decision. But, again, what could possibly motivate *this* decision?

We see that there is a lot at stake in this question. To desire is to be moved by something outside of the self, but the will is a self-determining power. It may be that this original desire is the *only* desire over which we have no ultimate control, as Locke seems to say in the passage we quoted above concerning the apparent constraint on freedom. But this is a desire that lies at the root of the will in all of its acts! To concede a self-transcending receptivity at the root of the will in all of its acts is to be forced to *define* it as something *other* than a self-determining power. Schouls, one of the strongest advocates of Locke's conception of freedom in its libertarian interpretation, admits that Locke's theory is basically incoherent on this point.[116] His interpretation is that "human beings are not determined to the greatest good unless they want to be so determined," though he then adds, paradoxically, that "they are under the necessity to want to be so determined."[117] As if this weren't paradoxical enough, he goes on to admit that this necessity is not that of desire (what we would call the immanent activity of a transcendent good), but specifically of *duty* (what we would call the law of an absent good), and of course we retain the *power* to refuse this obligation.[118] We cannot avoid persisting, however, with the same question: Why would we refuse this obligation—because we *want* to (by virtue of a desire that precedes choice) or because we *choose* to (by virtue of a choice that precedes desire)? In the end, what directs us to the proper good of total mastery, according to Schouls's interpretation of Locke, is a sheer act of will that would ultimately have to be understood as wholly unmotivated and therefore arbitrary. Again, Schouls himself concedes that this is basically incoherent, but he nevertheless insists that, once we allow this sheer act of unmotivated freedom at the outset, the rest makes remarkable sense. We thus subsequently have a motivation for every other act of will.[119] The problem, however, is that this is not a discrete act, which can be set aside once it has been conceded; instead, it is fundamental in the sense of lying at the ultimate basis of each successive act of the will as it is performed. In this sense, it is a problem that is properly pervasive.

Schouls is certainly right about one thing, namely, that Locke's theory is basically incoherent, but it is odd that he seems to make this a fairly minor concession, a relatively small price to pay for an otherwise remarkably coherent vision. It is odd because this "small" point concerns not just one issue among many, but it is a *basic* incoherence, which in fact radically problematizes the very essence of Locke's conception of the will—and thus, given the role of the will in achieving a concept of power, and given the centrality of power in Locke's thought, it problematizes the whole of Locke's philosophy, in all of its dimensions. Indeed, if Locke is in fact one of the founding thinkers of modernity, we have grounds to suggest that it problematizes modern thought generally. This is a suggestion we will develop in the chapters that follow. In his book *The City of Man*, Manent presents Locke as the author of the transformation in the development of the modern West by which power ceases to be human.[120] Hobbes may have been obsessed with power, but the very obsession is what, we might say, allowed it to retain a human character in his thought: there is in Hobbes a fundamental *desire* for power, which means that there is a certain connection, through desire, to the "real world," to which power always remains relative. But in Locke, even this desire—at least *apparently*—falls under the scope of power, and so enters into the reach of human control. Although this gives the resulting theory a much more tempered and rational appearance than Hobbes's, the appearance is actually deceptive: this simple difference from Hobbes makes Locke's philosophy of human nature far more radically revolutionary and epoch-making.

In spite of the profound implications of what is at stake in this question—Is the will ultimately determined by something outside of itself or is even this indispensable determination itself subordinated to the will's sovereign power?—Schouls sets it aside as marginal, a matter that should not distract us from the significance of Locke's achievement. The fact that he can dismiss it in this way turns out to be very much in the spirit of Locke himself: as we will propose shortly, the empirical perspective essentially brackets out the significance of such a fundamental question. Before we turn to this, however, it is good to note that Schouls's interpretation seems itself to be a sheer act of arbitrary will in the sense that the opposite interpretation is equally plausible, namely, that the desire for happiness is a necessity rather than a choice, and it is a necessity that operates in each of our choices. Locke insisted in the first edition of the *Essay* that a necessity determines volition: "This, then, is evident, That a *man is not at liberty to will, or not to will, anything in his power that he once conceives of*: liberty consisting in a power to act or to forbear acting, and in that only" (2.21.24.327).[121] When he subsequently revised the *Essay*, he *left* this insistence in the final text, and in a certain respect amplified it.[122] When he did at the very end seek to qualify this insistence, he nevertheless did not deny necessity in the operation of the will simply; instead, he suggested that this necessity is what governs only for the most part, insofar as we almost always make decisions in the context of immediate demands, and in this case follow what we could call automatic volitions.[123] Indeed, through his late correspondence with Limborch, Locke comes to conclude that the power of suspension does in fact allow a notion of volition as *itself* an act of freedom, but even this concession he presents as part of some notes to be added to the posthumous edition without requiring any other change to the text.[124] In the end, a basic ambiguity is never eradicated: Does the concession of exceptions change the rule generally? This leads us to the second basic problem.

The second problem is more obviously pervasive, and more commonly recognized.[125] Arguably, it is simply a further expression of the first problem we just described—as it were, the repeated horizontal instantiation of the first, "vertical" ambiguity. To put the problem in a nutshell: it is the power of suspension, as we have seen, that most decisively lifts the human mind above and beyond the chain of natural causes and allows the human being to make his choices freely. But what causes the operation of this power? What, in other words, *motivates* us to suspend the causal force of an impulse that happens to impose itself on us in every given case? Is it an uneasiness, and thus the result of some external force acting on the mind, that determines the suspension? Locke is clear that every choice we make is driven by some uneasiness, which would seem to imply that all of our volitions are produced in us by an external cause. And yet, it is just to avoid this that Locke introduced what we have called the mind's "veto power" over any, *and therefore all*, of the "desires" that solicit the mind at a given moment. The universality of this power would therefore necessarily include sovereignty over even the uneasinesses that would effect the operation of the power itself. But this of course leads to an infinite regress. Every desire that solicits the will can be trumped by the will's power to suspend, and every act of suspension is brought about by some uneasiness. Which, of course, can be trumped. But only by an act of suspension. Caused by another desire. And so on.

It is hard to believe that Locke himself would have failed to see this problem, since, as we saw at the outset of this chapter, he himself raises essentially the same objection with respect to the idea that the will can be said to be free, as opposed to what he suggested is the much more coherent restriction of freedom to the agent in his action.[126] But then, he does indeed use the expression "free will" with respect to the power to suspend, though he continues to resist allowing this expression without qualification, until, perhaps, his final revision.[127] The problem that faces Locke is the following: How is it possible to conceive the will and action in a coherent way once we have introduced a universal power of suspension as the foundation of freedom? Locke does not so much resolve the problem as set it aside. Let us consider, first, in a little more depth why this problem is inevitable, given a conception of will and freedom as power, and then why Locke is in fact able to set it aside.

We recall that Locke entered into his lengthy discussion of the will in order to show the derivation of our notion of *power*, which he defines in its active sense as the ability to produce a change. To elucidate the significance of Locke's particular understanding of power, it is useful to compare him to Aristotle on this point (we will elaborate Aristotle's view of potency and act and its significance in part 3 of this book). For the Stagirite, *dynamis*, "potency," is intelligible only in relation to *energeia*, "actuality." To speak of "capacity" or "ability" simply and in itself would make no sense;[128] one immediately demands a "to" or "for" to complete the thought, and this completion comes with the naming of some actuality: we don't simply say, without context, "I am able," but specify it through reference to an actuality: "I am able to play the piano." Moreover, though actuality generally has a reciprocal dependence on potency—except for the pure actuality of God, all other actuality is the realization of some potency—this reciprocity is asymmetrical. The *source* of whatever change is at issue is always for Aristotle an actuality, while potency represents that in and through which the change comes about. Aristotle, like Locke, does indeed distinguish an active potency from a passive potency—the active potency of my hand to write is different from the passive potency of paper to be written on[129]—but it is the dimension of actuality in the potency, so to speak, that brings about the change. According to the Scholastic axiom taken to be an interpretation of Aristotle on this point, potency can be reduced to actuality only by a being itself in a state of actuality.[130] In any given instance of change, for Aristotle, there is a relationship between potency and act that we may describe as that of an essentially differentiated unity and in which act accounts for the determination. For Locke, by contrast, potency or power is *itself* properly active, which means *it itself* is the capacity to bring about change; indeed, this is for him its essential definition.

But this way of defining power entails an extraordinary dialectic. On the one hand, power can now be separated from its intrinsic relation to actuality, and isolated as a thing in itself. We can recall that Locke presents power precisely as a simple idea (or a simple mode thereof), which means it is something that can be understood immediately, and without relation to anything else. Power is, for Locke, *not* a relative notion, essentially a part of a couplet (potency–act) that is indispensable to its own intelligibility. On the other hand, because this isolation deprives it of any reference to a particular actuality, power thus has no specificity in itself; it is strictly *formless* and so empty. In this respect, there is nothing there to understand! This means that we can *only* understand power in terms of the particular changes it brings about, which changes are in fact *other* than, external and so accidentally related to, the power in itself: "Power cannot be apprehended except in the past, once it has produced its effects, and is no longer."[131] Thus, Locke goes on to define substances as a collection of powers—the qualities inherent in things are powers to produce ideas, sensible impressions, in a subject, and it is those ideas, rather than the substances, that we know.[132] As far as we are concerned, Locke explains, things can be said to have powers *only to the extent that* they actually produce particular effects. To put the point more generally, a power is in fact nothing but the effect that it produces: "The power in any body *is nothing until it is actualized*, as the power in a bat is nothing until it hits a ball."[133] Note that what was a differentiated unity for Aristotle is separated by Locke into two isolated moments, each of which in a certain respect can claim to be the whole: power is everything as being the source of change, and it is also nothing but what is produced, which is to say that the actual effects are everything. Power thus is interpreted by Locke as a sheer effective force; it is not a communication of form, which is what the agent cause is in Aristotle and which implies a common form distributed between cause and effect, but instead an *acting on* something that is *strictly external* to the cause. It is, so to speak, purely transitive "energy." Power manifests itself as real only in the change it effects. This is, for example, why Locke does not describe the agent's *resting in a satisfaction or completion* as an act of will, as we observed in the first part of this chapter.[134] The will, as just power, is actual, that is, *real* at all, only to the extent that it brings about a change in something other than itself.

It is this notion of power that gives rise to the problem of infinite regress in the will's relation to itself. But at the very same time it is what makes the problem effectively disappear, so to speak. Power, as we have seen, is for Locke the essential quality of the will, and freedom, too, is nothing but a particular power. Locke rejects, in the first edition at least, the notion that the will is free because that would imply attributing a power to a power. But even more decisively, because a power is that which *acts on* something that is *external to it*, to say that the will wills itself would be to split the will into two separate things, external to one another, one of which *acts on* the other.[135] Once we begin to split the will thus, however, we can't stop: each will requires itself a further will outside of itself as cause. The moment we conceive of the will as effective power, the problem of infinite regress is inevitable. Locke initially terminates this regress, we saw, by denying that the will is a cause of itself, which means that there is some power outside of the will that sets it in motion. But this solution gives rise to an even more basic problem: if the will is not a cause of itself, it ceases to be itself a "beginning of motion," and it becomes instead an essentially passive transfer of power, a link in a chain of natural causes. It is clear, however, that Locke never intended to embrace such a complete naturalism.[136] He thus sought to clarify what he meant ultimately by introducing the notion of the power of suspension. But this additional dimension of the will is just that, namely, a *power*, which means that it too is an effective force that acts on what is other than itself. To the extent that one thinks of power as a univocal concept, as Locke does, the difference between powers necessarily remain differences within the same order, which means that different powers are necessarily in competition with each other.[137] It therefore follows that the introduction of a *new* power, the power to suspend, cannot possibly resolve the dilemma of the will's freedom, but only defer it. What causes the power to suspend but an act of will, and what in turn is the cause of *that* act? Power as sheer effective force means we think of causal relations precisely as a strictly linear chain of events, and any link in that chain is simultaneously a beginning and an end; it is passive and active, reducible in its effective force to what comes before it and in turn that to which what comes after can be reduced. Where we decide to start the consideration is altogether arbitrary.

But this is precisely why the problem disappears and why the dialectic can be *effectively* resolved. Note: the key word, here, is "effectively"; there is no logical resolution to the dialectic, but at the same time the dialectic nevertheless necessarily "resolves" itself in the practi-

cal order, though *only in purely pragmatic terms.* We are here arriving at
the very heart of the argument around which this book will turn. The
"source of all liberty" is the power of suspension (2.21.48.345). But the
effect of this particular power, unlike that of the will's normal exertion,
is not a positive actuality, but only the *negation* of what is already positively given. There is no introduction, as it were, of any novel content
with this power; nothing is *added* in its operation. Instead, something is
taken away. Even more specifically, no *thing* is removed: the positive
stimulus remains, but it is the status, or indeed the *effective power*, of
this stimulus that is canceled out. In this respect, the power is present,
after all, only as a kind of absence; it is either present only as a potency
that is not effectively bringing about a change (i.e., it is absent) or it
brings about a change that is the *removal* of something, namely, causal
force (i.e., it brings about an absence of what was otherwise present).

Indeed, when we realize that this power to suspend is the essence of
the will's freedom, which is the very paradigm of active power for
Locke, we see that pure power can be defined as the presence of absence,
or sheer negativity. However we formulate it, the point here is that the
power of suspension—precisely *as* power, rather than as an *act* of suspension—can perfectly coincide with any actually given natural stimulus, insofar as there is no real—that is, *effective*—difference between the
presence of an absence and the absence of an absence. To speak less
cryptically perhaps, if the power to suspend is not exercised, it has no
actual effect, which means that the greatest current uneasiness causes the
volition, so to speak, without any interference: the will is subject to natural causes. At the same time, however, it was always possible to "veto"
the stimulus that proposed itself, which means that in every case I *could
have* chosen otherwise. The very *presence* of the power, even if that
presence is without any effect *de facto,* entails an inevitable effect in
terms of the *meaning* of the volition: it makes that volition inescapably
mine, a volition for which I can always be called to answer. Though my
will is utterly passive in one respect, insofar as the uneasiness is produced in the will wholly from without, it is always the case that I *could
have* canceled the power that the stimulus exerted over me, and so the
preference that is produced in me is nevertheless my responsibility. I can
equally describe a preference as *natural,* that is, as caused in me by the
mechanical effect of an external stimulus, and as *voluntary,* that is, as an

effect that I "allowed." I am simultaneously a pure product of external causes and the unassailable master of my own fate.[138]

It is important to see that what makes this strange paradox possible is the essential *emptiness* of the notion of power that defines the will, an emptiness that arises from the severance of potency from actuality. It is just this emptiness that allows the will, as it were, to be hermeneutically laid over any particular cause without leaving any real trace. To ask what accounts for the particular acts of the power of suspension, when they do occur, is in one respect a perfectly legitimate question, and the moment we raise it we get caught in the infinite regressive series of volitions, which can be stopped, as Locke himself pointed out, only with a reference to something that is *not* the will and that acts on it from the outside, that is, a natural cause. But, practically speaking, we are nevertheless able to refer to the purely natural cause that breaks the chain of infinite regress as a voluntary cause, *not because it is the effect of an act of the will, but precisely because it is not*, insofar as the power to suspend was, even in this case, present—albeit ineffectively (i.e., it was not actualized, and so it was nothing). In this respect, there is no need to make any reference to the nonuse of the power to suspend, which renders the choice *free*, that is, a result of my own active power, in order to account for a particular volition. It seems that, if Locke does not raise the question of infinite regress with respect to the power of suspension, a problem of which he is perfectly aware in another context, as we have seen, it is because a nonevent does not need a positive cause. If no change is brought about, the power of the will has not been activated—even if it nevertheless always *could have been*. Logically, to make it an actual nonevent, to say that I have chosen in this case not to choose, just so far is to demand some cause. In the (immediate) practical order, however, the problem this represents simply does not impose itself.

It is well known that Locke was deeply influenced in his thinking by the empirical, positivistic turn in science that was occurring around him in England. We have suggested repeatedly that what is revolutionary in Locke's thinking on freedom and the will is not only the content of his particular interpretation but also, and in a sense more basically, the shift in perspective, which colors the content of all ideas, the meaning of all the terms in question. We may describe the shift as a sort of application of the positivism and pragmatism of modern science to the study of the mind.[139] One implication of this shift becomes apparent precisely in relation to the particular problem we are discussing. Roger Woolhouse remarks on the impact that Locke's meeting with the doctor Thomas Sydenham had on Locke's thinking about nature and the natural sciences, which had been Locke's primary intellectual interest until Lord Shaftesbury persuaded him to turn his attention to the political order. Sydenham dismissed efforts to understand things in theory and showed Locke that the important work of science consists, not in comprehension and explanation, but simply in the *description* of the behavior of nature.[140] This positivistic shift was reinforced by Robert Boyle, whom Locke greatly admired,[141] and whose influence on Locke's *Essay* has been shown to be more profound and pervasive than originally acknowledged.[142] According to Boyle, an investigation into ultimate causes is necessary only if one's interest in the natural world is a speculative or theoretical one. If one's interest is, by contrast, primarily pragmatic, it suffices to grasp immediate connections between things, "without ascending to the top in the series of causes."[143] *Practical* interest directs us to proximate causes and away from ultimate causes. Now, if reason is thus not ordered to the being of things, there is no intrinsic drive to get to the heart of any matter. Locke's interpretation of knowledge, as the perception of agreement between ideas, allows the mind to find complete satisfaction in the grasp of the immediate relation between two terms, without having to understand how this relation bears on the whole or how the whole bears on this relation. In other words, it allows us to abstract this relation from everything else, to bracket out the more remote relations and the larger issues they entail, and then to face these only when they happen to impose themselves in an immediate way.[144] In this respect, a *fundamental* incoherence, such as we have been describing, can be set aside as a primarily theoretical, and therefore marginal, problem, which does not need to be resolved in order for the theory to "work." This is the case insofar as the problem lies at the "top of the series of causes," as Boyle puts it. In other words, precisely because it is fundamental, it is not of immediate, practical concern. If we recall that the purpose of Locke's entire discussion of the will is not in fact in the first place to achieve insight into the nature of things, but is rather simply to account—in the manner of a "natural history"—for the origin of the "*idea* of the beginning of motion," the question of the ultimate truth of that idea fades away.[145] Locke's notion of freedom as power in a certain sense represents the paradigm of this positivistic turn specifically in the science of man, insofar as the very content of the notion is a "doing" rather than a "being": power is not a *substance*, it is a *force*. When we interpret freedom as power, one could say that a positivistic anthropology, eo ipso, *imposes itself*.

But this abstraction entails a hermeneutical dialectic. Though he is not talking about Locke specifically, and puts the matter in different terms, Hegel makes an argument about a peculiarly modern notion of the will in the introduction to his *Philosophy of Right*,[146] which is quite similar to the one we are making here, and helps to illuminate it. In sections 14 and 15 of the introduction, Hegel describes what he calls the "most common idea we have of freedom" as "arbitrariness" (*Willkür*), by which he means the purely formal relation the will has to itself: irrespective of any possible content, I am free insofar as what I do is something *I* will to do.[147] But because freedom in this case is itself without any content—what we have referred to as the sheer power to make a change—whatever determinate content the will chooses in a particular instance is related to the will as wholly foreign, wholly external. And so the pure indeterminacy of freedom coincides with what cannot but be a dependence on the determinacy of a particular material content. If form and matter are extrinsic to one another, pure arbitrariness of form can coincide with pure determinism of content: because they are absolutely unrelated, they do not exclude each other in any particular instance. If I choose something in a given case, I am combining the two: the determinate choice is both the necessary effect of an external cause and an expression of my arbitrary will, an option I can be said to have selected because I decided not to set it aside for the sake of something else, any one of the infinite other options available to me at that moment.

What Hegel says regarding the dialectic of *Willkür* can be said equally of Locke's conception of will and freedom as power. Precisely because Locke interprets power as separate from actuality, it is utterly without content: *in itself* it is nothing. Whatever content an act of will might have therefore comes to it from the outside. The notion of will as power thus bifurcates into two separate spheres that are "hermeneutically sealed" off from one another, so that they can perfectly coincide without contact, as it were: the very same event can be interpreted in terms of content, in which case we are able to account for the whole of it in terms of natural causes; or it may be interpreted in terms of its ultimate form as an expression of will, in which case it may be posited as a wholly spontaneous act—the power *to begin* an action. When I consider motivation, I think from the perspective of natural causes, but I am free at any point to think of those causes as wholly subject to my sovereign fiat: whatever it is that circumstances (necessarily) caused me to do, I always had the option of doing otherwise. However contradictory these interpretations may appear in theory, practically speaking they do not conflict as long as I can grasp the immediate connections that Lockean knowledge requires and keep the perspectives separate. In this case, the two perspectives are like the famous figures of the rabbit and the duck that displace each other in our perception of the single image as we choose a perspective and so mentally reorder all of the elements, which are equally constitutive of either figure. To switch metaphors, freedom in Locke is like Schroedinger's cat: simultaneously dead and alive.

And so we thus come to the end of our opening reflection on Locke's (re-)conception of freedom—a vision of freedom that is always a *revision*, which we will go on to suggest is the contemporary liberal notion "in a nutshell." We began by pointing to the unending controversy in interpretations of Locke between those who see him as a compatibilist, one who reconciles freedom of action with a naturalistic account of will, and those who see him as a libertarian, insisting that, no matter what the causal pressure from the outside at any given moment, the will always retains the final say over its choices, and so is ultimately master of nothing else but itself. We are not so much arguing simply for a more sophisticated kind of compatibilism, which may at first appear to be the case, as we are what may be called a "metacompatibilism," that is, the claim that both interpretations are valid in the order of praxis, even while they are logically exclusive and even self-subverting. Compatibilism and libertarianism, to the extent that they conceive of freedom essentially in terms of power not connected in an internal way with actuality, are themselves not really opposites but flip sides of the very same coin. And both are deeply problematic. The reason that each partial interpretation can justify itself, even while it collapses into the other, is that, at the very heart of Locke's conception of freedom—and therefore of power, of substance, of action, and of every other notion connected in turn with substance—is an absolute incoherence. Let us now turn to see what implications this has for his specifically *political* interpretation of freedom.

CHAPTER 2

The Political Conquest of the Good in the *Second Treatise*

Hegel observed that political order is, so to speak, the incarnation of the will: the political community is freedom made objective, actual, and real.[1] The shape of a particular community will therefore be determined by the conception of freedom to which it gives expression. If this is true, we are led to ask in the present context what Lockean political order looks like. We saw in chapter 1 that Locke's conception of freedom is shot through with a dialectical ambiguity, either because of the detachment of power from goodness or, in more strictly metaphysical language, of potency from act. But this makes our present question rather paradoxical: to put it bluntly, what can it mean to actualize what is *essentially* nonactual? What objective form can subjective nonform take? How does power become real precisely *as* power rather than simply as its effect or product?

Our intention in this chapter is to interpret Locke's political thought, as presented in his *Second Treatise*, as the social incarnation of the notion of freedom he developed in the *Essay*.[2] There is scarcely a single study of Locke's political thought that does not remark on the tension, inconsistencies, and paradoxes that seem so deeply embedded as to be inextricable.[3] As C. B. Macpherson put it succinctly, the *Second Treatise* is "full of ambiguities."[4] These ambiguities—like those in the chapter on power in the *Essay* (2:21)—are not simply the results of vague thinking or an obscurity of expression, but they seem to be more fundamental and even essential to the concepts he articulates. It is not, in fact, uncommon to observe that Locke not only tends to reverse his claims in the course of his exposition of them, but even on occasion to say in particular instances the very opposite of what he turns out, on closer inspection, to mean.[5] In a well-known study of Locke, Richard Cox has shown that this sort of (apparent) duplicity was already a problem that enraged his contemporary readers.[6] But whereas Cox himself interprets Locke in the usual "Straussian" style as attempting deliberately to conceal his real meaning to all but his most careful philosophical readers in order to avoid the persecution that inevitably falls upon radical political thinking, we wish to leave aside here any ad hominem judgments.[7] Such judgments are inevitably speculative and ultimately not very satisfying philosophically because they concern what we might characterize as subjective motivation rather than objective meaning. Our proposal here is that, regardless of Locke's own projects and intentions, the paradoxes that one regularly discovers in his thinking are due to the nature of the thoughts themselves. Let us assume that Locke is perfectly sincere in his endeavor to say what he thinks; we mean to show that it is his ideas themselves that are duplicitous. This is the case because those ideas represent an attempt to embody in the political order a notion of freedom that is inherently dialectical.[8]

We will not attempt to offer an exhaustive interpretation of the *Second Treatise*; our larger aim, after all, is not a study of Locke for his own sake, but rather an exploration of the meaning of modern freedom as it comes to a certain perfection of expression in Locke—similar to the way in which tragedy, according to Aristotle, attained its natural form in Aeschylus and Sophocles.[9] Our aim is to think through the principles of political order as Locke presents them, in relation to the view of the will we outlined in chapter 1. We will pursue this aim by focusing our investigation on a few representative notions—freedom, nature, war, property, consent, and authority—attempting to present what these mean and how they relate to one another in Locke's overall political vision.

FREEDOM, LAW, AND ORDER IN NATURE

In what is in some editions the opening sentence of the *Second Treatise*,[10] Locke describes the state of nature—man's original condition—

as a "State of perfect freedom." Freedom is in effect the very first characteristic he ascribes to man, and it is, moreover, just this original power from which political power is ultimately derived. We will not understand the political order correctly, as Locke sees it, unless we first understand what Locke means by nature and the freedom that essentially constitutes it.

Though the state of nature consists of perfect freedom, it is not anarchic; Locke interprets freedom *from the very first* as connected in a basic way with *law*. The connection between freedom and law may be the distinguishing feature of Locke's conception of political order, and so our first task is to ask after the precise nature of specifically political freedom and the relationship it bears to law. It turns out that the second part of this task is easier to accomplish than the first. Locke does not in fact define freedom in this *Treatise*, in spite of its evidently central role in the text; instead, he simply describes, so to speak, "how it works." But this is already significant and accords with what we saw in our chapter 1: freedom as power without an intrinsic relation to actuality cannot be defined in itself, strictly speaking, or perhaps we can say that it is defined by a nondefinability, insofar as the power, so conceived, is of its very essence the absence of internal form. We are therefore able to define only the parameters of its exercise. The closest Locke comes to a definition of freedom in this *Treatise* is in fact here in the opening sentence, and what he offers is just this sort of a delineation of the field of its proper use: men's original state is "a State of perfect Freedom to order their Actions, and dispose of their Possessions, and Persons as they think fit, within the bounds of the Law of Nature, without asking leave, or depending on the Will of any other Man" (2.4). Definition, as we see it here, is not a matter of articulating an internal order but rather of marking the outside border, so to speak, of the limit to which freedom extends, and therefore by the same token where it comes to an end. In this respect, it matters little whether we think of Locke's conception of freedom as most basically positive or negative.[11] The border marking the proper scope of freedom is also a boundary, which in addition to limiting its use at the same time protects it from outside interference.

The principal threat to freedom that Locke identifies here is precisely the *will* of another man. This too makes sense, given what we saw in chapter 1: if freedom is active power, what comes strictly into competition with it is in the end only that which cannot be made in some sense a function of this power, and that is most directly another power, which is itself active: "The *Natural Liberty* of Man is to be free from any Superior Power on Earth, and not to be under the Will or Legislative Authority of Man, but to have only the Law of Nature for his Rule," which means that in political society freedom is "A Liberty to follow my own Will in all things, where the Rule prescribes not; and not to be subject to the inconstant, uncertain, unknown, Arbitrary Will of another Man" (4.22). There is no essential authority over man but law, which, as we will argue further on, is not an *active* power, but a passive one.

For now, we need only see that, because freedom is defined by boundaries, its connection with law is *immediate*, since law just *is* the setting of boundaries in the order of human action. We might say that law and freedom are simply flip sides of the same political phenomenon for Locke: law is the outside of freedom, and freedom is what lies inside of law. The basic public articulation of freedom will thus turn out to be the enclosure of space, whether that be in the literal sense of designating property or in the broader sense of the determination of rights, which we could think of as the enclosure of political space. Locke describes freedom as a "Fence,"[12] and says that the function of law is "to determine the Rights, and fence the Properties of those that live under it" (11.136). This is essentially the structuring of freedom, without which freedom in the public order would not exist: "For in all the states of created beings capable of Laws, *where there is no Law, there is no Freedom. For Liberty* is to be free from restraint and violence from others which cannot be, where there is no Law" (6.57).[13] It is, incidentally, this conception of freedom that would make property, as we shall see, a kind of paradigm of political rights,[14] so that Locke can use the term "property," as scholars regularly observe, in a broad sense to cover even the person and his nonmaterial goods.[15] This conception of freedom moreover explains why Locke would describe the purpose of civil society precisely as the preservation of property.[16] From the perspective we have just articulated, this is another way of saying that political order is the actualization of freedom. We will come back to these issues in due course.

The essential connection between freedom and law in Locke is why Locke is able to present the state of nature, in stark contrast to Hobbes, initially as a *peaceful order*. Hobbes, of course, likewise affirms a law of nature that governs man from the beginning, but his law appears to be much more "naturalistic" than that of Locke, more directly analogous to the laws of physics and biology than to law in the political sense.[17] To simplify, Hobbes's fundamental natural law is in fact a natural *right*, namely, to self-preservation, and this right is *prior* to, and the ultimate *source* of, law in the normative sense. Hobbes does indeed acknowledge the fundamental importance of other-regarding activities, such as cooperation and compromise, but these activities for Hobbes are functions, in a straightforward manner, of self-preservation, which represents an absolute given. Man has a right to anything necessary to preserve himself, and so a right in principle to *everything* (including other people),[18] but this right, as multiplied, cannot help but undermine itself because of the self-destroying hostility it inevitably generates in its "raw" form. My claim on others, which is indeed a claim even *to* them, is the flip side of a vulnerability to their claim on (and to) me. Precisely in order to avoid that claim, I have to limit my own. Thus, the right itself, by its own logic, produces the constraint of law. Nevertheless, right and law for Hobbes are perfect opposites: "Law, and Right, differ as much, as Obligation, and Liberty; which in one and the same matter are inconsistent."[19]

For Locke, by contrast, law seems to come before right and provide its basis.[20] Self-preservation, indeed, "is a *duty* rather than a right."[21] Moreover, the law of nature that stands at the origin, prior to any civil compromises or agreement, is not mere self-preservation, but it is "larger" than that, we might say; it comprises the duty to preserve *mankind*, first in myself, but *also* in others:

> Every one as he is *bound to preserve himself*, and not to quit his Station wilfully; so by the like reason when his own Preservation comes not in competition, ought he, as much as he can, *to preserve the rest of Mankind*, and may not unless it be to do Justice on an Offender, take away, or impair the life, or what tends to the Preservation of the Life, the Liberty, Health, Limb or Goods of another. (2.6)

There is, therefore, from the beginning, a positive obligation in Locke's state of nature—individuals need not only to preserve themselves, but at the same time to preserve others, whenever others' preservation does not come into conflict with their own. We ought to note, however, that this obligation is "positive" only in a qualified sense: it is not an obligation to help promote the flourishing of others,[22] but rather the obligation to keep from hindering others in the pursuit of their own well-being.[23] Locke is quite clear about what grounds this obligation: we have a duty to preserve ourselves and others because man was created by God;[24] we do not belong first to ourselves but rather first to God. It is, as we shall discuss in a moment, *labor* that creates ownership. Because we are God's "workmanship," we are therefore God's "Property" (2.6). Though he qualifies this assertion later in his interpretation of labor, he says here that we are ultimately not our own for the simple reason that we did not make ourselves. Whatever rights we have, therefore, we have within the limits of the obligation to God and to others in God. Locke thinks through the nature of political community on the basis of the state of nature, to be sure, but it is not nature as a "naturalistic" given; instead, Locke presents nature from the beginning specifically as God's creation (even if he makes the meaning of this status essentially accessible to natural reason without a necessary reference to God).[25]

The second quality that Locke ascribes to man in this original state is *equality*. In positing this radical equality, Locke is in agreement with Hobbes; but whereas Hobbes interprets equality most basically in terms of *right*, which means each has an equal claim to the same resources and so is necessarily in a state of competition, that is, hostility, with others, Locke interprets equality most basically in terms of *law*. Thus, for Locke, equality means first of all that "all the Power and Jurisdiction is reciprocal, no one having more than another" (2.4). While Hobbes recognizes no authority in the state of nature as such, which means that there is no original law and therefore no distinction between the just and unjust,[26] Locke is able to affirm the priority of natural law even in the original state by presenting *each individual* as an *authority that is equal to all the others*. Each has, by nature, the power to execute the law of nature, which means that justice has a root in nature that precedes, and will provide the foundation for, the agreement that constitutes civil society. Justice is not, in other words, a "reality" that comes into being only *with* civil society, as it does for Hobbes, and as such only what we call today a "social construct." The original reality of justice in Locke's state of nature means that this is first and most basically a state of peace.

Finally, the freedom and equality that Locke sees as constitutive of the state of nature have implications for his particular interpretation of the original status of *property*. Once again, though Locke and Hobbes agree in denying private property in the initial state of nature, they are directly opposed to each other in their interpretation of what this means. As James Tully has shown in considerable historical detail,[27] private ownership for Locke is not natural, but conventional, which is to say that it is not an original "given," but instead that it comes about through man's action, even if it emerges prior to the existence of political community *as such*. The original condition is a state of *common property* or, more strictly speaking, common availability for use. Locke bases his view on both reason, which recognizes this common availability for use as a correlate of the universal right to self-preservation, and revelation, which teaches that God "has given the Earth to the Children of Men, given it to Mankind in common" (5.25). Locke interprets God's gift of the world to Adam, not as the establishment of exclusive rights to private property, which Adam subsequently bequeathed to his children, and from thence to subsequent generations,[28] but rather as a gift to man *simply*. Here we see a concrete expression of the "universalism" we noted above in Locke's conception of natural law. Each person has a right to *use* what nevertheless belongs to no one in particular but is rather available equally to all. As we will show in more detail later, this original condition will remain decisive for the meaning of property when it eventually comes about. Thus, as Tully puts it, for Locke, "the question of property must be answered within a context of positive duties to others."[29] This entails a certain *telos* in one's use: things are not subject to the whims of private owners, to be used—or abused—as they wish, but ought to be used in a manner that benefits humanity, first in myself but then also in others. Use must therefore be *justified*. In Locke's words, "The same Law of Nature, that does by this means give us Property, does also *bound* that *Property* too" (5.31). For Hobbes, by contrast, there is no *private* property in the state of nature, not because the world *belongs* to no one, as in Locke, but because it *belongs* equally to everyone. We might say that Hobbes's state of nature is characterized specifically by the oxymoron "common property," which creates an essentially tragic condition in which the world belongs in an exclusive way ("property") to each and every person ("common"): the world is simultaneously exclusively yours and exclusively mine, and this is a contradiction that necessarily entails war. By contrast, because natural *law* is primary for Locke rather than natural *right*, this means that the world is there most basically for all of us to share in a respectful way.[30]

The difference between Locke and Hobbes seems as clear as can be. Both emphasize as foundational for their political theory the absolute equality of all individuals as their starting point, though for Hobbes this means the "warre of every man against every man," while for Locke it implies mutual respect, and—why not?—even support. In chapter 1, we saw Locke's insistence on the necessity of reason for the proper use of freedom. If Hobbes notoriously makes reason the servant of the passions as their "scout and spy," Locke affirms the traditional aim of subordinating the passions to reason (even if, as we showed, he interprets this in a nontraditional way). The status that reason has for Locke in relation to passion corresponds politically to the status of law with respect to freedom. Locke takes reason and law to be a natural norm: we all wish most basically to live peaceably with others, because we recognize that this is a condition for our own pursuit of happiness. Locke makes peace and order fundamental, and he speaks in his opening pages of the "Obligation to mutual love amongst Men," which forms the basis of justice and charity. In this respect, Locke's conception of the state of nature seems much closer to Rousseau's idyll than to Hobbes's state of war. To be sure, Locke does make reference, even in this earliest state, to the power that each man has to punish anyone who might violate natural justice, but this power does not necessarily need to be used: it simply stands at this point as an entailment of the *law* of nature, qua law. The most natural reality is the law itself, which marks out the limit of each man's free action precisely so that each can carry out that action without worry about the transgressions of others. The more surely we *know* this law, the more genuinely free we become (6.59). To say it again, because there is natural law, there is natural justice, and therefore what appears most basic for human nature is the peace of order.

By presenting such a clear contrast to Hobbes,[31] Locke may be offering an attractive picture of the state of nature, but he loses what must be acknowledged as a logical strength of Hobbes's view: in Hobbes, man has every reason to leave the state of nature and become part of civil society. The very attractiveness of the state of nature in Locke weakens the attractiveness of civil society. If the natural condition is one of perfect freedom, peace, and harmony, what could there ever be to entice one to leave it behind? To make the emergence of civil society intelligible, Locke is required to darken the picture of nature. But it becomes clear that, to do so, he does not have to add anything to what he has already presented; instead, he only has to think through more deeply, and perhaps more "realistically," the implications of his fundamental principles.

The State of War as the *Actual* Form of Nature

In order to explain the transition from the state of nature to civil society, Locke follows his sketch of the state of nature with that of the state of war, which he presents as the very opposite of man's original condition. In contrast to those who might identify these, Locke insists that there is a "plain *difference*" between them (3.18). Nevertheless, however distant these two states may be from one another, it turns out that the transition from order to chaos occurs essentially in the blink of an eye. When it does, a path opens up directly into civil society, which Locke presents as, so to speak, the natural remedy for the "inconveniences" brought about by the state of war. Our aim, in this section, is to ask why the collapse of man's natural condition into war is inevitable.

Locke defines the distinction between the state of nature and the state of war thus: "*Want of a common Judge with Authority, puts all Men in a State of Nature: Force without Right, upon a Man's Person, makes a State of War*, both where there is, and is not, a common Judge" (3.19). Both states lack an authority that transcends individuals in their relations to one another, but in the state of nature the individuals avoid harming one another, while in the state of war, there is, if not actual harm, at least the intent to harm. Note that the difference is not that of a positive relation between individuals and a negative relation between individuals. There is no relationship referenced in the description of the natural condition (we will discuss Locke's view of familial relationships in the section on "Consent as a Transfer of Power" below). We know from the previous section that those living in the natural state are governed by the law of nature, which commands mutual respect, but we also saw that the law does not relate individuals to one another in an intrinsic and positive way; instead, it keeps them respect-fully apart. War is when the proper distance between individuals is transgressed.

What sort of action constitutes a transgression? Much of the lan-guage in this section of the *Second Treatise*, as one would expect, is the dramatic language of life and death, but it turns out that the instigation of war can have a surprisingly trivial cause. The transgression does not have to be life-threatening to justify killing the intruder in response; the simple attempt to take "my Horse or Coat" (3.19) suffices, if I do not have the actual protection of the law regulated by a recognized author-ity. Note that there is a certain progression in Locke's description of what instigates war: first, he speaks of the loss of the self (the threat of destruction, 3.16); then, the loss of one's freedom (the threat of enslave-ment, 3.17); then, the loss of property (theft, 3.18); then, a general refer-ence to "injury done" (3.20); and finally Locke concludes the whole section by saying that "every the least difference is apt to end" in war (3.21). How can it be that the "least difference" between individuals tends to precipitate war and so overturn the order that Locke had said was fundamental? Why should peace be so fragile? According to Locke, war is essentially inevitable in the state of nature because each individual is judge and executioner of the law of nature in that state, and judgment will almost certainly be biased by the self-love, the desire for self-preservation, that he insists is the strongest of all passions.[32] A person who is willing to transgress the rights of others, Locke explains, can hardly be expected to be willing to hold himself accountable for that transgression.[33] But then who holds him accountable, if not himself, if all in nature are equal? The evident answer is the injured party, "the damnified Person" (2.11), though of course he himself does not hold the scale of justice in his hand with a blindfold on. It is, indeed, difficult to distinguish in these circumstances between justice and revenge. But Locke in fact renders the distinction, even if it could be made, effectively irrelevant by making every act of revenge ipso facto an act of justice—even though this equally justifies taking revenge in retaliation.

As surprising as this move certainly is, there is an evident logic to it given Locke's understanding of the state of nature. It is worth quoting Locke at length on this point. According to Locke, any encroachment at all on my freedom not only *may* be interpreted as a willingness to kill me, but in fact *ought to* be so interpreted:

> This makes it Lawful for a Man to *kill a Thief*, who has not in the least hurt him, nor declared any design upon his Life, any farther then by the use of Force, so to get him in his Power, as to take away his Money, or what he pleases from him: because using force, where he has no Right, to get me into his Power, let his pretence be what it will, I have no reason to suppose that he, who would *take away my Liberty*, would not when he had me in his Power, take away every thing else. (3.18)

Indeed, it ought to be taken not only as a willingness to kill *me*, but in fact a willingness to kill *anyone*:

> And thus it is, that every Man in the State of Nature, has a Power to kill a Murderer, both to deter others from doing the like Injury, which no Reparation can compensate, by the Example of the punishment that attends it from every body, and also *to secure* Men from the attempts of a Criminal, who having renounced Reason, the common Rule and Measure, God hath given to Mankind, hath by the unjust Violence and Slaughter he hath committed upon one, declared War against all Mankind, and therefore may be destroyed as a *Lyon* or a *Tyger*, one of those wild Savage Beasts, with Whom Men can have no Society or Security. (2.11)

If we connect the dots,[34] we come to a conclusion that is as extreme that can be imagined: the slightest injury to me—indeed, the *perceived* injury, or even further, the perception of the very possibility of an injury to me—ought to be taken to be a crime against humanity, punishable by death:

> One may destroy a Man who makes War upon him, or has discovered an Enmity to his being, for the same Reason, that he may kill a *Wolf* or a *Lyon*; because such Men are not under the ties of the Common Law of Reason, have no other Rule, but that of Force and Violence, and so may be treated as Beasts of Prey, those dangerous

and noxious Creatures, that will be sure to destroy him, whenever he falls into their Power. (3.16)

To make this significance even more extreme, we need only add that any attempt to enforce this justice will of course be perceived by the other as a threat to his freedom and so is equally a crime against humanity punishable by death. Not only do we lose a distinction between revenge and justice, we also lose a distinction between justice and simple crime. Justice and injustice are *effectively* the same thing in the state of nature in which there is no common authority.[35] However different Locke is from Hobbes in principle, he begins to appear quite close to him in fact.

Now, it is clear that Locke himself is not, in these passages, attempting to make a positive argument on behalf of a conclusion that is patently absurd, though it is admittedly disturbing that he makes no effort to draw any lines or even to insist on the necessity that transgression concern some grave matter. To the contrary, he seems more intent on emphasizing its triviality.[36] Moreover, though he does not dwell on the implications, he seems aware of the chaos his argument implies. He raises just this point as an evident objection to his position, which he in fact acknowledges to be the function of what he offers as a "strange Doctrine."[37] Surprisingly, perhaps, he says not a word to contest the charge that "nothing but Confusion and Disorder will follow" from what he has presented (2.13). Instead of attempting to defend the principles he previously established as an argument for a *natural* foundation for order, he simply dismisses the problem because the remedy of "civil society" is ready to hand, and presumably sufficient: "I easily grant, that *Civil Government* is the proper Remedy for the Inconveniences of the State of Nature, which must certainly be Great, where Men be Judges in their own Case" (2.13).[38] We therefore end up in a situation scarcely different from Hobbes: a state of nature as total war, which therefore necessarily gives rise to the social contract. The difference is that, while total war is caused in Hobbes by unrestrained greed, ironically in Locke the case may be said to be just the opposite: it is man's natural law-abidingness, the desire to restrain (the other), that unleashes violence. These turn out to be flip sides of the same coin: one side is the Hobbesian "I want," the other is the Lockean "You shall not have," and neither of these has any *objective*, individual-transcending, limit.

Before we turn to consider what sort of remedy civil society pro-vides, we ought to dig a little deeper into what presumably lies behind these extreme conclusions. Perhaps the least plausible point made in the foregoing is Locke's claim that the slightest transgression of my freedom ought to be interpreted as a willingness to kill me (and anyone else). This claim, surprising in itself, is downright shocking when we recognize that it comes just a couple of pages after Locke's statement of the law of nature as the *obligation to preserve* mankind because we were all created by God, a law that is universally accessible to reason, and indeed even more obvious, Locke says, than any civil law insti-tuted by man. It is "writ in the Hearts of all Mankind," which would seem to imply that harming others is a betrayal of our own hearts. One would expect man's *first* instinct therefore to be to give benefit of the doubt and to avoid a "guilty until proven innocent" verdict. The law of nature, after all, states that man is not permitted to harm others in prin-ciple (2.6), and if natural justice demands punishment in a particular case, it also strictly limits its extent (2.12). But the moment the slightest difference between people rears its head, we might say, suddenly all hell breaks loose. What enables such an apparent inconsistency?

There are at least three aspects of Locke's view of the state of na-ture that explain the radical reversal, and each one of them concerns in a different way the primacy of potency or power over actuality: (1) the status of reason (see "Potential Reason" below); (2) the nature of legal order (see "Impotence of Law" below); and (3) the character of equal-ity (see "Equality as Unrealizable Possibility" below).

Potential Reason

The first is Locke's notion of *reason* as it exists in the state of nature. Locke refers to the law of nature as the "law of Reason," and we note that he means this genitive in both the subjective and the objective sense. In one respect, the law of nature *is* reason: "The *State of Nature* has a Law of Nature to govern it, which obliges every one: And Reason, which is that Law, teaches all Mankind" (2.7). What Locke seems to mean by this is that the law of nature—not to harm others in the case of no competition—is perfectly self-evident; it appears to derive, for him, in an immediate and automatic way from the original condition of absolute equality. In another respect, the law of nature is universally accessible to reason. As Locke explains, the existence of this law is "as intelligible and plain to a rational Creature, and a Studier of that Law, as the positive Laws of Common-wealths, nay possibly plainer" (2.12). These two descriptions—namely, reason as the instrument by which the law is discovered and reason as the law itself—may be said to converge to the extent that the law of nature is interpreted in a purely formal sense, indifferent in principle to any possible material content. Interpreted thus, the law of nature amounts to simple self-consistency (much like the categorical imperative, for example, in Kant's thought): I have the right not to be encroached upon by others because of our original equality, but to encroach on another is to deny just that equality that grounds my own right. In this sense, the law of nature shows itself to be nothing but the practical instantiation of Locke's definition of knowledge generally, namely, the agreement of ideas among themselves. What distinguishes what we might call Locke's "first principle of practical reason" from the classical one, which states that "good is to be done and pursued, and evil is to be avoided,"[39] is that Locke's principle makes no reference to the good, and the concrete actuality that goodness implies.

Now, it is reasoning itself that makes the law of nature *evident* and therefore allows it to be *binding* in fact. We are obliged by the law of nature because we are rational creatures. But in what sense and to what extent are human beings *actually* rational creatures, according to Locke? Macpherson has highlighted a fundamental ambiguity in Locke with respect to this question: Locke appears both to insist on the universality of reason in man and at the same time on the rarity of reason among men.[40] Our discussion of Locke from chapter 1 explains quite clearly why there would be such an ambiguity. Reason, as Locke understands it, is not in the first place an actuality, but a power, a power that is most originally empty of content.[41] To put it in Locke's language, there are no innate ideas. Reason, for Locke, is not what it most basically is for the classical tradition, namely, the *presence* of truth in us, but it is rather the *power* to achieve truth, or more precisely, the power to achieve a claim to truth (which may or may not be justified or even verifiable). Prior to this achievement, reason is simply an empty power—a "white paper, void of all characters" (*Essay*, 2.1.2.121)—and, as a power that is not yet actual, it is so far not real. A recognition of this ambiguity, incidentally, enables us to resolve the debate between John Passmore and Schouls over the question whether Locke's denial of innate ideas, with its corresponding exclusion of the knowability of intrinsic essences, entails a denial of any universal human nature:[42] we can affirm a "nature" precisely as a (contentless) *capacity* to reason, which both posits something *real* about human nature and does not posit anything real. Locke may affirm with consistency that all men are rational even if there is little positive evidence of that fact. Man is not born rational, but born *to* rationality, a condition that must be achieved (6.61); the law of nature that is a basic expression of reason in the practical order is not simply given in an actual way, we might say, but is only *potentially* there from the beginning: "for no Body can be under a Law, which is not promulgated to him; and this Law being promulgated or made known by Reason only, he that is not come to the Use of his Reason, cannot be said to be *under this Law*" (6.57).

It may seem that Locke thinks any otherwise unhindered person grown beyond adolescence would have achieved rationality and so would be expected to live within the confines of the law of nature, but the matter is in fact not so simple. In the first place, Locke says that the law is evident to one who has *studied* it, which implies that it is known only to those who have given it focused and sustained attention.[43] A far deeper problem, however, is that, even if the law is *known*, there is no guarantee that it will be "justly" interpreted and effectively enforced—the word is in quotation marks, here, because it is not clear how justice can in fact exist in reality in Locke's state of nature.[44] Where each individual is an absolute authority, one man's justice will always be another man's injustice, and, without any common measure, we have no way of determining who is correct.[45] Indeed, Locke seems to think that not only is there no guarantee of justice, but we ought rather to presume the bias of individuals' judgment.

It is important to recognize that Locke's assessment is not due (simply) to a pessimism regarding the general moral condition of mankind, but more basically to the logic of his view of human nature. To conceive reason most fundamentally as a power without any intrinsic relation to actuality is to give the *power* of individual judgment priority over the actuality of truth, and so inescapably to make the exercise of that power the ne plus ultra measure and authority.[46] To put the matter in plain English, we can never get outside of our own heads, and so we cannot help, no matter how pure our intentions, seeing things from our own perspective. (This inability, of course, will *tend* to make us egocentric and self-preoccupied, but what is at issue here is not in the first place a moral judgment.) We are inescapably logically self-referential no matter how much we might wish it otherwise. What all of this means is that there is no contradiction between Locke insisting on a clear and principled line of distinction between the state of nature and the state of war—"*Want of a common Judge with Authority, puts all Men in a State of Nature: Force without Right, upon a Man's Person, makes a State of War*, both where there is, and is not, a common Judge" (3.19)—and at the same time rendering the distinction altogether meaningless *in reality*. Without a common measure, it is not possible in fact to determine whether force is used with or without right. The distinction turns on what exists as a *potentia*, and, because power is for Locke intrinsically indeterminate, it can exist in this manner without ever having any significant implications for the way people live in the world. Locke, in spite of having insisted so clearly on the law of nature and its importance for understanding the relationships among human beings, does not hesitate to present it as impotent in its natural state:

> For the Law of Nature being unwritten, and so no where to be found but in the minds of Men, they who through Passion or Interest shall mis-cite, or misapply it, cannot so easily be convinced of their mistake where there is no establish'd Judge: And so it serves not, as it ought, to determine the Rights, and fence the Properties of those that live under it, especially where every one is Judge, Interpreter, and Executioner of it too, and that in his own Case. (11.136)

The law exists, but "only in the minds of Men," and so it "*serves not*" to do what it is meant to do. In sum, Locke gives three succinct reasons that the natural law is simply ineffectual in nature: first, men tend to be biased and ignorant; second, in judging and executing law, they tend to be moved by passion and revenge in their own case and negligent in others'; and, third, even if a correct judgment is made, there tends to be no overarching power to enforce it (9.124–26).[47]

The Impotence of Law

The second aspect of Locke's view is closely related to the first. Locke presents the obligations that individuals have toward each other, not in the metaphysical terms of the good, but in the juridical terms of law. As we saw in chapter 1, goodness indicates an actuality that therefore bears on me prior to, and as a condition for, my moving of myself in pursuit of it. In simple terms, I choose a good because it attracts me.[48] Natural law in the classical tradition is understood as an expression in the moral and legal sphere of natural teleology, the ordering to the good that is, so to speak, built into the very being of things. This is the classical conception of nature. It implies the notion of a "proper place": things "fit in" to a larger, concrete whole, which is an extraordinarily complexly textured fabric of ontological exchange. Things need each other and are needed in turn, usually in nonlinear sorts of ways. To speak of the good is necessarily (as we will elaborate in just a moment) to speak of order, and therefore of hierarchy.[49] But none of this forms the backdrop of Locke's notion of natural law. This is why it is not innate in the sense of being actually present, from the beginning, in all things. Instead, to borrow Kant's terminology, the law of nature for Locke is *regulative* rather than *constitutive*. It is, in other words, an extrinsic order, a limit on behavior *to which* persons must conform. The law of nature "hedges us in" from the outside rather than guiding us internally toward fulfillment.[50] This is why Locke does not use the language of flourishing or human excellence when speaking about the law. For him, instead, if free and intelligent "Agents" could "be happier without it, the Law, as an useful thing would of itself vanish" (6.57). Such a claim about the law of nature would simply make no sense to Plato, Aristotle, or Aquinas.[51]

As an order that is imposed externally, rather than, as it were, unfolded from the intrinsic intelligibility of agents, Locke's law presupposes that what falls under the law, as that onto which order is imposed, is in itself without order. It would be lawless if not for the extrinsic limitation. *Inside* of this limitation, Locke admits that freedom is "uncontroleable" (2.6). As we discussed in the beginning of the chapter, Locke is well known for presenting law—in contrast to Hobbes—as indispensable to true liberty. There can be no freedom without law, for

Locke, but this is *not* because freedom is of itself a kind of order.[52] Instead, freedom requires law for the very opposite reason, namely, because it is disordered, or at least "an-archic," in itself. In other words, law is not, for Locke, an explicit codification of an implicit order, which brings that internal order to a certain completion, but is rather prescribed to what is inherently lawless from the outside. The connection between liberty and law, however necessary, remains extrinsic. The reason I need to affirm a limit to my field of action is not first of all because limit is itself freedom, but rather because it is an unavoidable implication of restraining the action of others in my regard. The fence that I build to keep you out ends up also keeping me in. One of the implications of this point—though it certainly appears to lie beyond what Locke himself had in mind—is a vulnerability to what is often today called the "nanny state": if freedom is formless in itself, there can be no freedom without external regulation, but the very intrinsic limitlessness of freedom means that there is likewise no principle of constraint for regulation; the law, and the governmental machinery needed to prop it up, can intrude as deeply as deemed necessary into the lives of individuals *precisely in the name of freedom* (indeed, even in the name of privacy).[53] In chapter 1, we saw that Locke's conception of freedom as pure spontaneous power is perfectly compatible with the necessary imposition of external determination.[54] Though this threat would seem on the surface to run counter to Locke's view of civil society as formed precisely for the sake of preserving private property and *therefore*, one would presume, preserving privacy simply, it turns out, as we will presently show, that the logic of Locke's position points inexorably in this direction.

However this may be in the end, there is a more immediate implication that bears directly on our current discussion. We noted above the harshness of Locke's apparent "guilty until proven innocent" verdict: the reflection on law as the external imposition of order offers a reason for it. If external imposition is the origin of order, when it is absent then a condition of disorder would be the only logical presumption. As Locke put it, if a person disregards the law in any particular case "there is no reason to suppose" in fact any restraint on his action in my regard, that is, no reason to suppose any kind of order. In other words, if order is conformity to a limit, judgments about the existence of order become an either–or proposition: a limit is a boundary, a dividing line, and one is either on one side of the line or on the other. There is what we might call a subtle, legal version of the theological doctrine of "total depravity" here: underneath the show of respect for boundaries, every person is in reality a scofflaw; whoever does not *actually* prove himself to be in conformity to the law must be considered to be utterly lacking in self-restraint. According to Locke, if a person crosses the dividing line in any instance, it reveals that the limitation the line would imply simply does not exist for that person. But the one who fails to obey the law of nature does not live according to reason.

What are the implications of not living according to reason? One forfeits a claim to the title of human being. One becomes a "Beast of Prey," which necessarily poses a threat to humanity generally (3.16). To disobey the law of nature, which commands mutual respect, is, in short, to surrender one's own claim to the protection that this law promises. The ground of the obligation that this law entails turns out therefore to be remarkably thin. Indeed, it is *in reality* altogether nonexistent once we realize that, in the state of nature and the absolutized individualism this state implies, the forfeiture of the protection of the natural law does not require an actual transgression; even the perceived threat of a possible transgression suffices, and I am accountable to no one but myself in making that judgment. Indeed, in the given circumstances, it seems logical to conclude that, even if I am reluctant to judge others as a threat to myself, I ought nevertheless to assume the absence of such a reluctance in others with respect to me. In this case, they become willy-nilly a threat to my safety, since I am basically vulnerable to their preemptive retaliation for the potential transgression they perceive in me.

It is in this sense that Locke famously advocates what is called "ordered liberty":[55] the law of nature is what provides the regulation. As we have seen, however, Locke can affirm this law with as much clarity and insistence as one might wish, but it remains in itself a pure potency, which may perfectly coincide with its being utterly ineffectual in reality. This point is crucial in order to avoid falling into the Straussian position that has invited so much criticism, namely, the argument that Locke is just pretending to affirm natural law in its traditional sense in order to sneak Hobbes past his readers.[56] Locke was in fact personally critical of the narrow egoism associated with Hobbes, as he observed in his journal, "An Hobbist, with his principle of self-preservation, whereof himself is to be judge, will not easily admit a great many plain duties of morality."[57] Our interpretation, instead, allows at least the possibility that Locke fully intended to affirm natural law as fundamental, even as absolute, and that he interpreted this law not simply in the "raw" sense as the desire for self-preservation but in the more genuinely "just" sense as an obligation to preserve all human beings as far as possible.[58] But this is in itself never anything more than a possibility, as we have seen, and depends on external and contingent factors to give it *actual* significance. *In* nature, it remains a law that is unwritten, unknown, unjudgeable, and unenforceable. Having rendered the positive law of nature effectively impotent frees Locke in principle to affirm its traditional character all the more forcefully and to cite "the judicious Hooker" at length in support, without compromising the nontraditional contract theory of society he intends to propose.[59]

Equality as Unrealizable Possibility

The third aspect is the most basic, and perhaps the most abstract. Locke described the state of nature as a state of *equality* (2.4). It is important to see that this claim, as Locke interprets it,[60] is simply the anthropological and political instantiation of the principle of the primacy of potency over act. Actuality inescapably brings differentiation: in the real world that exists *in actu*, things are always already related to each other, relation implies giving and receiving, and these entail some sort of priority and posteriority, determination and receptivity of determination. There cannot be *order* without some sub-ordination and super-ordination, however paradoxical and nonlinear these hierarchies may turn out to be. Moreover, people are different ages, occupy different stations, have different histories, follow different paths, are not only born with different talents but develop them differently, and in different cultural contexts. When Locke affirms equality, he precisely *abstracts from* all of this actual differentiation. We are all equal because we are "promiscuously born to all the same advantages of Nature, and the use of the same faculties" (2.4). Notice: we are born *to* the advantages, which means that these are advantages we have *actually* to reach through our own efforts. Prior to these efforts, the advantages are only *possible*. Likewise with our faculties: we have all exactly the same *potential* to use our reason, will, and so forth, if we disregard all actual circumstances and the conditions they present. The equality of Locke's state of nature is what is often called today an equality of *opportunity*, rather than a real equality. We will return, in our discussion of property in the next section, to consider some of the concrete implications of this interpretation.

At the moment, the point we wish to highlight is that this particular interpretation of equality entails a radically nonrelational understanding of the human being.[61] It is in the actualization of potencies that we relate to others, or perhaps the relation to others inevitably actualizes our potencies.[62] But the actualization, as we just suggested, necessarily implies differentiation, and therefore the essential hierarchy of order. Order in the deepest sense is unity in multiplicity and multiplicity in unity. This deep sense of order, however, implies an inwardly differentiated—an *analogical*—understanding of unity. The positing of unrelated and undifferentiated units lying next to each other all at the same level is a kind of mechanical imitation of order: order is not given as a priori actuality, but is instead produced through the equilibrium of equal forces acting on equal objects at equal distances from each other. Unity and equality are in this case *quantitative*, rather than qualitative, terms. This order can be sustained, so it seems, only to the extent that the equality is maintained.

Now, insofar as this equality is taken to be original, it means that human beings are strictly unrelated to one another, and to the world in general, of their very essence. But this implies that the establishment of any relation becomes a disruption of order, a disequilibrium. We have seen that the "justice and charity" that Locke refers to as prevailing in the state of nature is just the preservation of distance that respects others. *Actual relation* is, from this perspective, necessarily a transgression of the boundaries that make order, and therefore freedom, possible. On the other hand, it simply cannot be denied that each person is born into this world as always already related: we come to be, first of all, in a family, in a particular place with a particular history, as inheritors of a tradition that precedes us. We therefore do not *begin* as "equal" in Locke's sense.[63] Instead, we have to achieve that equality precisely by abstracting from our relations, which means we are *positing* an equality

that is not actually given. This is an unavoidable implication of thinking of equality in the univocal sense of quantity rather than, say, in
terms of dignity, which is not in principle *opposed* to a great variety of
concrete "inequalities."[64] To think of equality in terms of dignity is to
posit something that *includes* all of the positive features and relations
that distinguish a person, even as it transcends any one of them and
also their sum, so that these features and relations become relative expressions of that dignity. To think of equality in terms of power is to
posit that equality as separate from all of these actualities, and indifferent to them. It is clear, for example, that a child and a man can be said to
have equal dignity, but they cannot *in actual fact* be said to be equal in
Locke's sense. To consider them equal in this sense, we have to think
away the concrete differences and consider the child precisely as a *potential* man, that is, as *not* in fact a child.[65] To use the language from the
previous chapter, we "suspend" the differences, and therefore turn
them into accidents, possibilities, or "options" (in the sense of the various packages of "add-on" features offered to a person buying a car), as
it were, even if they are then recognized as options a person cannot
help but have chosen, given circumstances. In other words, I take any
concrete qualities and relationships I have as options that were imposed on me, not in principle, but nevertheless with the necessity of
my contingent circumstances. Just as, in chapter 1, the power to suspend, even if merely ineffectually present, makes the (inevitable) natural determination a kind of choice, so, here, the principle of equality,
though in itself unreal, makes the actual differentiations of nature and
history functions of my freedom, insofar as it separates them from my
personal identity.

If political freedom is defined as the fixing of fences, then it follows that actual relations between human beings are encroachments on
freedom, which is to say: *human relationships have the a priori form of
hostility.* This a priori form can of course be transformed concretely
through an act of will in a manner similar, once again, to the power that
renders extrinsic natural determination a choice—to anticipate, this is
the deep sense of consent in Locke and what it means to think of *positive* human relations as having the form of a contract, not as a natural
given (which would mean hostile intrusion), but a reciprocal object of
freedom. Nevertheless, "positive" relationship is achieved in this case

as an overcoming of the form of encroachment that is most basically given. And this brings us to an extraordinary paradox. The very equality that grounds the law of nature therefore makes this law the regulation of essentially hostile forces: in this respect, *it builds antagonism into the meaning of real nature.* This is the case, not only because the natural imposition of law takes for granted a priori disorder, as we saw above, but also because this abstract equality renders man essentially nonrelational, which implies that all relationships have the form of encroachments on freedom—and this is just what Locke says instigates war. As we have observed several times already, the law does not affirm the a priori and so natural "belongingness" of individuals together in the relation to the good, but rather fences them off from one another. It therefore turns out that the state of war is not an overturning of the state of nature; instead, war represents, we might say, the inner form of that state, insofar as it has been brought into actuality. To interpret "justice and charity" essentially as the preservation of a respectful distance between individuals is to presuppose that for individuals to be actually related is for them to enter into competition with one another, in a way that is indistinguishable in fact from Hobbes's total war. If nature is a state of order, freedom, and peace only as an abstract potentiality, then reality is disorder. And reality is unavoidable.

PROPERTY AS THE POTENTIALIZING OF GOODNESS

Before Locke presents the social contract that is the remedy for the inconveniences of the state of nature, he inserts a chapter, "On Property." This chapter is the pivotal one in the *Treatise*:[66] on the one hand, it appears to introduce into the state of nature precisely the reality that triggers the antagonisms of the state of war, and on the other hand it presents in its substance the very purpose of political community. As Locke says repeatedly, the chief end of political community is the preservation of property.

If we step back and look at the matter from a more fundamental philosophical perspective, we see that the chapter on property has an even deeper importance. Several observations can be made in this regard. First of all, we note that Locke presents the chapter on property as the fifth, *before* he discusses the family ("On Paternal Power," chapter 6) or any other form of positive human community ("Of Political or Civil Society," chapter 7). The only forms of relation between individuals and the world outside of them that precede property are the putatively "neutral" form of natural equality (chapter 2), or the negative forms of war and slavery (chapters 3 and 4). Man's first positive relation is thus for Locke not to any *person*, but to *things*. This makes sense given Locke's definition of freedom, which we discussed at the outset of this chapter. Freedom takes political form most basically as the enclosure of space, and one can enclose *things* inside one's sphere of dominion, but not other *freedoms*, which as we saw represent other instances of active power. Since freedom is a defining feature of man's natural state, we can say that property is man's only natural relation, or at least the only relation that is not in a formal sense *contra naturam*. The free-floating atom of abstract equality—man in his potential state— first takes on concrete substance through the acquisition of property. Relations among human beings are therefore organized *around* property. If political order represents the actualization of human beings, the place wherein man takes concrete form, then, given Locke's view of freedom, it is only logical that he takes the preservation of property to be the ultimate purpose of political community. It is significant that this purpose is articulated in a primarily negative form: not the positive achievement of some good, but the keeping intact of what is already given prior to the formation of community.

To shed light on this point by means of a contrary example, Aristotle presents *human excellence* as the purpose of community (which of course includes, but is not limited to, property), and this conception follows from a notion of man as *naturally* political.[67] Locke conceives civil society as a *remedy* for the failings of nature, and his conception of the political good is correspondingly a negative one.

Private property represents for Locke the most complete realization of human freedom, or at least man's highest *worldly* achievement (as distinct from man's heavenly destination, to which, as we saw in chapter 1, there corresponds virtue as self-control). Just as power is the organizing center of his conception of "Human Understanding," property is the organizing center of his political theory—and there is a logical connection between these two conceptions.

Locke enters into his discussion of property by raising the classic question concerning the origin of private property, given the equality that we saw is implied by the law of nature. Let us first sketch out the basic features of his account before reflecting on their significance. In contrast to Sir Robert Filmer, who claimed that God gave the world to Adam qua individual man, a bequest that implies the primordiality of private property, Locke insists that God gave the world to *man*, in the universal sense.[68] Thus, the world originally belongs to everyone equally, not—as we explained earlier—in the sense that each person in principle possesses a share of the whole, but in the sense that there is an inclusive right, common to all, to *use* the world's resources as a means of pursuing the self-preservation protected by the law of nature. It is, then, precisely the actual use—or more specifically the *labor* involved in the use—that removes the thing from the common store, as it were, and transforms it into private property. The reason it does so is that, in precise contrast to the world, which belongs to *no one*, each person possesses *himself*, and indeed in an *exclusive* way: "Every Man has a *Property* in his own *Person*. This no Body has any Right to but himself" (5.38).[69] A man's labor likewise belongs to him as an extension of his person. It is by virtue of its extension of his person that the activity of laboring takes things out of the common store and makes it private property: "Whatsoever then he removes out of the State that Nature hath provided, and left it in, he hath mixed his *Labour* with, and joyned to it something that is his own, and thereby makes it his *Property*" (5.27). Because this appropriation, however, occurs within the context of the common property that God gave to all for the preservation of all, it is, as James Tully has shown at length,[70] limited by that context. Thus, appropriation is constrained by three principles:[71] (1) the "sufficiency limitation," which states that, in appropriating property, one is required to leave "enough and as good" to everyone else (5.33); (2) the "spoilage limitation," which states that one can appropriate only what one is in fact able to use: an accumulation of so many goods that they spoil in one's possession would not be a justified appropriation because it would offend the purpose for God's gift of the world to man; and (3) the "ownership limitation," which states that you can appropriate *only* what you have mixed with your own labor (5.32).

As straightforward as these limitations appear, it turns out that man has invented a means of transcending them without thwarting God's original intention, namely, money.[72] Money is a good that does not spoil, and never loses its potential for use (as long as people continue to value it). There is therefore no natural or intrinsic limit to its accumulation. Moreover, precisely because it has no natural limit, it can be multiplied in principle without end through the expenditure of labor. And finally, with respect to the third constraint, the invention of money allows the purchase of others' labor, so that this labor can be a part of my property and so an extension of my person, without having to come, as it were, directly from me.[73] In other words, I can come to ownership of a thing, not because I myself labored to produce it, but because I purchased the labor of another in my place. All of this means that the value of the natural world can be indefinitely increased, making more usefulness available in principle to everyone else: in contrast to the rare apple tree that nature provides on a particular plot of land, which would allow me to take only a few of the apples as long as there remain plenty for others, I can cultivate the land where this one tree originally happened to grow, indeed, hire laborers to plant and harvest hundreds of trees, and sell the apples, not only to be eaten, but perhaps to be transformed in turn by other laborers into further products to be bought and sold, and so forth.[74] The freedom from spoilage and the expansion of labor that money gives opens up the opportunity to expand the value of the world God gave and so leave "enough and as good" for more and more people. In appropriating this piece of land, which might be larger than I could have fruitfully used by myself naturally, through the existence of money I have actually given back in principle far more than I have taken. It becomes *good* for those who will use it well to acquire as much land as they can.

On the other hand, however, this legitimate use transforms the original equality *in potential* of the state of nature into an actual society differentiated into social classes, in which there are those with property and those who can sell nothing but their labor, and, because money allows accumulation unbounded by any natural limit, among those who own property the relative distribution of wealth can be infinitely disproportionate. But it is important to see that this radical inequality does not necessarily and in principle thwart God's original intention of the world for common use. As Gopal Sreenivasan has argued, Locke does not insist on the common *enjoyment* of the world (equal consumption), but only on common *use* (equal permission to produce); "enough and as good" pertains to the *means* of subsistence.[75] In the language we have been employing, what has to remain equal is the *potency* of resources, which individuals may or may not make actual use of. Thus, one can produce as much wealth as one wishes as long as this contributes to the greater store of available wealth and does not eliminate others' possibility of producing wealth.[76] Accumulation of money, in fact already, ipso facto, increases that potency: the more money I have, the more potential wealth others have because they are able to sell me either their goods or their labor. Locke's principles would seem to grant *more justice* to one man's appropriation of a large tract of land, for example, as long as he puts it to productive use, than to that land's distribution among many men who would simply allow it to waste away. The world is there for all equally, but it was never meant to stay that way. In Locke's words,

> God gave the World to Men in Common; but since he gave it them for their benefit, and the greatest Conveniencies of Life they were capable to draw from it, it cannot be supposed he meant it should always remain common and uncultivated. He gave it to the use of the Industrious and Rational, (and *Labour* was to be *his* Title to it;) not to the Fancy or Covetousness of the Quarrelsom and Contentious. He that had as good left for his Improvement, as was already taken up, needed not complain, ought not to meddle with what was already improved by another's Labour: If he did, 'tis plain he desired the benefit of another's Pains, which he had no right to, and not the Ground which God had given him in common with others to labour on, and whereof there was as good left, as that already possessed, and more than he knew what to do with, or his Industry could reach to. (5.34)

With the introduction of money, therefore, people will naturally tend to enlarge their possessions (5.41), and this will inevitably bring about a scarcity of land and an inequality among people. It is this situation that makes the state of war essentially inevitable. The perfect equality of free-floating atoms, each of which has in abundance what is necessary to live and so has no need of others, will not likely present a reciprocal threat, but the conditions brought by money make the threat inevitable: the boundless enlargement of possessions, on every side, cannot but lead to what will be perceived as an encroachment in some case.[77] If the state of nature is man "in potentia," man in the "real world," so to speak, is necessarily going to be entangled in antagonistic relations with his neighbors. And thus we have an effective transition to the state of civil society.

But before considering that transition, let us reflect more deeply on the significance of all of this in relation to our larger argument. The connection between Locke's conception of power and his notion of property, as expounded in section 6 of the *Treatise*, is quite clear. We saw in chapter 1 that, in order to present freedom as power, Locke had to revise the description of the cause of choice from the greatest good, which would make a claim on the will in some sense "from above," to unease, a propelling impulse "from below." Turning to the objective instantiation of Locke's theory in the *Second Treatise*, we can ask: In what sense is the world "in itself" a *good* that draws man into the world, so to speak, through attraction? What, in other words, is the "intrinsick value" of the world that it possesses by virtue of God's making as opposed to the value man gives it through his own making? Locke is admittedly *shifty* in response to this question. He initially presents the gift of the world as an abundance intended for human flourishing, but in short order he ends up saying that the value of the world, taken in itself, is "little more than nothing" (5.42). Perhaps to ease the shock of this claim—or perhaps to enact its content—Locke first calculates the intrinsic value of the world relative to the value it acquires through man's labor as one to ten (5.37), but then gradually revises it to one to a hundred (5.37, 40), and finally concludes with one to a thousand (5.43). The native, God-given goodness of the world dwindles, as it were, right before our eyes. For Locke, things do not originally represent a goodness, but "'tis *Labour* indeed that *puts the difference of value* on everything" (5.40).

The fact that Locke can make this claim in spite of the countless obvious objections[78] suggests that he is giving expression to a deep principle of his thought rather than drawing an evident empirical inference.

That principle is the *priority of potency over act*, to which the potency has no intrinsic relation. By virtue of this principle, the world is not first *given* as a good that implies some a priori claim on my will, but is in itself "little more than nothing." We do not have to interpret Locke as being deceptive when he originally describes the bounty of nature. Instead, we can see that this bounty exists at first only *in potentia*. Until someone labors on it—and we might add thereby *actualizes* it— "the common is of no use" (5.28). Note that this is simply an economic instance of the principle we have regularly affirmed, namely, that what is mere potential, in Locke's sense, is in itself nonexistent for all intents and purposes. The reality of the world's native goodness, in other words, has the same status as the reality of the law of nature. From one perspective, then, we can refer to "the plenty of natural Provisions" (5.31) and with consistency nevertheless say that, from another perspective, this plenty is *effectively* nothing. Even the "intrinsick value" Locke ascribes to things he nevertheless does not grant to them in themselves, but only relative to "their usefulness to the Life of Man" (5.37). The world, thus, is only what we make of it. Significantly, Locke describes the efforts that man makes as "annexed" to what was given, that is, added to it from the outside (5.27), rather than, for example, in terms of what Heidegger describes as the ancient sense of *technē*, namely, the essentially receptive activity that allows a thing to stand forth, from itself, as what it most genuinely is.[79] The will, for Locke, is precisely *not* receptive; it is not responsive to a good that elicits its activity from outside of it, but is instead a force that shoots up, so to speak, from below, or, perhaps better, shoots outward from an essentially nonrelational power source. The object of this will is therefore necessarily "little more than nothing" prior to the will's acting on it.

The will's activity, moreover, is precisely an exertion of power, and power is the ability to effect a change in something. In the prepolitical order, this power takes the basic form of labor; and the change that the power of labor makes is simultaneously the addition of value (*"Labour ... puts the difference of value* on every thing" [5.40]) and the reversal of its status from common to private (*"labour* put a distinction between [privately owned items] and common" [5.28]). Now, it is crucial to see that this addition of value is a strictly unilateral event, which follows from the simultaneity just mentioned. Though Locke uses the word "mixing" to describe man's work on the world, this work is precisely that, a working *on* the world, rather than, for example, a "joining with" it, so to speak. Locke may initially have described labor as man's "joyning" himself to what is given in creation, but he goes on to say that there is effectively "little more than nothing" given. As Tully explains, when Locke gradually shrinks the intrinsic value of the world to 1/1000 of the value added by labor, he is saying that there is nothing, or at least nothing of any significant value, that underlies the laboring, nothing that continues through the process, and so is left remaining at the end. Instead, the product in its entirety must be understood as a result of labor.[80] Though parts of a thing might be made by previous laborers, it is not the case that the final laborer adds a final bit of value to the partial value added before, but in fact the whole thing is the result of this labor, because the final labor transforms the meaning, and so value, of every single bit, making it an altogether new thing.[81] Each act of labor would seem in a sense to render the previous ones "as nothing" in relation to itself. Note that this accords well with a notion of will as essentially power: each act begins, in a sense, de novo, as we saw in chapter 1. In any event, what all of this means is that property takes on a decisively new meaning in Locke: rather than being an extension of the private person into the public sphere of the world, which is at the same time a bringing into oneself of the world,[82] it represents a unilateral privatizing of what was originally public.[83] It is interesting that Locke's initial example is the labor of *eating*, which is literally an incorporation of a thing into oneself. Thus, for Locke, man does not come out of himself and unite himself to the world through labor in property (which would imply the retention of an objective obligation toward the property as an intrinsic good[84]), but instead simply takes the world, as it were, into himself, or, more specifically, he takes it into the private space that his freedom encloses. Locke's interpretation of appropriation through labor represents, in short, a paradigm of what we indicated in the title to this chapter, namely, a political conquest of the good.

Let us now consider why this way of conceiving property gives it a logical propensity to "cash out," so to speak, in money. There is both a practical and a more directly metaphysical argument for this tendency. On the practical level, one might object to the suggestion that money for Locke is the logical end of property by pointing out the obvious derision in Locke's tone when he speaks of the "*little piece of yellow Metal*" (5.37), which seems to have such a profound effect on human relationships, and point to Locke's moral disapproval of man's greedy inclination to hoard.[85] Indeed, doesn't Locke also state clearly that money is essentially an illusion? "Money, and such Riches and Treasure," he says after all, "are none of Natures Goods, they have but a Phantastical imaginary value: Nature has put no such upon them" (16.184). But this apparent judgment reverses itself when we consider it in the context of Locke's general labor theory of value, which we just presented. It may be that money has little to no *natural* value, but we have just seen that Locke says *effectively* the same thing about everything. Whatever effective value things have has been added by man's actualizing efforts. It may be that, in the one case (e.g., the apple yet to be picked) there is a naturally given potency for this value, while in the other (the lump of yellow metal) the value arrives simply by conventional fiat, but this difference has only theoretical significance. Locke makes "intrinsick value" equal to the "usefulness to the Life of Man"; to the observation that a single apple is more directly useful to man than a pile of gold, because man cannot eat that pile, it takes very little imagination to see a decisive response: the apple is gone after its eating, but the pile of gold can buy any number of apples, whenever they happen to be needed, or indeed anything else one might wish to eat. The use-value of money thus in a literal sense *infinitely* exceeds that of an apple, precisely because there is no natural limit, no finite bounds to the use to which it can be put. If "intrinsick value" is measured by potential for use, money has a value against which no real goods in the world can effectively compete. Because money can be accumulated without limit, and preserved indefinitely, given alternatives it is almost always preferable to pursue money rather than some actual object (just as it is generally most rational to suspend desires for the sake of greater self-control, as we explained in chapter 1).[86] From a purely practical perspective, the drive to actualize freedom through the achievement of property in Locke's sense will logically tend to the acquisition of money.

At a more profound level, we can see that this conversion of property into money is simply an essential economic expression of the primacy of potency over act.[87] In speaking of the meaning the world has for man, it is significant that Locke rarely speaks, as we noted already in chapter 1, of the *enjoyment* of the earth's goods; instead, even when he mentions the "intrinsick value," as we have seen, he refers this not to enjoyment, but specifically to *use*. We saw in chapter 1 that enjoyment and pleasure is a kind of actuality; *use*, by contrast, is potency, insofar as it indicates the means by which an end, an actuality, is achieved. To call even basic natural goods such as fruits *useful* is to conceive of their value specifically as *productive* of further value: fruits are useful because they sustain life, that is, they produce further life. Man does not *receive* the world for Locke as a good, but *labors* on it, effecting a change that gives it value, and the highest value it can have from this perspective is quite logically the ability to make more change. As we just observed, this is precisely what causes money inevitably to eclipse basic natural goods on the scale of "intrinsick" value. Money is a symbol of productivity; it is nothing in itself, and so nothing but power. As Locke put it in his journal: "The chief end of trade is Riches & Power which beget each other."[88] Because money has no intrinsic goodness, the purpose of accumulation is not to have money in one's possession, but to have more than others; the disproportion is precisely what gives power. Speaking of *national* wealth, Locke makes just this point: "Riches do *not* consist in having more gold and silver, but in having *more in proportion than the rest of the world, or than our neighbors*, whereby we are enabled to procure to ourselves a greater plenty of the conveniences of life, than comes within the reach of neighboring kingdoms and states, who, sharing the gold and silver of the world in a less proportion, *want the means of plenty and power*, and so are poorer."[89] We note, here, the connection between money as means and as power, a connection we will develop in part 2 of this book.

Above we said that property, for Locke, is not an extension of the person into the world, but rather a kind of "incorporation" of the world into the person, a conquest of the good. Because a kind of objectivity, however, is inescapable with property, we have to modify this description: to have property at all is to be extended in some capacity into the world. But the reflection on money allows us to modify the description without in fact fundamentally revising it: money represents the extension of the person into the objectivity of the world *precisely in the form of potency*. In other words, money is a paradigmatic outward expression of the will interpreted as effective power. We will discuss the meaning and implications of this point at greater length in chapter 5.

In what is rightly regarded as a classic, though an endlessly controversial one, in Locke studies, *The Political Theory of Possessive Individualism*, C. B. Macpherson presents what he refers to as "extraordinary contradictions" in Locke's political theory, the primary one of which being Locke's affirmation of universal equality as man's natural condition, and his seemingly unhesitating assumption of a differentiation of social classes, founded on radical inequality in the possession of power, as likewise natural in the sense that it comes into being *prior to* civil society.[90] For Locke, the distribution of property that results from the use of money has a reality "out of the bounds of Societie, and without compact" (5.50), so that civil society takes this inequality for granted, and simply regulates it post factum. The natural state is therefore *both* a state of equality and a state of inequality. Macpherson argues that Locke was capable of such a contradiction because of his unwitting assumption of the universality of his contemporary social conditions.[91] In other words, Macpherson attributes an ultimately sociological cause to Locke's political theory. Although we tend to agree with the essence of Macpherson's analysis of the "extraordinary contradictions" in Locke's theory,[92] and the pivotal role money plays therein, we attribute it most fundamentally to a metaphysical and anthropological[93] cause rather than a sociological one: it is due to an assumption of potency as prior to, and inwardly dissociated from, act, and the related interpretation of freedom as power. This more fundamental level of analysis is important, not only because a sociological analysis in fact implicitly concedes the ultimacy of power, since it makes thinking a function of oppressive class structures—this is the basic flaw in Marxist approaches to cultural problems in general—but most basically it enables us in this particular case to see that the contradiction lies at such a deep level that the two conditions, total equality and severe inequality, can in fact coexist.[94] They are not mutually exclusive, such that one would have to deny the reality of one in order to affirm the reality of the other. *Inside* the actual conditions of inequality, for Locke, we still have essential cores of free-floating, unrelated atoms, that are, as pure potencies, identical to one another, and because of their abstractness they will inevitably remain identical regardless of actual conditions. It will always be the case that persons remain in principle free and equal, able to change their circumstances if they make sufficient effort, which means that, if they do not change their circumstances, it is because they have chosen not to exercise their will.[95] Of course, this is simply the flip side, as we have seen, of the interpretation of the will as wholly determined by external circumstances. In this case, change can be made only by reversing social structures, to which the individuals have no natural or ontological connection. The interpretation of freedom as power offers equal justification to laissez-faire policies and total revolution. Just as nature, with respect to the exercise of the will, is simultaneously nothing and everything, so too are the artificial superstructures of society nothing and everything at once.[96] However all this may be, Macpherson remains correct that it is the *actual* conditions of inequality that bring about the need for civil society to regulate these conditions, and to "preserve property" in the name of the law of nature that safeguards freedom. Indeed, the "preservation of property" *is* the law of nature, expressed in the political sphere.

CONSENT AS A TRANSFER OF POWER

The remedy for the volatility of nature in its actual condition is the transition into civil society, whereby the individuals in the state of nature surrender their power to judge and punish wrongdoings and jointly submit themselves to an agreed upon authority. They thus pass from being a mass of individuals, each absolute in himself, and therefore in a potential state of war with all the others, into one "Body Politick" (7.89). The transition from "heap" to "whole," to borrow Aristotelian language, is effected by the act of *consent*, the actual choosing to accept jointly the sovereignty of a common authority.

It is the very nature of this consent that it take an explicit, that is, an identifiable, external form in a manner analogous to law. Nature, for Locke, is in itself *a-political*; without the contingent necessity imposed by the state of war, man would never have left it. Because nature is not itself *internally* ordered to the political, the entry into the political is a leaving of the natural (rather than a fulfillment of the natural, so that man would be more perfectly natural in political community than he was prior to it).[97] As Locke explains, consent "*puts Men* out of a State of Nature *into* that of a *Commonwealth*" (7.89). Consent is thus an explicit borderline dividing one state from the other. In this case, there is a strict "either–or," just as there was regarding the law of reason. Crossing the borderline, for Locke, represents a definitive change, like the flipping of a switch: "He, that has once, by actual Agreement, and any *express* Declaration, given his *Consent* to be of any Commonweal, is perpetually and indispensably obliged to be and remain unalterably a Subject to it, and can never be again in the liberty of the state of Nature" (8.121). Prior to the consent, the positive obligations we have to others exist only *in potentia*, and so do not make an a priori claim on my freedom, but to the contrary depend on my prior willingness to undertake them. This is the import of Locke's fundamental position that no one is subject to the will of any other in the state of nature (2.4), but instead each represents an authority unto himself. Once the consent is given, on the other hand, the transformation is dramatic: one is henceforward *in fact* subject in a certain sense (yet to be explicated) to the will of others, and this subjection means that the social obligations now have an *a priori* claim on one's will. In other words, we no longer have the obligation *only because* we willingly accept it in each instance:

> And thus every Man, by consenting with others to make one Body Politick under one Government, puts himself under the Obligation to every one of that Society, to submit to the determination of the *majority*, and to be concluded by it; or else this *original Compact*, whereby he with others incorporates into *one Society*, would signifie nothing, and be no Compact, if he be left free, and under no other ties, than he was in before in the State of Nature. For what appearance would there be of any Compact? What new Engagement if he were no farther tied by any Decrees of the Society, than he himself thought fit, and did actually consent to? This would be still as great a liberty, as he himself had before his Compact, or any one else in the State of Nature hath, who may submit himself and consent to any acts of it if he thinks fit. (8.97)

Civil society is therefore in a strict sense a *reversal* of the state of nature.

Now, there are two evident difficulties with this doctrine of consent, as representing a "bright line" dividing the natural from the political state. First, isn't it the case that man enters into the world invariably as a child, subject to the will of others prior to any consent? Second, is explicit consent *in fact* the normal way people enter into a political

community?[98] Locke offers principles for a response to the first question
in chapter 6, "Of Paternal Power," which precedes his explicit discussion
of political community. The point of Locke's chapter is precisely to rebut
the notion—most immediately articulated by Filmer[99]—that patriarchy
is a natural form of government insofar as it is simply an extension into
the political sphere of the father's natural authority over his wife and
children. The aspect of this theory that concerns us most directly here[100]
is the implication that one is born *into* obligation, which would seem to
make subjection to authority man's natural and most essential state—
which of course presents a perfect contrast to Locke's theory. Locke
attacks this notion, first, by arguing that parental authority over children,[101] which is so obvious a fact that it cannot be denied, is nevertheless
only a *provisional* authority, necessitated by circumstances that are
meant ultimately to be left behind. Locke acknowledges that children
are not their parents' peers, and so do not possess the equality that he
had identified with the state of nature: "*Children*, I confess are not born
in this full state of *Equality*, though they are born to it" (6.55). This is
a concrete instance of the principle we discussed above, namely, that
equality is not a given reality, except as potency, and so is something
that has to be achieved—in this case, through the acquisition of the
actual use of reason. There is a certain irony in Locke's position, as it
comes to expression here: human beings are not born (*natus*) *into* the
state of *nature*, but have to achieve that state through their own, deliberate activity. It follows that familial relations and the inevitable *dependence* they imply are, strictly speaking, *un*-natural, since it is precisely
not being "Subject to the arbitrary Will of another, but freely follow-
[ing] his own" that represents the state of nature. The most properly
human form of positive relationship, for Locke, is the explicitly political one of cooperating with another through consent.

This inference is confirmed by the second aspect of Locke's attack. We saw that the position Locke sought to refute interprets political order as in some sense derived from what is taken to be the natural
order of the family. For Locke, by contrast, the family is not "a little
Common-wealth," but "very far from it" (7.80). He means to say that,
no matter what hierarchical structure may be given in the family, there is
no warrant for projecting an analogous hierarchy into the political community. These forms of obedience and responsibility in the family, after

all, exist only because of the practical needs of children and are therefore provisional. They do not express any essential truth of human nature.[102] But this generates another irony. If Locke rejects the idea that the commonwealth resembles the family, he nevertheless ends up affirming that the family resembles the commonwealth. Locke interprets the various relationships that constitute what Aristotle described as the *oikos*— husband–wife, parent–child, master–servant relationships—precisely according to the model of consent we discussed above (though of course the children's relationship to the parents is, in its essence, a consent waiting to happen). These relationships are presented in the chapter called "Political or Civil Community."[103] Here, for example, Locke insists that "*Conjugal Society* is made by a voluntary Compact between Man and Woman," and indeed goes on to explain that this compact has a *practical* purpose (just as does that of the political community), which means it ought to be dissolvable once its purpose is served. We see here that positive relationship is not affirmed as an intrinsic good, which exists in its own right and so *ought* to be cultivated for its own sake, but instead marriage is essentially a means for the promotion of the well-being of individuals. Incidentally, when Locke cites the scriptural passage in which man leaves his father and mother in order to cleave to his wife, he leaves out the phrase that follows regarding their becoming "one flesh," which would seem to give substance to the marriage bond. What Locke highlights instead in this text is the "Licence from Divine Authority" to cut one's ties to one's parents (6.65). Once again, we see that the *base reality* for Locke, is, to use Charles Taylor's term, "unbuffered" individuals, connected only by their deliberate will.

The second difficulty with Locke's theory of consent is its infrequency; the explicit declaration of consent to hand oneself over to the political authority of the community does not *in fact* seem to take place often, if it takes place at all. And yet there are and have been multitudes of people living in commonwealths and subject to their laws. There is a dilemma, here, for Locke, because he has fundamentally rejected any sense of obedience as something one is born into—as he puts it, something one inherits through one's father. If obedience requires consent, and explicit consent is rare, how can obedience in a commonwealth be generally expected and indeed demanded? Locke responds to this problem by formulating the principle of "tacit consent," which we can understand as a reinterpretation of natural obedience according to the model of deliberate consent. One does not inherit obligation to the state directly from one's father, but one *does* inherit property from him. Insofar as the father gave consent to the commonwealth, according to Locke, his property too (in a manner we will discuss in a moment) was given over to his jurisdiction. By accepting the property, one implicitly accepts the jurisdiction of the state, and so the membership in the commonwealth, that necessarily accompanies it. In a broader sense, but according to the same principle, whenever one makes use of property under the jurisdiction of the commonwealth—a public road, for instance (8.119)—one is giving one's tacit consent to follow its laws. *Any actual existence* inside a commonwealth, assuming one is not already a member of some other, implies tacit consent. Tacit consent can always be trumped at a later point by explicit consent—Locke affirms that if one is bound to a particular commonwealth only implicitly, one is yet free explicitly to pledge one's commitment to another (8.121)[104]— because it is only explicit consent that is definitively binding, for the reasons we gave above. Tacit consent, then, is taken to be binding, one might say, for all intents and purposes otherwise.

Locke's notion of consent, as just presented, poses additional problems, which are insurmountable because they turn out to be symptoms of the dialectic we have been arguing lies at the root of Locke's thinking. It is not just that the notion of tacit consent is unsatisfying as an account of political membership, though that is undeniably true. Attempting to make a case in defense of Locke, John Dunn says that the best statement one can draw out of his principles is the following: "Men must be supposed expressly to consent to their nationality, their membership in a given society, by their settled disposition to identify themselves as such," though he himself admits that this remains weak.[105] Dunn's formulation is more than weak; it is self-contradictory, insofar as "supposed expressly to consent" means the consent is implicitly explicit. But this just points us to the deeper problem: the explanation Locke offers for one's tacit consent presupposes that one's father gave *explicit* consent—or at least *his* father did, or *his*, and so on—such that the property I inherit or otherwise make use of *in fact* lies under the state's jurisdiction.[106] The theory of tacit consent does not solve the problem, but simply pushes it back, perhaps beyond the horizon of evident relevance, but not out of existence. We can nevertheless explain how nonexistence does not mean irrelevance from a Lockean perspective by appealing to what we saw in chapter 1. The active power that defines the will does not have to be actualized in order to bear on any particular determination of the will, insofar as the sheer fact it *could have been actualized*, at least in principle, *already*, at least in principle, changes the meaning of that determination. The fact, in other words, that one always could have actualized one's will by joining another commonwealth means that one's remaining in this one can be taken to be an actual expression of one's will. Thus, there only ever needs to be tacit consent. The empirical facts, then, do not need to be any different, so to speak, but they now come to have a different meaning. The social relationships, and all of the benefits and obligations they entail, into which one is born and which therefore precede one's deliberate choices, no longer need to be interpreted in relation to nature, but may now be interpreted in relation to explicit consent. Note that these do not really represent symmetrical alternatives: nature—in the classical view—is actual as an internal principle that has analogous expressions (so that, for example, the child's relation to his parents, though it is decisively natural, does not represent nature in a univocal fashion that is imitated in every other relationship, even if its significance bears intrinsically on all others), whereas (explicit) consent, representing as it does a kind of borderline or threshold, just *is* an extrinsic model, against which various relationships are measured. As extrinsic, it represents a univocal concept that is not inwardly differentiated in real instances, but it is a model as a nonactual ideal. Why would Locke take such a nonactuality as a model for relationships? The answer to this question is that it is a function of the abstract equality he assumes at the origin. And so we come to the most basic issue: Locke posits explicit consent—which is never actually given—as a norm for all positive social relationships because he posits equality—which never actually exists[107]—as man's most original and so essential condition.

Coming back to our exposition, we may now ask after the shape of the political community that arises from the act of consent. Political community, as we have seen, is not natural but is instead achieved through the will. The essence of the will, on the other hand, is *power*. We may thus view the act of will that gives consent as a *transfer of power*. Significantly, Locke describes man's original condition in terms of power: "In the State of Nature, to omit the liberty he has of innocent Delights,[108] a Man has two Powers. . . . The first is to do whatsoever he thinks fit for the preservation of himself and others within the permission of the *Law of Nature*. . . . The other power a Man has in the State of Nature, is the *power to punish the Crimes* committed against that law" (9.128). Through his consent, man gives up the first to the extent required by civil law (9.129), which means he retains this power in areas that civil law does not reach; and the second he "wholly *gives up*" (9.130). It is, in political society, *only* the political authority that has the right to carry out punishment, except in circumstances that preclude its possibility (for example, an emergency that requires an immediate act of self-defense).

Now, it seems that his transfer of power through consent concerns not simply his possible actions but also his very property. As Locke explains,

> Every Man, when he, at first, incorporates himself into any Commonwealth, he, by his uniting himself thereunto, annexed also, and submits to the Community those Possessions, which he has, or shall acquire, that do not already belong to any other Government. For it would be a direct Contradiction, for any one, to enter into Society with others for the securing and regulating of Property: And yet to suppose his Land, whose Property is to be regulated by the Laws of the Society, should be exempt from the Jurisdiction of that Government, to which he himself the Proprietor of the Land, is a Subject. By the same Act therefore, whereby any one unites his Person, which was before free, to any Commonwealth; by the same he unites his Possessions, which were before free, to it also; and they become, both of them, Person and Possession, subject to the Government and Dominion of that Commonwealth, as long as it hath a being. (8.120)

Our first impulse is to think that this "annexing" of property does *not* mean that property ceases to belong to the individual, and instead comes to belong, through consent, to the commonwealth. As we have seen, for Locke the very purpose of political community is the preservation of property, which means it would be self-contradictory to surrender property in order to form such a community. Locke insists resolutely on the absoluteness of private property. He for example states clearly that "no Body hath a right to take [people's] substance, or any part of it from them, without their own consent" (11.138). As strong as this statement is, we cannot overlook yet another ambiguity. Does the "consent" mentioned here refer to a discrete act in response to a request for the transfer of a particular property, or is the condition that the statement describes satisfied by the basic act of consent by which one enters into the community? The longer passage we cited seems to suggest the latter. In this case, the social contract would put a claim, not just on the use of my powers, but indeed on all that I possess, unto my very person (insofar as this, too, is a possession).[109] If this fundamental consent is a transfer of all the power in one's possession, and property, not only as ownership of things, but also as ownership of one's person, is a kind of power, then what is surrendered in consent is quite comprehensive. The reason that this surrender does not undermine the ultimate purpose of political community is that this transfer is not into the hands of some other private person (cf. 11.139), but rather into those of the community generally.[110] The (putative) act of consent thus entails a rather dramatic transformation: from the state of nature, in which I was absolute authority over myself, I am now *wholly* subject to an external authority, namely, that of the political community. This transformation is striking insofar as it is taken to be something I have always already consented to insofar as I exist at all inside of a particular commonwealth. The significance of this point stands out clearly when we contrast it with the classical view. If man is naturally political, if the duty of obedience that follows from his participation in a structured order that precedes him, is part of his nature, then membership in a political community, with the obedience it entails, is not a surrender of his nature. Instead, civil relations and obligations always remain relative to what he is by nature. But the social contract theory implies that entry into political relations is a relinquishing of the state of nature. When we consider this fact along with Locke's theory of tacit consent, it means that every inhabitant of a commonwealth is taken for all intents and purposes always already to have wholly surrendered his natural liberty.[111]

The way this subjection to a higher authority occurs becomes evident when we consider how the political order functions, according to Locke. For him, the political order is not an organic whole, which would require the acknowledgment of an a priori form, but instead it arises "from below." This is just what it means to say that community is the product of will, which for Locke is an active power that moves itself from below. Political order is thus brought about precisely through aggregation; it has the *form*, in other words, of the "will of the majority," understood in a mathematical sense. Given Locke's notion of will as power, it is therefore not surprising to see him describing the acts of the "Body Politick" in terms of a corpuscular theory of physics: "For that which acts any Community, being only the consent of the individuals of it, and it being necessary to that which is one body to move one way; it is necessary the Body should move that way whether the greater force carries it, which is the *consent of the majority*" (8.96). On the one hand, Locke's theory of consent makes the majority will an expression of the individual's freedom: the individual's "consent is permanently implied in all the events of its political life and in all the acts of the public authority. Each one of these acts is transformed into free acts *de jure* consented to by each one of the citizens."[112] By the same token, the majority will is, on Locke's terms, essentially irresistible: a single unit can never count mathematically more than a quantity of units, and, because the individual has definitively handed over his person and power to the community and now is subject to them a priori, he is effectively subsumed into the larger "Body Politick." In relation to the integrity of the larger whole, his individual integrity cannot hold any weight. If the individual holds onto a power to judge the majority, then in fact this would indicate that he has not entered into the "compact"; the individuals in society, therefore, "must be understood to give up all the power, necessary to the ends for which they unite into Society, to the *majority* of the Community" (8.99); as Willmoore Kendall puts it, the proper interest of the individual becomes "unquestioning obedience to the will of the majority."[113] This explains the observation one finds that a kind of social collectivism in Locke comes to supplant his natural individualism. At the same time, however, because this collective is nothing but the aggregate of individuals, each individual remains in a certain sense absolute in its own right. The significance of this point will become evident at the end of this chapter.

The power of the will of the majority is not wielded as such, but is once again transferred through the institution of the government. The distinction between the social community and the government (which is a forerunner to the eventual liberal distinction between the civil society and the state per se) is crucial for Locke for reasons that will soon be evident. Locke does not insist on any particular *form* of government: the majority can "freely" dispose its power into the hands of one person, a few, or a majority (10.132), but no one of these forms is ever definitive in itself. What *is* essential, for Locke, is that the government be articulated into what we now call three "branches," which not accidentally represent compensations for the three deficiencies Locke had identified in the state of nature: the legislative, the judicial, and the executive (cf. 9.124–26). Locke says, in fact, very little about the judicial, focusing his discussion on the executive, and above all on the legislative. It makes sense for Locke to emphasize the legislative as he does: if the will is active power, and the only unco-optable challenge to it is another active power not under the control of a contract—what Locke calls an "arbitrary will"—it is crucial that ultimate authority lie not in a person, but in an impersonal law. The inconveniences of the state of nature arose from the fact that the natural law had no effective authority over individuals, and this state of affairs cannot be remedied by making a single person the final authority. This would be "to think that Men are so foolish that they take care to avoid what Mischiefs may be done them by *Pole-Cats*, or *Foxes*, but are content, nay think it Safety, to be devoured by *Lions*" (7.93). Here is a decisive difference between Locke and Hobbes, who was unable to conceive of an ultimate power that did not lie in the hands of a single person. In strong contrast to the notion of the divine right of kings—which, Locke says facetiously, "we never heard of among Mankind, till it was revealed to us by the Divinity of this last Age" (8.112)—Locke refers to the *legislative power* as "sacred and unalterable" (11.134), though of course this usage changes the meaning of "sacred." In any event, Locke constantly calls the legislative the "Supream Power," to which all owe complete obedience as long as it is exercised within its proper bonds.[114]

Of course, there arises here the familiar problem in a new form: the law cannot execute *itself*, and so in itself the law established by the legislative power remains a mere potency awaiting an actualization to give it authority. Locke acknowledges the tension here. He admits that there is a certain sense in which the executive power, even in the hands of a single individual, in fact stands higher than the legislative, and so most deserves the name "Supream Power," but he insists that this is *only* the power to execute law, not *make* it, and that the people owe obedience to the legislative power rather than to him (13.151). He concedes at the same time it is inevitable that the executive power retain a "prerogative" (chapter 14), that is, a freedom with respect to the body of law, cautioning sternly that this ought to be used for good. And if it isn't? The complex textures of Locke's political order have only deferred, but not yet solved, the central problem of modern political philosophy, namely, the question Locke asked in the *First Treatise*, which we quoted last chapter: If freedom is active power, then the *ultimate* political question is, who finally *wields* it?[115]

Before we look directly at Locke's explicit wrestling with this question, which we will see produces yet another "Supream Power," in conflict with the executive and the legislative, it is helpful to see in summary form a basic pattern that emerges in Locke, due, we suggest, to his conception of the will as active power. When we think of consent as a transfer of the will's native power, we see that a dialectic establishes itself at every level. To put it in the most concise metaphysical terms, which will have to be elaborated more concretely: if potency is dissociated from act, the two are extrinsic and so indifferent to one another. In this case, the transition from potency to act represents a supplanting of the former by the latter. The actualization is extrinsic to the potency and so not in any inward sense measured by it, which means that it is arbitrary with respect to that potency. On the other hand, however, because the potency is inwardly indifferent to the actuality, it is at the same time unaffected by it and so left in place in the transition. Each then is absolute on its own terms, and this means they enter into competition with one another as juxtaposed absolutes. Thus, more concretely, we have natural law supplanted by actual individual wills, nature gets supplanted by civil society, civil society gets supplanted by the legislative, which in turn gets supplanted by the executive. But then the executive comes into conflict with the legislative, which then comes into conflict with the "people" of civil society, who end up being nothing but the individuals in the disordered state of nature. If power is interpreted as wholly self-activating and so without an intrinsic connection to anything outside of itself, the transfer of power necessarily creates a vulnerability of subjection to arbitrariness, which will then call on power to overcome the vulnerability. The irony is that the very notion of *free consent* meant to protect against this vulnerability is just what sets it ultimately in place. The solution is the cause of the problem: this will be a basic theme of our chapter 4.[116]

THE TRANSFER OF IMPOTENCE

Let us consider in some detail the most representative instance of this conflict in Locke, namely, between the people and the government, and see why his principles make this conflict unresolvable. We see that, although Locke generally says that the legislative is the "Supream Power" of government, he nevertheless insists that this power is not without bounds. Instead, it is *"limited to the publick good of the Society,"* which means that it never loses its measure in the law of nature it was originally formed to make effective. As Locke explains, "the Law of Nature stands as an Eternal Rule to all Men, *Legislators* as well as others" (11.135). This is indeed an essentially traditional perspective: in Aquinas, for example, positive law is essentially a translation of the natural law into the concrete terms of a particular political community, and the natural law thus presents a measure for civil law.[117] But we have seen that Locke interprets nature and its law in a radically nontraditional way because of his having removed it from the context of a natural teleology ordered to and by the good. It makes sense from a classical perspective to point to the normativity of nature because the political order is precisely the highest expression of nature, but it is not clear what this normativity could mean in a social contract theory of politics. For Locke, the political order is not an enhancing expression of nature, but a substitute for it because of its deficiency. The law of nature, for Locke, is impotent *in* nature; it can be actualized, in fact, only in the nonnatural state of civil society. Moreover, the law of nature as a pure potency is not only compatible with radical, hostility-generating inequalities, but it has the a priori *form* of hostility since its content is limited to the separation of individuals from each other. There is therefore a certain paradox in appealing to the law of nature as a standard by which to judge the legislative power of civil society. Who in the end has the authority to make this judgment? In the state of nature, each individual has complete authority, but we have seen that this amounts to saying there *is* no authority *in fact*. The law of nature in its natural state, as it were, *cannot but* be subject to the "arbitrary will" of individuals. They thus give up authority to make this judgment by entering into civil society. It would be a contradiction to say, then, that they retain this authority, since this would amount to saying that there is no submission to a common authority, which is the essence of civil society. So what could it mean to insist that the law of nature stands as an "Eternal Rule to all Men"?

It is in response to this question that we see the importance of the distinction Locke had drawn between civil society and the government proper. This distinction is meant to protect the people from possible abuses of power by those in government. When an individual gives his complete and permanently binding consent to enter into civil society, he does not necessarily consent to any particular form of government or to any particular holders of power: the deputizing of government represents a *subsequent* transfer of power, which can be measured by the extent to which it carries out the purposes of the original consent. Locke therefore insists that "the *Community* perpetually *retains a Supream Power* of saving themselves from the attempts and designs of any Body, even of their Legislators, whenever they shall be so foolish, or so wicked, as to lay and carry on designs against the Liberties and Properties of the Subject" (13.149). Locke's repeated return to the point underscores its importance: he comes back to it in his discussion of executive prerogative (14.168), and then, with great emphasis, in the concluding paragraphs of the *Second Treatise*. In this latter context, he explicitly raises the problem we are reflecting on:

> Here, 'tis like, the common Question will be made, *Who shall be Judge* whether the Prince [i.e., the executive power] or Legislative act contrary to their Trust? . . . To this I reply, *The People shall be Judge*; for who shall be *Judge* whether his Trustee or Deputy acts well, and according to the Trust reposed in him, but he who deputes him, and must, by having deputed him have still a Power to discard him, when he fails in his Trust? (19.240)

Note that Locke seems to indicate, here, that the transfer of power is an ineffectual one, because the original power is never in fact relinquished. We will return to this point in just a moment. First, however, we ought to see that Locke goes on in the passage, presumably because he feels the inadequacy of this claim, given the inherent problem of authority he recognized in the state of nature, to provide this judgment with what would seem to be an absolutely objective basis: "But further, this Question, (*Who shall be Judge?*) cannot mean, that there is no Judge at all. For where there is no Judicature on Earth, to decide Controversies amongst Men, *God* in Heaven is *Judge*: He alone, 'tis true, is Judge of the Right" (19.241). The inadequacy of this solution to the problem will become obvious in what follows, and we will see that it manages to unravel the very foundation of political order that Locke sought to put in place.

First, let us consider the implications of Locke's surprising attribution of "Supream Power" to the community. This is the very phrase he uses repeatedly to describe the legislative power on the one hand and the executive power on the other—precisely those bodies in relation to which the community is here being distinguished. We seem thus to have two (or even three) supreme powers set against each other. But Locke defuses the threat of this obvious contradiction by rejecting the possibility of a coincidence of these powers, at least with respect to the powers of the people and the government; the one begins, he explains, only when the other one ends: "The *Community* may be said in this respect to be *always* the *Supream Power*, but not as considered under any Form of Government, because this Power of the People can never take place till the Government be dissolved" (13.149).

There remain two fundamental problems, however, with this attempt at resolution. First of all, what could Locke mean by describing the people's power here as *perpetual*, and then saying it does not exist so long as there is an acting government? It would seem that the only explanation of this claim would follow the resolution we saw in chapter 1 of the problem of free will, which depends on the "power to suspend." In this case, the power the people have to resist the government, *as* a power, is effectively absent when it is not in use. In this sense, it can coincide with the actualization of an opposed power without in any sense entering into competition with it. We saw that the effective nonpresence, or nonpresent effectiveness, of the power to suspend transformed the character of the purely extrinsic determination of the will by making it something for which I become responsible, making it something I can—and in a certain sense *must*, whether or not I wish—call my own.

In the present case, we can say that the people's power to resist, even if it is not actualized, allows one to describe the government as in fact a function of the people's will, even if the content of its judgments has no relation to or even runs directly against that will. The acts of government remain theirs because, one might say, they always had the possibility of overthrowing it for another. The nonactualized possibility makes the obligation more fully binding. In this respect, the power to resist ironically strengthens the power of the possible object of resistance.

But this power to resist at the same time means that power was never in fact truly transferred. Locke observes that one cannot be said to have something as property that can be taken away at any moment: "I have truly no *Property* in that, which another can by right take from me, when he pleases, against my consent" (11.138). Moreover, he said that consent, and the relinquishing of individual judgment it implies, has to be taken to be definitive and absolute, or else the "*original Compact*, whereby he with others incorporate into *one Society*, would signifie nothing, and be no Compact" (8.97). A consent that retains the power to judge in each case is a straightforward contradiction.[118] Along these same lines, we can say that, insofar as there exists a positive right to revolt, governing power cannot be said finally to *belong* to the legislature, even for the period it is ostensibly given, because it can in principle be rescinded at any moment. It is not clear whether it would make sense, in these circumstances, to use the words "consent" and "compact" in relation to the establishment of government. Has one given consent when one can take it back at any moment? To this question, the obvious answer is that Locke is saying that the power given to the government can be rescinded *only if* the government fails to execute its trust; if the party to whom one pledges oneself in a contract does not fulfill his obligation, the contract itself is broken and one is released from one's own duties in its regard. But the question arises once again here: Who is the authority to judge whether the contract has been broken? The authority cannot *ultimately* lie in one of the contracted parties without that very fact rendering the contract meaningless.

This leads us to the second problem with Locke's attempt at resolution. The power of the people comes into effect, Locke says, only when "the Government [is] dissolved": But who has the power to declare the government dissolved? There is a logical difficulty here. It would seem to be the case that the people themselves would have the power to dissolve the government or to declare it dissolved, because it would seem unlikely, if not logically impossible, for a government effectively to declare that it is not a government.[119] Though he was referring to the limited situation of a particular dispute and not the replacement of government, Locke says that "if a Controversie arise betwixt a Prince and some of the People, in a matter where the Law is silent, or doubtful, and the thing be of great Consequence, I should think the proper *Umpire*, in such a Case, should be the Body of the *People*" (19.242). Extending this point, we might think that it is the people who have the power to dissolve government. But the people do not in fact have the power until *after* the government is dissolved. Locke repeats this condition in section 220: "*When the Government is dissolved*, the People are at liberty to provide for themselves, by erecting a new Legislative, differing from the other, by the change of Persons, or Form, or both, as they shall find it most for their safety and good."

Once again, Locke appears to give the people an extraordinary power over the authority to which they submit themselves, though it is in this case under the qualifying condition that the government be dissolved. This would seem to imply a successive shifting of absolute power: first the people have it, but then they transfer it to the legislative to which they are unconditionally subject, and then when it dissolves, they once again have absolute power to elect, and submit to, a new government. But when Locke repeats the point in this later context, he changes the condition quite dramatically:

To tell *People* they *may provide for themselves*, by erecting a new Legislative, when by Oppression, Artifice, or being delivered over to a Foreign Power, their old one is gone, is only to tell them they may expect Relief, when it is too late, and the evil is past Cure. This is in effect no more than to bid them first be Slaves, and then to take care of their Liberty; and when their Chains are on, tell them, they may act like Freemen. This, if barely so, is rather Mockery than Relief; and Men can never be secure from Tyranny, if there be no means to escape it, till they are perfectly under it: And therefore it is, that they have not only a Right to get out of it but to prevent it. (19.220)

It is not only an actual transgression of trust that dissolves the government and thereby liberates the people to establish a new one; instead, the perceived threat of such a transgression already provides grounds for resistance. This power must therefore be understood as always implicitly present, and so able to become effective whenever necessary. In this respect, the people, even when establishing a government with the ability to make laws to which they will necessarily owe obedience, can be said never actually to lie under "the Power of another" (19.217), which is precisely the motivation that drove them out of the state of nature in the first place.

We see that a "perceived threat" suffices to justify an overthrow of government. To say this would seem to entail a radical instability in any given political community that would exactly mirror the instability of the state of nature. Locke, however, gives a number of plausible reasons that revolution, even if it is recognized as a *right*—and indeed *precisely because* it is recognized as a right—will remain quite rare, the principal one of which is human indolence: "People are not so easily got out of their old Forms, as some are apt to suggest" (19.223). The pain of radical change outweighs the pain of occasional inconveniences, and so governments need not fear that the slightest mistake will precipitate revolt (19.225; cf. 18.207). Our concern, here, is not primarily the actual danger of instability, but rather the underlying nature of political order and the principles of authority or power in Locke's understanding. The notion of a "perceived threat" puts us in mind of the earlier description of the state of nature as inevitably a state of war. What generates this state, we saw, is the absence of an effective common authority, which leaves individuals to judge for themselves.

It would seem to be possible to avoid this collapse into disorder because of the difference between government and civil society: the dissolution of government would seem to leave us yet with the individual-transcending unity of the community, which is distinct from it. If there is any bond that Locke insists is indissoluble, it is the social contract.[120] Locke admits, however, that a community cannot exist if its government dissolves: "'Tis in their *Legislative*, that the Members of a Commonwealth are united, and combined together into one coherent living Body. This *is the Soul that gives Form, Life, and Unity* to the Commonwealth: From hence the several Members have their mutual Influence,

Sympathy, and Connexion: And therefore when the *Legislative* is broken, or *dissolved*, Dissolution and Death follows" (19.212).[121] It may be that the will of the people is distinct from the governmental institution, but this does not mean that the former can survive the latter. Can the people act as a "Body Politick" without some kind of organization, and therefore something at least analogous to government? Locke gives the "*Community*" the power to judge the justice of the government, but if there can *be* no community without government, what does it mean to say that the people judge that their trust has been abused other than that *each individual* makes the judgment for himself? Indeed, isn't it the case that the "will of the people" is just a manner of speaking, which indicates only the collective force generated by individual wills?[122] Locke himself ultimately points to just this individual judgment, which seems to present for him the final tribunal. When he raises the appeal to heaven as the last resort against an unjust government, after saying that "God alone . . . is Judge of the Right," he goes on: "But every Man is Judge for himself, as in all other Cases, so in this, whether another hath put himself in a State of Ware with him, and whether he should appeal to the Supreme Judge" (19.241). And again:

> Force between either Persons, who have no known Superiour on Earth, or which permits no Appeal to a Judge on Earth, being properly a state of War, wherein the Appeal lies only to Heaven, and in that State the *injured Party must judge* for himself, when he will think fit to make use of that Appeal, and put himself upon it. (19.242)

Locke states quite clearly that, when the holder of governmental power oversteps the bounds of his charge, he enters into a state of war with the people (chapter 18). This would seem to imply that, if he remains within his bounds, there is no state of war, but peace. The point we are making, however, is that because the people, that is, each individual, necessarily retains the power to judge the legislative power—and *therefore* the obligation, since the existence of the power inescapably means its nonuse is an actual choice for which one has responsibility—the individuals remain in truth in the state of nature, which has the inner form of the state of war, and this inner form cannot but be actualized to one degree or another. There may be an explicit "appeal to heaven" mentioned here, while in the original state of nature the appeal was only implicit, mediated through the appeal to natural justice, but the effect in both cases is the same: because, in both cases, there is no basis for judgment other than one's own individual perception, the appeal to heaven or to justice can mean only making the judgment for oneself. Individuals abandoned the latent hostilities of the state of nature in order to submit to a *common authority*, but because this submission is safeguarded by nothing more than a natural law, impotent in itself and so dependent on individual judgment and power, the common authority remains finally subject to individuals.[123] And this is a contradiction: the individual has submitted his will to a supreme judgment, over which he has the final say; he has given his irrevocable consent, which he retains the right to take back.

THE DISSOLUTION OF COMMUNITY

Once we see that the "Power of the People" means "every Man is Judge for himself," then we realize that we have to radicalize Locke's discussion of the "dissolution of government." This last chapter of the *Second Treatise* ought to have been followed by a chapter entitled "The Dissolution of Community," which Locke never wrote but which his principles imply by an inescapable logic. This chapter, if written, would describe, we suggest, not some possible catastrophe, but the constant state of things, the normal condition of political order as Locke understands it. To see why, it is helpful to begin with the final paragraph of Locke's *Second Treatise*:

> To conclude, The *Power that every individual gave the Society*, when he entered into it, can never revert to the Individuals again, as long as the Society lasts, but will always remain in the Community: because without this, there can be no Community, no Commonwealth, which is contrary to the original Agreement: So also when the Society hath placed the Legislative in any Assembly of Men, to continue in them and their Successors, with Direction and Authority for providing such Successors, *the Legislative can never*

revert to the People whilst that Government lasts: Because having provided a Legislative with Power to continue for ever, they have given up their Political Power to the Legislative, and cannot resume it.

Thus far in this passage, we see that Locke refers to two moments of consent, the first by which individuals constitute community through a transfer of their natural power, and the second by which the community constitutes government. There is a parallel between these: both transfers of power are definitive and irrevocable. But then Locke goes on to qualify the second transfer:

But if they have set Limits to the Duration of their Legislative, and made this Supreme Power in any Person, or Assembly, only temporary: Or else when by the Miscarriages of those in Authority, it is forfeited; upon the Forfeiture of their Rulers, or at the Determination of the Time set, *it reverts to the Society*, and the People have a Right to act as Supreme, and continue the Legislative in themselves, or erect a new Form, or under the old form place it in new hands, as they think good. (19.243)

The bond of obedience that society gives to the government dissolves when the political authority miscarries (which we have seen means also when such a miscarriage is perceived to be a threatening possibility). But Locke, curiously, does not add any condition to the first consent, which seems to remain absolute and without any measure outside of it. What justifies the *absolute* absoluteness in the first case (as opposed to the *relative* absoluteness of the second)? No satisfying response to this question is forthcoming. Indeed, quite the opposite is true. Locke says that the first consent has to be really irrevocable (as opposed to apparently irrevocable) because to revoke the consent would be "contrary to the original Agreement," but of course the very same can be said for the second agreement. We might appeal to the natural justice that Locke says necessarily makes all promises binding (2.14),[124] which might be said to apply more directly to the first agreement than to the second, insofar as this latter is more properly conventional. But even if we grant this rather dubious point, there are two rejoinders to make: first, Locke claims that a promise made in duress is not binding (16.176), and what is the state of war, out of which the original social contract arises, but a state of duress? This would seem to make the second pact more binding than the first, because it presupposes, at least ostensibly, that the state of war has been left behind. The very necessity that Locke insists compels man to form civil society renders the act by which it is formed entirely unreliable; this promise is worth as much as the paper it is written on. Locke's social contract is in fact no more real than the law of nature, which he concedes exists "no where but in the minds of Men" (11.136)—that is, in the varying perceptions of individuals.

But the second rejoinder is even more decisive: we are obliged by our promise only if the other party satisfies its own obligations. Thus, everything that Locke said about the power of the people remaining perpetually supreme even in the apparent transfer of authority to the legislature—Who, asks Locke, has the power to judge but the one who deputes?—can be said about the individual in the apparent transfer of authority to civil society. We observed earlier that the individual is necessarily subject to the will of the majority, which is mathematically irresistible. But according to the principles he has established, it turns out that the individual cannot but have a power of judgment over that will, and so a responsibility regarding the use or nonuse of that power. The positing of the power to resist is in the end same as the positing of consent (and since these are conceived as *powers*, they may be imputed in fact without having to be real). But did they not all agree to give the power of judgment to a "common judge" precisely in order to end the dispute, in order to produce some grounds that would allow one to distinguish justice from revenge, and indeed from simple violence? Yes, but the agreement that set this judge in place is a contract, the terms of which are the self-preservation of each individual. It follows that, though we agreed on a common judge, we cannot surrender the right, and so the duty, to judge in each case whether in fact justice has been done or instead my freedom has been encroached upon, which would mean that I have been forced, willy-nilly, to remain in a state of war. Thus, it is not the executive, the legislative, or even the community that has "Supream Power," in the end; there is, in addition, a fourth, namely, the individual in himself (though this does not in the least imply that this power has any effective force). The position we arrive at here coincides perfectly with Locke's fundamental argument in the *Essay*, namely, that the ultimate judgment of truth falls to each individual for himself. But Locke insists that, to the extent that individuals retain the right to judge over the terms and execution of a contract, there *is* no contract. What this means is that the social contract that forms the basis of Locke's political vision necessarily fails in its purpose.[125] The very condition he sets for the existence of community at the beginning (8.97), he denies at the end (19.241).

CIVIL SOCIETY AS A STATE OF WAR

The point we intend to make here is not that civil society, for Locke, is inevitably a war zone in any immediately recognizable sense. Locke's response to the objection that his establishment of a right to revolt would undermine the substance of political authority and so destabilize society would seem to apply with equal, or perhaps even greater, force at this more basic level: human beings are creatures of convenience and habit, and they can be expected to prefer the occasional missteps in the distribution of justice in their regard to the radical disorder that would come with explicitly breaking the social contract. An individual would generally have little reason to want to make the attempt, except perhaps in the most extreme circumstances. Reassurance can always be found in the fact that, in a reasonably ordered society, laws are "standing" and are impersonal and universal (even if they require *persons*, finally, in order to be made effective). Those who break the law can be expected for the most part to be apprehended and punished, and the power to punish grows immensely when the perpetrator, in breaking the law, thereby in principle forfeits its protection. Moreover, the "power to resist" increases the effective force of government regulation in two ways: on the one hand, the principle that one is obliged to obey only the authority to which one consents entails the principle that one is positively obliged to obey that authority, because one has consented, and so the imputation of consent deepens the claim that the authority has on the individual; on the other hand, one is more willing to obey an authority if one feels one has the power to judge it, just as one is more willing to commit to a purchase when one is told one has the right to

return it at any time for a full refund. Finally, the fact that individuals retain the right and obligation to judge the will of the majority in every
case does not *in fact* mean that the will of the majority becomes any less
irresistible. To the contrary, the transformation of politics into the distribution of power both imposes this right (and so obligation) onto the
individual and at the very same time (in a manner we will elaborate further in chapter 5) makes the majority will a force against which the individual simply cannot stand. The right to resist it only serves to make the
majority will less and less intrinsically meaningful for the individual, because it makes that will essentially alienating in the strict sense of the
term. In short, the failure of the social contract need not entail any *manifest* breakdown of society. Increasing disorder can coincide with increasing efficiency and organization (one might say that this is the very
definition of bureaucracy). The artificiality of political order does not
necessarily make it any less stable; in this respect, it may be like the
Twinkie, which can last forever precisely because it no longer has any
organic ingredients, being made up of synthetic substitutes.

Again, the dissolution of community need not be overt. The point
we wish to make is much more subtle, and, indeed, dialectical. The
state of war, in Locke, is never actually remedied but simply driven underground, as it were. This is another way of saying that, in Locke,
there *is never any community in reality*, but *only* in appearance. Social
bonds have no substance, but are rather shared illusions, the strength of
which depends on the force of the individual wills that agree to share
them, and indeed so depends at every single moment. The point of these
social bonds, in fact, turns out not even to be safety, as Locke contends,
but only the feeling of safety. Order becomes itself a social construct,
which means it is a figment of the collective imagination generated
from below. Because it is mere appearance, it is not even the case that
people have to conform to the order of law; they need only *appear* to
conform, which means they must seek to keep others from perceiving a
threat to their safety. The main energy of government is spent on keeping people from appearing to be threats to each other, and from appearing, itself, to be such a threat. If community is not in the first place an
intrinsic good, supremely worth pursuing even if it generated no extrinsic benefits, if, in other words, it is justified ultimately by some external end—for example, the preservation of property of the individu-

als that constitute it—then community can be substituted for by anything else that might accomplish this end. And it *ought* to be replaced by anything that can accomplish it better. In his journal, Locke observed that "the principal spring from which the actions of men take their rise, the rule they conduct them by, and the end to which they direct them, seems to be credit and reputation, and that which at any rate they avoid in the greatest part shame and disgrace. . . . He therefore that would govern the world well had need consider rather what fashions he makes than what laws, and to bring anything into use, he need only give it reputation."[126] As Plato judged many centuries before Locke, a social order that is produced by consent will play itself out at the level of appearances, which is the sphere of existence governed by the force of power.[127]

We saw at the end of chapter 1 the dialectical implications of Locke's conception of freedom: as pure power, the will can be indifferently described in any instance as wholly a master of itself and as wholly a passive function of external determinants. This paradox must be kept in mind in order to appreciate the full scope of the implications of political freedom as Locke articulates it, and to keep us from the misleading complaint that an overemphasis on freedom will weaken the force of law. The murky formlessness of human interaction can coincide with a social order that is hard as steel, and it will continue to clank away in perpetuity, with all of the reliability of a machine. The essentially insubstantial character of social bonds in Locke's political philosophy does not necessarily make them any looser. Quite to the contrary, eliminating their reality can tighten them to the point of becoming all but inescapable. If the fear for one's safety generated in the state of war is what drove one to hand authority, through consent to join others in the social contract, to the will of the majority and the law-making body it deputizes, any sense at all that the state of war lingers will only compel one to hand oneself all the more unreservedly over to that authority. If the object of one's addiction fails to satisfy, one's most immediate response is *not* to give up pursuit of that object. In the political sphere, the recognition that law does not succeed in binding all the members of society tends to make people cling more desperately to it, though of course by the same token it cannot help but generate a certain cynicism regarding law and the authority behind it. In a society formed by Locke's principles of political order, one would expect to find law simultaneously wielded as a personal weapon and appealed to as a kind of untouchable absolute that is superior to us all.[128] Given this dialectical character, it represents no contradiction for a culture to proliferate endless legal regulation precisely in the name of freedom: "*The end of Law*," as Locke says, "is not to abolish or restrain, but *to preserve and enlarge Freedom*" (6.57)—and therefore necessarily to enlarge the scope of regulation, without which freedom cannot exist.

If we keep the dialectical character of Lockean freedom in mind, we realize that interpreting Locke as *either* an individualist who has no place for social relations *or* as a "collectivist" who relentlessly tramples on the rights of individuals fails to see the heart of the matter, and we see why these two aspects are simply flip sides of the same coin.[129] Richard Cox, for example, explains that "the individual's right to self-preservation . . . is necessarily absorbed by and subordinated to the commonwealth's right to self-preservation."[130] This is certainly true, and one can find expression of this principle in the text, but one can also find clear statements in which Locke subordinates the commonwealth to the individuals that constitute it.[131] We do not have to see these claims as competing if we understand that, when the individual surrenders power to the majority, which thereby becomes irresistible, he always simultaneously retains it "in potentia," and this is a potency that in principle could be actualized in any given circumstances, so that the actuality becomes trivialized. We have been arguing that the individual is both absorbed into the community and remains the final judge over its legitimacy. To sharpen the dialectic further: the individual's being the final judge is just what absorbs him into the community, and his absorption into the community is what imposes on him the obligation of standing outside of it as a final judge. We will spell this dialectic out further in chapter 6.

This same dialectic complicates the classic debate concerning the relative priority of rights and duties in Locke's notion of natural law. Thus, John Dunn says that rights for Locke are always a function of obligations, so that the fundamental right to self-preservation is a result of our being created by God, and so has the form of a *duty* to preserve ourselves and then by extension a duty to preserve everyone else.[132] Cox, by contrast, argues that, in Locke, rights are "by nature absolutely superior to duties, because man's natural desires are prior to any theoretical and therefore unnatural restrictions on them."[133] The absolute priority of duty over right or of right over duty is interchangeable depending on context. As we saw in chapter 1, no matter how "natural" a desire is, for Locke, it only ever has a *potential* effectiveness, which is actualized according to choice and whatever "theoretical and unnatural restrictions" choice happens to set (though of course this is not to deny that every choice is in turn driven by desire). If the will is pure power, duties can be actually imposed without eliminating the will *as* potency. As we have shown, pure potency can always coincide with its actual opposite. The preservation of persons and their property is the final end of political society, but even this purpose tends to lose an actual, objective foundation. It is true that Locke generally acknowledges that the person's basic right to self-preservation is inalienable because the person himself, as it were, has no rights over this right: he has a *duty* to preserve himself that trumps any rights he has potentially to destroy himself. This means in turn that he cannot transfer a right over his person to any other person, or to the community at large. But to the extent that the person is conceived most basically in terms of power, we fall into the same dialectic here that we have seen everywhere else. Insofar as the person is a power, his relation to others will take the form of a conflict of forces, and this conflict can be adjudicated only on these terms. One side or the other has to win, and that side will tend to be the strongest.

Moreover, a power is real, for Locke, only to the extent that it actualizes itself, and, since there is no connection between the actualization and the power, that power is in itself impotent, lacking any claim on the actualization, and so wholly dependent on the relatively arbitrary will of what lies outside of it. Those who cannot actualize themselves (the sick, the disabled, the infirm, the enslaved) and those who have *not yet* actualized themselves (children and the unborn) have only an ineffectual claim on the respect of others.[134]

In the end, for Locke, there is no organic unity between the natural individual and the civil community, which would imply that each brings the other to an internal perfection; instead, both simply collapse without resistance into the other, while at the same time they exclude each other, never coming into contact, like parallel lines that can be extended into infinity. Civil society never rises above a naturalistic horizon, even while nature is rendered altogether artificial.

A regular refrain of our analysis of Locke has been that he substitutes a primacy of potency over actuality for the primacy of actuality one finds in classical thought. This is an oversimplification insofar as the actual cannot help but be primary *in fact*. More adequately formulated, then, we ought to say that potency itself becomes in Locke the highest actuality, in which all things participate. In other words, power becomes the actual horizon, and everything within the horizon takes on the character of power as its most basic form. The implications this form has for the nature of relationships between and among persons and things has become evident: political community is human relationship writ large, and if political community is deprived of internal substance, so too will be the various relationships that are meant to grow within its defining borders.[135] Plato describes the good as a kind of metaphysical glue that binds things internally together.[136] As we will see in part 3, this notion of the good lies at the foundation of classical political order, and it is what gives that order, and so all of the relationships that constitute it, a certain ontological depth. Locke precludes the good from the outset, and he then fabricates a substitute that aims to fulfill the various functions of the good, but now on fundamentally different terms. Instead of enjoyment, there is labor, instead of goods, there are uses, instead of substance, we have property, instead of property, we have money, instead of bonds, we have boundaries, instead of connection, we have contract, instead of order, we have regulation, and so forth. Locke's political theory represents a conquest of the ordering principle of human life, which then allows that principle to retain its rule only if it changes its meaning.

The final word of Locke's *Treatise* is "good." But this no longer indicates that which has intrinsic value, and so presents an a priori claim on all human beings, and the communities they form. Instead, Locke has reduced this good to what "they think good" (19.243), and this "they," in turn, is reduced to the individuals' will and the effective force they are able to give it.

CONCLUSION: ZERO TOLERANCE

Let us return to the question we articulated in the opening of this chapter and summarize our answer to it. The question was this, given Locke's interpretation of freedom as power, which is disconnected from actuality: What does the realization of freedom in the political order look like? Power that is disconnected from actuality can be made actual only by turning into its opposite, but at the same time remaining present as an ineffectual potency.[137] We have seen this occur in Locke's political philosophy in two essential ways. First, Locke articulates a person's positive presence in the social sphere in terms of *property*. But rather than seeing property as the individual's being brought into the world, the extension, so to speak, of one's freedom *into* the actuality of the social order, or perhaps the objective "publicizing" of one's subjective inner being, Locke interprets it in exactly the opposite direction: property is the annexing of the actuality of the world into the inner, subjective sphere of private ownership. There is thus an inner tendency for ownership to take the form of money, which is when, we might say, actual goods become abstract power. As we will explore in more detail in chapter 5, money is the *appearance* of property. If freedom is conceived as power, then a basic form of the exercise of freedom on the world is the conversion of the world into money. The way freedom is exercised in relation to people, on the other hand, is through the setting of boundaries (rights and the laws that protect them). The proper crossing of these boundaries, and so the positive relationship with other human beings, takes the form of a contract, which represents the aligning of otherwise mutually indifferent, if not opposed, forces. But insofar as contracts, without any sense of a transcendent good that is actual as their foundation, remain a function of the individual wills that constitute them, they are in reality an accidental coincidence of private interests and only present the *appearance* of social bonds. Forming a relationship, in this case, becomes identical with fixing the boundaries that keep us separate: good fences make good neighbors.[138] Contracts are a kind of objectification of relationships that does not have ontological actuality any more than money does. In short, the political actualization of power *qua* power takes the form of the accumulation of property that is unreal and the entering into bonds that are unreal. The more fully freedom is exercised in this way, the more deeply one is driven into an isolation from both the world and other people (not to mention from oneself), which is coincident with an abject vulnerability to being swallowed up impotently into these relations. We will see in part 2 of the book how freedom, thus conceived, locks one in a very dark place.

We have seen that Locke's interpretation of the will and its free-dom as power requires the neutralizing of the good and any a priori claim it might make on my will before its exercise. We have described this as a "potentializing" of the good, a reinterpreting of its actuality as possibility. Along these lines, we may understand in a more generalized way the importance of nature in Locke's political thought. Nature rep-resents for Locke the "original" from which political authority is de-rived (2.4) and is the "Eternal Law" against which everything is finally measured (11.135). For Locke, nature thus stands as a kind of authority that is in a certain respect *universal* insofar as it transcends individuals and so promises to provide a principle of political order, but at the same time it does not have an *actual* authority over individuals insofar as it cannot, as it were, speak for itself. Nature, paradoxically, is a supreme authority that ranks lower than the individual will, and so can always be trumped by it in any particular instance. It is just this para-dox that generates the various dialectics we have sought in this chapter to make clear.

It may seem that, in Locke's appeal to nature as an authority, he is returning to the classical tradition. But as we hope to discuss at greater length in a future study, nature has a radically different status prior to the claim of Christian revelation and after that claim. In the first case, nature is understood in relation to the actuality of the ultimate, namely, the good (or God), *as far as it is actual in fact.* The status of nature is al-together different when, after the fact of revelation, that actuality is ex-plicitly denied. It is illuminating, specifically in this context,[139] to con-sider the significance of the other great text that Locke published more or less simultaneously with the two we have studied in this book, namely, the *Letter Concerning Toleration.*[140] This text is of course one of the charters of Western liberalism. As is well known, in response to the religious persecution that poisoned the political communities in Locke's age, the *Letter* argues for the acceptance of any religious doc-trine or form of worship that does not disrupt political order.[141] In other words, it champions what we would today call "openness" in re-ligious matters. Following the logic of our interpretation, we can say that Locke's call for political toleration amounts in fact to a "potential-izing" of the ultimate. Locke does not deny the existence of God or the truth of religion;[142] indeed, he affirms these as indispensable, to the extent that atheists have to be excluded from toleration.[143] What Locke *does* deny, however, is the *actuality* of religion—in other words, he denies the objective authority of any concrete, historical form that religion might take.[144] But of course a religion cannot exist except concretely in history. If a religion, which means the effective manifestation of *ultimate* meaning, exists concretely in history, it necessarily makes a claim on me prior to my act of will, because it makes a claim on everything without exception. To recognize this claim is to see that actuality precedes potency, and if this is true ultimately, it will be true, so to speak, all the way down. And this will mean that freedom will necessarily have to be interpreted as sharing in actuality, a response to the good that precedes me and makes my choice of it possible; the actualizing of the will in this case comes to mean being brought into an actual world, a tradition, and a hierarchy of goods. *Actual* religion is therefore incompatible with an interpretation of freedom primarily as active power. Locke can affirm freedom as power only by transforming at the same time the status of religion.[145] It can no longer be a single truth that precedes political agents, but it has to become an array of possibilities, any one of which individuals are free to accept, at least within the constraints of political order. Within these constraints, I am permitted to affirm any religion as true, and practice it thus in public, as long as I recognize that this has a new meaning that would strike an ancient thinker as confusing, if not simply confused: it is true *"for me."* Notice that the potentializing of religion in this way allows one to neutralize the implications of the existence of God without having to shoulder the burden of responsibility that would come with rejecting God outright.[146] In short, the precondition for the emergence of the modern concept of freedom is not the denial of God, but the denial of his actual self-revelation in history. Modern liberty, at its core, is a rejection specifically of the incarnation, God's coming *in the flesh.*

PART TWO

Modern Liberty as
a Flight from the Real

CHAPTER 3

The Basic Shape
of Modern Liberty

Our first two chapters have explored the thought of John Locke, but our interest in that thought is primarily as an expression of a dominant trend in modern and contemporary understanding. We thus in this chapter begin to reflect on the concept of freedom, as it appears in modern thought, in a more general way. Our aim here is to distill the basic pattern, to give it a name, and to capture its significance, as far as such a thing is possible, in a concrete image.

Before we enter upon that reflection, however, it will be good to show that Locke's notion of freedom is not an isolated case, the interest of which would be apparent above all, if not exclusively, to intellectual historians. The features of Locke's interpretation of freedom as active power, we trust, will have struck anyone inhabiting the modern Western world as at least remotely familiar, and this impression will no doubt grow as we begin to generalize. But it is worth pointing out the echo of what we have detected in Locke's thought in other representative thinkers of modernity, who are not usually thought of as belonging to the same intellectual stream. Let us make clear that, in having selected Locke as our focus in the two preceding chapters, we do not mean to claim that he is especially influential in the specific sense that his works were widely read and his ideas about freedom in particular were found to be persuasive to people in high positions (though this is clear in certain parts of the English-speaking world), so that one could identify a particular following and perhaps even trace the impact of this following on actual historical events and political or philosophical developments. However much truth there may be in any of this, our interest in Locke is not as an "efficient" cause of historical or intellectual developments, but rather as a *formal* cause, one might say. Regardless of what notions preceded or followed him, Locke sums up and crystallizes a particular understanding of freedom that has been decisive for the Western world. Accordingly, what we wish to show, in these preliminary observations, is that the basic form of Locke's idea of freedom can be found in other landmark modern thinkers, who might be said to represent opposite poles of modern thought. Considering them will thus provide a simple glimpse into the broad sweep of modern thought generally. If Locke is taken to be a representative of the "empirical" school of modern thinkers, Spinoza is a good representative of the "rationalist" school, and Kant one who attempted to reconcile the two traditions.[1]

We ought first to identify the basic form that we have discerned, with the proviso that this basic form is a simplifying specification of the work of our first two chapters: we will have to give nuance to this form in the rest of this chapter and the one that follows. The essential feature of modern liberty that has emerged from our exploration up to this point is *power*. We saw that Locke interpreted freedom as a question of (productive) power in the ontological sense (and, indeed, in the political sense), that is, more specifically, an ability to cause a change in something external to that power. According to this view, freedom is a transitive activity, an "acting *on*," a transfer of energy from a source (cause) to a recipient (effect). It is important to note, immediately, that the act need not be a physical one, that is, a change in matter and/or motion; the act of will may instead give rise to thoughts, judgments, decisions, and so forth, that never come to bear on what is called the "outside world." Nevertheless, change in the physical sense (*metabolē* as *kinesis*) appears as the paradigm, which is expressed analogously in all other acts of will, including the exclusively "internal" acts. Our thesis has been that the conception of freedom as power in this sense entails a dialectic, whereby freedom ceases to have actual being or bearing on the "real" world—reality *in se*—and becomes instead a question above all of subjective appropriation, interpretation, or disposition—reality only *quoad me*. We will argue that the various forms by which such a conception of freedom is embodied in the objective, social order turn out, then, to display analogous dialectical tendencies, which we intend to explore at greater length. Our first concern, however, is to see how something similar to the essential form of freedom that we discerned in Locke is manifest in the thought of Spinoza and Kant.

In fact, the presence of the basic features of what we have distilled as the concept of modern liberty is not difficult to recognize in these two philosophers, however different the ethos of their philosophies may be or how divergent the concepts of freedom may become in their details. It is the well-known and basically uncontroversial understanding of freedom that both thinkers straightforwardly present (uncontroversial in terms of *what* they claim, not, of course, in terms of the justice, value, or implications of their claims, which have been endlessly disputed). However numerous and weighty may be the differences between these theories of freedom, there are five features the thinkers all turn out to share in common. On the anthropological level, (1) they conceive of freedom as a kind of active power, and (2) they affirm that this freedom is incompatible with heteronomy, paradigmatically in the form of an opposed active power, insofar as anything else that is external can be appropriated in such a way that it loses its heteronomous character. On the political level, we have (3) a reduction of political order to the preservation of the individual's natural rights through the regulation of external behavior, and (4) a rejection of any a priori *specific* religious claim, that is, any *authoritative* affirmation of God as revealed in an actual, historical form and so as presenting a claim on obedience—that is, on the will not only in its external activities but above all in its internal action—as a prior context for all other political determinations. Finally, (5) for all of their emphasis on spontaneous power, there is a tendency in all of these thinkers for freedom to collapse into the objectivity of some form of determinism, whether it be natural, logical, psychological, metaphysical, or political.

To reiterate: we are not claiming that these three thinkers have the same theory of freedom, but rather that, amidst their significant differences, they have five features in common, all of which we take to be essential aspects of what we are calling "modern liberty." Having dwelt at length on Locke, let us now briefly consider the other two thinkers in turn.

SPINOZA

Freedom and its essence lie at the heart of Spinoza's philosophy.[2] Matthew Kisner has recently argued that we can gather the various aspects of Spinoza's view of freedom, at both the philosophical and the political level, into a unity when we see that the whole turns on the concept of *power*: "Freedom amounts to acting from one's power, what [Spinoza] calls *conatus* or striving, while he understands the good as whatever promotes one's power."[3] Spinoza offers a succinct definition of freedom in the beginning of his *Ethics*: "That thing is said to be free which exists solely from the necessity of its own nature, and is determined to action by itself alone."[4] God is absolute freedom, insofar as there is nothing external to him, and so nothing but what is an expression of the necessity of his own nature. Human beings, however, are finite, and so subject to a great many things outside of their control. The key to achieving freedom for Spinoza is understanding: we internalize things by grasping their causes. To have an adequate idea of a thing is to grasp in an exhaustive manner the totality of causes that bring it about. To the extent that one succeeds in attaining an adequate idea, one becomes *active power*, one achieves a freedom with respect to that thing.[5] By contrast, to have an *inadequate* idea of a thing is to be affected by it as something external to oneself, which means one is *passive* with respect to it and just so far unfree. The possession of freedom coincides with the internalizing of what would otherwise be the imposing force of external causes, and so the elimination of heteronomy.

It is important to note that, because of the identification of freedom and proper understanding, there is evidently not a trace of arbitrariness in Spinoza's conception of freedom; to the contrary, freedom comes to mean a conformity of the mind to an absolutely necessary order of things, an order that remains identical regardless of whether one has appropriated it intellectually or not. Thus, in his correspondence, Spinoza explains that freedom is typically associated with indeterminacy, but he claims that this amounts to an identification of freedom with ignorance of the cause that inescapably determines one's actions.[6] Spinoza defines freedom as just the opposite: "I place freedom, not in free decision, but in free necessity."[7] Genuine freedom consists in the renunciation of will, since its arbitrariness is inseparable from a subjection to external causes. Spinoza explains, therefore, that it is wrong to suppose even that God has a "will" that is in any real sense distinct from perfect, eternal, and unchanging understanding of the natural order of things. Spinoza's identification of freedom with perfect understanding of what is eternally unchanging—the famous "amor intellectualis"[8]—may seem to be an utterly "quietistic" conception of freedom, but it can at the same time be interpreted as wholly spontaneous, since it views actions as produced wholly by the precedent causes, now identified through knowledge with the agent. It is therefore consistent for Spinoza to conclude, at the end of the *Ethics*, that freedom *excludes* any receptive condition with respect to what is other: "The more perfection a thing has, the more active and the less passive it is. Conversely, the more active it is, the more perfect it is."[9] Although the ethos of Spinoza in this regard is so evidently different from that of Locke, and he betrays no concern to retain some aspect of "free decision" (as Locke does in his correspondence with his Dutch Arminian friends), we see that they arrive at a similar point in the end: a simultaneity of freedom and determinism, interpreted as the acquisition of power *over* what might affect one from the outside.

As for the political expression of this notion of freedom, we see that Spinoza and Locke are also very much of one mind. Freedom as power, thus conceived, translates into a natural right of self-preservation. Thus Spinoza: "Now since it is the supreme law of Nature that each thing endeavours to persist in its present being, as far as in it lies, taking account of no other thing but itself, it follows that each individual has the sovereign right to do this, that is (as I have said), to exist and to act as it is naturally determined."[10] In the state of nature, there is no justice or injustice, because everything belongs equally to all, at least *potentially*: "for there is nothing in Nature that can rightly be said to belong to one man and not another; all things belong to all, that is, to all who have the power [*potestatem*] to gain possession of them."[11] Insofar as the impetus to exercise this authority lies in *individuals as such*, the state of nature tends to set people against each other as enemies: "Whatever every man, when he is considered as solely under the dominion of Nature, believes to be to his advantage, whether under the guidance of sound reason or under passion's sway, he may by sovereign natural right seek and get for himself by any means, by force,

deceit, entreaty or in any other way best he can, and he may consequently regard as his enemy anyone who tries to hinder him from getting what he wants."[12]

To escape from the fear that this state-of-nature-cum-state-of-war
entails, the people must *all* either "tacitly or expressly" transfer their
natural right *entirely* to the "body politic."[13] Because the entry into civil
society occurs through an act of will conceived as a transfer of power, a
dialectical relationship obtains between the part and the whole, the individual and the political authority of the state. On the one hand, the
individual is eclipsed by the state: he hands over "the whole of his
power" to the body politic, which thus represents an accumulation of
individual instances of power. Against this accumulation, the individual
unity is effectively nothing. As Spinoza puts it in his later *Theologico-
Political Treatise*: "If two men come together and join forces, they have
more power over Nature, and consequently more right, than either one
alone; and the greater the number who form a union in this way, the
more right they will together possess,"[14] and so "each of them has that
much less right the more he is exceeded in power by the others collectively. That is to say, he has in reality no right over Nature except that
which is granted him by the communal right. For the rest, he is bound
to carry out any command that is laid on him by communal consensus,
or else he may be rightly compelled to do so."[15] Note that right, here, is
not being defined by a reference to any transcendent principle of justice, but rather by power, and indeed by power as determined quantitatively. On the other hand, because the state is *democratic*, the individual retains a share of this power, which is to say that the authority is
not simply something alien to him that descends on him from above.
There is no figure of authority who stands *above* any particular individual: "Nobody transfers his natural right to another so completely
that thereafter he is not to be consulted; he transfers it to the majority
of the entire community of which he is part. In this way all men remain equal, as they were before in a state of nature."[16] But if all remain
equals, all remain standing opposed to one another: "Men are by nature enemies, and even when they are joined and bound together by
laws they still retain their nature."[17] This state remains even when individuals enter into contracts willingly, which means that these contracts
never *actually* bind anyone: "Everyone has the natural right to act de-

ceitfully and is not bound to keep his engagements except through hope of greater good or fear of greater evil."[18] Just as in Locke, so too here, there is an absoluteness of the state into which the individual, along with the rights that define him by nature, is wholly absorbed by the artifice of the social contract, and at the same time one could justifiably argue that man never in fact escapes from the state of nature, and its implicit universal war, insofar as the transfer of power rests on the consent of individuals, who thus always retain the right to break the contract whenever necessary. The individual is completely eclipsed by the state, and the state is wholly subject to the individuals.

It may seem, on the surface, that Spinoza's view of the church–state relation is the exact opposite of Locke's mature position,[19] since Spinoza grants to the sovereign power supreme authority to regulate the worship of God by force of law. But his position turns out to be quite similar: Spinoza does indeed give the sovereign power authority in regulating external practices, but he insists that these practices have virtually nothing to do with true religion, which is wholly a private matter. Thus, on the one hand, the state is to have complete authority in matters of religion: "When I said above that only those who hold the sovereign power have an overall right and that all law is dependent on their decision alone, I intended not only civil but religious law; for in the case of the latter, too, they must be both the interpreters and guardians." On the other hand, "inward worship of God and piety itself belong to the sphere of individual right which cannot be transferred to another."[20] This absolute piety of the individual concerns not only religion but also, and indeed *therefore*, everything at all: as is well known, Spinoza was above all a champion of individual freedom of thought and speech.[21] The best way to preserve control of the public sphere is precisely to cede complete power over the private sphere of thought and belief to the private individual: "If honesty is to be prized rather than obsequiousness, and if sovereigns are to retain full control and not be forced to surrender to agitators, it is imperative to grant freedom of judgment and to govern men in such a way that the different and conflicting views they openly proclaim do not debar them from living together in peace."[22]

It may seem strange that Spinoza would champion individual freedom politically when *in fact* by freedom he means the total conformity of the individual to the objective, necessary order of the cosmos. But our argument regarding Locke applies analogously to Spinoza; we need to see that these apparently opposed notions are simply flip sides of the same coin. What we have with Spinoza, in the end, is an absolute dualism: complete (natural and political) determinism regarding what is external, objective, that is, "real," and complete supremacy of the individual regarding what is internal, subjective: "The state can pursue no safer course than to regard piety and religion as consisting solely in the exercise of charity and just dealing, and that the right of the sovereign, both in religious and secular spheres, should be restricted to men's actions, with everyone being allowed to think what he will and to say what he thinks."[23] Here there appears once again the simultaneity of power and impotence, which we have described as the essential dialectic that comes into effect when one interprets freedom as power. For all of their differences, Spinoza and Locke end up in essentially the same place.

KANT

Kant is well known for rejecting the sort of rationalist, compatibilist view of freedom that one finds, for example, in Spinoza: to think of action as subject to necessary causes but as free merely because the cause is *internal* to the agent's nature is to posit what he says is nothing more than the freedom of a turnspit, which operates mechanically according to the pushing and pulling of automatic components, once it has been wound up.[24] For Kant, we cannot consider ourselves free unless we are the *authors* of our actions, their absolute and unconditioned first cause ("absolute" in the sense of one's being able to stop the causal chain of explanation at the point of the agent's will), so that we can *finally* attribute responsibility for a person's actions to the person himself, regardless of circumstances. To be free is to be "active power," to use Locke's term, that is, to be the source of the change we call an action; in Kant's terms, freedom is the faculty of "unconditioned causality," so that being free means having "a principle in which reason does not call upon something *else* as the determining ground with respect to its causality but already itself contains this determining ground by that principle, and in which it is therefore as *pure reason* itself practical."[25] At the same time, however, Kant affirms—like Locke and Spinoza—the inescapable causal determinism of nature. The most fundamental theoretical problem of his practical philosophy is to reconcile free agency with that natural determinism. It is the conflict between these two theses that Kant articulates in his famous third antinomy of pure reason.[26] His solution to this antinomy turns out to be essentially a translation into the terminology of transcendental idealism of precisely the resolution we described in Locke in the face of the very same problem—with the difference that Kant worked out the resolution more explicitly (while Locke left off trying to resolve it and so left the resolution implicit). This is not surprising given Kant's relentless logical clarity. In his account of this idea in Kant, Allen Wood describes Kant's ultimate position in just the same terms we used to describe Locke in chapter 1: Kant does not seek simply to reconcile freedom with natural determinism—that is, he does not adapt "compatibilism." Instead, he seeks to reconcile an interpretation of agency that is compatible with natural determinism with an incompatibilist interpretation, that is, with one that denies the sufficiency of determinist natural causes in bringing about human action. Kant seeks to show, in other words, "the compatibility of compatibilism and incompatibilism."[27] Let us look briefly at how he does so.

According to Kant's transcendental idealism, there are two perspectives from which one can interpret any given matter, the *noumenal* (that is, according to things as they are in themselves and beyond experience), and the *phenomenal* (that is, according to things as constituted in our experience of them). These perspectives are absolutely distinct, so that there is no possibility of reconciling them, but at the same time there is no need to do so. With respect to reason in its practical mode, that is, with respect to the will, Kant explains that any given choice can be wholly explained *either* as a determined result of antecedent natural conditions *or* as a result of nothing other than the purely spontaneous determination of my own will: "It is . . . possible to regard one and the same event on the one hand as a merely natural effect [i.e., as the necessary result of antecedent causes in a temporal series], yet on the other hand as an effect of freedom."[28] We know that this latter view is valid because of the experience, and indeed the logical necessity, of moral responsibility that cannot be explained away by extenuating circumstances; Kant points to the voice of conscience that we cannot silence no matter how many natural causes we could adduce to excuse our action.[29] As he elaborates in the second critique, *Critique of Practical Reason*, although it would be possible in principle to predict a person's outward actions "with as great a certainty as the occurrence of a solar or lunar eclipse" if we had sufficient empirical knowledge of the conditions of those actions, from the inward or transcendental perspective we may nevertheless see that "this whole chain of appearances . . . depends upon the spontaneity of the subject as a thing in itself, for the determination of which no physical explanation can be given."[30] We might consider the example of stealing a watch. On the one hand, I can show the necessary series of causal events that account for the theft—that is, I can point to the natural and psychological mechanisms at work in producing the choice, the history of events that made this choice strictly inevitable. On the other hand, however, I can reduce these mechanisms themselves, and the entire antecedent history, back to my transcendental freedom as its sole cause, and view the whole as an expression of my unconditioned agency. No matter what excuses there may be that would explain away the choice, it remains, from the transcendental perspective, altogether my responsibility because it is ultimately due to my decision. Kant is saying that both accounts are true, and they would contradict each other only if we assumed that the noumenal and the phenomenal perspectives were competitors in the same philosophical order. Once we see that they are not, we are able to switch perspectives depending on the nature of our interest in any given instance: Are we viewing the action as the behavior of a natural entity or as the deed of a moral agent? The explanation of the action's causality differs accordingly.

Kant admits that his resolution might seem implausible to common sense, but he simply defies anyone to produce a better way of reconciling the evident truth of ethics, on the one hand, and natural science, on the other:

> It will be said that the solution to the difficulty given here involves even greater difficulty and is hardly susceptible of a lucid presentation. But is any other solution that has been attempted, or that may be attempted, easier and more apprehensible? One might rather say that the dogmatic teachers of metaphysics have shown more shrewdness than sincerity in keeping this difficult point out of sight as much as possible, in the hope that if they said nothing about it no one would be likely to think of it.[31]

Wood explains that, in any event, Kant is not concerned to *explain* freedom—which, as pertaining to the noumenal realm can be merely *thought* but never *known*—but only to argue for its necessity, along with showing it cannot be positively disproven.[32] The distinction between the noumenal and phenomenal, moreover, allows him to elude, once again, Hume's problematic—in this case, Hume's identification of what is called the "naturalistic fallacy"—and so establish the practical sphere of morality and politics as a wholly autonomous field of study.[33] Freedom has no natural constraints, but only the constraint of reason, and in the end it is *only* in submitting to the constraint of reason that the will can be free from any subjection to nature.[34] This, too, echoes a principle we saw in Locke.

That Kant thinks of freedom in terms of effective, spontaneous causality[35]—that is, power—comes to light especially clearly when he defines freedom, in the political sphere, as "independence from being constrained by another's choice."[36] What formally resists power is not in the first place a *thing*, which can be acted on by the power, or even, as we have just seen, an inescapably necessary causal chain of events, which ought to be posited as an effect of the will as free cause, but only another spontaneous source of so acting or causing, that is, another power. Political order is therefore most properly conceived as the separating of wills from each other. Kant identifies political freedom with right, the "universal principle" of which is the following: "Any action is right if it can coexist with everyone's freedom in accordance with the universal law, or if on its maxim the freedom of choice of each can coexist with everyone's freedom in accordance with a universal law."[37] This is similar in effect to Locke's conception of the natural law, which amounts to a "noninterference" in the rights of others, a mutual respect for others, which may arguably imply at some level a set of positive duties, but which takes the primary form of safeguarding negative space. As Arthur Ripstein puts it, the foundation of Kant's political theory is "a simple but powerful conception of freedom as independence from another's choice."[38] Also like Locke, Kant conceives of rights—the objectification of freedom—as analogous to property, the demarcation of the boundaries of arbitrary use. The various rights that Kant ascribes to man by nature may be interpreted as articulations of the different ways a person may be said to *belong to himself*, as opposed to belonging to another: for example, Kant's "natural rights include the right to one's physical, psychological, mental, and moral integrity, the right to obey only laws to which we have given our consent (or ought to have done so), and the right to acquire property."[39] This is nothing but the political expression of Kant's view of reason, embodied in the categorical imperative that lies at the basis of the critical philosophy in general and whose principle is "that reason must answer only to itself, rather than to anything outside of it."[40] Whereas Locke conceives political order as founded on, and at the service of, the more basic right of property, Kant interprets property, not as man's relation to *things*, but already from the first as an organization of the relationship *between* persons, with regard to things, and so as essentially a matter of public authority.[41] The determination, recognition, and organization of property is thus ultimately a negotiation of freedoms, conceived as instances of individual self-agency. The purpose of the political order, for Kant, is therefore precisely the protection of autonomy.

Kant's answer to the classic question, whether man has a social nature, is ambiguous (just as it was for Spinoza).[42] One aspect of the ambiguity turns on the relation of reason to man's nature generally: Is reason an expression of human nature or opposed to it? Thus, Kant explains that "men do no wrong at all when they feud among themselves" in the state of nature, since mutual opposition just *is* that state. And yet "they do wrong to the highest degree by willing to be and to remain in a condition that is not rightful, that is, in which no one is assured of what is his against violence."[43] But Kant holds that even man's rational condition requires at another level some form of hostility. On the one hand, man needs interaction with others to develop the rational capacities that lie at the foundation of his freedom and dignity,[44] and yet, on the other hand, that interaction is inevitably contentious, not only (negatively) because of the "radical evil" that Kant ascribes to human nature, but also (positively) because antagonism is a necessary engine of creativity. Thus, Kant famously spoke repeatedly of man's "unsocial sociability."[45] Human nature, Kant says, can achieve its purpose only in a condition of externally regulated antagonism:

> Just as trees in a forest, precisely because each of them seeks to take
> air and sun from the other, are constrained to look for them above

themselves, and thereby achieve a beautiful straight growth; whereas those in freedom and separated from one another, that put forth their branches as they like, grow stunted, crooked and awry. All culture and art that adorn humanity, and the most beautiful social order, are the fruits of unsociability, through which it is necessitated by itself to discipline itself, and so by an art extorted from it, to develop completely the germs of nature.[46]

For Kant, political order is founded on autonomous reason, which is to say that it has an a priori as opposed to a merely practical justification. Whereas the standard social contract theorists interpret the civil state as arising from the dangers posed by the state of nature, Kant presents the political order as a necessary consequence of a rational incoherence in the state of nature: man is free, which means independent of the choice of others, but the state of nature is one in which each is subjected to the choice of others without buffer.[47] There is thus a rational duty, rather than a merely practical need, to enter the political state, namely, the preservation of the human dignity that is tied to man's reason. An interesting problem, however, arises here for Kant, given his understanding of the a priori, no natural, empirical condition or act can generate rational order. Political order cannot be produced, as it were, by causes that stem "from below," which means that the state cannot arise as a result of real problems generated by the natural condition, nor can there be any transition from one condition to another through a particular act. As Kant puts it, man as an animal needs a master, but if it is simply another man who is made master, he too will be an animal in need of a master in turn, and this remains the case whether the contrived authority is one man or the collective will of a majority.[48] There must therefore be a kind of impersonal authority that is recognized by all as absolute, and that means as independent of the arbitrary will of any person or persons. This means, of course, that Kant clearly dismisses any historical reality of a state of nature, out of which man departed through some concrete act of actual consent.[49] But he is not content to posit, in its stead, a merely "tacit" consent, as Locke and Spinoza do, since even this remains too empirical. On the other hand, however, to deny consent and the social contract altogether would seem to undermine the principle of freedom and autonomy it is the very purpose of political order to protect. Kant's solution to this problem is to conceive of political order and its laws *modally*, that is, as the *possible* object of consent of all rational persons, and thus just so far an a priori form imposed on all from above.[50]

Reducing the problem of consent to the problem of political authority through appeal to possibility entails a dialectic quite similar to the one we found in Locke, and then again in Spinoza. Because it is enough for consent to be possible in order to impose it, there is no actual condition that would limit the scope of the claim political authority can make on individuals, given of course that it is taken (by whom?) to be rational. Inspired certainly by Rousseau here, Kant argues that all must give up, not just a *part* of their freedom, but the *whole* of it, precisely qua *naturally* (and therefore, according to Kant, individualistically) possessed, so as to receive it back as lawful. But precisely because the authority of law is objective, that is, not an expression of personal will, it can be posited as *wholly* an expression of the freedom—the rational autonomy—of the individual:

> The act by which a people forms itself into a state is the original contract. Properly speaking, the original contract is only the idea of this act, in terms of which alone we can think of the legitimacy of the state. In accordance with the original contract, everyone (*omnes et singuli*) within a people gives up his external freedom in order to take it up again immediately as a member of the commonwealth, that is, of the people considered as a state (*universi*). And one cannot say: the human being in a state has sacrificed a part of his innate outer freedom for the sake of an end, but rather, he has relinquished entirely his wild, lawless freedom in order to find his freedom as such undiminished, in a dependence upon laws, that is, in a rightful condition, since this dependence arises from his own lawgiving will.[51]

Thus, law is *nothing but* an expression of my will, and so a reflection of my freedom, and at the same time it has an authority over me that is absolute and irresistible as a matter of principle. In contrast to Locke and Spinoza, Kant famously rejects the notion of a "right to rebel," since political authority has to be unconditional if it is to serve its function at all.[52] This does not mean that Kant is blind or unrealistic about the temptations to corruption that always seem to dog political power, but he nevertheless insists that the anarchy that would result *in principle* from the assertion of such a right—which annuls the very principle of right, since it places law under the judgment of individuals—is a greater threat to rational autonomy than the possibility of power's abuse.[53] It is not essential, for us, to determine whether Kant is correct in this judgment, or whether the position taken by Spinoza and Locke is more consistent with a notion of freedom as power. The point, here, is simply to show that, when nature is not understood analogically, but rather as the dialectical opposite of society—as pure subjection to arbitrary will versus subjection to impersonal authority—then society cannot help but take the form, externally, of the absorption of the individual.

It is important to see, however, that this external absorption of the individual coincides even in Kant's thought with an "internal" absolutizing of the individual, just as it does in Locke and Spinoza. One might wonder how Kant's insistence on the incontestable authority of the state, to which we owe complete obedience, can be reconciled with his paean to free thought and individual autonomy in "What Is Enlightenment?": "Have courage to make use of your *own* understanding!"[54] In fact, we see that these imply one another once we interpret them properly. In the most obvious sense, Kant insists on an absolute independence of conscience, which means that one is free and so (Kant would say "and *therefore*") obliged to offer publicly one's scholarly opinion in criticism of what one takes to be a corruption of power, unjust laws, and so forth. The key, however, is that one can and ought to do so *only as an independent thinker*, and so only as one continues to fulfill the duties of one's office and obey the external regulations of the law. The criticisms can have *objective* significance only to the extent that the political authority recognizes them and modifies its laws accordingly. Kant himself says that the freedom of thought is "the least harmful of anything that could even be called freedom," that is, the least disruptive of public order.[55]

But there is an even deeper level at which the "private" absolutizing of the individual in Kant's practical philosophy comes to expression; to see it, we have to return to the notion of transcendental freedom we explained above: any given act of will may be interpreted either as an exhaustively determined natural causal event or an effect of spontaneous moral agency. The transcendence of this moral agency, however, and its essential indifference to the horizontal dimension of natural conditions, makes it equally indifferent to political conditions. But this means that the question of moral autonomy is logically independent of the question of the particular quality of the existing political order, which is to say that one can be completely free, one can achieve absolute moral autonomy, *internally*, in spite of any degree of external unfreedom, whether that unfreedom is imposed by natural causes or by political structures. As Beck puts it: "Autonomy, for Kant, refers to a wholly internal state of the agent, does not require the translation of autonomous acts of volitions into external actions, and its realisation does not presuppose the agent's external freedom. It cannot therefore provide the normative basis for man's right to external freedom, nor does it support the liberal conclusions of limited government ensuing maximum equal liberty for its citizens."[56] Absolute individual freedom, understood as power, can coexist in principle with an absolute authoritarian government. This coincidence comes to expression in the maxim that Kant repeats in his "What Is Enlightenment?" as a paradigm of the enlightened state: "Argue as much as you will, and about what you will, only obey!"[57] Clearly, this conclusion conflicts with the thesis that the purpose of civil society is the preservation of individual freedom— if freedom is so radically individualized, and thus so completely privatized, that it becomes indifferent to political order, then that order can no more preserve freedom than eliminate it—but our aim here is not to try to resolve this dialectic. We wish only to indicate it, and we suggest that it follows from an identification of freedom and power, and the concomitant bifurcation of the internal, subjective sphere from the public, objective one.

The same bifurcation underlies Kant's response to the "theologico-political problem." In fact, Kant suggests in "What Is Enlightenment?" that the theme of freedom and public order comes to a head in this problem, so that, to solve the proper relation between church and state is to solve everything else.[58] We should not overlook the importance of the theologico-political problem in the formation of modern liberty.[59] The aim, for Kant, is to remove any a priori claim of truth from religion that would impose a heteronomous obligation on reason, external to its otherwise immanent function. He thus separates religion altogether from what Hegel calls its "positive" dimension, namely, from any particular ecclesial institution, and from any dogmatic content.[60] Religion thereby becomes a purely "internal" reality—that is, wholly a matter of morality, which, as we suggested above, concerns exclusively in the end reason's internal relationship to itself. The various "churches" become relative, and essentially exchangeable, instruments of moral improvement. Without recognizing that this, too, is a dogmatic theological claim, Kant says that the existence of Christian *dogma* (as distinct from praxis) is an adulteration of pure religious belief, the result of the influence of paganism.[61] It is contrary to human dignity for the political authority to embrace any "eternal" religious truth, because this would impose intellectual content on individuals that they had not chosen themselves on the basis of their own reason. It would make them cattle. On the other hand, there is no obstacle at all, in principle, to the state's regulation of religious *behavior*.[62] Once again, we reconcile conflict through an absolute separation of the subjective and the objective. The individual-political authority and the church–state relation turns out to be a manifestation of the relation between transcendental freedom and natural causality. The two can coincide in the same place because they have essentially nothing to do with each other.

SUMMING UP

For all of their differences, Locke, Spinoza, and Kant thus appear to share a common core in their conception of freedom, which we may justly characterize in general as "modern liberty": a view of freedom as spontaneous and unconditioned causality, or as active power that produces effects as a result of self-originating energy *rather than* receiving determination from outside of itself. What we wish to suggest at this point is that such a conception of freedom, because it relentlessly separates potentiality from actuality, represents, in its depths, a flight from reality. Specifically, it represents a priority of potency over actuality, which reverses the classical order. What this means is that possibility comes to extend beyond actuality, to engulf it and thus to outflank it; at every point, actuality comes to be interpreted in relation to a prior and more basic potency, rather than the reverse. Thus, for example, the actuality of goods, which in the classical understanding implies a real claim on the will of individuals and so an order to which the individual desires to, and is obliged to, conform, becomes a set of options, which depend for their goodness on the will's own determination; relationships are not taken to precede the individual will and thus suffuse that will, from the first, with responsibilities (again, both in the sense of the responsive attractions of beauty and goodness, and also the weight of duties), but are now reinterpreted, even if *in reality* they precede the will, as products of rational choice and consent, that is, as having the form of contracts; the coming-to-rest of attainment, achievement, acquisition, and so forth is instrumentalized for productive purposes, so that every end is systematically transformed into a means, and affirmed as good in itself *only* in that particular form (which is to say that means become isolated as ends), and so forth.

Because man has no relationship with anything—other people, the world, God—that is not mediated at some level through the will, a reinterpretation of the meaning of the will and its freedom will inevitably be what Nietzsche called a "revaluation of all values." What is at issue is not simply a new hierarchy of values, a replacement of higher values by things previously held in lower esteem, but indeed a transformation of what it means to value and be valuable *tout court*, or, more adequately put, a transformation of the meaning of goodness and its principal mode of manifestation. It has been said that Darwin's late modern interpretation of evolution stands as a "universal acid":[63] the inner logic of his idea eats away at all other traditional ideas, not only on the biological level but also on all levels of human existence; it dissolves everything in its wake. One might say that the notion of modern liberty we are discussing is even more radical and therefore more subtle in its effects. It is not so much an acid as a sort of alchemical reagent. Instead of dissolving things, it leaves them standing, but eliminates their original essence, their native goodness, transforming realities into gold—that is, a conventional representation of value without any organic relation to its own given nature. There is *nothing at all* left untouched by this transformation. In presenting modern liberty as destructive in this way, it is important to emphasize here that we do not mean to suggest that Spinoza, Locke, and Kant—or any of the founders of modernity—self-consciously took the dissolution of culture to be a sort of goal. To be sure, it is clear that they had a general awareness that their ideas were revolutionary, but it would be silly to suppose that they had anything in mind other than the improvement of the human condition, as they understood it. They were, presumably, responding to the problems that confronted them with the means that were available. We have no intention here of making any individual thinker responsible for the problems of modernity. Instead of blame, we are seeking an understanding. It is for this reason that we seek to enter into the inner logic of the ideas and consider the consequences of this logic, intended or not.

In the introduction to his *Philosophy of Right*, Hegel presents what he calls "negative freedom"—which is similar to, but not identical with, what we are calling "modern liberty"—and argues that, though it contains an essential element of a proper conception of freedom, it becomes problematic when taken to stand for the whole.[64] In his "Remark," he offers two historical examples that illustrate what it would look like to *actualize* this pure potency and render it a reality. One is the hyper-spiritualization of what he takes to represent the Hindu concept of freedom, namely, the total detachment from the world and retraction into inwardness, which is expressed objectively as a political quietism. On the other hand, there is the Terror of the French Revolution, which he says made negative freedom real *as negative* through the relentless razing of public institutions (and persons!), even those it had established and seated itself. In both of these cases, we see an inability to extend the subjective potency into the objective order, either because it remains excluded from it or because, by contrast, it itself excludes any objective order. This negative view of freedom "may well believe that it wills some positive condition, for instance the condition of universal equality or of universal religious life, but it does not in fact will the positive actuality of this condition, for this at once gives rise to some kind of order, a particularization both of institutions and of individuals."[65]

We would like to propose that the notion of freedom in modern liberalism, typified in Locke, manages to achieve a certain reconciliation of indeterminate potency with a particularized objective order. Liberalism represents an uncanny combination of the two historical examples that Hegel presents: it combines the public worldliness of the

French Revolution with the total detachment of Eastern mysticism; it is a freedom that is *of* the world, but never *in* the world. It enters into the public sphere (unlike Hindu detachment, as Hegel interprets it), but is so thoroughly negative that (unlike the French Revolution) it does not displace any of the positive realities, the actual institutions and real human goods, that are there; instead, it transforms them in the image of its own negativity by rendering them variations of potency, structures of power that are contrived for the sake of absolutizing private freedom, without encroaching on its private character. Modern liberalism is in this sense an even more perfect illustration of this inadequate notion of freedom than Hegel had been able to conceive himself.

In order to make this suggestion concrete, we will gather up the various aspects of freedom we have indicated under a single heading: instead of the "dialectical," which, at least according to Hegel, generates life, we will sum things up under the "diabolical," which represents a radical subversion of natural order.

CHAPTER 4

Symbolical Order and Diabolical Subversion

Root Meanings

We will begin our exposition of the meaning of the "diabolical" by considering its etymology, which we will set into relief through juxtaposition with the "symbolical." After a consideration of the etymologies, we will offer a metaphysical interpretation that connects the terms with the theme of freedom as we have been exploring it.

The words "symbolon" and "diabolon" are etymological opposites: συμ-βάλλω literally means "to throw together," "to collect," "to join or unite," and "to come together"; δια-βάλλω means "to throw over or across," and "to set at variance." Διά, in composite words, means "in different directions," and "asunder" (compare the Latin *dis-*). The more extended meaning of the verb διαβάλλω thus includes "to slander," "to misrepresent," and "to deceive by false accounts."

Symbolon (or also *symbolaion*) originally meant the *tessera hospitalis*, the half of an object (usually a bone or die) that a host had broken in two and delivered into the safekeeping of his guest while holding onto the other himself. It was a token of the friendship that was formed through the act of hospitality. This preserved token represented the abiding character of the bond; as Gadamer has explained, "If in thirty or fifty years' time, a descendent of the guest should ever enter his house, the two pieces could be fitted together again to form a whole in an act of recognition."[1] We see this original sense of the term in Plato's *Symposium*, specifically in Aristophanes's speech about love. As is well known, Aristophanes relates a myth about the nature of love: human beings were originally in the form of perfectly contented spheres. Their contentedness led to a hubris, which provoked the gods to cut them in half. Eros is the search to rejoin one's other half and restore unity. The "halves" are called "symbols": "And so each of us is a symbol of (a) man" (ἕκαστος οὖν ἡμῶν ἐστὶν ἀνθρώπου σύμβολον).[2]

From this original signification, we get various derivative meanings, which we list here without any particular arrangement:[3] "symbolon" can indicate any token serving as proof of identity or credentials; it is used to stand for a treaty or contract formed between nations or other divided parties; it can even refer to the actual bond or union itself, or can be used as the technical term for the marriage contract. The Nicene Creed, or analogously any unifying confession, can be referred to as a "symbol of the faith." The term also designates a ticket, entitling the bearer to participation in political discussion, to vote, or to attend a spectacle; "symbolon," moreover, can be used to indicate contributions to a common meal, or the meal itself; the term generally came to mean a sign, omen, signal, symptom, or secret code. In an extended sense, it can therefore represent a standard of measurement.

"Diabolon," on the other hand, originally meant false accusation or slander, charges that discredit or prejudice. In a derivative sense, it can indicate a quarrel, enmity, fear of or aversion to, or withdrawal from. Finally, it came to mean simply fraud or deceit. The word has become especially significant in the Judeo-Christian theological tradition, associated with the agent of evil: the devil, the tempter, the Father of Lies, the deceiver who seduces to self-destruction. In folk tales, the devil is the one to whom a person sells his soul in order to obtain some worldly success.

The Symbolical

Let us consider these terms from a more speculative perspective. Paul Ricoeur offers an illuminating analysis of the characteristics of the symbol.[4] As he explains, a symbol is a sign, which means it points to a meaning that is other than itself, but it relates to that meaning in a distinct way: the meaning, though indeed *other*, is nevertheless manifest *in* the symbolic reality, the *thing*, so that the meaning cannot be simply detached from the thing in which it resides, as it were. This manifestation gives the thing an extraordinary density: "The manifestation through the thing is like the condensation of an infinite discourse; manifestation and meaning are strictly contemporaneous and reciprocal; the concretion in the thing is the counterpart of the surcharge of inexhaustible meaning, which has ramifications in the cosmos, in the ethical, and in the political."[5] A symbol thus differs in an important sense from allegory: while allegory points away from itself to a separate meaning (ἄλλος-ἀγορεύω, "to tell of what is other"), which, as separate, can be grasped apart from the sign that leads to it, a symbol *makes present* a meaning that cannot be simply translated into other terms, that is, replaced by a concept or a set of concepts. Ricoeur speaks in this regard of a "double intentionality"[6]—that is, a first, literal meaning that simultaneously presents a second meaning, which is not separate from the first. Though the term "tautegory" (ταὐτο-ἀγορεύω, "to communicate what is the same"— as opposed to pointing to what is other), which Schelling uses to characterize the symbolic presentation of mythological meaning,[7] is perhaps too one-sided; it indicates an essential element, namely, that a symbol *contains* the meaning it signifies, so that form and content are organically bound together in it.[8] One who "reads" a symbol, then, does not simply record the information it indicates, but instead enters into the symbol; he is *assimilated* to its essentially latent sense, so that he can be said to "indwell" the meaning and "live" in it.[9] To the extent that he does, the meaning becomes transparent to him, even while it remains resistant to complete conceptual translation. Symbolic meaning is present and given analogously (literally: ἄνω-λέγω), which is to say that the meaning draws one up into itself. This is what Ricoeur has called the "donative" character of the symbol, a character he articulates in the well-known phrase, "la symbole donne à penser," inadequately translated as "the symbol gives rise to thought."[10] The symbol, in other words, communicates meaning in a *generous* form; the unity of the meaning that it contains, which is not grasped in abstraction as a discrete, explicit concept, but is rather assimilated through what can be called a concrete indwelling, generates a kind of boundless wealth of significance.

Given the donative character of the symbol, it is perhaps not an accident that the term originated in a ritual of friendship. If we turn back to the *tessera hospitalis*, in the light of Ricoeur's description of the symbol, a number of insights open up. First of all, in turning back to the original usage, we see that there is a certain reversal here of the relation of generosity that Ricoeur had described: rather than the symbol being donative, in this original instance, the symbol is the *result* of generosity, which belongs, first, to the principle of meaning that comes to reside in the thing (and is the reason for the generativity of the symbol itself). In following this reversal, we are shifting to an ontological perspective, as distinct from, and indeed as undergirding, the primarily epistemological/phenomenological perspective that Ricoeur adopts.[11] What, we may ask, is the relation between the friendship and the token that comes to represent it in the *tessera hospitalis*? On the one hand, we can say that the friendship achieves a certain objectification in the *tesserae*; these represent a certain "condensation," to use Ricoeur's term, or a "crystallization," of the friendship, a kind of embodiment, incarnation, or realization. This objectification in a thing gives the friendship a public significance and a certain permanence; the event of hospitality gives rise, in the *tesserae*, to a significance that goes beyond the particular event, even though it remains always connected to that concrete event as its origin; it creates a bond that bears even on future generations, providing both privileges and responsibilities. On the other hand, this objectification is not an actualizing of what was previously merely *in potentia*. Instead, the actual reality of the friendship is the prior condition for the *tesserae*; they are created *in* and *as* an act of friendship that is already established, already in existence. We might say that the *tessera* puts a certain *seal* on the friendship, which simultaneously "crystallizes" it, closing it as a complete reality in itself, and at the same time opens it up to future possibilities by objectively disseminating its significance. These possibilities may thus be said to represent *extensions* of its actuality.

Thus, the symbols themselves, the distinct *tesserae*, are sharers in a unity that precedes them and makes them possible. What they "add" to this unity, however, is an external form, an embodiment, an *objective presence*, that the friendship, as an inward relation, a meaning, does not immediately have itself. The symbols, in their signifying reference, do not immediately point to this presence, but in the first place they point directly *to each other*. Each symbol, as a broken half, refers to the other, in which or with which it fits; in their unity, they give rise to, or rather, they *make "really" present*, the meaning they signify, which, as Ricoeur puts it, in its generosity exceeds the bounds of any discrete formulation or formulations. It is as part of a ritual of friendship that the bone is broken into complementary halves, and it will be inside of another ritual of friendship that they are rejoined. We see a simultaneous openness and closure in the symbols, which correlates to the "double intentionality" that Ricoeur described: in being joined together, the symbols form a complete whole, and so are resolved into unity, but this resolution is precisely a participation in a meaning that remains transcendent even in its immanent presence, and so always generative of more receptions, embodiments, or actualizing objectifications, of that meaning.

When we at this point go on to speak in this context, not just of a symbol, but of a *symbolical order*, we mean not just a particular phenomenon or ritual, individual instances of the communication of meaning. Instead, we take the form of the symbol to be a description of the nature of things generally. There is no room, in the present context, to develop an entire metaphysics, of course; we will have to be content for the time being with a general sketch of what this means, and the assertion of a number of claims that would require, in another context, much more elaboration and justification.[12] Our primary purpose here is to describe the symbolical sufficiently in order to set into relief the meaning of the diabolical, which represents the most basic alternative.

The classical conception of the cosmos may be appropriately described as "symbolical." What this term is meant to articulate in this context is, briefly put, "an ordered whole that has its foundation in a transcendent cause, understood as most perfect and so as most essentially generous."[13] According to Plato, the ultimate cause of being is the good, which transcends all things, even the very being of the world, as its originating principle.[14] Above we saw that symbols come to be in a gesture of friendship; Plato understands friendship, not simply as a relation between persons, but analogously as ontological, as constitutive of the nature of all that exists.[15] (One might say that the friendship found between persons is a recapitulation, a completing expression, of the basic meaning of reality.) As he puts it, the whole cosmos and everything in it is joined together ontologically by a bond of friendship: "The heavens and the earth, gods and men, are bound together ontologically by fellowship and friendship (τὴν κοινωνίαν συνέχειν καὶ φιλίαν), and order and temperance and justice, and for this reason [wise men] call the sum of things the 'ordered' universe (κόσμον) . . . not the world of disorder (ἀκοσμίαν) and riot."[16]

We might think of the "parts" of cosmos as so many symbols, which is to say that things are *signs* of the good that is their always prior principle of unity; that, understood in this way, they are seen to "fit together" by virtue of their most basic nature,[17] to be suited to each other, and so to have a proper place, thus taking part in a larger order (which is for that reason always hierarchical); and, finally, that, in their "symbolic" joining together, they make really present the transcendent good, they are "transparent" to it in their interrelation without ever exhausting its meaning. Aristotle says that the good exists both as a transcendent principle and, immanently, as the order itself of the cosmos: "The world is not such that one thing has nothing to do with another, but they are connected. For all are ordered together to one end."[18] Those who deny a transcendent unity, by contrast, "make the substance of the universe a mere series of episodes (for one substance has no influence on another by its existence or non-existence), they give us many governing principles; but the world refuses to be governed badly. 'The rule of many is not good; one ruler let there be.'"[19] It is important to see that an order founded on goodness is *essentially* symbolical and that, conversely, the essence of symbol is goodness. These two principles are not related in a merely accidental way—they cannot be separated.

What it would mean, then, to speak of freedom in terms of the symbolical is—briefly to anticipate a more elaborate discussion in part 3 of this book—to see it as a participation in goodness, which is to say, a sharing in a larger, ordered whole, a sharing that naturally tends to objectify itself in public realities, and thus to join people together, to join man and nature, God and the world. We might say, from this perspective at least, that the *polis*—the most complete political community[20]— is itself a "cosmos" in miniature, a unity and so an outward manifestation of the good, the unity of which is constituted through the relations between all the various members, parts, of various orders: the symbols.

This includes not just the relationships between persons, but quite concretely the land, the architecture, the customs, rituals, practices, institutions, artistic traditions, the language and literature, the stories, the markets, the system of labor and exchange, and so forth. Freedom is an objective status that gives one membership and the privileges and responsibilities entailed by that membership. Each aspect is a sharing in the whole, a member of the common good, a contribution to that good, and so an expression of the whole that reinforces its wholeness. If freedom is a participation in the good, then all of these *symbols*, all of these constitutive elements, are concrete realizations of freedom. They are extensions of actuality rather than being primarily the expressions of mere *potentia*. Freedom becomes *essentially* symbolical; the forming of relationships—the bonds of friendship, marriage, and family, the building of a home, the sharing of the life of the community, with the reciprocity of benefits and responsibilities it entails— becomes a multiplication of freedom, or perhaps a better image: its fructification. These fructifications of freedom are realities that join persons to the whole, to other people, and properly to themselves. Because of the "double intentionality" of symbols, its reciprocity of manifestation and meaning, and its simultaneity of openness and closure, each realization of freedom, as symbolical, is both a genuine completion in itself, which gathers together what has preceded, and a greater capacity for what is more. Freedom thus has depth and extension; it is not an instantaneous flash that volatilizes the moment it becomes real, but instead crystalizes and gives abiding witness to a unity of past, present, and future, a genuine integration of actuality and possibility. As Ferdinand Ulrich has shown, freedom is an opening up, in the present, of the originating source (past), so as to enable a genuine future.[21] In an understanding of freedom in terms of symbolical order, potency always takes its bearings, so to speak, from actuality, whether that be the real order that comprehends it and in which it participates, or the internal actuality of which it represents a generative expression of power. It is actuality, in fact, that is most potent, full of possibility; these are not dialectically opposed. All of these affirmations need to be justified and elaborated, of course, but the purpose at this point is simply to provide a contrast that will accentuate the meaning of the diabolical.

The Diabolical

Drawing on the etymology and the traditional associations with the "diabolical," we may distinguish six features as particularly relevant to our theme.

1. The first and most essential is the notion of dissemblance, which we interpret in the present context as a deceptive image. In Platonic philosophy, an image is an *expression* of a reality in an order that differs radically from that of the original: a painting of a bed—to use Plato's example[22]—is an image of a physical bed; though the painting, too, is a physical object, it nevertheless does not exist in the same order of being as the physical bed, since its reality *as image* consists in its *appearance*. It is the presentation of the aesthetic form of a bed, which, no matter how realistically portrayed, will never be something on which one would sleep. For Plato, the physical bed on which one sleeps, in turn, is itself an image of the *idea* of bed, which is what Plato finally takes to be most real. The point, for our present purposes, is that the idea and the physical bed represent radically different ontological orders, which is why there is no competition between them, even though they *are* the same in the sense of having the same quiddity or essence, which is given immediately with the idea.[23] Although Plato is often taken to disparage the image, in fact for him there is nothing *intrinsically* bad about an image *qua* image; it is instead good insofar as it is an *expression* of something good, and ultimately of the good itself.[24] Using the language we discussed above, we might say that the image is essentially symbolical, which is to say that it makes the reality accessible in itself (both meanings of that phrase are intended: reality in itself is accessible, and the locus of this accessibility lies precisely in the image). An image is bad only if it comes to *replace* what it signifies. In this case, instead of pointing beyond itself to what is real, and *thereby* becoming in itself good, it takes on a reality of its own, becoming opaque, so to speak, and so losing its image-character. This is the heart of the diabolical: an image that is not an image, but presents itself as the real thing—indeed, in a certain sense (as we shall see), as *better* than the real thing precisely because of the immediacy or the lack of transcendence that the dissemblance implies. What we mean by the "diabolical," in this regard, bears a certain similarity to William Desmond's illuminating notion of the

"counterfeit double," which he illustrates by pointing to the falsely printed banknotes dropped by plane into Germany with the aim of precipitating an economic crisis during World War II: the forgeries were finally able to be identified because they were too perfect.[25] We will come back to this point.

For the moment, it is important to note the essentially parasitical character of the diabolical: it remains, in spite of everything, an image, which is to say that the whole of its intelligible and axiological content derives from the reality that it imitates. If this were not the case, there would be no deception, nothing fraudulent about it. It is not a simple alternative to the reality, but a *substitution* for it, one that promises to fulfill the same function as what it replaces. The interest in the fraudulent image, therefore, presupposes and so actually draws on a more basic desire for the reality that it imitates. We observed above the complex intentionality of the symbolical: it is not a mere disposable vehicle that conveys the subject to what is *simply* other than itself (but which could just as well be attained without it), as in the typical allegory, but mediates that other in an intrinsic way: it becomes good in itself *because* it points beyond to a good that is other; it is an intrinsic means to this end, so that one already shares in the end by abiding with the means. This is what makes it symbolical: one "joins with" (συμ-βάλλω) the reality *in* the image. Plato speaks appropriately of the "presence" (παρουσία) of the reality in the image and the "communion" (κοινωνία) it involves.[26] The key is the *absolute* priority of the end, the reality, which then gives rise in its "donative" character to a *relative* priority of the image, insofar as the reality is accessible only in and through the image. With the diabolical, the priority is dialectically inverted: it is a specifically dialectical inversion because the image cannot help but presuppose the reality, even as it constantly seeks to overcome the priority it is relentlessly obliged to posit. The image, in the overcoming, detaches itself from the reality precisely by pointing to it while at the same time refusing to transcend itself; instead, it *captures* the reality within its own borders (or at least claims to). It *pre-tends*, that is, claims to have (*tenere*) the reality always already, and so prior to (*pre*), any intrinsic relationship, which would subordinate it to that reality. In this way, the diabolical truly "sets apart" or "drives asunder"; it points in two directions at the very same time: to what it derives parasitically from and to itself as the reality. Instead of the "both/and" of the image and reality that constitutes participation, the "joining with" of the symbolical, we have, not just the "either/or," but more specifically the "either *and* or," which inevitably turns itself into the "neither/nor," as we will suggest below.[27]

2. Precisely because of its parasitical character, the diabolical is defined by negativity; as Goethe put it, the devil is a "verneinender Geist."[28] The symbolical has an essentially *receptive* structure, since it (positively) presupposes the reality in which it shares. The diabolical is a rejection of just this reality, which it nevertheless cannot avoid presupposing. It is therefore primordially negative; its essence consists in its separating itself (δια-βάλλω) from the reality. The reason this separation is a negation, rather than a neutrality, is that the reality against which it defines itself cannot but continue to come first. Image as such includes a negation (it is *not* the reality it manifests); but the symbolical includes this within the positivity of the givenness of the good, which gives the negation the character of gift and generosity, while the diabolical makes this negativity primary, or at least seeks to do so, by reducing the primary reality to an empty significance. To acknowledge the primacy of that reality, as the symbolical does, is to become a part of a larger order, to be situated in a whole and so have one's own reality, so to speak, enlarged. The symbolical is always more than itself; it shares intrinsically in the order that it helps constitute and so what lies beyond it at the same time lies within it. This is why it is a "joining-together," and why it is characterized by bonds. The diabolical, as we have said, cannot cease to be an image even as it refuses to be secondary. It thus includes the reality, but no longer as an actuality, which would necessarily imply some form of a priori claim. Instead, it includes the reality only as a possibility, which depends on the image, so to speak, to be actualized. In this case, the actuality of the reality is *accorded to* that reality rather than *received from* it. Instead of being inwardly present as a genuine, real other, that to which the image points is included inside of its boundaries as a possibility, the realization of which arrives on the image's terms. Since it remains present as a possibility, the diabolical creates the appearance of neutrality, since the content at least seems to remain intact even if it loses its form as an actuality with an a priori claim. At a deeper level, however, this "letting be" represents an even more radical negation, since an outright rejection would at least grant the reality an *actual* significance that it then

denies. Diabolical negation simply nullifies this significance while leaving the thing more or less in place. A perfect, that is, complete, negativity is one that remains invisible: it not only negates, but at the same time it refuses to allow the negation to stand as a positive claim, and so it negates even this positivity. It therefore appears to restore the original, positive reality, but it does so now only on its own terms. The dissembling image is no longer in any *ontological* sense beyond itself, more than itself, but instead merely *signifies* the other as one of its own possibilities. There is a connection, which we will explore in a moment, between the potentializing of a thing and its functionalization, that is, the reduction of the thing to the effects it produces. The link between these two is power.

Whereas the symbolical presents itself in the form of internal bonds, connection, intimacy coupled with generous respect, the diabolical is by its very nature *divisive*. It participates in the good precisely in the mode of separating from it, and since this radical negation is its defining essence, it turns up everywhere else in the mode of antagonism. In the diabolical order, things come together precisely in the form of mutual exclusion, which can appear negatively as hostility or "positively" as respectful indifference ("live and let live"). In the symbolical order, external realities become tokens of intimacy, real mediators of unity; in the diabolical order, external realities are protrusions of self that cast out from within. Externalization becomes an occupation of space that would otherwise be taken by something else, so that *to be is to evict*; mutual exclusivity lies at the core of the diabolical. The deceptive image of unity is compromise, which is a sort of reciprocal self-negation, or perhaps at best (from the perspective of the beneficiaries) cooperation, which is a reciprocal instrumentalization that amounts to self-promotion; this joint venture, this harnessing together of individual instances of self-interest, in turn, to the extent that it succeeds, necessarily entails the negation of some third party. The diabolical, as the *verneinende Geist*, is quite literally a *zero*-sum game. It produces nothing, but transforms through subtraction.

3. What is communicated by the diabolical is everything but the internal essence, that is, everything but the reality *in* itself *qua* real. The diabolical is not an intrinsic participation in the real, but an extrinsic imitation of it: it *mimics*, rather than *mediates*, reality. There are two aspects to this nonessential simulacrity. On the one hand, the diabolical

is all about *appearances*. This means, moreover, that it concerns subjective perception above everything else. The real tends to be reduced, in its significance, to what we make of it. On the other hand, the real, as we suggested above, is reduced to the *effects* it produces; in other words, it is functionalized. We might say that the diabolical confers all of the benefits of reality, but it relieves one of the burden of reality in itself. In both aspects, what is communicated is something external to the real, however immediate it may be in any given case.

In that it represents benefits without the burden, the diabolical might be thought of as an improvement on the real. This "improvement" occurs most specifically under two aspects: convenience and efficiency. Both of these notions are meant here specifically in the impoverished modern sense.[29] Convenience—*con-venientia*, "coming together"—means fittingness. The sense of fittingness depends on that to which a thing is adapted. In contrast to the basic medieval sense of *convenientia*, which means conformity to an objectively logical or aesthetic measure—or, more adequately, let us say conformity to the standards of truth, beauty, and goodness (and ultimately to the mind and will of God)—convenience here means adaptability to the perceiving subject.[30] It is important to see that this is an *essential* part of the diabolical, precisely because of its mimetic nature. We said above that potency separated from act is diabolical, since potency thereby loses any intrinsic relation to, and therefore any essential claim on and accountability to, reality, but instead depends on what is external to itself for that reality. In this respect, the *form* it takes does not arise organically from within the reality; instead, it comes to be outside of the reality— above all in subjective perception—and so its actuality is defined by the horizons of that alien space. The medieval thinkers repeated the saying, "That which is received is received in the mode of the recipient" (*quidquid recipitur ad modum recipientis recipitur*); they understood, however, that the thing received nevertheless has its own *substance* distinct from the mode of its reception. The reception therefore inevitably entails a kind of reciprocal relationship. Such a thing occurs when reception means in some basic way "joining with" a reality that remains abidingly other. In this case, the reality continues, so to speak, to stand in and emerge from a center that lies in itself and in that respect remains forever distinct from the center of the recipient, no matter how intimately the centers may intertwine. When everything is communicated *except for* the internal essence, by contrast, there is no presence of a distinct center to which the recipient ecstatically conforms itself; there is no abiding substance that makes an ongoing demand on the one who binds himself to it. Instead, the "reality" is collapsed into the recipient. The diabolical, in this sense, fits the subject, so to speak, like a glove. It is not only convenient, it is convenience itself.

Something similar can be said regarding the *efficiency* of the diabolical. The collapse into the mode of the recipient is a collapse into subjective power. The primacy of actuality means that there is something beyond power, and indeed that it is precisely *that something* which is most significant. The transcendence that power claims is a horizontal transcendence, a "beyondness" only along the lines of the relationship of causality interpreted in a linear form of succession.[31] This relationship falls under the scope of *ratio*, that is, of discursive, calculating reason, as distinct from *intellectus*, the intuitive and contemplative aspect of the mind.[32] Accordingly, the act of the mind in classical philosophy that grasps actuality is not calculation, the determination of effects in relation to causes, and of causes in relation to effects; instead, actuality is most basically *seen* in an affirmative act of consent. If "determinatio est negatio,"[33] then *intuitio*, we might say, *est affirmatio*. Rather than derive actuality from a hypothesis, we recognize it in its reality, which means we responsively acknowledge its presence: *it is*. The reduction of actuality to potency is a subsumption of reality into what can be calculatively determined. From this perspective, potency reduces at least in one respect to the power possessed by a subject. If we know how effects are produced, we can control those effects, and so if we identify what something is with the effects it produces, that is, with its functionality, then what things are lies in a certain sense within our power. In the diabolical order, then, reality becomes little more than what we want to see, as it were. It is a matter of appearance and products of manipulation; in this sense, reality seems obvious and easy. Of course, because the diabolical can never finally overcome the fact that it is an imitation of what it is not, the impression of efficiency and convenience can never altogether eliminate a liminal awareness of the reality beyond its borders, so to speak, which is thereby transformed into its alienating opposite. Reality in the diabolical order is both easy and impossible, the subject is simultaneously full of presumptuous self-confidence and radically insecure. The diabolical points in both directions at the same time. And all of this is the result of its communicating everything but the essential sense of things, their intrinsically abiding actual meaning.

4. The collapse into subjective perception and power, however, does not make the diabolical a reality that is merely relative to the individual. Instead, because any given individual is *real*, in its separation from reality the diabolical is at the same time a separation from each and every individual. It may collapse into subjectivity, but it essentially eludes the possession of any actual subject. It is a detached subjectivity, which necessarily falls short of each and every real individual. There is a kind of transcendence here, but it is a pseudotranscendence, insofar as genuine transcendence requires some reality, some actual principle, which means a common *good* that is *really distinct* from that which it transcends. This is why genuine transcendence is always unifying, which is to say it is always symbolical. A real transcendence includes the reality of what it transcends, which means the parts are therefore affirmed in their uniqueness, even while they are never confined, so to speak, to the limitations that uniqueness inevitably entails. The diabolical "transcends" by simply disregarding those limits, annulling their actuality. It has been said that the devil is a "personal being" only in a qualified sense, and that what is, so to speak, most devilish about him is that he hides his personality.[34] Interpreting this metaphysically, we could say that the diabolical is "supra-individual" in the sense of being more than any of the constitutive subjects, but without having a subjectivity of its own. It is "impersonal." Benedict XVI describes the devil as an "Un-person, the disintegration of and collapse of personhood, and that is why he characteristically appears without a face and why his being unrecognizable is his real strength. In any case, the fact remains that this 'in between' is a real power, or, more precisely, a collection of powers and not just the sum of human selves."[35] The form that this impersonal, pseudotranscendence tends to take is *system*. It is a configuration of pieces that acquires a certain intrinsic logic that makes it operate, as it were, with a mind of its own—much like a disease, for example, which is a kind of paradigm of a disorder. Hannah Arendt famously described this phenomenon as the "banality of evil,"[36] apparently mean-

ing that in the modern age evil takes the form of small, characterless personalities simply "doing their job" in the service of a destructive machine, more or less oblivious to the larger meaning of what is going on: what is most inhuman is not the terrible roar of the tyrannical beast, but the relentless clamor of a million clacking keyboards.

One of the crucial dimensions of such a system is that it is self-perpetuating, in a mindless, automatic way. It is nonsymbolical in the sense that it does not move generously from within to an order that lies beyond it, but points instead relentlessly to itself in a merely successive way. The diabolical system does, indeed, aim at producing effects, but these do not truly transcend the system. These ends are not affirmed in their (transcendent) actuality, but become in turn mere means that justify and promote the continued existence of the system itself, even while this remains nothing real in the sense of a genuinely subsisting whole. Because the ends and means are extrinsic to one another, the system and its products become mere instruments, exhaustively subordinated to each other.[37] This is a simulacrum of the living organism, which Kant described as a reciprocal subordination of parts and whole, because in the case of the organism, these are intrinsic to each other.[38] Likewise, the self-perpetuation of the diabolical system is a translation of eternity into its possibilistic, horizontally contained, image: it is not a self-transcendence, but a constant repetition of self into the future without meaningful limit, or in other words without the limit of meaning. An example of a system that mimics the intrinsic life of the organism is the modern economic system (which we will elaborate in chapter 5): in one respect, the economic system is nothing more than individual agents making decisions to buy and sell according to their own private criteria, but in another respect, the system is something like an independent organization that moves and develops according to laws internal to itself, with respect to which individual agents are organs that behave in more or less predictable ways.[39] Another example of a system in this sense is a bureaucratic administration, which has no reality in itself insofar as it exists solely to enable its institution to function smoothly and productively, and at the same time evidently operates as the tail that wags the dog. The diabolical is just such a system, which, as nothing real in itself, is reducible in a certain respect to its subjects and at the same time makes use of these subjects as its instruments.

People speak of *progress* in general terms. But progress means advancement; as Robert Spaemann has pointed out, progress can be determined only in relation to a *telos*, a destination, and thus the term makes sense only in relation to specific, determinate realities.[40] One might say that, when a person uses the term "progress" without intending any specific, concrete, actual, and end-directed reality or realities, then the implied subject of progress is the diabolical.

A further dimension of this pseudotranscendent impersonality that is worth describing is its "anti-incarnational" character, that is, its resistance to embodiment and the flesh. Actuality is always concrete, and so *both* universal *and* particular. Symbolical universality arises from the depths of the particular; the more completely and profoundly one involves oneself with a particular reality, the more fully one is acquainted with the reality it makes present: further up, further in.[41] Diabolical universality, by contrast, overrides particularity. There is a connection between this and the absence of the internal essence of reality, discussed above. One has access to the internal essence of a thing only by entering into it, which is to say, sharing in its actuality, and this is located in time and space. Moreover, it can be entered only by taking time and giving space. Aristotle, for example, said that genuine friendship can arise only through individuals' living together (i.e., being in the same place) over a protracted period of time.[42] Real ontological unity cannot be imposed or effected, nor can it be systematically programmed; instead, it can only be allowed to grow quite literally *on its own*, and we bring about this growth only by creating propitious circumstances for it to happen by itself, as it were. We plant, we water, and we hope. Similarly, according to Plato, the genuine communication of knowledge, and the intimacy with reality this implies, differs from the mere persuasion aimed at by sophistry by requiring the patient introduction of seeds that must be allowed to take root and grow on their own. These genuine ideas are opposed to the technological manipulation of words and exchange of commodified, or in any event commodifiable, information.[43] Because the diabolical is about separation rather than unity, and about appearances rather than intrinsic reality, it is not essentially, but only accidentally, constrained by time and space. It tends toward abstraction from limiting conditions and circumstances and privileges immediacy both temporally and spatially. In grasping this immediate presence, individual subjects at the same time become functions of a larger process, over which no one has any direct control. There is, thus, a simultaneous omnipotence and impotence; in one's unbounded activity, one remains a cog in a comprehensive machine, but without any of the intimacy of participation. In this respect, the individuals are, each of them, ghosts in the machine, disembodied members of a corporation without a corpus.

The distinguishing sign of the antichrist, according to St. John, is not that he denies God, but that he denies his "having come in the flesh" (ἐρχόμενον ἐν σαρκί; 2 John 1:7).[44]

5. The correlate of this anti-incarnational aspect of the diabolical, and its communication of everything but the essential, is that it abrogates what is essential in the recipient subject. A real center makes contact with a real center; this is the communication of being that occurs in the symbolical. But if the reality is only imitated, in such a way that what is communicated is precisely separate from the essential, original, and originating center, then it, so to speak, calls on nothing more than the surfaces of the subject for its appropriation. The subject is involved in every way but *essentially*; his center is removed from this relationship. In other words, he loses his soul. Here we have what is called the "devil's bargain"—the exchange of one's soul for worldly success—but interpreted in an ontological manner. We normally think of this transaction as a mythical deal done at the crossroads, and we take this deal to represent allegorically a moral decision: instead of taking care of one's soul and helping others (*cura animae*), one resolves to pursue fame and fortune, by hook or by crook. But we mean here something more basic, a kind of exchange that is in a certain respect prior to any moral consideration,[45] so much so that it can even coincide with a conscious intention—as we saw in Locke—to live virtuously and be "right with God." In chapter 1, we referred to Weber's discussion of the accumulation of capital as an objective sign of holiness that compensates for the sacramental presence of God that gets lost in modernity. The point we wish to emphasize in the present context is that this sign, though putatively bearing witness to one's virtue and thus to one's sincere endeavor to live in harmony with God, is a sign *specifically of God's absence* from the world, that is, of God as separated from (δια-βάλλω) the world as it actually exists.

We are able to enter into this more basic sense of the devil's bargain by pondering the connection between losing one's soul and specifically *worldly* success. The adjective indicates an achievement that is not essentially connected with the intrinsic meaning of things, but rather with their effects and how they are perceived (see above); intrinsic meaning, by contrast, is the reality of things that remains distinct from, and transcendent in relation to, these external dimensions, regardless of how inseparable they may be at another level. "Success," moreover, is a measure of precisely this sort of external achievement, the mark of having produced an impressive quantity of effects,[46] or managed to earn the esteem of colleagues, and so forth. As is well known, one of the central notions of the ancient Greeks, a guiding light to thinking, and an endlessly fruitful source of culture, was ἀρετή, "excellence."[47] The notion tended to include the aspect of success, but one of the great problems, perhaps *the* constitutive drama of classical Greek culture, from Homer to Plato, Aristotle, and the tragedians, was to make, indeed to cultivate, a distinction between the two, a distinction that ultimately concerned in some respect the difference between being and seeming. If we understand the soul to be the internal essence of an individual, the unifying and therefore "animating" (from *anima*, "soul") center of a being, we see that there is a necessary connection between the loss of soul and the pursuit of worldly success, and this connection holds even if the pursuit of worldly success is intended to be a means of some further virtuous activity. We will return to this point especially in chapter 5. In any event, the point here is that, to the extent that one's relation to the world is mediated by and through the diabolical, one not only *will* lose one's soul (as a future danger), but one has already surrendered it.

It is good to see, moreover, that the loss of soul that coincides with the diabolical is not only subjective, but it has in addition an analogous objective expression. This expression is connected with the self-referential system that we described above. One often hears a principally bureaucratic operation described as "soulless," and it is important to recognize that there is something genuinely—that is, not-merely-metaphorically—true about this description. There is a tendency to subjectivize and sentimentalize the meaning of this description, to take it as a claim that those who sit in the various offices that constitute the system are not very "personable," that is, they reduce you to a number and a problem to be resolved, rather than treat you as a person, and perhaps make conversation with you as they carry out their task. This, however, is an inadequate moral critique, which fails to see that the tendency to reduce people to a number and such things is an expression of the inner logic of the system rather than simply an accidental character of the individuals who happen to operate it. As we have suggested, a soul lives "soulfully" in a *real* relation to what is actually and abidingly *other* than itself, even as intimately present: this is the symbolical order. The essence of the diabolical, in contrast, is a *separation from* what it signifies and thus a (tragically perpetually frustrated) self-enclosure. The diabolical itself therefore has no genuinely animating center, but only a relentless external logic. The "system" to which it gives rise has no inner heart, as it were, which is what would make it genuinely open to (and inwardly participant in or reciprocally generated by) an end outside of itself, and so respectfully affirmative of any persons involved.

There is obviously a connection between the self-referential order and the "worldly success" we just described: both are essentially *introverted* ("turned within") activities—or, better, *per-verted* ("completely and radically turned"), because there is no *real* interiority into which to turn. The *curvatio in se* is at the same time *extra se*. Because there is no genuine center, each part is in a sense merely a function of other parts, and so there is no real, internal guidance. We have here a fragmentary division (δια-βάλλω) of tasks, so that none of the laborers share in the whole, or join together with one another (συν-βάλλω) by virtue of such participation. Instead, they are drawn to their particular work, if not merely by the self-interest of external reward, at best by a certain thought, which remains necessarily abstract, of the final product of the collective activity, a product that is just as extrinsic to their individual labors. We might think, again in this context, of the banality of evil that Arendt saw in Eichmann, who in the extreme violence he helped perpetrate seems to have been driven, not by any personal *animus*, so to speak, but rather by a sense of the citizen's moral responsibility to do his duty. No one is in control, which is why nothing in the activity of the system is an expression of ontological and personal depth. It is *in this sense* soulless.

6. Finally, the diabolical is essentially self-subverting. In a way, this aspect is the summation of all of the features we have described. There

is a contradiction "built into" the diabolical, insofar as it is defined both by the reality that it imitates and at the very same time by its opposition to that reality. It is crucial to see that this contradiction lies at the very heart of the diabolical; it is not, for example, a subsequent problematic into which it may happen to fall or even to which it is ineluctably driven. Contradiction *constitutes* the diabolical. It follows that self-contradiction will turn up in all of its other features and all of its effects. The diabolical presents as essential what it simultaneously denies or renders impossible, so that we could say that it is the very essence of the diabolical, ontologically considered, to make "empty promises." The diabolical proffers an object of desire while at the same time undermining the conditions under which that object could be attained in actuality. It is not only perverse; it is perversity itself, because its turning toward what is other than itself is *in fact* nothing more than a turning toward itself. This is what we have meant by saying that it points in two directions at the same time: δια-βάλλω. The essential *per-versity* of the diabolical comes perhaps most intensely to light in the fact that it is, so to speak, precisely the nature of the diabolical to present *just itself* as the solution to the problem that *it itself* generates. The absence of the reality that is imitated, which is precisely what draws one to the imitation, is fulfilled by the absence of the reality that is imitated. The need is therefore satisfied, if at all, only in appearance, which means in reality that it is deepened and intensified, but what the need relentlessly demands is more of the same problem.

The diabolical has the structure of despair. It signals a kind of desperate neediness, the response to which tends to take the repetitive and self-reinforcing form of addiction. This neediness is desperate in the strict sense of the term, that is, it lacks the inward openness in response to the other that is the form of hope, as Gabriel Marcel, for example, has characterized it.[48] In the place of such other-centered hope, we have the reversion to self to solve the problem that *is* the self, which Kierkegaard, to take another example, has described as the essence of despair.[49] The symbolical likewise bears the openness of desire, but in principle it is a generous desire, insofar as the object of its desire, as actual, is inchoately but really present already, so that the openness of this sort of desire will always coincide with a certain kind of completeness.[50] This desire is therefore of its essence *joyful*: according to the original usage, "joy" is the opposite of "frustration"; it signals an achievement, a success, a fruitfulness as opposed to the barrenness or sterility of a desire that is empty.[51] The Latin term for enjoyment, *frui* ("to enjoy") designates the completion of finality, but it is also the root of *fruit*: a fruition, an excess that is an opening to what is more. This is the generosity of the *symbol* that we described above, and which we will elaborate in part 3 of this book.

LIBERTY AS DIABOLICAL

We may now turn to consider the way in which modern liberty, as expressed paradigmatically in Locke but not limited to him, is diabolical in the sense that we have described. It does not take long to see that the adjective fits quite naturally, though some of the elements won't be fully apparent until our reflection on contemporary cultural forms in chapter 5. The heart of the matter is the definition of freedom as active power, which subsumes actuality into the potency and so eliminates any *internal* reference to the real order that transcends, and so informs and orients, the potency. If power is active in this sense, it is by itself the causal source of the actuality to which it gives rise, which means that that actuality is most radically produced rather than first recognized and received.

Here we see the diabolical in a pure form: the actuality that is subsumed into potency is thereby, as it were, retranslated into the terms of potency; this power thus becomes an imitation of "real actuality," and then carries out that imitation by functionalizing the actuality. The functionalizing breaks into a dual form (δια-βάλλω), each part of which claims reductively to be the whole even as it opposes itself to the other. The "parts" both tend simultaneously to collapse into each other and to remain mutually exclusive.

The two forms of the functionalization are, on the one hand, a kind of "activism," insofar as the potency cannot imitate the actuality in its *being*, since this would make the actuality genuinely immanent to it, but because the actuality remains extrinsic, the power can imitate it only in its acting, specifically by "actually" achieving the ends of what it imitates. On the other hand, the being that is distinct from the acting takes the form of a kind of *storing up* of power, a making of the means that it is into a separate end either through accumulation or through rationalization (in the sense of the systematized perfection of the efficiency of methods). We recall that Locke subordinated knowledge—which is privileged in the symbolic order since it is the *recognition* of and *intimate indwelling within* what is really real—to the twofold practical end of contriving conveniences for life in this world and acquiring virtue (i.e., accumulating the power of self-control) for the sake of reward in the world to come. The contemplative rest that would be given in knowledge becomes a restless praxis or potency for such, elevated to the status of the highest achievement.

In general, modern freedom tends to actualize itself as a kind of power *over* the real, which cannot avoid becoming at the very same time a flight *from* the real. Let us consider how this happens with respect to Locke's "re-conception" of what determines the will. As we saw, Locke comes to reinterpret the more traditional determination of the will by the good as a self-determined choice that posits the good in question as essential, or at least conducive, to my happiness as I see it. This is diabolical. Why? On the surface, this reinterpretation may seem to represent a negligible difference: one could say, with a certain justice to be sure, that the content of the choice remains the same whether I choose something as a good that has an a priori claim on my will or instead as something that I have identified as important, and so worthy of my selection—indeed, perhaps so worthy that any right-minded person would *have* to choose it in the given circumstances. In this latter case, one might even say that, in this hypothesis, the object of choice is presented as equally necessary in the two instances and thus as imposing the same sort, or at least a comparable degree, of obligation. But there is a subtle difference between the two, which turns out to have profound and infinitely extensive implications. In the first case, we understand the will as participating in an essentially symbolical order. The will therefore most fundamentally *receives* its determination, though, of course, *precisely because* it is an internal determination, that reception is not the passive affection by something wholly extrinsic but instead necessarily takes an active form of sharing in a mode proper to it. The power of the will in this case is a sort of "enablement" by the actuality of the good, which means that the will's *own* power, so to speak, exceeds its own borders. The will in this case is constitutively ecstatic; it genuinely "reaches" beyond itself, and so from its most inward core makes real reference to a larger order. The will is what it is as always already having participated in what is more than it is. In *seizing*, taking possession of, this particular good, it is even more profoundly seized by the embracing order, and it thereby joins in an ontological unity with all other members of this order: "to own" something means both "to have it belong to one" and "to confess its truth." The exercise of the will in a genuinely symbolical order is always a kind of intimate exchange of being, which at the same time deepens the individual reality of the participants in the exchange.

By contrast, if the object of choice presents itself from within the notion of freedom as active power, the *goodness* gets eliminated from the good, even as everything else is left firmly in place. As we saw in chapter 1, the thrust of uneasiness is the diabolical substitute for the attraction of goodness. Indeed, this substitute presents a kind of paradigm of the diabolical, because it consists of a re-description of the same relation or event according to a different point of reference, which covers the exact same ground functionally but gives the whole an entirely different meaning. This subversion occurs when the choice of the will, understood as active power, is given priority: in this case the (abstracted) content of the particular good is affirmed even as the primacy of its actuality is rejected or, to use the language we just introduced above, you get everything but the internal essence. All the parts are there, but serially rather than organically interrelated in a whole that is greater than their sum and is present intrinsically to each even in its discreteness, since such organic wholeness depends on an essential center, which is the *forma totius*. Thus, the particular object is taken to be a good, and in this sense there seems to be a perfect identity with the symbolical choice: the thing is not rejected outright, interpreted as an evil, but is rather *affirmed* as something choice-worthy. The *nature* of its choice-worthiness, however, is subtly transformed. It is now affirmed precisely as an option, which means that the choice is not a receptive recognition of, and so an ontological participation in, its prior actuality, but is instead *just what actualizes it as good*. Before the choice, it is simply a possibility, that is, an option that stands alongside other options. It may be that none of the other options seems to offer sufficiently compelling warrant for pursuit, so that only this one is in the end capable of "imposing" itself, but it remains the case that it thereby imposes itself only as an option, which the will makes actual in its choice. In this respect, the "goodness" of the option is effectively—that is, in the order of efficient causality—a function of the will. The option is not actual in itself ("internal essence") but has its actuality *in* the will that chooses it. What is chosen is therefore an effective imitation of the good rather than the good itself.

It is in this context that the full significance of Locke's clarification of the proper terminus of the act of the will in his second and subsequent editions of the *Essay*, which we discussed in chapter 1, comes to light. As we recall, Locke somewhat enigmatically summed up the essential point of revision of the *Essay* with the formulation that the act of will, properly speaking, does not terminate in *things*, but in *actions*. Here is the diabolical in a nutshell. To say that the will terminates in things—that is, in actual goods outside the soul—is to conceive of freedom in essentially symbolical terms as a "joining-with," a sharing in goodness, by uniting with a reality that evokes desire and at the very same time responsibility. To deny this, as Locke came to see he must, is *to deny that the will connects with reality* in any genuine sense; it is to lock the will within its own boundaries, to replace the ontological union of the soul and reality with the power to carry out an activity that seems, for all practical purposes, to represent an adequate translation of that enjoyment or union: to take a rather trivial example, instead of saying that my will terminates in the plum, and the activity of eating is the means by which it does so, I say that my will terminates in the eating, and the plum happens to get consumed in the action. My act of the will comes to its completion, not *in re*, but in the motion it is able to produce in my body.[52] My will in this case never actually reaches (συν-βάλλω) the plum, but the plum nevertheless effectively disappears in the process—and so does its goodness: the willed activity of eating takes the place of the actuality of the plum that is enjoyed or consumed. However slight this distinction may appear, it is in reality sufficiently large to accommodate an infinite difference, namely, that between the goodness of the world and its counterfeit double.

Now, in speaking of an effective imitation that replaces the good itself, we are setting the order of efficient causality into relief here, which means there are other dimensions that are *not* simply produced by the activity of the will. A failure to grasp this point would lead to a serious misunderstanding of the critique being developed and therefore a facile dismissal of what turns out to be a straw man. One sometimes hears the rather glib complaint that modern freedom represents a rejection of all constraints: people think you can just do whatever you want, whatever "feels good," regardless of the consequences it might have for oneself or for others. This is not the criticism we are making; the point here is more subtle. To say that the goodness of the options is effectively a function of the will's choice is compatible with a recognition of all sorts of constraints on that choice; it is simply a denial of the very specific "constraint"—which we have suggested is at the same time an "empowering"—of *actual goodness*. What survives the reinterpretation is the formal content, but now in an abstract mode.[53]

There are several dimensions to this new mode of the formal content. First, though the formal content retains a certain normativity and so a priority over the will, there *is* in the "optionizing of the good" actually a relative control over the content, since the will, as what grants actuality, becomes the arbiter of what formal content it chooses to acknowledge. The content, here, is selected from a number of options. At the same time, this arbitration is compatible with a recognition of objective norms. In this case, the norm takes the form specifically of a *law, as opposed to* an actual good. On the one hand, it is the nature of law, so conceived, to be specifically impersonal. Obedience to the law in the modern context of Locke (but equally in Spinoza and Kant, not to mention others in the liberal tradition), is not only compatible with the rejection of heteronomy, understood as subjection to the "arbitrary will" (*Willkür*) of another, but it represents the surest safeguard against such a threat to autonomy. In this regard, in strict contrast to the ontological intimacy of the symbolical order, there is no real encounter with an actual *other*, but rather a "filtering" of all the content of otherness, so to speak, through the potency of power. The ideal then becomes mere formal constraint as potency, which is actualized either by my own will or by an impersonal system (as we will unfold further below), but in any event *not* in the will of another active power, an "arbitrary will." On the other hand, this obligation, precisely because it has been detached from any real actuality of a good, is as it were *unable to enable*. As nothing but a formality, and so a pure potency, the law or obligation in general is impotent in itself and so lacks any capacity to communicate actuality to the will that is governed by it—to render the yoke sweet and the burden light. The will therefore becomes itself impotent, in turn, with respect to the law. This does not mean that the will is incapable of following the law, but only that the law is precisely imposed from outside as an extrinsic rule to which the will attempts *extrinsically* to conform, more or less, through its own efforts to control behavior. There is, in other words, no deep participation in the intrinsic meaning of the good, to which the law gives a certain formal expression, but rather an exhortation to exercise will power backed by the threat of punishment.

Thus, to return to the difference we indicated above: if I choose something precisely as a good in the full sense, I recognize (re-cognize, i.e., I come to know it precisely as something I always already knew) it as real, which means it is already present to me—or better, "in" me—in a certain respect, so that my choice is a *consent* to its given reality. As such, the activity of the will is quite concrete: it is responsive to a real good that is actually present, and in its concreteness actually related in a complex and organic way to a host of other goods within a comprehensive order. (For the very same reason goods are *never* simply commensurable, and so the determination of what is to be done is never a quantitative calculus.) In a field of mere options, by contrast, the will is simply left on its own to choose what it will and what it can. It is not, so to speak, liberated to make its particular choices. The form that is *imposed on* the will in the law is, as we have seen, an extrinsic limitation, which is necessarily general—that is, it concerns classes of choices rather than particular choices—because it is abstracted from the concreteness of actuality. Within those limits, there is no positive in-formation or internal guidance, which means that the acts are completely indeterminate and arbitrary, that is, they are preserved as expressions of formless "power." On the other hand, in relation to those limits, the will is utterly passive, and so helpless: the limits prescribed by law, or, analogously, the sphere of objectivity in general, represent an order that is radically distinct from the order that belongs to the will in itself, and so the will has no relationship to them other than acquiescence—or, of course, rebellion. A basic result is a tendency toward the subjectifying or privatization of freedom on the one hand, and, on the other hand, a kind of fatalism with respect to what is "objective," "public," "natural," or comprehensive.

Benjamin Constant, writing in the early nineteenth century, famously pointed to this privatization as precisely what distinguishes the modern conception of freedom from the ancient one[54]—and it is interesting to note his claim that the notion has undergone such a transformation in the modern era that the use of the same word in the two contexts simply invites confusion. Liberty, in the modern era, represents a separation (δια-βάλλω) of a sphere of one's own over against the public order, the isolation of an arena over which one has more or less complete control, which implies a concession of the surrounding area to the "powers that be," powers that are therefore alien to my freedom. We may observe, here, that this isolated private arena, however much it is protected politically, cannot help dwindling, even inside of the preserved private sphere, to the unreality of an abstract mathematical point in relation to the objective laws, not this time of the social order, but of nature, so that there is a schizophrenic split within the private sphere: it is pure aimless power and indeterminate freedom and at the same time the absolute givenness, and deterministic behavior, of biology and neurochemical physiology.[55] It is not surprising, then, that this novel form of modern liberty comes explicitly onto the scene at more or less the same time that sociology emerges: sociology is a science that studies human behavior collectively as a system that operates according to laws analogous to those governing physical objects. In a certain sense, this sociological eclipse of the concrete individual is a further extension of the Enlightenment dream of constructing a political order as a machine (Hobbes), which transforms human freedom, as it concerns the objective order, into a force—self-interest, *conatus* (Spinoza)—that is taken to be absolute precisely so that it can be reliably calculated and so harnessed. Freedom is absolutized *precisely* by being abstracted from the conditions that are inseparable from the actual order, which is to say that it is cut off from any reality that would give it an internal weight and substance. It is therefore the absolutizing of individual freedom that makes it vulnerable to external control. Modern politics, then, tends to become a system that is indifferent to the substantial quality of the souls that constitute it, and so it necessarily takes the form of the extrinsic manipulation of forces. On the "inside," modern liberty is formless, while on the "outside" it is nothing but (mechanical) form and negotiations of power. Here we have a compelling case of the *diabolical duality* of (subjective) appearance and (objective) being.

Because of the nature of the liberty in question, the attempt to mediate between these two spheres—actualizing subjective freedom in the objective sphere through civil and political institutions—likewise takes a diabolical modality. We reflected on two forms of this mediation in Locke, though these forms are certainly not exhaustive: property as money (with respect to things) and contracts as the exchange of rights (with respect to persons). To be clear, it is worth pointing out that property, money, contracts, and rights are not of themselves and in principle diabolical. The claim we are making, instead, is that they become such only when they come to represent the primary form of objectivity or public relation to the things in the world and other people. If they are secondary forms, relative to a primary actuality, an encompassing order that embodies a concrete hierarchy of goods, these institutionalized embodiments of freedom can be genuinely *symbolical*. But we are concerned with these realities, here, in the characteristically modern form that we explored in Locke. Lockean property is perfectly diabolical: it just *is* the division of the world as a keeping apart (δια-βάλλω). Property is the enclosure of previously public space, marking it off as mine precisely *as opposed to* anyone else's.[56] To claim property in this case is to establish a boundary that shows, one could say, where the world ends, and it is at just this point that *I* begin in my sovereign subjectivity. As we recall, prior to this enclosure, for Locke, the world is strictly *common*, which means it belongs to no one, and for this reason it has no value—it is "little more than nothing" to me (or anyone else) because it is not mine (or anyone else's). Its goodness does not precede any private possession of it. Exclusivity is the essence of property, in the sense that this is precisely what the word "property" means for Locke. We recall that his paradigm of property is the eating of an apple (diabolical indeed!): when it enters into me it is mine and mine alone.

It is not the fact of "dividing" the world that is at issue here—after all, distribution of the world's goods is inevitable, indeed, it is very good, and part of any political order and philosophy of that order—but rather the interpretation of distribution as the establishment of the boundaries of mutually exclusive rights.[57] According to such an interpretation, property is inherently divisive (though this divisiveness can of course coincide with all sorts of cooperation and effective harmony, as we will explain in a moment). What is particularly diabolical about Locke's view of property, however, is not only that he defines it in terms of mutual exclusion, but that he makes just this the foundation and goal of political community. As Locke theorizes, community takes property for granted as a reality established prior to civil order and that thus provides the context in which civil order emerges. This means that political community, as Locke understands it, presupposes as an absolute given ("ab-solute" in the sense of "separated from" the conditions of actuality of the real order) the isolation of human beings from one another, and it takes as its end the protection and preservation of this isolation. Again, this is simply a translation of the diabolical into the sphere of interpersonal relations.

It is, moreover, because of his conception of property that politics becomes for Locke essentially a matter of power, that is, the regulation of force, understood as effective energy acting *on* things from the outside. Locke's notion of property turns human beings into political agents that are essentially opaque to one another, and so they interact as so many quantifiable and externally regulatable forces. Political order, in this case, cannot penetrate into the inner essence of a person—as it does in the classical understanding in which politics is most basically a matter not of power, but of education, even though it does not of course exclude power—but "at best" imitates this ontological penetration by aspiring to exhaustive regulation unto the minutiae of human existence. Because it is only an imitation, however, such an attempt at regulation has always already failed to give form. As we have seen repeatedly in our investigation thus far, when power is severed from actuality, it becomes essentially unreal, which means it acquires an absolute quality in one respect simultaneous with utter impotence in another. In this case, founded on exclusively possessed private property and aimed at its preservation, "political order" is neither genuinely *political* nor actual *order*; it is instead a deceptive substitute for both. This is a diabolical conception of political freedom.

We will explore the diabolical character of money at greater length in the following chapter, but it is worth indicating a couple of points in relation to Locke and the origins of modern liberty. First of all, as

Locke himself observes, money is not in any sense an actual good, that is, it presents no real value to man: not only is it meaningless with respect to man's so-called natural desires but moreover fills no higher needs, in the sense that it holds no aesthetic value (collector's coins, which one would indeed put on display, bear only a residual relationship to money as an economic unit precisely to the extent that they are put on display). Its value derives only from what it *can do* rather than what it intrinsically is, and this "rather" is absolute: what it *can do* has nothing to do with the intrinsic capacity of actual potency, but is altogether a function of what it is "taken to be" by collective subjectivity. In other words, it is wholly an unreal appearance of value, and this value consists entirely of power, precisely as dissociated from actuality. It is interesting to recall in this context that Goethe has Mephistopheles introduce the institution of money in the *Faust II*, which is an epic of modernity;[58] the devil urges it on an emperor whose kingdom is falling into financial ruin, arguing that there will no doubt one day be many actual treasures dug up from under the existing kingdom to back up the bills: the money is wealth *in potentia*, which effectively substitutes for the gold that is absent. We saw in the previous chapter that property, as Locke interprets it, has an inherent tendency to "cash out," as we tellingly say, or in other words to reduce to money, the quantified means of exchange. This is an essentially diabolical logic: the actual goodness of the world is gradually converted into what is unreal. As we saw, inside of this logic, money infinitely outweighs any actual goodness, and so that goodness has no power to resist this incursion into actuality. Once one surrenders the primary vantage of actuality, the transformation of reality into unreality is inexorable.

The flip side of this transformation—though the phenomenon appears on a cultural scale only later—is "substanceless" possession, that is, a tendency toward the immediacy of private consumption, which corresponds to the formless character of freedom we just described. The classical tradition recognized three fundamental kinds of good— the *bonum honestum* (intrinsic goodness), the *bonum delectabile* (pleasure), and the *bonum utile* (utility)—and saw that the latter two were ultimately derived from, and so dependent on, the first.[59] We might say that the Lockean sense of political freedom represents an elimination of the foundation of actual goodness and so ends in the private sphere with a dialectical relationship between the other two: accumulation of pure means, money, on the one hand, and formless consumption ("entertainment") on the other hand. These cease *to be* good precisely because they no longer bear any internal relation to the intrinsic goodness that gives them their proper status as actualities, and so they now bear the burden of compensating for its loss. They become substitutes for the good itself.

The other aspect of money to point out in this context is its *divisive* character. Precisely because it does not have intrinsic value, its value is so to speak achieved through differentiation, or, more precisely, opposition. In a manner we will explore further in chapter 5, money has only *comparative* value, which means its worth to me depends in an essential way on the amount others have. This is not just a subjective valuation but is "objectively" the case (insofar as we can use that term in the present context): money is devalued the more it is distributed. Money is a symbol of power, and it has this power only through relative inequalities. For money to have value requires scarcity, people in need. If all people had an overabundance of money, the system would fall into crisis, while the same cannot be said of intrinsic goods, such as food, clothing, shelter, and so forth. These goods become economic goods precisely inside a system in which their value is measured against need, which is to say assigned a quantified value through the comparative relations of supply and demand, and otherwise converted into exchange values. In this sense, the "enough and as good" principle that Locke proposed as a constraint on private property can hold *only* in principle, which means here, in potency. It cannot be actually true without rendering money just so far ineffective and meaningless. For money to be effective, then, requires if not the preservation, and indeed in certain respects the exacerbation, of conditions of scarcity, then the artificial generation of effectively similar conditions through the invention of new desires (which, indeed, *have* to be unreal precisely to the extent that they are simply invented).[60] The very functioning of money as a system of objective value therefore depends upon pitting people in a basic sense against each other as competitors. In other words, it is strictly speaking diabolical. If property, understood as an expression of freedom as power, is the end of political community, and if property, thus conceived, tends logically to reduce to money, then political community has as its formal end to foster opposition between its members, even if it does so through objective (and soulless) regulation. Kant's "society of devils" in this case becomes not a test case but a cultivated ideal.[61]

With respect to the relations between and among people, we have seen that the principle of freedom as active power requires the model of the contractual exchange of rights, which, even when not explicitly instituted, remains the implicit, analogous form of every human interaction insofar as it represents the encounter of two (or more) active powers: it is a form that is *imposed* on all relations, even those that are naturally given, inherited, and so forth. This exchange is a simulation of the unity that subsists in a genuine reciprocity, and indeed acts as a substitute for it. The condition for unity is a common good, that is, an actual reality that is ontologically prior to the parts that constitute it, the members that join together in relation to it. The priority of the whole is what makes the members *sharers* in a reality that exceeds in some respect each of them and all of them together, a whole that, as actual, is implicitly present a priori in each of the members and so enables the members to be present in some sense in one another. There is no intimacy without metaphysical transcendence. The form in which the members share cannot be *merely* a potency subsequent to the actual reality of the members, which would have its actuality, if at all, solely as a result of the *action* of the members, because this fundamentally betrays the logic of unity. A connection that arises only from consent can only imitate unity.

The truth of this principle becomes evident when we consider what it means to speak of an exchange of rights, which is the form of the contract understood in liberalism to lie at the foundation of community. A right, in the Lockean sense, is a kind of legal boundary strictly analogous to the notion of property as the excluding enclosure of space. We might think of a right as an enclosure of a field of power. Thinking of it in this way brings its essentially diabolical character immediately to the fore, in two respects. First of all, to the extent that it is detached from any a priori form, power is nonactual, *unreal*, in itself. Before it acts, it is nothing. In this respect, power needs something on which to act, something that resists it; it depends on what is external to itself in order to be actual, as we have seen. This means that power comes into being only in a fundamental sense through the very enclosure that sets it off from what it is not. This intrinsic unreality of right as power is the first aspect of its diabolical character.

The second aspect is the *essentially* oppositional nature of right that this implies. The right depends not only on what is other than itself, but on what is opposed: it *needs* precisely what it excludes by definition. This is even more profoundly diabolical. The internal reality comes into being only by *separating out* and *standing against* (δια-βάλλω) what is other. To see how this is the case, let us imagine a world in which there existed a single human being—Adam prior to the creation of Eve. Note that, in this scenario, it would still make sense to speak of the good making a claim on Adam, entailing an order to his activity, but it would not make sense to speak of Adam having rights. One has rights only with respect to real or potential competing claims. Adam participates in goodness even alone, but he has rights only in relation to other rights-bearing agents.[62] This is because goodness concerns the inner nature of reality, whereas liberal rights concern only external behavior (as we will explain in chapter 5), precisely as dissociated from any consideration of internal nature and moreover in relation to other external behavior posited as potential threat or intrusion. Rights thus *require* opposition in principle to exist, and so to found social existence on rights is to define human relationships as fundamentally antagonistic. This is why Hegel, for example, says that to talk about the rights of family members with respect to one another is already to presuppose the dissolution of the family.[63] As we saw in chapter 2, although Locke insists on a clear difference between the state of nature and the state of war, the latter not only turns out to reveal the *inner truth* of the former, but it is also the indispensable cause of political community. And so we have the diabolical in a nutshell: it is our opposition that brings us together, and because this opposition is the cause of our political "unity," it cannot help but characterize that unity from the ground up.

Let us consider how covert this antagonism may be. A contract would appear to be the overcoming of opposition through cooperation, but insofar as it is a negotiation of rights, understood in the sense we have just indicated, the antagonism is not overcome here, but simply driven underground. Every right that is retained remains a separating out of what is in my exclusive control from what is *not* in my control, and so I remain opposed to what is other than myself. But

every right that I agree to surrender is henceforth to that extent alien-
ated from me, and it now lies under the power of the *other* rather than
my own. In this case, what was mine as opposed to others' is now others' as opposed to mine. The exchange preserves the opposition. This
remains the case even if those who are contractually bound are granted
rights to the same thing (for example, rights to use the same beach):
what we have here is the simultaneous presence of what is mutually exclusive, which presents only a dialectical contradiction in the place of
the paradox of genuine unity.[64] It is simply a unity "for all intents and
purposes," rather than being a unity in actual fact, and that means it effectively imitates unity. It can never get beyond mere simulation except
by conceding what it necessarily denies, namely, an obligation that *precedes* and provides the proper context for any contractual consent. We
ought to recall here Locke's sense that social obligation is exclusively
occasioned by consent—you don't have to do anything you haven't
obligated yourself to do (Kant would say, "anything you *shouldn't*
have obligated yourself to do, as a rational being"), and so forth. We
have here another instance of the will never exceeding itself, never
"joining-with" (συν-βάλλω) the real, never terminating in an actual
good in which others may actually share, but only in actions belonging
strictly to individuals that happen to overlap with the actions belonging to others, in the same time and place: a *coincidentia oppositorum*, if
you will. This imitation of unity entails the dialectic we saw in chapter
3: the individual loses himself in the consent, that is, gives away his
rights in some determined respect, but at the same time never *really* lets
go of himself, and so never really "joins-with" the other. Reality and
appearance essentially diverge, and this is an expression of what we
have been calling the diabolical. We might add, here, that the failure to
have community in actuality will tend to encourage a subjectivizing of
intimacy, a sentimentalization of friendship,[65] the almost infinite elevation of an unreal romantic ideal: its very absence of substance is what
causes it to rise above any and every "mundane" reality.[66] When the
ontological ground of unity gives way, love is undermined and exaggerated at the same time.

   In the diabolical order, the political agent—the subject of property, rights, contracts, and, in short, of freedom—is himself rendered
unreal, and for that very reason a reliable unit of organization. If *in re-*

ality actuality precedes potency, then one can give primacy to potency and power only by theoretically annulling all of the relationships inside of which concrete individuals always-already necessarily find themselves and reconstructing them as functions of power. The liberal political agent, then, is not connaturally a member of any larger whole. In fact, qua liberal political agent, he is impotent to achieve any such membership, since it can only come to be on the terms of the sort of political agency that founds it, and that agency excludes the priority of actuality. There is an analogy between the liberal political agent, which is an abstraction, a fiction posited hypothetically in order to make calculations, and the fictitious mathematical entities posited to make calculations in modern physics. The reality of flesh-and-blood humanity is transformed into the unreality of abstract political agency, and it is only the latter that is given public significance, since it is only the latter that presents itself as a possessor of power.[67] But even this power is never given *in reality*, since a gift can only ever be *actual*; power is instead only attributed to the individual units of the state, and increased to the extent that it is accepted *as appearance*—that is, as essentially private, with significance for the subject alone. Modern liberty, in a word, is a deceptive substitute for freedom, which subverts the very reality it promises.

To provide some evidence for this description of modern liberty, we may leap three centuries beyond Locke and consider one of the few deliberate attempts to define modern liberty in an explicit, official way in the context of the modern United States. In 1992, the U.S. Supreme Court took the occasion of a challenge to abortion rights (*Planned Parenthood v. Casey*, 505 U.S. 833) to articulate what it took the word "liberty" to mean, as the basis for its arbitration of a fundamental case concerning how human beings relate to each other. Rather than determining in a narrow sense the application of law to a particular situation or the balance of limits and allowances, the Supreme Court in this situation quite unusually ventured self-consciously into the sphere of philosophy, insofar as it tried to express an *essence*: specifically, it sought to define the reality that lies at the foundation of modern liberal society. It is significant that what occasioned this effort was an issue that reaches to the core of human relationship, the relation between mother and child. "At the heart of liberty," according to the Kennedy-Souter-O'Connor plurality opinion, "is the right to define one's own concept of existence, of meaning, of the universe, and of the mystery of human life." We note that liberty is being described here in terms of the possession of a right, which, as we have seen, represents in the Lockean sense the delineation of the scope of one's power to choose, as one wishes, unobstructed by the power of the will of others.

The scope of the power granted by this formulation strikes one initially as breathtakingly broad. The formulation has often been criticized for pretending to grant to man a power that any reasonable person would have to recognize as *superhuman*: Who in history, even in the periods of the greatest confidence in man's capacity for achievement, would ever have dreamed of having the power to determine the very meaning of existence, of the universe, of life itself? The very idea not only taxes the imagination, it kills it. This power, which exceeds the gargantuan aspirations of the most megalomaniacal of ancient tyrants is hereby not only offered to, but thrust upon, all people without exception, however meek and unassuming. What we need to understand, however, is that this claim to power is a devil's bargain: it comes at a cost, and the price paid is the elimination of precisely what is promised. One can have the absolute power to determine the meaning of existence as one wishes *only* on the condition that one's determination of that meaning amounts to *nothing at all*. This is most clearly evident if we consider this to be a universal right granted to everyone, which is what is being claimed here: you and I can both have the absolute power to determine the meaning of existence *only if* your determination means absolutely nothing to me (or anyone else) and my determination means absolutely nothing to you (or anyone else), unless we so choose in turn. We can all have this power only if it concerns ourselves alone in each case, and indeed ourselves only with respect to ourselves. This restriction, of course, immediately changes what power means, but it serves to bring to light what was in a sense always lurking inside of Locke's concept as its essential logic. If power means the capacity to bring about change, the power claimed in the Supreme Court's definition of freedom can be absolute only if it ceases to be power: one can have absolute power only if one agrees that it cannot effect any actual change.

We have just said that the self-subversion of absolute power is most evident at the level of a universally possessed right, which would seem to imply that, if I cannot determine the meaning of existence for anyone else, I can at least determine it for myself. But even this is not true. The devil is crafty indeed! If it is an absolute power to determine the meaning of existence, then I can have that power only if I am never *in actual fact* bound to any of my previous determinations. Indeed, we have to go further: I am not even bound to the determination of meaning that I happen to be giving to existence at this very moment. The determination volatilizes the very instant it is made, unless I "freely" choose to make it again the next instant, and so on. Indeed, a decision is therefore *required* of me in every instant. But this simply means that my determination of the meaning of existence cannot have any actual significance even for myself. The only way that I can possess freedom in the sense that the Supreme Court defines it is by dissociating it altogether from any contact with reality. In this case, to *be* free can only mean to have a purely subjective feeling of freedom with no implications for anything outside of that feeling. The feeling is, to be sure, an overwhelming one, because it seems that, in possessing such freedom, one possesses everything—or at least, one possesses *potentially* everything, and this potentiality is absolutely incapable of ever being realized. Note that the further it gets from reality, the greater the potency becomes, so that it increases in its (apparent) capacity to compensate for the reality that it occludes. That reality, then, becomes in turn unconstrained in principle on the other side by any limits of freedom, because freedom conceived as nothing but power presents no *real* limits. It is crucial, in this respect, that the power be absolute, that it be given to determine the meaning of everything, of existence, because it is just that absoluteness that removes it from reality; if the power were articulated in an apparently more modest form, for example, as the power to determine one's own concept, say, of this cup, or of water, or of financial responsibility, the absurdity would immediately become evident. We might say that the "sleight of thought" works only if the power is to determine the meaning of the whole at once: you can have the power to determine *only* the meaning of everything, and *not* of anything in particular.

To the extent that freedom is here reduced to a merely subjective feeling, it is perfectly compatible with *any* objective circumstances.

The absolutizing of the power of determination therefore at the very same time encourages and reinforces a fatalistic passivity with respect to the mechanical determinations of physics, biology, and psychology, to political and market manipulation, to the soulless machinations of bureaucratic institutions, to the oppressive weight of proliferous regulation, and to the inexorable movement of history—that is, the "forward march of progress." Modern liberty is, in sum, a deceptive and ultimately self-destroying illusion, which cuts one off from, and indeed sets one in opposition to, God, the world, other people, the community as a whole, and in every analogous expression, and even oneself, so that one's inner being, in its congenital blindness to the inner reality of everything else without exception, is smothered by endless layers of dissemblance. But if one is willing to pay this price, one can have everything. Modern liberty is not merely an instance of the diabolical, but is, we might say, diabolicality itself. If symbolic order is at its highest expression a love *even of* one's most extreme enemies (since the cause of unity is *in fact* universal), its perfect opposite is a "turning against" (δια-βάλλω) *even those to whom one seems to be most closely united*—indeed, unto one's very self.

THE GARDEN AND THE CAVE

The story of the devil's intrusion into the ordered life of the cosmos through his entry into the life of man is of course not a new one. It is fitting to end this chapter with a brief consideration of the original drama, which offers a summary paradigm of what we have been discussing and reveals its appropriately cosmo-historical dimensions. God's creation of Adam and his placing of Adam in the garden of Eden, his subsequent creation of the animals to which Adam gives names, and the culmination in the fashioning of Eve from his side, ought to be seen as the model of the symbolical order. There is the intimate presence of God ("breathed into his nostrils the breath of life," Gen. 2:7), the first principle of all things, in what is genuinely *other* than God ("of dust from the ground," 2:7), and this simultaneous intimacy and distance is the basis for man's status as "image and likeness" of God (1:26). There is a differentiated hier-archy, a "holy order," of all things: each created reality has its proper place in the larger whole, and each is, in itself, "good" (κάλον in the Septuagint), while the whole, capped by man, is "very good" (1:31). That man, who is given dominion, and so a certain responsibility, for the whole, nevertheless has his place *in* this order as a member, rather than simply *above* it, is indicated by the fact that what is highest, knowledge of good and evil, or ultimate judgment over the whole, does not belong to him but is placed outside of his reach.[68] This is what gives him a symbolical relation, as part of a whole. There is a natural community of things: the world is not created *by* man, which would reduce it to him, but nonetheless *for* him, to such an extent that he is invited to give the animals their proper names. (Moreover, the animals are certainly created for man in the sense of being for his use, but in the first place are analogously companions in the world.)[69] And, finally, in radical contrast to the atomism of Locke's state of nature, the original human relationship is presented as symbolical in the most literal sense: the woman is fashioned from the side of Adam—which is the place of the heart, and represents, according to Aquinas,[70] equal dignity—so that the two may *join together* and become one flesh (2:24; emphasis added). Note that it is precisely an *a priori* principle of unity that allows the real unity to come to be, just as the original act of friendship created the *tesserae hospitales* and allowed them to be "redeemed" at a historically later point. In their intimate joining, the man and woman fulfill the commandment to be fruitful and multiply; this obligation is not simply imposed as an external law but represents a fruition of their immanent activity. This is the essence of the symbolical.

The serpent upsets this order in several respects. We will briefly indicate three. First, we note that the serpent deceives, not by introducing a positive falsehood, but by recasting what is true in a "new light," so to speak, which changes its meaning. Instead of making a positive claim that would present an actual denial of what is given in reality, he raises a question that simply overturns its significance: "Did God say, 'You shall not eat of any tree of the garden?'" (Gen. 3:1). The question implies a universal extension and immanentizing of the limit that had originally presented a seal, as it were, on the totality of the symbolic order. Even if the reversal is rejected in its extreme form, Eve's response does allow a false extension of the proscription ("neither shall you touch it," 3:3), which implies a consent that establishes the "reinterpretation" in principle.

Moreover, the serpent reinterprets God's claim regarding the consequences of eating the fruit: God implied it would make Adam and Eve *mortal*; the serpent takes this in a narrow sense to mean they will immediately drop dead, and then correctly says that this is false. He is right, of course, in this restricted sense, but God is thereby made to take on the appearance of a deceiver.

Second, most decisively, what occurs in this moment is a transformation of the intrinsically hierarchical order of goodness into the terms of power. God's command regarding the tree of knowledge becomes the pronouncement of what Locke would call an "arbitrary will."[71] It ceases, in other words, to be a creative statement of the truth of things, a limit that makes the whole a whole, and instead becomes an imposition that is not in any way measured by goodness: this may be good for you, but it is off limits. The moment the will becomes an expression not of goodness but of arbitrary power, an essential opposition is introduced. Wills founded on goodness are intrinsically related to one another (συν-βάλλω), even if they happen in a particular case to be opposed, but wills founded on power have an essentially competitive relationship to each other (δια-βάλλω), even if they happen in a particular case to coincide or cooperate. In the serpent's reinterpretation of the order of creation, God's will and man's become reciprocally exclusive. Man is thus left to express his will precisely by rejecting God's ordinance.[72] It is interesting to note that the serpent promises to man precisely what God had forbidden, but he, so to speak, takes away everything that God had given as the result of fulfilling that promise.

Third, the negative relation with the ultimate principle of all things generates negativity in all other relations. The symbolical, once again, becomes diabolical. The first act of Adam and Eve after eating the fruit is the self-protective gesture of fashioning a covering for themselves (Gen. 3:7). (This appears, incidentally, to be the first instance of acquisition in the story, of taking, holding, and using, as opposed to immediate enjoyment.) They hide from God "among the trees of the garden" (3:8): those things that had initially mediated an intimacy between God and the creature have now become means to keep the creator at a distance. The opposition to God introduces a tension into the most basic human community, insofar as the symbolical unity is recast in terms of needy desire and power (3:16), and a tension into man's relation to the world generally,

which now *resists* man's work. In short, a denial of the truth, a reinterpretation of goodness as power, immediately makes what had been a
symbolical unity into an internal strife. Man is cast out of the garden.

Exile from the garden in the most extreme sense is separation from
the good; the furthest distance from the garden may be said to lie at the
bottom of Plato's cave. Plato's allegory offers another succinct image of
what this exile looks like, taken to perfection and viewed specifically in
relation to its implication for man's relationship to the real. It is an intuitive expression of modern liberty, as we have been describing it. The
essence of the allegory is the distinction between being and appearance;
Plato presents it as an attempt to visualize what human life looks like in
as complete a separation from the good as can be conceived. The prisoners are trapped in the pit of the cave, forced to watch the shadows
thrown up on the back wall (thus at the opposite extreme of the sun, the
image of the good).[73] The shadows are a reduction of the reality of
things to how they most immediately appear *to me*, independently of
what they may happen to be in reality.[74] This reduction is logically connected to the dissociation of things from the good: instead of real things
being manifest to all in the open light of the sun, the shadows of the images of reality have only what we might call "private" significance. The
prisoners viewing these shadows in a certain respect have everything,
and have it cheaply: there is no reality in the world that is not *available*
to them in an immediate way; from their vantage, there is nothing that
does not fall effortlessly into their passive field of attention. Or more
specifically, there is nothing except for reality itself, the "internal essence" of things as actual. It is not an accident, then, that the immediate
possession of all things in appearance coincides with a complete oblivion
with respect to their real situation, namely, that they are bound, motion-
less, to that particular vantage. We have here a perfect description of the
Lockean dialectic that we have been unfolding: *pure* power by its nature
collapses into the infinitely small space of merely subjective appearance,
which coincides with a passive surrender to the actual as impassible objective determination. In being dissociated from the actuality of goodness, the captives in Plato's cave are simultaneously isolated from the
real world, from other people, and indeed even from themselves and
their most basic desires. These desires are *perfectly* satisfied, but only in
a transformed mode, namely, in appearance.

The prisoners are thus vulnerable to the puppeteers, those who manipulate the figurines that cast the shadows on the wall. But they lack even the resources to be dissatisfied with this state of affairs if it could be communicated to them, insofar as genuine dissatisfaction would require a view from the perspective of actuality. Without this perspective, the communication could be received only as yet another image to be subjectively consumed, as it were, yet another shadow to be passively observed. (It does not require the genius of a Swift to ridicule the market campaigns that promote challenging authority, breaking all conventions, and being oneself.) The feeling of impotence, wherever it happens inchoately to emerge, is quieted by the offer of more power, and there is nothing that cements the bonds more securely. We see that what Plato describes in his allegory of the cave fits surprisingly well the liberal conception of political order and the individual wills that constitute it.

Let us consider now in more detail the institutional and cultural forms that the offer of political power takes in the contemporary world. As we shall see, what is perhaps most diabolical of all is that we become our own most vigilant jailors,[75] since the imprisonment is subjectively experienced as the *most complete* liberation, offered in the place of the inevitable burden of the real. It is precisely its being a bargain that reveals its provenance from the devil.

CHAPTER 5

A "Society of Devils"

Kant famously suggested that a proper organization of political community ought not to depend on the virtue of its citizens, but it should be able to keep the peace even in the case of a "society of devils."[1] We observed in passing in chapter 4 that the form of liberalism, in spite of anyone's deliberate intentions, tends to make the "society of devils," not a test case, but a cultivated ideal. In other words, it imposes what we have described as a diabolical form on all of its elements and refashions those elements in that mold. The point of this chapter is to elaborate this observation in greater detail. More specifically, we mean to argue here that the various ideals, values, and institutions that we associate with freedom in the contemporary West, or that we identify as its conditions or essential expressions, are *diabolical* in the technical sense we have just set forth. That is to say that the things we protect and foster ostensibly in the name of freedom and its flourishing tend as a matter of intrinsic logic to undermine freedom, dissolving its substance.

If we were to ask an average twenty-first-century U.S. citizen to play "free association" with the word "freedom," he or she would no doubt at some point mention the following: on a personal level—choice, self-determination, and autonomy; on a political level—equality, freedom of the press, the power to vote, rights, and privacy; at the cultural level—power, technology, academic freedom, access to information, and the free market. We will discuss all of these in the following pages, after a preliminary reflection on the relationship between means and ends, since this relationship enters in a certain respect into all of the phenomena we will address. Finally, in order to show the all-encompassing character of this diabolical form in liberalism, we will close the chapter with a reflection on the presence of this logic in the most transcendent sphere and the most intimate one: God and the body.

The thesis we are proposing may be seen as analogous to the well-known argument presented by Horkheimer and Adorno in their 1947 book, *Dialectic of Enlightenment*,[2] namely, that when reason is systematically instrumentalized—that is, interpreted as concerned with means irrespective of ends—the "hyper-rationalism" that results can no longer be distinguished from wholesale irrationalism: According to the authors, the Enlightenment, meant to be a self-liberation from the darkness of mythology, inevitably reverts to a new mythology, which is even blinder than the previous one because it has already exhausted its alternative. By analogy, we are proposing, here, that a freedom that has been impoverished by a reduction to power, potency, and possibility turns out to be perfectly compatible with, and even to encourage, substantial forms of slavery. In this respect, we see the connection between the broader cultural reflection we offer in this chapter and the more formal exploration of Locke's revolutionary re-conception of freedom in chapter 1.

There are two caveats that need to be noted before we begin. The first is that our exploration will be forced to remain relatively superficial: any one of the features we will discuss deserves a much more thorough study in itself. If we investigate such a broad and apparently eclectic array of phenomena in the stretch of a single chapter, it is with the hope of thereby setting a form into view, which will illuminate a certain unity among these otherwise disparate realities. On this score, it is important to emphasize that we are studying a basic pattern running through the variety of phenomena; we are *not* investigating the phenomena for their own sake, each of which would receive more attention and detail if it were the subject of study by itself. As far as possible, we will draw on classic or well-known discussions, rather than attempt to break new ground. It is not our aim to account for every aspect of the admittedly very complex realities in their historical circumstances or to suggest that the aspect we highlight is the only one of significance. Instead, our claim will be that the aspect we describe is the one that tends to dominate in a liberal political order, but the very point of our discussion is to recognize that these phenomena could take a rather different form inside of a more properly human order.

Second, and even more importantly, it should be noted that, to describe the various values and institutions as diabolical is *precisely not* to argue for their simple elimination. Quite the contrary: to interpret the charge thus would be to fail altogether to understand the nature of the diabolical. As we will explain in more detail in part 3 of the book, the response to possession is not *execution* but *exorcism*, which is not a rejection but a reorientation, from the innermost depths, to the good.[3] To think otherwise would be to make the diabolical a positive reality in itself, which represents, we might say, a diabolical interpretation of the diabolical. It remains caught in the very trap it is attempting to dismantle.

Meaning the End and Ending the Means

At the heart of all human action (whether *praxis* or *poiēsis*) and, analogously, all human institutions, is a relation between means and ends. This is simply another way of saying that human action is teleological, undertaken for a purpose, whether that purpose is conscious or unconscious, external to the action or immanent within it. Although, in a "symbolical" cosmos, all activity of whatever sort is likewise teleological, what distinguishes specifically *human* action from subhuman activity is that, in human action, the agent is able to pursue ends in a self-conscious and deliberate manner and also that the means to the designated end are not given with an automatic necessity. Instead, they are selected from a number of possibilities, which implies that they can be varied, improved, and developed in an intentional way.[4] There is clearly a connection between these two features, which we merely indicate here without further analysis: the self-relation implied in self-consciousness is connected to the capacity to abstract an end from a particular means, and thus the capacity to envision *other* means to achieve it. There is, in other words, a connection between (self-)transcendence and freedom of choice. Whatever the details of this connection may be,[5] the point in the present context is that the nonnecessity of the relation between means and ends in human action makes that relation *an issue*, that is, something that needs to be decided and so *is* (freely) determined in a particular way in any given action. What we wish to do here is penetrate beyond the obvious sense of this claim—namely, that in every human action a particular means is chosen with respect to a given end—to a more fundamental implication: not only is a particular means chosen, but also the *mode* of the relation between means and ends in general is likewise codetermined to one degree or another with the choice made. In other words, each human action is a presentation of the meaning of human action simply—it both presupposes a sense of how means relate to ends in general and codetermines that sense through its free enactment of a particular instance.

What all of this means is that all human action is *revelatory*; it makes manifest a meaning that transcends the significance of the accomplishment of the particular end on which it is set. Human action inevitably reflects an order that transcends it. It is in this respect an embodiment of the good, a manifestation of the complex structure of goodness in its particular way. Recognizing the transcendence of the meaning of human action beyond itself allows us to see, in turn, what we might call the *organic* relationship between the action of individual human beings and the cultural institutions within which, or in relation to which, those individual actions unfold. Plato famously presented the city as the soul "writ large": what he meant is that the order of the community, its way of integrating the one and the many in the relationship between and among citizens and the world in a greater whole, reflects the order, the one-manyness, of the individual souls that constitute the community. The order of the community and the order of the individual souls that comprise it, in other words, are reciprocally cause and effect of each other; as Plato puts it, they share a "form."[6] Analogously, we may say that the order of particular human action reflects and amplifies the order of public institutions, or, even more directly, institutions represent a kind of objectification of the *form* of human action. In this case, the personal and the public illuminate each other. Such in any event is the presupposition of this chapter, which seeks to set into relief the particular form that comes to expression in contemporary liberal culture.

In chapter 4, we sketched in broad strokes the distinction between a symbolical ontology and the diabolical perversion of the same. In this chapter, we wish to argue that this distinction bears also on cultural form. More specifically, we propose that there is a *symbolical* sense of the relation between means and ends and a diabolical perversion of this relation, and that the diabolical form of the relationship has come to dominate in contemporary culture. What does it mean to speak of the relation between means and ends as *symbolical*? As we explained in chapter 4, συμ-βάλλω means a "joining together" that makes really present a meaning that transcends it. The *sym-bol* is not in the first sense a joining together with the transcendent good, but a joining together of realities *in* the good; the transcendent becomes present in the differentiation of the unity and a unification of the diverse. The friendship is both enacted and manifest, presupposed and generated, in the uniting of the *tesserae hospitales*. Participation is an essential dimension of the symbolical order.

With respect to the relationship between means and ends, we may say that, from a symbolical perspective, means ought to be seen as participating in the end and thus as possessing an intrinsic relationship to that end. The end is *other* than the means—indeed, it is radically other, of a different order—and this implies that there is a genuine distance between them: the end is in a certain respect *absent from* the means. But if the means is a real means, that is, if it is a medium, or mediator, that conveys in reality to the end, and indeed if this relationship to the end defines it, what is other is in some sense already *co-present in* the means. Its reference to the other, in other words, is not a mere superadditum, but it constitutes its very identity as a means. In a certain respect, we thus have to recognize that the end *precedes* the means insofar as the means *is* just that, namely, a means. Here we see why the symbolical order always implies the relative priority of actuality over potentiality:[7] potency comes before act only in a chronological sense, and, even there, only in a specific respect, namely, in individual instances *qua* individual; one must have the potential for something in order to realize that potential, which is to say that one must pass through a means to get to the end. But in every other respect, actuality comes before potency; the potency is a potency *for* an actuality, and this actuality defines that potency (while the reverse is not true). Indeed, whatever power potency has, to the extent that the power is at all real, is received from actuality (though this is not to deny that the potency *itself* is potent). In the symbolical order, actuality, we might say, "enables" potency, which is thus a potency *for* that actuality. Understood thus, the actuality is always-already present in a particular way *in* the potency, not of course *as* actuality, but in the mode of symbol. To put it another way, the actuality is not present only conceptually as that which may or may not be achieved by the potency, as that which the potency simply "ought" to achieve, but is rather transcendentally immanent, so to speak, as the inner form of that to which the potency is ordered.

With respect to the means/ends relation, we have to see that the means participate in the end ontologically, which means that the end is always-already present in the means as its inner (and transcendent) form. This way of interpreting the relationship *enriches* the means: understood symbolically as participation, it implies that the means already has something of an end character in its mediation, which is to say that it has a kind of intrinsic goodness, even though we may not forget that its intrinsic goodness is a participated goodness, so that this character belongs to it precisely in its pointing beyond itself. As we discussed in chapter 4, classical philosophy makes a distinction between intrinsic goods (*bonum honestum*) and instrumental goods (*bonum utile*). The modern mind is apt to interpret the latter as "mere" means, an otherwise indifferent instrument that allows one to achieve something other than itself. But to interpret it thus would be to deny that it is a good, to think that the means is a "neutral," which perhaps *ought* to help achieve a good, but that is it. Assuming that we may genuinely refer to a thing as a "*bonum*" *utile*, we must nevertheless recognize a certain paradox in this: "bonum" has the "ratio finis";[8] to call something a *bonum utile* is to say that it is a means that is an end. In other words, it implies that goodness is analogical, in the sense that its perfection can come to expression in a radically differentiated manner, and not *merely* univocally, in being a final terminus of relation or movement. If we are to avoid a simple contradiction in describing a means as a *bonum utile*, we would have to say that it is a good by virtue of its intrinsic participation in the end, which is thus made in a genuine sense part of it, without depriving it of its mediating character.[9] An implication of this symbolical interpretation of the means/end relation is that there is no opposition in principle between an affirmation of the means *in itself* and a movement *beyond* the means to the end. Quite the contrary, once we recognize the real participation of the means in the end, we see that a desire for the end (in the sense of a genuine ordination to the end) can liberate one to dwell, so to speak, *in* and *with* the means, even while such an indwelling is just what moves one beyond, conveys one to the end.[10] Moreover, if we see that there is a real, *intrinsic* relationship between the means and the end, we recognize that, not only is the end always-already present in the means, but also the means may *therefore remain present* in the end that comes to be achieved. In other words, attainment of the end does not necessarily render the means obsolete. It does not require leaving the means behind, using it *up* rather than just using it. The presence of the end liberates the "bonicity" of the *bonum utile*, so to speak. Its presence can mean that the means is now most fully enjoyed *as good* (without ceasing to be, of course, a mediation of what lies beyond it). If potency already includes act as the form to which it points, actuality in turn includes potency: it may be understood as the liberation of possibility.

It is just at this point that we can see what it would mean to interpret the relationship between means and ends *diabolically*. The heart of the matter is that means and ends are set apart (δια-βάλλω) from each other, so that they may "connect" only in an extrinsic fashion. In this case, the end is not already present in the means as the prior actuality in which the means participates as a potency thus ordered radically from within. The means therefore ceases to be an instrumental *good*, and becomes instead merely an instrument. But here we get a dialectical inversion: a mere means is no longer *in truth* a means at all, except accidentally, as a matter of appearance. If the means does not presuppose the prior actuality of the end it is meant to mediate, it is no longer defined by its relationship to that end, which is to say that its essence is not constituted *as specifically* a participation in the end. Precisely to the extent that the means does not point to an other *in* itself, it simply turns into an end by itself, that is, it becomes its own relatively independent reality. We saw a similar phenomenon in chapter 4 in the reflection on (Lockean) active potency, which has its own power to realize an effect in itself, without "drawing," so to speak, on a prior actuality outside of itself to bring it to act. The same thing happens here: the means becomes a kind of reified potency that is first pursued discretely for its own sake in abstraction from possible ends. What is particularly diabolical about this inversion is that it *hides* by an internal logic its having "usurped" the character of end precisely by claiming to be a *mere* instrument: the more "merely" it is an instrument, the less it makes genuinely present an actual end by virtue of its participatory character, and so the more it becomes a place where the human will that is engaged in it comes to a standstill. To will a genuine means, which of its very essence mediates an end beyond itself, is simultaneously to affirm a thing in itself and to transcend it in concord with its own intrinsic movement toward the actuality to which it points. But a mere instrument is opaque: to will such an instrument is to will *just that instrument*, and nothing more.

What then becomes of the "end," access to which the mere means makes ostensibly possible? Here again we find an inversion. Though actuality is prior to potency absolutely speaking, we mentioned that there is a respect in which actuality follows potency, namely, in the individual instance chronologically considered. Actuality in relation to this aspect of potency indicates a kind of arrival into reality (ἐν ἐργεία), which presupposes a prior not-yet-being-there; as perfection, it indicates the accomplishment of a potency (*per-fectio*, "being made completely") rather than a static state of affairs (which is of course redundant). In this case, we see that actuality exhibits a certain dependency on potency in order to be actual in the fullest sense, even if this dependence remains relatively hidden.[11] While one can understand an actuality absolutely in itself without reference to the potency it realizes (to define "skiing" does not require reference to the ability to ski, whereas one cannot define the ability to ski without reference to skiing), one cannot understand it in its mode of being actual—that is, the *actuality* of its actuality—without seeing it as completing a potency. Similarly, an end can be affirmed as an end only as the proper termination of a "movement" that, as a movement, in some analogous sense passes through a *means*. Given such a reciprocal dependence, if the means does not point to the end in its very essence as its own intrinsic meaning, it necessarily transforms in turn the meaning of the end. The end ceases to be the realization of the means, which means that it ceases to be an end in an essential sense.

Let us put this more concretely. To the extent that the means is a *mere* instrument, it is ontologically indifferent to any end, which means it can be "applied" to any number of possibilities. It is accidental to the means what end it happens to convey or enable. Because it does not actually presuppose an end as prior to itself, in which it participates, the human will that is engaged with this means, as we explained, stops at its borders, and this implies that a new act of will is required to make the connection with the "end." In this case, however, the end is not willed as the natural fruit, the genuine fulfillment, of the means, but it becomes instead a discrete object that is willed *subsequent* to the willing of the "means." As we will explain in the next section, to *choose* something is to select it in light of an end, and therefore to make it a means. If we thus choose an end in a discrete act of will, it can be only as a means in relation to a more basic end. What is the more basic end in this case? Because the willing of the end is subsequent to the willing of the means, the means becomes the reason for which the end is chosen. In other words, the end becomes a relatively indifferent means that is subordinated to the more immediate end of exercising the means. The "end" becomes a function of the power of the means and is determined by the terms that the means set. The means therefore becomes *in fact* the governing end, the reference point in relation to which the end makes sense, which means that the end has become a mere instrument, a relatively arbitrary object, of the means. The inversion is complete.

We said at the outset that a relationship between means and ends lies at the core of human action and institutions. An extrinsicist understanding of that relationship, whereby means and ends lie simply outside of one another, is a *disordered* relationship. We have just described, in fairly abstract terms, the dialectical inversion the relationship undergoes when means and ends are separated from each other. The proposal is that, because liberal society was essentially founded on the separation, on the idea that liberation can be achieved by isolating means and rationalizing them, while leaving the end to be determined in each case *ad libitum*,[12] the inversion we presented will tend to show up in analogous ways throughout our contemporary anthropological phenomena and cultural and political institutions. We now turn to look at these features in some detail.

Varieties of the Diabolical

Choice

When one speaks of freedom in the contemporary situation, what is most commonly meant is the power to choose: I say that I have done something freely when it was my *choice* to do it, meaning that there was nothing forcing me to do it and that I could have done otherwise if I had chosen differently. The effort to explain why I did what I did arrives at my act of choice, and there is no need to go further. The decision was ultimately mine, a function of my own will. Now, there is of course an undeniable truth to this interpretation, even if the matter grows quickly complicated the moment we push beyond the surface and begin to ask after the source of the options with which I was presented or, even more deeply, the source of the criteria according to which I deliberated, and ultimately the source of the particular desire that led me to make the choice that I did. The fact that such an inquiry will inevitably and without any exception lead me to some factors outside of my will's deliberate activity and so beyond my control is why there will always be a plausible compatibilist interpretation of free choice, such as we discussed in chapter 1. But our focus here is simply on the *meaning* of choice and the relation it bears to freedom.

In classical philosophy, choice is understood as the selection of means in relation to an end that is *given* rather than *chosen*. In the contemporary context, this understanding is taken to mean that I am free with respect to the means I adopt, but that I am not free with respect to the end, precisely because the end is something *imposed* on me, concerning which I have "no say," as it were.[13] A modern mind that is friendly to the classical tradition might go on to say that it is all well and good that ultimate ends are imposed on me, because freedom needs to be seen as a relative good, rather than an absolute one; freedom is right and proper if it is subordinated to higher goods, such as truth, respect for the law, for the well-being of others, and so forth. A modern mind not so friendly might respond that such a view is ominous, liable to abuse, and threatening to the human dignity that lies in autonomy. But the argument we are making here is that both sides of this particular debate in the terms it is usually set share an essentially diabolical conception of freedom. The reason is that both conceive freedom as *defined essentially* by choice and so measure the freedom of any particular act by the degree of unobstructed choice involved.

This charge requires of course an elaboration of the nature of choice. To interpret the classical view as admitting freedom with respect to certain things—means—but not with respect to other things—ends—is to confuse orders, and subsequently to reduce the act of will to what we could call a univocal, a nonanalogical, form. For Thomas Aquinas, for example, the act of will is not, so to speak, a unidirectional ray of psychic energy that passes from a subject to an object, but it is always, in every single instance, complex and multidimensional, both on the side of the subject and on the side of the object: the will, he explains, is always moved simultaneously by sensible appetite, the intellect, the will itself, the object, goodness, and ultimately God.[14] Each of these works in consort, contributing to the *single* motion of the will to its object (not in the sense of pieces coming together to form a whole, but irreducibly distinct causes of a single actuality greater than the sum of its parts), with God of course acting as the cause of all these causes.[15] We hope to enter into the details of Aquinas's account at much greater length in a future study, but in the present context we wish to point out that, for him, the will that is directed (without its choosing) to an end and the will that chooses the means are not two separate powers, which would be brought into operation through two separate spiritual acts. Instead, they represent two irreducibly distinct dimensions of a single power—the willing of the end and the choice of the means occur as a single act of will.[16]

We wish to propose that this distinctness in unity is due not to the structure of the human soul, first of all, but rather to the complex nature of reality itself. To put the point in the language we have been developing in this book, it is due to the essentially symbolical character of being. Goodness, which forms the necessary end of every act of will, is transcendent of its very nature, however immanently present it may be in every given instance. There is always a "for the sake of which" in every particular thing chosen, but the *telos* is (at least formally, if not also materially) *distinct* from that thing. In chapter 4, we discussed Ricoeur's observation that a symbol represents a double intentionality, a reference simultaneously to the thing itself and to the meaning signified. In the present context, we may interpret this double intentionality in the order of the will as the profound interrelationship of means and ends. When I choose something, I am setting my will on it, but always at the very same time in relation to a further telos, which the means is thus taken to mediate. This structure, which in its simplest form is twofold, is an inevitable feature of every act of will, precisely insofar as it is an act of choice. In this respect, it simply does not make any sense to say that I choose a means, but for some reason—whether it is a good reason, as conservatives tend to say, or a bad reason, as liberals tend to say—I can't choose the end. In fact, I *can* in a separate act of will choose a different end (as long as it is not the *last* end)—but in this case, that "end" is now a means chosen in relation to a more fundamental end. To choose freely is to select the means conducive to a given end.

Once we put the matter in these terms, we see that, to make a judgment concerning the freedom of a choice, we will inevitably have to go beyond merely formal criteria. We cannot finally evaluate the act of choosing in abstraction from its "why." If choice is always made with respect to an end, we need to consider the actual nature and meaning of the end in our assessment of the choice. This very fact illuminates one of the constant themes of this book, namely, the relative priority of actuality over potentiality, and it is worth dwelling on its significance for a moment. If one identifies freedom with the mere power to choose, one tends to remain within a formal framework. We often find, in contemporary discussions of freedom, a fairly arbitrary choice of examples, or a privileging of the counterfactual, sometimes to the point of absurdity (zombies, often manipulated by remote control, have become a regular feature of such discussions). Formal abstraction is typical: the assumption is that one can say everything one means by saying, "S is free at t with respect to p iff it is up to S at t whether p or not-p,"[17] and so forth. The reason is that it is only the form of the act that is at stake in this sort of analysis, a form that is meant to be empty precisely in order to be universal. But to raise the issue of ends insofar as they are ends, and not simply as *possible motives of action*, is to raise the question of *goods*, and therefore of the good simply. What "end" means *in fact* is "*good*."[18] Goodness is actuality. It is therefore not a mere cosmological accident that choices are made with respect to ends that are *given* prior to choice, because actuality is essentially prior to potency. The potency, or power, to choose is responsive to the good that is *already present in a decisive respect*. From this perspective, one's investigation of the freedom of choices, if it is to be genuinely explanatory, always has to take its bearings from reality, to start from the actuality of the world *as it is given*.[19] To speak instead of choice in itself as if it represented, alone, the essential dimension of freedom is to abstract from reality, and so to lose an intrinsic connection to the good. Here we have an instance of the separation of the means from the end, which ends up reifying, and so absolutizing, the means and therefore relativizing the endness of the ends.

Although he approaches the matter in different terms, this is essentially the point Plato is making in Socrates's famous sparring with Polus in the *Gorgias*. In this argument, Socrates is discussing the nature of power, which we will address more directly at the end of this section, but what he says applies immediately to the issue of choice as we have framed it here. The basic point of his argument turns on the distinction he draws between the things we do—which, as particular actions, may be beneficial or harmful depending on their context, and which he refers to as "intermediaries" (τὰ μεταξὺ)—and that for the sake of which (οὗ ἕνεκα) we do them, insisting that the will that is directed to the intermediaries is *most fundamentally* directed to an end in them.[20] He puts the matter plainly: "So the reason we walk when we walk is that we are pursuing the good, believing it better to walk, or on the contrary we stand still, whenever we do so, for the sake of the same thing, namely, the good."[21] Note, by calling the end sought simply the *good*, Plato retains a certain universality in his formulation, even though this universality is not a merely formal sort in the abstract and empty sense. Instead, it is the universality of an actual quality, one that is opposed to another quality, namely, the bad (or evil), and so one that will necessarily exclude an endless range of possibilities. In this respect, the good, even in its transcendence represents a *limit*, but of a particular sort: it is, we might say, *concretely* universal; it will include anything at all, as long as it is good. It is open and indeterminate in this sense, not because it is vague or formless, but because it transcends the determinateness of particular goods in their particularity. But this is why it can be, and in fact will *necessarily* be, present as ultimate end *in* every particular good chosen. It is because of the simultaneous unity and distinctness of means and end—because the end transcends the means but is at the same time "co-intended" in the very act of intending the means—that it is possible to will to do something that one nevertheless does not really want. Interestingly, Socrates does not infer from this implication that one therefore needs to will good ends, but rather that one needs to do what one sees fit *with intelligence*;[22] in other words, one needs to make choices in light of an understanding of what is, as he always puts it, "really real." The good is not what *ought* to be chosen as an end (in preference to other possibilities), but it is always-already actual in some respect as the end pursued, insofar as actuality precedes potency (even the choice of evil is evil by measurement against the good most basically and invariably sought). It follows that, to reduce the good immediately to an object of choice, even if one means to affirm the good as what one most ultimately wants, is to eliminate its end character, which is just another way of saying that, paradoxically, by directly *choosing* the good, one ceases to recognize it *as* good.

At this point, it is easy to imagine an objection to the insistence that one cannot properly understand choice except in relation to the end sought in it. The objection would run as follows. The purpose of focusing on the power of choice itself, "bracketing out" a reference to the good, is precisely to avoid excluding any possibility a priori. Choice in itself is "neutral," and we can promote its conditions of possibility as a discrete task, before the broader consideration of purpose. That consideration is essential, but it is a separate concern. The power to choose can, and indeed *ought*, to be used for the good, which means only that we need to accompany a cultivation and preservation of this power with an education about how properly to use one's freedom, along with institutionally supported incentives to encourage proper use. In any event, the objection continues, the power to choose remains a crucial piece of the puzzle of freedom no matter what else one wants to say about it, and so we may as well start with this while we work on the rest. One is perfectly right to criticize the *use* of choice in particular cases, but no one can object to simply having the *ability* to choose. And so on.

From the perspective of the understanding of choice we have just presented, the problem with this objection becomes immediately obvious: to think that we *first* have the power to choose, and *then* "apply" this power to the achievement of one end or another, as if the means were simply extrinsic to and so separable from the end, is already to have a diabolical conception of freedom. There is a profound deception in the notion that the power to choose is open to anything, and so in principle at least more available for proper use the more it presents itself as *mere* power, which is as yet undetermined. To think of choice as a *mere* power, a mere potency, is to think of it as isolated from actuality, which is to say from goodness as such (even if the intention is subsequently to overcome the separation in the *exercise* of choice). A *mere* power to choose that has been so isolated is *impotent to choose a good qua good.* Whatever good it chooses *qua* isolated power ceases in the very choosing to be good in the metaphysical sense (even if it remains something one wants). We might recall here the alchemical image we used in chapter 4: to have the *mere* power to choose is to have, as it were, the "Midas touch": the good things Midas *really* wants—a bite of meat, a sip of wine, the embrace of his son—turn willy-nilly into infinitely more "valuable," but utterly "good-less," gold.

But let us set aside the image. What do goods become when they are made the object of the mere power to choose? They become *options*. Options in other words are the diabolical substitute for goods. The notion of option is especially fitting insofar as it sets into relief, and indeed *fixes*, the dimension of possibility, that is, nonactuality. That to which I am already committed or otherwise *actually* bound, even though it may remain good, is no longer an option. From inside a diabolical conception of reality, this means that my relationship to the thing is no longer in itself a matter of freedom. At best, I remain free only with respect to the further options I have regarding the use I may make of it. Now, from this same perspective, if I say that my commitment itself remains free, what I mean is that it is something I choose in every moment, which is to say that it is not in itself *actual* but is always an option that I continue to take. But this of course is a commitment only in appearance; I may carry out all of the activities associated with or entailed by the commitment, but I am not *in reality* committed. I do not dwell *inside of* a bond, which in its actuality would present a reality that embraces me, along with my will and its power to choose. An option is something I always stand *outside of.* Thus, to live in the world *by means of* a freedom understood as mere power to choose is to be *of* the world, perhaps, but never *in* the world. Because it implies an absence of *intrinsic* relation to actuality or reality, to be free in this sense is to be a slave to appearances.

From this perspective, the effort to be free is the effort to "keep one's options open." Options are kept open by preventing any particular possibility from being actual in any definitive way. If a possibility becomes actual in some sense, we can keep it from becoming a *real good* and preserve its "free" character as an option by prying it open and inserting alongside it other alternatives that remain possibilities.[23] *Its* actuality is necessarily "infected" by their possibility. Keeping options open means granting actuality to possibilities precisely and abidingly *as* possibilities. It is not an accident that this statement echoes in an uncanny way Aristotle's definition of motion: the actuality of potency precisely *qua* potency;[24] there is a constant movement here that is repelled by the actuality of rest but that *imitates* the actuality it excludes precisely through *the constancy of activity*. In any event, we see that there is a logical tendency toward multiplicity in the specifically negative sense of a breaking away from unity. We speak of keeping *options* open rather than "keeping option open." To actualize a possibility precisely *as* a possibility, rather than simply an actuality, requires a "co-positing" of *other* possibilities along with it. Freedom, as mere power to choose, becomes real in an objective sense through the multiplication of options. The quantity is more important than the quality, if we are speaking of the quality of a single good.

But it is just here that the self-subverting character of this power becomes once again evident: the psychologist Barry Schwartz has observed that the multiplication of options surprisingly often impairs one's capacity to choose.[25] One might wish to explain this phenomenon in reductively psychological terms by saying that having too many options can be overwhelming and create a certain confusion regarding the proper criteria to make one's choice and so on, but we ought to see that, however true this point may be in principle, more fundamentally this confusion has an objective cause: the multiplying of options, insofar as this is interpreted as the essence of freedom, necessarily eliminates any criterion as an *actual* good preceding and informing the power to choose, and it thus renders any given criterion itself an option, set alongside other possibilities. This is not *first* a subjective confusion, but the subjective experience of confusion is itself an expression of a radical, objective disorder. The mere power to choose is not diabolical (only) because it tends to eclipse other goods but in an even more basic sense because it undermines itself. A mere power to choose is not in fact a power to choose at all, if we take the meaning of those terms—"power" and "choice"—in the proper sense. It is instead the fraudulent image of such a power.

Self-determination

More briefly, we may contrast two interpretations of self-determination. The concept presents a fundamentally different sense depending on whether primacy is given to actuality or to potency. If actuality is recognized as primary, then self-determination means the power to conform oneself to a given good, which is to say to internalize the form of a good as part of one's own form. One can imagine different degrees of capacity in this regard, depending on the depth of one's docility, one's desire and openness to receive, and the disposal one has over oneself. Self-determination, in this sense, is a kind of ontological transformation, and it has an essentially receptive modality. A free choice, in this sense of self-determination, is a reception of form. As Karol Wojtyła emphasized in his early philosophical work, one inevitably becomes different through one's choosing and acting; the action of the will not only changes something "out in the world" but necessarily also changes the agent himself.[26] To make certain kinds of choices is to become a certain kind of person. From this perspective, the more one commits oneself in an act, the more one determines oneself, and so the *freer* the act is. The vow by which one all at once and definitively determines oneself becomes, from the perspective of this interpretation, a paradigm of freedom.[27] We see here the way in which self-determination, thus conceived, is *essentially* symbolical, that is, a joining of the self to what is other. We also see why the question of the power of self-determination cannot be answered in abstraction from the actuality of the content of the choice under consideration. The random waving of my arm, though it is altogether arbitrary and unpredictable in its motion (even by me!), is far less free, for example, than the pronouncing of the marriage vow, since there is very little determination of the self, that is, reception of a form that is other than myself, in this trivial gesticulation.

Finally, we see that, with respect to the object of the will in its choosing, there is an almost *inverse* relationship between power in the sense of control and actual self-determination. A thing is *in my control* precisely to the extent that it is subordinate to me, that is, to the extent that it does not present to me an actual form *to which* I must rise in conformity. I am therefore *not* changed by a thing in my control to the precise extent that it lies *within* my control. The more control, the less self-determination; the more control, the less freedom. This does not at all imply an identification of freedom with the *lack* of control. Obviously, one cannot determine oneself if one has no disposal over oneself—self-mastery, self-possession, and so forth. "Control" of this sort is an indispensable dimension of self-determination. The point is that, for this particular kind of power to be genuinely self-determining, it must occur, as it were, *inside* of the receptive relation to a form that lies beyond that power. The more comprehensively the form chosen *lays claim* to the self, the more complete is the self-determination in response. In *this* respect, the degree of self-determination and therefore freedom corresponds to the degree of transcendence beyond the control of power.

The diabolical "version" of self-determination becomes apparent along just these lines. Instead of beginning with the actual order, in which the power to determine oneself takes its bearings from the good, the prior form to which it rises, one begins with the means taken in isolation. In this case, the abstract *power* becomes the essential feature; self-determination reduces to the capacity, or at least the *right*, to determine oneself in whatever way one happens to choose. From this perspective, self-determination is entirely a matter of control. For just this reason, it is defined specifically in opposition to being determined by another; if it is one, it is *not* the other. We can easily see how this is diabolical in the etymological sense of the term we explored in chapter 4; the power of self-determination in this case *separates* the self from everything else, all that is *not* the self. Though it may be possible, just as with choice, to emphasize the neutrality and so indeterminateness of this power in a way that would seem to enable all sorts of relations to others as long as the power is used appropriately (i.e., my exclusive self-determination is used to place myself in relation to various people and things), in fact the very *essence* of this power is self-separation, an exclusion of the other. To have this power at all, no matter how apparently positively it is able to be exercised, is to be so far cut off from an *internal* relation to what is other. But we need to see that the alternative—*either* self-determination *or* determination by the other—is a deceptive illusion. As we saw with the reflection above, one can *be determined at all* only through the acquisition of some new form, which necessarily entails a subordination, in some respect, to what is other. Self-determination and determination by an other, if this means a genuine transformation of the self, a becoming different—and what else could determination mean?—can *only* occur simultaneously. If self-determination is isolated as a power in itself, a form of control rooted in an exclusive way in the self, not only is it fundamentally opposed to the reception of an *other* form, it is fundamentally opposed to self-determination. The power to determine oneself is thereby rendered impotent to effect any actual change. Absolutized, self-determination becomes a self-subverting illusion.

Autonomy

The principle of autonomy is in truth a variation of the power of self-determination, such as we just described it. According to its etymology, "autonomy" means "self-governance." This may be interpreted as the *appropriation* or internalization (an οἰκείωσις), of a given *nomos*, a norm, law, or custom. In this case, if we acknowledge the traditional teaching according to which all law has its roots in the natural law,[28] and ultimately in the eternal law, then autonomy coincides with taking one's proper place in the order of things, which is to say autonomy is essentially symbolical. One might say that autonomy is *necessary* for there to be a proper order of things, insofar as this order depends on intrinsic participation and therefore on the active assumption, analogously, in each part of the meaning of the whole. No one part can appropriate that meaning simply in the place of the other.[29] It also follows that, the truer this participation in the whole, the more perfectly each becomes a unique and self-standing part. Here is the key: a symbolical cosmos, and thus social order, requires *profound* autonomy; that each part *so* appropriate the meaning of the whole that that meaning arises, so to speak, from the part's own inner being. The law, then, becomes an internal, ontological principle of the self (*auto-nomos*) rather than a limit imposed merely from the outside. Moses characterizes the—premodern—law thus:

> For this command that I enjoin on you today is not too mysterious and too remote for you. It is not up in the sky, that you should say, "Who will go up in the sky to get it for us and tell us of it, that we may carry it out?" Nor is it across the sea, that you should say, "Who will cross the sea to get it for us and tell us of it, that we may carry it out." No, it is something very near to you, already in your mouths and in your hearts; you have only to carry it out. (Deut. 30:11–14)

Autonomy in the premodern sense of ap-propriating (etymologically, "taking a thing into oneself and making it one's own") a law is therefore not a rote conformity to an external order, but an internal ordering, which takes what is given and symbolically re-presents it, reenacts it, in a way that inevitably exhibits an irreducible novelty in each case. Autonomy is in this respect inseparable from analogy, which is why genuine law will always have both a "letter" and a "spirit" dimension, and will coincide with space for prudence. True autonomy is thus *always* a "relative autonomy," that is, an independence that is both fruit of and condition for a proper dependence on everything else—and it is more fundamentally fruit than condition. There is no opposition in principle in this sense between independence and dependence, between self-relation and relation to others.[30]

Autonomy is diabolical, by contrast, the moment it is absolutized, that is, the moment it ceases to be *relative* to an encompassing order from the ground up.[31] It is important to see how an absolutizing of autonomy coincides with an inversion of the relationship between act and potency. In the "symbolical" version, autonomy *presupposes* a given order, a determinate actuality, which it takes *analogously into* itself; there is no autonomy without there being first a *nomos*, and this by nature must be a priori, and so actual. If we ab-solutize autonomy (that is, sever it from any relation), which means we deny that there is a prior *nomos* to which it is relative, then self-governance comes to mean the *power* to give oneself a rule, whatever one might determine that rule to be. The inversion of means and end that we spoke of at the outset comes into play here. As we saw above, autonomy in the sense we are describing is the power that one has *over* oneself, but because it is by its nature devoid of determinate content, this power receives its defining contours, not from any *actual reality*, but instead precisely from one thing alone, namely, its *exclusion* of the *power of an other*. This exclusion becomes its formal meaning. The very essence of autonomy, in other words, is the rejection of heteronomy, neither *nomos* of which has any given essential intelligible content, but both of which instead are reduced to a form of indeterminate active power, distinguished only by the point of origin. We recall that Locke can tolerate subordination to *anything but* the "arbitrary will" of another. Thus, autonomy, interpreted as a power, is *essentially* diabolical: it has no other meaning than the keeping at bay (δια-βάλλω) of what is other.

But the trumping of actuality by potency means, further, that there can never be in truth a *nomos*, to which the self conforms or corresponds; from the diabolical perspective, the moment the self *actually* subordinates itself to a law, even if it is one it has given to itself, it ceases to be autonomous, because the law cannot in this context be an internal ontological principle, but only an external regulation. To the extent that the law is established, however it is established, it *actually* sets limits to power and therefore to one's capacity to determine oneself. The self can retain autonomy, in this sense, only if it retains power over even the law it gives itself, which means that this is a law in no real sense at all. Autonomy is self-governance only in the sense of constantly subjecting the self to its own arbitrary power. This is not autonomy, but rather a kind of *auto-krasis* ("exercise of power over oneself"), or perhaps even more appropriately, *auto-tyranny*.

But diabolical autonomy subverts itself in an even more fundamental way. Because autonomy defines itself as the repulsion of heteronomy, it actually presupposes a larger order of which it remains a part. The inversion of the act–potency relationship is essentially diabolical because it cannot ever *be true*; it is inevitably a falsifying hermeneutic, a distortion of reality, a perversion of what cannot help but remain ultimately valid. In the present case, we see that autonomy is the assertion of the self's own power *against* the reality in which the self, "will-he nill-he," already exists. As mere force, this self-assertion, however, cannot acquire any substantial reality because it volatilizes in every moment. It can become real only through the recognition of another. But because the other's recognition itself, if it is conceived only as an expression of force—in this case a *yielding* to one's self-assertion—will also volatilize at every moment, the recognition will have real substance only if it is made official and enforceable. In other words, it can be "real" only if it acquires the institutional force of regulation: a pure phenomenon of intersubjectivity can become "objective" only through legal support. The diabolical irony ought to be clear: autonomy as the rejection of heteronomy, as the self's power over itself, requires subjection to law if it is to avoid collapsing into impotence. Moreover, law in this context becomes coercive of its very essence because, as we pointed out above, it ceases to have its roots in an ontological principle of order that can be internally appropriated, and instead can be only an actual rule in relation to which the self surrenders its autonomy. If autonomy is not an organic relation to the order of the whole, an internal participation in a prior actuality and so a genuine joining together (συμ-βάλλω) with all other things in relation to a transcendent principle, then it becomes a dialectical subjection to the extrinsic regulation of behavior, a need for the imposition of law—which is now exclusively *positive*, that is, an essentially arbitrary super-position "from above," from the arbitrary "powers that be"—on anything that it would want to claim for its own power. Absolute autonomy and limitless subjection to the coercive force of law imply one another.

Rights

One of the most basic ways that autonomy is regulated in the modern political order is through the granting of rights. In our previous chapters, we have already discussed the basic reason that rights, conceived in a modern, Lockean fashion, are essentially diabolical: they represent the demarcation of political space, the *division* (δια-βάλλω) of power, which is by the necessity of its own logic competitive. The overlapping of spheres of rights entails a conflict in principle, though this does not mean that the conflict cannot be resolved, as we saw, through compromises and cooperation. Cooperation, however, is not at all contrary to diabolical opposition, since it can occur between merely extrinsically related agents, and indeed this is the normal sense of the term. In the present context, we wish to extend the discussion a bit further by reflecting for a moment on the issue in relation to the question of potency and act. To do so requires reference to the controversial question of the origin of the modern notion of rights, though we can only touch on one aspect of what is admittedly a dense and thorny issue.

Rejecting a common view that the "invention" of natural rights in the modern era represents a decisive departure from the classical tradition,[32] Brian Tierney has argued that modern rights have medieval roots, from which they can be shown to grow organically.[33] Tierney, however, neglects the significance of the novel metaphysics—late medieval nominalism—in which what he recognizes as the distinctively modern formulation of the notion of rights occurs.[34] He therefore fails to attend to the inversion of potency and act, which, as we have seen in the previous pages, is liable to give the same word a radically different meaning. Thus, though it is true that medieval legal texts speak of rights, and indeed interpret such rights as *subjective powers*, we need to see that subjective powers have a distinctive meaning when they are viewed from the perspective of a classical metaphysics. From this perspective, subjective powers always have their sense as a function of some more basic actuality. In other words, rights in the premodern context are *determinate* powers, claims made by virtue of a given nature, or a given office (which is itself understood as service of an order given by nature). Just as a nature possesses capacities entailed by that nature, capacities that have a determinate shape and teleological order, so too does human nature possess rights in the political order that are entailed by that nature, and are likewise teleological. We might consider rights to be the social extension of natural powers,[35] the translation of natural powers into the sphere of organized community with others. To the extent that the natural power is extended into the political order, it enters into the sphere of free human interaction, and this entails recognition, the provision of protections, and a variety of forms of support, all of which require some sanction in positive law. Note that the formulation we are proposing—rights as the social extension of natural powers—is different from the early modern language of "natural rights," insofar as it recognizes that rights are essentially social and political entities. Our formulation acknowledges that rights have their proper place in the objective sphere in which the common good is determinative as the given context in which particular goods subsist. On the other hand, this recognition coincides with an acknowledgment that rights are *rooted* in nature, just as political order is more generally— and, indeed, this rootedness takes the form of a relativizing of rights, as powers, to the actuality that makes them intelligible. We may set this point into relief by contrasting it with the distinctively modern notion: the pioneer of modern natural rights, William of Ockham, asserted natural rights *over against* the positive political order.[36]

Now, a "symbolical" interpretation of rights sees them as the means by which persons fulfill their nature and the social obligations entailed by that nature or, to put the same point conversely, by which they fulfill their social obligations and thereby fulfill their nature. The subjective claim, which a right represents, thus coincides with an objective responsibility to the common good of the whole. In the symbolical order, as we have seen, nature is inherently social, and the social order is the flourishing of human nature.[37] What all of this means is that, from the symbolical perspective, rights are precisely the indispensable means by which persons join profoundly with others—the world and other people—and so come to teleological perfection. It is for just this reason that rights are to be protected and defended.

Diabolically conceived, rights are defined as protections *against* the intrusive, or obstructive, actions of others. There is an extraordinary convergence of confusions built into the modern conception. First of all, if a right is interpreted most fundamentally as a protection against the intrusive action of others, it always comes too late: there is no such thing as a self that is not always-already radically related to others, from conception, through the existence and development of the child, on until the very end. Relations that come to be as the pure result of choice, of the purely spontaneous action of the self, if they exist at all, are only a rare and relatively insignificant subset of relations. It is not possible to determine where the self ends and where relation to others begins, and indeed attempting to draw such a line on these terms betrays a misunderstanding of reality. If rights are understood, as in the premodern era, as the social extension of natural powers, there is no need to fix a dividing line between self and other; moreover, rights have thereby a determined content and meaning, from the beginning. But if rights are interpreted in an essentially *negative* way (negative, that is, with respect to the other, whether we are talking about "innate" rights or what are called positive rights as claims to some object), the dividing line has to be *invented*, and indeed in a basically arbitrary way. In other words, the division between the self and the other can be nothing more than a legal fiction.[38] Right here, however, we see another incoherence. The modern thinkers insisted on the natural character of these powers and protections: hence the emphatic language of "natural rights" and the "rights of man." But this insistence was self-consciously opposed to the idea that rights are essentially social realities, established in positive law, as they were in the premodern era. This insistence implies that rights belong to individuals *prior* to any relation to others. As we just observed, however, there is no *actual* prior moment, because there is no "prerelational" self, and never has been. As became clear in modern political thought, which eventually came to recognize that the "state of nature" was a theoretical hypothesis rather than a historical fact, there is no natural place wherein the self is isolated from everything that is "other," though this is just what the notion of natural rights requires. Purely natural rights are therefore quite evidently social constructs.

Is this a construction *by* society or a construction *of* society? As in all things diabolical, the movement goes in both directions at the same time (δια-βάλλω). As a protection *against* others, a right has reality, as we have seen, only to the extent that it is recognized by others. But if there is no actual reality to give rights real determination, that recognition is arbitrary—that is, it becomes a matter of social decree. It is thus logical that there would be a multiplication of rights according to the ideological evolution of society, that we would regularly discover the paradox of *new* "innate" rights that never would have made sense to earlier ages. At the same time, and for basically the same reason, the things *to* which rights grant claims of one sort or another are necessarily recast, so to speak, in the image of the agent who is himself essentially a bearer of rights, that is, of relatively indeterminate power. The best example of this is what has become in the course of just a few short years the "burning" legal issue of our time, namely, the granting of the legal status of marriage to same-sex relationships. According to the premodern, *symbolical* conception, the right to marriage is the social extension of a natural power, and that *to* which the right grants privilege and protection is itself a natural reality: the one-flesh union of man and woman, a union that is in principle procreative. Much of the debate—to the extent that there has been any at all of any substance—has turned on the procreative dimension, which is part of the traditional understanding but absent in principle from same-sex coupling, even if this absence might be compensated for through some artificial means. But in reality the one-flesh dimension is at least as fundamental as the procreative dimension, if not more: traditionally, a person is able to contract marriage if he is knowingly infertile, but he cannot contract marriage if he is unable to consummate the union. The right, as we can see, is a social extension of a natural power; if there is no natural power, it simply makes no sense at all to speak of a right. If it *is* based on a natural power, that power is by its essence ordered to a natural fulfillment, which has definite features. To grant same-sex couples the right to marry is to change the meaning of marriage, and indeed the meaning of rights simply, in a radical way: marriage is no longer a one-flesh union, since such a union is possible only in the case of sexual complementarity. But if the meaning of marriage is wholly uprooted from any actual, naturally given reality, the constraints that allow definition disappear. There is no reason in principle why marriage in this transformed sense would require any physical contact at all, why it cannot be contracted by siblings, groups, religious orders, corporations, and so forth. The point in all of this is that, from a diabolical perspective, rights can be understood only as sheer indeterminate power: both because they have sense only in relation to the opposition of forces (rights as protections), and in the sense that they cannot be *real* insofar as all actualities are selves in relation, natures in society, from beginning to end. As pure powers, their reality is arbitrary, which means that no person or reality, as it were, has any protection against the sheer fiat of any given social order. All institutions, and indeed all selves, in this case, are subject in principle to redefinition according to prevailing interests, and "rights," as abstract powers, lack any actual substance that might provide resistance to the incursion of others or of the arbitrary, and so coercive, force of positive law. In short, rights as natural self-protections collapse into their opposite, purely positive social fictions that automatically trump all naturally given realities on which any protections could be based. Such a collapse once again follows from the nature of the diabolical.

Privacy

We single out the "right to privacy," here, since it has come to be so closely associated with freedom as to be in some contexts effectively identical with it. Benjamin Constant defined the modern view of liberty, which he took to represent a radical departure from the ancient view, as "the enjoyment in security of private pleasures."[39] The right to privacy represents a curious paradox: on the one hand, it is one of the "newly discovered" innate rights, which would not have been recognized when natural rights were first being championed, while on the other hand it arguably captures the very essence of the modern conception of rights as an enclosed space protecting arbitrary power. What explains this paradox is no doubt the metaphysical dictum that what is *in reality* first comes to *appearance* last. However this may be, it is worth reflecting for a moment on the nature of the modern notion of privacy insofar as it brings the diabolical to fairly direct expression. The word "privacy," it should first be noted, designates something essentially *negative*: the Latin "*privatus*," meaning "set apart," "belonging to one-self rather than to the state," is the past participle of *privare*, "to separate" or "to deprive." In contrast to the word "intimate," or perhaps "personal," which may point to more or less similar matters or concerns, the word "private" designates these concerns precisely as set *off* from, or *opposed* to, something else, namely, other subjects and finally *the public*.[40] But in the typical modern sense this opposition is not in the first place the recognition of an actual reality, that is, something already given (namely, the reality of public life, the *res publica*), which possesses its own meaning prior to the act of recognition. As we have just argued, a recognition of this sort is fundamentally at odds with the modern concept of rights, insofar as that which lies within the scope of a right, so conceived, is at the disposal of precisely *arbitrary* power, which means it does not in the first place have an actual reality that would *determine* that power, but instead it is subject to determination *by* that power. We will come back to this in just a moment. The point that we wish to make here is that the establishment of a "right to privacy" *creates* a new kind of reality; it necessarily transforms both the nature of the intimate and personal sphere that is designated to lie within its sphere and at the very same time the nature of the "public" realm that lies outside of that sphere.

There are several "levels" to this transformation. First of all, the separation of the two spheres means that each is now precisely *outside* of the other: that which happens "inside" the walls of my private personhood for that very reason is "none of the state's business"; it has no public, no common, no universal significance. Correlatively, the public as such, to the extent that it concerns the sorts of matters that have been marked off as "private," have no claim on me. To take a simple example, what John Rawls calls a "comprehensive doctrine of the good" is taken to be a paradigmatically "private" matter, which means that it belongs to individuals precisely *qua* individuals.[41] The private individual has no a priori obligation to regard any state-sanctioned doctrine as binding, even if he is nevertheless required to follow the law that may have been generated under such a doctrine to the extent that the law governs external behavior. If belief is private, behavior that impinges on others is public.

The example we have considered reveals immediately the radical character of the transformation involved. The idea of a *private* comprehensive doctrine of the good—that is, a comprehensive doctrine that has no significance outside of the mind that holds it—is of course ludicrous on its face. We already discussed in chapter 4 how the elimination of public significance removes all constraints to the determination of this "doctrine," so that the power diabolically increases with its impotence, but in the present context, we wish to point out how the right to privacy undermines substance on both sides of the dividing line. In a symbolical sense of reality, there is of course recognition of what we might call the "secret depths of the heart," the intimacy of personal relations, such as friendship, marriage and family, and one's ultimate relation to God, realities that at least in some respects grow best outside of the direct sunlight, so to speak, of public view. But this recognition can coincide with the recognition that these realities, personal decisions, familial interactions, are not "private" in the modern sense;[42] they have a universal significance, that is, they have an actual reality, an objective meaning, they touch on the common good, involve the transcendent principle that makes all joining-together (συμ-βάλλω) possible. There is no opposition in principle between the personal and the common, the intimate and the external or objective.

Clearly, given an inseparable unity, some matters may be more personal and less universal, or more "public" and less personal, but it does not follow that more of one implies less of the other: in fact, arguably there is nothing more personally significant than the universal meaning of reality. Once we see the unity in principle of the personal and the common, we understand that certain duties and obligations follow in both directions. What one does in one's home, for example, is not some matter sealed off from the rest of mankind and handed over to arbitrary subjective power, but it has an internal order from the beginning, and therefore always in itself entails a call to conform with meanings that are given, that is, not "self-created." Conversely, the public order has a duty to protect what is intimate and personal, precisely because that is what it really, actually is: it too must *conform* in turn to the actual reality of the properly personal. What is really real has a substance of its own, which means that it has an interior depth that does not come to ("public") view. Note: noncoercion in personal matters therefore does not necessarily stand or fall with the existence of a "right to privacy," which sets the personal sphere off *against* the public. Instead, it follows more basically from the very same thing that entails responsibility in intimate matters, namely, the recognition of the real, conformity to what is given.

Another level of the transformation comes into view when we register the anxiety that we spontaneously feel, no doubt, at the critique of a right to privacy, which would seem to imply that government would be a given a "say" in our personal affairs. It would seem to invite the machinery of the state, as it were, into the intimate community of our most personal relationships, and indeed ultimately into even the "secret depths" of our own heart. But this anxiety reveals an ignorance regarding the deep and subtle implications of "modern rights" simply. Insofar as a right is *not* understood as the social extension of a natural power, and so one rooted in and ordered to an *actuality*, it becomes, as we have already argued, an external boundary set to fix the legitimate extension of the arbitrary powers of autonomous subjects. But power, in the Lockean sense, as we have also argued, is analogous to a force, which has reality only in relation to opposed force. What this means in the present context is that the establishment of a right to privacy not only separates the private from the public, but it simultaneously transforms the public, giving it the form, most fundamentally, of *coercive power*. In other words, the right to privacy makes this coercive power the essence of political governance; the very right gives rise to the "machinery of the state." This right gives me control over certain matters, and by that very fact *removes* these matters from the control of the state, which implies that the state's relationship to these matters is precisely that of control, if no longer actually, then still potentially. In other words, from this perspective, the government comes to represent in principle an ever-present threat of control, which can be protected against only by the establishment and reinforcement of boundaries. It is not at all accidental that where these boundaries are set is determined through the negotiation of interest: public interest versus private interest. Public order, thus, is established through *competing interests*, which is just the form the conflict of powers takes.

But what exactly does the phrase "public interest" mean? It is in fact oxymoronic, at least according to the modern sense of "interest," which in contrast to the classical language of the "good" indicates the benefits that one party in a negotiation hopes to achieve as distinct from, if not opposed to, the benefits that the *other* party may derive. Interest is thus always *particular*, the concern of one *part* (party) in contrast to another *part*. "Public interest," then, does not mean the good of the whole qua whole, but the benefits to the "whole" qua collection of individuals, now conceived in a quantitative fashion, and *opposed to* the benefits to certain individuals as individuals. "Public interest" is the advantage to the greatest number, or simply the majority. From the perspective of the right to privacy, in order to show that something has significance *outside* of the private sphere, one has to show that it entails benefits or damages to individuals severally, which means in effect showing that it impacts the private lives of many. To the extent that this can be shown, the state has the right to determine the matter accordingly.

Conceived in terms of the opposition of powers, of competing interests, what belongs to the public order can only be a diminishment of private power, an encroachment on what would otherwise be the dominion protected by the right to privacy. The public can exercise authority, indeed can be effectively present at all, only in a coercive form. What is strictly excluded is the possibility of a common good, which would be intrinsically present to all and so a principle of genuine unity.[43] The transcendence of the good, as we have seen, is what generates a *symbolical* order, in which the parts "connect" in a manner simultaneously perfective of each severally and of the whole commonly. The right to privacy reduces the common good to public interest, which becomes a diabolical substitute for it. Public interest is diabolical, in this regard, because it only *apparently* enables unity: as essentially tied to coercive power, it can do no more than ensure external conformity of behavior, and, more profoundly, even this conformity of behavior serves not the good of the community as such, but ultimately only the individual advantage of a preponderance of its members. The idea that one finds, for example, in the work of Martin Rhonheimer, who seeks, in line with the later Rawls, to "rehabilitate" modern political thought for the classical and Catholic understanding, namely, by arguing that a liberal sense of rights encourages at least a partial sense of the common good—the virtues of respect, fairness, and so forth—which can then be privately, or perhaps at best "civilly," supplemented through comprehensive doctrines of the good, ultimately fails to grasp the implications of this point.[44] What would traditionally have been recognized as goods are forced to take the form of interests, which are evidently not the same thing: however much they may appear to overlap in content, the difference in form changes their nature from the ground up, so radically that they may justly be characterized as opposites.[45]

To understand the difference, we may take as a concrete example the very thing under discussion, namely, the "right to privacy." From a symbolical perspective, we would affirm, say, the intimacy of the marital union *as a good*, indeed, as representing a fundamental truth that discloses a basic dimension of the meaning of human existence. To say that it is a true good is to acknowledge it as having a real nature, an actual form, which entails certain obligations and protections if it is to thrive and flourish. Because it touches on the meaning of human existence, even in its inviolably intimate character it is nevertheless a *common good*, worth defending by all, even by those who are not married and so in some obvious way are not strictly "interested" parties. One of the rights entailed by its nature is that its intimate character be safeguarded, which means for example that the state would be entitled to use coercive force to prevent a person from installing hidden cameras in a husband and wife's bedroom. From a diabolical perspective, by contrast, "privacy" is not an actual good to be respected, in the sense that it does not arise from some essential nature. Instead, it is a positivistically established sphere of arbitrary power. The only thing respected in this case is the *power* itself, which as we have seen is inherently ambiguous: it can mean everything and nothing. Thus, in principle, no action would be a betrayal of intimacy as long as the interested parties gave their consent to that action (whether the consent is explicit or imputed as implicitly given). Here we have a perfect instance of the diabolical: *precisely in the name of privacy*, one has the right to disclose details of one's most intimate relationships to absolutely anyone, for example, via the Internet. The diabolical self-annihilation is especially evident when what another person is not permitted to do to a person, that person is fully entitled to do to himself. We might sum up the modern doctrine of rights by the old quip: "You can pick your friends and you can pick your nose, but you can't pick your friend's nose." Note that, from a sense of reality rooted in actuality, a person would have no "right" to expose details of his intimate relationships, even with the explicit consent of everyone involved, *because intimacy is a real good.*[46]

On the other hand, even though the power granted by the "right" to privacy appears absolute insofar as it is unmoored from any intrinsic relation to an actuality, it is at the same time *in principle* perfectly impotent in the face of public interest. If a compelling public interest can be shown—which ultimately means nothing more than a majority of people in a given community become persuaded of some fact or indeed that the governing powers determine that they ought to be so persuaded— the "right" to privacy can always be trumped. It may be difficult to make a persuasive case, for example, that there is a compelling public interest that would enable the government to mandate secret cameras in every bedroom, but that is the only thing preventing it: there is no *principled* reason, because there is no *actual good* to protect. It is perhaps not quite as difficult, given certain historical circumstances, to argue for the necessity of the government's tapping of phone lines and tracing people's movements and activities through communications technologies, satellites, and drones.

We need not enter here into the radicalizing of privacy in the diabolical "order" to the point of being purified of any objective significance, and being reduced to a mathematical point of subjectivity, since we touched on this at the end of chapter 4 in our discussion of the Supreme Court's characterization of what it called the heart of liberty.

Equality

Another political feature closely associated with modern liberty is a "value" that lies at the heart of that political form, which in many minds virtually coincides with freedom in the political order, namely, democracy: that value is equality. For a consideration of the diabolical character of equality, we turn to the classic discussion of the theme in Tocqueville. It is true that Tocqueville sees a clear distinction, and even a tension, between equality and freedom, but this is in part due to an interpretation of freedom as active participation in political institutions, which is no longer the best description of the modern view.[47] According to Tocqueville, the dominant passion in the democratic society of America, to which all other desires are subordinated, is the desire for *equality*.[48] Whereas Tocqueville confesses a difficulty in determining *why* this would be the case—it is enough, he says, simply to observe that equality is the defining characteristic of a democratic age[49]—our reflections up to this point seem to cast an additional light on the topic. Tocqueville tries to find a compelling reason why this particular *good*, namely, equality, would hold an appeal that manages to outweigh that of other goods, and though he offers a few,[50] this approach seems to miss the essential point: it attempts to interpret equality first as an actual good. But the significance of equality in specifically modern democracy stands out only when we shift from actuality to potency as the primary point of reference. It is one thing to see equality as a relatively abstract feature of complex, real wholes: two very different things, an apple and an orange, may be equal in a certain respect—for example, the ability to satisfy a craving for fruit after a meal. But this equality concerns their adequacy to an extrinsic measure; it is not an essential quality of the ontological reality of the things in themselves. A decisive, *metaphysical* shift occurs when equality is absolutized, and, as it were, ontologized, since this implies that the actual reality gets effectively subordinated to what is in truth a relative abstraction, and indeed one dependent on an external measure.[51] Such a shift is inevitable when we interpret order, the organization of a multitude, principally in terms of *power*. If power is not differentiated in terms of concrete *quality*, which would be the case only insofar as it was subordinated to, and took its bearings from, actual ontological realities, it can be distinguished only quantitatively. But in this case, for one unit to have even a slight degree more power than the others is to deprive each individually of power altogether, since a power that cannot *over*power is ineffectual, which is to say that it is not in reality a power: it cannot effect change.[52] A balance is ensured by the separation of powers, and a separation is ensured by balance: each remains in itself a power by being set off over against equivalent powers.[53] We see here a connection between the absolutizing of equality and the rise of privacy as the separation of individuals, discussed above, which we will turn to in just a moment.

Equality does not dominate in a modern democracy primarily because it is taken to be a better good than others,[54] but because it becomes indispensable once the *power* to attain any good in principle is given priority over any *actual* good in particular. From inside this in-version, the more purely potent a power is, so to speak, the more it can include within itself the attractiveness of not just any good, but all of them at once. In this case, it does not have to compete with other goods, and so outweigh them in actual goodness, but instead co-opts their goodness, as it were. If the passion for equality is connected with an interpretation of political order in terms of power, then this value will tend simply to trump any other political good. This observation suggests not just that the rise of modern democracy as a political form, as Tocqueville describes it, represents a shift in political preferences, or even evidence of an increased sense of the value of the individual; even more, it suggests that all of this, true as it may be, is itself an indication of a more profound change at the metaphysical level, a shift in the un-derstanding of the nature of reality.[55]

The specifically diabolical character of the predominance of equal-ity comes to light when we recognize how the notion of equality, ideal-ized in an abstract form, *requires* an opposition to reality as actual. The actual order is always real-ly differentiated, and therefore it exhibits hi-erarchies, however diverse and organically interrelated they may be. The desire for equality as an end in itself, an ontological condition, will coin-cide with a tendency to detach from, disregard, or eliminate the signifi-cance of reality as it actually is. We see this for example in *choice*: options can be balanced over against each other insofar as they remain possibili-ties, but to choose any one of them is to acknowledge, or in any event, to establish, a preference and therefore a hierarchy: this is better than that, and indeed this represents a whole host of things that outweigh what are represented by the options that were not chosen. If choice is not a re-sponse to a real differentiation of goods,[56] it can only be arbitrary and so meaningless, but it will nevertheless still be effectively a denial of equal-ity. One can preserve equality in principle by emphasizing, not the *ac-tual making* of a choice (or indeed the actual reality of social conditions, etc.), but simply the *power* to choose, as we discussed above. Moreover, as we observed in chapter 4, to be is always to be in relation: the concrete order of existence is made up of real things in real dependence on and in real responsibility for other things. Actual diversity necessarily implies that some things are better or worse than others, that different people have different degrees of talent, different qualities, and so forth. It is interesting in this regard to compare Locke's description of the original condition of nature, which, we recall, presents equality as the essential feature, to Aquinas's description of the same: presupposing what we have called a "symbolical" sense of order, Aquinas is unable to see any *real* equality in the original state, though this does not present for him any problematic imperfection.[57] Not coincidently, the primary reference that Locke uses in his presentation is the distribution of *power*, while for Aquinas the governing principle is *beauty*.[58]

Now, as we saw in the previous chapter, the insistence on the absoluteness of equality can, and in fact inevitably *will*, coincide with the most extreme inequalities of actual conditions. The reason for this is precisely that equality can be absolutized (as opposed to recognized as a relative aspect of an actual whole) only in detachment from reality, only as "potentialized" into nonexistence. The principle of equality thus entails the logic of detachment from relations, a tendency toward isolation, forms of separation, a kind of uprootedness. This tendency is a basic focus of Tocqueville's discussion. For example, Tocqueville indicates the connection between the cultural drift toward equality in American democracy and the rejection of the "old regime's" law of primogeniture:[59] *landed* estates, a form of wealth that is of course rooted in a place and so has a kind of fixed reality, belongs not principally to individuals but to families. In such a culture, one seeks to honor one's family more than to make a name for oneself.[60] But such an inheritance cannot be divided *equally* among descendants; landed wealth has its own actual reality, and the members of the family relate to that wealth in distinct and "unequal" ways. To privilege equality requires a division of inheritance. It is not possible to divide land *strictly equally* (who gets the piece with the house on it?), and so the property is—as they say—"liquidated." Money *can* be divided equally, precisely because of its abstract nature, which we discussed in chapter 4. The point, here, is that money is not a good *to which* one devotes oneself—in contrast, for example, to a landed estate—but is a power taken into one's possession. This form of inheritance, rather than drawing the inheritors together *to* a reality that has its own substantial being, *separates* them as discrete units. Over time, estates get "chopped up" and mobilized, and those who make up a political community are increasingly sorted out, as it were, in their individuality.

Tocqueville goes on to distinguish individualism from egoism: the latter, he says, is a moral vice that has afflicted to some degree all people of every age and every sort of order. The former, by contrast, is specific to the modern age. Tocqueville does not use these terms himself, but it accords with his description to refer to the individualism encouraged by equality, not as a moral vice, but more basically as an ontological, and so objective disorder, prior in some respect to any moral action and so even compatible with what one might want to call altruistic, or other-centered, behavior. The issue is not whether one privileges one's own self or that of another in one's behavior. Instead, the more basic question is whether one understands one's self as ontologically a part of a greater whole—a "symbolical" sense of the self—or primarily as a separate agent, who has the *power* to connect to others in a broader community if he so chooses—a "diabolical" sense of the self:

> Egoism is a passionate and exaggerated love of self which leads a man to think of all things in terms of himself and to prefer himself to all. Individualism is a calm and considered feeling which disposes each citizen to isolate himself from the class of his fellows and withdraw into the circle of his family and friends; with this little society formed to his taste, he gladly leaves the greater society to look after itself. Egoism springs from a blind instinct; individualism is based on a misguided judgment rather than depraved feeling. It is due more to inadequate understanding than to perversity of heart. Egoism sterilizes the seeds of every virtue; individualism at first only dams the spring of public virtues, but in the long run it attacks and destroys all the others too and finally merges in egoism. Egoism is a vice as old as the world. It is not peculiar to one form of society more than another. Individualism is of democratic origin and threatens to grow as conditions get more equal.[61]

Tocqueville describes individualism as a tendency of the self to settle into the "private" circles of one's most immediate relationships with family and friends, but we may see that the radicalized notion of equality requires even more complete isolation, since even these immediate relations are unequal to the extent that they are actual. We recall here how important it was to Locke's basic proposal to provide a complete reinterpretation of family structure. In an order of radicalized equality, the only proper resting place is *inside* of abstract subjectivity, the pure *power* to relate, the totally undifferentiated and indeterminate—utterly *void*—moral agent: the abstract "chooser."[62]

Such a radicalizing of equality, and so absolutizing of the separation from all things real, might initially seem to imply political chaos: the opposite of hierarchy is anarchy. But, as Tocqueville famously shows (and in doing so "channels" Plato's classical critique), the privileging of equality tends to coincide with the *centralizing* of power in the political order.[63] The essentially diabolical character of equality comes once again to light in this seeming paradox. This centralizing takes both an objective, institutional form, and a more general, cultural form. We will close this subsection by looking at the institutional form, before turning to the cultural form in the next subsection. As for the former, the city—to borrow Plato's idiom—is the soul writ large. If the individual is understood, not as an actual reality embedded, so to speak, in a variety of relationships that precede, and so are ingredient in, his very unique individual being, but instead as an abstract quantity of indeterminate and undifferentiated power, this vision of the order of the whole will tend to be that of a "single central power." Connected to this vision is a notion

> of uniform legislation [which] equally spontaneously takes its place in the thought of men in times of equality. As each sees himself little different from his neighbors, he cannot understand why a rule applicable to one man should not be applied to all the rest. The slightest privileges are therefore repugnant to his reason. The faintest differences in the political institutions of a single people give him pain, and legislative uniformity strikes him as the first condition of good government.[64]

The tendency for extreme individualism to coincide with a kind of political collectivism in the modern era is something that thinkers have observed from a variety of perspectives, from Hobbes and Hegel, to more recent thinkers, such as Robert Nisbet.[65] The logic behind this tendency is twofold: on the one hand, from a practical point of view, the disorder of extreme individualism, lacking an internal and organic principle of organization, calls on an imposition of order from the out-side, an external imposition that extends as far as the potential disorder, and that reflects the undifferentiated abstraction of the equal units on which it is imposed: it is thus absolute and monolithic. On the other hand, at a deeper level, we see that the principle of equality, when it is made absolute, demands a single, universal measure, applied in princi-ple uniformly to all "across the board." The inherent diversity of a va-riety of centers of organization with regional roots—for example as implied in the notion of subsidiarity[66]—offends this principle: what-ever diversity of centers of organization may exist, they have to be lev-eled out in turn by an absolute measure above them to the extent that equality needs to be maintained, which is to say to the extent that we conceive of politics as the distribution of power. The absoluteness of individualism and the absoluteness of centralized governmental power inevitably coincide, which means that an insistence on equality tends to subvert itself, once again, into a mass capitulation to power imposed mechanically from above.

Freedom of Thought

The tendency of equality toward tyranny is perhaps more immediately experienced, though more subtly, at the broader cultural level: the ten-dency, that is, for the people to be controlled irresistibly by popular opinion. According to Tocqueville's well-known diagnosis of the mat-ter, the phenomenon of the tyranny of the majority comes about as a re-sult of "the theory of equality applied to brains."[67] The logic is straight-forward: if all opinions are equal, there is no intrinsic reason why any one opinion should be allowed to prevail over any other; in fact, strictly speaking, on these terms, it is impossible for any to do so on its own merits. The only "reason" for the dominance of any view at all that the principle of equality as applied to minds permits is quantitative accumu-lation, or the sheer force of expression, or both together. Note that, to appeal to the possibility of prevailing through argument is *either* to sur-render the principle of equality of all opinions (because it implies that one opinion might be more correct than another, which means that opinions are measured by *actual reality* and equality is not a relevant consideration), *or* to reduce meaning ultimately to the force of rhetorical manipulation.[68] The very same principle that makes this latter the only means of prevailing makes the force of majority opinion strictly irresistible. As Tocqueville points out, in a democratic age in which equality is absolute, there is in principle no actual reality to which one might appeal that would be higher than majority opinion.[69] Nothing can gainsay it. It is for this reason that Tocqueville is able to make the somewhat surprising observation: "I know no country in which, speaking generally, there is less independence of mind and true freedom of discussion than in America."[70] The reason it is shocking is that in America we believe we have more freedom to think what we wish than perhaps any other nation, not only now but at any point in history. We are virtually absolutely free in this regard. But that is just the point: an absolute freedom of opinion, the right to think whatever one wants to think, is itself the cause of abject subservience to popular opinion. The freedom of thought, understood in this way, is essentially diabolical.

Let us take a step beyond Tocqueville and look more closely at the philosophical dimension of this issue. If we understand "free thinking" as the *right* to think whatever I wish, this implies a very definitive interpretation of the nature of the mind. Specifically, it represents a denial of the classical view of the mind as bearing what we could call a "constitutive" relationship to reality, which means the mind is not first and most basically a power that has its reality in itself as any empty instrument and is only subsequently applied to reality, indifferent in its essence to its content. This denial is a paradigmatic expression of the separation of means and ends we discussed at the beginning of the chapter. Instead, in accordance with the principle that actuality precedes and so gives order to potentiality, the classical view understands intelligence as always-already involved with the real. We cannot explore what this means in the present context,[71] but the point here is to see that there is an essential connection between equality of opinion as a principle and a view of the mind as a pure instrument, a power that is essentially detached from reality. The connection rests on the constitutive indifference to content—freedom to think "whatever I want"—which means that the relation to reality does not enter into the mind in itself, determining it in an intrinsic way and (ontologically if not also chronologically) prior to any deliberate use. This is why one can be so readily seduced by the power of public opinion: one always feels secure in the impenetrable subjectivity of one's own mind, which is free to think otherwise, or any way at all, whenever it chooses, and so feels unthreatened at one level by the force of popular opinion. But it is just the feeling of safety, of having the "power" to reject popular opinion at any time, that causes it to accede to that opinion so readily. If abstract subjectivity is not threatened by the force of public opinion to think whatever it wants, it is also the case that the power of public opinion is not in the least threatened by individuals having this power; tyranny is rather strengthened by divided (δια-βάλλω) subjectivity.

A couple of years ago John Kerry explained to the German people in Berlin, with regard to the question that had just arisen of whether neo-Nazis should be allowed to demonstrate publicly, that, in America, we have "the right to be stupid." The observation says more perhaps than Kerry realized. Such a phrase makes no sense at all, of course, from a classical perspective, which views rights as a social extension of a natural power (which in turn is defined by an actuality). But from a modern perspective, the phrase is not only evidently true, it is redundant: freedom of thought is the right to think anything at all, which means that this right defines the mind as a power *separated* from and indeed in a certain sense set over against reality. A mind that is detached from reality, to the very extent it is so detached, is what the ancients would call *ignorant*. To use the modern word, such a mind is "stupid." Freedom of thought *is* therefore the right to be stupid, not just as one of its many options, but as its constitutive and therefore *inescapable* condition, no matter what option it happens to take. The right imposes itself as an obligation. This is not a freedom at all in reality but an unbreachable prison.

To be sure, we ought to recognize the "good intention" that motivates the protection of a "right to be stupid": it is human to make mistakes, and one ought to be protected from oppression or ostracism as one strives to "figure things out." Human frailty and fallibility need to be acknowledged, and human development needs to be given space. We should remain modest with respect to our capacity to make definitive truth claims.[72] Moreover, the notion of a public "space" in which only "correct opinions" are allowed is oppressive in the extreme. But we have to see that such things can be recognized and protected *in fact* only if we surrender the absoluteness of equality and the correlative notion of rights as power and freedom of thought as the right to think whatever one wishes. The dignity of the person, which belongs inherently to the being of each and so does not depend on the proper "achievements" of intellect and will, or on the welcome of popular opinion, is an *actual good*, a reality to which any right as power would have to conform. To accept this is to accept the priority of actuality over potency, which in turn implies that a grasp of truth is better than a failure to grasp truth.

To protect human dignity requires denying the absoluteness of abstract equality. To affirm that a grasp of truth is better than a failure to grasp truth, it ought to be pointed out, is not to say that the claim of truth allows one to impose one's views coercively on others. This is no doubt the most common objection to the critique of the equality of all opinions, an objection that persuades people to cling more tightly than ever to that equality, but we have to see that this objection is quite diabolical. It first of all imposes a diabolical perspective on the classical alternative (namely, that opinions are measured by the truth of reality), by interpreting this as the forcing of what is cast as a single, purely subjective, "equal" opinion on all other minds. But, in reality, if truth has priority, not only is it not a particular opinion that is being forced on others, since *all* opinions, even the one under consideration, are measured by something that transcends them, but it is also the case that coercion is for that very reason necessarily ruled out in principle with respect to the consent to truth. As Plato showed over and over again, the only way that truth can be "imposed" is through persuasion, understood in the Platonic sense not as rhetorical manipulation, but as argument ordered to enabling others to see the matter for themselves. To resort to coercion is to abandon the claim of truth.[73] Conversely, to insist on equality is to require coercion in all cases without exception, as a matter of course, because there simply is no alternative. The only question is how explicit the coercion becomes. The principle of actuality, of truth, *invites* public discussion and ensures that such discussion is meaningful, because all judgments can be right or wrong, and so are in principle correctable. By contrast, far from protecting genuine freedom of thought, the insistence on equality is *precisely* what makes it that *only* "correct opinions"—understood in this case as conformity to dominant public opinion—are permitted. To see this we need to follow out further Tocqueville's argument regarding the tyranny of the majority and see its connection with what is called "freedom of the press."

Freedom of the Press

Tocqueville observes that the press becomes centrally important in a democratic society, understood as consisting of equal—and that means, as we have been arguing, essentially isolated—individuals:

> When no firm and lasting ties any longer unite men, it is impossible to obtain the cooperation of any great number of them unless you can persuade every man whose help is required that he serves his private interests by voluntarily uniting his efforts to those of all the others. That cannot be done habitually and conveniently without the help of a newspaper. Only a newspaper can put the same thought at the same time before a thousand readers. A newspaper is an adviser that need not be sought out, but comes of its own accord and talks to you briefly every day about the commonweal without distracting you from your private affairs.[74]

What Tocqueville says about newspapers applies, of course, to the Internet and other communications technologies to a degree greater by many orders of magnitude. It is interesting to note that when we speak of freedom of the press, in the contemporary context, we typically do not mean principally the production and distribution of books, say, but most immediately newspapers, and much more commonly any communication of news through the electronic media, including the "freelance" reporting and commentary by bloggers. What we wish to suggest, here, is that this fact is evidence of the diabolical character of freedom of the press, so understood. The decisive aspect is the *immediacy* of this sort of communication, especially when we connect that immediacy with the reflection on the "theory of equality applied to brains," which we just discussed. Reality, in its transcendence of mere subjective opinion, makes a certain demand on those who would know it precisely because of its rooted depth. One has to take time, to exercise great patience and persistence, in short, to undergo a genuine sort of labor, in order to achieve insight into what is real. (This does not imply of course that work is all that is necessary, or that the more work the better the insight; it is rather a rule of thumb.) And one must likewise work to give such insights proper expression, a form that is adequate to their content. The very concrete and material conditions of that expression are not a matter of complete indifference: the content of "content on demand" is in subtle but profound ways different from the ostensibly similar content that appears, say, according to the order of the seasons; content that is as nearly as possible injected directly into the brain is likewise different from content that appears in a real, heavy, and beautifully bound book. If we mean by freedom of the press the freedom to express any opinion whatsoever, regardless of content or form, we are saying that this freedom has nothing to do in principle with reality (which is not the same thing as saying it has nothing to do with *accuracy*).[75] The point here is similar to the one above; it is the theory of equality applied not only to brains but now also to typing fingers. The very immediacy of the medium reinforces the tendency toward superficiality. If all opinions are equal, there is no reason why one ought to waste one's energies by taking the time to *form* one. Moreover, it is easier to give vent to immediate and unreflected impressions than to think some matter through to the end, so one can expect the "media market" to be flooded much more by examples of the former than examples of the latter.

Moreover, one tends to believe one is better informed, given the sheer quantity of material, by reading many (short) things than by reading one thing in depth. The average time spent reading what are considered content-heavy websites hovers at about a minute and a half. Can one reach to the center of some reality, in its ontological depths, in under two minutes? The point is that this sort of "freedom" does not encourage habits of contemplation and reflection; it does not bring a soul *out*, *into* the world, and engage it in reality, but instead tends to package "reality" small enough so that it can fit into the shrunken space of contemporary attention. Although he meant to be generally positive about the meaning of the press in an economic age, Tocqueville already observed this character of newspapers. Note the last line of the passage we quoted above: "A newspaper is an adviser that need not be sought out, but comes of its own accord and talks to you briefly every day about the commonweal without distracting you from your private affairs."[76] Because of its objective depth, reality by contrast *does* need to be "sought out" and involves more than a daily brief consultation. It also does not simply fit neatly inside one's "private affairs." As we have seen repeatedly, the mark of the diabolical is that it gives everything, apparently, without making much of a demand on the recipient.

The only qualification of Tocqueville's observation we would have to make here regards the subject matter. Tocqueville refers to the press as reporting on the "commonweal." But if there is indeed a connection between form and content, a medium designed to enter unobtrusively into the narrow space of one's "private affairs" will naturally tend to cater above all to private interests, which touch on the commonweal more often only incidentally. The phenomenon of the "tyranny of the majority" arises when minds are radically isolated from each other, and from reality, the "common world"[77]—rendered, that is, purely "equal,"[78] which means transformed into the pure power to think, anything or nothing at all ("to think" in this case means simply to set the machinery of the mind in motion; it does not mean—to provide a contrast—to gratefully receive the being of what is: *thinking as thanking*).[79] A press that "freely" serves such minds, in the sense of submitting to their condition, will not generally "speak of the commonweal," as Tocqueville supposed, except insofar as this happens to form part of one's personal—that is, private—interests, or to use Tocqueville's language, insofar as it does not "distract you from your private affairs." In the modern context, the commonweal certainly does not *define* personal interest, as it essentially does in a symbolical order, which recognizes that the universal good is the ultimate object of desire in any particular good sought.[80] Instead, the commonweal has to fit itself to the *form* of private interest. This means that the good that belongs to the whole *as such*, a good that always also is present to and in the parts, but in such a way that the parts *mediate* what transcends them, reduces in this case (we might say diabolically) to the *im*-mediacy of its presence in the parts. In other words, the "content" of the impoverished communication will not come in the form of mediated wholes, but rather in disconnected parts, flashes of meaning, or "sound bytes." These will not be *integrated*, which would of course imply the hierarchical ordering of actuality, but will instead be leveled out into a monotonous series of "equally" important bits of information.

One of the principal characteristics of the technological transformation of "news"—though, if our interpretation has some merit, one would have to say this feature was logically implicit in the notion of popular news from the beginning[81]—is the chaotic juxtaposition of the most disconnected, indeed utterly discontinuous, "realities." There is no intrinsic reason why—to pull up a webpage at random—a celebrity's choice of shoes at an event is any more or less important than the discovery of some new feature of the constitutive elements of matter.[82] And why should any of this, we might ask fancifully, with Thornton Wilder, be any more newsworthy than a beautiful sunrise at a particular spot over the landscape,[83] or at a more profound level (perhaps), the evolution of the meaning of freedom in the Western world? The response that would be given today is that there is no reason in principle that any of these should be considered any more or less important, and that the very point of freedom of the press is to keep from excluding any such possibility. The relative importance is left up to the choice of individual consumers. But the response fails to come to grips with the implications of the "theory of equality applied to brains": when all notions carry equal weight in principle, the effective criterion of selection becomes the sheer accumulation of quantitative force. There is an irresistible tendency for things that appeal most directly and immediately to the senses and to the analogously sensual interest to crowd out the sorts of things that call on patience and a certain depth of attention, one that gathers up the self into a focused, docile whole. This logic gets intensified through the "im"mediacy of mass media. A vicious circle thus arises:[84] things become important because they are important. The sign of their importance is that everyone is talking about them, or even more basically because of the frequency of their repetition on social media ("trending" stories); and they are so frequently repeated because they are important. Mass media most basically reports on itself. In a very straightforward sense, this is the phenomenon of tyranny of the majority as expressed *in* the medium itself. The medium is, indeed, the message.

The amplification of particular notions, which would otherwise be no more important than any other "equally" important realities, that occurs by virtue of the medium's diabolical tendency to mediate, above all, the medium itself, that is, its infinite self-reference, has both personal, psychological implications and, more ominously still, public, cultural ones. Regarding the significance of newspapers in a democratic age, Tocqueville writes: "As equality spreads and men individually become less strong, they ever increasingly let themselves glide with the stream of the crowd and find it hard to maintain alone an opinion abandoned by the rest. The newspaper represents the association; one might say that it speaks to each of its readers in the name of all the rest, and the feebler they are individually, the easier it is to sweep them along."[85] But the reason it becomes "hard to maintain alone an opinion abandoned by the rest" is not just because of the psychological pressure that results from the flood of images and sound bytes; there is also a public, coercive dimension to this tyranny, which Tocqueville described in an unforgettable manner. We see here why it is the case that "free press," interpreted in a modern liberal way, diabolically entails the official permission of nothing but the "correct opinions," a permission enforced through coercive power. It may seem that a military, fascistic government would represent the paradigm of such a stricture on thought and speech, but as Tocqueville observes, in such cases, to resist a fascist government one can always appeal, at some level, to the people's support, however persecuted, or at the most extreme limit to the truth of one's own conscience in the face of all else. To the extent that there is a priority of the actual over potency, there will always be some foundation in reality *beyond* the scope of power, whether that power be the top-down might exercised by a dictator or the "grassroots" force of popular opinion. By contrast, to the extent that one insists on the equality of opinions, and subordinates everything to that equality through a so-called freedom of the press, there is in principle no basis at all for any appeal, there is nothing at all, no prior actuality, outside of the sphere of sheer power. One is utterly at the mercy of majority opinion, most directly because this tyranny remains so often invisible.

But it does not have to remain invisible. Tocqueville's description of the manner of such coercion is worth quoting in full, because of its eerily prophetic quality; what was no doubt an occasional event of some moment in Tocqueville's time has become a weekly occurrence in ours: the phenomenon of the tyranny of the majority that he had in mind, we might say, awaited the invention of social media and communications technologies to find its proper expression, just as the tragic drama had to await the appearance of Aeschylus and Sophocles to reach its natural form:[86]

> Princes made violence a physical thing, but our contemporary democratic republics have turned it into something as intellectual as the human will it is intended to constrain. Under the absolute

government of a single man, despotism, to reach the soul, clumsily struck at the body, and the soul, escaping from such blows, rose gloriously above it; but in democratic republics that is not at all how tyranny behaves; it leaves the body alone and goes straight for the soul. The master no longer says: "Think like me or you die." He does say: "You are free not to think as I do; you can keep your life and property and all; but from this day you are a stranger among us. You can keep your privileges in the township, but they will be useless to you, for if you solicit your fellow citizens' votes, they will not give them to you, and if you only ask for their esteem, they will make excuses for refusing that. You will remain among men, but you will lose your rights to count as one. When you approach your fellows, they will shun you as an impure being, and even those who believe in your innocence will abandon you too, lest they in turn be shunned. Go in peace, I have given you your life, but it is a life worse than death."[87]

The Power to Vote

Before turning more directly to some of the cultural dimensions of the problem we are exploring, we ought to make a brief comment on the power to vote, because this power is generally considered the essential vehicle of freedom in the modern political sphere. We would like to suggest that this power, too, is fundamentally ambiguous. We can be brief here because the phenomenon is simply an iteration of the same form we have been discussing all along.

To *define* one's participation in the political order *precisely by* the power to vote, as an abstract power, is to cut off political agency from any *intrinsic* relation to the whole, any true participation in the community, insofar as the very existence of a whole implies its actual priority with respect to the parts, which means that the actuality has to be a part of the participation. In other words, that participation in the political community cannot be essentially defined as a power without a prior reference to the nature of the whole. To define it as essentially a power in abstraction from this reference, and thus as a power that *acts on* the whole as it were from the outside, is just so far to make it diabolical *as opposed to* symbolical. Its diabolical character becomes most evident when we see that the promise of this power is that it gives the individual a certain leverage over (δια-βάλλω) the rest of the community, but this very leverage renders the individual totally impotent with respect to the political power that dominates de facto. The reason is that the very separation of the individual from the whole in the granting of the power reduces the individual's *political* significance to an abstract quantity, a mere unit of power, which now disappears in the face of the massive collection of such units. As we observed above regarding equality, an abstract power that is less than the power on which it is meant to act is not actually a power at all, but an impotence. If the political order is taken to be a matter of power determined by the tallying of votes, then what is decisive in political deliberation is nothing but essentially quantitative force, and the individual qua political unit is meaningless in comparison to that force. It is not an accident that the liberal mind cannot conceive of the right to vote as anything but universal in the positivistically empirical sense, because this "right" simply coincides in such a mind with the rejection of any intrinsic principle of organization, which would reflect a priority of an actual whole. Analogously to the principle of equality we discussed above, the power of each individual must be strictly identical—in mere potency, of course—with the power of every other individual or it ceases to be power in any intelligible sense at all.

But ironically it is the very same universality that empties it of genuine meaning: political power can be equal only by being equally meaningless, because to reduce it to quantity is to render its particular content irrelevant. The question of the significance of a political idea is replaced by the question of the number of people who consider it significant, or even more simply by the number of people who can be persuaded to vote for it. The very elimination of *qualitative* significance invites "extra-political" forces—above all, money and the power it generates—to become all but decisive in political deliberation. It would be a very different matter if political participation were interpreted qualitatively in terms of actuality, rather than merely quantitatively in terms of power: in this case, a single insightful voice, recalling us perhaps to a forgotten truth, could have genuine political significance.[88] Such a significance is eliminated the moment the person is told simply to cast a vote like everyone else.

The reason this power is an impotence, and so becomes totally pliant to external manipulation, is that, not only is it vulnerable to the tyranny of popular opinion,[89] but also that it can be summarily preempted or cut off by the coercive force of political process. As we were saying, if political participation is reduced to the sheer "power to vote," the *content* of participation becomes irrelevant: no one has any need to *listen* to what is being expressed, to hear the voice as a disclosure of reality, which may need to be further corrected by appeal to reality, or which may entail for all of us a rethinking of things because we are all accountable to what is real. Indeed, to insist on *deliberation*—as opposed to *dialogue*, in the contemporary sense, which amounts to little more than the serial voicing, and acknowledging, of particular opinions—is to deny the equality of opinion in principle. If the actual content of a voice is irrelevant, its significance *is exhausted by* its actualization of power as mere unit, registered along with the rest. At committee meetings, one of the best ways to silence a dissident voice raising unexpected considerations is quickly to put the matter to a vote; the untimely character of the consideration will itself ensure that the proposal will be overridden. In the Iraq War, when the United States had—as it turns out, only superficially—defeated the enemy with a speediness that astonished everyone, but then was left to find some way to bring order to the internal political chaos of warring factions vying for power, government officials explicitly presented the efforts at bringing the "extremist" parties into the democratic process by giving them seats in the new parliament as a *strategy for controlling them*. The diabolical irony becomes evident right here: we control agents precisely by giving them power. Tocqueville makes an observation that reflects a similar phenomenon.[90] In an election he witnessed in Pennsylvania, Tocqueville was surprised to discover that, though the slaves had been liberated and given the right to vote, almost none of them turned out to exercise that right. In answer to his questioning, he learned that the freed slaves recognized that their votes were relatively meaningless, and that casting them would have more immediate political costs in the community. Receiving the right to vote in those actual circumstances did not in the least elevate their political relevance. In fact, ironically it might be said precisely to have diminished it. No one has to be concerned anymore about their condition, because it has now become simply a private interest, which acquires significance only when the number of individuals who have this private interest reaches a certain threshold. Granting the right to vote can be a devious way of canceling out political significance. Malcolm X saw something of this in his resistance to being co-opted *into* the system; but one might argue that his attempt to gather up the power of violence to combat the power of the intrinsically manipulative political system represents a surrender to that system, insofar as it simply translates into more crudely physical terms the inner logic that always governs in that system. The problem is the absolutizing of power itself, a problem that cannot ever be resolved by means of power, but only by the relativizing of power to actuality. It is only the truth of reality that can grant freedom from the power to vote.[91]

Technology

Now we turn to more general cultural phenomena. There are few things in the contemporary world more immediately associated with freedom at the cultural level—that is, at the level of a general, shared mode of existence—than technology. For some, the development of technology and the development of freedom go hand in hand: "The history of human technology, which covers hundreds of thousands of years, is closely linked with the history of human freedom."[92] This association is not an accident if we think of freedom as active power, a kind of store of "capacity" that has not yet been designated for any particular use, and so able to be discharged in any number of ways. To adopt a Hegelian notion, we could say that technology represents a kind of perfect objective realization or embodiment of the subjective notion of will, such as we find it in Locke, or, in other words, technology represents what such a notion of will looks like when it is turned into a thing in the world.

Practically speaking, technology enhances freedom, insofar as freedom is the capacity to effect change in the world. The very point of technology in its most general sense is to mediate between the human agent as cause and the thing in the world that is meant to be brought about, modified, or transformed as effect, and to do so in a way that amplifies the effective power of the cause. A hand with a hammer in it can drive a nail into a board; a bare fist cannot. We do not have the space here to enter into a reflection on this matter to the extent it warrants, but drawing on Heidegger's classic work on the subject, we may observe that there is a decisive difference between the ancient understanding and use of tools and the modern mode, which is most properly designated by the (modern) term "technology."[93] To use the language we have been developing, we may refer to the premodern tool as "symbolical" and technology per se as "diabolical." What is the difference exactly? Some believe that the essence of the tool is the same in the ancient and modern world, and that modern technology is simply a more advanced and sophisticated version—that is, technology just does what tools have always *wanted* to do, but it does it almost infinitely better—but there is a radical difference in the reality itself. We can point to two aspects of the difference, both of which rest on the inversion of actuality and potency, and the subsequent dialectical relationship of means and ends we discussed at the beginning of this chapter.

The first is a difference that Heidegger, and in a somewhat different way Romano Guardini, make evident concerning the relationship between nature and artifice (or as Heidegger puts it in another context, between "earth" and "world"[94]), both in the tools that are fabricated and in those things *on* which the tools work.[95] At the heart of Heidegger's notoriously obscure reflections is a profound and relatively simple point that finds an echo in Guardini: in ancient *technē*, human activity is fundamentally *responsive* to what gives itself by nature, a giving that the human activity takes for granted as its condition of possibility. This means that a kind of "gratitude" is built into *technē*. This activity is creative and transformative, to be sure, bringing something *new* out of what gives itself and so transforming it (even to the point of enlisting it in the service of ends that are not anticipated by it naturally),[96] but, to use Robert Spaemann's formulation, this transformative activity *recollects* the natural reality at its root,[97] which is to say that it draws on the reality of that nature and affirms that nature as what it is *in* itself, even if that affirmation is not the final point, but is itself, as affirmed, lifted up into a new context in relation to what one in principle can call higher ends.[98] In modern technology, by contrast, what gives itself naturally is not positively and integrally affirmed as a foundational *part* of the activity, but it is only acknowledged to the extent necessary for use; otherwise, it is disregarded. Heidegger points to the difference between a windmill, which for example derives the "energy" to grind wheat into flour from a natural motion, and a hydroelectric plant that converts the forces of water from a flowing stream into electricity.[99] (We note here the difference in what is produced in the two cases, an actual human good and a store of power to be used for any possible good in the future; we will expand on this difference below.) Guardini points to the difference between a sailboat, which harnesses the wind as it blows, and a motorboat, which moves by its own propulsion, in spite of weather conditions.[100] Along these lines, we might compare a stone wall and a concrete wall, which could be poured from concrete that was made out of the very same stones. Again, it is a simple point: in the former, the stones are used *as* stones; in the latter case, the stones are eliminated *qua* stones. Their usefulness is derived from them in spite of their natural form rather than *because* of it.[101] There is no doubt that this objective gratitude, built into the wall, so to speak, is a significant part of the reason why we find stone walls in general more beautiful than concrete walls. In looking at a stone wall—to use Christopher Alexander's expression—we feel our own humanity enhanced, which is generally not what we feel when faced with a concrete wall.[102]

One might worry about the apparent Romanticism behind the examples chosen,[103] but we ought to see that the difference being elucidated is not at all a merely sentimental one, and it is not a matter of one being old and the other being new; the difference is quite objective, and indeed directly related to the theme we have been developing in this book. To use a thing *because* of what it is is precisely to acknowledge the relative priority of actuality, and to derive potency or capacity *from* that reality.[104] To go *behind* or *under* a thing's natural form, as it were, to extract a usefulness from it *in spite of* what it naturally is, is to subordinate its actuality to potency. It is not an accident that the kinds of potencies one finds in premodern *technē* tend to remain in some direct way dependent on nature; they are for the most part not able to be *stored*, as independent things in themselves, but require the actual energy, analogously in every case, of the natural reality giving itself. We might think in this case of the sailboat that can move only in the presence of the wind (and of course someone managing the sails). Similarly, as we mentioned above regarding Heidegger's example, these natural realities tend to *produce* real goods meant directly for use or enjoyment (flour for baking) rather than a power to be stored (electricity). To use the language developed above, we see that the potency in *technē* is a participation in, or otherwise directly related to, the actuality, or in other words that the potency in this case is suffused with the actuality it presupposes and depends on. This is just what makes such *technai* symbolical: you *connect*, rather directly and necessarily, with the weather and natural conditions in a sailboat, and so *you connect with nature* simply, whereas one is relatively "free" of such dependence in a motorboat.[105] In this latter case, the actuality is more or less irrelevant. The natural reality is what governs the artifice in ancient *technē*, in contrast to technology, in which the cart pulls the horse, as it were. Technological devices "dissolve the coherent and engaging character of the pre-technological world of things. In a device, the relatedness of the world is replaced by a machine, but the machinery is concealed, and the commodities, which are made available by a device, are enjoyed without the encumbrance of or the engagement with a context."[106] Note that the *very point* of modern technology, the very benefit that is indicated as the explanation for its development, is its overcoming of dependence on natural conditions. We will return to this point below.

On the other side of the relationship, that is, the human agent who uses the technological instrument, we find the second difference, which is perhaps more subtle, but no less significant. If the first point we just discussed concerns the separation of potency from the actuality of nature, the second is the separation from the actuality of the human agent. Technology tends not so much to enhance or amplify human agency as to displace it. A hammer doesn't swing itself. Not only does this tool depend on the actual reality of the wood and the iron or steel, but at the same time on that of the human agent, whose animal strength enables the hammer's own contribution. We might compare the mediating presence of a hammer to that of a nail gun, which does not amplify man's natural movement, but substitutes for it. It may seem to be the case that tools *always* substitute for human agency to one degree or another, the difference between ancient and modern technology turning only on just *that*, the degree. After all, it is the machinery of the water mill, for example, that grinds the wheat *rather than* the human hand. But the ideal that technology aims at is an elimination of human involvement. Though there may be marginal cases in which the truth of the claim we are making is not as immediately evident, a fundamental difference between *technē* and technology on this point is clear in relation to the difference we just indicated: the very presence of nature qua actual requires the actual presence of a human agent, and just as the potency of a premodern means remains a participation in the actuality of the natural reality that suffuses it, so too in *technē* actual human intelligence pervades the means in its exercise. A person can't sail a sailboat without a knowledge of how the winds work, the function of the various ropes, pulleys, and boom, and a constant attention to the actual quality of the wind and weather; indeed, it is the very nature of the *technē* that one constantly learns more about, not only the elements that make up the mediating instrument itself but also the nature in which it is involved, in the use of it.[107] By contrast, one doesn't need to have the slightest understanding of how a motor works internally to be able to operate a motorboat, as long as one knows how to start it and where to put the gas, and operating such a motor never has to mean understanding it better. Because the *technē* is both an extension *of* nature *beyond* nature and *of* man *beyond* man, this *technē* represents a genuine *encounter* between man and nature in their reality, a true "joining-together" (συμ-βάλλω). The experience of being "at one" with the wind and the waves in the act of sailing is no mere metaphor or purely subjective impression, but the experience of a reality. In the nonmodern sense, it is a flourishing of freedom.

A recurrent theme in discussions of the cultural impact of technology, exploited to sometimes great effect in science fiction, is the tendency for man to become the servant of the machine he created. It is helpful to see that this is a logic "built into" technology. Because of its detachment from the actuality of given ends and from the actuality of any particular user—a detachment we reinforce precisely to the extent that we define technology as "neutral"—the technological device takes on a pseudosubstantial reality of its own. Following the logic we outlined at the outset of this chapter, human activity becomes, in this case, accidental to the machine; man becomes an external operator, like the Deist God. Once started, the machine takes over; the ideal machine propels itself. In this respect, it is a mimic of a natural reality, a living organism, according to Aristotle's classic definition.[108] The diabolical character of this tendency comes especially to expression in the drive to produce a machine that imitates not only life but the analogically higher level of being, namely, *thought*.[109] Though some well-known figures in science and technology have begun to express their concerns regarding the prospect of Artificial Intelligence, there are tellingly no illusions regarding the possibility of ceasing the efforts being made in this regard. The unstoppable necessity of this drive, too, is due to the very nature of technology. Because technology is abstracted from any given ends, it is not defined, and so naturally limited, by any reality; it is not intrinsically ordered by what actually is. This means it is not able to be "inserted," properly speaking, into any given order. Instead, technology is defined only by the limits of its own capacity, which are therefore meant to be expanded as far as possible in principle. One makes a computer chip with the *maximum amount of storage* capacity as the material will bear, and once the limit is reached one seeks a "better" material. It runs against the meaning of technology to aim for a "good enough" standard, relative to the actual realities it is meant to serve. Technology in this respect has no "appropriate" place; it has an inherent drive to take over in any given context.

Matthew Crawford has written about what we might call the "forgetfulness of work" in the contemporary world, which has lost a sense of the encounter that occurs between man and reality in manual labor, an actual working on things with one's hands.[110] (Aquinas, incidentally, points to the *hands* as the specifically *bodily* expression of intelligence, and so as a distinctive mark of humanity.)[111] Crawford's discussion, which helps reveal why a critique of technology does not have to be Romantic, centers on his own trade, fixing motorcycles, though his account harmonizes beautifully with the argument we have been making: he observes, for example, the transformation of the meaning of such work that occurs with the introduction of a diagnostic computer, which replaces the mechanic's function of figuring out problems by going in and looking for them. What is especially illuminating in his book is how *genuine* hands-on work *connects* the worker, not only with the object worked on, but with a particular place, with a community, with the ideals that bring a community together, and, in short, with reality itself. There is "a paradox in our experience of agency: to be master of your own stuff entails also being mastered by it."[112] This is what it means to give priority to actuality over potency, to understand a reception of

what is actually first as giving form and energy to, and indeed as liberating, one's capacity. To say that such work *connects* one in all of these
ways is to say it is *symbolical*, to conceive of freedom in real terms.
One of the basic points of Crawford's book is to distinguish genuine
agency from the modern ideal of freedom as "autonomy":

> [A tradesman's] individuality is thus expressed in an activity that,
> in answering to a shared world, connects him to others: the cus-
> tomers he serves and other practitioners of his art, who are compe-
> tent to recognize the peculiar excellence of his work. Such a socia-
> ble individuality contrasts with the self-enclosure that is implicit in
> the idea of "autonomy," which means giving a law to oneself. The
> autonomy denies that we are born into a world that existed prior
> to us. It posits an essential aloneness; an autonomous being is free
> in the sense that a being severed from all others is free. . . . When
> the conception of work is removed from the scene of its execution,
> we are divided against one another, and each against himself. For
> thinking is inherently bound up with doing, and it is in rational ac-
> tivity together with others that we find our peculiar satisfaction.[113]

It is crucial to see that the technological device, insofar as this detachment from the actual conditions and qualities of both man and nature is built into its essence, reveals itself to be diabolical in its very
structure or inner logic. Let us spell this out further. A *technē* mediates
between man and nature in a manner that depends on their actuality,
their real presence. Technology, by contrast, tends to stand alone, in
relative independence, not as a *mediator* between an agent and patient,
but as a pseudoagent itself. The typical emphasis on the essential "neutrality" of technology only underscores this detachment and independence: it is *not actually* ordered to some reality, but in itself a potency
with its own intelligibility separate from any possible such ordering. In
this respect, the technological device is indifferent to any number of
possible uses, some good, some—perhaps—bad. But, as we suggested
at the outset of this chapter, this relative indifference to ends, this separation and isolation of means, tends to make the means an end in itself.
In its subordination of actuality to potency, a technological machine or
device becomes a kind of *suppositum* of energy; it is not accidental that

such things represent a kind of storage of capacity, to be used whenever and wherever needed. For just this reason, they tend to bring the movement of the intellect and will of the person employing them to a halt in themselves; they draw our interest to themselves and keep it there, in abstraction from the world around (compare the use of a sailboat to that of an iPad). To be sure, a "symbolical" tool also tends to acquire the character of an end, it tends to become itself an object of love: we might think, for example, of the trusty old saw in the hand of Charles Péguy's woodcutter, or perhaps an outfielder's favorite mitt. But the end-character, and the reason for it, are profoundly different in the "natural" tool and the technological device. The love one develops for a real tool grows over time precisely on the basis of actuality, what we might call the accumulated actuality of history. In this case, the thing is loved precisely in its connectedness, not for its abstract power first of all. The technological device, by contrast, tends to separate, to draw attention *to* itself and *away* from reality. One of the reasons for their capturing of attention—the word "fascination" is often and justly used in this context—is precisely the indeterminate power that such devices contain in themselves.

We wish to set into relief the specifically diabolical character of this power. Because it can be indifferently used for any number of things, one might say that all of these possibilities are in some strange way *present* in the device, and they can *all* be present *at once* precisely because they are *only* possibilities—that is, not yet real. A kind of bargain is being made here: one can include the whole wealth of possibilities in one's intentionality, so to speak, which is directed principally to the device itself, rather than resigning oneself to the relative "poverty" of a single focus, which occurs when one privileges actuality. The price one has to pay for such universality, however, is reality itself. In the indeterminacy of its power, technology represents a deceptive image of the comprehensive good, in a way that is similar to money.[114] This deception becomes apparent, for example, if we juxtapose the almost literally infinite possibility of the "World Wide Web"—one often hears access to the Internet described as having the world at one's fingertips—to the total self-absorption of the person lost in his smartphone, which has become essentially a cultural type. The devil himself would have to smile at this irony! A friend who had moved to a big, new house showed me around during the visit and, towards the end of the tour, pointed out with a particular satisfaction the amazingly technologically advanced grill on the deck (if I recall correctly, one could check the temperature of the meat from inside the house, using one's phone!). He told me, of all the things he and his wife bought to furnish the house when they closed on it two years before, this grill was his favorite. I asked him how well it worked, and he sheepishly admitted he had yet to find an occasion to use it.

Today (April 21, 2015), as it turns out, has been dubbed—with the great hyperbole that comes with an overweening sense of self-importance—by the techno-media as "Mobilegeddon," the day the world changes because Google is going to begin to enact a new policy it had announced apparently a month earlier: from now on, websites that are designed specifically with small, mobile devices in mind—sites, that is, with big and simple text, easy to read at a glance (while driving?), without any sophisticated internal articulation—will be privileged over more "traditional" sites in searches. Here we have a paradigm of the diabolical turn whereby the *means* becomes the *measure*, that which is meant to facilitate movement to an end becomes the standard to which the end is required to conform itself. It is a perfect instance, too, of the "tyranny of the majority": no coercive force is used to impose this conformity, but it is evident that there is little freedom, except in the most superficial (i.e., merely *apparent*) sense, in this matter. A website that would want to communicate substantial intelligible content, rather than merely make an impression, is not at all eliminated, of course, but left in "peace"—not, however, in the original, symbolical sense of the word as your being in communion, but in the modern sense of the word, as your being set apart so that no one will bother you. For small businesses, this is the sort of peace in which one can only *rest*.[115]

We should ponder how this diabolical mediation actually transforms the relationships at stake. A study was recently reported in the news that—as such studies so often do—demonstrated a phenomenon regarding the use of cameras that one would have anticipated through a little reflection on the matter: in visits of various tourist attractions, it was discovered that those who took pictures of the sites were less able than those who did not to recall details of what they had seen. In a sense, this phenomenon is simply a variation of Plato's critique of writing in the *Phaedrus*: instead of representing an "art of memory," as its inventors claimed, it is better understood as a tool for forgetting, because, in putting something down on the fixed medium of paper, one has less need to retain it in one's soul, and so less inclination to make the requisite effort to internalize it.[116] But the study then took the point a step further: it was found that, years later, the ones with the cameras, and now with the photo albums, were *still* less capable of describing details of the sites compared to those without. Here is the astonishing point, which reveals the diabolical character of the matter: it is not simply the case that, because one can take a picture, one does not have to view the reality now, but can view it at greater leisure later, for as long as one wants, but *because* one has the photo, there never arrives a time when one *needs* to look at the picture. The very potency that trumps the actuality of the initial visit is a permanent potency, which therefore *always* tends to trump the actuality at any given moment. It is similar to the value of money always trumping the value of an actual good, which we discussed in chapter 4. The *possession* of the reality in a photo defers one's ever coming into significant contact with that reality. This is diabolical. Though we cannot unfold the matter in any depth here, it becomes even more weighty when we consider the analogous point in social media: the immediate and effortless contact that such devices enable with all of one's friends, acquaintances, and even strangers, in one respect seems to affirm all of them: unlike the past, when it was difficult to remain in contact except with a very few, I can now sustain and rekindle any and all relations at any time. But the very convenience and intrinsic distance transforms the quality of these relations. If I can only write a letter a year to my family, as for example in the case with cloistered Carmelites, every word I write will be meaningful, or at least that is my hope and my aim; I will say what most needs to be said, and I will pour *myself* into the writing. If, by contrast, I can "text" something to my friends at any moment, a thousand times a day, there is never any need to say much that is substantial, because the next moment will always provide another opportunity. But when would that need *actually* arise? When will there be a moment in which I would not be able to "text" if I so chose? There is an almost inevitable tendency, once again, for the potency to trump the actuality at every turn. And it is just not possible that one's relationships can avoid suffering as a result. It is the very "freedom" of the connections that threatens genuine intimacy.

We will leave aside here any discussion of the economic exploitation, which seems to be inseparable from communication technologies,[117] but it is fitting to point out, before moving on, the essentially coercive force that has come to stand behind these technologies. Schools now as a rule *require* their students to use technological devices—and the flood of virtually unanimous studies that show how such technologies impair students' intelligence and degrade their capacity to learn for some reason seems only to increase school boards' enthusiasm for these programs, which are often funded by the technology companies themselves.[118] We have all remarked on the ubiquity of these devices in what used to be recognized as the public realm, but which ought perhaps now to be described as a merely externalized and socialized private realm, and we have all sensed—some of us to excruciating degrees—how addictive these technologies tend to be. There are two ways in which the addiction to technology differs from addiction to drugs: it seizes on the mind directly rather than through the body, and it is fully encouraged and constantly reinforced by all of the cultural and political forces available. The forces are typically mustered under the banner of freedom.

Free Market

Tocqueville said that the tyranny of modernity leaves the body free and targets the soul instead, but we ought to see that the body itself—and the extension of the body into the world in material property and the like—is not as free as it would seem in the modern era. In chapter 4, we considered the meaning and implications of the transformation of property into money, which is inherently divisive; here, we will look at the phenomenon in a broader, cultural perspective, on the basis of Karl Polanyi's classic work *The Great Transformation*.[119] In this book, Polanyi, referencing William Blake's poem, describes the modern free market as a "satanic mill" that "grinds men into masses."[120] We cannot follow out the thorough historical details of his account, or pass judgment on his own conclusions and proposals, but wish here only to set into relief the logic of his diagnosis, which we will see supports the argument we have been making here. According to Polanyi, Adam Smith's apparently self-evident observation regarding man's natural "propensity to barter, trade, and exchange one thing for another" was in fact entirely anachronistic, and it served to bring about the reality it described: "No misreading of the past ever proved more prophetic of the future."[121] As Polanyi explains, there is a fundamental difference between the economic system we take for granted today as an expression of what is natural to man and the economic configurations of premodern societies. Before the modern era, the notion that an economic system should be founded on *gain* as its governing principle was simply inconceivable. In these societies, *exchange* was always in the service of social and human ends. The word "economy," of course, means something like household management, the ordering, cultivation, and sustenance of one's home or estate.[122] The very asking of the question that Aristotle poses in the *Politics*—Does economics have anything to do with money-making?[123]—is perhaps no less surprising than the answer he gives: properly speaking, the answer is clearly *no*.[124] What distinguishes the modern view of economics, according to Polanyi, is (significantly for our argument) an *inversion* of what might be called the natural order: now, society conforms to the market, rather than the reverse. And the results, he says, are devastating.

At the heart of Polanyi's argument is what he calls the "free" or the essentially self-regulating market. What he means by this is a market that is not, as it were, embedded in a larger order, but instead draws its governing principle from its internal necessities alone. Markets have existed, of course, more or less as long as man has, but in premodern societies the form of exchange was always conditioned by more fundamental realities and actual social relationships. Markets were always "contextual." The modern market, by contrast, is a disembedded system that operates according to its own laws, which is to say that *it* provides the context for the realities of man in the world and in society. According to Polanyi, the emergence of the self-regulating market becomes evident in the transformation of three things in particular into market commodities: labor, land, and money itself. The reason these are significant is that, according to Polanyi, none of them can *be* commodities in reality. Polanyi calls them "fictitious commodities"; they are fictitious because none of them was actually produced for sale:

The crucial point is this: labor, land, and money are essential elements of industry; they also must be organized in markets; in fact,
these markets form an absolutely vital part of the economic system. But labor, land, and money are obviously *not* commodities;
the postulate that anything that is bought and sold must have been
produced for sale is emphatically untrue in regard to them. In other
words, according to the empirical definition of a commodity they
are not commodities. Labor is only another name for a human activity which goes with life itself, which in its turn is not produced
for sale but for entirely different reasons, nor can that activity be
detached from the rest of life, be stored or mobilized; land is only
another name for nature, which is not produced by man; actual
money, finally, is merely a token of purchasing power which, as a
rule, is not produced at all, but comes into being through the
mechanism of banking or state finance. None of them is produced
for sale. The commodity description of labor, land, and money is
entirely fictitious.[125]

There would be much to explore here, but we must limit ourselves
to quoting a few passages from the text to elaborate the implications of
this fiction: "Labor and land are no other than the human beings themselves of which every society consists and the natural surroundings in
which it exists. To include them in the market mechanism means to
subordinate the substance of society itself to the laws of the market."[126]
On the one hand, this subordination tends to refashion all of the relationships that constitute society in the image of the market:

To separate labor from other activities of life and to subject it to the
laws of the market was to annihilate all organic forms of existence
and to replace them by a different type of organization, an atom-
istic and individualistic one. Such a scheme of destruction was best
served by the application of the principle of freedom of contract.
In practice this meant that the noncontractual organizations of kinship, neighborhood, profession, and creed were to be liquidated
since they claimed the allegiance of the individual and thus re-
strained his freedom. To represent this principle as one of noninterference, as economic liberals were wont to do, was merely the ex-

pression of an ingrained prejudice in favor of a definite kind of interference, namely, such as would destroy noncontractual relations between individuals and prevent their spontaneous re-formation.[127]

On the other hand, this fiction tends to "cancel out" the givenness of the things of nature, and the actual interrelatedness that make it up, and to break natural relations down and mobilize them in the service of the market:

> What we call land is an element of nature inextricably interwoven with man's institutions. To isolate it and form a market out of it was perhaps the weirdest of all undertakings of our ancestors. . . . To detach man from the soil meant the dissolution of the body economic into its elements so that each element could fit into that part of the system where it was most useful.[128]

Polanyi, moreover, observes that calling the self-regulating market *free* is a misnomer:

> Just as, contrary to expectation, the invention of labor-saving machinery had not diminished but actually increased the uses of human labor, the introduction of free markets, far from doing away with the need for control, regulation, and intervention, enormously increased their range.[129]

As we have seen repeatedly, the broadening of freedom as self-determining power separated from actual ends always coincides with the proliferation of external constraints arbitrarily imposed.

The convergence of Polanyi's account of *The Great Transformation* with the drift of our own argument should be apparent. What he describes as the essentially *fictitious* transformation of land and labor into commodities is a concrete expression of the diabolical inversion of potency and act that we have been exploring. Man's labor is an outward extension of his being, an expression of his reality in a way that effects a change in the world. To the extent that labor is rooted in, and responsive to, the complex reality of nature—"land"—the change that labor introduces is inherently meaningful. This meaning is eroded, by contrast, when the whole is instrumentalized to the market. When such a system came to be in England, Polanyi says, the meaning of production changed at its roots. The real, human meaning of work was subverted:

> The creation of goods involved neither the reciprocating attitudes of mutual aid; nor the concern of the householder for those whose needs are left to his care; nor the craftsman's pride in the exercise of his trade; nor the satisfaction of public praise—nothing but the plain motive of gain so familiar to the man whose profession is buying and selling.[130]

To transform a reality into a commodity is to subordinate actuality to potency: the thing ceases to be in the first place a reality in itself, with its own intrinsic goodness, and becomes instead a token, an exchange value, a quantity of purchasing power. The value of a commodity is determined entirely by the market to the extent that the market is free (i.e., unbounded by any natural reality or limit), which is to say it is determined *extrinsically* by the system of relationships of buyers and sellers, supply and demand. In such a system, there is no meaningful difference between real demand—generated by actual goodness in relation to human nature—and artificial demand, and this lack of difference underscores the detachment from actuality that occurs in this context.

There are two consequences of this "commodification" of reality that we wish to highlight here. First, the subordination of actuality to potency entails a subordination of complex wholes to their various parts. Thus, as we saw above, there is a certain priority given to the discrete *elements* composing production and sale, which have been isolated and thus rendered serviceable for the broader system. We witness here a kind of fragmentation, not only in the "land," which becomes now a store of separate "raw materials," over against the labor that will be applied to them, which in turn is the raw material to which the separate activity of management will be applied, and so forth. But there is also a dissociation of man from his labor: it ceases to be an extension of the reality of man into the world, and becomes an object in man's possession, something he is able to buy or sell. Labor thereby loses any trace of "praxis," immanent human action in which man finds fulfillment (which depends on intrinsic participation in the actuality of the end), and reduces to a pure *poiēsis*, a productive power that is transitively exercised *on* something external to the self.[131] Second, because these fragmented elements do not have an *internal* and a priori unity, they tend to stand over against each other and to resist each other. We can see this not only in the competition that ensues between the individual participants in the free market but also among the very structural elements of the system that have been dissociated from each other and from the whole as such. The elements "turn against" (δια-βάλλω) each other. Having been reduced *essentially* to commodities, land and labor are meant to be *exploited* as a rule, and labor, in turn (land of course has no say in the matter), resists such exploitation to the point of deforming its own essence:

> As long as labor lives up to this responsibility [of finding its price on the market], it will behave as an element in the supply of that which it is, the commodity "labor," and will refuse to sell below the price which the buyer can still afford to pay. Consistently followed up, this means that the chief obligation of labor is to be almost continually on strike. The proposition could not be outbidden for sheer absurdity, yet it is only the logical inference from the commodity theory of labor. The source of the incongruity of theory and practice is, of course, that labor is not really a commodity, and that if labor was withheld merely in order to ascertain its exact price (just as an increase in supply of all other commodities is withheld in similar circumstances) society would very soon dissolve for lack of sustenance.[132]

What we have here is a paradigmatically diabolical system: it is founded on an unreality ("fictitious commodities"), and it results in pitting all of its elements against each other as a matter of their basic logic.

The third "fictitious commodity" Polanyi mentions is *money*. This one is significantly different from the other two, though Polanyi does not make much of the difference.[133] Whereas the other two are actualities by their nature, money is not: it is, in the conventional meaning of the term, not a reality but a "symbol." In a natural economic system, its function consists in the facilitating of an exchange of (real) goods. To make money itself a commodity, as precisely *what* is exchanged, is we might say the very *expression* of the inversion of potency and act in the economic order. In this case, the power to purchase is quite directly made a thing in itself, an *end*, no longer relative to the real goods whose exchange it was originally meant to facilitate. This relation remains, of course, as a kind of lingering memory, a ghostly appearance, since money would lose all value without some reference to what it could be used *for*, but that reference can remain a distant one; it need not be effective in its actuality for money to acquire the "shine" (*Schein*) of value. The unnaturality of money's capacity for self-reproduction—the generation of "interest"—has been recognized from the beginning.[134] It is this very unnatural inversion that entails the swallowing of the substance of society into what Polanyi refers to as the "mechanism of the market." The reference to the free market as a "mechanism" recalls the point we made above regarding the inherent tendency of a machine to subordinate man. We might think of the free market as a technologized version of economy: here we have a putative means (money), which is separated from any actual good in particular, and then "rationalized," or perfected as a system in itself. This system in turn tends to reduce all of its constitutive elements (land and labor) to its *own* instruments, accidents of its substance.

There is an "either–or" in the relationship that the elements of an economy bear to one another. If land stands for the givenness of natural reality and labor for human activity, we could say that *either* labor is rooted in the land, in which case money has an always-merely-relative value as the fruit of real participation in the meaningful order of the world, *or* labor is subordinated to money, and both labor and land are transformed in the process into things that are essentially *unreal* ("fictitious commodities"), things that are forced to try to achieve some reality, or at least recognition, by creating demand on the market.[135] It is not difficult to see the implications of all this, which both Polanyi and Hegel described in different ways: we end with the global market standing de facto as the organizing principle of human society, which is what Hegel meant by civil society engulfing the human community of the state in itself. But what does it really mean to say that the market controls the state? There is no ruler in the free market. "Conspiracy theories," which place the puppet-strings in the hands of the few, unfathomably wealthy, although perhaps not altogether false, fail to see that even the wealthiest are but gears—large ones, no doubt—in a more comprehensive mechanism. And so it is an order without any ordering principle, a system without genuine organization, a mechanism without any human purpose, a force without a human face. To say that civil society engulfs the state is to say that symbolical community has been ground up in the satanic mill of the free market.

Academic Freedom

One aspect of the essential unfreedom of the free market demonstrates itself every time a teenager goes off to college. He is no longer seeking primarily a *liberal* education—that is, an education that frees precisely by deepening and forming a person's love of reality in its goodness, truth, and beauty, through an introduction into a tradition—but now, above all, to acquire what "marketable skills" he can.[136] Indeed, the first reason he needs such skills is to be able to pay off the debt incurred while acquiring them (again, diabolical self-reference!). Education itself has been turned into a commodity, and this fiction strikes even more directly at the root of humanity than the commodification of labor, since labor, arguably, is already instrumental and productive by nature, even if it ought to be understood as more than just this. Education is first of all a school in humanity: becoming human by learning to affirm in a profound way what is real.[137] As commodified, however, education has to justify itself as a *market* value. To answer the question, What is it worth?, one has to point to what the particular program of education produces—ultimately to the average salaries of graduates. Even the ostensibly "internal goods" of education, that is, what were known in the premodern world as virtues or human excellences, are reduced in this context to essentially instrumental substitutes. The apparent defenders of traditional liberal education today say that education is not about getting a job, but about acquiring the skills of writing, speaking, and critical thinking. There is an enormous pressure here that bears directly on the freedom to teach and learn. It falls not only on students, who are as a rule compelled to prioritize the question of marketability in choosing their major (responsible students are precisely those that picture their job resume when selecting not only the course of studies but other extracurricular involvements, a skill they mastered already in high school in view of their college applications). But the pressure falls equally on the professors and administrators; it is communicated through all the channels in the structure of the academy. If education is a commodity, students are customers, and the "customer is always right"—an awkward axiom for the teacher responsible for assigning grades to papers. Programs of study, course descriptions, and even the performance of every class lecture are advertisements that make an often hysterical, desperate pitch to students' attention. Education, in a word, has come to be measured by something radically extrinsic to itself, and this is diabolical. We will forgo a reflection on the transformation of the meaning of "academic freedom" in this context, but suffice it to say that what today goes by the name of "academic freedom" will inevitably entail a wholesale, if unwitting, capitulation to the pressure we've described to the extent that it rejects a need to represent, and so serve, the truth of reality.[138]

Freedom of Information

Information is associated with freedom in the modern era in two ways. The more immediately evident of the two is perhaps the demand that freedom makes to have access to information; the assumption behind this demand is that to limit such access is in principle a threat to freedom. The second is a positive formulation of the same principle; it lies in the translation of the already quintessentially modern dictum "knowledge is power" into hypermodern terms: information is freedom. The notion here is that possessing information allows one to make intelligent and responsible choices. Prima facie, it may seem as if nothing could be more obviously true and good than the insistence that choices be made intelligently and responsibly, but we must be attentive to the meaning of the terms and their implications. We would like to suggest that having information—*qua* information, that is, precisely *to the extent that it is information* (which does not rule out information accidentally being something more profound)—in every instance undermines freedom. Our thesis is that information excludes the possibility of genuine freedom in the symbolical sense of the term. What does this mean?

Behind the demand for access to information, for what is called "transparency," is a refusal to be subject to the arbitrary will of another, to use Locke's phrase. If one does not have access to information "on demand," one sees only what the other chooses to disclose. In this case, one is bound by limits the other sets; one is thereby *dependent* on the other, who is not an object under one's control, but who instead has control himself, at least in this particular matter. That control is, of course, limited by the degree of access he himself has, in turn, to the information possessed by *his* other. Here is a perfectly diabolical situation, in which "freedoms" are pitted against each other; they are diametrically opposed in principle even if they happen to cooperate or agree to compromise. The more freedom one has, the less freedom the other has. This is because freedom is being interpreted here in terms precisely of control or power, which, as we have seen repeatedly, entail a zero-sum logic. If, by contrast, freedom is understood most basically in relation to the good, and so in symbolical terms, it *necessarily includes* dependence in its essential structure, so that *an absence of dependence would indicate a lack of freedom.* One cannot be *joined-with* another in a *real* sense without this entailing some dependence, and freedom as a participation in the good is always in some respect a joining-with. In this case, to await the disclosure of the other in a patient dependence is not a threat to freedom, but an *expression* of it, an essential characteristic of it. It lies outside our capacity to explore the issue here, but it bears remarking that the positive dependence that comes to light in the symbolical interpretation of reality implies a certain coincidence of transparency and mystery, light and darkness, in perfect freedom. The key, in any event, is to see that, from the modern perspective, transparency *cannot* be left as a matter of someone's arbitrary choice, but it must be coerced, or coercible in principle (cf. the Freedom of Information Act). Information, in other words, from this perspective is a matter of "freedom" only ever on one side of the relationship, the side that can lay claim to it as a legally protected right.

But so far we have remained on the legal level of the right to information; we need to reflect further on a more profound, and so more universal, dimension to the issue, though still related to the first. One of the assumptions in the association of information and freedom is that information means the same thing as knowledge. But this assumption betrays an ignorance of the transformation that occurs, not only in the object of knowledge but simultaneously in the knower and the mode of knowing, when knowledge is reduced to information. Information is a particular form of intelligibility, which is distinguished, for example, from the classical principle of intelligibility (namely, form) in two respects. First, information is a breaking down of intelligibility into discrete units, which can be quantified (and indeed in this sense commodified[139]): the term adopted to name the unit of measure of information was "bit."[140] Whereas the classical notion of form indicates an internal principle of order that transcends the various parts that it gathers up and unifies into an irreducible *what*, information concerns the various parts themselves that still need to be gathered and processed into a whole, the "bits of data" with respect to a thing.

The second more precisely characteristic respect in which information is distinct from the classical principle of knowledge lies in its essential "transferability," not only to a multiplicity of knowing subjects (which is *also* a feature of form in its transcendence of matter) but into a variety of contexts of use.[141] The reduction of intelligibility to information is analogous to the commodification of land that Polanyi described: it is dissolved into its elements for the sake of utility. Information is *detachable* from any organic relation to its source; for that reason, it represents a kind of processed and packaged intelligibility.[142] It is in this form that it is delivered, and expected to be received. The recipient, then, is primarily a processor of information, and it is not an accident that the human mind is increasingly described in such terms. Information has an inner drive toward a particular kind of simplification, in the first place for the sake of ease and speed of communication, through the most basic possible mediation: ones and zeros. Distance is the very presupposition of information. We speak of "knowing a thing from the inside," or "having intimate knowledge of a person," but we would not use the word "information" in this context—or if we did, it would be with almost the exact opposite meaning.[143] In classical thought, by contrast, the principle of intelligibility is in a basic sense identical with the principle of the being of a thing, namely, form,[144] which means that knowledge always implies a kind of contact with reality. Knowledge is the mediation of actual presence. Hence, the frequent reference to ontological intimacy in premodern descriptions of knowledge: one *becomes* in a sense what one knows (*fieri aliud in quantum aliud*); to understand a thing is to enter into its innermost essence with the mind (*intus-legere*); knowledge is an erotic union between the soul and being, and so forth.[145] We might contrast all this with the frequent reference, in the context of information, to speed, convenience, storage capacity, and power.

The point, here, is that, if freedom is connected with knowledge in the *premodern* sense, then it is certainly *not* a matter essentially of power, because the reception of form, which is actual in being whole (perfection) and in being *present*, entails a privileging of act in its givenness, though of course such actuality is profoundly "enabling." This very privileging, moreover, entails an awaiting of the other, and so setting aside a demand for disclosure. Knowledge is a surrender of power *over* and instead a submission *to*.[146] Knowledge as freedom in this case entails a deep unity between subject and object. But if freedom is understood, instead, as increasing with the possession of information, then the meaning of freedom is altogether different. It becomes essentially self-referential; freedom is the control I have over my own actions and whatever my actions might be directed to, the "active power" over what I do. I need information so that I can make responsible choices, that is, so I can be protected as far as possible from unforeseen consequences, and ultimately from your attempts to control *me*.

We already pointed out the oppositional relation this notion of the "freedom of information" entails, but we can now dig a little deeper. Because of the inherently reductive fragmentation it implies, and even more basically because of the *distance* it takes for granted, the information I might have about a reality *is not at all* the reality itself. The unsurprising truth that information gathered through torture—violent coercion rather than free disclosure—is rarely reliable might be taken as a metaphor for a fundamental dialectic that concerns the nature of reality all the way down: "bits" of information, that is, parts separated from an organic whole, are never capable of expressing the whole as such, even if they are "reassembled," because the communication of a whole, and so a genuinely intelligible form, requires its actual presence. But all of this means that the more *control* I have *over* information, as power exercised by my isolated subjectivity, the less that information tells me what I "need to know"—or, in other words, the less meaningful it is. The *distance* that such information implies is itself a lack of the very power I identify with my freedom.

It is most directly at this point that the diabolical character of information comes to light: the literal flood of information available has rendered meanings unstable and has multiplied exponentially the possibilities of confusion that can be introduced into relationships. The more *access* there is to information, the more uncertain it becomes, because its accessibility—to the extent that it is "free" or in other words *without limit*—implies a detachment from any absolute anchor in reality. Inside of the dialectic that has taken hold of the contemporary field of communication and data exchange, we are on the one hand being *reduced* to the sum of our information;[147] on the other hand, we now have a variety of identities according to different contexts, a variety because the separation from reality allows us to *present* ourselves in an arbitrary fashion.[148] It is not an accident that the primary place wherein this dialectic between information and nondisclosure plays itself out is a medium that simultaneously absolutizes distance and eliminates it. The Internet is a place where one can feel free to be oneself.

Power

The many facets of the modern notion of liberty can no doubt be summed up in a single word: power. And so it is appropriate to conclude this chapter with a brief reflection on what it means in a diabolical context. We have argued that at the root of the cultural patterns we have been discussing is an interpretation of the will as active power, and each turn of our argument has encountered power under a certain aspect. It is customary to critique power most basically in moral terms: it seems more than obvious that power is neutral in itself—it is nothing but a means, nothing but the ability to do something or other, something as yet undetermined and so at this point *either* good *or* evil; as power, simply, it is indifferent to the options and equally capable of either—and so the critique is leveled at the *use* that is made of it. It focuses on the moral character and intentions of the one who possesses power and chooses to use it for self-interested ends of one sort or another. The critique, in other words, aims to unmask the abuse of power in a particular case, in the spirit of a "hermeneutics of suspicion," to show that, though on the surface it may seem that some innocuous transaction is taking place, there is actually a subtle manipulation or coercion of one party by another, through the use of means to which only that party has true access. At the heart of this critique is the claim, whether spoken or not, that the principle of equality has been betrayed, and this betrayal is identified as an injustice. Now, the problem with such a critique is not that it is false, but that it does not go deep enough; it does not reach to the essence of power, but takes that essence for granted and judges only its exercise. The unmasking, though it *seems* at least to penetrate below the surface appearances, is in reality therefore only a deceptive imitation of radical depth. Because of this lack of depth the terms of power remain absolute, and it is only the direction of the leverage, so to speak, that gets shifted.

A more radical critique must consider power in its essence. While we cannot carry out such a critique here, we can at least indicate some basic aspects with respect to our general argument. Our concern in the present context is simply to bring out its diabolical character, to show that its indifference to actuality (its "neutrality") implies an actively antiactual impulse. To see this, we ought to turn to the point from which we began this chapter, Plato's *Gorgias*, which is a critique of sophistry, but specifically as a form of power. The critique of sophistry unfolds first as a very simple question, a question that Gorgias constantly resists answering in a simple way (by pointing to a *form*): "This is what causes me to wonder, Gorgias, and what has caused me to ask you from the very beginning: *what is the power of rhetoric* (ἡ δύναμίς ἐστι τῆς ῥητορικῆς)? For, as I look at it, its greatness comes over me as something demonic (δαιμονία)."[149] Gorgias's enthusiasm is sparked by this description, and he responds: "Ah, yes, if only you knew the whole of it, Socrates—as the saying goes, it sums up all powers in itself (ἁπάσας τὰς δυνάμεις συλλαβοῦσα ὑφ' αὑτῇ ἔχει)!" The reason it sums up all other powers in itself is that it is not a particular activity or a trade, juxtaposed to others, but rather it concerns a way of doing any or all of them "successfully"—what this means, here, is that it gives one power over other people and so puts one in a position to manipulate interactions so as to achieve whatever it is one wishes. In this respect, sophistry, for Plato, *is an emblem of power*; it represents a disposition toward the world as a whole, and ultimately the one perfectly opposed to the philosophical.

The question of the nature of rhetoric is in fact a question of the nature of language, and the reason this question represents the heart of the matter, as it were, is that man's relationship to reality comes to expression most basically in the *word*. To simplify what is rather a complex and profound issue, for Plato, a word has its roots, so to speak, in (actual) being; it is an expression of *what is*: the word discloses the truth of reality. In this case, a "true word" is a redundancy. Being true is not an accidental condition of a word, but its *proper* condition. Along these lines, it becomes evident that *being false* is not therefore the "other alternative," the other condition that the word, which is indifferent to truth or falsity in itself, happens to find itself in, but represents a *failure* of the word, a betrayal of its authentic nature. This understanding of the nature of language lies behind what might otherwise seem to be an annoying refrain in Plato—annoying not only because it is relentless but also because it does not seem to be directly relevant when it arises: Socrates regularly says that he cannot understand how it is possible to speak *well* (καλῶς) about something unless one has *knowledge* of that about which one wishes to speak. Note that this insistence is an expression of what we have been calling the classical principle of the priority of act over potency and ends over means: knowledge (as distinct from *information*) implies a reception into the soul of the reality as it *actually is*, that is, as it is *in act*, in its complete form. If speaking well is a power (or more specifically a *habitus*, a perfected power) of the soul, to say that one has to have knowledge in order to speak well is to say that the *power* of the soul is ordered *by* and *to* the actuality of reality. The beauty (τὸ καλὸν) of the word is a reflection, an image, of the reality in itself.[150] In this case, to learn to speak well is to be drawn more and more deeply into reality; it is an acquired power, but one which is ordered from the beginning, and its order is a reception of a principle that lies beyond it, outside of its control. We might call this even more basically an example of *authority*, as distinct from power simply: it is an author-ship, that amplifies (*augere*) the reality to which it is entrusted.[151] There is a natural subordination, here, of rhetoric to philosophy, and the power to *speak well* takes on in a basic way an inherently "martyric" aspect: to speak is of its very essence to bear witness to the truth.[152]

The trafficking of rhetoric, that is, the commodifying of the specific skill of speaking well, which is the distinct mark of sophistry, reveals its deeper significance in contrast to the "Platonic" notion of the word. Plato is reluctant to categorize rhetorical power (in the sophistical sense) as a *skill*, or a *technē*, since *technē* is a form of knowledge, which means that, of its essence, it implies a subordination of a power to the good of the object to which the power is directed.[153] He calls it instead an "ἐμπειρεία,"[154] a word difficult to translate in this particular context but meant to represent a kind of practical capacity acquired without knowledge, that is, in relative abstraction from the intrinsic meaning of any particular object. It is crucial to see that Plato is not making a point ad hominem; in other words, he is not criticizing the sophists *personally*, charging them with possessing less knowledge than other people (for example, the philosophers!). Instead, the point concerns the very nature of rhetoric, conceived as power—and thus of words, and thus of human nature, of the soul, of justice, and thus of the cosmos simply, and thus of man's ultimate relation to God[155]—as the sophist understands it. In the sophistical view, rhetoric is a marketable skill, and it is marketable because it is in itself a power that can be applied to whatever the possessor may wish. You first learn how to speak well, the sophist explains, and then you are free to learn other subjects to which you can apply this skill, or you can use it to be successful in any other pursuit or profession.

What, then, does "speaking well" mean in the context of sophistry? It does *not* mean making manifest the truth of the reality it seeks to express, except perhaps *per accidens*. One of course hopes that this skill would be used to say true things.[156] But truth does not belong to its *essence*; it is not intrinsic to the *kalōs* character of speech. Instead, to speak well means here to speak *persuasively*—about whatever it is one happens to be speaking (let us hope it is the truth). What does *this* mean? It is not the Platonic sense of persuasion: to persuade for Plato is to enable one to see what is true and assent to it freely, rather than to coerce one into the acceptance of an idea. To persuade in the abstract rhetorical sense, by contrast, simply means to *succeed* in causing a person to hold an opinion that one wants him to hold. The essence of persuasion, in other words, is not just "active power" as the ability to bring about an effect, but indeed essentially *blind* power, because knowledge is not an indispensable ingredient in it. Instead, if knowledge is present at all in this power it is only because it happens to accompany that power incidentally. To the extent that it is nonessential, however, it cannot *be* knowledge in the authentic sense, and likewise persuasion, so understood, cannot ever communicate *truth*, because if it does so it is only incidentally, and this is contrary to the nature of truth. One can coercively persuade a person to a true opinion, but, to the extent that the holding of it is the result of coercion, the person does not hold it *precisely as true*.[157]

Here we arrive at the heart of the matter: power, so conceived, is essentially averse to truth. Truth, in the end, means a priority of actuality as what is, as giving a context, a greater whole, *into* which human agency, as intellect and will, and in all of the political institutions and cultural phenomena in which that agency is embodied, is inserted, so that the "power" of this agency may magnify that order. If instead potency is *removed* from this context as something *intelligible in itself*, as producing its own ends, determining its own form, and actuating its own effects, then actuality cannot but represent its opposition. In this case, it has to eliminate actuality, whether it be by dissolving it, by outwitting it, or by rendering it neutral and defusing any a priori claims it might present. The problem, of course, is that these strategies cannot help but backfire: they not only make power empty but also make that emptiness in a sense the only thing power has left going for it, which leads power to cultivate its own downfall.

There is a tendency, with power, to detest any limit. John Dewey described the difference between the ancient and the modern world as a replacement of natural limit by power:

> Our present feeling that associates infinity with boundless power, with capacity for expansion that knows no end, with the delight in a progress that has no external limit, would be incomprehensible were it not that interest has shifted from the esthetic to the practical; from interest in beholding a harmonious and complete scene to interest in transforming an inharmonious one. One has only to read the authors of the transition period, say Giordano Bruno, to realize what a pent-in, suffocating sensation they associated with a closed, finite world, and what a feeling of exhilaration, expansion and boundless possibility was aroused in them by the thought of a world infinite in stretch of space and time.[158]

The feeling of "suffocation," however, is not just a response to an outer limit, a boundary at the furthest regions. Instead, once the principle of limit, and therefore intrinsic order, is denied, then *any* limit, no matter how small, becomes an oppressive burden. Goethe illustrated just this point in his portrayal of Faust, the symbol of the modern man, at the end of his life, surveying his accomplishments. Faust had managed to subdue the world through a relentless exercise of power—"Before my eyes my realm is boundless" (Faust, line 11153)—but there remains on the horizon a tiny little cabin, with a wind chime on the porch, inhabited by an aged couple who offer hospitality to the strangers who wander the land. It is the one thing in his line of vision that is not under his sway, and he cannot bear it. He becomes obsessed with the cabin, not because it represents something he desires, but only because its very existence stands as an affront to his power, a boundary placed on what would otherwise be a boundless ocean: "The will's omnipotent command / Like surf it breaks upon the sand. / How can I rid myself and breathe! / The bell but tinkles, and I seethe!" (11255–58).[159] And so, suffocating like the founders of modernity that Dewey described, he orders his men to burn the little cabin to the ground, with the elderly couple and their guest within.

Power, as such, cannot integrate or join with what is other than itself in a larger whole. To accept any limitation at all is therefore to change the very nature of power. This is why, for example, the most modest critique of technology, the slightest proposal for an a priori limit on the scope of medical research, the slightest hint of "censorship" of the press, and so forth, is inevitably greeted with a reaction one would have to call "unhinged."[160] This is because at issue is never the desirability of any particular thing in itself—this possible medical procedure, which does not yet show much use,[161] this little bit of pornography, and so forth—but the very meaning of the world. Because of this necessary contempt for limits and the rejection of order, the refusal to participate in a whole greater than oneself, the possessor of power, thus understood, is at odds, not only with himself but with all other things: "For neither to any of his fellow men can such a person be dear (φιλῆς), nor to God; for he is powerless to participate in community (κοινωνεῖν γὰρ ἀδύνατος), and where there is no community, there is no friendship."[162] Without community, such a person remains essentially outside in every context. Such a person is turned in opposition (δια-βάλλω) to anything and everything real. Radicalized internal opposition is the essence of power once it is severed from actuality. And this severance from actuality is what defines power when it refuses to define itself in terms of the order that precedes it. No matter how well regulated, a society of such people is, to use Kant's phrase, "a society of devils."

GOD AND (IN) THE FLESH

We will end this chapter by pointing to the extreme ends of the concrete realization of modern liberty, both in the outward, public sphere, and the most inward and private: on the one hand, we have what is called "freedom of religion," and, on the other, the freedom with respect to the meaning of one's own body. As John Paul II intuited almost a generation ago, there is a profound connection between God and the body.[163] Our purpose here is to set this connection at least somewhat into relief.

Our argument has been that a genuinely symbolical order—an acknowledgment of a radical generosity at the heart of things and the subsequent implication of things' *belonging together* in principle—rests on the recognition of the relative priority of actuality over possibility, which means in turn a re-cognition of the priority of the *given qua given*. It is not an accident that classical thought culminates in a notion of God as pure act: this ultimate principle of the cosmos cannot, itself, lie in a state of potency, which as such would require an even more ultimate principle to raise it to actuality. Now, there are to be sure many further and *decisive* questions raised by the notion of God as pure act—for example, whether pure act excludes potency, and, if not, how potency and act are related in God—which would require further exploration in another setting. The point in the present context, however, is simply to see that a meaningful cosmos depends on a principle of absolute meaningfulness, however else it may be qualified. This principle, by its nature, is absolutely first, which means it precedes all other considerations without exception and thereby represents a necessary reference point for those considerations.[164]

Given this absolute priority, there can be no more momentous claim than the Christian one; it is that-than-which-nothing-more-decisive-can-be-thought: God has become incarnate, which is to say that the pure actuality of the absolute first principle, the radical generosity that is the source of *all* things, has entered into history, and indeed as a "powerless" child. The implications of this claim are overwhelming in both their breadth and depth, and we make no claim at all to sound them out. We intend only to point out that, as a consequence, the absolutely first, which represents the given reference point for all other considerations, is in Christianity no longer *merely* a transcendent first principle (though it *always* remains *also* that[165]) but also a particular history, an event in time, which makes all other events meaningful in relation to it.[166] God is eternal, as pure act, but not as timeless; instead, the Incarnation represents the "fullness of time" (πλήρωμα τοῦ χρόνου; Gal. 4:4). The point for our present purposes is that actuality, even in its supratemporality, now also and decisively has a historical form. This claim raises the stakes, as it were, for there cannot be a response to this event without ultimate metaphysical implications. It is no longer possible to reflect adequately on fundamental questions, such as the meaning of human freedom, without reckoning with the significance of historicity, not in the rather abstract Heideggerian sense, but quite concretely in the form of a recognition of tradition.[167]

It is not an accident that the birth of liberal political theory occurs precisely as a response to the claim of the Christian event, and even more specifically the significance of the tradition that grows from it, in the aftermath of the so-called wars of religion.[168] It purports to solve the problem of violence, at least at the level of political order. But we have to see that liberalism is *not* a solution to violence, however it may seem on the surface, and that it turns out to destroy infinitely more than it pretends to preserve. It is said that there is no other fair and peaceable response to the problem of religious pluralism, which is an undeniable fact of the modern world. But we must already be wary of characterizing the issue here as the problem of "religious pluralism," because doing so threatens to push one outside of the tradition and its given claims in order to survey the historical situation from above—the "view from nowhere," which is in fact and in spite of its self-understanding a radically presumptuous "God's-eye view"—as presenting a variety of "religious options." In other words, to frame the problem as the potential violence of religious pluralism is *already* to accept liberalism as the solution, because it is to accept the terms that liberalism itself sets.[169] Instead, a solution to the problem of violence must be sought *within* the tradition, and so always with reference to the priority of actuality: in subordination to the standards of truth, goodness, and beauty rather than most basically as a negotiation of power. We cannot of course enter into this reflection here, since it must be recognized as a profound, delicate, and weighty issue that requires a great deal of patience and care,[170] but we can at least point out why liberalism, the opening up of options, is itself, so to speak, *not an option*. However one works out the details, one thing is clear: to render what is ultimate—the nature of God as first principle of the cosmos—a matter of options, to be decided privately by the individual, is to *reject* as a matter of principle, and without any further recourse or possibility of discussion, God's *actual entry into history*, and so indeed God's nature as supreme actuality. To reject this is to reject the priority of actuality simply. It is a powerful deception to insist that liberalism in its merely political or juridical form is not a rejection of the Christian claim,[171] because that claim remains a protected possibility for the individual to recognize in freedom, but this is indeed a deception: it is a contradiction, a deep and epoch-making contradiction, to render absolutely actual a possibility *as merely possible*.[172] What becomes absolutely actual, in this case, is the power to choose, but *only as a power*, and never as a really real actuality. In this case, one may indeed be able to recognize Jesus as one's personal Lord and Savior, but it is not possible, no matter how sincerely one may intend it, to recognize him *as God*. The deception succeeds, however, because the very elimination of actual significance, ontological depth, and so genuine objective, political *form*, allows such a profession of faith to proliferate without any real (!) obstacles.

But religious freedom in the sense just described—namely, as the rendering of the nature (and eventually the existence) of God a possibility to be "actualized" by the private wills of individuals—represents *the ultimate seal of the diabolical*. Human dignity rests on the fact that, when the social order breaks down, in the face of oppression and the blind force of power, one can always take a stand on truth. But if the ultimate ground of truth is itself suspended in the empty space of possibility, if it is thus made nothing more than an option, then there *is* no place to stand. There is nothing outside of liberalism, no reality beyond its borders, to which it is subordinate.[173] Its very form is such that it (paradoxically) has no limits. Here we are back inside Plato's cave. The essence of the diabolical, we have suggested, is a co-opting of the reality it pretends to represent: as distinct from the image that points beyond itself and so becomes, as it were, more vividly real in itself the more transparent it is to what transcends it, the diabolical is a self-enclosed system that parasitically derives the energy for its self-enclosure from the reality that it essentially excludes even as it cannot cease to reference. There is thus no incompatibility between the deep neutralizing of religion and the surface cultivation of it.[174] The freedom of religion that speaks everywhere of God, or at least a "higher power," that promotes worship and charitable acts, above all "social justice," that encourages a spirituality, though evidently not a religiosity, is the devil's final triumph.

Power, in this case, becomes—to all appearances at least—limitless by its very (natureless) nature. Not only is there no transcendent reality that would present, so to speak, an outermost boundary, but for the same reason there is no immanent or internal boundary that can be taken as given. A direct expression of this dissolution of limit even with respect to what is most intimate is the evacuation of the body of any meaning of its own, any symbolic depth of significance that would present itself as a prior reference point for the intelligibility of choices. With the rejection of the transcendent entering into the flesh comes the rejection of the flesh entering into the transcendent—that is, presenting deep and substantial significance. The body is no longer recognized as manifesting an *order*, a given meaning, possessing a unique eloquence, but has become dumb stuff, which is either passively submitted to as a kind of oppressive power (to the extent that it is actual), or it is taken to be a matter able to be manipulated in the service of purposes external to it. The proposal that gender has nothing to do with the body, that gender is not given as an innate dimension of one's reality, but is a matter left up to the individual to decide, would have seemed absurd only ten years ago but has now gathered a sort of momentum. One senses in this momentum a kind of restless energy, which evinces a deep-seated anxiety. The political movement is quite tangibly *not* witnessing to a self-evident truth, but the desperate and relentless repetition that comes from the effort to bring about something that is, in the end, intrinsically impossible: a complete deception of oneself and others concerning what is real. The desperate urgency of this force is due to the fact that such a view of the body—and the whole of reality implied in it—can never acquire the support of objective and all-embracing truth, since it is precisely this that has been excluded in principle.

It is important that we see how diabolical is this apparent power over ourselves. What is at stake is not the well-being of the few, those who for whatever reason, beyond their control, suffer from what is called "gender confusion," who ought to have the right to the same "comfort with one's identity" that the majority possess who are free from such confusion. Instead, the stakes are universal: to make gender simply a matter of choice for some—in fact, for any at all—is to eliminate the meaning of the body for everyone. The existence of "transgender" transforms the act of *not* changing one's gender into the taking of a political position: one becomes "cisgender." Just as an optional religion can never actually *be* a religion at all, no matter how enthusiastically affirmed, so too an "optional" gender can never be a gender as the *truth* of one's body, because truth represents an actuality that necessarily precedes choice. But to present the changing of one's gender in any case as an option is to transform the acceptance of gender in every other case as the exercise of a *different* option, rather than the straightforward response to what is given as real. *Transgender* thus becomes the standard for sexuality in general—and "trans" here is meant in the sense of actively effecting a change.[175] Thus, Bruce Jenner, as he unveiled himself to the world as "Caitlyn," announced that "I am the new normal." Of course, "new normal," properly understood, is an oxymoron, and what is in truth "normal" does not have to announce itself as such and insist on that fact—except perhaps in an age in which order is fundamentally under siege. It is significant that this, the *real* "sexual revolution," is above all a political movement, on the one hand, and a paradigm of coercion through "freedom of the press," on the other. What is not an organic expression of reality, emerging freely from roots in nature, has to be imposed from the outside and regulated through the force of purely positive law.

At the most fundamental level, the submission of the flesh to empty power comes to expression in biotechnology, more specifically, in the possibility of manipulating the human genome, which is just now making its cultural appearance.[176] If there is no basic reality that is given, and which as such presents a prior claim on our freedom, then even our biological origins fall in principle under our control, regardless of how much this possibility may continue to elude us practically speaking. There is a deep connection between the givenness of our theological origin and the givenness of our biological origin: one cannot stand for long once the other has been denied. When our very genetic code, the actual order at our foundation, is turned into an *option*—which like everything else we have seen carries with it a totalizing logic, changing the nature even of what is left apparently untouched and in place—we reach a kind of perfection of the diabolical: the paradigmatic figure of the diabolical is a self-consuming substance. Here we allow to the essence of man only power over the essence of man, which is to say that man is dissolved in unhuman power, and he becomes the animal that cancels itself out.

And so we come full circle. We began this book with an exploration of Locke's notion of the will as something simultaneously omnipotent and impotent; in the phenomenon of the "transhuman," man appears simultaneously as the all-powerful technician and the helpless product.[177] This is a kind of antiredemption, a diabolical inversion of the perfect sacrifice of Christ, who is at once priest and victim. Pure power and utter powerlessness now converge into one, and man becomes the abject servant of his own limitless freedom, a passive object of active power: a slave of modern liberty.

PART THREE

Retrieving the Origin
as the Essence of Freedom

CHAPTER 6

Starting Over and Starting After

A First Foundation in Plato and Aristotle

THE ANCIENT SOURCE OF HOPE

In an interview he gave toward the end of his life, Heidegger was asked whether there was any hope for the world, given his fundamental critique of Western civilization as an absolute technological state, and he famously responded, "Only a god can still save us!"[1] As he sees it, there is nothing that any individual can *do* to save the world from its fate, and even thinking itself has become in this respect powerless: its highest function can now be nothing more than "preparing a readiness . . . for the appearance of the god or for the absence of the god in the decline."[2]

Heidegger is often, and certainly with some justice, criticized himself for advocating a kind of ultimate quietism with respect to the movement of history.[3] It may seem that the more radical the critique of a culture and its institutions, the less possibility of hope, so that one who wishes to avoid falling into a sterile contempt and paralysis of will would want to mitigate, if not the sharpness of cultural criticism, at least its depth. But, however reasonable this judgment may appear to be, we wish to suggest that it turns out to be self-defeating, because it is the very *radical* character of the criticism, in this case, that opens up to genuine hope. We make this suggestion not because of the putatively regenerative capacities of crisis, of the "nothing," which seems to be Heidegger's position—"But where danger is, grows / The saving power also"[4]—but for the exact opposite reason: the absoluteness of actuality. The reason for hope is that an ontological critique, rather than a merely moral one—or in other words, a critique of the understanding of reality that lies at the root of all our acting, rather than simply a critique of certain choices, values, and so forth, which would take the modern understanding of reality as a necessary given, if not also as a positive good—does not allow the problem itself to set the ultimate terms for its resolution. Instead, such a critique *essentially* relativizes the problematic terms by placing them up against the measure of reality in itself.

Gabriel Marcel made the profoundly insightful observation that hope is fundamentally excluded to the extent that we limit possibility to the power of our own action; hope does not depend ultimately on us alone.[5] This does not mean that hope is a function of a divine intervention in the mode of magic, wholly discontinuous with the nature of reality itself, which would reduce us to emptying the stage for the possible *deus ex machina*: "Only a god can save us!" Quite the contrary, hope in the deepest sense does not depend most fundamentally on us because it is first rooted in truth itself, in the very *nature* of reality as already given. And this leads us to see why a genuinely ontological critique, in spite of its radical depth, is more hopeful than a merely moral one. It may seem that, if nothing else, I can at least have some confidence about changing *myself* and *my* actions, and so limiting my critique to such things as I can effect through my own discrete choices would allow me to have a certain optimism regarding the future. But there is a paradox here: a moral critique looks ultimately to the practical consequences, and perhaps the implications of ideas, rather than ultimately to the intrinsic meaning of things: and practical consequences—even of our *own* actions *alone*—are never in our control. To base hope on what we ourselves are able to change is to seal ourselves in a self-undermining dialectic. We are, here, back inside a diabolical conception of freedom, and despair is the very "essence" of the diabolical. By contrast, the recognition of a reality that transcends my actions, and by implication, anyone's and everyone's actions, is itself already an act of hope. Such a recognition is a kind of entrusting of ourselves to a goodness that, so to speak, has always already conquered every attempt to subjugate it.

It is interesting to return for a moment, in this light, to the confrontation between Socrates and the sophists in the *Gorgias*, which we discussed at the beginning and end of chapter 5. Socrates shows a re-markable freedom in the midst of the onslaught from his three aggressive interlocutors, and he calmly acknowledges Polus's point—which was made with the intention of *forcing* a concession—that, regardless of the question of the truth, Socrates's position is simply ineffectual: *no one* is going to accept his view that power is impotent and that it is better to suffer injustice than to commit it. In the court of popular opinion, he will always lose, and whatever may speak in his favor is impotent in relation to this particular juridical body.[6] His position, in other words, is practi-cally speaking *hopeless*. But Socrates responds that, if one clings to the truth alone, one can never be separated from it,[7] and so he reveals the im-potence of coercive force as what it is *in truth*. For Socrates, the point is not in the first place to persuade the many but to avoid being divided in himself—*not* because his own integrity is his primary concern, but be-cause this internal harmony itself bears witness to objective truth.[8] Moreover, to the extent that the position Socrates holds is in fact the truth, he can calmly show that his interlocutors always-already agree with him, which means that his task is not to persuade them of one alter-native rather than another, but to call them to recognize what they al-ready know to be true in spite of themselves. Thus, he begins, *in friend-ship*,[9] by explaining to Polus that he will show how Polus's disagreement with Socrates is actually a disagreement with himself. And after he suc-ceeds in doing so (a point that Polus concedes only with great reluctance, of course[10]), he responds in turn to Callicles's outraged intervention:

> Either refute [philosophy] . . . or else, if you leave this unrefuted, then by the Dog, the god of the Egyptians, *Callicles will not agree with you, Callicles*, but will be dissonant with you all your life long. And yet, for my part, my good man, I think it's better to have my lyre or a chorus that I might lead out of tune and dissonant, and have the vast majority of men disagree with me and contradict me, than to be out of harmony with myself, to contradict myself, though I'm only one person.[11]

Note that Plato gives priority to an internal transformation, through recognition of what is true, over the outward production of practical effects, or a concern with popular influence.

The point is more significant than may initially be apparent with respect to the general argument we are making in this book. Socrates does not first aim at *persuading* his interlocutors, in the sense of *producing a change*, that is, bringing about through his own causal activity a new state of affairs that differs from the previous one. To make this one's principal aim, to think that this is the essential issue, is already to concede a notion of will, and so freedom, akin to Locke's, which we have sought to show is diabolical insofar as it gives primacy to potency *over* act. If, by contrast, actuality is recognized as having relative priority over potency, then *change is not the first concern*. Instead, the most fundamental act is understanding, which is first a receiving of what is rather than a production of something new. To say this is not at all to deny the importance of bringing about change—after all, Socrates does want to convince Polus and the others—but only to insist that change be a kind of natural fruit of understanding, not simply in the sense that one must have correct information in order to be able to work most effectively; instead, as we will argue in this last part of the book, liberation is most basically a reawakening to our rootedness in reality, so that truth, goodness, and beauty can become effective *in us*. In this regard, coming to a proper understanding of the true nature of freedom is not just the first step in a larger project, to be filled out with the more obviously urgent concrete applications and concrete proposals. Instead, it is already everything; it is the whole aim, the essential task—though this is not to say that our work simply ends here. Coming to understand freedom, in other words, is not just a necessary condition for the efforts to *become* free, but properly understood it is already itself an essential act of freedom. Understanding freedom and being free are all but inseparable from one another.[12]

What we have said has implications for the approach required for a proper critique of modernity, and it also explains why we end this book, as we do, specifically with a discussion of Plato and Aristotle. As for modernity, we mentioned at the beginning of chapter 5 that the essential response to the diabolical is not execution but exorcism, which, we argued, means a reorienting of the given reality to what is good and true. This observation takes on a greater weight in light of our point above: to think that we can stray absolutely from reality is to fail to grasp what reality is. According to the classical tradition articulated in the Middle Ages, the transcendentals—unity, truth, goodness, and beauty—are convertible with being: all things are good, true, beautiful, and one *insofar as they exist*. We do not have to re-create truth and goodness as a response to the diabolical: as we already observed, we absolutize it to the extent that we think we do. Darth Vader persuaded Luke to attack the Dark Side precisely as a way of bringing him over to it. Our response to cultural crises must always first take the form of a grateful affirmation of what is given. This is the perennial human task, though it takes on different forms in different ages according to the principle of analogy.

Modernity poses a special problem in this regard, insofar as it does not represent simply one historical period among others (antiquity, Middle Ages, Renaissance, etc.). What is distinctive about modernity is that, in contrast to other periods, it *defines itself precisely as breaking with the tradition*.[13] The importance of this point cannot be exaggerated. One might think that a critique of modernity necessarily arises from nostalgia, a sentimental attachment to the old simply because it is old. But to think this is to misunderstand completely the argument we are making. Romantic nostalgia is silly; it makes no sense to oppose the old to the new, because the old only ever exists in a new form or new context, and the new is always ultimately the fruit of the old. To think that a critique of modernity is necessarily nostalgic, a kind of idiosyncratic preference for the old, is to adopt as absolute the terms set by modernity, according to which old things and new things are various options, detached from context—which means, uprooted from tradition—from among which one then makes an arbitrary choice. To affirm the goodness of modernity, in an ontological sense, requires a recovery of its roots in the tradition. But because modernity defines itself against tradition, affirming the goodness of reality in it involves a much more radical "no" to it than the other periods: as Spaemann has so insightfully put it, saving modernity requires us to "interpret modernity against itself."[14] We bring to light the *good reality* of modernity fruitfully by reinserting it, so to speak, back into the tradition, of which it nevertheless remains a part, willy-nilly, in spite of its self-deception. To reconnect (συμ-βάλλω) the notions, values, and institutions of modernity with their roots in the tradition is precisely to liberate modern liberty.

It should be evident, from all of this, why we end this book with Plato and Aristotle: though they are not, of course, the first philosophers—quite significantly, they understood *themselves* already to be heirs of an ancient tradition[15]—they nevertheless represent, we

might say, the two great doors of the gateway into the philosophical tradition, and they are in any event the first to reflect philosophically on
the meaning of freedom.[16] A radical critique, which is for just that reason genuinely hopeful, must go back to the origins *both vertically and
horizontally*, both in ontological depth and in time. Though we cannot
explore the matter here, there seems to be a connection between the
openness to metaphysics and openness to the philosophical tradition
precisely as such.[17] We end with the beginning *because* actuality is prior
to potency, and the negation implied by the isolation of potency as
such—the negativity of the diabolical—therefore cannot stand as the
last word. The last word must always be given to what is in truth first:
the good.[18]

   If it is evident why we end with the beginning in classical Greek
thought, it may be less evident why we address Plato *and* Aristotle,
rather than just the latter alone. This question may arise because so
many of the discussions of the origin of the notion of freedom and the
will in Western thought begin with Aristotle and leave Plato out of the
discussion altogether, or present Plato primarily as a foil.[19] We suggest
that the tendency to conceive of the origin of freedom in this way is a
symptom of the very understanding we mean to criticize. In a word, the
intellectual histories that begin with Aristotle tend to take for granted a
diabolical concept of freedom, to one degree or another, as normative—
not because Aristotle himself has a diabolical conception (far from it),
but because he introduces what may at least be interpreted as the begin-
nings of a sort of spontaneous arbitrariness, which comes to full flourishing only later (perhaps in St. Paul,[20] or in the Stoics,[21] or most often
and most evidently in Augustine[22]). To simplify the issue somewhat, the
argument typically assumes that to be free means to have a power to determine ourselves *as opposed to* (δια-βάλλω) being determined by something outside the power of the self, and so one looks for evidence of a
break with the given, evidence of this assertion of power over against
the "heteronomous" causality.[23] In this approach to the origin of freedom, a disproportionate place is given to the phenomenon of *akrasia*,
the choosing *against* what one sees to be good, and the internal division
such a choice entails. It is worth meditating on the implications of this
(all-too-common) approach: divergence from a good order is supposed
to be an unmistakable sign of freedom, to reveal something about its

essence. Aristotle, from this perspective, opens the way to the modern notion because of the importance he gives to self-determining "choice" (προαίρεσις), in relative distinction from our "theoretical" knowledge of what is good, and Augustine, with his great existential crisis, is offered as a kind of *paradigm* of freedom in its mature form, to such an extent that one defines freedom precisely as the capacity to sin.[24] Such a formulation is quite obviously diabolical, but it simply makes explicit the implicit drift of the most common view of freedom, among scholars and lay people alike: namely, the view that freedom has something to do *most basically* with the ability to *change* what is given, and so to disrupt a given order. We recall that, for Locke, remaining in a particular state is not an actual act of will, which always produces a change in response to some *unease*.

As we hope to make clear, the reason we go to Plato first is that we are seeking to get behind, so to speak, the distinction between autonomy and heteronomy, so that each of these dimensions—which are not meant to be simply *con-fused*—can be understood in a sound and sane way as intrinsically related. Moreover, in a sense that will turn out to be inseparably connected with the first point, we wish to show that the question of freedom is an ontological one before it is a matter of psychology, or a moral or political reality. It is true that neither Plato nor Aristotle has a notion of a *will* as a separate faculty of the soul, but we wish to suggest that the lack of this separation, though not by itself an adequate final statement regarding the nature of freedom, nevertheless bears witness to a dimension that is indispensable to such a statement. The faculty can be properly understood only secondarily, principally as a kind of fruit of the relation to reality, rather than as the spontaneous cause *by which* the soul relates itself (or not) to reality, which is conceived of as lying outside of, and so at a distance from, the self-contained self.[25] In other words, we propose that the soul is first of all constituted *in* relation to reality, and that the notion of the will, the distinctness of which does indeed require affirmation, needs to be unfolded *from inside* the soul's reception of reality in reason and desire, rather than through the introduction of a separate power from the outside, as a *mere addition to* the powers that, for example, Plato and Aristotle recognized in the soul. Finally, and implied in all of this, we ought to see that the interpretation of the nature of freedom is most basically an interpretation of the nature of the good. And so it is with Plato that we most properly begin.[26]

It is worth pointing out, however, that if we conclude this book with Plato and Aristotle, we do not mean thereby to suggest that they represent by themselves a fully adequate response to the problem we have sought to bring to light in the preceding chapters.[27] This can hardly be the case, given the genuine development in thought since their time. We intend to show that there is *indeed* in the Greeks an insufficient sense of the genuine novelty of human action, as Arendt so memorably showed,[28] and that this inadequacy is due to an inadequate conception of the primacy of actuality, a conception that tends to reduce potency to act in such a way that potency, so to speak, "adds nothing" *simpliciter*. In *this* respect, it is quite true, and importantly true, that, as Hegel observed, Plato and Aristotle failed to understand and appreciate that man as such is free.[29] It would be possible to show that modernity arose in part as an attempt to compensate for this inadequacy in the classical tradition. One might show that the cluster of tensions that arise around this point ultimately bear on, and require a certain resolution of, the Trinitarian and Christological controversies that were faced in the early Church; indeed, they ultimately require the drama of God's own assumption of the negation of the diabolical in himself for the sake of re-orienting it to the good—the most comprehensive interpretation of modernity against itself. But it nevertheless remains the case that all of this would be misconceived if we interpret it as *overturning* the primacy of the good, of the metaphysical dimension of freedom and its inseparable connection to reason, that we have in Plato and Aristotle, rather than transforming all of that *from within*. If there is a "discovery of the will" as something genuinely new in the history of thought, it will nevertheless be the uncovering of a reality found inside of human reason. In this respect, attempting to re-conceive freedom, after Locke, requires our receiving the classical Greek tradition.

FREEDOM AT THE ORIGIN

As Plato famously observed in the *Meno*, you cannot look for something unless in a certain respect you have already found it;[30] we must accordingly have some sense of what freedom is before we can explore its meaning in Plato and Aristotle. The tendency in this endeavor, as we just mentioned, is to take a conventional contemporary notion as a norm by which to measure ancient thought. The classic text in this area is also a classic example of this problem: for all of its great insight and matchless erudition, Albrecht Dihle's book takes for granted a very modern view of the will, which could be called "libertarian."[31] Ironically, Michael Frede, who points up this problem in Dihle and writes a series of lectures of his own to correct it, quite clearly falls into the same trap, as one of his reviewers pointed out.[32] The reason he does so is simply because the trap is unavoidable, as the *Meno* paradox makes clear. Best, then, to *sin boldly*, to step into the trap with eyes open, so to speak: we will articulate the notion of freedom we are seeking but will go to the roots to get our bearing, and then aim at a view based on the ancient sense of reality, which anticipates the further development in specific thinkers and stands as a genuine contrast to the Lockean notion of freedom and the will, rather than trying to identify a "universally acceptable" notion, through a minimalistic methodology, which cannot help landing on the liberal view we have been criticizing.[33] The view we propose will therefore be "maximalist," one might say, an attempt to begin with a *full* sense of freedom, in the light of which we are able to interpret and judge the developments, even as we unfold that sense in turn in their light. Such a view of freedom cannot justify itself, perhaps, in abstraction, but will have to show its worth over the course, not only of the rest of this chapter, but also of the two that follow.

As different from each other as the words "freedom," "libertas," and "ἐλευθερία" appear to be at first glance, they actually share an original principle. In contrast to an older hypothesis, according to which ἐλευθερία arose from the root ἐλυθ-, ἐλευθ- (the future perfect of ἔρχομαι), meaning "to go where one wishes," scholars are now generally in agreement that the Greek word derives from the Indo-European root *leudh-, from which comes the old Slavic and Germanic word for "people" (*Leute*, etc.).[34] This root also gave rise to the Gothic (*liudan*) and Indo-Iranian (Sanskrit: *rudh–*; Avetic: *rud–*) verbs for "grow" and "develop."[35] The general consensus, thus, is that the adjective ἐλεύθερος means "belonging to a people or a common stock."[36] It is not hard to see the connection between this etymological root and the sense of the term most familiar in Greek literature,[37] namely, the political distinction between the freeman and the slave: the freeman belongs to the city, and the slave was, so to speak, imported from elsewhere. The determining factor is origin. Metics, who do not have the condition of life we normally associate with slavery, nevertheless are not free men;[38] the distinguishing mark of the freeman is not first the content of a person's activity (in many ways nobles did the same work as slaves[39]), but the relation of blood, of birth, and the status that it implies. In this context, what defines a political community, in which one participates as a freeman, is not just the external organization that brings various individuals into coordinated activity, but first internal relation: that is, it has natural roots in the organic unity of a people. This natural origin is what gives freedom its most basic *positive* sense: "The first meaning is not, as one might be tempted to suppose, 'to be relieved of something'; it is that of belonging to an ethnic stock designated by a metaphor of organic growth."[40]

Robert Muller insightfully connects this positive meaning with the relatively common associations of freedom in its negative sense—freedom from constraint, and so forth—by emphasizing the organic sense of the term: freedom, he explains, means "unimpeded growth," the attainment of the full development of one's seed, as it were. To grow means to exceed limits, and therefore in a sense to transgress a set, external boundary.[41] We see immediately how this sense of freedom as a sort of internal impulse would imply "nonconstraint," though it is also clear that this negative sense is the derivative one, founded on the positive notion of an inward principle of growth. Nevertheless, the common association of freedom with a kind of independence becomes evident, since the achievement of growth implies a relative completeness, an individual integrity. If this is true, the unity of the people and the strength of the individual share a common source. With the organic sense of the term, in other words, we see the unity between the political sense (freedom as growing from the same stock) and the individual sense (freedom as a particular flourishing, which demands its own space).

But we can go deeper. The Latin adjective *liber, libera, liberum* ("free") bears an etymological connection with ἐλεύθερος,[42] and, like the Greek, is related to *origin* or *birth*. According to Richard Onians's brilliant study, what we might call the "natal" sense of the term brings unity to what would otherwise appear to be unrelated words: "*liber*, the term applied to a man or to his head when the procreative spirit in him was naturally active thus, and *Liber*, the word used to designate the procreative or fertility god . . . were one, and . . . it originally expressed a natural state, a distinctive activity or attribute of the procreative spirit or deity."[43] The reason for the reference to the *head* is due, as Onians shows at length at various places in his book, to what we might call the ancient anthropology: the life seed, or fertile liquid, was thought to be contained in the head. It is this liquid, a sort of life spirit, that is poured out in joyous desire, in sexual intercourse, and it serves to unite the people of a family or tribe.[44] There is thus, in turn, a connection between *liberty* and *libation*, the pouring out of liquid in a celebratory religious ritual, and indeed between liberty and the "cognate libet or lubet, libido, etc., and German *lieben*, our own 'lief,' 'love,' and their obvious kin."[45] Further, this interpretation reveals a connection, which would otherwise be hard to make sense of, between *libertas* and the English "freedom" (and German *Freiheit*):

Anglo-Saxon *freó* not only means "free, noble" (of rank) but also occurs in the sense and must mean in the first place "having desire, joy"; for it is clearly related to *fréon*, "to love" (our "friend," German *Freund, Freier*, etc.). We may relate no less the variant *fri*, "free, noble," and *fria*, "lord, master," with *fria*, "to love"; and *frig*, "free, noble," with *frig*, "love, affection," and *Fríg*, the goddess of sexual desire or love and of fertility. The connection is not less clear in old Norse or Icelandic. There the word applied to those who are not slaves is *frjáls* (= *fri-hals*, where *hals* = "neck" . . .) or *frí*, but *frí* also means "lover" and *frjá* "sweetheart," and the physical aspect appears in *frjó, freó*, "seed" (Eng. "fry"), *frjór*, "fertile," etc. *Freyr* and *Freyja* (cf., *Fríg*), the names of the god and goddess of love, procreation and fertility . . ., are currently explained as merely expressions of rank: "lord, master" and "lady"; but we have seen that in these formations above (Anglo-Saxon *freó, fria*, etc., so Germ. *Frau*, etc.), those meanings are secondary to the sense "desiring, loving" and it is natural to believe (as in the case of *Liber* and *Fríg*) that these deities originally were singled out, from others no less exalted, to receive these names because the latter described just them, the powers of love and fertility.[46]

For his part, Onians intends to highlight the "physical" aspect of this etymology (though of course he has a rather profound sense of the meaning of matter), and this insistence is one of the standout features of his book. But we may propose a philosophical interpretation of this etymological archeology, and it is this interpretation that we adopt for the rest of our study. There is an evident connection between the organic imagery of growth and development that Muller evokes and the image of love and fertility that Onians presents. The connection is a life-expressing and -giving "super-fluity" or superabundance. A seed is a principle of life: it grows because, we might say, it contains in itself more than it is at any given moment. The classic image is emanation, a flowing out, an out-pouring, a spilling over, from a superabundant origin. The crucial point is an *excess*, which wells up *from within*, giving rise to a movement that passes from inside out. The notion of fertility is clearly implied in this: fruitfulness, so conceived, is an inner exuberance, which *generates*, multiplies, proliferates. The notion of generosity is likewise directly implied here, and of course the etymological connection with fertility is not an accident: generosity, generativity, generation, genitals (and so, for example, the French *gens*, "people"; cf. *Leute*, **leudh-*). This connection explains quite neatly a usage, found not only in Greek and Latin but still in modern European languages generally: namely, "liberality" as magnanimity, the spirit of unconstrained giving. The attempt to explain the connection between freedom and generosity by interpreting generosity as a typical characteristic of wealthy nobility, and associating nobility with the political class of freemen, is superficial and unconvincing (generosity is not obviously the defining characteristic of the noble taken simply as a social class[47]); the connection is spontaneous, however, the moment we see the procreative meaning of freedom: generosity as superabundance.

The notion of freedom as fruitful inner abundance also gives a natural interpretation of some of the more derivative senses of the term. If the heart of this interpretation is an excess that wells up from within, we understand immediately how self-movement would come to be seen as an expression of freedom; it is simply the translation of freedom into the terms of locomotion. There is an obvious connection here, which we will expand below, between freedom and nature, which, according to Aristotle's definition,[48] is an internal principle of motion and rest. A further positive sense that stems from this is the notion of *perfection* or *completion*.[49] Growth is not just an outward movement, mechanically conceived, as it were; it is instead teleological. Growth is an ordered movement, which flows *from* an internal principle and *therefore* toward an end. There is in fact no such thing as an internal principle of motion that would not *also be*, of necessity, a principle of rest. Purely mechanical motion, in contrast to organic development, is always imposed from the outside in some respect. To pick up on a point made by Muller, the growth implied by freedom can be interpreted with respect to its outcome, the achievement of full stature. In this sense, freedom represents the full flourishing of a nature.[50] We see here the "normative" dimension of freedom that is recognized at least in some expositions of classical views of freedom.[51]

From this positive sense of freedom, it is easy to render intelligible the negative sense, as we already noted above, namely, the absence of external constraints: anything that "stunts growth," or in other words that imposes itself from the outside, in such a way as to impede the natural flow, so to speak, from an internal principle, can be understood as a limitation of freedom. Thus, not only physical constraints but coercive laws, subjection to a master in slavery, or even the necessity of meeting needs that are imposed from the outside or that arise from internal deficiencies are all challenges or threats to freedom. It is a misunderstanding, but an intelligible one, that would associate freedom with a kind of lawlessness. Life has a certain "uncontrollable" quality to it, because it is not measured first by some external standard, but rather regulated by its own intrinsic principle. In any event, the basically positive sense of freedom also explains the derivative usage in the term "liberal arts": these are activities that are *intrinsically* good and so justify themselves without having to appeal to some external purposes. The practice of such arts, then, is an expression ultimately of internal exuberance rather than principally an effort required to meet some extrinsically imposed need or to bring completion to an internal deficiency.[52]

If we now attempt to account for the sense of freedom as choice, in the sense of "arbitrary" selection of some option rather than others, in other words, if we try to explain the meaning of "free will" in its usual connotations, along the line of the notion of freedom we are proposing here, we come up against a profound tension, which we will record at this point but will deal with more extensively later.[53] How do we account for the spontaneous novelty that such choice seems to imply? The tension is already implicit in the account we have just been giving, which can be formulated in a number of different ways. The source of this tension can be identified quite directly: the notion of an *internal excess* represents a paradox. If it is internal, it is contained and so cannot represent any real excess; if it is excess, it must go beyond what is already present internally. It is not an accident that the description we have offered of the original notion of freedom coincides perfectly with the classical understanding of goodness, which likewise exhibits a twofold character—indeed, a character that, at the limit, itself suggests a tension that might even be seen as a contradiction. On the one hand, in what seems to be the more ancient view, and which, as we will see, is more appropriate to associate with Plato,[54] we have the notion of goodness as a self-diffusive first principle, the ultimate cause of generation: goodness as generosity. On the other hand, we have the dimension that is more evidently associated with Aristotle, namely, goodness as finality. In this sense, goodness represents the *telos* toward which things strive, by which they are attracted, and in which they rest. And so we can formulate the tension thus: How do we reconcile the "Platonic" and the "Aristotelian" senses of goodness? The two senses are not simply opposed to each other, to be sure, but the tension between them is hard to deny. Is the outpouring of freedom *genuinely generative*, in the sense of giving rise to something *genuinely new*, or is the movement outward simply a "catching up" with what has always been the case, a simple unfolding of what is already priorily given?

We propose that the ultimate philosophical problem of freedom lies right here. The question of the origin of the will, as the faculty of spontaneous self-direction and choice, can itself be articulated in terms of this problem. Let us say, as we will below, that the foundation of freedom is the principle of an *original* and *eschatological* generosity, a generative outpouring that gives order to all existing things. The question, then, is the following: Is the first principle generative of what is radically other than itself, so that its actuality is productive of possibility, in the sense of allowing to the human soul the capacity to determine things actively, things that have not simply been determined "beforehand," straightforwardly prior to its existence? To put the matter more simply: Is God creative, and indeed so creative that he allows the goodness he gives to be codetermined by what is other than God? Or more simply still: Does God allow us to share in his fruitfulness? Our suggestion is that a proper notion of the will would have to be rooted in just this; properly understood, it is the active capacity to share in the intrinsic fruitfulness of the good, and *just so* is able to bring goods into being that are truly new and unanticipated.

As we just said, this is a problem that deserves to be studied in much greater depth in the context of Christian thought, a project we hope to take up in a future study. With respect to Plato and Aristotle, we intend to show the following. In the end, neither affirms the possibility of a truly radical novelty, and this is why neither can be said to have a notion of *will* in the fullest sense we have described. Curiously, Plato clearly affirms the first principle as *generous*, but he is quite explicit about denying the goodness of novelty and change,[55] and Aristotle famously gives a positive account of change to supplement the apparent lack in Plato, but he describes the First Mover, not principally as a "beginning," but as an *end*, the "first" mover only as that which draws all things to itself.[56] Nevertheless, we conclude this study with Plato and Aristotle, not in order to criticize them, but, as the chapter title has it, because they provide—we will suggest—the first foundation for a proper understanding of novelty and will. Without rooting this discussion of the will inside the ultimate priority of the good, and the relative priority of actuality over potency it implies, a collapse into an essentially diabolical conception of freedom is virtually inevitable. What Plato and Aristotle reveal about the nature of freedom, though not the final word, is a permanent word; it will remain indispensable for everything that will follow.

CHAPTER 7

Plato

The Golden Thread of Freedom

BELONGING TO THE GOOD

We offer here, not a study in the history of philosophy, but an *interpretation* of Plato on the question of freedom. Plato did not himself explore the question in any systematic way, though the theme is arguably more central in his thought than is typically assumed.[1] However this may be, it lies beyond our present scope to follow out a close analysis of each appearance of the term or its cognates in Plato's work, both because the questions that occupy us concern more than what Plato explicitly connected with the specific word himself and because our principal aim is to evoke a general sense of freedom in ancient philosophy, to stand as an illuminating contrast to what we have seen in Locke and in the cultural forms of modernity.

As many have observed, the most common usage of the term "freedom" in the classical Greek period is the political one,[2] which distinguishes between those who belong to the city in reality—the citizens, or "free" men—and those who do not: the slaves or foreigners of various sorts.[3] The key factor distinguishing them, as we pointed out in chapter 6, is, we might say, "lineage": the political status is the recognition of a natural belongingness, due to a common stock or blood line, which on the one hand binds the people together through a genuinely organic unity of "substance"—a unity expressed most memorably in

295

the "noble lie" of Plato's *Republic*, the purpose of which is to communicate in mythological form an underlying truth, namely, that the
members of a city are in a certain respect a *family*⁴—and on the other
hand enables the proper growth and flourishing of each individual. The
common origin and the resultant growth is freedom. Thus, in this conception, which we can call the traditional Greek one, the notion of the
οἰκεῖον becomes paramount, and so, too, the attendant notion of φιλία.
What is highest, here, is what belongs to one, what is one's own. Φιλία
is the "force" that binds things together and so binds one to one's own;
Homer, for example, speaks of φιλία as holding together the limbs of
one's body, an image that Empedocles famously takes over in his cosmology. The emphasis on "one's own" implies at least in some respect
the exclusion of what is "other." Given the twofold aspect of freedom—
belonging together by virtue of a common source and standing in relative independence by virtue of one's consequent flourishing—we see
that a certain problem therefore becomes almost inevitable. It is one
of the classic problems of political order: Which has primacy, the unity of
the *polis* or the integrity of the individual? Is one's bond (φιλία) first with
oneself or first with the community of which one is a part? Does οἰκεῖον
refer to one's self-relation or the self's relation to a larger οἶκος? How
"large" is, or what is the scope of, the "one" in the phrase "one's own"?

One of Plato's major accomplishments with respect to this question
is that, rather than simply taking sides, so to speak, he pushes the question to a deeper level, which radically transforms its terms. This shifting
of terms is, arguably, the very point of his masterpiece, the *Republic*, but
also runs through the rest of his work as one of its unifying threads. A
clear, explicit example can be found in the *Symposium*, where Plato reinterprets the conventional term οἰκεῖον as relative not to a particular individual, but *first to the good*: "I don't think an individual takes joy in
what belongs to him personally unless by 'belonging to me' (οἰκεῖον)
he means 'good' (ἀγαθὸν) and 'belonging to another' (ἀλλότριον) he
means 'bad' (κακὸν)."⁵ This reversal resonates throughout Plato's corpus; the point is to show, relentlessly, that truth has priority over the
inevitable partiality of merely particular perspectives.⁶ This point is a
way of putting the question that animates much of Plato's thought
from the center: What is justice?⁷ As Plato shows through the well-
known drama of the *Republic*'s opening book, the moment one charac-

terizes what is οἰκεῖον in the merely relative sense as highest, as the measure for everything else, even if one intends the higher unity of friendship or of the city, a collapse into polemical individualism is inevitable.[8] If one wanted to formulate Plato's notion of ultimate disorder in a single phrase, a strong candidate would be "the absolutizing of private interest" (τὸ ἴδιον), and therefore the prioritizing of this interest over the good of the whole.

It is in response to this particular problem that we can perhaps best understand Plato's transformation of the traditional political notion of freedom. In a nutshell, freedom for him is not first of all belonging to oneself, or even simply to one's city; instead, *freedom is belonging (with others) to the good.* In other words, more basic than our natural relations to city, family, and even self is the relation to *goodness simpliciter.* We need to add, immediately, that this relation is not meant simply to substitute for, or otherwise exclude, the natural relations without qualification (we will show in a moment that it makes them indispensable);[9] but the reorientation nevertheless relativizes them, that is, trumps their spontaneous tendency to absolutize themselves, by providing the proper context—let us call it the "free space"—in which to live these relationships fruitfully. As the passage from the *Symposium* makes clear, the issue is not to reject what is one's own, but to reveal that what is *most* one's own is . . . *the universal good*—which is "ownmost" for everyone.

What sort of relationship is this relation to the good? One is tempted to think that, if it transcends the relationships given in nature (κατὰ φύσιν), it would best be characterized as a moral bond rather than a "real" one, or in other words it would represent the obligation implied by a certain (unreal) ideal, rather than any sort of "physical thing." But while the relation to the good certainly is not a "physical thing" in the sense of a tangible object existing in time and space, this way of characterizing it is anachronistic and misses what is crucial. Plato does not, first of all, identify the natural with the sensible.[10] As he shows in the central books of the *Republic*, the intelligibles stand higher than the sensibles in the order of reality; the latter, in fact, *image* the former, in a manner analogous to the way a mirror presents an image of the reality it reflects. This is not to say that the image is unreal, but only that its reality is secondary, dependent on the causal presence of the reality being imaged.[11] The "divided line" he draws to articulate the hierarchy of being, the degrees of reality, from the most purely intelligible to the most purely sensible, represents a chain of ontological dependence.[12] Commenting on Plato, Proclus calls this chain of dependence the "Golden Chain" of *love*, associating it with the thread from which the world as a whole is suspended—the other end of which lies in the hand of Zeus.[13]

Proclus's interpretation is an apt one, for two reasons. First, it is not only the case that the various sensibles are bound to the various intelligibles in ontological dependence, but rather there is ultimately a single "chain" that binds *all* together (συμ-βάλλω) to a single principle, the sole absolute cause, namely, the good. As Plato puts it in the *Republic*, the good is the cause of the being and truth of everything that exists.[14] He illustrates this by pointing to the sun, an "analogy" that is generated by the good itself as its "real offspring."[15] Just as the golden rays of the sun pour forth from it, simultaneously illuminating all things in the cosmos and giving them life, so too is the good the principle of intelligibility and existence. We have here the very paradigm of the original notion of freedom, an overflowing superabundance, and we have to keep in mind through everything that follows that there is nothing more ultimate, for Plato (and, indeed, for Aristotle also, even if it is not as obvious) than this absolute principle of liberality. It is finally in reference to this principle that everything else makes sense.

Second, for reasons that are evident from the foregoing, Plato considers the good divine; it is his understanding of God. Of course, it is difficult to know the extent to which Plato adopted the mythological language of the gods and expressed the need for a pious deference—"the gods should be first in every man's words and thoughts"[16]—for the sake of his interlocutors and audience, but it is not at all obvious that we should assume a sort of Straussian separation between religion, for the masses, and philosophy, for the elite.[17] We will not enter into the controversy here, but it is worth pointing out that, if Plato does refer to God as the Father of all,[18] and if he identifies the divine craftsman (*Demiurge*) with goodness that does not refuse to share its perfection with all,[19] at the very least he is indicating an ultimate common origin in the good, the first principle of all things, the ultimate philosophical parentage of which the "noble lie" of the political family is itself simply an image (and which therefore becomes dangerous when absolutized). Can we say that the good is "personal"? The term itself is of course anachronistic here. In any event, though Plato hesitates, it seems, to speak of the good as an intelligent agent, he also hesitates to deny it, because, insofar as life and intelligence are perfections, they must *somehow* belong to the first principle of all things itself.[20] It is interesting to note that, when Plato speaks of our relationship to the first principle, he describes it, not as being a mere effect of some "impersonal" cause, but instead specifically as our *belonging* to the gods.[21]

In the *Laws*, Plato presents this "belonging to the gods" in a notorious image: we are, he says, *most ultimately* "play-things" (παίγνιον) of the gods or, more directly, *puppets* tied to their hands.[22] We can hardly read this passage without immediately taking offense at the indignity of being compared to a mere puppet, insofar as it seems to imply that man is a passive object, subject entirely to the "arbitrary will" of an "other."[23] But instead of interpreting this image directly in the typical modern terms of power and control, it is important to attend to the principal point Plato is trying to make here: the relationship to God is an ontological reality that, so to speak, enters into our very core and is "causally present" to and in us. It is not a mere unreal ideal or a mere object of moral intention, but instead lies as an actual reality at the foundation of our being. All of our desires, hopes, and fears, he says, are "strings" that attach our soul to things outside of it. But if these strings are hard and inflexible, the golden thread in the hands of the gods is unique precisely because it is "pliant."[24] The word "pliant" is clearly meant to soften the sense of control from the outside, but the question of "passivity" in this relationship remains an important one, and we need to give it more scrutiny.

The relation to God enters into the core of our being because the "puppet string" that places us in the hand of God, that binds us to the good, is not attached, so to speak, to our arms and legs, as a "physical" string would have to be; instead, it is attached to our *reason*, or more adequately put—and this is the heart of the matter for Plato—*it is our reason itself.*[25] The ray of the sun,[26] so to speak, that enters into the human soul *is* that soul's reason.[27] Plato does not think of reason in the first place as a "privately" possessed faculty, but rather as a power in the soul generated by the actual presence of the good. The good is the cause, or indeed originative source, not just of intelligible reality, but also specifically of the soul's "active power" to know.[28] The good thus, in what we might describe as a "symbolical" fashion, "yokes together" the soul with the things that it knows.[29] In his divided line, Plato shows, in a manner that strikingly anticipates the notion of intentionality in phenomenology, that there is a connection between the "powers" of the soul and levels of reality. Though he presents this as an epistemological connection in the context of the divided line image, it is clear that, in a moral or axiological key, something similar can be said for the three "parts" of the soul that he enumerates elsewhere in the text. Every desire is a desire for the good,[30] but the desires can be differentiated according to the particular *aspect* under which the good is desired in each case, and the "parts" of the soul can be distinguished accordingly: the "desiring" part of the soul (*epithumia*) corresponds to the good as expressed sensibly, the "spirited" part (*thumos*) corresponds to goodness as expressed in honor, and the "reasoning" part (*logos*) corresponds to . . . goodness simply.[31] In other words, the "rays of the sun" constitute the soul as a whole and in all of its parts, insofar as the powers respond to modes of being,[32] but reason is the good recognized precisely as such; it is the reception of goodness in its actual truth.[33] We might think of reason as the "organ" by which the soul perceives the good—or receives the good, since it does not simply refer to it across a distance as a "separate" object.

Resisting Freedom

With this characterization of reason, we are obviously separated by an almost infinite chasm from Locke's conception of reason as a subjective power by which we deliberate and come to our own conclusions. But the foreignness of the Platonic view might incline one immediately to *prefer* Locke's, even if only because it is more familiar (οἰκεῖον!), but also because it seems to allow more genuine freedom, as we typically understand the term. The Platonic notion of reason seems to take reason, so to speak, out of our own heads, and—how else to put it?—turn us into a mere puppet of the gods. It is true that Plato does indeed wish to insist—and not just *verbally*, as does Locke[34]—that we belong to

God more than to ourselves, but we need to recall not only that Locke's view leads *in reality* to the total destruction of any possibility of freedom, in spite of appearances, but also that Plato's intention is not to eliminate freedom; instead, his purpose is, so to speak, to *liberate* it. The concern about passivity stems both from the fact that our reason is a participation in actuality as an emanation from God and from the absolute significance that Plato ascribes to reason, which seems to take all control out of our own hands. Reason appears, in Plato, to be an almost tyrannical power, which cannot be contradicted, much less disobeyed.[35] This fear seems to find its realization in the *Protagoras*, for example, a dialogue in which Plato takes up Socrates's notorious dictum that virtue is knowledge, and, giving it a rigorous defense beyond even what some say Socrates intended, insists not only that reason *ought* to be obeyed, but in fact that it is strictly impossible *not* to obey it.[36] Reason is simply "stronger" (κρεῖττον)—the word seems inescapably to imply coercive force—than any other power, and cannot ever be gainsaid. According to Plato, this incontestable power of reason leads to the paradox that, contrary to our normal experience of things, we *invariably* choose what we think is best, so that, if we choose the bad, it is due simply to ignorance, a lack of knowledge. To put the classic Socratic phrase succinctly: οὐδεὶς ἑκὼν ἁμαρτάνει.[37] Here, Plato appears to fall into an obviously problematic intellectualism, and he offers what many take to be the clearest evidence of his failure to recognize the reality of the will and its freedom.

Several things ought to be said in response to this common complaint, but the very first has been said definitively by Julius Stenzel.[38] At the heart of Plato's surprising claim that to know the good is to do the good, Stenzel explains, lies a particular understanding of the nature of reality itself. Reality, for Plato, is not inert; it is not a cold and lifeless fact. Instead, in its essence, reality is good, *radiantly* good, indeed, *compellingly* so. Plato's interpretation of the relationship between knowledge and virtue is not first of all a judgment about the structure and function of human psychology, but rather a recognition of what we might call the overwhelming goodness at the heart of things: "The unknown power that enigmatically renders the decisions of the individual will unnecessary is the actuality and effective force (*Wirklichkeit und Wirksamkeit*) of the things themselves that radiate from them in the very moment we come to know them; this radiance, which is laid bare in that particular moment, is an unfolding of the life of things in the 'medial' sphere [of language]."[39] While Zeitler suggests that Stenzel's description borders too closely on the mystical,[40] it is in fact a necessary implication of a basic principle of Plato's—indeed, we must say, of Western—metaphysics: reality must have a first principle, which as such must be absolute, not relative to anything else; but because this principle is evidently generative (i.e., there exists more than just the first principle, and the world cannot have come from anything else without denying the first principle itself), it must also be good. Its goodness must therefore ultimately be irresistible in principle:[41] to deny the good would be to exert a power over it, a power that would thus have to be superior to it, and this is simply not possible. We see in this precisely the source of hope described at the beginning of this chapter: reality *helps* us adhere to it in the sense that the power to choose the good is not first self-generated, but first given to us or, in Stenzel's words, "the world's own power of grace in general is objectified" in the energizing actuality of things.[42]

But to say that the good is irresistible is not—however paradoxical it may sound—to say that it cannot be resisted. What Plato rejects is that the good can be *actually* present to us, which means known, and be ineffective, but this does not exclude the possibility that we can fail to know it or, in other words, act in a way that "blocks" its presence to us. The good does not act *on* us, which would compromise its transcendence by reducing its effectiveness to an agency in competition with our own, but it can act only *with* us, which is to say simultaneously as a transcendent and immanent cause of our action. This is why Plato says that the golden thread is not violent but "gentle" and that we ought to *cooperate* with it.[43] The verb he uses here, συλλαμβάνομαι, is the middle voice of συλλαμβάνω, and means "to take part with someone in something." The verb is quite close in meaning to our key concept of συμβάλλω.[44] If Plato does not include a distinct "will" as part of his psychology,[45] it is not because he recognizes two different faculties, reason and will, and decides that only one of them, reason, is essential, disregarding the significance of everything the other faculty represents. Instead, what he understands by reason includes within itself—more or less—what the modern mind typically understands by will. In other words, he does not define reason *over against* some other power, namely, will, and then leave the will out of the picture, so to speak. Reason, we recall, is the "organ" by which the soul affirms the good as such. The mind's *highest* object is not truth, simply, but truth in relation to its originating cause, the good, and this means that reason attains truth in the fullest sense only by receiving it in an "adequate" relation to the good, which relation is not separate from reason but part of the meaning itself of reason. Platonic reason, in other words, does "double duty," fulfilling the functions of both what we normally mean by reason *and* what we normally mean by will—and thus Plato sees these functions as ultimately converging into one.

It is not an accident that he uses interchangeably terms that are often strictly distinguished from each other: *nous*, as mind in its theoretical aspect, and *phronesis* as mind in its practical aspect.[46] He does not want to divide knowing and acting, contemplation and action, theory and praxis, as fundamentally separate activities, but views them in unity.[47] If Plato identifies knowledge and virtue, it is because he has a particularly *robust* sense of knowledge. As Zeitler puts it, knowledge in the proper sense, for Plato, "is a knowing that has passed over 'into flesh and blood,' which generates a relatedness to the object known, and is thus a knowing that transforms the entire person."[48] It follows that, with respect to the good, every failure of virtue is always also a failure of knowledge, and vice versa: if one acts contrary to one's good sense, it means only that one's "superficial belief" that the thing one ought to have done but didn't does not qualify as genuine knowledge. Genuine knowledge of the good necessarily includes the doing of it, because there is no proper knowledge of the good that is not an assimilation to the good in one's "flesh and blood."[49] The good is irresistible in itself, but there are all sorts of things one can do to resist its presence in one's soul, which is to say one can resist having proper knowledge of it. *This* is the deepest sort of ignorance.

There are two things to point to that clearly justify this interpretation. First, Plato does not infer from the inability to do evil willingly that people should not be held responsible for vicious acts; quite the contrary, he not only speaks everywhere about praise and blame for virtue and vice, and depicts the internal struggle one faces when one's desires do not correspond to one's reason,[50] but he also proposes increased punishments for *deliberate* acts of injustice, that is, those done "knowingly."[51] To be sure, the explanation he offers for his position on this latter point represents a real twist with respect to our general understanding: punishment is not for him essentially retributive, even in the sense of "justice," nor is it meant to be "remedial" in the usual sense—that is, causing the person to "learn" from his mistakes so that he will be able to act better in the future. Instead, punishment is the accomplishment of something the unjust person was unable to bring himself to effect, namely, an entering into relationship with goodness. "Punishment," properly understood, is the form that the relationship to goodness takes when the term of the relationship is an unjust soul (and this will turn out to be a *healing* relationship, perhaps in spite of immediate appearances). With respect to the "deliberate" acts of injustice that Plato discusses in the *Laws*, he argues that the punishment ought to be greater, not because of a greater "willfulness," but because of a greater ignorance: one *thinks* that one chose against what one takes to be best, but this is wrong. The distinction between incidental wrongdoing and fully deliberate wrongdoing is at bottom, for Plato, a distinction between "simple" ignorance and "double" ignorance, the latter of which is doubly bad.[52] Again, it is not that Plato denies we can fail to do the good that we "know"; it is rather the case that this failure is not a failure of "moral character" *rather than* reason, but if the one then always also the other. A failure to do the good is always also a failure to know the good. What this means is that we bear responsibility, not just for our moral character, but for our knowledge: knowledge is a way of *being good*, and so to know requires all the "purity of heart," the nobility of a true way of life, the conformity of the whole of one's being with the good, that we usually take virtue alone to require.

Second, the complaints about Plato's "rationalism" in the *Protagoras* typically fail to reflect on the implications of how this particular dialogue turns out. Socrates remarks with astonishment after his long "debate" with the sophist, that their respective positions got apparently reversed over the course of the discussion: Protagoras denied that virtue is the same as knowledge, while Socrates insisted on the opposite. But, curiously, Protagoras started the discussion out by arguing that he can teach virtue, while Socrates insisted that no one can. What is the proper inference from all this regarding Socrates's position? If virtue and knowledge are one and the same, and virtue cannot be taught, *it follows that knowledge cannot be taught.* Why can't knowledge be taught? Because it is not the same as information, which can be commodified and peddled on the market, a set of items or "techniques" that can be inserted into the soul without any particular preparation, as the sophists thought.[53] Instead, for Plato, knowledge is the result of a formation in goodness;[54] it is the fruit of a relationship between the soul and reality,[55] an elevation of the soul into the actuality of the order of things. This relationship cannot be produced by a professional teacher, but instead can only be *mediated*, as by a *midwife*.[56] Knowledge, in other words, is a relationship that must be lived, as the order of the soul to, in, and from the good, a relationship that one must *enter into*, or be brought into, though as we will explain in a moment, this will always take the form of discovering its "a priori" character. As Stenzel puts it, "the grasping of a particularly existing thing *draws* us *into* the particular order of things"[57]: "This order is, for the Greeks, good, indeed, it is identical with the good, into the power of which man abandons himself in knowledge and thereby freely fulfills his innermost desire and duty."[58]

Let us look at this aspect more closely, because it will open up a further dimension in relation to the problem we posed. Coming to know the good—which Plato calls the "highest study," indeed, the foundation on which all other learning rests[59]—is not a discrete task, something begun at a definite point, concluded, and then left behind as a fait accompli. Instead, it is a point around which the whole of one's life is organized (and, as we will see shortly, the whole *polis*, as a reflection of the cosmos simply). One does not "take in" the meaning of the good, as if it were a determinate object, a "piece of information": if this were possible, then knowledge and virtue could be taught as a set program with a fixed price. (The price will end up being freedom itself: a devil's bargain.) Instead, education is the ordering of the self *to* the good, and a necessarily slow, because *organic*, reception of order from the good.[60] Plato is notoriously elusive regarding the possibility of providing a definition for, or adequate description of, the good. While some adduce political strategies as a reason for the reticence, or suppose that the good represents a mystical reality that is foreign to thought, or perhaps simply assume that it is something vague and indeterminate, we have argued elsewhere that the reticence is due to the perfectly intelligible nature of the good as the first principle of being and truth: the cause of all things and all understanding cannot be adequately defined by any of its effects, but this is because it cannot be understood in its truth in terms that are less intelligible than itself.[61] We alluded to this point above as the reason for the good's essential "irresistibility." In the present context, we can translate this absoluteness into the language we have been developing and say that the good as perfect actuality precedes all potency of understanding, and so cannot be "captured," as it were, finally *in* that power, as merely circumscribed within its horizons. In this respect, the good both *precedes* and *exceeds* the soul that would know it.[62] This is the transcendence of the good.

This transcendence bears directly on the question of freedom and the will in Plato. As we have noted, Plato does indeed use a term that eventually gets translated as "will," namely, βούλησις, but the term does not designate a discrete faculty that might be numbered alongside the intellect. In fact, βούλησις can often be translated in Plato simply as *reason*. The term seems to designate reason in its specifically appetitive aspect, its *tendency towards*. Muller describes βούλησις in Plato as "the dynamism or activity of the soul, or, more precisely, the movement that carries the soul toward objects in general."[63] Zeitler even more pointedly defines Platonic βούλησις as *"vollstreckende Vernunft,"* or reason in its *effective* character as actually stretching out toward and connecting with its object.[64] He goes on to identify this striving of reason, reason qua βούλησις, as the proper meaning of *eros*, insofar as it represents the whole soul in its movement specifically toward the beautiful and good.[65] In the light of our discussion of the good, we might distinguish reason as such, that is, as the organ of knowledge, from reason as βούλησις by saying that reason as such is a reflection of the good as immanent to the soul, while reason in its striving aspect, or as βούλησις, is a reflection of the good in its transcendence of the soul. But just as these two aspects, the immanence and the transcendence, are not two "parts" that are put together to form the whole good, but are rather two different implications of the single absoluteness of the good, so too the reception and striving after are not two separate actions of distinct powers, but flip sides of the soul's single reason in its relation to the good.[66]

Recognizing βούλησις as an essential dimension of reason in its relation to the good, which is never transcendent without being immanent or immanent without being transcendent, allows us to see the fundamentally receptive dimension at the root of action, but also to see that this receptivity is nevertheless truly active. Desire for the good is not only generative of "spiritual" motion but also of physical motion. Indeed, Plato insists that the motion that fills the cosmos ought not to be understood mechanically as the collision of matter—this, he says, is an essentially atheistic conception of reality—but instead to be recognized as "the reasoning (διάνοια) of the will (βούλησις) aimed at the fulfillment of good."[67]

Whose will, and whose fulfillment? One translator renders this passage from the *Laws* thus: the events of the cosmos "are directed by the intention of a benevolent will,"[68] implying the image of a God moving things from above the cosmic order, according to his plan. But, setting aside the question of whether God has a will, and what this might mean, the context of the passage in the *Laws* makes it quite clear that, for Plato, the reasoning connected with the good does not act on things from the outside, as it were. In fact, this is the very notion Plato means to reject, since such an "acting on" represents the force of *necessity*, of compulsion, or—in political terms—the "coercion" of a mechanistic physics.[69] What he insists on, in contrast to this notion, is that all things are "animated" in some sense *from within* by the good. To use Plato's language, all things share in soul, which is to say that they are ultimately moved by goodness and beauty.[70] The *transcendence* of the good is crucial here, though, to say it again, this may not be detached from or otherwise juxtaposed to its immanence, since the transcendence is an expression of its being *first* and therefore always already present.[71] The good is not simply *outside* of the soul, as it would be in Locke's "blank page," but transcends the soul even while being present *in* it. As Plato explains in the *Republic*, in discussing the significance of the famous allegory of the cave, the power to see does not have to be introduced *into* the soul in order for it to be able to see what is real, but that power already belongs to it; the soul simply needs to be "turned around," converted, which is the essence of education.[72] But the power to see, we have to recall, is not for Plato an empty potency; it is, as he explains, the eye's share in the light of the sun. Just as, he explains, the sun not only illuminates objects to make them visible but also gives eyes the power to illuminate, so too does the good make intelligible the things to be known and empowers the mind, enabling it to know.[73] And we can say something analogous is the case in the order of freedom. Just as the soul's learning is a recollecting of what it has already known, its "choosing" is a willing of what it has always already "chosen": namely, the good, and therefore anything that reveals itself as such in its light. Not only knowledge, but freedom, too, is a kind of "recollection," though perhaps with the emphasis on the movement outwards, a "recollection forward," so to speak.[74] It is the presence of the good that sets the soul in motion, and it is the absence of the good that sets the soul in motion. The dynamism of the soul, its *eros*, is precisely the "between" inside of this paradox, the intermediary, we might say, between the good as beginning and the good as end.[75] *Eros* is the child of *penia* and *poros*, poverty and plenty.

FRUITFULNESS AND SELF-DETERMINATION

The question we must press further in relation to this point is whether, or to what extent, the soul's dynamism can be called "self-movement." The answer to this question is quite simple and straightforward, though the "how" and the "why" of it require some reflection. Plato is unequivocally clear that the soul moves itself: ἑαυτὸ κινεῖν, self-movement, "is the definition of that very same substance which has 'soul' as the name we universally apply to it."[76] But he is also unequivocally clear that the good is the cause of everything that happens in the cosmos; it is for the sake of the good—that is, in pursuit of the good that draws us to itself—that we do everything we do, without exception.[77] Moreover, we recall that man belongs not first to himself, but to God, a belonging so real it calls forth the image of a puppet, the strings of which lie in God's hands. How are we to reconcile being *essentially* a self-mover, and being a puppet in God's hand? Part of the answer we have just seen: the good causes in the mode, not of power, which acts *on* things by imposing the force of necessity (ἀνάγκη), but of *generosity*. It causes by giving agency, we might say. We recall that the reason Plato presents for God's creating the world is that he is *good*, and goodness is not jealous but seeks to make others like itself, as good as possible.[78] The good is not moved by something outside of itself, but from within, which is why it represents the perfection of freedom, why its "making things good" is a communication to them of varying degrees of self-motion. To use Plato's own language, the good causes not by necessity, but by *persuasion*. And this leads to the other part of the answer: to persuade is to give reasons instead of coercing or, to put the point more basically, *to give reason*, which, as we argued above, is a share in goodness itself. Reason is, we could say, the very presence of the good in what is other than itself.

Let us explain this point further. All things are moved by the good, and all motion is ultimately derived from self-motion,[79] which is the essence of the soul. The *reason* that the soul is capable of self-motion is just that, namely, *its* reason. As we observed earlier, the different parts of the soul are all able to be described as different kinds of desire, which is to say that they all correspond to the good in different respects. What distinguishes reason qua βούλησις specifically is that it is a desire that corresponds to the good *precisely as such*. This, then, is exactly why the soul's self-motion is tied to νοῦς: Whereas the other parts of the soul— ἐπιθυμία and θύμος—receive goodness as something "external" in a certain respect, reason receives the good *as such*, which means it represents the presence of the good *in* the soul *as* good. The movement that the good generates, it generates *from within* the soul (though not exclusively), which is in a nutshell why the soul is a self-mover. The good— and indeed the "golden thread" by which we are bound to God—is not a threat at all to this self-motion, but its very condition of possibility, or indeed the "actual substance" of the movement. Muller is quite right to say that, for Plato, when the mind thinks, insofar as it thinks, it is not subject to anything outside of itself, not even to the good or the true as a transcendent principle,[80] though we need to qualify this by saying it is moved by the transcendent principle in this case precisely *as* immanent to it, or else we end up bringing Plato too close to a Kantian sense of autonomy.[81] This will have great implications, as we shall see in a moment. In any event, though all things in the cosmos are moved by soul to a certain extent, and so are not *simply* forced by extrinsic necessity, man alone *is* his soul,[82] and so man alone is capable of moving himself, which is to say: he alone is free in the strict sense. If the good is the paradigm of freedom, man is free because of the *intrinsic* and indeed *active* participation in the good that his reason allows, or indeed that his reason *is*.

We see quite clearly here an echo of the original sense of freedom as the outpouring of an inner fullness, represented on the one hand in the good as ultimate source and on the other hand in the soul as moving itself from out of its internal principle, which is its *reason*, its participation in the good precisely *as such*. Earlier we mentioned Socrates's description of his role in communicating wisdom: he is not a (sophistical) teacher that introduces pieces of knowledge into the soul from the outside, but the *mediator* who brings transcendent wisdom from out of the interior of the soul: the midwife, who is both a "matchmaker" providing the conditions of fertility and the one who delivers the resultant issue.[83] The language of pregnancy is significant for Plato. It reappears in a central place in his philosophical vision, in which he describes, yet again, man's ultimate relationship to the good as beauty.[84] Man desires the beautiful-as-good above all other things, and yet comes to "possess" it not as an acquisition that enters into the soul's "stores," so to speak, but precisely in being made fruitful by it: "τῆς γεννήσεως καὶ τοῦ τόκου ἐν τῷ καλῷ," begetting and giving birth in the beautiful.[85]

In this context, Plato extends the notion of pregnancy in a remarkably broad way. "Natural" pregnancy and birth is a "real image" of the "spiritual" fruitfulness of noble ideas and actions. The reference to noble ideas and actions suggests the classic Greek couplet, "words and deeds," that represents the paradigm of genuinely human action. It may seem that, by describing what is borne in beauty in terms of the loftiest virtue, Plato is offering this account to explain only the most distinguished and "inspired" human activity. We wish to suggest, however, that "birthing in beauty" is the model for all human action *tout court*, from the noblest to the most trivial, insofar as it is human at all.[86] We have to recall that Plato had insisted on such universality at several points in the *Symposium*: we reserve the word "poet" for one who creates in a special sense, he points out, but all human making is analogously "poetic"; so too, the word "*eros*" is used to distinguish great human love, but all action without exception is moved by the beautiful-and-good, and so all is a mode of *eros*.[87] The special instance, we might say, reveals the (hidden?) truth of action generally. And so we arrive at the heart of the matter: if *eros* ordered to the good underlies all human action, it follows that all human action ought to be conceived as analogous expressions of birthing in beauty.[88] In other words, every human act is generated in a relation to the transcendent principle, which brings us to the decisive formulation: I am free to the extent that the beautiful-and-good is "productive" or "effective" in me. Freedom is fruitfulness.

But let us return to our earlier line of questioning in light of this point. Can this action, a self-motion now recognized as a fruit of the good, be understood in any sense at all as self-determination, a capacity to choose in any genuinely spontaneous sense and make unconstrained decisions? In one respect, Plato does not focus his attention on this question, but in another respect he most certainly does: a constant theme in the Platonic dialogues is the "choice" between justice and injustice. Plato describes the soul in a dramatic condition as a charioteer driving a pair of horses with apparently divergent impulses in an attempt to find their way home. He exhibits no trace of fatalism,[89] but instead presents both reason and exhortation for following goodness and beauty, and serving the truth in spite of obstacles. One of the clearest expressions of this drama is the "eschatological contest," so to speak, that Plato depicts at the end of the *Republic*,[90] in which souls paradoxically make *a basic choice* about what lives they *will be fated* to lead, and, not accidentally, the quality of their choice depends on their degree of both intelligence and virtue.[91] It would make no sense to talk about a final judgment upon death, as Plato regularly does in a variety of myths, usually of his own making (i.e., not because he is gratuitously referencing common beliefs[92]), unless there were some sort of *decision* made at the core of one's existence. If one would object that the choice Plato seems to allow is nevertheless only whether one will conform to reason, and so is not really "free," one shows a misunderstanding regarding the unity of reason and will in νοῦς/φρόνησις/βούλησις that we explained earlier: one's reason depends on one's choice just as one's choice depends on one's reason. The two dimensions, for Plato, are interdependent, even if there is not a simple symmetry between them.

But one might nevertheless insist that there is no room, in this unity of reason and will, for the "free" spontaneity we normally associate with self-determination, for one is always "bound" to choose whatever option one sees as best in any given case. How can Plato's notion of freedom account for the choice that must be made between equal goods, or between genuinely incommensurable goods, such that neither is in any determinative sense better than the other? In fact, our daily decisions are not between good and evil in a general sense, but more often between better or worse, or even effectively indifferent, possibilities, and we are constantly faced with alternatives whose goodness cannot simply be measured against each other.[93] It must be acknowledged, in response to this objection, that Plato did not explicitly address what came to be known as the problem of "Buridan's ass," and his neglect of the question of the spontaneity of the will required to decide between equal goods, or indeed more generally incommensurable goods, is not insignificant; we will return to this in the conclusion. Nevertheless, Muller makes an argument that seems quite consistent with Plato's principles, even if Plato doesn't make this particular argument himself. The argument turns on the transcendence of the good: its absolute transcendence implies, as we observed above, that it is not defined by a determinate content. It is *goodness* itself, which is distinct from any particular definable goods, and indeed from all of them together. This means that, as we ourselves mentioned in chapter 6, the absolute necessity of the good does not "limit" the possibilities of goodness in its determinate forms. Any particular thing is possible, in other words, *as long as it is good*; what "counts" as good is not positively determined beforehand, even if it remains true that the good does not make a bad choice possible *as such*. Plato points at this "limitlessness," without making the point explicitly himself, when he muses on a curious puzzle of justice applying to everything, and therefore to nothing in particular,[94] and similarly when he observes that *sophrosunē* represents a kind of fundamental knowing that is not identified with any discrete body of knowledge.[95] As Muller explains, "the openness to all possibilities" that the transcendence of goodness implies "is not a negative indeterminacy; it contains at the same time the possibility of a positive self-determination."[96] Muller thus concludes that Plato's ethics can be summed up by varying the well-known phrase from Augustine: it is not a directive to do one thing or another in particular, but rather a claim about how all shall be done: "Be good, and do what you will!"[97] We might say that the law of goodness opens an area for genuinely free action. From a Platonic perspective, a good man is a free man, and of such a one we can say with complete confidence that he will never do anything evil, but this does not limit at all the possibilities of what he might do. A person driven by greed, for example, is rather predictable, and, because of the external, and indeed, "material," character of the ends he pursues, can be controlled. But one who is in love with beauty for its own sake—we might think here of the figure of Socrates in the *Symposium*[98]—constantly surprises; his actions spring from within, with all of the "newness" we associate with birth.

FREEDOM AS THE BESTOWAL OF FORM

An emphasis on the "surprising" character of freedom is a kind of speculative development of Plato, though arguably implicit in his description and consistent, as we said, with his principles. Nevertheless, Plato himself tends most often to connect the notion of goodness with order. It is thus fitting that we conclude our study of Plato with a brief reflection on the crucial relationship, in his understanding, between freedom and order, especially since this represents such a fundamental contrast with the view of freedom in Locke.

Let us first consider the "internal" order of the soul, before looking at the "external" order of political community. The *Phaedo*, which was given the subtitle "On the Soul: Ethical," presumably by Thrasyllus, the original "editor" of the Platonic corpus, could just as easily have been subtitled "On Freedom." The reason this latter subtitle is especially fitting is the setting in which the dialogue takes place, a setting that Plato presents with an evident sense of irony. Socrates is sitting *in prison*, while the friends who came to speak with him in his last hours are *free*—or at least this is how it seems. The actual reality, of course, is that Socrates is free and his friends are imprisoned. Being free even inside the condition of physical constraint and limitation is one of the principal themes of the dialogue, with Socrates's situation representing what Plato takes to be the proper relationship of the soul to the body.[99] In relation to our present discussion, we wish to highlight a single dimension of this theme, namely, Plato's identification of freedom with the condition of ordered love (*ordo amoris*).

The *Phaedo* evidently takes for granted Plato's general "tripartite" anthropology that we described above, according to which the soul has three "parts," each of which is an *orektikon*, or is characterized by a certain kind of desire. As we argued above, this is just another way of saying each "part" of the soul is ordered to the good under a certain aspect: the base level is the love of the sensible, which Plato characterizes in different contexts as love of gain, love of pleasure, or even love of money;[100] the second is love of honor; and the highest is love of wisdom, that is, philosophy. In a nutshell, Plato shows here that the only way to *fulfill all three*, or in other words to complete the soul as a whole, is through respect of the proper hierarchy. This means that the measure, the reason for, the lower loves must come principally from the higher, rather than the reverse. A love of wisdom, for example, that is driven most fundamentally by a love of honor, will not in fact be a love of wisdom at all, but rather a desire for the appearance of wisdom, which can turn out to be the very opposite of the reality. Moreover, it will also inevitably lead to a betrayal of honor, since, unless the honor sought is founded on *truth* (the object of the love of wisdom), the desire will itself degenerate into merely a love of reputation and public approbation. Similarly, if the love of pleasure is absolutized to the extent that a concern for the *truth* of pleasure is excluded—if this love, in other words, loses any connection to reality—not only is wisdom or honor eliminated, but pleasure itself is finally undermined. Hence, the pointed question that Socrates invariably raises in conversation with the champions of pleasure of various stripes: Do you want to do what *seems* to bring pleasure or what does so in reality?[101] The point is that if either honor or pleasure is made primary, it not only eliminates the other goods, but also itself. We might say that honor and pleasure are *partial* accounts of the good, and so limited, and so *exclusive* of the good as such insofar as they are made fundamental, which ultimately means that in this case they undermine their own foundation.

By contrast, if wisdom is absolutized, which is to say if what is absolute is taken to be absolute, then nothing is lost in principle and, as it were, by definition, because wisdom means reality, the whole of it, in all of its dimensions.[102] To love wisdom is therefore *also* to love honor and pleasure, but to love these precisely in their truth, in their proper place in the whole.[103] In other words, to love wisdom absolutely is to love everything else *in freedom*, because as we have seen, the love of wisdom is the fruitful presence of the good itself *as such* in the soul, which is the very meaning of freedom. To adopt Plato's image, if the soul is like a city, the responsibility of the ruler is distributive justice;

the ruler is in this sense the channel through which goodness passes to the various parts and extremities of the city and, by analogy, of the organism. Again, we have here an echo of the original meaning of freedom as abundance poured outward. In a free soul, in the Platonic sense, the "golden thread" through which goodness communicates itself, precisely because it is goodness as such that is thus received, causes every other part not simply to survive, that is, to meet the demands of (externally imposed) necessity, but properly *to thrive*, to become itself abundant and so free in the manner appropriate to it.

Plato's likening of the soul to a city in the *Republic* is not at all accidental, in the sense that he just happens to choose a metaphor that presents certain similarities. For Plato, in general, likeness arises from ontological dependence. This is especially clear in the relationship between the soul and the city, if we consider these precisely in light of the meaning of freedom we have been elaborating. For Plato, as for the classical Greek mind generally, goodness is inseparable from order. In Stenzel's words, which we quoted above, to know is to "abandon oneself" to the order of things, and, through the attraction of goodness, to be taken up *into* that order. The order of love that we just discussed is not a "subjective" set of values; it is a recognition of the way things are in truth and a conformity of the soul to that truth. If this order of love is rooted in the interior of the soul, it nevertheless "freely" spills over into the world of human community. Political order is generated by the order of its constitutive souls. Or, viewed from the other side, the order that lies within the soul is one that it receives into itself as the fruit of its participation in the community. Political order generates the order of souls. There is a reciprocal, if asymmetrical, dependence between the soul and the city. One might say that objective order is just as "natural" to freedom as the subjective order of desire.

It is true, of course, that Plato often presents the well-ordered soul, the philosopher, *precisely in conflict with* the disorder of the actual *polis*, but it ought to be recognized that this conflict is tragic, contrary to the nature of things, and tends to distort the nature of the philosopher himself.[104] Even if he ultimately subordinates the statesman to the philosopher, Plato regularly insists on the importance of political life.[105] Because freedom is most basically an internal abundance that pours itself out, it is natural that the interiority of the soul in its relation to the good would have a certain priority over the external organization of community; it remains the case, however, that Plato never conceives that interiority in the manner of modern privacy: the philosopher living in corrupt times nevertheless remains a member of a *polis*, obedient to its laws,[106] even if in the end historical circumstances force that *polis* to be, as it were, only the one written up in the sky.[107] If freedom is conceived in terms of fruitfulness, it will always tend to properly social expression, not only in the words and deeds of pregnant souls, but also specifically in the organization of political community. In fact, Plato gives a certain primacy to this dimension:

> There surely *are* those who are even more pregnant in their souls than in their bodies, and these are pregnant with what is fitting for a soul to bear and bring to birth. And what is fitting? Wisdom and the rest of virtue, which all poets beget as well as the craftsmen who are said to be creative. But *by far the greatest and most beautiful part of wisdom deals with the proper ordering* (διακοσμήσεις) *of cities and households*, and that is called moderation and justice.[108]

Freedom, we might say, is fruitful in the sense of *giving rise to order*, or *giving form*, and the most comprehensive instance of this is giving form to human life in all of its aspects, in the community of the city and the household.

COMMON LAW

From this perspective, let us return to Plato's image of the "golden thread" from the *Laws*. Plato calls the "golden thread" of relation to God *both* man's reason *and* the "common law" of the *polis*: the reference to the specifically *common* law (κοινὸν νόμον) evokes the theme of the original sense of *logos* in Heraclitus, and the latter's assimilating of reason to common law.[109] We cannot attempt to present Plato's political philosophy here, or even his understanding of the nature of law, but we can at least give a general characterization, which serves our purpose of presenting a contrast to Locke. The first thing to point out, in this regard, is that, in contrast to the modern hypothesizing of a state of nature as essentially a state of war (based already on a certain interpretation of freedom and rights we have called diabolical), Plato describes the original state in terms that evoke the original meaning of freedom: it is a state of abundance and peace.[110] It is *this* abundance that Plato identifies with man's nature (though this does not exclude a constant tendency to betray one's nature, which Plato evidently also takes for granted).[111] Thus, at the outset of the dialogue, the Athenian Stranger criticizes the Cretan and Spartan political order for taking *war* for granted as the basic human condition, and thus determining the city's laws and practices principally with a view to protection and victory.[112] Instead, the Stranger insists on subordinating war to peace—we might say, subordinating the diabolical to the symbolical, which radically transforms its nature. He thus founds public order most basically on the principle of celebration. Accordingly, the first matter of business, which occupies essentially the whole of books 1 and 2 of the *Laws*, is the proper organization of drinking, singing, and dancing! The most immediate reason that Plato presents the essence of human existence as being a puppet or plaything in God's hands is not to raise the question of who has ultimate control, but to make clear that, because the relation to God is the foundation of human existence, the most fundamental characteristic of human existence is *play*.[113] *Seriousness* (σπουδή) is always connected with the service of external ends. (One recalls Chesterton's line: anything worth doing is worth doing badly, or in other words, if a thing is *intrinsically* good, it does not have to justify itself by what it produces or accomplishes.) It follows with strict philosophical necessity, so to speak, that interpreting life in relation to God, who has no external purpose, requires the relativizing of seriousness.[114] (Note that there is a connection between the notion of goodness as irresistible and the notion of existence as play.) In other words, to view human existence in relation to what is absolute, namely, the good, is to make play central to human existence in its social expression and concrete form.[115] This is what it would mean to found a city on freedom. Accordingly, the activity that lies at the center of political existence, for Plato, is *the praise of God*: this is a condition of freedom (both the subjective and objective genitive is intended here). As Plato puts it with his characteristic irony, the only *serious* thing is praise of God; it is the *unicum necessarium*.[116]

Anticipating our analysis of Locke's self-subverting political philosophy, Plato shows that supposing the preparation for war to be the purpose of political order makes division, as it were, fundamental in principle, and this schism will eventually fragment and set in opposition not only the members of a society in relation to each other, but each individual in relation to himself.[117] Thus, in the place of this purpose, Plato claims that there are three things at which a statesman must ultimately aim, and he has the Athenian Stranger state this explicitly three times in the space of a single page: freedom, friendship, and wisdom (φρόνησις) (or community of mind [νοῦ κοινωνία]).[118] We wish to propose that, understood properly, these name one and the same thing according to a different aspect in each case; they are each a way of describing the political order, which is social order as an expression, an outpouring, of goodness. Plato himself says that friendship and wisdom are the same (ὁ αὐτός),[119] and we have already suggested how wisdom and freedom are the same.[120] It follows that, as Dieter Nestle puts it simply, for Plato "Freiheit ist φιλία."[121] The point is they all indicate a kind of order, a way of integrating the one and the many, which is a way of expressing goodness itself.[122] The sort of political order envisioned by Locke, in which space is created through regulation so that one can pursue private gain or private friendship in relative "peace," does not qualify, for Plato, as a political order in the strict sense, but it is a deficient imitation of such an order. He calls an organization of this sort a "nonpolity" (οὐ πολιτεία) or a "republic of factions" (στασιωτεία).[123]

In this context, law ought to be interpreted itself as an expression of goodness; we might think of it as the extension of freedom into the social sphere.[124] Such an extension is natural to freedom in its original sense, which relates generativity to the notion of belonging to a people. We might say that the golden thread that binds us to God necessarily *passes through others*, so that one cannot receive goodness, and so be free, as an individual except as bound to others in community. Indeed, the principal community for Plato is the family, because of its own foundation in nature.[125] Here we see a far more intimate connection between freedom and law than is seen in even the most "positive" conception of freedom, which would make freedom a *consequence* of following the law, or describe law as a necessary precondition for freedom. For Plato, the law, properly understood, itself *is* freedom, just as reason is freedom: reason and the common law are the golden thread of relation to the good.

This identification, of course, changes our usual sense both of freedom and of the law. On the one hand, in light of this identification, it becomes apparent that freedom is not a merely subjective power to change or control, but has an objective structure or form. On the other hand, we see that law is not principally about control or regulating behavior. Instead, the law—like political order in general—has most fundamentally a positive purpose: it is the golden thread that binds people together into a whole, a thread that *just is* relation to God or the good.[126] Having a law is a basic part of what it means to belong together, to comprise a whole that is more than any single individual or any collection of mere individuals. It is for this reason that law existed according to Plato even in the original state of perfection, though it was not then "codified": a state of perfection is not conceivable except as a harmonious whole, and such a unity requires law as a principle of order.[127] In this respect, obedience to the law is not simply a proper way to exercise freedom, but it is itself an *enactment* of freedom, properly understood, or indeed a *realization* of freedom. If Plato explicitly contrasts genuine freedom at one point in the *Laws* with "voluntary slavery to the law," which he presents as the typical Athenian attitude, it is not, as Muller suggests, because obedience to law is a "noble substitute" for freedom, whereas the truly free man needs no laws.[128] Instead, it is because the Athenians had an essentially "lawless" concept of freedom and so related to the law as an external constraint, to which they willingly yielded insofar as they saw it as a necessary condition for freedom; but this is just why it is a form as slavery, no matter how *willingly* it is undergone. True freedom and true law are one and the same in the social order: they are both a belonging to the good, which is itself essentially generative, but specifically *of order*. It is this coincidence that explains a remark from Plato that would otherwise seem utterly nonsensical: it is in accordance with nature, he says, that *free* men ought to have a law ordering every activity of their daily lives, from sunup to sundown.[129] The existence of a free man, in other words, is more thoroughly ordered by law than the existence of a slave; it represents a perfect expression of order to the extent that it is free.[130]

Because law is not principally about regulating behavior but, we might now say, *articulating generosity*, its pedagogical function must have priority over its coercive function. One of the primary images in Plato's *Laws* is the contrast he draws between the free doctor treating freemen and the slavish doctor treating slaves. The image makes little sense from the perspective of a modern conception of freedom, but it is quite intelligible from the perspective of the Greek conception that we have been elaborating. The free doctor does not simply impose instructions and prescribe medicine, as the slavish doctor, but instead *explains* and *persuades*.[131] The free doctor himself derives his knowledge *from nature*, from reality, rather than slavishly learning to imitate procedures simply for the sake of producing an effect (τέχνη vs. ἐμπειρία), and he connects the patient to reality, we might say, through *persuasion*, the communicating of reason, which is a participation in the good. Plato says that the free doctor *philosophizes* with his patient, which the slavish doctor cannot help but consider a waste of time.[132] The free doctor thus possesses authority in the proper, "martyric," sense of the term we described in chapter 6: he gives orders in the very same way that a genuinely free mind does, that is, by witnessing to the truth of nature.[133] The law is meant to have exactly this sort of authority, and, like the free doctor who heals by mediating a connection between the patient and nature (συμ-βάλλω), it is true law to the extent that it mediates reality, and the generative power native to it. Law is authoritative in that it brings about free growth (*auctoritas, augere*). Plato does indeed accept that the law will necessarily be coercive with respect to those who refuse to listen to reason and take no interest in the meaning of things.[134] Nevertheless, he insists that the codification of law ought *not* to be a mere issuing of commands, so to speak, but ought instead to begin with a prelude, which affirms reasons—and indeed philosophical ones—before laying out the regulation that translates that reason, the golden thread, into the public sphere of common interaction. Laws, he says, "should resemble persons moved by love and wisdom, such as a father or a mother."[135] Ultimately, like the free doctor, the free ruler ought to derive his understanding of order from the nature of reality itself. Here is the reason for Plato's regular insistence on the importance of an ultimate coincidence of philosophy and power.[136] The word "prelude" (*ludere*, "to play"; "prelude" is "foreplay") to describe the free context in which the order of law is best presented is the right one,[137] insofar as it highlights the fundamental playfulness that follows from the subordination of necessity to intrinsic goodness. In any event, we may understand that Plato's composition of the *Laws* is meant precisely to be such a playful philosophical prelude, with the purpose of transforming law by making manifest its freedom, its ordered participation in the good.

It is, finally, from this perspective that we can understand the various judgments Plato makes in the *Laws* regarding what represents *unfreedom*, illiberality. Once again, these judgments are difficult to understand if one takes the modern conception of freedom for granted, but they are quite intelligible if one thinks of freedom along the lines we have been describing. First, Plato describes the "peddling of trades," especially of the servile type, as "unfree."[138] We already remarked generally on the understanding behind this judgment regarding servile as opposed to "liberal" arts. In this context, we wish to observe that the practice of any activity that most basically serves an external purpose, and responds to an imposed necessity rather than proceeding most basically from an internal principle of celebratory abundance, will naturally tend to measure itself by an extrinsic standard. Thus, according to Plato, there is an inherent tendency for the practice of trades to take its measure from the wealth that the trades produce, and wealth in turn has no intrinsic measure.[139] Although Plato does not reject the trades simply, he does recommend *imprisonment* for the freemen who engage in them,[140] and he insists that they be integrated into the freedom of the city by being ordered as fundamentally as possible to the good of the whole.[141] Second, Plato describes money-making itself as "unfree," as he does for the tendency to hoard possessions.[142] And, third, he suggests that the paradigm of unfreedom is *theft*.[143] What all of these curious observations have in common is most directly expressed in this last: each represents the trumping of the common good by *private interest*, the privileging of the part over the whole, the refusal of the part, we could say, to take its proper measure from, and so proper place in, the whole, but instead to impose its own measure with force. They each, in other words, represent a diabolical mode of being rather than one that is symbolical—the latter term indicating, as we know, both a "sharing in" and a "making a contribution to." The very individualism that Locke understands as the essence of freedom in the political order is just the opposite for Plato. For the latter, it represents the very collapse of freedom, not because individualism tends to create conditions that might threaten private peace, which thus requires the protection of law, but because individualism is already in itself an overturning of freedom even when the law succeeds in eliminating any such threats. Plato makes what would seem to be an un-Greek judgment near the beginning of the *Laws*, though it fits in well with what we have been arguing: the "root cause of sin," he says, "is excessive love of self (τὴν σφόδρα ἑαυτοῦ φιλίαν)."[144] This excessive love is a dis-order, an offense against the good, which is the very principle of generative generosity. But for that very reason, it is a loss of freedom. In short, Plato identifies unfreedom with opposition to the community that law creates: the illiberal man is ἀκοινώνητος νόμων, that is, "hostile to the community of law."[145] This opposition is a detachment, we could say, from the golden thread that gathers all together in the good. If this detachment is unfreedom, then the deepest meaning of freedom in Plato is fruitful attachment to all others in the good, a being bound by the liberating golden thread of reason and the common law.

CHAPTER 8

Aristotle

Freedom as Liberality

PICKING UP THE THREAD

It is common to present Plato and Aristotle as essentially different, if not even diametrically opposed, on many of the most fundamental philosophical questions: *either* Plato *or* Aristotle. The question of freedom seems to be an obvious one on which the two great thinkers part company: Plato defends Socrates's notion that one cannot willingly commit injustice, while Aristotle tries to show precisely *how* this is quite possible indeed. And though Plato insists that to *know* the good is always therefore to *do* the good, Aristotle clearly states that "knowledge alone does not suffice to motivate action."[1] But we have already observed that, in the final analysis, whatever differences there may be between them on this point are relativized, and in some cases disappear altogether, once the terms are clarified. This is not to say that there *are* no significant differences between them, as we shall see in a moment, but the position we adopt here is that their differences fall within a greater unity, such that we may see them as part of a (genuinely) growing tradition, rather than as discrete options at a philosophical buffet. By interpreting Aristotle ultimately in continuity with Plato, we mean to pick up the "golden thread" of freedom, as it were, which lies deep in the tradition and binds the thinkers together.

As has been conclusively shown by a recent prominent scholar, the ancients took for granted that Aristotle was a Platonist, and that the (sometimes quite serious) criticisms he raised, not only against certain Platonists, but even against Plato himself on occasion, were debates *inside* the general school of Plato.[2] Specifically, in relation to our general theme, our position is that Aristotle developed some of the basic Platonic insights we have just presented, that he differentiated to a certain extent what was a unity in Plato without undermining that unity, and that he shifted the focus of inquiry. In general terms, we could say that whereas Plato emphasizes the absoluteness of the good, Aristotle underscores its *appearance* to each of us as the principle of our action; whereas Plato emphasizes the ruling power of the good in what we think and do, Aristotle highlights the way we move ourselves, and the individual responsibility that is entailed in this self-motion; and whereas Plato emphasizes our *knowledge* of the good as the principle of action, Aristotle foregrounds the power of choice, or discriminating judgment (προαίρεσις),[3] as decisive (so to speak). But a proper understanding of freedom requires all of these aspects. In the end, it seems that the specific interests and aims are different in Plato and Aristotle, and this implies a strikingly different *ethos*, as it were, but there is apparently no crucial point in this regard on which they differ so far as to exclude the position of the other in principle: if, for example, Plato says emphatically that no one commits injustice willingly, it is because by "willingly" he means "in accordance with man's ultimate end"—which Aristotle does not deny;[4] and if Aristotle says emphatically that one *can* commit injustice willingly, it is because, by "willingly," he means "as the result of a deliberate act for which one can be held to be genuinely responsible and therefore accountable"— which, as we have seen, Plato does not deny. In short, the significant differentiation that Aristotle introduces into the notion of freedom is a differentiation *from inside of* the Platonic conception, and so, whatever its novelty, Aristotle's thought on the matter does not represent an overturning of Plato's position, or even a merely extraneous addition, but— to carry forward the meaning of freedom—a "new birth," a movement *beyond* that originates *from within*.

What Aristotle contributes to the deepening and growth of the Platonic conception of freedom is the notion of *actuality*, or more specifically, the rich distinction between potency and actuality, a notion that Hegel justly observes is Aristotle's great contribution to the intellectual treasury of philosophy.[5] If Plato identifies being with perfect completeness, Aristotle, accepting this identification in principle, nevertheless recognizes the significance of a kind of "real nonbeing" in potency, though of course it remains always relative to real being. We have all along pointed to the reversal of the classical priority of act and potency as the essential formulation of the diabolical conception of freedom, and we may now, at the end of the book, explore that classical notion in some detail.

THE UNFOLDING OF PERFECTION

For Aristotle, the soul is in different ways formal, first, and final cause:[6] with respect to the body, and indeed the organism considered as a complete substance, the soul is the form, or formal cause, the intrinsic organizing principle that makes the organism a real unity, and indeed gathers its aspects together in an intelligible "what." But, with respect to what is *other* than the organism, the soul is a potency or power; it relates to such things, as we will explain in a moment, as an ἀρχή, an originating principle or first cause, though, again, in this very relation to the other, the soul relates to itself in turn as a *telos*, or final cause. Let us sort all of this out.

To understand the complex relationship of causes that constitutes an organism, and how it bears on what we can call (somewhat anachronistically[7]) "the freedom of human action," we need to understand the relationship between potency (δύναμις) and actuality (ἐνέργεια), as Aristotle interprets it. Aristotle defines δύναμις in terms that sound at first strikingly like Locke's notion of will as "active power." Though δύναμις has a range of analogous meanings, the principle sense, the definition, is the following: a potency is "an originative source of change in another thing or in the thing itself qua other (ἀρχὴ μεταβολῆς ἐν ἄλλῳ ἢ ᾗ ἄλλο)."[8] What distinguishes Aristotle's definition of power from Locke's is his insistence that this meaning is intelligible only in relation to a more basic actuality of one sort or another. We recall that power, for Locke, is a simple idea, or at most a "mixed mode," which means it does not require reference to another idea for its own intelligibility. It is not too much to say that the entire contrast between ancient and modern freedom grows from this apparently minor difference, as we will come to see as our argument unfolds. Potency's basic relation to actuality, in Aristotle, has immediate implications for the way we must interpret the essence of potency: if Aristotle goes on to distinguish, again just like Locke, an active and a passive sense—a power to act upon and a power to be acted on—he nevertheless adds a crucial qualifier in the very next sentence: potency implies *also* acting or being acted on *well* (καλῶς). To take an example, if we say a person "can" play the flute (i.e., has the "potency" for flute-playing), we might mean simply that, like just about anyone else, he can get sounds to come out of it by blowing, but we most likely mean to communicate his special *competence*.⁹ There is a certain ambiguity that is "built into" the notion of δύναμις: as a capacity to effect some change, it has to do with what can be other than it is, and so with what will admit in a certain respect of its contrary: "Every potency is at the same time a potency of the opposite."¹⁰ On the other hand, because, for Aristotle, change has intelligibility only in relation to form,¹¹ and so actuality, δύναμις is *not* indifferent in relation to alternatives, but we might say represents a "preferential option" for the good.

The ambiguity is deepened with respect to the potencies that Aristotle calls "rational" (μετὰ λόγου), in contrast to "irrational" (ἄλογοι) potencies, the former being those that reside in the human soul.¹² (It is worth noting here, though we will address it only later on, that Aristotle connects the capacity for self-movement, and the "free" choice of options, specifically with the possession of *reason*.) The capacity to reason implies a greater detachment from the way things happen to be at a particular moment, and so in this respect a *greater* indifference to possibilities: "Every rational potency admits *equally* of contrary results."¹³ Whereas a potency without reason is ordered to a single effect (heat has the power only to warm), a rational potency is capable of effecting contraries (the rational soul can decide either to warm or chill a thing). The former, as a potency, remains a "potency also of the opposite" only in the more limited sense that it warms what could also be cold if the heat were left unapplied, but the latter is actively capable of either effect. The example that Aristotle gives in this context is the scientist who, by virtue of his knowledge, is able to produce *either* health *or* disease, because disease, as a privation, is governed by the same *logos* as health (though of course in a different way).[14] Note that the specifically *active* aspect of potency is due to knowledge, that is, a perfection or actuality: for Aristotle, in contrast to Locke, indeterminacy has no power to effect change. Thus, although a rational potency is in one respect more indifferent to "what is" than a nonrational potency, at the same time, a rational potency implies a greater determinacy to excellence since it is precisely defined by the intelligibility of (perfect) form. Thus, rational potency opens up a greater scope of possibilities, but this is principally because a *logos* includes its privation, and the infinite variations thereof, by implication. For this reason, we have to say that the rational capacities are ordered to perfection in an *essential* way (καθ' αὐτὰς), and ordered to any other possibility *nonessentially* or *accidentally* (μὴ καθ' αὐτὰς or κατὰ συμβεβηκός).[15] In other words, the capacity to play the flute is essentially, of its own internal *logos*, a capacity to play it perfectly, and so if one fails to play it perfectly, or if one makes mistakes, whether deliberately or not, the failure cannot be understood as an expression of that potency itself, even though the failure is possible only because there is a rational potency. We will come back to this important notion in the section "Action as a Communication of Goodness" below and unfold some of its implications. To summarize the point we are making here, a potency considered simply in relation to itself as the ability to change or be changed, in abstraction we might say from reality, implies an indifference with respect to contraries, but taken concretely and in its proper intelligibility, we understand potency as ordered to a proper fulfillment. The positive ordering to fulfillment is not something *added* to potency but belongs to its essence.

As we have observed at a couple of points in this book, Aristotle insists that "actuality is prior to potency and any principle of change,"[16] which means both that actuality is in principle *better* than even a good potency[17] and that potency in a certain respect "*proceeds from* actuality" (ἐξ ἐνεργείας).[18] Potency in other words is "derivative" of actuality in both the axiological and the ontological sense of that term; it is essentially *relative* to actuality. We can differentiate this relativity further. To recapitulate the observations we made on this score in previous chapters, actuality precedes potency logically, ontologically, and in one respect chronologically, while potency precedes actuality in another chronological respect.[19] Actuality, we could say, comes both before and after potency, giving it order, while potency has a certain place *between* actualities. Let us consider each of these priorities in turn. First, logical priority. Even though our understanding of actuality *simpliciter* is illuminated in a profound sense by the relation to potency,[20] no *particular* actuality requires reference to the related potency for its *logos*, while the reverse is not true (to use our example from chapter 5: we can define skiing without explicit reference to the power to ski, but we cannot define the power to ski without explicit reference to skiing). Second, ontologically considered, potency derives its "being" from what is actual: a seed comes from a mature plant, and one learns to play music from someone who already knows how to play (or if self-taught, from listening to music or from studying sheet music, all of which derives from the actual playing or from a mind accomplished in music). Indeed, one does not first acquire the potency and *then* proceed to engage in the activity, but instead one learns by actually *doing*. Aristotle says we would not call a person a builder, for example, who had never actually built anything before;[21] to help illuminate this point, we might think of Hegel's famous one-line devastation of Kant's entire philosophical project: the critical philosopher is like the man who refuses to go into the water until he has learned to swim.[22] Finally, the chronological priority follows evidently from the ontological priority: all coming to be, Aristotle says, arises for the sake of an end, which is an actuality, and the final cause is what sets the other causes, so to speak, in motion. If each of these actualities can be shown to be preceded by some potency, that potency itself will always turn out to be the expression of a more fundamental actuality. We thus eventually arrive, in chronological series, regressively at a "first mover," which is pure act and preceded by no potency: "One actuality always precedes another in time right back to the actuality of the eternal prime mover."[23] In the relation between potency and act, act is relatively absolute, and potency is always relative to what is absolute.

Let us now consider some of the implications of the primacy of actuality for Aristotle's interpretation of change. Given the mechanistic physics to which the modern imagination has grown so accustomed, with its linear sense of time as the succession of discrete moments and its sense of space as coordinates on a grid, we have difficulty conceiving a change in anything but what we could call *horizontal* terms, and we interpret the causality that determines the event accordingly: if A (happens), then B (happens); A acts on B at a certain moment, so that, *at* that moment, B becomes altered, transitioning from one condition or quality to another. But this strictly "horizontal" way of understanding change makes it impossible to understand what Aristotle means by the term *metabasis*, and indeed by the proper relation between act and potency. Because potency is a capacity for change in some *other*, its exercise involves a horizontal transition of some sort, but because potency is always derived from actuality, that horizontal transition never suffices on its own to account for the change. Once we see the fundamental relativity of potency to act, we come to see that the *horizontal* movement, which has a connection to potency, is always relative to a more basic vertical "movement." In other words, change in the most proper sense[24] ought to be understood essentially as a descent of actuality into potency, or an ascent of potency to higher levels of actuality (these are two different ways of describing the same thing): the horizontal motion that passes *from* one thing *to* another is always an "unfolding," in some respect, of a higher intelligibility from above. Change can never be adequately analyzed all the way to the bottom; it can never be, in other words, broken down into a sequence of discrete moments, so that the change might be identified with the mere sum of such moments. Instead, there is always some intelligible whole at the foundation of change, which resists this sort of reduction. One cannot reach this whole through the accumulation of partial bits following one another in a process. The sequentiality of temporal moments in any change is therefore always relative to, and indeed embraced by, the supratemporal condition of form. "Horizontal" movement is always the internal condition of arrival of some intelligible reality, which transcends that condition.

Let us explore this a little more concretely. Local motion is the closest thing in Aristotle to a purely "horizontal" change, insofar as it is a transition in space, from point A to point B, that occurs in time. Local motion is essentially temporal because it is, according to Aristotle, essentially incomplete, as fully bound to potency, insofar as this means its end lies outside of it: hence the horizontal "from/to" structure of such change. Nevertheless, even local motion, for Aristotle, is not *mere* potency, in spite of the fact that potency constitutes its essence. Instead, as Aristotle puts it in his famous definition, motion is ἡ τοῦ δυνάμει ὄντος ἐντελέχεια ᾗ τοιοῦτον, "the actuality of a thing in potency qua potential," and so it is potency in a kind of active mode.[25] Thus, even the crudest sort of physical motion is for Aristotle relative to an actuality that cannot be reduced to its parts. On the one hand, Aristotle argues, against Zeno's paradoxes, that motion is a continuous whole that is *actually* undivided even if it is *potentially* infinitely divisible, which means that the parts into which it may be divided are not themselves *actually* real, but always relative abstractions from the actual reality of a particular instance of motion *in toto*, and have to be understood as such.[26] On the other hand, and along these lines, Aristotle shows that it is impossible to identify a *first moment* of motion: at any given moment, the motion has either *not yet* or *already* begun.[27] This observation makes clear that the intelligible whole that any given motion actually is transcends its merely "horizontal" conditions; even the crudest of changes, physical motion, is a kind of "breaking in" to time of a supratemporal actuality, an irreducible wholeness, and so even this cannot be finally accounted for in merely horizontal terms.

The truth that flashes through here, so to speak, becomes much more manifest in action proper. Aristotle distinguishes proper action (ἐνέργεια) from simple motion (κίνησις)[28] by saying that, while the latter is defined paradoxically by its imperfection (κίνησις is an ἀτελὴς ἐντελεχεία, "an imperfect perfection"),[29] the former has its end in itself and so is *essentially* complete. But this is just what lifts it, we might say, from the horizontal axis of mere motion. To say that an act has its end in itself is to say that it is already whole or, in other words, that it does not have to cross a span of time to reach its end but is "already" what it is the moment it is at all. Thus, Aristotle says that activities in their proper sense are complete the "moment" they are begun, and so we can use both the present tense and the present perfect tense equally to describe them ("I am seeing" and "I have seen").[30] Any complete action therefore just so far transcends the passage of time and the multiplicity of moments that constitute it. This does not mean that it happens *outside* of time, but only that it is in time specifically as a "transtemporal" whole.[31] This transtemporal quality, however strange and even "mystical" it may seem, is a part of ordinary experience. Aristotle observes, for example, that the experience of pleasure, which is a kind of bloom on a complete animal act, is not a movement that can be broken down into a sequence of temporal moments:[32] the experience of transcendence we have in pleasure, the sense of "time flying" in "fun," or the temporal density of moments of real joy, can be said to be simply the subjective resonance of this metaphysical truth. If this experience of transcending the mere sequentiality of discrete temporal moments occurs in physical pleasure, it is most perfectly evident in the activity proper to intellect, which appears to lie altogether beyond physical distension: even the eternal motion of the heavens is, for Aristotle, just an image of the absolute supratemporality of pure thought.[33] Though this divine activity lies at the furthest extreme from crude locomotion, it is important to see that there remains an analogy between them, and that, in the light of this analogy, we ought to interpret the lower kinds of activity from the perspective of the higher, rather than the reverse, which is the more common approach of modernity. In other words, to say it again, all change, even in its horizontal coming to be, remains in some respect the unfolding of an actuality "from above." We see here a fundamental difference between Aristotle and the reductively mechanistic materialism that lies at the basis of Locke's thought.[34]

This understanding of "change" as ultimately a kind of unfolding "from above" of a complete wholeness, which we take to be the necessary implication of the priority of actuality over potency, will turn out to be the *hinge* of our interpretation of freedom in Aristotle. The reason it is the crux of the matter is that it is what will allow us to avoid reducing activity in general, and so human action in particular, to a merely unilateral transaction of one thing acting on another or being acted on by it. Instead, as descending "from above," actuality serves to gather up the various principles in any given event into a unity, relating them internally to each other, rather than leaving them as separate things that can only connect through collision, as it were. To descend "from above" is, we might say, to enter "from within" rather than to act on extrinsically. Merely colliding things can never succeed in bringing about anything *real*. As we have seen, this latter frustration constitutes the endlessly self-subverting essence of the diabolical. The primacy of actuality, by contrast, is what enables us to understand freedom symbolically, to gather up constitutive parts into a genuine unity.

THE ACTIVITIES OF LIFE

We discussed act and potency in general terms above. Let us now explore the significance of the priority of actuality in relation to the activities specific to the soul. Vegetative growth, the most basic activity, is clearly not a mere *motion* but the unfolding of an internal form, an actuality, a movement of the organism, so to speak, from its potential state to its actual state. As a general principle, Aristotle observes that the transition from potency to act is either *not* a change or is a change only in a very special sense.[35] This motion necessarily involves what is outside of the soul—nutrients from its environment—and, for this reason, entails a *physical* alteration, namely, a change in size (and in some sense in shape), but from another perspective there *is* no alteration: a frog remains a frog, from the very beginning to the very end of its growing, and through all of the—sometimes quite significantly—different stages of the process. Already here, we have a radical contrast to Locke's sense of the identity of a being, which he makes entirely dependent on empirical conditions.[36] We do not have, in Aristotle's account, a movement from what *is not* a frog to what *is* a frog, a transition that occurs at a discrete moment, when just enough "bits" of matter have been added "to the pile" (σωρὸς),[37] so to speak, from the outside. Instead, the new matter is taken up *into* the actual form, which is always-already present, so that it may unfold, expand from within. The horizontal expansion occurs, in other words, inside of a "vertical" transition from potency to act, or more properly speaking, from a first level of actuality, which represents potency in relation to the higher level of fulfillment, to a second level of actuality.

Aristotle places the local motion of which animals are capable at a higher level of activity. We discussed local motion in a certain respect already above. In the present context, we wish to focus on the activity that makes such local motion essentially, rather than merely accidentally, animal movement, and this is the activity of perception and imagination that provides its root. Perception and imagination open up the possibility of animal locomotion because they represent a remarkable expansion of the soul's potency, beyond the horizon of the animal's own form (to which the potency for growth is limited) to something that transcends it; we might say that the potency of the animal soul in this case *in some respect exceeds* the actuality, insofar as perception is an openness or "power for," not only more material for the animal's own form, but for a form different from the animal's own. Perception implies not a change in quantity, like growth, but now a change in *quality*. What brings about this change? In responding to this question, Aristotle articulates a principle that we may justly say is *definitive* of the classical tradition, and he makes concrete one of the implications of the primacy of actuality: "Everything that is acted upon or moved is acted upon by an agent which is actually at work" (πάντα δὲ πάσχει καὶ κινεῖται ὑπὸ τοῦ ποιητικοῦ καὶ ἐνεργείᾳ ὄντος).³⁸ Or as the subsequent tradition has it: potency can be reduced to act only by something in a state of actuality.³⁹ Precisely because the potency of perception proceeds from, but nevertheless *exceeds*, the form that is the animal soul, the soul alone cannot be a sufficient cause of the actualizing of this potency. Instead, the motion of sensation has to be initiated by an object *outside* of the soul, a real actuality that presents itself to the soul from beyond it and elicits its own activity: "The objects that excite the sensory powers to activity, the seen, the heard, etc., are outside."⁴⁰

This dependence on what is exterior does not mean, however, that the object of perception is *merely* outside of the soul, and acts on it in a mechanical way, as one thing exerting force on another; it is not as if the sensible object were a complete reality already in itself and the soul a mere passive recording device. It is important to note that some medium is always necessary in sensation, which implies that both the subject and object have to come out of themselves to a certain extent in order to be joined in the activity of perception.⁴¹ We remarked that the soul is itself an ἀρχή, an originative source, of its motions, and this includes perception. *Both* the soul and the object are *principles*, and that means potencies or powers, of perception in different ways, and as potencies, they are necessarily relative to some actuality: in this case, the actuality is the act in its most complete form, namely, actual sensation. Does this word indicate here the *activity* of sensing or *the thing itself* being sensed? The appropriate answer to this question is yes.⁴² According to Aristotle, the power and its object are identical in the actuality of the sensation, which is to say that the actuality represents a perfect unity of two irreducibly distinct principles or powers. We see here what we have referred to as the essentially "symbolical" character of actuality.

The actuality of perception ought to be understood not first as an extrinsic acting on of one thing by another, but rather as a kind of intimate exchange, a communication of form—which, we might say, is a reflection of the general classical principle of generosity that we discussed in chapter 6. The change that occurs in the act of perception, whatever it might entail, can always also be described as the raising of a potency, by actuality, to actuality: "We cannot help using the incorrect terms 'being acted upon or altered' of the [transition that occurs in perception]. As we have said, what has the power of sensation is potentially like what the perceived object is actually; that is, while at the beginning of the process of its being acted upon the two interacting factors are dissimilar, at the end the one acted upon is assimilated to the other and is identical in quality to it."[43] Let us take full note of the paradox indicated here: the activity of seeing is *not simply the result* of one power acting on another or vice versa; instead, as the complete actuality in the order of the particular act of perceiving and being perceived, there is a sense in which the "result" *precedes those powers*. The powers are relative to the actuality more basically than the reverse. In other words, drawing on the language we used above, the temporal change that can be described "horizontally" as a transition from not seeing to seeing (or being unseen to being seen) can also, and even more properly, be described "vertically" as the descent of sensation, or the ascent of the principles *into* this actuality, which is shared between them as a real unity. The actuality unfolds itself from above in the sequential motion of seeing and being seen.

The priority of the actual unity, which *allows* the principles to join together, explains each level of Aristotle's account of animal motion: from perception, to the imagination it makes possible, to the appetite that results from imagination, and finally to the actual movement itself engendered by appetite.[44] This unity is why Aristotle is able to describe animal movement simultaneously as a being-moved by what is good and a self-motion, a motion that originates *in* the soul itself. Perception is a reception of sensible form as it actually is, in its givenness, though it implies some transcendence of that form with respect to the sensible thing insofar as it is able to be present *in* the soul of the perceiver. But this transcendence naturally grows beyond itself: sensible form gives rise to imagination, which is a kind of transcendent sensibility. It is transcendent in that it indicates a perception not only of what actually is but of what could be, and as such engenders appetite—since desire can be only for what is in some respect not yet actual: a squirrel sees an acorn and desires it specifically *as food*.[45] To say that it is not yet actual, however, is not to say that it is a mere potentiality, because as such it would be unable to move the appetite, and, thus, the animal as a whole. Instead, it has to be already actual in a certain respect in order to elicit this motion. Here is the significance of imagination: it represents, we might say, the anticipatory presence of the particular good to be sought, and as such that which moves the appetite by making the object sought in a certain sense actually present to the soul *prior* to its reception in fact.[46] Without this presence, the soul would not be able to move itself *to* the object, because a power can be actualized only by an actuality; the isolated power of the soul *cannot* move itself. We might recall here the absence of a good, immediately felt as unease, which is for Locke the only causally effective propellant of the will. For Aristotle, by contrast, self-motion is never the irruption, *ex nihilo*, of an empty and indeterminate power, imposing force on what is external, but is always an unfolding of an original fullness, which makes itself present incipiently in the self-moving soul as the energy that draws it to realization. The fact that such "free" self-movement requires this presence of a form that transcends actual conditions without being, for all that, simply unreal, is incidentally why a pure materialism, which denies any distinction of form from matter, cannot in the end have any place for freedom.[47] More directly related to the present point, we see that the "really imagined" good is a kind of simultaneity of immanence and transcendence of the sensible form in relation to the soul that *sets* it in self-motion (as an *immanent* transcendence) and sets it in *self-motion* (as an immanence of *what is transcendent*).

It is as a result of what we might call a "symbolical" sense of actuality that Aristotle can refer to the goodness of the object as the "unmoved mover" of the soul's appetite,[48] the *ultimate* and so *original* cause of the movement, and at the very same time affirm that the final cause of the soul's movement is the soul itself: the soul is a genuine *archē* and *therefore* a genuine *telos*; it is the paradigm of nature, which Aristotle of course defines as a principle of both motion *and* rest. The soul thus comes out of itself—toward its other—and returns to itself in this motion. These are not separate activities that occur seriatim but relatively distinct dimensions of the unity of all activities originating properly in the soul. The activities of life thus always exhibit a kind of interplay of giving and receiving, self and other. To be sure, in the directly "natural" acts of a soul, there is a priority of the self: life seeks to sustain itself; the purpose of the soul's motion is not, most fundamentally, to realize a sensible object, to look at a tree in order that the tree might be seen, but this purpose—though not excluded[49]—is itself ultimately integrated into the soul's more *definite* purpose of realizing itself.[50] Perception, and its attendant motions, is genuinely different from mere growth, which is the development of a form from within through the "addition" of matter, insofar as perception involves reception of another form as such, and a more complete movement *out towards* what is thus other, but such things are not absolutely different from growth. An analogy remains.

The quality of the soul's activity acquires a new dimension with respect to the actuality of intelligible form. A curious paradox lies within sense perception and the physical movement that arises from it: this motion is in one respect fundamentally ordered to the soul's own organic completion, while in another respect it represents a fundamental dependence of the soul on what lies outside of it. In such activity, the soul is especially concerned with itself and at the same time especially dependent on what is not itself. A soul cannot perceive when it wants, but only when a sensible object presents itself to it, only when the sensible object is *there* to be perceived. The motion of the intellect differs from sense perception and its related activities in a decisive way: on the one hand, the intellect does not depend fundamentally on what is other than itself for its actuality, and on the other hand it is not specifically concerned with itself in its activity. We will return to the second point later. Let us first explain in what sense the intellect is relatively independent for Aristotle. This relative independence is manifest in several ways. First of all, Aristotle says—and here he is identical with Plato on a point that many presume a fundamental difference—that the acquisition of knowledge, the act of intellection, *is not a change*; the soul is not altered in learning:

> Again, the states of the intellectual part of the soul are not alterations, nor is there any becoming of them. In the first place it is much more true of the possession of knowledge that it depends upon a particular relation. And further, it is evident that there is no becoming of these states. For that which is potentially possessed of knowledge becomes actually possessed of it not by being set in motion at all itself but by reason of the presence of something else.[51]

There is here a "becoming-present" of an object of knowledge, but this does not *affect* the soul from the outside. If there is a "change" here, it can be described only as the soul's coming to be what it always already has been, as we will explain further in a moment. Second, the intelligible form that it thus "acquires" is one that *it* is able to take fully and completely into itself, unlike the sensible form that always retains a direct connection with actual things. Aristotle explains both the nonalteration in knowing and the capacity to take complete possession of an intelligible form with that form's *universality*, by which it transcends in a decisive way any and every particular sensible thing. Finally, once a soul has acquired knowledge, precisely because of the completeness of that possession, it is able to know whenever it wants, and not only in the actual, physical presence of the thing: I can smell a rose only when it is close by, but I can think about what a rose is and ponder whether it would smell as sweet by any other name, even in its absence. If it depends on an external object for sense perception, the soul is able to *move itself* to knowledge.

A potency can be actualized only by what is already actual; it cannot produce its own actualization (merely) from inside itself. But we just now said that Aristotle describes the act of knowing, or let us say, the power to know, as in a certain respect "self-activating." Given his apparent refusal of such a description to any other potency, which is always brought into activity by something (else) already actual, we need to see what makes the intellect unique in this respect. Here, we enter into a theme that is quite mysterious, but must be recognized to be a central point for the coherence of Aristotle's thought as a whole, and, we would argue, ultimately a condition of freedom simply. The nonalteration in the event of coming-to-know is due to the universal nature of intelligible form. Everything that one may encounter through sense experience, and so be in some sense physically altered by, is *particular*. One cannot have sense experience of an intelligible form simply *as such*, and no accumulation of experiences will ever "add up" to an intelligible, even if the process were extended into infinity, for it represents a radically different order, a different "kind" of being. This does not make sense experience simply extraneous to knowing, as the opening pages of the *Metaphysics* make clear, but it does mean that knowledge is not simply *derived* from such experience (as it necessarily is in Locke).[52] We might say that, just as the passage of time is the internal condition for the arrival, in motion, of an intelligible whole that is not reducible to that condition, so too is sense experience that *by which* an object is attained that transcends such experience. In any event, whatever knowledge one has of the particular rests on a "prior" knowledge of the universal. As Aristotle puts it here, "it is when [the intellectual part of the soul] meets with the particular object that it knows in a manner (πως) the particular through its knowledge of the universal."[53]

If there is to be an *actual* intelligible, it cannot come merely from the principles of sense objects. So where does it come from? According to Aristotle, intelligibility comes in a basic way from the soul itself, understood as *nous*, or mind, though it comes *not* in the (Kantian) sense of the mind's supplying in a purely spontaneous, or an abstractly "a priori," way what it fails to receive from the sensibles. What we have here is Aristotle's notoriously enigmatic conception of *agent intellect*, the controversies surrounding which we will not attempt to resolve here. Instead, we will rest content with a couple of observations. Agent intellect represents the soul's most complete transcendence of motion; it clearly has something to do with absolute Mind itself, God as "self-thinking thought" (νοήσεως νοήσις), though at the same time Aristotle explains its function in the *De anima* as enabling the human soul—the *individual knower!*—to know. There are clear grounds for interpreting this relationship, thus, in the Neoplatonic sense as the soul's participation in God, the presence in the soul of divine perfection—Plato's golden thread.[54] The point in the present context is simply to make clear that, whatever else we eventually have to say about the soul's learning, its coming to know, that activity cannot be the passive imposition of a "datum" of experience, but must *arise* in the soul precisely *in the form* of always already having been there. In other words, the powers of the soul must always be interpreted in relation to some actuality. If the actuality of sense experience is as it were given most basically by an external object in its actual presence, the actuality of intelligence arises most basically from within the soul itself. And just as the dependence on the external object does not exclude, but rather includes, the "principal agency" of the perceiving soul, the origin *in* the soul of knowledge does not necessarily imply the exclusion of the contribution of the object's intelligibility as something other than the soul in itself. If we keep in mind the transcendence of actuality, and the implication that what descends "from above" emerges "from within," we see that there is no need to pit potencies or principles against each other: an actuality can be seen to belong to both principles, differently, and indeed requiring in some sense their union.

Any "horizontal" change in Aristotle may be described as an unfolding from above of what is already complete in itself. In the case of intellection, we have a perfectly complete actuality, which thus at the limit does not require *any* unfolding in time and space, any "horizontal" passage from a cause to an effect; instead, there is as it were no (real) distinction between the descent of the intelligibility from above and its arising directly from within the soul. The act of knowledge, in other words, is not the production of an object, intelligible form, through the temporal activity of powers acting on each other from the outside, but the unfolding of an "a priori" perfect actuality *through* the reciprocal activities of knowing and being known, which reveal themselves as a kind of intimate exchange between reciprocally but asymmetrically dependent principles in a real unity. All of this is what Aristotle means by saying that "the soul is in a certain sense all existing things" (ἡ ψυχὴ τά ὄντα πώς ἐστι πάντα).[55] The soul, we might say, is a "moving image" of God's self-thinking thinking, a participation in the pure actuality of all things, an expression, in time, of what is always already perfect in itself.[56] If Aristotle likens the mind to a wax tablet,[57] it is not because it is primordially *empty*, like Locke's white page, but because it is a *full* openness: a wax tablet *receives* characters, not by having something added from the outside, but paradoxically by having something *removed*. Learning is thus not the addition of new bits of knowledge, but, however novel may be any particular insight, learning is always also the mind's "catching up" in a sense to what it already is; in other words, learning is recollection.

ACTION AS A COMMUNICATION OF GOODNESS

We see here, once again, how similar Plato and Aristotle are on this score. But Aristotle, as we observed, lays particular emphasis on the dimension of individual agency. In our account thus far, we have devoted most attention to the primarily theoretical powers of perception, imagination, and knowledge. Let us now explore the implications of the primacy of actuality for Aristotle's account of human action. The *Nichomachean Ethics*, which attempts to make clear the comprehensive human excellence identical with happiness, is concerned in large part with virtuous action, and action can be called virtuous, Aristotle explains, if it not only meets a certain objective measure, which gives it a completeness and intelligibility, but if it also meets certain conditions of human agency. We might summarize Aristotle's point, here, by saying that a truly virtuous action is a good action in which man fully and inwardly participates.

In order to understand the "mechanics" of human action, as it were, we need to interpret *praxis* as a deepening of Aristotle's discussion of animal motion in the *De anima*, a deepening due to the presence of intellect, such as we have just laid it out. We recall that the soul's self-motion is nevertheless itself moved by a good that lies outside of the soul as an "unmoved mover," and that the coincidence of causality in this case is possible because of the priority of actuality, which, in descending "from above," is able to include and integrate within itself a complex "horizontal" transaction. In human *praxis*, that transaction involves the kind of creative spontaneity we associate with self-conscious self-determination, though this self-determination—in Aristotle, just as in Plato—takes place always "inside" of the causality of the good. It is just reason, as ordered to the good, that opens up this self-determination. Whereas in animal movement, the appetite generative of motion is awakened by imagination, we have at this level a deeper and more sophisticated relationship, which reason itself entails. There are two basic differences between imaginative self-movement and rational action. On the one hand, because intellect is in a certain sense all things, and so receives without being "affected" from the outside, the end to which reason is ordered springs more directly *from the center* of the agent than does merely imaginative motion; and, on the other hand, because of the universality that is "congenital," as it were, to reason, and the essential particularity of action, reason's object, in contrast to the relative simplicity of the phantasm that informs imagination, divides "naturally" into an irreducible duality of ends and means (as we will explain more fully below), a duality that gives rise to the phenomenon of choice.

The two features of Aristotle's thought that are generally taken to bear most directly on the question of freedom are his account of "willingness" or "voluntariness" (ἑκουσία), and his account of "choice" (προαίρεσις). Let us consider each of these in turn in the light of the above. Aristotle defines a willing act as one whose moving principle proceeds from inside the agent.[58] In this, we see a reflection, in the order of *praxis*, of the act of intelligence, which emanates from the interior of *nous* itself. Aristotle's description of a willing action arises from a contrast with *compulsory* action, which he defines not simply as an act whose moving principle is outside of the agent (ἡ ἀρχὴ ἔξωθεν), as if all externally caused actions were ipso facto compulsory; instead, this designation includes only those externally caused actions "in which nothing is contributed by the person who is acting or is feeling the passion, e.g., if he were to be carried somewhere by a wind, or by men who had him in their power."[59] Aristotle repeats this qualification consistently.[60] Note that the qualification implies that an action can have its cause or principle simultaneously inside and outside the agent. The verb that Aristotle uses to describe this simultaneity is nothing other than συμβάλλομαι, the middle voice of συμβάλλω. The middle voice is the mode of a verb that has a passive form but is translated in an active sense; it presents specifically an action in which the agent has something done to himself or allows it to be done, and it stresses more the inward participation in the action than does the active voice, which is why the middle voice occurs so often, for example, for mental acts.[61] The verb συμβάλλομαι is rendered here as "making a contribution to," but we ought to hear this, not as adding something simply from the outside, but as adding something (namely, one's own agency) from *inside* of one's participation in the thing given "prior" to that addition: it is a joining-with, in the sense of realizing an internal relation, such that we can speak of a real unity, and so of a single cause with irreducibly different facets. Aristotle's account of willingness, in a nutshell, translates what we have been calling the "symbolical" into a verbal form.

The question that arises at this point is whether willingness, so conceived, has anything to do with reason. It may seem, initially, that reason has only an accidental role in bringing about the condition Aristotle calls "willingness," because he himself says explicitly that animals and children are said to act willingly, which is why we can also call certain acts done out of anger or appetite, beyond the control of reason, nevertheless as willing.[62] But it is crucial to see that this impression, namely, that willingness is not essentially a matter of reason, is wrong, for two reasons. First, and most fundamentally, we need to recall that, for Aristotle, there is always an analogy between nature and reason: nonhuman nature, too, acts "with reason" in an important respect, even if it does not possess that reason strictly as its own, insofar as it acts for the sake of an end.[63] Aristotle's definition of the voluntary, in fact, closely resembles his definition of nature in general—an internal principle of motion and rest—and this definition in turn resonates with our description of the action of the intellect as an emanation from within that remains immanent. These resemblances are not, of course, accidental. But we ought to see that the analogy between nature and reason goes, so to speak, both ways, and the other side of the relation is particularly illuminating with respect to our present line of argument. Those who oppose nature and reason tend to do so because of an assumption that reason is a faculty of the human soul that is at our complete disposal and through which we can exercise control over other things to one extent or another, and that nature is by contrast a kind of brute fact that we can't control.[64] But just as Aristotle sees nature as an analogously inwardly self-directing life ordered to what is good specifically in its regard, rather than as a "brute fact," so too does he understand reason as *rooted*, so to speak, in a natural way in reality, rather than seeing it as a mere psychological faculty, a "neutral" instrument of calculation that "applies" itself to reality. It follows from the analogy between nature and reason that any genuinely natural act is a rational act in an important respect—the notion of "willingness" that includes the activity of animals and children presents, we might say, an analogous extension of reason.[65]

Second, because the extension of reason is *analogous*, it implies the affirmation of a principal sense (*per prius*) to which the extended meanings are related (*per posterius*). It is thus natural, though he extends willingness even to agents that are in an obvious sense nonrational, that Aristotle would identify a paradigmatic instance of willingness, which is of course that of reason in its fullest, deliberate exercise: "The things men have done on rational principle (τὰ μετὰ λόγου) are thought most properly their own acts and voluntary acts (αὐτοὶ καὶ ἑκουσίως)."[66] In the context in which Aristotle makes this observation, he is arguing that our reason is most truly ourselves: "That [reason] is the man himself, then, or is so more than anything else, is plain, and also that the good man loves most this part of him."[67] This follows from the argument we have been making ourselves, namely, that the more fully rational a thing is, the more it proceeds from the very center of the soul, descending "from above" rather than acting on it from the outside. As we recall from the preceding, to descend from above is to enter from within, and reason's relation to its objects is the paradigmatic expression of this. If the primacy of power, which entails a dialectical relation of one thing acting *on* another, plus the reverse, is essentially diabolical, then the primacy of actuality, which implies a descent from above that expresses itself in the internal unity between what is outside and what is inside, is symbolical.

What, more precisely, is reason's relation to its objects specifically in the realm of action? It is in just this context that we can understand Aristotle's notion of *prohairesis*, or "choice." Aristotle's conception of choice is often cited as one of the roots of the modern conception of will as a spontaneous, self-directing power, essentially independent of the reason or desire. This interpretation, we suggested, is "Whiggish": it takes the modern conception of liberty for granted as normative, and projects it, or at least its prototype, "back into" Aristotle. What we seek to do here, by contrast, is to read Aristotle in the light, not of contemporary thinking, but of his own tradition, which is eventually also ours. According to Aristotle, the originative principle (ἀρχή) of our actions is choice, but choice is not absolute, a power that acts from itself. Instead, it itself has in turn an originative principle, which Aristotle identifies with "desire and reason directed to some end" (ὄρεξις καὶ λόγος ὁ ἕνεκά τινος). Indeed, this is why he specifies that choice is the "moving" (or efficient) cause (ἡ κίνησις) rather than the final cause (οὗ ἕνεκα), which is always in Aristotle the controlling cause: Aristotle's description "inserts" the causal role of choice inside of the more comprehensive causality of reason in its more basic sense. Now, to be sure, Aristotle clearly states that reason "by itself" does not motivate action; instead, it is always appetite or desire that does so. Nevertheless, when it comes to human action proper, the appetite that moves us is not something *other* than intellect, but simply intellect specifically in its ordination to an end—that is, intellect in its appetitive aspect, namely, as βούλησις:[68] "for βούλησις is appetite, and when movement is produced according to reasoning, it is also according to βούλησις."[69] *Choice*, as operating inside of the intellect in its appetitive aspect, is likewise not something "in addition" to reason, but the specific form that reason takes in relation to a particular kind of object. Aristotle therefore says that choice is "either desirous mind or reasoning desire (ὀρεκτικὸς νοῦς . . . ἢ ὄρεξις διανοητική)."[70]

What exactly is that object? To understand the object of choice, we need to consider more precisely the relationship between βούλησις and προαίρεσις. We observed above that the object of the intellect as such is essentially universal. Βούλησις, then, which is the intellect in its practical orientation, that is, in its orientation to the good, aims at the good precisely in its universal sense. But a certain paradox arises here, insofar as actions are inescapably particular:[71] practical reason, as practical, is concerned with particulars, but as reason, it is concerned with the universal. The only way that it may attain its end, then, is by choosing and bringing about a particular in which that end is to be found, or at least best achieved in given circumstances. Thus, the "faculty" of choice arises, we could say, from the transcendence of the good with respect to man's "historical" condition. Or, in other words, choice represents the soul's best effort to be reasonable, given its specific condition, which is its dwelling in a symbolical cosmos, a reality that makes present a transcendent principle.

We can understand better how *prohairesis* works, in this respect, if we recall what we saw at the outset of our discussion of Aristotle in relation to rational potency, of which we would have to say that *prohairesis* represents the paradigmatic instance. As we explained there, a rational potency is "equally" capable of different effects because of reason's transcendence of what is immediately given. Reason can see the end, in other words, beyond what is immediately given, and it is precisely *because* of this vision that it can give its assent to one particular action rather than another. Note that this assent is neither a unilateral imposition of the "will," that is, a purely spontaneous choice, nor a compulsion from outside, but a συμβάλλομαι, and it is such because the soul is joining itself to something it *receives* as good. In other words, it is a coaction, the dual character of which is reflected in the very structure of choice. As Aristotle explains in the *Eudemian Ethics*, the reason that initiates action (i.e., βούλησις), *begins from the end* (ἄπὸ τοῦ τέλους), which means that, as we said the priority of actuality implies, the act of reason (as βούλησις) itself originates in a decisive way from the good being sought, and then, inside of this, reason (as προαίρεσις) determines the best way to connect the agent to that end: "either what tends to enable him to bring the end to himself or how he himself can go to the end."[72]

We have to recall in this context the decisive principle that we cited earlier, namely, that, for Aristotle, a power is able to be exercised only by virtue of what is already actual. If we were to ask, in light of this, what enables the exercise of the power of *prohairesis*, there is only one possible answer, namely, the end, or the good that is sought, not as some object lying "out there somewhere," but specifically as "apprehended" by the intellect (βούλησις, i.e., intellect in its practical aspect). This point is *crucial* for a proper understanding of Aristotle. It is not the case that we "project" an end as a possible result of our action, or even as an un-real ideal toward which we choose to strive. In such a conception, the power to choose would have to actualize *itself*, drawing on its own resources insofar as the alternative resource is something that exists only in its intention. Here, we have a version of the modern understanding of will. Instead, for Aristotle, it is the actual goodness of the end, upon which reason as βούλησις draws, that "energizes" the choice. It is in other words the "prior" presence of the good in our reason that enables us to seek it in a "free" way in the always particular circumstances that face us. The possibility of deliberate action is given by the soul's intrinsic relation to all things that we described above. In this respect, Jonathan Lear's description of the act of προαίρεσις as a "transmission of desire" is especially apt: it is not an irruption of force from below, but a kind of free channeling of the actuality of the good it receives from above, and so *is*. The *actual* desire for the good, we might say, is in a certain sense all desires, just like the intellectual soul is "in a certain sense all things": choice, then, is the *narrowing* of this desire to one particular thing, at a given moment, cutting out so to speak all other possibilities just as the stylus removes wax from the tablet of the soul to allow the particular figure to emerge. True desire thus is not a void that desperately seeks to fill its own lack, but, rooted in actuality, has at its heart a basic generosity, which makes it a *free* seeking.

It would take us too far afield to explore in any detail Aristotle's wrestling with the problem of *akrasia*, which naturally arises in this context of choice as the transmission of desire for the good, but we can at least make the observation that, because the means cannot simply be deduced from any grasp of the end, the soul has to determine the means in a basic way "for itself." Such a determination can go astray, as it were, and because it is due to the soul's own choice, the soul is itself responsible for such straying.[73] As we observed at the outset, the emphasis on this aspect is one of the distinctive characteristics of Aristotle's theory of action. It should be noted, however, that Aristotle remains closer to Plato than to Locke on this point: it is *not* the case that we have a power to choose various options, which has its own functional integrity in itself, but ought to be used to make good decisions. Instead, the proper way to put it, for Aristotle, is that we have a power, a "rational potency," that is defined by its capacity to choose the good, and this power includes in itself *nonessentially* or *accidentally* the possibility of failing in that choice. We recall that a rational power is capable of contrary effects only because a *logos* implies its privation. In the *Metaphysics*, Aristotle illustrates this point by saying that the doctor can also produce disease because of his ability to produce health—though this possibility does not *define* him (it would be absurd to define the doctor as one who can produce either health or disease). In a moral context, we can see that the *logos* of any given type of action is its perfection, its virtue, but this *logos* implies the two corresponding vices, the defect and the excess, as privations (and indeed the infinite variations thereof).[74] As Aristotle says, the soul can direct its self-motion, a motion necessarily "energized" by the good, to a means only by "linking" it (περιέχεται) to the desired end.[75] The power for a vicious act therefore ultimately derives from desire for the good, which means it is a fundamental perversion, a twisting of nature against itself.[76] But what Aristotle says about the selection of means to an end does not apply only to moral acts, because the good is more than just moral: it also manifests itself in pleasure and utility. The acts directed to the good in these particular respects, however, still possess a governing norm in some analogous sense, which means one can also "hit" or "miss" with respect to pleasure and utility. (Indeed, any act we choose always aims at the good in *some* respect and can thus succeed or fail in any case: even one who tries to act randomly, or in complete disregard of any standard or purpose, cannot avoid either succeeding in this or failing to do so.) In any event, the *anchor* of all our activity in the good is not an oppressive limitation, but it opens up endless possibilities and even permits possibilities that run contrary to it in some respect.

The distinctive point of emphasis in Aristotle's approach to freedom lies on the individual as a kind of generative source of action. It is worth dwelling on this for a moment. Though it is ultimately the good that "energizes" our action, for Aristotle as much as for Plato, it is important to recognize that the primacy of actuality does not at all mean that man is somehow nothing but a passive channel, directing a current that originates from outside of himself. As we have insisted, this source emerges *from within* the soul. Thus, even though Aristotle echoes the imagery we saw in Plato, according to whom free action is a "birthing in beauty," by comparing man's being an originative source of his actions to the fertility that runs through nature,[77] he does so principally to highlight the *origination* of action from within man's soul. There is something truly generative in this, even if it always remains a fundamentally receptive creativity. In action, a particular good comes to be that did not exist before. As Aristotle explains, deliberation, appetite, choice, and action *always* concern something that can be *other* than it is, something "changeable," contingent, or able to be brought into being. If the good at which reason ultimately aims is absolute and unchanging, the "practical good" (τὸ πρακτὸν ἀγαθόν), the contingent good of the means, which cannot be simply deduced from the end, becomes actual only as a result of the choice.[78] The good itself is not "up to us," but it can only ever be attained *in* actions, which contain matter that is inescapably "up to us." In this respect, there is always a unity *in action* of what is received as given and what is positively generated in the receiving: action is a *symballomai*. The universal good can be *possessed* only in the inevitable particularities of (creatively) *doing*.

And here we meet up with yet another distinctive quality of Aristotle's notion of freedom. People often remark on Aristotle's concept of happiness, because it differs so markedly from our own conventional view of happiness as essentially a subjective state: a sense of contentment, good feeling, and so forth. For Aristotle, happiness is an *activity*. Our reflection on the nature of action reveals why this is so, and why it is crucially important. It results from the very transcendence and immanence of the good, the irreducible difference between the universality of the end and the necessary particularity of the means in which the end is sought, which we have described as features of a "symbolical" cosmos. The attainment of the good, for Aristotle, is *not* the end in the sense of being the last step in a series, upon reaching which one would simply stop. If it were, one could, so to speak, take the good into one's soul once and for all. But the transcendence of the good means, as we suggested a moment ago, it can be "possessed" only in a doing, and this doing is both essentially *complete* in itself and at the same time continually renewed in the particular acts (it warrants simultaneously the present and the present perfect verb tenses). Becoming good is therefore not identified with the *acquisition* of virtue, Aristotle explains, but, beyond that, with its *exercise*.[79] Aristotle's model of freedom is thus an entering into the actuality of the good, which always requires the soul's coming out of itself in action, and indeed action that is born from within the soul through deliberate and rational choice.

LIBERALITY AS THE PARADIGM OF FREEDOM

The notes of the unity of giving and receiving that have emerged in our description of the proper sense of action evokes Aristotle's description of a particular virtue, namely, *liberality* (ἐλευθεριότης). We suggest that this is not an accident. At the beginning of this part, we mentioned that the original sense of freedom bore a connection with fruitfulness, a kind of outpouring or spilling over, which we pointed out resonates quite clearly in the virtue of liberality, in Aristotle's description. The sense of fruitfulness has appeared often in our discussion of freedom in Plato and Aristotle. At this stage, we wish to point more directly to the virtue of liberality as a paradigm of what we have been discussing and show how this reverberates through Aristotle's notion of human perfection. We do so not because liberality is the highest virtue for Aristotle, for it clearly is not: after all, it is principally concerned with one's external possessions, which Aristotle, like Plato, considers the lowest sort of goods.[80] Instead, we highlight this virtue because it is the one that bears the name of freedom. Our suggestion, then, is that Aristotle's description of this virtue characterizes in a nutshell the basic form of human freedom, which we find expressed in all the fundamental dimensions of human existence. The virtue of liberality presents the basic pattern of freedom that we have been elaborating in this chapter. Specifically, liberality is a simultaneity of receiving and giving, in contrast to meanness, which is receiving without giving, and prodigality, which is giving without receiving.[81] At the heart of this virtue is not a vague altruism, a moralistic exhortation to think of others rather than oneself, but rather a respect for the primacy of actuality, here specifically in the sphere of material goods. Liberality takes delight in receiving (from the right source), not in order to hoard possessions, but so as to be able to give—again, specifically when such giving is *noble* (i.e., in relation to the true good).[82] The goodness received is a goodness passed on—and thus the energy, we might say, of actuality remains actual, rather than settling into mere potency. (We recall that the diabolical tendency is precisely to *store power*.) So too a free action is a good action that pours forth from the soul, without the soul's preoccupation with itself.[83] A self-preoccupation would be akin to the privileging of (self-centered) power. Along these lines, free action reveals itself to be a kind of giving and receiving of the soul's own inner substance, its internal goods. Truly free *praxis* is as it were the reflection of liberality at a higher level. The more *complete* an action is, the more it simultaneously wells up from within and receives from without, in a beautiful unity of self and other. This is freedom.

In the light of this model, we can look at the particular actions that Aristotle describes as essentially whole and complete[84]—and so identifies with human happiness, and thus with freedom. Contemplation, clearly, is for Aristotle the "freest" sort of action, not in the first place for the reason one might initially think, namely, that it represents a kind of detachment from the world and from the various pressures of practical concerns: an escape. Instead, this "detachment" is just the outer surface of freedom, so to speak, and its negative formulation. To see the heart of the matter, we need to return to the point made in our discussion of intellect above. Intellection is "freer" than perception because the principles of the act are *at once* transcendent and immanent, which is to say that, in the contemplative act, one knows an object as if that knowledge "welled up" *from within* the soul, as distinct from the act of perception in which the principles have a certain distance between them that has to be "horizontally" crossed.[85] The *action* of contemplation can thus be described as unfolding from the interior of the soul (though in saying this we can never exclude the transcendence of its object—that is, never oppose its movement from within to its being received from without). It is important to see that Aristotle contrasts contemplation with inactivity, indeed, to the point of identifying contemplation with the highest sort of activity, with the most "practical" action.[86] This is because it is not an action directed at achieving an end, but an action that *is* most purely its own end outside of itself, and so has always already been achieved in the doing of it. Action in general, for Aristotle, is complete in the sense of containing its end within, but contemplation represents a sort of "supercompleteness" insofar as the end of the act is not only *in* the act but is in an essential respect identical with it.

But to say that the act of contemplation has thus always already been achieved in its enactment does not mean it is finished. Instead, contemplation is an (endlessly) ongoing activity. To recognize the *ongoingly active* dimension of contemplation is to see that it is not a knowing that one simply takes into oneself and stores away,[87] but it is indeed a knowing in which one dwells, which suggests it is a knowledge that the soul has to rise up to meet, as it were, and in this sense to come out of itself, to be fully active. It is a taking in, then, that coincides with a certain "spending" of the self, which is why contemplation has an essentially self-forgetful character.[88] In this emanation, we have the echo of the original sense of freedom, as the outpouring of fruitfulness. We thus ought to see contemplation as a kind of mirror image of liberality. They both represent a (symbolical) unity of giving and receiving. Liberality means taking delight in the activity of communicating, passing on, rather than in an acquisitive or possessive hoarding. Contemplation is more fundamentally receptive, but its wealth is nevertheless "possessed" only through the soul's active self-transcendence. Contemplation is the freest action in the same way that philosophy is, in Aristotle's words, the only free science (μόνην ἐλευθέραν . . . τῶν ἐπιστημῶν):[89] it unfolds from within, as a self-originating principle, and this emanative actuality results in a free relation to its objects, which are received in wonder, and affirmed for their own sake rather than instrumentalized in relation to an end that is *external* to them. Contemplation, then, is productive, but in a primarily *internal* way: *Sophia* and *phronēsis*

> are necessarily desirable in themselves, even if neither produces any effect. Secondly, they do in fact produce an effect: Sophia pro-

duces happiness, not in the sense in which medicine produces health, but in the sense in which healthiness is the cause of health. For wisdom is a part of virtue as a whole, and therefore by its possession, or rather by its exercise, renders a man happy.[90]

If contemplation exhibits a priority of the "receiving" dimension of liberality, a virtuous action expresses more directly the self-outpouring dimension, though in doing so it seeks the completeness of activity that exists perfectly in contemplation. To say, as Aristotle does, that every action aims at something beyond itself, that is, that every action is a means to an end that transcends it,[91] is not to say that every action is a means in the same way, or that it makes present the end that transcends it in the same way. Indeed, a great deal of Aristotle's reflection on human existence in its aiming at the good concerns a clarifying and ranking of these very differences. We might think of these as a ranking of degrees of freedom. To go back to our earlier discussion, sheer physical movement, no matter how unrestricted it might be, is the least free, since it is defined precisely by the externality of the end—by its being "*a-telēs.*" At the other extreme, contemplation is the freest, because, as we have seen, it is the *most* perfectly immanent action. Specifically human movement, in distinction from these two extremes,[92] is *praxis*, which represents a paradigm of the activity (ἐνέργεια) that Aristotle distinguishes from κίνησις because of its containing its end within itself, though of course *as* an action it nevertheless aims at an end that, even in its immanence, remains distinct from that action.[93] There is an analogical range concerning the specific mode of this immanence, however. On the one hand, we have ποίησις, productive activity, in which the actuality lies most basically in the thing made,[94] and this distinguishes it from *praxis* proper. On the other hand, *praxis*, genuine human action, can be directed to a variety of things, which Aristotle ultimately distributes into three groups in the opening book of the *Nichomachean Ethics*: pleasure, honor, and virtue. All three are objects of *leisure* (σχολή) in the sense that they all represent intrinsically good ends,[95] but they do not represent them in the same way: pleasure is an internal state, but rooted principally in sense experience (which does not exclude analogous extension to "intellectual pleasures"), which as we have seen has a certain "external" character; honor is, likewise, intrinsically good, and transcends mere sense experience, but is nevertheless dependent, in a certain respect, on the judgment of others, external to the self; and, finally, the exercise of virtue is the best human action because it concerns actions that are complete in themselves, choice-worthy for their own sake, regardless of whether another sees them and recognizes them as such.[96]

It is crucial, for our purposes, to see that it is just this quality, the *intrinsic goodness* of the act, that allows the act to emanate from the center of the soul in a manner that is analogous to contemplation. It is in other words precisely the goodness of an act that allows it to be free, a generous self-outpouring of the soul. The analogy holds, here, once again because the principle of such action is reason. To pursue pleasure or honor as absolutes in themselves is to become in some respect a slave, subject to ends that always remain outside of one's action. But to pursue them *from the principle of reason*, which is to say to love them exactly in the way that they ought to be loved, no more but also no less, which is to say again to engage them virtuously, is to have a free relationship to them, to "possess" them generously, in the way that philosophical wonder possesses its objects; it is to enjoy them thus in a contemplative way, to enact them as pouring forth from one's very center: "The things men have done on a rational principle are thought most properly their own acts and voluntary acts. That [reason] is the man himself, then, or is so more than anything else, is plain, and also that the good man loves most this part of him."[97] In a word, the more truly good an action is the more it proceeds *from* the soul in the soul's pursuit of a reality that remains distinct from it; the soul receives the good by doing the good, making its own contribution (*symballomai*) from its own inner substance. Once again, we hear the echo of the original sense of freedom, namely, the streaming forth of superabundant goodness that generates something truly other.

THE PERFECTING OF FREEDOM IN FRIENDSHIP AND COMMUNITY

It may seem that to emphasize the self-originating aspect of free action would threaten to set the individual in opposition to others, and thus in a way to anticipate the diabolical notion of freedom that defines itself *precisely by* the exclusion of any sort of heteronomy. After all, Aristotle seems to deny the liberty of an action to the extent to which that action has an "external" origin. But, though there may well be a certain ambiguity on this point,[98] we have to recall that the goodness that the noble soul takes for itself, so to speak, in virtuous action is not at all what we could call private interest (τὸ ἴδιον), even if it is the condition of individual happiness. Just as contemplation has a self-forgetful character, so too does virtuous action, which is why Aristotle can point to the deed of self-sacrifice, as, paradoxically, a kind of fulfillment.[99] In fact, the goodness in which the free man generously and actively participates is for Aristotle necessarily a common good—"the good of the individual and the good of the community are one and the same"[100]—which is to say that freedom has for Aristotle, just as it did for Plato, an essentially social character: to be free is to be bound to others, "symbolically," in the good. We will close with a brief exposition of this point.

Although books 8 and 9 of the *Nichomachean Ethics*, on friendship, are among the most loved of Aristotle's works and no doubt among the most read, few people remark on the strangeness of their presence in a study of human virtue. To explain this presence, it is certainly true but nevertheless inadequate simply to observe that Aristotle's primary purpose in writing the text was to describe human happiness, and friendship is one of the things we need to be happy. The notion of friendship is more essential than this explanation suggests: the heart of the matter is that the goodness that man pursues as his freedom is essentially a *shared* goodness, by its very nature. To put the point directly: the goodness that one comes to possess as emanating from one's own soul comes to a higher perfection when one *also* contemplates and receives that same goodness as emanating from the soul of another. If contemplation is a doing that is a perfect receptivity, and virtuous action is a self-outpouring in the perfect deed, friendship might be seen as a kind of synthesis of the unity of receiving and giving that is expressed in the virtue of liberality; friendship combines action and contemplation, and so it is fitting that Aristotle treat it at a culminating point of his book on human excellence, just before the final book dealing with happiness in general.

To preface his explanation of the significance of friendship, Aristotle sets into relief what we could call the essentially relational character of nature, life, and existence simply, and he does so in a way that directly confirms the argument we have been making. There is an astonishing paradox in his description of life here, but we would like to conclude with the proposal that it represents the life-giving paradox of freedom itself. On the one hand, Aristotle defines life as a paradigm of nature, which is an internal principle of motion and rest, that is, an activity that emanates from within a being. On the other hand, however, Aristotle says that "life is defined in the case of animals by the power of perception, in that of man by the power of perception or thought; and a power is defined by reference to the corresponding activity (ἡ δὲ δύναμις εἰς τὴν ἐνέργειαν ἀνάγεται [literally, "the potency is led up into actuality"]), which is the essential thing; therefore, life seems to be essentially the act of perceiving or thinking."[101] We must recall that the "corresponding activity" by which the power is defined and to which it is ordered (ἀνάγεται, "passively" led up), is the *sameness*, the perfect unity, of perceiver and perceived, knower and known. If living is the "being of living things,"[102] and, now, perceiving and thinking is the living of animals and man, then man enacts his being in the activity of thinking. It follows that the fullness of being is the unity of the soul with what lies *beyond* it (or else it would not represent an actuality, a "movement" from potency to act), which is to say that that which most fully arises from within the interior of the soul is its relation to what transcends it. We might say that the actuality that defines life *in itself* is an actuality *into* which (εἰς plus accusative) a soul enters by being raised up (ἀνάγεται) *beyond* itself, and so in union with an other, and in this movement it most fully rests in itself in free self-possession.

It is in light of this characterization that we can understand Aristotle's description of friendship. One is most fully alive, one most fully enjoys one's own existence, in good activity, which reaches a (new) perfection in being shared with another:

> If life is desirable, and particularly so for good men, because to them existence is good and pleasant (for they are pleased at the consciousness of the presence in them of what is in itself good); and if as the virtuous man is to himself, he is to his friend also (for his friend is another self)—if all this be true, as his own being is desirable for each man, so, or almost so, is that of his friend. Now his being was

seen to be desirable because he perceived his own goodness, and such perception is pleasant in itself. He needs, therefore, to be conscious of the existence of his friend as well, and this will be realized in their living together and sharing in discussion and thought; for this is what living together would seem to mean in the case of man, and not, as in the case of cattle, feeding in the same place.[103]

If there is a tendency for contemplation and virtuous action to be "one-sided"—contemplation as a purely receptive taking into oneself and action as a purely generous giving to others—friendship presents a remarkable unity that reverses these tendencies. One does not only contemplate, but one shares "in discussion and thought," and one not only performs good deeds, but one takes joy in the good deeds a friend does for oneself in turn. It is important to note that mere appreciation of or awareness of the goodness of the other is insufficient: Aristotle distinguishes friendship from "good will" by pointing to the *actuality* of friendship, by which he means an *intimacy*, a real presence of the other—which ought to be heard in an *organic* sense, as a springing from the real depth of nature.[104] It is not enough to have goodness in oneself, and it is not enough to see goodness in an other; it is "necessary," rather, for the other to be intimately present to the self, and the self to itself in the other:[105]

> For friendship is a partnership, and as a man is to himself so is he to his friend; now in his own case the consciousness of his being is desirable, and so therefore is the consciousness of his friend's being, and the activity of this consciousness is produced when they live together, so that it is natural that they aim at this.[106]

And this is not a necessity imposed from the outside, but what we might call a "gratuitous necessity," the kind of necessity "native" to goodness: the necessity of *freedom*.[107] We recall the etymological connection between the words in many languages.

To draw many threads together: the "voluntary" action is in general one in which one "symbolically" shares in and makes a contribution to an "external" causal principle. In friendship, a person actively and receptively joins, not just to a principle or cause, but to another *agent*, not just to a good *thing*, but to a lover of goodness simply—and indeed, does so not just in thought, but body and soul in a shared existence. Moreover, in the ideal friendship, which defines the rest, the other agent is himself *actively actual*, a complete whole in himself, but for that very reason, precisely because it is the (nonprivately possessed) good that makes him complete, is reciprocally open in turn to oneself. The two together show forth the meaning of the good in its most good mode: one alone might suffice, but goodness requires more than what is necessary. If this is the most good good, it is also the fullest expression of liberality, not just with respect to possessions, but with respect to one's very self. It is thus a paradigm of freedom. To interpret freedom in terms of the priority of actuality, rather than the priority of power, is to understand its realization in community, to understand it, that is, *symbolically*.

As if to underscore this point, Aristotle ends the *Nichomachean Ethics*, his treatise on human happiness, by indicating the incompleteness of that book on its own. He does so by making reference in the closing pages to the discussion to follow, which is his *Politics*. Happiness, we might say, as *free*, necessarily spills over into community.[108] It is in light of Aristotle's interpretation of friendship that we can understand the importance he gives to the *political*. Whatever differences there may be between them in the details, Plato and Aristotle are "joined together," as it were, on this point. We can end with just a brief characterization of the essential point in relation to our theme. The good that one most desires as an individual soul is a good that is "possessed" best, we have proposed, in the virtuous activity of a good community. In contrast to Locke, Aristotle affirms that the state is a "creation of nature"[109]—which is *not* to deny that it is (also) a work of reason,[110] because reason itself is rooted in and ordered to nature.[111] The state is moreover not an (unfree) function of the necessities of bare existence; instead, even if its empirical origin can be explained by such necessities, its *existence*, its actual reality, cannot: "A state exists for the sake of a good life, and not for the sake of life only."[112] The state therefore does not have the essential purpose of protecting citizens from each other, and from foreigners, so that individuals can pursue their private pleasures and private goods, which is to say that its *end* is not war, or even peace as the productive harnessing of hostile forces (the "society of devils"); instead, the purpose of the state is *noble activity*:[113] a state that is simply a place wherein individuals can enjoy their own lives, in a merely external companionship with others—in what we would call today "civil society," a situation Aristotle would liken to "cattle feeding in the same place"—is *a state only in name*,[114] in exactly the same way that a finger cut off from a body is a finger only in name.[115] For a finger to be real requires its sharing in the actuality of the soul, relating as a part intrinsically related to other parts as members of a greater whole. Similarly, a *polis* has a "soul" only in a living relationship to the good. This soul extends, as it were, to the citizens that constitute the community. According to Aristotle, citizens belong to the city more basically than they belong to themselves,[116] and this is not a compromise of their individual freedom, but its precondition, or indeed its very essence. Just as the actuality of a sensation fulfills and unifies the perceiver and the perceived, preceding them in a certain respect so as to make them possible, and the actuality of knowledge precedes and makes possible the unity of knower and known, so too is the actuality of the common good the condition for the generous and intimate interaction of citizens. The *polis*, in its objective, social character, represents, we might say, an analogous extension of the synthesis of giving and receiving, contemplation and action, which we saw in the paradigm of friendship. As we mentioned at the beginning of our discussion of Plato, the key to political freedom is not external organization, or merely social status due to birth,[117] but relation to the common good. Almost as if Aristotle were responding directly to Locke, he writes:

> It is clear then that a state is not a mere society, having a common place, established for the prevention of mutual crime and for the sake of exchange. These are conditions without which a state cannot exist; but all of them together do not constitute a state, which is a community of families and aggregations of families in well-being, for the sake of a perfect and self-sufficing life. . . . Our conclusion, then, is that political society exists for the sake of noble actions, and not of mere companionship.[118]

If Aristotle affirms that political rule is a great human good—so much so it would be fair to say that the life of the statesman is second only to the life of the philosopher[119]—this is not because "active power" is a supreme good in itself, worthy of being made an organizing principle of life. In fact, Aristotle says that if supreme power of this sort were the "best of all things, because the possessors of it are able to perform the greatest number of noble acts," then robbers or plunderers ought to be held in the highest esteem.[120] To make power supreme, he says, is necessarily to pit neighbor against neighbor, father against son, friend against friend, and oneself against everything else—in short, to found "community" on what we have called the diabolical. Instead, Aristotle explains that power over slaves is empty, and he distinguishes it from genuine rule over free men.[121] How is "rule over free men" not a contradiction? Only if we recognize that ruling is not a controlling of others, but a *liberation*, and this is because, to rule, for Aristotle as for Plato, is to communicate the generosity of actuality, the liberation of form. The reason Aristotle, like Plato, subordinates the statesman to the philosopher is that the essence of *strictly political freedom* is to receive, and so pass on, a goodness that transcends both the individual and the *polis*, because it transcends all things simply. Freedom in its specifically political form thus reflects the same sense that resonates in contemplation and genuine action, as expressed in the virtue of liberality: a coincidence of giving and receiving, which creatively receives what is good "from above" and passes it on to others. Once again, freedom is goodness made fruitful.

Conclusion

In the introduction, we spoke of the need to recover a fundamentally ontological conception of freedom, one that is rooted, at its core, in goodness. As we have come to see, the goodness at issue here must be understood first of all not as a mere ideal, but as a wellspring; it is a moral concern only because it is more basically a metaphysical reality, an actuality that is fruitfully present to all things as their ultimate source and destination. We have suggested, in the course of our investigation, that, because of its nature, a genuinely ontological goodness cannot be simply posited as a concept, or constructed as a useful instrument. Instead, it must be *recovered* through a retrieval of the tradition that is actually given. We thus explored the etymological roots of the ancient words for freedom and then studied the first flowering of the notion in the thought of Plato and Aristotle. In these thinkers, the "organic" notes of the original concept were grafted, so to speak, in an explicit way onto a more universal, and directly philosophical, notion of goodness as the first cause of all existing things. Freedom in this context comes to appear as the full flourishing of being, a completeness that is not sealed up in itself like a treasure locked and stored away, but is rather an exuberant superabundance, ordered from within to generous and generative relation to what is other. We identified this premodern sense of freedom as *symbolical*, which is to say that it celebrates its reality in the endlessly renewed unities that come to be, at every level of being, between members of the friendship lying at the origin of the cosmos.[1] The spontaneous acts of choice and self-determination, the framing of contracts, the exchange of goods, and the creation of laws and institutions in the organization of the political order are not events that happen somehow outside of this fundamental meaning—perhaps in the best cases with the aim to protect and promote freedom—but instead ought to be understood themselves as already analogous expressions of the friendship that freedom simply is.

A greater contrast can scarcely be conceived with the notion of freedom that we explored in Locke and the political and cultural institutions and phenomena to which it gives rise. Here there is no original fullness of being; to the contrary, we have an effort to clear space, to excise as radically as possible whatever is already given a priori, *precisely* in order that the individual might have the power to make choices, to determine himself, to acquire property and pursue his own happiness, to have his *own* voice in political matters, and so forth. The very condition of this power is the elimination of a truly ontological good, a generous and abundant first cause. Goodness can be retained only as a moral obligation, which comes to expression in the form of empty laws and neutral procedures. We discover the absence of real goodness not just in Locke's explicit ideas about the nature of the will, but already in the methodology of the *Essay*, which aims to rethink all of the basic concepts of thought anew, from the ground up, from the vantage of pure subjective immanence—that is, as far as possible without appealing to what is first given a priori. There is a connection, in Plato and Aristotle, between the affirmation of an original goodness and the recognition that the acts of human freedom always begin, as it were, from the completeness of the end and take the form of choosing what one has in a certain respect always-already willed. There is likewise a connection, in Locke, between the "active power" that characterizes the will and the various dialectics that ensue when one makes the impossible attempt to begin "from nowhere." The total spontaneity of will that one seeks to establish invariably reverts, again and again, to naturalistic determinations and political impositions of various sorts: Locke is the father of both modern compatibilism and modern libertarianism.

We identified the attempt to "empty" freedom in order to make it self-originating as "diabolical," in the strict sense of the term, which indicates a division or driving apart. Such an attempt can be found not only in the modern approach to human nature in itself but in the political theory that grows from that approach. Pierre Manent has described liberalism as the organization of separations. We might call this organization the "essence" of liberalism—though of course liberalism resists any talk of essences precisely by virtue of its effort to begin without any "given" form. In any event, it remains the case that the hallmark gesture of liberalism is to *keep things apart* as the principal mode of setting them free. It is just this separation, this "ontological emptiness" of liberalism, in direct contrast to the "ontological abundance" of freedom in its original form, that causes the political aspect to come to dominate in the modern period. As an inwardly indeterminate potency, there is not much to say, in the end, about *what* freedom is, and so attention is directed at how it functions and how it is regulated.[2] On the one hand, this seems to let individuals have protected space to give their freedom whatever content they feel is necessary or desirable, and this is supposed to be the great, and in our age finally the victorious, advantage of what Isaiah Berlin called "negative freedom." But our argument has been that a purely negative freedom will always be encroached upon by the now purely positive—that is, essentially arbitrary—apparatus of regulation, even while it is never thus brought to any order. We thus have in Lockean liberalism what Erich Przywara called an "explosive" unity of dialectical opposites: a revolution always waiting to happen. Of course, if a revolution is *in fact* always waiting to happen, it never has to happen in reality to achieve at least a part of its goal, namely, to nullify, if not to subvert altogether, the given order, insofar as order calls on an *inward* participation (*autonomy*).

From the premodern perspective, freedom is not simply something we need to protect and regulate; it is something we can *deepen*. The proper way to deepen freedom, moreover, is not to separate and keep apart, but rather to reconnect, especially to origins, to what is authentic and real. The priority of actuality over potency, which lies at the heart of the premodern view of freedom, entails a privileging of nature, of what is given a priori, and therefore of what one receives from those who come before one. In a symbolical order, freedom is rooted in a pattern of life that has its center in the truth of reality, a truth that gets amplified through the generative diversity of analogy, through relations and activities that reflect gratitude in their basic form. The "energy" (ἐνέργεια) of the origin is thus communicated, and it is crucial to see that this communication depends in some respect on genuine presence, on contact with real things, on our actual tradition. At the same time, because it is precisely an "energy" that is communicated, none of these realities is essentially self-referential, but instead they all point "liberally" beyond themselves to what is other and greater.

Privileging the natural and original does not entail the disparagement of human art, culture, and ingenuity, but demands it: because the origin is a superabundant source. The appeal we make here to tradition is therefore not "backward-looking," however it may appear. Our argument has been on behalf of a *living* tradition; the point is that a "reconnection" (συμ-βάλλω) with tradition is a *sine qua non*, not just for a truly human order in the present, but indeed for any genuine novelty in the future. Deep creativity is always a reappropriation of roots, a reentry into the original energy that is itself, of its essence, a moving beyond. In this respect, reconnecting with the tradition is not an attempt to resurrect something dead and gone, to pick up again something long abandoned. If it is living, which is to say, if it is *in fact* tradition rather than something else, it cannot but remain alive, though perhaps in perverted forms in the present. These forms must be liberated precisely by being reappropriated, and this can occur only if we undertake the patient labor of reliving the actuality at their roots by taking them up into a genuinely free existence.

One of the greatest critics of the Western tradition, who was also one of the greatest critics of modernity (and indeed criticized the tradition above all because, in his view, it produced the modern world), was Friedrich Nietzsche.[3] It is astonishing to discover, then, that even he bore deep traces of the tradition we have identified here, as it were, in spite of himself in the very alternative he sought to engender in his overcoming of modernity. At the heart of Nietzsche's response to the pusillanimity of the modern world was the cultivation of the *Übermensch*, the "super(abundant)man." This supreme artist is one who creates, in a spirit of play, out of his inner wealth, in noble indifference to extrinsic demand—in imitation of the sun (!), that great star who pours out his substance daily without envy or need.[4] It is, indeed, an image of genuine freedom—and not a new one. The novelty is perhaps just that there is no reference in any of this to the good (or indeed to the transcendentals that are inseparable from it: namely, beauty and truth).[5] We might say that Nietzsche represents an attempt to recover the "self-diffusiveness" of the good in spite of the good itself, because the good itself cannot be separated from the Christian Neoplatonic tradition that lies at the roots of Western civilization. He thus ends up, as Heidegger has compellingly shown, with an emptiness of the will to power, sheer willing, which does not overcome modernity but rather consummates it.[6]

Heidegger's response to the final triumph, in Nietzsche, of the particular kind of power that characterizes the modern project is especially illuminating in relation to our own proposal. To the "no" that defines modern liberty at its core, or more adequately put, the radical "no" to which modernity aspires as what it takes to be the proper condition of freedom, he himself says *no*—and thus his thinking, for all of its depth, and for all of its promise of being a truly "other thinking," becomes a function of the same project in spite of itself. As Arendt explains, Heidegger counters Nietzsche's will to power finally with a "will not to will"; specifically, he offers the stillness of *Gelassenheit*, which he describes not as the attainment of some *actual* good, but as a calmness that "prepares for" a "thinking that is not a willing." The renunciation of the will, however, is a concession to the problem, an attempt to discover an *even purer* form of potency—that of a pure openness to the *freedom*, that is, the *open space*, of being itself[7]—than Locke could ever have imagined in his entanglement with politics, and thus to evade ever more fundamentally the claim of the good. The problem of the primacy of (empty) power cannot be resolved simply by positing the absence of power. Instead, the response can only, finally, come from a rekindling of the embers of love for the actual good, embers that can never altogether die out.

NOTES

INTRODUCTION

1. G. K. Chesterton, *Heretics* (Rockville, MD: Serenity, 2009), 20–21.

2. Along these lines, we might describe the postmodern as "hyperpolitical" in that it retains the primacy of power negotiations, but it extends them, beyond the sphere of the public order, into all social relationships, even into one's intimate relation to oneself. Our characterization of the evolution in the understanding of freedom is not unlike Nietzsche's description of the movement in conceptions of "value" from the premoral (ancient) to the moral (modern), a movement he seeks to drive toward the final step, the "extramoral." Nietzsche explains the extramoral essentially as the "psychological," in his peculiar interpretation of the term, meaning the realm of impulse that lies deeper than deliberate intentions. See Friedrich Nietzsche, *Beyond Good and Evil* (Cambridge: Cambridge University Press, 2002), §32, pp. 32–33. Our aim is, like Nietzsche's, to discover the deep roots of freedom beyond mere deliberate choice originating in the self-conscious individual, but our approach differs from his in two ways: we seek these roots in the metaphysical rather than the psychological, and we intend to include the dimension of deliberate intention rather than marginalizing it as a mere symptom. As will become clear by the end, we do not mean, in our efforts to recover the roots, to throw out the plant itself.

3. We hope to follow up the present book with two connected volumes, which together will form a relatively complete argument: after the present book, we project a genealogical volume that seeks to account for the emergence of the distinctively modern conception of freedom from the complexity of the Christian appropriation of the classical tradition, and then a largely constructive "metaphysics of freedom" that would articulate the various dimensions of an adequate conception of freedom in response to the deficiencies brought to light in the preceding two volumes.

4. As we will eventually argue, the absolute priority of actuality does not exclude a relative priority of potency. Though this aspect is recognized in

classical philosophy, it gets radicalized in the Christian appropriation, as we hope to demonstrate in our projected volumes 2 and 3.

CHAPTER 1. LOCKE'S (RE-)CONCEPTION OF FREEDOM

1. Lee Ward, *John Locke and Modern Life* (New York: Cambridge University Press, 2010), 8. Indeed, he goes on to say that, if after the end of the Cold War we are all liberals, one could say we are all Lockeans. According to Edward Feser, "Of all modern philosophers, John Locke has had the profoundest influence on the world we live in, and most embodies its guiding principles"; Feser, *Locke* (Oxford: Oneworld, 2007), 1.

2. Bolingbroke, "Fragments or Minutes of Essays," Essay XLV, quoted in James Harris, *Of Liberty and Necessity: The Free Will Debate in Eighteenth Century British Philosophy* (Oxford: Oxford University Press, 2008), 19. As a description of the complexity of his friend Locke's explanation of freedom, Phillip van Limborch wrote succinctly: "materia est intricata"; quoted in Tito Magri, "Locke, Suspension of Desire, and the Remote Good," *British Journal for the History of Philosophy* 8, no. 1 (2000): 55.

3. We will be citing from Locke's *Essay* as it appears in the following edition: John Locke, *An Essay Concerning Human Understanding*, 2 vols., ed. Alexander Campbell Fraser (New York: Dover, 1959). This edition is an unaltered and unabridged reprint of the Oxford University Press edition of 1895, and it contains all of the variations that Locke made in the different editions of the *Essay* that appeared in his lifetime. All parenthetical references in the present chapter refer to this book, according to the following format: book, chapter, section number, and page number.

4. The date inscribed on the book was 1690, but Locke completed it in fact in late 1689. See the discussion of the various editions in Vere Chappell, "Power in Locke's *Essay*," in the *Cambridge Companion to Locke's "Essay,"* ed. Lex Newman (Cambridge: Cambridge University Press, 2007), 137.

5. In addition to the revisions Locke made, he also added several new chapters, the most significant of which was no doubt the treatment of personal identity (chapter 27, "Of Identity and Diversity"). Etienne Balibar has argued that this new chapter may be read as the introduction of the distinctively modern notion of the *self*; see his groundbreaking, Balibar, *Identity and Difference: John Locke and the Invention of Consciousness* (New York: Verso, 2013). There appear to be grounds for suggesting that this new understanding of the *self* as founded on consciousness, that is, on a power rather than on a sort of substance, bears a relation to the reconception of freedom that we discuss in the present chapter.

6. Locke wrote that his view prior to composing the chapter tended "to the contrary side to that where I found my self at the end of my pursuit. But doubting that it bore a little too hard upon man's liberty, I shew'd it to a very ingenious but professed Arminian [Jean Le Clerc, whom Locke befriended in Holland during his exile, which is where he composed the *Essay*], and desired him, after he had consider'd it, to tell me his objections if he had any, who frankly confessed he could carry it no farther": Letter 1592, January 20, 1693, published in *The Correspondence of John Locke*, ed. E. S. de Beer (Oxford: Clarendon, 1979), 4:625. (Hereafter cited by volume and page as *CJL*).

7. Letter 1579, December 22, 1692, *CJL*, 4:601.

8. Notes enclosed in Letter 1544, October 15, 1692, *CJL*, 4:540.

9. As Chappell points out, the changes were almost all "additions" to the earlier text rather than rewrites of existing passages (Chappell, "Power in Locke's *Essay*," 148). One must concede, however, that in his opening epistle, Locke says that the changes to the first edition were all clarifications, *except* for those made in chapter 21, which signal in fact a new opinion on the matter.

10. In 2.21.73.366, Locke mentions that the whole change of view from the first to the second edition turns on a single word; in Letter 1643 to Molyneux, July 15, 1693, he clarifies what the change was (*CJL*, 4:700), and indicates where the change was needed. But it is a matter of some controversy what Locke in fact has in mind here. Chappell confesses that it is hard to determine what Locke could mean by this suggestion; see Chappell, "On the Intellectual Basis of Sin," *Journal of the History of Philosophy* 32, no. 15 (1994): 198n5. Cf. Matthew Stuart's discussion in *Locke's Metaphysics* (Oxford: Oxford University Press, 2013), 457 ff. Although it is indeed hard to explain how this observation accords with the specific changes he made (he changed, after all, quite a bit more than a single word in his revision), there is a certain logic to the switch he alludes to here: it indicates a move from a fundamentally *receptive* notion of will to one that is fundamentally *productive*. We will discuss this at some length later.

11. On Locke as libertarian from the beginning, see Peter Schouls, *Reasoned Freedom: John Locke and Enlightenment* (Ithaca, NY: Cornell University Press, 1992), 119. Chappell generally follows one of the classic interpretations of Locke (typically associated with Locke's radical disciple, Anthony Collins, and the Calvinist Jonathan Edwards) by presenting him as a "volitional determinist." See his overall account in Chappell, "Locke on Freedom of the Will," in *Locke's Philosophy: Context and Content*, ed. G. A. J. Rogers (Oxford: Clarendon, 1994), 101–21. But Chappell does concede a fundamental change in view from the first to the second editions, and allows that Locke eventually took on elements of a more libertarian notion of free will through his correspondence with Limborch, though he maintains that Locke was never com-

pelled to surrender the essence of his "volitional determinist" view, even if he may have thought he was in the end. On a basic change in Locke's position from the first to the later editions, see Magri, "Locke, Suspension of Desire." Stuart acknowledges fundamental changes in the first and subsequent versions, but he judges that, in spite of rhetorical concessions he made as a result of correspondence with his friend van Limborch, he did not make a fundamental change in his position over the course of his repeated revisions; see Stuart, *Locke's Metaphysics*, 443–92.

12. Harris, *Of Liberty*, 18.

13. See Peter Walmsley, *Locke's Essay and the Rhetoric of Science* (Lewisburg, PA: Bucknell University Press, 2003), 59.

14. If reflection is required for the acquisition of an idea, one might contest its simplicity or immediacy, as Hume would go on to do.

15. Of course, there is a reciprocal dependence, insofar as the production of change requires something that *can be changed*, but the reciprocity is nevertheless asymmetrical. Locke calls the active sense "the more proper signification of the word power" (2.21.4.311).

16. Pierre Manent, *The City of Man* (Princeton, NJ: Princeton University Press, 2000), 115.

17. Locke made this distinction explicit in handwritten marginal notes in a pamphlet written by Thomas Burnet, which sharply criticized his *Essay*; see Fraser's introduction to the *Essay*, xliv.

18. Locke, "First Treatise on Government," 11.106, in John Locke, *Two Treatises of Government*, ed. Peter Laslett (Cambridge: Cambridge University Press, 1960), 218–19.

19. 2.21.21.325. Cf. pages 316, 367, et passim.

20. See comparable statements: to be free is to have "the power of doing, or forbearing to do, according as the mind shall choose or direct" (2.21.10.317); "*Liberty* . . . is the power a *man* has to do or forbear any particular action according as its doing or forbearance has the actual preference in the mind" (2.21.15.320); "as far as any one can, by the direction or choice of his mind, preferring the existence of any action to the non-existence of that action, and *vice versa*, make *it* to exist or not exist, so far *he* is free" (2.21.21.324); freedom is "being able to act, according as we shall choose or will" (2.21.27.329); and so forth.

21. Letter 2925, May 21, 1701, *CJL*, 7:329. The original reads: "consistat in sola potentia agendi vel non agendi consequenter et congruè ad determinationem voluntatis." All of Locke's correspondence with Peter van Limborch, a Dutch Remonstrant theologian whom Locke met during his exile in Holland, and who became a lifelong friend, was in Latin.

22. Letter 2979, August 12, 1701, *CJL*, 7:406.

23. Stuart shows that there was an initial ambiguity in Locke's thinking whether volition indicates a state of "being pleased with" or an occurrent "action," but that Locke strengthened this latter sense in his revisions (*Locke's Metaphysics*, 444–51). Of course, positing the will specifically as a discrete action, which Stuart suggests Locke comes to do, brings it under the scope of freedom, which Locke resists for reasons we will discuss below. The basic ambiguity in his thought, which we will be presenting here, can in fact be formulated as a question of the extent to which he conceives of volition as a discrete action in itself, as opposed to being always only a *part* of an action.

24. See Stuart, *Locke's Metaphysics*, 398.

25. E. J. Lowe refers to this act, helpfully, as a "trying"; Lowe, *Locke on Human Understanding* (New York: Routledge, 1995), 120. The notion of willing as trying distinguishes it from the common interpretation of willing as giving assent to a proposition.

26. We see an example of Locke's distinction in Bernard of Clairvaux, *On Grace and Free Choice* (Collegeville, MN: Cistercian Publications, 1977), 72. Bernard's purpose in introducing the distinction is to allow God's grace to "co"-operate in the achievement of the will's act, but in order to open this space, he sets off and secures that dimension of the act that lies in man's own power. In this respect, his distinction resembles Locke.

27. A host of objections could legitimately be raised here regarding Locke's example and its sufficiency for the point Locke wants to make (see Stuart's discussion of various objections and possible responses, *Locke's Metaphysics*, 403–18), but the issues these objections entail are not our primary concern here. We wish only to retain the simple point that there is a distinction between the voluntary and the free, and that the latter is founded on the former.

28. Hobbes, *Leviathan*, ed. C. B. Macpherson (New York: Penguin, 1982), chap. 21, pp. 261–74. Hobbes says plainly that the notion of freedom "may be applied no less to irrational and inanimate creatures than to rational."

29. It is also the case that the possibility of *forbearance* is essential to freedom in Locke's view, whereas Hobbes speaks only of the positive ability to act on one's desires. The significance of this possibility will become apparent when we discuss the "power to suspend," below.

30. *Essay*, 2.21.18–19.322–23.

31. One might raise a question about this dismissal, saying that one can in fact be pleased with what one is pleased with: for example, I can be pleased with the fact that reading pleases me more than watching television. Locke,

however, is not considering whether such willing to will is possible in certain cases, but whether this in fact constitutes the structure of every genuinely free volition.

32. Locke made this point explicitly in the version of the argument in section 23, which was included in the first through fourth editions, but it is implicit in the shorter version from section 25. This version, as we indicated, remained in the fifth edition, and all subsequent ones. Jonathan Edwards famously embraced this argument as central to his own view of freedom; see Edwards, *Inquiry respecting that Freedom of Will which is supposed to be essential to Moral Agency* (1840), pt. 2, sec. 1.

33. See Fraser's observation in this regard: *Essay*, 1:331n1.

34. Chappell notes this problem in passing, but then continues on—"Be that as it may, . . ."—without reflecting on its implications for Locke's conception of freedom as a whole (see "Power in Locke's *Essay*," 149). We will suggest at the end of this chapter why such a fundamental difficulty can be simply noted in passing once one adopts a Lockean perspective.

35. See Vere Chappell, "Locke and the Suspension of Desire," in *John Locke: An Essay Concerning Human Understanding in Focus*, ed. Gary Fuller and Robert Stecker (New York: Routledge, 2000), 236. Chappell refers to *Essay*, 4.10.3 and 4.620: "bare nothing can no more produce any real Being, than it can be equal to two right Angles"; and "what had its Being and Beginning from another, must also have all that which is in, and belongs to its Being from another too." Stuart raises a question whether this in fact constitutes a theory of universal causality (*Locke's Metaphysics*, 468), but it is not essential to our argument to resolve this dispute.

36. Cf. section 33 of the original edition, in which he states that "the preference of the mind be *always* determined by the appearance of good, greater good." It should be noted that here Locke already adds that man retains the capacity to carry through, or not, this preference in action, and therefore remains free (2.21.33.377). This may be read as an initial formulation of his notion of the power of suspension.

37. Harris has judged that Locke's important contribution to the debate on free will in the eighteenth century was not primarily a matter of *content*, but rather of style and method—namely, his approach to the operations of the mind as an object of scientific inquiry (*Of Liberty*, 12–13).

38. It is known that Locke studied the work of Malebranche in order to respond to the criticisms a student of Malebranche, John Norris, had made of the first edition of the *Essay*, see Fraser, *Essay*, "Prolegomena," xlii–xlvii.

39. Jean-Michel Vienne, "Malebranche and Locke: The Theory of Moral Choice, a Neglected Theme," in *Nicolas Malebranche: His Philosophical Critics*

and Successors, ed. Stuart Brown (Assen: Van Gorcum, 1991), 94–108. Vienne is the modern French translator of the *Essay*.

40. This is Chappell's phrase, which he takes to express the essence of Locke's position on the question of free will (see "Locke on Freedom of the Will," 101–21).

41. "Good and evil, present and absent, it is true, work upon the mind. But that which *immediately* determines the will, from time to time, to every voluntary action, is the *uneasiness of desire*, fixed on some absent good" (2.21.33.334).

42. Tito Magri refers to the contingency between perception of the greater good and its moving us as "motivational externalism," and he cites this as the essence of Locke's attempt to respond to Molyneux's critique of intellectualism ("Locke, Suspension of Desire," 58).

43. The necessity of a qualifier here will become apparent below.

44. Letter 2979, 12 August 1701, CJL, 7:403.

45. Lee Ward observes that what is notable about Locke's view of happiness is its lack of content (*Locke and Modernity*, 43); Magri makes the same point: "The desire for happiness has no particular content" ("Locke, Suspension of Desire," 67).

46. For example, Locke speaks of "the eternal law and nature of things, which ought not to be altered to fit one's ill-conceived choices" (2.21.57.353). Schouls rightly insists that Locke is *not* a "relativist" in this particular sense (*Reasoned Freedom*, 136–37). We will return to this judgment below. It is interesting to note here that the norms Locke articulates do not refer to concrete goods but are instead formal rules of behavior.

47. See Ward, *Locke and Modernity*, 17–18.

48. In the second through fourth editions of the *Essay*, Locke wrote, in the opening "Epistle to the Reader," of a Mr. Lowde, who mistook his point: "If he had been at the pains to reflect on what I had said," Locke explains, "he would have known what I think of the eternal and unalterable nature of right and wrong, and what I call virtue and vice. And if he had observed that in the place he quotes I only report as a matter of fact what *others* call virtue and vice, he would not have found it liable to any great exception" (18).

49. Gideon Yaffe, *Liberty Worth the Name: Locke on Free Agency* (Princeton, NJ: Princeton University Press, 2000).

50. Locke's description recalls Aristotle's distinction between the ordered activity of the free man and the random activity of the slave (*Metaphysics* 12.10.1075a15 ff.), though the metaphysical principle at the root of each is fundamentally different, as we will see in the course of this chapter, and in our discussion of Aristotle in chapter 8.

51. Yaffe constantly adds this qualifier, which echoes Locke (see 2.21.48.345); it indicates a reluctance on Locke's part ever to embrace a straightforward libertarianism—at least until the end: as Chappell has shown, Locke seems finally to have conceded the notion of free will in his discussion with Limborch, though he did not propose any obvious changes in the *Essay* as a result (Chappell, "Locke on Freedom of the Will," 119–20). Yaffe claims with some reason that the apparent change he made can be explained according to principles he had already established himself; see Gideon Yaffe, "Locke on Refraining, Suspending, and the Freedom to Will," *History of Philosophy Quarterly* 18, no. 4 (2001): 390n13. See Letter 3192, September 28, 1702, *CJL*,7:680. For a detailed account, and an argument that Locke's position remained consistent on this point in spite of rhetorical adjustments, see Stuart, *Locke's Metaphysics*, 481–92.

52. Yaffe, *Liberty Worth the Name*, 118.

53. Ibid., 68.

54. Yaffe adds, however, that there is a connection between God's will and individual fulfillment: "God arranges things in such a way that all good things are achieved . . . when the agent acts in a way that maximizes her overall personal pleasure" (*Liberty Worth the Name*, 33). Yaffe interprets Locke's ethics as a combination of hedonism and divine command theory.

55. We note that Yaffe's view, which presents Locke's notion of freedom essentially as "self-transcendence" in relation to the good (*Liberty Worth the Name*, 8, 118, etc.), is unique, and in itself one of the most interesting among readings of Locke. It represents an attempt to view Locke as offering a notion more apparently in continuity with the classical account we will be presenting in part 3 of the book. It differs from the classical view, nevertheless, among other things, most notably by coming to rest finally on potency rather than actuality: it is the *ability* to order choices, not the actual self-transcendence in the good, that most decisively defines freedom in Yaffe's interpretation (see ibid., 54, 63). Whatever merits the conception of freedom Yaffe presents may have in itself, as *an interpretation of Locke* specifically it is problematic for several obvious reasons: Locke never adverts to this relation to the good in any of his summary statements of what freedom is (which we cited above, in note 21; moreover, the whole thrust of the *Essay* is to deny that the human spirit transcends itself at all: it presents a thoroughly "self-referential" notion of reason; the metaphysics of participation that necessarily underlies the classical view of freedom as self-transcendence is resolutely denied by Locke's nominalism; and Yaffe's insistence on the importance of the content of choices (ibid., 5) is ultimately irreconcilable with Locke's divine command theory of ethics, which founds the moral goodness of the act on something extrinsic to its content. A

thorough assessment of Yaffe's view, however, is not possible in the present context.

56. We will, however, give reasons later on why it in fact does not matter: the extrinsicism of the dependence gives the internal logic of the will as power a self-enclosed structure.

57. This is not to deny the positive necessity for *reason* in one's choices, which we will address below.

58. Plato describes the good as "what every soul pursues and for the sake of which it does everything" (*Republic* 505d), and, indeed, he presents justice—which includes of course moral obligation to others in relation to the community as a whole—as "a thing more precious than a great deal of gold" (*Republic* 336a), and as "the most desirable kind of good" (*Republic* 357b–358a). Aristotle states in the *Nichomachean Ethics* that the good is "what all things desire" (*NE* 1.1), and Aquinas often cites this quasi-definition axiomatically in his discussions of the meaning of goodness (see, e.g., *Summa theologica* 1.5.1). What has been called classical "eudaimonism" is often profoundly misrepresented by being juxtaposed to benevolence, or duty to others, even by otherwise very careful interpreters of classical philosophy, see, e.g., Robert Spaemann, *Happiness and Benevolence* (Edinburgh: T&T Clark, 2000).

59. On the necessary coincidence of transcendence and immanence, which is the heart of Platonic metaphysics, see the compelling account presented by Eric Perl, "The Presence of the Paradigm: Immanence and Transcendence in Plato's Theory of Forms," *Review of Metaphysics* 53, no. 2 (1999): 339–62.

60. According to Michael Zuckert, "Locke's transcendent natural law position is that neither the content nor the obligatoriness of the natural law is immanently present in nature, but each can be known only through knowledge of God the creator and legislator," Zuckert, *Launching Liberalism: On Lockean Political Philosophy* (Lawrence: University Press of Kansas, 2002), 189. Zuckert goes on to show that Locke, having made this affirmation, quietly introduces elsewhere in his work arguments why such knowledge of God is impossible, thus paving the way for a substitution of traditional natural law by modern natural right.

61. Yaffe, *Liberty Worth the Name*, 33; cf. 66.

62. Aquinas, *De veritate* 21.1.

63. "The motive for continuing in the same state or action, is only the present satisfaction in it; the motive to change is always some uneasiness: nothing setting us upon the change of state, or upon any new action, but some uneasiness. This is the great motive that works on the mind to put it upon action, which for shortness' sake we will call determining of the will" (2.21.29.331). Note that, if will is a power, and power is the ability to produce a change, then

there is no act of will whenever there is no change. This view of will could be compared to Aquinas, who sees the will as most *in act* in its resting in the good.

64. Vienne, "Malebranche and Locke," 101.

65. Hannah Arendt, *The Human Condition* (Chicago: University of Chicago Press, 1998), 309–10.

66. Manent, *City of Man*, 132.

67. William Desmond, *Hegel's God: A Counterfeit Double?* (Burlington, VT: Ashgate, 2003), 9.

68. Not even the actual consideration of a remote good in itself removes one from the chain, as Hobbes shows: for him, thought enables us to see beyond what immediately presents itself, that is, to consider future consequences, but this ability does not in the least entail a qualification of his strict determinism.

69. On this, see Yaffe, "Locke on Refraining, Suspending, and the Freedom to Will," 373–91, esp. 390n13, where he argues that we are free (as opposed to determined) in willing only with respect to (temporally) remote goods, but are determined with respect to every immediate choice (though he affirms the point of his general argument that this determinism is not in principle a threat to full-fledged agency).

70. This text first appeared in Coste's French translation (which was produced under Locke's direct supervision and discussed with him, line by line), and then in posthumously published editions. On the reliability of the French translation, see Locke's statement of this fact in Letter 2979, to Limborch, August 12, 1701, *CJL*, 7:412.

71. There may be extreme instances of passion in which the possibility is lessened to the point of disappearing, but it remains the case that we could have led the sort of life that would render such occasions rare, and so we are still in some sense responsible.

72. This is modern language, because the classical (Aristotelian) view speaks of choice only in the context of rational deliberation regarding multiple means available.

73. This passage comes from a section that first appeared in Coste's translation. See note 65, above.

74. For objections to Hobbes from a more or less traditional perspective, see the classic debate between Hobbes and John Bramhall: *Hobbes and Bramhall on Liberty and Necessity*, ed. Vere Chappell (Cambridge: Cambridge University Press, 1999).

75. Schouls (*Reasoned Freedom*, 147) describes Locke's sense of freedom thus. He refers to the classic libertarian text, Roderick Chisholm, "Freedom and Action," in *Freedom and Determinism*, ed. Keith Lehrer (New York:

Humanities Press, 1966), for the particular phrasing of the point: "Each of us, when we act, is a prime mover unmoved."

76. Schouls, *Reasoned Freedom*, 8.

77. Ibid., 19.

78. Ibid., 113: to be critical, Schouls explains, means that one must *initially reject* one's received beliefs, and only subsequently affirm them according to one's own criteria.

79. Ibid., 114.

80. Hobbes does indeed include deliberation in his account of freedom, but the act seems to be more a mechanical than a rational process: the evidence of this is that even though he admits that man possesses reason and that free human action follows upon rational deliberation, he nevertheless insists that human beings are no more (and no less) free than anything else, animate or inanimate, that is not forced or constrained (see *Leviathan*, chap. 21). Locke is quite clear on the fact that only man is free, whereas a tennis ball in flight is not, and ascribes this difference to reason: this implies that reasoning is not a purely mechanical process.

81. Schouls, *Reasoned Freedom*, 143.

82. Note Locke's characterization of the profitability of virtue in *The Reasonableness of Christianity*: "The philosophers, indeed, shewed the beauty of virtue: they set her off so as drew men's eyes and approbation to her; but leaving her unendowed, very few were willing to espouse her. . . . But now there being put into the scales on her side, 'an exceeding and immortal weight of glory,' interest is come about to her, and virtue now is visibly the most enriching purchase, and by much the best bargain"; Locke, *Reasonableness of Christianity*, ed., I. T. Ramsey (Stanford, CA: Stanford University Press, 1958), 70.

83. Locke urges Limborch to consider, in his insistence on the will's essential indifference, "whether, while you want in this way to make a man free, you are not simply making him a blind agent; and whether in order to make him free, you are not taking away from him understanding, without which any sort of Liberty cannot exist or be supposed to exist" (Letter 2979, August 12, 1701, *CJL*, 7:408).

84. See Raymond Polin, "John Locke's Conception of Freedom," in *John Locke: Problems and Perspectives*, ed. John Yolton (Cambridge: Cambridge University Press, 1969), 3.

85. Descartes writes that "the more I am inclined toward one direction—either because I clearly understand that there is in it an aspect of the good and the true or because God has thus disposed the inner recesses of my thought—the more freely do I choose that direction"; Descartes, *Meditations on First Philosophy*, 4th ed. (Indianapolis: Hackett, 1998), 84.

86. See, for example, Servais Pinckaers's classic presentation of freedom in Aquinas on this point: Pinckaers, *Sources of Christian Ethics* (Washington, DC: Catholic University of America Press, 1995), 381–86.

87. It should be noted that we are asking this question in this form in order to bring out a feature of Locke's view of the will, and not because we accept the idea that reason's necessary determination of the will represents a compromise of freedom. We will see in part 3 why the necessity of the good, perceived by reason, enhances freedom.

88. Schouls, *Reasoned Freedom*, 79.

89. See G. A. J. Rogers, "The Intellectual Setting and Aims of the *Essay*," in *Cambridge Companion to Locke's "Essay,"* 7–32.

90. We will elaborate this in part 3 on Plato and Aristotle.

91. For a strong argument that even our sensitive knowledge regarding the external world (which scholars often point to as inconsistent with Locke's general conception of the nature of knowledge) reduces ultimately to agreement between ideas, see Lex Newman, "Locke on Knowledge," in *Cambridge Companion to Locke's "Essay,"* 313–51.

92. Vienne, "Malebranche and Locke," 103. To say that Locke substitutes process for content does not mean that Locke is not concerned with truth; we are suggesting only that Locke's concern for truth specifically takes the form of care for the proper "use and exercise" of the reasoning faculty, as he says repeatedly in the *Conduct of the Understanding*. In the beginning of that text, after stating the supreme importance of the understanding, insofar as the will cannot help but follow it in all its choices, rather than concluding to the importance of coming to a proper understanding of the truth of reality, Locke says, "It is therefore of the highest concernment that great care should be taken of the understanding, to conduct it right in the search of knowledge and in the judgments it makes"; see *Some Thoughts Concerning Education and Of the Conduct of the Understanding*, ed. Ruth Grant and Nathan Tarcov (Indianapolis: Hackett, 1984), 167. In other words, truth is ultimately a consequence of *proper procedure* in the exercise of reasoning: this is the "via moderna" in philosophy, of which Locke was one of the most influential pioneers. We may describe this philosophical *via moderna* as the accordance of primacy to matters of logic and method. This approach follows naturally if one defines knowledge, not in terms of the soul's intimacy with being (see Plato, *Republic* 478a; 490a–b), but rather as "agreement or repugnancy of ideas."

93. There are occasional passages in Locke that would seem to contradict this interpretation; perhaps the most direct in this regard is in section 54: "We should take pains to suit the relish of our minds to the true intrinsic good or ill that is in things" (2.21.54.350). Here, Locke seems indeed to be measuring our

judgment by a truth that lies in things and so beyond their appearance to us. But insofar as Locke does not provide an epistemology that would lend any support at all to such assertions—quite to the contrary, his epistemology actively undermines any sense that a statement such as this could have—these comments only serve *to give the appearance* of not straying too far from the classical tradition. As Zuckert (*Launching Liberalism*, 82–106) persuasively demonstrates, this is the defining characteristic of Locke's "way of writing." Locke's exhortation to conform our minds to the intrinsic good in things ought to be read in light of his constant insistence, namely, that the mind never has access to the reality of things, to which it may wish to conform itself: see his claim that our knowledge inevitably falls "short of the reality of things" (4.3.6.191).

94. Walmsley, *Locke's Essay*, 94–95.

95. David Hume ends up making this judgment explicitly. As he famously puts it, "Tis not contrary to reason to prefer the destruction of the whole world to the scratching of my finger"; Hume, *Treatise of Human Nature*, ed. David Norton and Mary Norton (Oxford: Oxford University Press, 2000), 416.

96. For Plato, as a contrary example, it is *in principle and in fact* impossible rationally to choose what is evil, regardless of how carefully and deliberately one makes the choice. As we will argue in chapter 8, it is not always noticed that the identification of knowledge and virtue goes, as it were, both ways: it means not only that knowing the good entails doing the good, but also that one does not know the good unless one actually does it.

97. We might associate Locke's rationally free agent with the sophist in Plato's *Phaedrus*, who distinguishes himself from the (essentially Hobbesian) sensualist that blows in the winds of his immediate desires by his clear-eyed pursuit of self-interest. Socrates nevertheless goes on to distinguish this rationally self-interested agent from the philosopher, who is carried by love of the beautiful and good beyond himself to the truth of things. It is only the latter, for Plato, who represents the life of reason.

98. "Whatever necessity determines to the pursuit of real bliss [i.e., the enjoyment of eternal reward in the next life], the same necessity, with the same force, establishes suspense, deliberation, and scrutiny of each successive desire" (2.21.53.349).

99. Locke, *The Reasonableness of Christianity*. On Locke's understanding of the determinative role reason plays in religious matters, see Nicholas Jolly, "Locke on Faith and Reason," in *Cambridge Companion to Locke's "Essay,"* 436–55. Although Locke is careful not to deny divine authority and the normative status of scripture, he nevertheless maintains that "*reason must be our last judge and guide in everything*" (4.19.14.438). This interpretation of reason as having a self-referential form prompts a review of Locke's claim that God is

absolutely free and yet cannot but will what is good (2.21.50.347). Even though this assertion would seem to imply at first glance that Locke is affirming a certain kind of heteronomy, since it apparently *subordinates* the will to what is good in this supreme case, we need only ask what determines goodness for God as Locke sees it. Anything but the nominalistic answer would be unthinkable: a thing is good because God wills it to be so. In raising this question, we see how important is a reflection on the relation between God's will and God's goodness for an understanding of freedom even in human beings. This is a task we hope to pursue in our next volume. Zuckert has shown that Locke affirms Christianity only as radically reinterpreted, in a manner that makes "self-ownership" absolute (see *Launching Liberalism*, 129–68).

100. Polin, "John Locke's Conception of Freedom," 3. Cf. Schouls, *Reasoned Freedom*, 164.

101. According to Vienne, because Locke eliminates any metaphysical "relation of participation" between finite pleasures and the Supreme Good, what is left is "only a purely quantitative relation" ("Malebranche and Locke," 97).

102. Locke, *A Letter Concerning Toleration*, ed. James Tully (Indianapolis: Hackett, 1983), 47.

103. We see here a certain version of the problem that underlies Nietzsche's radical criticism of the dualism he took to be inherent in the Western tradition, a dualism that eventually gave rise to nihilism. The key, for Nietzsche, is the tendency to deify precisely what is not real; see, e.g., *Twilight of the Idols*, in *The Portable Nietzsche*, ed. Walter Kaufmann (New York: Penguin, 1976), 479–80, 485–86.

104. Max Weber, *The Protestant Ethic and the Spirit of Capitalism* (New York: Charles Scribner's Sons, 1976).

105. Man's end ultimately lies in the knowledge specifically of what is highest, i.e., the beatific vision of God, which is a way of sharing in God's own inner life.

106. See Locke, 1677a Journal MS f.2, 100-01 (held at the Bodleian Library); cited in Roger Woolhouse, *Locke: A Biography* (Cambridge: Cambridge University Press, 2007), 133.

107. Leo Strauss, *Natural Right and History* (Chicago: University of Chicago Press, 1965), 251.

108. Denis de Rougement, *L'amour et l'Occident* (Paris: Librairie Plon, 1972).

109. Schouls, *Reasoned Freedom*, 109.

110. Robert Spaemann, "The End of Modernity?" in *Spaemann Reader*, 211–29, and Spaemann, "Das unsterbliche Gerücht," in *Das unsterbliche Gerücht* (Stuttgart: Klett-Cotta, 2007).

111. See Zuckert, *Launching Liberalism*, 159–62, on Locke's grasp of the various ways Christianity is politically useful, even if it is not tenable by the genuinely reasonable (at least according to its traditional form).

112. He writes to Molyneux (Letter 1592, January 20, 1693, *CJL*, 4:625–26) the following: "I own freely to you the weakness of my understanding, that though it be unquestionable that there is omnipotence and omniscience in God our maker, and I cannot have a clearer perception of any thing than that I am free, yet I cannot make freedom in man consistent with omnipotence and omniscience in God, though I am finally perswaded of both as of any truth I most firmly assent to. And therefore I have long since given off the consideration of that question."

113. For example, St. Anselm showed that the will cannot move itself to will unless it is "already" willing to do so, which means that every elicited act of will presupposes a natural will that is always-already directed to happiness, a first act of willing that the will cannot give to itself but must be given by God; see Anselm of Canterbury, *The Fall of the Devil* (Minneapolis, MN: Arthur J. Banning Press, 2000), chap. 12, pp. 235–39.

114. We are affirming this point here as axiomatic, but we will elaborate it in greater detail in our discussion of Plato and Aristotle in part 3.

115. With respect to a remote good: "A man may *suspend* the act of his choice from being determined for or against the thing proposed, till he has examined whether it be really of a nature in itself and consequences to make me happy or not. For, when he has once chosen it, and thereby it is become a part of his happiness, it raises desire, and that proportionably gives him uneasiness; which determines his will, and sets him at work in pursuit of his choice on all occasions that offer" (2.21.57.352–53). This passage was introduced in Coste's translation and appeared in the English versions of the *Essay* only in posthumous editions.

116. Schouls, *Reasoned Freedom*, 168. Schouls's terms are a bit different from the ones we are using, and he distinguishes between the natural desire for happiness and the "master passion," which might be called the rational version of this natural desire.

117. Ibid., 151.

118. Ibid.

119. Ibid., 164.

120. Manent, *City of Man*, 115.

121. Cf., also, 2.21.23.325–26.

122. In the fourth edition—i.e., after the major revisions in the second that were intended to increase the self-determining character of the will—Locke added the following to section 23: "The act of volition, or preferring one of the

two [proposed actions], being that which he cannot avoid, a man, in respect of that act of willing, is under a necessity, and so cannot be free; unless necessity and freedom can consist together, and a man can be free and bound at once" (2.21.23.326).

123. Locke seems to concede a freedom of will, finally, only with respect to *remote goods*; see 2.21.57.352–53 and the qualifiers he added in this regard to section 23, restricting the assertion there to things "presently to be done" (2.21.23.325–26). On this issue, see the article by Yaffe, "Locke on Refraining, Suspending, and the Freedom to Will."

124. In the brief note he left to be ascribed on the sixth edition, he explained to his readers that the final changes could be written into the margins of the edition they already owned, and didn't require the purchase of a new edition.

125. It has been a classic problem insofar as Fraser "wrote it into" the text as a result of copious footnote commentary in what is a commonly used edition; see, e.g., *Essay*, 1:345n1: "Free agency with Locke thus consists at last in 'power to suspend' volition. But unless this man rises above a merely natural causation of motives, he is no more ethically free in suspending the voluntary execution of a desire than in any other exercise of will. A power to suspend volition, necessarily thus dependent, leaves man still a part of the mechanism of nature."

126. "To make a man free after this manner, by making the action of willing to depend on his will, there must be another antecedent will, to determine the acts of this will, and another to determine that, and so *in infinitum*: for wherever one stops, the actions of the last will cannot be free" (2.21.23.326). Locke eventually removed this sentence in Coste's French translation and in the editions following the fourth, but he left the more succinct statement of the same argument in section 25.

127. See 2.21.48.345, and then the passage first introduced in the French edition: "But yet there is a case wherein a man is at liberty in respect of willing" (2.21.57.352).

128. See Aristotle, *Metaphysics* 9.9.1049b10 ff.

129. Ibid., 9.1.1046a10 ff.

130. One might consider in this regard Aristotle's definition of motion, which has the curious quality of presenting the actuality of potency that so to speak retains its character as potency. Motion, he says, is the "actuality of potency *qua* potency": ἡ τοῦ δυνατοῦ ᾗ δυνατόν ἐντελέχεια φανερὸν ὅτι κίνησίς ἐστιν (*Physics* 3.1.201b5–6). In this case, if motion is what brings about a change, it does so *without the communication of form*, that is, without an internal determination. This is precisely how Locke seems to conceive cause and effect generally. From an Aristotelian perspective, we may thus interpret Locke's understanding of power as having lost any metaphysical sense of potency and as

therefore representing a reduction of potency to physical force. We will discuss the meaning of motion in Aristotle's philosophy and its significance for the question of freedom at some length in chapter 8.

131. Manent, *City of Man*, 135.

132. See *Essay*, 2.23.7–11.

133. James Gordon Clapp, *Locke's Concept of the Mind* (New York, 1937), 65.

134. See, again, *Essay*, 2.21.29.330–31.

135. It follows from this that, to insist on the will as something that is self-caused, as King does in his criticism of Locke (see Letter 1544, October 15, 1692, *CJL*, 4:540), ultimately entails, at a more fundamental level, rejecting the definition of will as *power* in Locke's sense. King doesn't raise his criticism at this level; to the extent that he does not, Locke must be said to be in the right in this particular controversy. In part 3, we will attempt to articulate a notion of freedom that is not first defined by power.

136. We recall that Locke worried sufficiently about such a naturalism in his writing of the *Essay* that he showed a draft to one of his Arminian friends in Holland, Le Clerc, for approval.

137. It is because of Locke's univocal conception of power and his identification of freedom as the paradigm of power that he is necessarily unable to reconcile human freedom and divine omnipotence: one cannot affirm any power at all in competition with omnipotence in the strict sense.

138. As an anecdotal illustration: I had a student once object strenuously in class to the proposal that there might be natural differences between men and women by saying that we are totally free to disregard whatever inclinations our biology may present, and then literally minutes later oppose the idea of monogamous love because we have evolved to be promiscuous—i.e., our biology keeps us from being faithful. Nature means both nothing and everything: this is the dialectic that necessarily emerges from a conception of freedom as pure power.

139. See, again, Harris, *Of Liberty*, 12–13. Cf. Walmsley, *Locke's Essay*, 23.

140. Woolhouse, *Locke*, 80–81: "The first-hand experience Locke gained with Sydenham and what he learnt of Sydenham's methods and ideas completely transformed his thinking not only about medicine but about our knowledge of the natural world in general."

141. Locke refers to him as one of the "master builders"—along with Sydenham, Huygens, and Newton—in relation to whom he is a mere "under-labourer"; see "Epistle to the Reader," 14.

142. See G. A. J. Rogers, "Boyle, Locke, and Reason," *Journal of the History of Ideas* 27, no. 2 (1966): 205. Rogers explains that Boyle's influence on Locke can

be seen not only in discrete notions, such as the separation between primary and secondary qualities, which is commonly recognized, but more generally in "his account of reason and the possible extent of human knowledge."

143. *The Works of the Honourable Robert Boyle* (London, 1772), 1:310. Cf. Edwin Arthur Burtt, *The Metaphysical Foundations of Modern Science* (Mineola, NY: Dover, 2003), 167–88, esp. 168.

144. Of course, the classical conception of reason also permits the relative abstraction of aspects from a broader context. The difference is that the grasp of the truth of any given matter becomes increasingly *rational* in the classical concept the more the part is seen in its relation to the whole. For Locke, by contrast, the grasp of immediate connections suffices in itself, and this understanding is indifferent to the larger context.

145. *Essay*, 2.21.4.313 (emphasis added).

146. Hegel, *Elements of the Philosophy of Right*, ed. Allen Wood (Cambridge: Cambridge University Press, 1991).

147. Ibid., 47–49. Hegel explains that this dialectic arises from a conception of the power of the will as pure, indeterminate possibility, which has been our argument also.

CHAPTER 2. THE POLITICAL CONQUEST OF THE GOOD
IN THE *SECOND TREATISE*

1. See Hegel, *Elements of the Philosophy of Right*, Introduction, §4 (plus addition and remark) and §27.

2. There is some controversy over how legitimate it is to read the *Essay* and the *Second Treatise* in light of each other, a controversy that turns on what seems at least on the surface to be an incompatibility between the two: in a nutshell, the nominalism and radical empiricism of the *Essay* seems to undermine the philosophical basis for natural law, and natural law seems to be a basic presupposition of the *Second Treatise*. Raymond Polin refers to the traditional interpretation, which takes the *Essay* and the *Second Treatise* to represent "two radically contradictory doctrines" (Polin, "John Locke's Conception of Freedom," 1). For an example, see Peter Laslett, "Introduction," *Two Treatises of Government* (Cambridge: Cambridge University Press, 1988), 82–83; cf. a contrary view in S. B. Drury, "John Locke: Natural Law and Innate Ideas," *Dialogue* 14 (1980): 531–45. For a general account of the problem, and the different attempts to solve it, see Zuckert, *Launching Liberalism*, 25–56. It is often pointed out, in this context, that Locke quite insistently hid his authorship of the *Second Treatise* (and indeed many of his published works), whereas he put

382 Notes to Pages 65–67

his name on the *Essay*. Whatever Locke's own intentions may be, we will show in this chapter that the two texts are quite evidently compatible.

3. Charles H. Monson, Jr., "Locke and His Interpreters," in *Life, Liberty, and Property*, ed. Gordon J. Schochet (Belmont, CA: Wadsworth, 1971), points out a series of tensions that he identifies as constitutive of Locke's political theory (46–48). According to Laslett, "Locke is, perhaps, the least consistent of all the great philosophers, and pointing out the contradictions either within any of his works or between them is no difficult task" ("Introduction," 82).

4. C. B. Macpherson, "Editor's Introduction," *Second Treatise of Government* (Indianapolis: Hackett, 1980), vii.

5. See, for example, Samuel Zinaich, Jr., *John Locke's Moral Revolution: From Natural Law to Moral Relativism* (Lanham, MD: University Press of America, 2005), 159–60.

6. Richard Cox, *Locke on War and Peace* (Oxford: Clarendon, 1960), 21–25.

7. This does not mean that we are positively denying any conscious attempts at deception in Locke, but only that we are setting that particular question aside as beside our present point, and leaving it open.

8. It is worth noting here that we do not mean by this term precisely what Hegel and Marx do. For these thinkers, "dialectic" entails movement, process, and development, insofar as the tension of dialectic seeks to resolve itself in its *telos*. In Locke, as we will see, the dialectic is so radical and essential that there is no tension, or at least not an evident one: it is rather the coincidence of what is so opposed as to be unrelated and so noncompetitive, i.e., inert. In this sense, there is a kind of static quality to Locke's basic notions, in contrast to those in Hegel and Marx.

9. Aristotle, *Poetics* 4.1449a.

10. Although Locke originally wrote what are called the "two treatises" as a single book, the division into two books seems to have been decided in the course of the first printing. It was not long before the second part was separated and published as a self-standing work. In the first French edition of the *Second Treatise*, and some others, the text begins with what has become the standard edition's chapter 2. This chapter is prefaced, then, by a very brief summary of the conclusions of the *First Treatise*. In our treatment, we will be citing Locke according to the following edition: *Two Treatises of Government*, ed. Peter Laslett (Cambridge: Cambridge University Press, 1960). All parenthetical references in this chapter are to the *Second Treatise*, according to the following format: chapter, section.

11. This distinction is most often associated with Isaiah Berlin; see Berlin, "Two Concepts of Liberty," in *Four Essays on Liberty* (Oxford: Oxford Uni-

versity Press, 1969). Laslett claims that there is not only a negative sense of liberty in Locke—as the "absence of restraint"—but also a positive sense, namely, "the progressive elimination of the arbitrary from political and social regulation" ("Introduction," 112).

12. I ought, Locke says, to consider him an "Enemy to my Preservation, who would take away that *Freedom*, which is the Fence to it" (3.17).

13. The passage continues: "But Freedom is not, as we are told, *A Liberty for every Man to do what he lists:* (For who could be free, when every other Man's Humour might domineer over him?) But a *Liberty* to dispose, and order, as he lists, his Person, Actions, Possessions, and his whole Property, within the Allowance of those Laws under which he is; and therein not to be subject to the arbitrary Will of another, but freely follow his own."

14. Ryan, "Locke and the Dictatorship of the Bourgeoisie," 105. Though Ryan concedes that property rights are the paradigm of rights, he insists that they are not necessarily the most important.

15. Laslett, "Introduction," 102–3.

16. It is also behind Locke's interpretation of justice, that is, the principle of political order, essentially in terms of property, however broadly this may be interpreted; see John Simmons, *The Lockean Theory of Rights* (Princeton, NJ: Princeton University Press, 1992), 318–27. David Miller has called this a "proprietary theory of justice"; see Miller, "Justice and Property," *Ratio* (June 1980): 1–2.

17. Van Leyden contrasts Locke's primarily *moral* sense of natural law to the physicalist sense one finds in Galileo and Newton. Van Leyden, "John Locke and Natural Law," in Schochet, *Life, Liberty, and Property*, 13.

18. As he puts it, "every man has a Right to every thing; even to one anothers body" (*Leviathan*, 1.14, p. 190).

19. *Leviathan*, 1.14, p. 189.

20. Locke first mentions "right" in §7, after having presented law in §§4–6. The "right" that he mentions here is specifically the right to punish, which is wholly a function of the law of preservation. We will return to a discussion of the relation between rights and duties in Locke at the end of the chapter. It is worth noting that there is a certain ambiguity here, if we identify right and freedom in some respect: it does not seem to be the case that freedom *derives* from law, but rather that freedom and law are two sides of the same political phenomenon. See David Gauthier, "Why Ought One Obey God? Reflections on Hobbes and Locke," *Canadian Journal of Philosophy* 7, no. 3 (1977): 432.

21. John Dunn, "Justice and the Interpretation of Locke's Political Theory," *Political Studies* 16, no. 1 (1968): 82n3. Contrast this with the reading of Strauss, who claims that, for Locke, right derives, not from duty, but from

the desire for happiness, which is the only innate law. Thus, there is no innate duty (*Natural Right and History*, 226–27).

22. To be sure, there is a (unique) place in the *Treatise* in which Locke posits the *positive obligation* that natural law enjoins on people, namely, the duty parents have to promote the well-being of their children (6.56). There are two things to note about this duty, however. First, it is provisional, arising in the contingent circumstances that do not present the equality that Locke says is the essence of the state of nature. Second, though this would require more discussion to show, a substantial sense of duty depends on a substantial conception of human nature, which is lacking in Locke. Moreover, Locke *does* argue that those who lack the basic means to subsist have a *right* to the surplus of others (see *First Treatise*, 4.42). Given such affirmations, Simmons has expressed bewilderment that critics (such as Strauss, Macpherson, or Cox, for example) could interpret him as denying the principle of political charity (*The Lockean Theory*, 327–28). Note, however, that Locke in the passage from the *First Treatise* speaks only of a right and not directly of a duty, and says that it arises only in extreme cases of the most "pressing Wants." As we will discuss in the section on property below, this claim can consist with the belief that there is in general no need to help those who are capable in principle of helping themselves, and there is scarcely a soul not capable of helping himself *in principle* if we have a sufficiently abstract sense of capability, or potency.

23. Locke presents, at least ostensibly, a priority of law over right, but this remains profoundly different, even in its most robust articulation, from a priority of *good* over right. Such a priority would entail a positive duty to promote flourishing. Robert Goldwin observes that Locke's notion of natural law differs from the medieval version because it makes no reference at all to human excellence, love of God, or love of neighbor; see Goldwin, "John Locke," in *History of Political Philosophy*, 3rd ed., ed. Leo Strauss and Joseph Cropsey (Chicago: University of Chicago Press, 1987), 484. A case can certainly be made on behalf of some form of positive duties on the basis of Lockean principles (see, for example, Simmons, *The Lockean Theory*, 336–52); our point is not to deny this possibility in principle, but simply to acknowledge Locke's explicit articulation here and the logical drift of his understanding generally.

24. On the "theocentrism" of Locke in contrast to Hobbes's "anthropocentrism," see David Gauthier, "Why Ought One Obey God?" 425–46.

25. The significance of faith for Locke is debated: opinions span from the belief that the Christian faith was the heart of Locke's thinking (Richard Ashcroft, "Faith and Knowledge in Locke's Philosophy," in *John Locke: Problems and Perspectives*, ed. John Yolton [Cambridge: Cambridge University Press, 1969], 194–223) to the belief that Locke hid his disbelief in Christianity in order to avoid persecution (Cox, *Locke on War and Peace*, 9–11, 45–65).

What seems unarguable is that he took the principles of social order to require a rational defense, even if they also might have support from revelation; see Hans Aarsleff, "The State of Nature and the Nature of Man in Locke" in *John Locke: Problems and Perspectives: A Collection of New Essays*, ed. John W. Yolton (Cambridge: Cambridge University Press, 2011), 104–5, and Zuckert, *Launching Liberalism*, 147–68.

26. See *Leviathan*, 1.14, p. 188.

27. James Tully, *A Discourse on Property: John Locke and His Adversaries* (Cambridge: Cambridge University Press, 1983).

28. This is precisely the view that he writes the *Two Treatises* to criticize, since he takes it to lie behind the old regime's patriarchy.

29. Tully, *Discourse on Property*, 104.

30. One may reasonably ask how Locke can claim the existence of justice in man's original state even while denying the existence of private property, insofar as he himself insists in the *Essay*, in line with Hobbes, that "*where there is no Property, there is no Injustice*" (4.3.18). In response to this question, one might point out that, if there is not yet any property in the strict sense at the origin, there is nevertheless property in the broader sense of the rights of natural freedom, and one could also point out that private property does indeed come to exist in the state of nature, prior to civil society, even if it is not man's original condition. However one decides this question, we will argue that it is not ultimately significant, insofar as Locke is actually going to remove any effective distinction between justice and injustice.

31. There is of course controversy over the extent to which Locke *sought deliberately* to distinguish his thought from that of Hobbes. Though there is what seems to be a direct reference (e.g., he mentions that "some Men have confused" the state of nature and the state of war; 3.19), Locke was explicit in denying any knowledge of Hobbes. Cox proposes that Locke was clearly being disingenuous here, because of the dangerous reputation Hobbes had (*Locke on War and Peace*, 1–44; cf. also Laslett, "Introduction," 67–92). But this question is irrelevant to the argument we are making here.

32. Cox, *Locke on War and Peace*, 88. Indeed, if reason is essentially self-referential, as we saw in chapter 1, this bias is not only due to corrupt moral character but also expresses the nature of reason, which necessarily fails to attain to the reality of things (i.e., fails to reach *beyond* the self), as Locke says in the *Essay*.

33. Locke observes that "he who was so unjust as to do his Brother an Injury, will scarce be so just as to condemn himself for it" (2.13).

34. The dots are in fact not very far apart from each other: as extreme as this inference is, it is worth observing that it is simply the straightforward meaning of the text.

35. Jeffrie Murphy argues, along similar lines, that Locke's notion—crucial for his *Treatise*—of the natural right to punish is unintelligible, since punishment as such requires the sort of codification of law, explicit authority, and institutions of enforcement available only in civil society; see Murphy, "A Paradox in Locke's Theory of Natural Rights," *Dialogue: Canadian Philosophical Review* 8 (1969): 256–71.

36. It is undoubtedly the case that Locke emphasizes, perhaps even exaggerates, the misery of the state of nature at this stage in the text in order to make the transition to civil society intelligible, but we are concerned with the inner logic that allows him to do so. We reject the idea that Locke would say something he took to be completely false simply for rhetorical purposes, for this suggestion would wholly cast away any reliable anchor for interpretation.

37. 2.13. The "strange doctrine," specifically, is the authority to execute the law of nature that Locke accords to every individual in the state of nature.

38. The main thrust of his response is not to defend the order of nature but, specifically, to point out that defenders of patriarchy or indeed of the divine right of kings offer no remedy in fact to this precarious state, since they leave authority in the end to an individual arbitrary will rather than to the impersonal universality of the state of nature.

39. See Aquinas, *Summa theologica* 1-2.94.2.

40. Macpherson, "Editor's Introduction," xiv.

41. This does not entail a rejection of self-evident truths, which is why it can be harmonized with his teaching on natural law; see David C. Snyder, "Locke on Natural Law and Property Rights," *Canadian Journal of Philosophy* 16, no. 4 (1986): 726–29. In Locke's own words: "There is a great deal of difference between an innate law and a law of nature; between something imprinted on our minds in this very original, and something that we being ignorant of, may attain to the knowledge of, by the use and due application of our natural faculties" (*Essay*, 1.3.13). Locke's position does, however, entail an alternative interpretation of self-evident truths, which no longer represent the inescapable primacy of actuality over potency in the epistemological order, but are now instead merely functional necessities that are impossible to deny in practice.

42. John Passmore, "The Malleability of Man in Eighteenth-Century Thought," in *Aspects of the Eighteenth Century*, ed. E. R. Wasserman (Baltimore: Johns Hopkins University Press, 1965), 21–46, and Passmore, *The Perfectibility of Man*, 3rd ed. (New York: Scribner's, 2000), chap. 8. Cf. Schouls, *Reasoned Freedom*, 39–40; 65–66. As Schouls explains, what is at stake in this question is the extent to which man becomes a mere passive receptacle of cultural influences.

43. See Strauss, *Natural Right*, 225–26, and Cox, *Locke on War and Peace*, 80–81. Aarsleff is no doubt right to judge that they make too much of this point in Locke; see Aarsleff, "The State of Nature," 136n1.

44. Consider the argument by Martin Rhonheimer, for example, that a social contract already presupposes an inherently social nature in man, even if that nature exists in a distorted way in the original state. We do not mean in the least to deny that Locke affirms natural justice. It could not be clearer that he does make this affirmation; we noted above, for instance, Locke's insistence on the implicit reference to this affirmation in his distinction between the state of nature and the state of war (3.19). The problem is that, within Locke's nominalist metaphysics, this distinction is *effectively meaningless*. There is justice, but it can't be realized, as we are attempting to show. The difference then amounts to that between justice being absent and being utterly ineffectually present.

45. See our presentation of this problem, as Plato discerns it, in D. C. Schindler, *Plato's Critique of Impure Reason: On Goodness and Truth in the "Republic"* (Washington, DC: Catholic University of America Press, 2008), chap. 1.

46. This problem is insurmountable, and can be resolved only by the imposition of the civil authority, which is either the judgment of an(other) individual or the collective preponderance of a majority of individuals. In this respect, we never rise above individual judgment, even if the mechanics are such that the implications of this limitation cease to be felt.

47. These three deficiencies eventually produce the three branches of government—legislative, judicial, and executive—as we will see below.

48. This does not necessarily mean that the object I choose moves me *sensibly*; it is of course possible to choose something that, on some level, I don't want to do. If one does so, however, it is not because one is choosing something one does not perceive as good, but because one is, so to speak, attracted at a deeper level: I understand that this good, however unappealing to me in some respect, is truly worth doing. The good as understood thus proves to exceed the good as sensibly perceived. On this point, see Aquinas, *Summa theologica* 1-2.10.3ad3.

49. Goodness is unity in multiplicity, which means that there is a connection between goodness and *order*; furthermore, order, which necessarily entails a first, second, and so forth, is always in some respect "hierarchy" (the word, after all, literally means "sacred order"). Hierarchy, however, is not necessarily unilateral; the insistence on order does not exclude a recognition that order is always relative to some principle, which means that it can display paradoxical leaps (of some sort) and reversals. Indeed, an *organic* sense of order arguably requires such things.

50. The sentence in 6.57 seems to suggest otherwise: "For *Law*, in its true Notion, is not so much the Limitation as *the direction of a free and intelligent Agent* to his proper Interest, and prescribes no farther than is for the general Good of those under that Law." But this seems to be an instance of Locke using traditional language, while giving that language a nontraditional meaning. When he elaborates what he means, it is clear that he is thinking of this guidance not as an internal principle of order, but an external establishment of boundaries "that ill deserves the Name of Confinement which hedges us in only from Bogs and Precipices." In other words, he is not denying in the least that law is of its essence an external limit, but only that this limit ought to be recognized as beneficial.

51. See Aquinas, *De regno*, chap. 1. Cf. Paul J. Weithman, "Augustine and Aquinas on Original Sin and the Function of Political Authority," *Journal of the History of Philosophy* 30, no. 3 (1992): 353–76. We will discuss Plato and Aristotle on this point in part 3.

52. In this, there is a direct contrast between Locke and a basic current in German philosophy. For a presentation of this alternative view of freedom, in which determinate limit is part of the inner essence of freedom, see D. C. Schindler, *The Perfection of Freedom: Schiller, Schelling, and Hegel between the Ancients and the Moderns* (Eugene, OR: Cascade, 2012).

53. See Michael Hanby, "Absolute Pluralism: How the Dictatorship of Relativism Dictates," *Communio* (Summer-Fall 2013): 562.

54. Along these lines, Hannah Arendt makes a similar observation: "Modern discussions of freedom, where freedom is never understood as an objective state of human existence but either presents an unsolvable problem of subjectivity, of an entirely undetermined or determined will, or develops out of necessity, all point to the fact that the objective, tangible difference between being free and being forced by necessity is no longer perceived"; see Arendt, *The Human Condition* (Chicago: University of Chicago Press, 1998), 71.

55. Feser, *Locke*, 28.

56. See, for example, A. John Simmons, *The Lockean Theory of Rights* (Princeton, NJ: Princeton University Press, 1992), 68–69.

57. Locke MS, quoted by John Dunn, *The Political Thought of John Locke* (Cambridge: Cambridge University Press, 1969), 218–19. To be sure, Locke may not be expressing a criticism of the egoism here, but only a worry about the political consequences of "publicizing" this truth—in which case, Strauss's basic way of reading Locke remains in place.

58. Contrast this, for example, with Goldwin, who claims that Locke's sense of natural law is ultimately identical with Hobbes's, as the drive to self-preservation ("John Locke," 485).

59. According to Zuckert, "the evidence seems very strong that Locke's doctrine is in serious disagreement with traditional authorities such as Hooker and also the Bible, but that Locke nonetheless attempts to enlist these authorities on his side, using them in misleading ways so as to obscure the very real differences between them and him" (*Launching Liberalism*, 95).

60. Locke's interpretation of equality is not, of course, the only one possible. We will suggest below an alternative, which is based on the priority of actuality.

61. See John Milbank's description of the liberal conception of man in Milbank, "The Gift of Ruling," *New Blackfriars* 85 (March 2004): 212–38. Richard Aaron judges that Locke's "individual is artificial. He has no family ties. He tends to be conceived as a somewhat isolated being even when he enters into social relations with others" (Aaron, "Authority and the Rights of Individuals," in Schochet, *Life, Liberty, and Property*, 165).

62. This does not mean, of course, that the potencies precede the actualizations in any simple fashion, for this is precisely the abstraction we are critiquing. Behind all of this is the profound metaphysical issue of the relation between substance and relation; on this, see David L. Schindler, "Norris Clarke on Person, Being, and St. Thomas," *Communio* 20, no. 3 (1993): 580–93. Without entering into the details of this discussion, we wish to affirm only the intrinsic connection between relation and actuality, and the relative priority of actuality over potentiality.

63. Aarsleff's interpretation of the state of nature in Locke seems to be correct, namely, that its primary significance is not to describe some actual historic condition (though Locke does not seem to want to exclude this as a possibility), but rather to describe human nature such as it is *presupposed* by political existence ("The State of Nature," 100).

64. Locke admits in a later chapter that men as they exist concretely possess all sorts of inequalities in relation to each other, but he says that "all this consists with the Equality, which all Men are in, in respect of Jurisdiction or Dominion one over the other, which was the *Equality* I there spoke of, as proper to the Business in hand, being that *equal Right* that every Man hath, *to his Natural Freedom*, without being subjected to the Will or Authority of any other Man" (6.54). This may seem to be similar to the point we are making about dignity, which "consists with" actual inequalities. But the difference, though subtle, is profound: Locke is saying that the right to natural freedom, which is in essence an isolation from others, can coexist with the duty I owe to "pay an Observance," as he puts it here, to others of higher rank, i.e., to my *superiors*, those to whom I am not equal in fact. But this can mean only that I affirm my equality by abstracting from this actual relation of obligation.

65. Locke admits that children are not born in the state of equality, but *to* it (6.55). We will come back to the implications of this point.

66. Cf. Macpherson, "Editor's Introduction," xvi.

67. Aristotle, *Politics* 7.1–2.

68. He says we learn this both through *reason* and through *revelation* (5.25). Tully helpfully lists the specific differences between Locke and Filmer on natural property thus: (1) Locke claims the right to property is possessed by all, while Filmer says it belongs to Adam exclusively; (2) Locke takes it to be a right only of *use*, while Filmer understands it as a right of use, abuse, or alienation; (3) for Locke the right expresses common property, while for Filmer it is private; (4) Locke conceives it as a right to use something that belongs to all, while Filmer takes it to be a right of ownership; and (5) Locke interprets use in relation to a specified end (namely, the preservation of everyone), while Filmer does not conceive of use in relation to some specified end; see Tully, *Discourse on Property*, 61.

69. According to Manent, Locke affirms self-ownership at the cost of all other ownership (*City of Man*, 125). There is some tension in Locke's affirmation of self-ownership here, since he had insisted at the outset that we do not belong to ourselves but are God's property. Tully makes a distinction between God's ownership of the *man*, and the individual's ownership of his own *person* (*A Discourse on Property*, 105), and he suggests, further, that there is no necessary inconsistency here: God owns the man, but the person has "tenants rights" to make full use of what belongs most fundamentally to God (ibid., 114). In this case, it is *use* that causes ownership, which is analogous (as we will see below) to Locke's general theory of labor. Following that theory directly, however, leads us to say that man comes to be nothing but what he makes of himself. As Zuckert helpfully observes by referring back to the *Essay*, "The 'I' is not, Locke argues, anything given in nature. It is made by the self in the course of its operations of sensation and reflection" (*Launching Liberalism*, 195). The "I," in other words, is not *given*, but *achieved*; more generally, substance gets reduced to the *impact* it has on what is other than itself. What God owns in me is therefore, effectively, *nothing*. This position becomes especially significant in the political sphere.

70. According to Tully, the "question of property must be answered within a context of positive duties to others" (*Discourse on Property*, 104).

71. We are drawing the names of these principles from Ryan, "Locke and the Dictatorship of the Bourgeoisie," 89.

72. "This I dare boldly affirm, That the same *Rule of Propriety*, (*viz.*) that every Man should have as much as he could make use of, would hold still in the World, without straitning any body, since there is Land enough in the World

to suffice double the Inhabitants had not the *Invention of Money*, and the tacit Agreement of Men to put a value on it, introduced (by Consent) larger Possessions, and a Right to them" (5.36).

73. Locke indicates this in a notorious passage: "Thus the Grass my Horse has bit; the Turfs my Servant has cut; and the Ore I have digg'd in any place where I have a right to them in common with others, become my *Property*, without the assignation or consent of any body" (5.28). Locke indicates this principle of extension *before* money; money just extends it in principle indefinitely.

74. The limits of this multiplication depend on the extent to which Locke allows money to function, not simply as a means of exchange, but specifically as capital. Macpherson has argued that Locke subordinates money as a medium of exchange to money as capital: see C. B. Macpherson, *The Political Theory of Possessive Individualism: Hobbes to Locke* (Oxford: Oxford University Press, 2011), 204–8. Tully, on the other hand, claims that there is no evidence of Locke interpreting money as capital (since the concept had not yet been explicitly formulated by Locke's time; *Discourse on Property*, 149); cf. Patrick Kelly, "All Things Richly to Enjoy: Economics and Politics in Locke's *Two Treatises of Government*," *Political Studies* 36 (1988): 292–93. For our purposes, Locke's intention doesn't matter: it cannot be denied that the logic of his position *clearly* points in this direction, as we will argue below.

75. Gopal Sreenivasan, *The Limits of Lockean Rights in Property* (Oxford: Oxford University Press, 1995), 43–44.

76. As Kirstie M. McClure observes, the law of nature that operates here is "silent" on the question of distributive justice and concerns instead only the "prohibition of injury and the imperative of worldly preservation per se"; see McClure, *Judging Rights: Lockean Politics and the Limits of Consent* (Ithaca, NY: Cornell University Press, 1996), 255.

77. On the inherent tension in Locke's theory, which makes the following of the original law of nature lead to the undermining of that very law once money is introduced, see Snyder, "Locke on Natural Law and Property Rights," 749–50.

78. Though there are things that speak in its favor (something that we have worked hard on tends to mean more to us than something we achieve with little effort), it is quite easy to come up with problems in the labor theory of value and counter examples: we all cherish things that are *there* without effort: the beauty of nature, for example, or our parents and familial relations, or talents that we are born with, or things we have received as a gift from others. Something can require an abundance of effort and not amount to much, while we might produce something else of great value with surprising ease. On this

score, we might ask whether the effortless work of genius is worth less than the laborious efforts of a mediocre artist. Such questions can easily be multiplied. Compare Aristotle's much more commonsensical account of what makes things good in the *Rhetoric* (1.6–7).

79. See Heidegger, "The Question Concerning Technology," in *Basic Writings* (New York: Harper, 2008), 311–41.

80. Tully, *Discourse on Property*, 117.

81. For example, I may chop down a tree to make wood; clearly, there is a substrate in this case that persists amidst the change from tree to lumber. But Locke's theory suggests that the lumber is a radically new thing with respect to the tree: it is now wholly an object of use, whereas the tree was not such an object in the least. A similarly radical transformation occurs when the lumber is turned, through labor, into a chair. In making a chair, it may seem that I am adding to a value that was already given through labor insofar as my labor presupposes the wood. The raw materials I have either acquired or purchased, and in either case I own the labor that went into making it what it is: either it *is* mine or it *became* mine through the purchase.

82. According to Hegel, the primary significance property has is the fact that it represents a "superseding of mere subjectivity of personality" (*Philosophy of Right*, §41, addition). Though the language is modern, Hegel is giving expression here to the classical understanding of property.

83. See Goldwin, "John Locke," 487–88.

84. Locke rejects this intrinsic obligation implicitly in his interpretation of freedom as the right to dispose as one wishes within the confines of law. One might insist that the law—of nature, if not of civil society—imposes constraints even on private use, which would preclude any right to abuse or alienate. Even if this were fully granted, however, it remains the case that this constraint is precisely *imposed* on property as an external regulation rather than representing the very meaning of property in itself.

85. Tully, *Discourse on Property*, 147.

86. Macpherson puts it thus: "Locke's disapproval of covetousness is plain enough. Yet it is not at all inconsistent with his belief in the moral rationality of unlimited accumulation. On the contrary, it was rational, i.e., industrious, appropriation that required protection against the covetousness of the quarrelsome and contentious who sought to acquire possessions not by industry but by trespass" (*Possessive Individualism*, 237). Similarly: "Not only is the desire for accumulation rational, according to Locke, but accumulation is the essence of rational conduct" (C. B. Macpherson, "The Social Bearing of Locke's Political Theory," in Schochet, *Life, Liberty, and Property*, 73).

87. This is not the *only* expression: one could also show that Locke's notion of rights is also a political actualization of power qua power, or his interpretation of freedom as boundary, or his view of law, and so forth.

88. Quoted in Macpherson, *Possessive Individualism*, 207. Locke is speaking here of international trade, but the logic of his notion would certainly extend in an analogous sense to trade between individuals.

89. Locke, "Considerations of the Consequences of Lowering the Interest and Raising the Value of Money," in *The Works of John Locke in 9 Volumes* (London: Longman et al., 1794), 4:13, quoted in Cox, *Locke on War and Peace*, 177 (Cox's emphasis).

90. Macpherson uses this phrase in "The Social Bearing," 74.

91. Macpherson, *Possessive Individualism*, 221–47; cf. Macpherson, "The Social Bearing," 74.

92. James Tully's *Discourse on Property* is no doubt the most comprehensive rebuttal to Macpherson. The basic argument Tully makes—namely, that Macpherson fails to give due importance to the "common use" principle as prior to, and limiting of, private property—we have in principle answered above: there is no contradiction between the affirmation of this principle as pure potency and the disregarding of it in actuality. Moreover, Tully's insistence that there is no direct evidence in Locke of money ever functioning as capital is beside the point, however true it may be as a historical matter. We have shown how money will have an inexorable tendency to acquire the role of capital given a labor theory of value. The most compelling objection Tully makes to Macpherson, in our judgment, is his observation that Locke insistently proscribes self-alienation, which lies of course at the basis of a capitalist economics. However extensive the rights may be that Locke accords to the person, Tully argues, those rights are always rooted in a given *self* that is essentially inalienable. One of the inferences Tully makes from this point is that, though a man can sell his *services*, he cannot sell *himself* into slavery. Analogously, Tully takes this to mean that a man can sell his work (that is, as a set of actual activities), but not his indeterminate power to work (*Discourse on Property*, 141). This latter, however, is pivotal for capitalism, and Macpherson claims that Locke allows this (by reference to 5.28). Tully's objection, here, is a strong one insofar as it stems from the logic of Locke's clear assumption of the individual as a subject of rights, and quite illuminating with respect to the principles of capitalism. Rather than resolve this point of the dispute, we will simply say that there seems to be an essential tension in Locke, who, in spite of the truth of Tully's observation regarding self-alienation, does indeed affirm man as possessing *himself* (a claim that Tully has to qualify in a rather artificial way in order to sustain his objection to Macpherson: as we

pointed out above, in a nutshell, Tully says that man does not own his *self*—which belongs to God—but only his *person*, and the actions of his person; see *Discourse on Property*, 105, 114), which would seem to give him the ability to alienate himself. In addition, Locke also makes freedom "uncontroleable" within the bounds of law. However ambiguous this issue remains in Locke, it is clear that modern liberalism has come to take for granted the self's absolute right over itself. There is, indeed, a radical question that inevitably arises at the center of the liberal conception of the person and his rights: Does a person have the right to commit suicide? If we answer yes, it would seem to undermine the absoluteness of the principle of rights, and if we answer no, it would seem to do the same. Is pure power (understood as indeterminacy) a logical contradiction?

93. The cause is certainly also theological, but this has not been our focus: we will address it briefly at the end of this chapter.

94. As his critics have pointed out, Macpherson seems to think that Locke meant the equality he posits as fundamental to remain in actuality in all circumstances; see, e.g., Simmons, *The Lockean Theory*, 84.

95. This is the central theme of Locke's notorious essay on the proposed poor law reform; see H. R. Fox Bourne, *The Life of John Locke* (London: Henry S. King and Company, 1876), 2:377–91.

96. It is interesting to note that, according to Tully, though Locke tends to represent on the contemporary scene a defense of capitalism, he was originally taken to be the founder of socialism, then of the economics of limited private property, and then that of unlimited private property (*Discourse on Property*, x). Our argument is that he fits all of these quite well, ultimately because they share a similar view of freedom, indebted to the modern disassociation of political order from nature.

97. This is Aristotle's view; it presupposes an analogous sense of nature; see Robert Spaemann, "Nature," in *A Robert Spaemann Reader: Philosophical Essays on Nature, God, and the Human Person*, ed. D. C. Schindler and Jeanne Schindler (Oxford: Oxford University Press, 2015), 22–36.

98. This question can be amplified by raising essential correlate questions: To whom is consent given, unless there is already some authority? Doesn't a contract require already a common authority? When is consent meant to be given? Is it written, a public oath? Do we have any evidence of a single instance of such a thing? But to engage all of these would take us too far afield.

99. This is not to say that Filmer represents the traditional view in fact. For a presentation of Locke's critique of Filmer, see Gordon J. Schochet, "The Family and the Origins of the State in Locke's Political Philosophy," in Yolton, *John Locke: Problems and Perspectives*, 81–98.

100. There are many aspects of his proposal that would require some reflection and response, but this is not our present task; we are addressing only a single aspect.

101. Note that Locke addresses the question of "parental" rather than "paternal" authority: one feature of his critique of patriarchy, which derives political authority from the natural order of the family, is that authority in a family has always been shared by the father and mother.

102. As a dramatic contrast, one might consider Antonio López, *Gift and the Unity of Being* (Eugene, OR: Cascade, 2014), esp. chap. 1, 11–50.

103. They are *not* political relationships strictly speaking, because they have their own specific ends, different from the end that defines political community, namely, the preservation of property. But these relationships are also not *natural* strictly speaking, as we have just seen, insofar as the state of nature is defined as perfect equality of power. Familial relationships seem to represent, in Locke, a kind of transitional relationship, defined according to the model of consent.

104. This is certainly an implausible aspect of his theory, which does not seem to accord with any actual historical practice, but we are most concerned only with its implications for the nature of political membership.

105. John Dunn, "Consent in the Political Theory of John Locke," in Schochet, *Life, Liberty, and Property*, 145.

106. As Kilcullen puts it, "If some people in the neighborhood did not join when the community was formed . . . their property was not submitted, and the community's territory may have gaps. To know who has tacitly consented would need more knowledge of the history of particular properties than is usually available"; see John Kilcullen, "Locke on Political Obligation," *Review of Metaphysics* 45 (1985): 339.

107. Or at least not as Locke means it; as we noted earlier, there are alternative interpretations of equality that can posit its actuality as coincident with the inequalities that are an essential part of the concrete order.

108. Note that the enjoyment of delights—which we explained in chapter 1 is a form of actuality—is set aside by Locke as politically irrelevant.

109. Kendall suggests that, in this apparently total self-alienation of the transfer of power, Locke is more "Rousseauian" than Rousseau ("The Right of the Majority," in Schochet, *Life, Liberty, and Property*, 169). Cf. Polin, "Locke's Conception of Freedom," 9–10. Rousseau seems to have an almost mystical sense of the unity of a political community, which is embodied in the inerrant "General Will." One misses this sense in Locke, but on close inspection the differences between the substance of Locke's position and that of Rousseau are relatively small.

110. Simmons argues (in part against Tully) that the entry into civil society does not make property conventional rather than natural—in other words, it does not cancel one's natural claim to own what one has properly acquired— but only gives the state jurisdiction over one's *land*, which remains in one's possession (*The Lockean Theory*, 307–18). Though Simmons's limitation of the scope of jurisdiction to land alone is unconvincing, one ought to accept his judgment regarding ownership, at least in the sense that one's property rights are not transferred through the social contract to some other individual. Nevertheless, Tully is certainly truer to Locke's text when he judges that, for Locke, *all* of one's possessions come to belong to the community (*Discourse on Property*, 164). Even if one were to concede Simmons's point that private ownership remains intact in the state of civil society, one must still ask what *actual significance* ownership has given the state's right to use that property as deemed necessary, a right that, given the social contract, trumps the individual's right to private use.

111. We will see in the end that nature will nevertheless return in the form of a conflict of powers.

112. Polin, "Locke's Conception of Freedom," 10.

113. Kendall, "The Right of the Majority," 169. Cf. Willmoore Kendall, *John Locke and the Doctrine of Majority-Rule* (Urbana: University of Illinois Press, 1941).

114. Locke presents four limits to the legislative power: (1) it cannot be an *arbitrary* power over the lives of the people (which they do not in any event have the power to alienate); (2) it must distribute justice according to "promulgated standing laws"; (3) it cannot take property from individuals without their consent; and (4) it cannot transfer its power of making laws to any other body; see chapter 11 of the *Second Treatise*.

115. *First Treatise*, 11.106, in *Two Treatises*, 218–19. It is common today to think that this has *always* been the political question because one believes that politics is most essentially a matter of distributing power. To think this way, however, is to concede the notion of freedom that is being criticized. In fact, the most basic political question is, What is the truth of man? This question is implicitly asked, and answered, willy-nilly even by those political theories that consider politics to be a matter only of juridical order and not at all of truth.

116. This is not to say that modern politics is the *cause* of the abuse of power, which would of course be an absurd claim. Instead, we must make a distinction between abuse as a *betrayal* of political order and abuse as its normal form, even if that form is tempered through regulation.

117. See Aquinas, *Summa theologica* 1-2.95.2: "Every human law has just so much of the nature of law, as it is derived from the law of nature. But if in any point it deflects from the law of nature, it is no longer a law but a perversion of law."

118. Kilcullen acknowledges this contradiction, but then attempts to alleviate it by drawing a distinction between *making* a judgment and *acting* on it. He explains that individuals give up their right to *act* on their own judgment in joining civil society (except in the extreme case of social breakdown or otherwise irremediable corruption), but they always retain the right to their own opinions. But this distinction, which is not Locke's in any event, fails to resolve the deep problem; it simply eludes some of the more obvious practical implications of it ("Locke on Political Obligation," 338).

119. This is a version of the liar's paradox: the declaration can be effective only if it is not effective.

120. We recall that, according to Locke, once one has given one's consent to enter civil society, one "is perpetually and indispensably obliged to be and remain unalterably a Subject to [the Commonwealth], and can never be again in the liberty of the state of Nature" (8.120). By comparison, the marital bond ought to be dissolvable once it has served the purpose of providing a framework for the rearing of children.

121. Goldwin observes that Locke "barely uses or does not use at all, in the *Second Treatise*, such words as *charity, soul, ethics, morality, virtue, noble*, or *love*" ("John Locke," 484). Ironically, the passage we cite, which is one of the only ones that appeal to a certain depth of connection among the members of a commonwealth, concerns precisely the "Dissolution and Death" of that unity.

122. Rousseau recognizes just this problematic implication of any social contract theory, and he attempts to avoid it by conjuring a "general will" that is distinct from "the will of all"; see book 2, chapter 3 of the *Social Contract*, trans. by G. D. H. Cole (New York: E. P. Dutton, 1913). Hegel is right to observe, however, that Rousseau cannot sustain this distinction because it requires a sense of individual-transcending "political substance" that Rousseau simply does not have. But we have shown elsewhere that, as correct as his judgment of Rousseau's (implicit) criticism of Locke may be, Hegel too fails on this point insofar as he attempts to recover the classical sense of politics on modern terms (see D. C. Schindler, *Perfection of Freedom*, 238–372, esp. 251–53).

123. According to McClure, "the revocation of consent becomes in Locke a matter of individual judgment, no more dependent on universal agreement than is the appropriation of individual property in the state of nature" (*Judging Rights*, 3n3).

124. As we have seen, however, natural justice is in itself ineffectual since it is always subject to the judgment of necessarily biased individuals.

125. That is, if the purpose is indeed to resolve the political problem. It may be the case that Locke was simply using this rhetoric in order to shape imagination in a way that effectively ensures a certain amount of peace. In other words, he may have intended to manage the political problem rather than solve it. This

interpretation would accord well with the pragmatic evasion of the problem of the freedom of the will that we discussed last chapter. I am indebted to Mark Shiffman for this observation.

126. Quoted in H. R. Fox Bourne, *The Life of John Locke* (London, 1876), 1:403–4.

127. Plato, *Republic* 358e–362c.

128. One could describe legal order in this case quite well in terms of Nietz-sche's notion of *ressentiment*.

129. Macpherson makes a similar observation (*Possessive Individualism*, 255–57), though he accounts for the paradox in terms of social conditions. Cf. Schochet, "Introduction," in *Life, Liberty, and Property*, 10–11.

130. Cox, *Locke on War and Peace*, 120.

131. See, for example, the limits Locke sets to the scope of legislative power: 11.134–42.

132. Dunn, "Consent in the Political Theory of John Locke," 133. Snyder likewise observes a "correlation" between duties and rights in Locke, but says that, for Locke, duties have priority ("Locke on Natural Law and Property Rights," 730–31).

133. Cox, *Locke on War and Peace*, 169.

134. We might consider the significance, in this regard, of Anthony Krupp's study, which shows that Locke at least implicitly denies personhood to chil-dren, and denies humanity simpliciter to "changelings," i.e., the handicapped; Krupp, *Reason's Children: Childhood in Early Modern Philosophy* (Lewisburg, PA: Bucknell University Press, 2009), chaps. 2 and 3. We might also consider the fact that Locke was invested in the slave trade; see Macpherson, "Editor's Intro-duction," x; cf. Maurice Cranston, *Locke: A Biography* (New York: Macmillan, 1957), and also the *Fundamental Constitutions of Carolina*, which Locke drafted in 1669, and which provided both for what was at the time a radical guarantee of religious liberty coupled with a right to own slaves (http://avalon .law.yale.edu/17th_century/nc05.asp).

135. Goldwin rightly observes that there is no discussion in Locke of the *bonds* between citizens ("John Locke," 508).

136. In the *Phaedo* (99c), Plato uses the verbs ξυνδεῖν ("to bind together") and συνέχειν ("to enclose" or "keep together") to describe the ontological function of the good.

137. Manent has observed that, for Locke, "the capacity to produce ef-fects, far from revealing the powers of human nature, on the contrary, testifies to its impotence and poverty," ultimately because man himself becomes a pure product of arbitrary will (*City of Man*, 116–17).

138. Along similar lines, Wendell Berry has famously observed that mar-riage in the modern world exhibits the form of divorce: "Marriage, in what is

evidently its most popular version, is now on the one hand an intimate 'relationship' involving (ideally) two successful careerists in the same bed, and on the other hand a sort of private political system in which rights and interests must be constantly asserted and defended. Marriage, in other words, has now taken the form of divorce: a prolonged and impassioned negotiation as to how things shall be divided. During their understandably temporary association, the 'married' couple will typically consume a large quantity of merchandise and a large portion of each other"; Berry, "Feminism, the Body, and the Machine," in *The Art of the Commonplace* (Berkeley, CA: Counterpoint, 2002), 67.

139. A larger study would be warranted in itself; in the meantime, we have explored the general question of the liberal interpretation of religious freedom in D. C. Schindler, "Liberalism, Religious Freedom, and the Common Good: The Totalitarian Logic of Self-Limitation," *Communio* (2013): 577–615.

140. Locke wrote the *Epistola de Tolerantia* (in Latin) in 1685–86, and it was published anonymously in May 1689 in Holland. The contract date of Locke's *Essay* was May 24, 1689, though he seems to have done further editing before the first publication. The *Two Treatises* were published, again anonymously, in October 1689, though this text, like the *Essay*, had 1690 as the nominal year of publication; see J. R. Milton, "Locke's Life and Times," in *The Cambridge Companion to Locke*, ed. Vere Chappell (Cambridge: Cambridge University Press, 1994), 14–17. Dunn's judgment that we may see "the issue of toleration as the axis of Locke's intellectual development, and the *Letter* as in some sense a summary of his final attitude towards the place of politics in human experience" supports our proposal here, namely, that the basic decision to "potentialize" what is in fact ultimate is the foundation for everything else (see John Dunn, "Justice and the Interpretation of Locke's Political Theory," 74). Laslett judges that Locke's political ideas developed slowly in subordination to the theme of toleration ("Introduction," 35). According to C. H. Bastide, Locke was formed by the Puritan mystical status of the individual, and the "latitudinarian" conviction regarding the inviolability of thought, so that there was for him nothing more objectionable than an outsider watching over one's relations to the Creator. This sense of the absolutely private character of religion was behind his insistence on separating it from politics; see Bastide, *John Locke: Ses théories politiques* (Paris: Leroux, 1907), 227: "Locke's political work is a long battle against Anglican theocracy."

141. Locke, *A Letter Concerning Toleration*, ed. James Tully (Indianapolis: Hackett, 1983), 41–42.

142. In fact, Locke defends his position by appealing from the outset to what he refers to as the "chief Characteristical Mark of the True Church" (ibid., 23).

143. Ibid., 51.

144. It is interesting to note that, though Locke allows any Protestant form of Christianity, at least in principle, he rejects *Catholicism*: what distinguishes the latter is precisely what we might call the objective manifestation of actual authority (tradition, magisterium, pope), as opposed to the authority of scripture, specifically *as* actualized in individual judgment. Cf., ibid., 50–51.

145. This is essentially the argument Zuckert makes (*Launching Liberalism*, 147–68), though Zuckert presents it as a very positive development.

146. We come back once again to Nietzsche's assessment of Western civilization: it would be possible to read his well-known "Madman" aphorism (*The Gay Science*, ed. Kaufmann [New York: Vintage, 1974], 181–82) as an expression of just what we are describing here: affirming God while at the same time rendering him actually ineffectual, so that the human being is forced, willy-nilly, to replace him in the form of power.

Chapter 3. The Basic Shape of Modern Liberty

1. We do not necessarily accept the typical classification of modern thinkers as "empiricist" and "rationalist," in part because a more adequate understanding would recognize how much their differences are flipsides of more or less the same coin. We choose Spinoza and Kant here, but there is scarcely a significant modern thinker who could not be shown to exhibit the same basic form, whatever further inferences they might make: Descartes, Leibniz, Hobbes, Hume, and so forth. Relative exceptions, such as Malebranche, for example, can be shown to retain some aspect of a classical metaphysics (as we suggested in chapter 1) and so not to belong so wholly to modernity.

2. According to Steven Nadler, *A Book Forged in Hell* (Princeton, NJ: Princeton University Press, 2011), 33, freedom is the essential subject matter of Spinoza's two main books, *Ethics* and the *Theologico-Political Treatise*.

3. Matthew Kisner, *Spinoza on Human Freedom: Reason, Autonomy, and the Good Life* (Cambridge: Cambridge University Press, 2011), 3. Kisner goes on to show that, in Spinoza, all claims about the good finally reduce to its capacity to increase power (88, 110). We might say that the production of power is, for Spinoza, precisely what constitutes the *goodness* of the good.

4. *Ethics*, pt. 1, definition 7; see *Spinoza: Complete Works*, trans. Samuel Shirley (Indianapolis: Hackett, 2002), 217. (Hereafter cited as *CW*.)

5. On the way in which achieving knowledge of a thing gives one power over it, see Don Garrett, "Spinoza's Ethical Theory," in *The Cambridge Companion to Spinoza*, ed. Don Garrett (Cambridge: Cambridge University Press, 1996), 267–314, esp. 279–82.

6. See Spinoza, Letter 58, to G. H. Schuller, October 8, 1674 (*CW*, 909).

7. Ibid.

8. Spinoza, *Ethics*, pt. 5, prop. 33 (*CW*, 377).

9. Ibid., pt. 5, prop. 40 (*CW*, 380).

10. Spinoza, *Theologico-Political Treatise*, chap. 16 (*CW*, 527). Spinoza is drawing out here the political implication of the desire for self-preservation he articulated in the *Ethics* (pt. 3, props. 6–7 [*CW*, 283]). Right, for Spinoza, comes to mean therefore the extent to which the individual has the *power* to assert himself without regard for others: "Each individual thing has the sovereign right to do all that it can do; i.e., the right of the individual is co-extensive with its determinate power" (*CW*, 527). On Spinoza's view of the coextensiveness of right and power, see Edwin Curley, "Kissinger, Spinoza, and Genghis Khan," in Garrett, *Cambridge Companion to Spinoza*, 315–42, esp. 318–22.

11. Spinoza, *Theologico-Political Treatise*, chap. 2, sec. 23 (*CW*, 689).

12. Ibid., chap. 16 (*CW*, 527–28).

13. Ibid. (*CW*, 530).

14. Ibid., chap. 2, sec. 13 (*CW*, 686).

15. Ibid., sec. 16 (*CW*, 687).

16. Ibid., chap. 16 (*CW*, 531).

17. Ibid., chap. 8, sec. 12 (*CW*, 727).

18. Ibid., chap. 16 (*CW*, 531). Spinoza repeats this same principle at the international level: "This treaty (*foedus*) of alliance [i.e., between commonwealths] remains effective for as long as the motive for making the treaty—fear of loss or hope of gain—remains operative. But if the fear or the hope is lost to either of the two commonwealths, that commonwealth is left in control of its own right, and the tie by which the two commonwealths were bound together automatically disintegrates. Therefore every commonwealth has full right to break a treaty whenever it wishes, and it cannot be said to act treacherously or perfidiously in breaking faith as soon as the reason for fear or hope is removed"; ibid., chap. 3, sec. 14 (*CW*, 694).

19. It is good to recall that Locke was originally in favor of "nontolerance," i.e., the strict enforcement of the practice of a particular religion by the state, and came to his better-known position later. While this may seem to be an about-face, in fact Locke was quite consistent in changing his mind: the reason he was in favor of state regulation originally was not because of a conviction regarding the truth of a particular church, and the obligation to reflect this truth in the political order, but because strict regulation seemed to be the best way to protect the state from civil unrest. Later, he came to see that this same end would be better served by allowing as free an exercise as possible (except for Muslims and Catholics, since these religions did not allow for such a division between the theological and the political).

20. *Theologico-Political Treatise*, chap. 19 (*CW*, 557–58). Earlier in the treatise, Spinoza says: "Therefore, as the sovereign right to free opinion belongs to every man even in matters of religion, and it is inconceivable that any man can surrender this right, there also belongs to every man the sovereign right and supreme authority to judge freely with regard to religion, and consequently to explain it and interpret it for himself. The supreme authority to interpret laws and the supreme judgment on affairs of state is vested in magistrates for this reason only, that these belong to the sphere of public right. Thus for the same reason the supreme authority to explain religion and to make judgment concerning it is vested in each individual, because it belongs to the sphere of the individual" (chap. 7 [*CW*, 470–71]).

21. Spinoza explained to a friend that one of the main motives for his writing of the *Theological-Political Treatise* was in order to champion "the freedom to philosophise and to say what we think. This I want to vindicate completely, for here it is in every way suppressed by the excessive authority and egotism of preachers"; Letter 30, to Henry Oldenburg, fall of 1665 (*CW*, 844).

22. *Theological-Political Treatise*, chap. 20 (*CW*, 570).

23. Ibid. (*CW*, 572).

24. Kant, *Critique of Practical Reason*, in Kant, *Practical Philosophy*, trans. Mary J. Gregor (Cambridge: Cambridge University Press, 1996), 218 (5:97); hereafter *PP*. Parenthetical references for Kant refer to the volume and page number from the standard edition, the *Gesammelte Schriften*, ed. the Royal Prussian (later German) Academy of Science (Berlin: George Reimer [later Walter de Gruyter], 1900—). In fact, it is clear that Spinoza would not, at a certain level, object to this comparison: he himself compares free human action to that of a stone that has received into itself from an external cause the impulse of projectile motion. If this stone were conscious, he says, it would think of itself as perfectly free in its endeavor to continue the motion. But man is conscious in just this way; see Spinoza, Letter 58 (*CW*, 909).

25. *Critique of Practical Reason*, in *PP*, 224 (5:105).

26. Kant, *Critique of Pure Reason*, A 444 ff. = B472 ff.

27. Allen Wood, "Kant's Compatibilism," in *Self and Nature in Kant's Philosophy*, ed. Allen Wood (Ithaca, NY: Cornell University Press, 1984), 74. See also Henry Allison, *Kant's Theory of Freedom* (Cambridge: Cambridge University Press, 1990), 28.

28. *Critique of Pure Reason*, AS543 = B571.

29. *Critique of Practical Reason*, in *PP*, 218–19 (5:98).

30. Ibid., in *PP*, 219 (5:99). See Wood's discussion of the "timeless" agent that is presupposed by this account ("Kant's Compatibilism," 89–93).

31. *Critique of Practical Reason*, in *PP*, 222 (5:103).

32. Wood, "Kant's Compatibilism," 99.

33. On this, see *Groundwork of the Metaphysics of Morals*, in *PP*, 61–66 (4:406–12), in which Kant clearly distinguishes the a priori aspect of duty from any empirical conditions.

34. See Katrin Flikschuh, *Kant and Modern Political Philosophy* (Cambridge: Cambridge University Press, 2000), 81; Wood, "Kant's Compatibilism,"80.

35. Wood says that Kant thinks of freedom as *effective cause* ("Kant's Compatibilism," 74).

36. See *Groundwork of the Metaphysics of Morals*, in *PP*, 393 (6:237).

37. Ibid., in *PP*, 387 (6:230).

38. Arthur Ripstein, *Force and Freedom: Kant's Legal and Political Philosophy* (Cambridge, MA: Harvard University Press, 2009), 29.

39. Gunnar Beck, *Fichte and Kant on Freedom, Rights, and Law* (Lanham, MD: Lexington Books, 2008), 194.

40. Ripstein, *Force and Freedom*, 355.

41. See Kant, *Groundwork of the Metaphysics of Morals*, in *PP*, 409 (6:255–56). Nevertheless, Kant does not have a positivist conception of civil rights, for he insists that these are founded on natural rights, which he considers to be in themselves "provisional" (ibid., 6:256–57 [*PP*, 409–11]).

42. See Spinoza, *Theologico-Political Treatise*, chap. 2, sec. 15 (*CW*, 687).

43. Kant, *Groundwork of the Metaphysics of Morals*, in *PP*, 451–52 (6:307–8).

44. G. Beck, *Fichte and Kant*, 202–3. As Beck explains, this is a basic insight that Kant received from his reading of Rousseau.

45. See Michaele Ferguson, "Unsocial Sociability," in *Kant's Political Theory: Interpretations and Applications*, ed. Elisabeth Ellis (University Park: Penn State University Press, 2012), 158–69.

46. "Idea for a Universal History with a Cosmopolitan Purpose," in Kant, *Anthropology, History, and Education* (Cambridge: Cambridge University Press, 2011), 113 (8:22).

47. Ripstein, *Force and Freedom*, 39.

48. "The human being is an *animal which*, when it lives among others of its species, *has need of a master*. For he certainly misuses his freedom in regard to others of his kind; and although as a rational creature he wishes a law that sets limits to the freedom of all, his selfish animal inclination still misleads him into excepting himself from it where he may. Thus man needs a *master*, who breaks his stubborn will and necessitates him to obey a universally valid will with which everyone can be free. But where will he get this master? Nowhere else but from the human species. But then this master is exactly as much an

animal who has need of a master. Try as he may, therefore, there is no seeing how he can procure a supreme power (*Gewalt*) for public right that is itself just, whether he seeks it in a single person or in a society of many who are selected for it. For every one of them will always misuse his freedom when he has no one over him to exercise authority over him in accordance with the laws" ("Idea," [8:23]).

49. See Wolfgang Kersting, "Kant's Concept of the State," in *Essays on Kant's Political Philosophy*, ed. Howard Lloyd Williams (Chicago: University of Chicago Press, 1992), 143–65.

50. See Onora O'Neill, "Kant and the Social Contract Tradition," in Ellis, *Kant's Political Theory*, 25–41.

51. Kant, *Groundwork of the Metaphysics of Morals*, in *PP*, 459 (6:315–16).

52. The debate over the meaning of Kant's notion and its practical implications has a long and continuing history. See, for example, Sven Arntzen, "Kant on Duty to Oneself and Resistance to Political Authority," *Journal of the History of Philosophy* 34 (1996): 409–24; Julius Ebbinghaus, "The Law of Humanity and the Limits of State Power," *Philosophical Quarterly* 3 (1953): 14–22; Katrin Flikschuh, "Reason, Right, and Revolution: Kant and Locke," *Philosophy and Public Affairs* 36 (2008): 375–404; Sarah Williams Holtman, "Revolution, Contradiction, and Kantian Citizenship," in *Kant's Metaphysics of Morals*, ed. M. Timmons (Oxford: Oxford University Press, 2002), 209–33; Christine Korsgaard, "Taking the Law into Our Own Hands: Kant on the Right to Revolution," in *Reclaiming the History of Philosophy: Essays for John Rawls*, ed. C. Korsgaard, A. Reath, and B. Herman (Cambridge: Cambridge University Press, 1997), 297–329; Reidar Maliks, "Kant, the State, and Revolution," *Kantian Review* 18, no. 1 (2013): 29–47; Thomas E. Hill, "Questions about Kant's Opposition to Revolution," *Journal of Value Inquiry* 36 (2002): 283–98; Peter P. Nicholson, "Kant, Revolution, and History," in Williams, *Essays in Kant's Political Philosophy*, 249–68; Lewis White Beck, "Kant and the Right to Revolution," *Journal of the History of Ideas* 32 (1971): 411–22; Sidney Axinn, "Kant, Authority, and the French Revolution," *Journal of the History of Ideas* 32 (1971): 423–32.

53. Kant explains that the "formal execution of a monarch *by his people*," "like a chasm that irretrievably swallows everything, . . . [is] a crime from which the people cannot be absolved, for it is as if the state commits suicide"; *Groundwork of the Metaphysics of Morals*, in *PP*, 464n (6:321).

54. Kant, "What Is Enlightenment?" in *PP*, 17 (8:35).

55. Ibid., in *PP*, 18 (8:36).

56. G. Beck, *Fichte and Kant*, 211. Beck says that the justification of a liberal political order, which Kant does indeed seem to champion, therefore re-

quires a different order of explanation, namely, the anthropological and historical (as opposed to the moral). Beck's position, here, however, just begs the question, since it is clear that Kant would never allow in the end a historical account to trump a rational a priori. Rather than attempt to resolve the problem, it seems more prudent simply to indicate the ambiguity, and in any event this suffices for our present purpose. It is nevertheless worthwhile to note that this ambiguity echoes another, more commonly noted, one concerning Kant's notion of transcendental freedom generally: on the one hand, Kant argues that we are inevitably free by nature, insofar as any choice at all can be interpreted as a result of the unconditioned causality of the will, and yet, on the other hand, he makes subjection to reason, and transcendence of natural causes, something we must strive to achieve rather than being automatically given. One of the best discussions and resolutions of this problem can be found in Henry Allison, *Kant's Theory of Freedom* (Cambridge: Cambridge University Press, 1990). Again, we do not need to assess any proposal for resolving it but wish only to point to the problem as an illustration of the ambiguity we have identified running through the modern concept of liberty generally.

57. Kant, "What is Enlightenment?" in *PP*, 22 (8:42).

58. Ibid., in *PP*, 21 (8:41).

59. Cf. Pierre Manent, *An Intellectual History of Liberalism* (Princeton, NJ: Princeton University Press, 1996), 3–9. Manent seems to assume that the modern "theologico-political problem" is an essential, and therefore inevitable, one which would make liberalism inescapable, rather than recognizing that the problem arises from assumptions about the nature of religion that are already modern. For this, Manent has been justly criticized; see John Milbank, "The Gift of Ruling: Secularization and Political Authority," *New Blackfriars* 85, no. 996 (2004): 212–38.

60. See Hegel, *The Positivity of the Christian Religion*, in *Early Theological Writings*, ed. T. M. Knox (Philadelphia: University of Pennsylvania Press, 1971), 67–181. For Kant's separation, see *The Conflict of the Faculties* (7:36–37), in *Religion and Rational Theology*, ed. Allen Wood and George di Giovanni (Cambridge: Cambridge University Press, 1996), 262–63. In his *Religion within the Boundaries of Mere Reason*, Kant explains that "the principle in an ecclesiastical faith which rectifies or prevents every religious delusion is this: ecclesiastical faith must contain within itself, besides the statutory articles which it yet cannot quite dispense with, another principle as well, of bringing about the religion of good life conduct as its true goal, in order at some future time to be able to dispense with statutory articles altogether"; in *Religion and Rational Theology*, 194 (6:175). For an interesting reflection on the differences between Kant and Hegel on this question, see George di Giovanni, "Faith without

Religion, Religion without Faith: Kant and Hegel on Religion," *Journal of the History of Philosophy* 41, no. 3 (2003): 365–83.

61. Kant, *Conflict of the Faculties*, in *Religion and Rational Theology*, 273 (7:50).

62. In his *Religion within the Boundaries of Mere Reason*, for example, Kant explains that outward acts of religion can be objectively required and regulated, provided that they are not thought, in their externality, to have any real religious value; in *Religion and Rational Theology*, 206–15 (6:190–202). In *Conflict of the Faculties*, he explains that the state has an interest in regulating doctrines, but only to the extent that they bear on the production of "useful citizens, good soldiers, and, in general, faithful subjects" (281n [7:60n]).

63. Daniel Dennet, *Darwin's Dangerous Idea: Evolution and the Meaning of Life* (New York: Simon and Schuster, 1995), 61–84.

64. Hegel, *Elements of the Philosophy of Right*, ed. Allen W. Wood (Cambridge: Cambridge University Press, 1991), §5, pp. 37–39.

65. Ibid., 38.

Chapter 4. Symbolical Order and Diabolical Subversion

1. Hans-Georg Gadamer, *The Relevance of the Beautiful* (Cambridge: Cambridge University Press, 1986), 31.

2. Plato, *Symposium* 191d.

3. This list is drawn from the relevant entries in *Greek-English Lexicon* by Liddell and Scott.

4. See Ricoeur, *The Symbolism of Evil* (New York: Harper and Row, 1967).

5. Ibid., 11.

6. Ibid., 15.

7. As Schelling puts it, "Mythology is not *allegorical*; it is *tautegorical*. To mythology the gods are actually existing essences, gods that are not something *else*, do not *mean* something else, but rather *mean* only what they are"; F. W. J. Schelling, *Historical-Critical Introduction to the Philosophy of Mythology*, trans. Mason Richey and Markus Zisselsberger (Albany: SUNY Press, 2007), 136. Schelling explains that Coleridge is the one who coined the term to describe his own (i.e., Schelling's) understanding, but he also expresses approval of the term.

8. Ricoeur, *Symbolism of Evil*, 17.

9. On knowledge as indwelling, see Michael Polanyi, *Personal Knowledge: Towards a Post-Critical Philosophy* (New York: Harper Torchbooks,

1964), and Polanyi, *The Tacit Dimension* (Chicago: University of Chicago Press, 2009); cf. Esther Lightcap Meek, *Longing to Know: The Philosophy of Knowledge for Ordinary People* (Grand Rapids, MI: Brazos, 2003).

10. Ricouer, *Symbolism of Evil*, 347–57.

11. In what is no doubt one of the most influential texts on the "symbol" in the twentieth century, Karl Rahner likewise insists on the *ontological* character of symbol that underlies, and makes possible, the epistemological function, but he interprets this character more directly in terms of the relationship between form and matter *in* particular beings, while (without excluding this dimension in principle) we propose that even this dimension has its roots in the "symbolism" of the act of creation; see Karl Rahner, "The Theology of the Symbol," in *Theological Investigations*, Vol. 4 (Baltimore: Helicon, 1966), 221–52.

12. Some of this elaboration and justification will be given in part 3 of this book.

13. Plato, *Timaeus* 29e.

14. Plato, *Republic* 508d–509b.

15. The idea of love—whether *eros* or *philia*—as a constitutive principle of the cosmos was of course common in ancient Greece. Plato gives the idea expression in Eryximachus's speech in the *Symposium*, but it is also explicitly found, for example, in Empedocles, and indeed in Hesiod's *Theogony*.

16. *Gorgias* 507e–508a. Cf. *Timaeus* 32c.

17. In his remarkable essay, "Plato's Lysis: A Re-enactment of Philosophical Kinship," *Ancient Philosophy* 15, no. 1 (1995): 69–90, Francisco Gonzalez shows that, for Plato, friends belong to each other precisely by belonging together to the good, which necessarily transcends them.

18. Aristotle, *Metaphysics* 12.10.1075a12 ff.

19. Ibid., 1076a1–5. For a beautiful account of the classical/Christian understanding of the cosmos, see Michael Hanby, *No God, No Science: Theology, Cosmology, Biology* (Malden, MA: Wiley-Blackwell, 2013), 49–104.

20. See Aristotle, *Politics* 1.1.1252a1–6; Aquinas, *De regno* 1.2.14. Aquinas calls the city the "perfecta communitas."

21. See his profound reflections in Ferdinand Ulrich, *Gegenwart der Freiheit* (Einsiedeln: Johannes Verlag, 1974).

22. Plato, *Republic* 596eff.

23. This description requires many qualifiers, but they are not necessary in the present context. For a fuller exposition and interpretation of Plato's notion of form, see D. C. Schindler, *Plato's Critique of Impure Reason: On Goodness and Truth in the Republic* (Washington, DC: Catholic University of America Press, 2008), 85–138.

24. For an argument on this point, see D. C. Schindler, *The Catholicity of Reason* (Grand Rapids, MI: Eerdmans, 2013), 120–29.

25. See Desmond's brief presentation of the meaning of "counterfeit double" in William Desmond, *Hegel's God: A Counterfeit Double?* (Burlington, VT: Ashgate, 2003), which we mentioned in chapter 1. Desmond has referred to the event in World War II in public presentations.

26. Plato, *Phaedo* 100d.

27. In his *Journals*, Kierkegaard relates the story of an awkward exchange he had with the queen, in which she makes reference to his books "*Either* and *Or*"—revealing that she missed the point. It is said that Kierkegaard's nephew, always in the shadow of his great uncle, in a state of despondency referred to himself as "Neither/Nor."

28. See J. W. Goethe, *Faust* (Munich: Deutscher Taschenbuch, 1979), ll. 336–39.

29. In the classical understanding, *convenientia* (from *convenire*, "to come together" or "to suit") meant harmony, an internal connection between things due to something other than logical necessity; efficiency (from *efficere*, "fully to bring about") designated the creativity of bringing about something new, a generativity that implied a communication of form and therefore an ontological unity between cause and effect.

30. Heidegger famously criticizes the Thomistic notion of truth as *adaequatio* precisely because he interprets it as implying a "convenience" in the modern sense: see Martin Heidegger, "On the Essence of Truth," in *Basic Writings*, ed. David Farrell Krell (New York: Harper and Row, 1977), 113–41, esp. 118–22. But this is a reading of medieval thought through the lens of the modern. Heidegger's tracing of the line from imperial Rome, through the Catholic Church, to the modern mind is asserted without any argument, and it turns merely on the linguistic link of the "Roman–Romantic"; see Heidegger, *The End of Philosophy* (New York: Harper and Row, 1973), 12–13, in which the connection is made in the space of a single short paragraph.

31. This would be *efficient* causality in the strictly modern sense, and in a certain respect final causality, again in the impoverished sense of a merely extrinsic aim.

32. See Josef Pieper, *Leisure: The Basis of Culture*, trans. Gerard Malsbery (South Bend, IN: Saint Augustine's Press, 1998), 9–14.

33. See Spinoza's Letter 50, to Jelles Jarig, June 2, 1674 (*CW*, 891–92). Hegel adapts this idea as a general principle of dialectic, *omnis determinatio est negatio*; see Hegel, *Science of Logic* (Atlantic Highlands, NJ: Humanities Press International, 1969), 113.

34. See, for example, C. S. Lewis, *The Screwtape Letters* (New York: Macmillan, 1982), 32–33.

35. Benedict XVI, *Dogma and Preaching: Applying Christian Doctrine to Daily Life* (San Francisco: Ignatius, 2005), 204.

36. Hannah Arendt, *Eichmann in Jerusalem: A Report on the Banality of Evil* (New York: Penguin Classics, 2006).

37. See Arendt's presentation of the dialectic between means and ends in Arendt, *The Human Condition* (Chicago: University of Chicago Press, 1998), 153–59.

38. See Kant, *Critique of Judgment*, trans. Werner Pluhar (Indianapolis: Hackett, 1987), §§64–65, pp. 248–55. The intrinsic relation of parts and whole is nevertheless ambiguous in Kant, since he qualifies the perception of this relation as a merely regulative judgment.

39. See Hegel's description of the "System of Needs," in *Philosophy of Right*, §§189–208, pp. 227–39, with the corresponding additions.

40. Robert Spaemann discusses this problem in Spaemann, "Ende der Modernität?" in *Moderne oder Postmoderne? Zur Signaturdes gegenwärtigen Zeitalters*, ed. Robert Spaemann et al. (Weinheim: VCH, 1986), 19–40.

41. Spaemann contrasts the ancient notion of universality with the modern, more abstract one: on this, see Robert Spaemann, "A Philosophical Autobiography," in *Spaemann Reader* (Stuttgart: Philipp Reclam, 1983), 12.

42. Aristotle, *Nichomachean Ethics* 8.31056b24–32, and 8.5.

43. Plato, *Phaedrus* 276a–277a.

44. Traditionally, the fall of the angels has been understood as caused by the angels' choice, coincident with their creation, not to reject God simply, but to reject the debasement of God implied in the Incarnation. The fallen angels' sin of pride is in other words understood in a basic way as contempt for the flesh (of man). It is interesting to note that Christ pronounced his well-known rebuke to Peter, "Get behind me, Satan!" (Matt. 16:23), after Peter asserted that Jesus, who had just revealed himself to the apostles as the Messiah, was so to speak "too good" to have to suffer incarnation to the extreme point of crucifixion.

45. This does not at all mean that it is "a-moral"; Heidegger makes this mistake, in his insistence in *Being and Time*, for example, on driving analysis always to the ontological level, to disastrous effect.

46. It may be suggested that success, even in its conventional meaning, often intends the *quality* and not just the quantity of effects: one might point to a doctor who has healed thousands of patients, or a philanthropist who has donated millions of dollars to some cause, as examples of success that people generally acknowledge. But note that even these examples present a "quality" that is still conceived in terms of quantity. We do not spontaneously use the term "success" for someone, perhaps through a single profound gesture, who permanently changes the life of a particular person, opening his eyes to the good, or a long life of quiet devotion that remains unknown to "the public."

47. The classic treatment of this theme is Werner Jaeger, *Paideia: The Ideals of Greek Culture*, 3 vols. (Oxford: Oxford University Press, 1945).

48. See Gabriel Marcel, "Sketch of a Phenomenology and a Metaphysics of Hope," in *Homo Viator* (New York: Harper Torchbooks, 1962), 29–67. We will return to this in chapter 6.

49. See Søren Kierkegaard, *Sickness Unto Death* (Princeton, NJ: Princeton University Press, 1980), 13–14.

50. C. S. Lewis has Psyche explain: "It was when I was happiest that I longed most"; see Lewis, *Till We Have Faces: A Myth Retold* (New York: Harcourt, 1956), 74.

51. This is the problem with Levinas's interpretation of *eros* in Plato, which he characterizes as a desire, not for any fulfillment, but rather for the absence of fulfillment: Levinas proposes that *eros* is simply for desire itself, the desire to go on desiring: see Emmanuel Levinas, "Philosophy and the Idea of the Infinite," in A. Peperzak, *To the Other: An Introduction to the Philosophy of Emmanuel Levinas* (Ashland, OH: Purdue University Press, 2005), 114. Plato's view is more paradoxical, insofar as he presents *eros* as lying *between* fullness and emptiness, *poros* and *penia*, rather than simply on the side of the empty (*Symposium* 202b–204b). We will return to this in our discussion of Plato and Aristotle in part 3.

52. By contrast, according to Aquinas, the will, or rational appetite, terminates specifically "in the thing" (*in re*): see, for example, *Summa theologica* 1.16.1; cf. 1.27.4.

53. It is important to note that, though the material object in some respect (!) remains the same, the nature of that object has changed, as we just suggested above. Moreover, the order of finality may be said to be left in place, insofar as in the two cases the object is referred to as an end, but the *nature* of the finality has likewise changed, from an intrinsic end to a merely extrinsic one. Ultimately, nothing is in reality the same in the two cases; it only "seems" alike.

54. Benjamin Constant, "The Liberty of the Ancients Compared with That of the Moderns," *Political Writings* (Cambridge: Cambridge University Press, 1988), 310–11.

55. Iris Murdoch describes the modern sense of the person along just these lines: "What I am 'objectively' is not under my control; logic and observers decide that. What I am 'subjectively' is a foot-loose, solitary substanceless will. Personality dwindles to a point of pure will"; Murdoch, *The Sovereignty of Good* (London: Routledge and Kegan Paul , 1970), 16.

56. It is illuminating to note that the controversial practice of enclosure, which produced protests and revolts throughout the sixteenth to eighteenth centuries, insofar as it implied a fundamental reorienting of existence (from

feudalism to capitalism, in a word), found its theoretical justification in Locke's chapter on property in the *Second Treatise*.

57. As opposed, for example, to interpreting it as individual ownership for the sake of common use, as we find in Aristotle (*Politics* 2.5.1263a38–40) and in the Catholic Social Teaching (see, e.g., *Laborem exercens*, 14).

58. Goethe, *Faust*, pt. 2, ll. 4925 ff., pp. 147 ff.

59. Aquinas, *Summa theologica* 1.5.6.

60. Consider in this regard the fashion industry: the *content* of fashion is nothing but its novelty, its *difference from*, what was worn, drunk, eaten, etc., "last year."

61. See Kant, *Perpetual Peace and Other Essays*, ed. Ted Humphry (Indianapolis: Hackett, 1983), 124. We will return to this at the start of chapter 5.

62. This claim follows from the Lockean *liberal* sense of rights, founded on a notion of freedom as active power. The matter is more ambiguous in the older sense of right in the Middle Ages that presupposes the primacy of actuality: in this case, right flows from some real condition, an actual reality (for example, a nature), as an expression of that reality, and so is not created simply in the opposition to competing claims. We will elaborate this idea in chapter 5.

63. Hegel, *Philosophy of Right*, §159 (p. 200).

64. Note, again, we are not criticizing the notion of a contract *simply*; contracts have an indispensable place in any social order. Contract, however, ought to presuppose a more fundamental unity that is not the result of reciprocal consent but precedes it. What we are criticizing is a view of political order *founded* on consent, and so on the presupposition of mutually opposed spontaneous wills as what is most originally and naturally *given*.

65. We see a paradigmatic instance of this in Montaigne, who describes his famous friendship with Étienne de la Boetie in beautiful—but altogether unreal—terms, as based on nothing essential ("because he was he, because I was I"), insofar as he had eliminated any natural or social reality as a foundation for friendship earlier in the essay; see Montaigne, "Of Friendship," in *The Complete Works of Montaigne*, trans. and ed. William Hazlitt (Philadelphia: William T. Amies, 1879), 104–10.

66. On this, see Samuel Kimbriel, *Friendship as Sacred Knowing: Overcoming Isolation* (Oxford: Oxford University Press, 2014), esp. 23.

67. On all of this, see John Milbank's critique of liberalism in Milbank, "The Gift of Ruling: Secularization and Political Authority," *New Blackfriars* 85, no. 996 (2004): 212–38.

68. This knowledge lay, not outside of his capacity, but nevertheless outside of his proper exercise, which is why there is a drama. It is necessarily the

case in a symbolic order that capacity exceed proper exercise, since intrinsic participation in a larger whole implies that one's power is greater than the limits set by the particularity of the self: the participation makes one *be* more than oneself.

69. It is not often noticed that God creates the animals in the first place because "it is not good that the man should be alone," though the need for companionship is not fully met, of course, until the creation of the woman (see Gen. 2:18–19).

70. Aquinas, *Summa theologica* 1.92.3.

71. Clearly, God's proscription is not simply an impersonal statement regarding a universal state of affairs (though it is in some respect *also* that), but it includes the personal involvement of a genuine act of will. This, though, does not necessarily make it "arbitrary" in the modern sense.

72. We recall, here, Polin's observation that "for Locke, . . . freedom represents a freedom for evil," which we discussed in chapter 1 (Polin, "John Locke's Conception of Freedom," 3).

73. Plato, *Republic* 515a.

74. See the broader discussion and textual justification of this interpretation in D. C. Schindler, *Plato's Critique of Impure Reason*, esp. 125–29.

75. Cf. Plato, *Phaedo* 82e–83a: "Philosophy sees that the worst feature of this imprisonment is that it is due to desires, so that the prisoner himself is contributing to his own incarceration most of all." Plato is referring, in this passage, to the soul's "imprisonment" in the body. What he means here by "body," however, is not the soul's enfleshed presence in time and space, but more specifically the subordination of intelligible reality to the sensible, which is a reversal of proper order.

CHAPTER 5. A "SOCIETY OF DEVILS"

1. See Kant, *Perpetual Peace and Other Essays*, 124: "As hard as it may sound, the problem of organizing a nation is solvable even for a people comprised of devils (if only they possess understanding). The problem can be stated in this way: 'So order and organize a group of rational beings who require universal laws for their preservation—though each is secretly inclined to exempt himself from such laws—that, while their private attitudes conflict, these nonetheless so cancel one another that these beings behave publicly just as if they had no evil attitudes.' This kind of problem must be *solvable*. For it does not require the moral improvement of man; it requires only that we know how to apply the mechanism of nature to man so as to organize the conflict of hostile attitudes present in a people in such a way that they must compel one another

to submit to coercive laws and thus to enter into a state of peace, where laws have power."

2. Max Horkheimer and Theodor Adorno, *Dialectic of Enlightenment* (New York: Continuum, 1969).

3. On this point, see Benedict XVI, *Dogma and Preaching*, 205.

4. See Robert Spaemann, "What Does It Mean to Say, 'Art Imitates Nature'?" in *Spaemann Reader*, 193.

5. The details will be pursued in our discussion of Aristotle in chapter 8.

6. See Plato, *Republic* 369a.

7. It is worth pointing out that, by calling this a "relative" priority, we mean to avoid a reductive interpretation of the relationship between act and potency, such that potency can be reduced altogether to act, essentially without remainder. What we would want to affirm—though this would need further development in a different context—is that potency also "adds" something to actuality, and that the difference between them is itself in principle *good*. For an illustration of such an affirmation, see Edith Stein's presentation of the relationship between act and potency, which in the ontologically higher being of living organisms reveals not only a greater unity *but also a greater difference* than in inanimate being; Stein, *Finite and Eternal Being* (Washington, DC: ICS Publications, 2002). For a profound metaphysical argument concerning the internal relationship between actuality and possibility, see Ferdinand Ulrich, *Homo Abyssus*, 2nd ed. (Freiburg im Breisgau: Johannes Verlag Einsiedeln, 1998), 153–68. The tensions that this difference generates is one of the great dramas of the development of the meaning of freedom. The point, as we will see in part 3, is the recognition of actuality as *generous plenitude*, rather than simple "terminus" of potency, a point that was not sufficiently explicit in the classical articulations of the relationship and led to problematic attempts to compensate. The key is a *reciprocal*, though asymmetrical, relationship between act and potency, in which each reinforces the other. This affirmation requires a supraformal notion of actuality and a radically analogous notion of being. In any event, in the present context, we limit ourselves to the classical conception of the matter.

8. See Aquinas, *De veritate* 21.2.

9. Augustine, who famously argued that only God is to be enjoyed as an end in himself (*frui*), and all other things are to be "used" as a means to this end (*uti*), nevertheless understood that we are meant properly to *love* the things used, which implies an affirmation of intrinsic goodness (see *De doctrina christiana* 1.23.22).

10. An example of a genuine means would be the *word*, properly understood. For an incomparably profound exploration of the nature of the word

along these lines, see Ferdinand Ulrich, *Der Mensch als Logo-Tokos*, in *Logo-Tokos* (Freiburg im Breisgau: Johannes Verlag Einsiedeln, 2003), 1–163.

11. Schelling had a deep insight into this point, which lay behind his attempt to reinterpret the pure actuality of God as a kind of *life*; see, e.g., Friedrich Wilhelm Joseph von Schelling *System der Weltalter: Münchner Vorlesungen 1827/28 in einer Nachschrift von Ernst von Lasaulx*, ed. Siegbert Peetz (Frankfurt am Main: Klostermann, 1991). He arguably did not, however, have a sufficient sense of analogy to make this point without falling into another dualism.

12. For penetrating observations on this score, see Max Horkheimer, *The Eclipse of Reason* (New York: Oxford University Press, 2013), 3–57.

13. See, e.g., John Peterson, *Aquinas: A New Interpretation* (Washington, DC: Catholic University of America Press, 2008), 198: "The will is unfree with respect to something when reason sees it only as end and not possibly as means."

14. See Aquinas, *Summa theologica* 1-2.9.1–6.

15. The intellect presents the object to the will, which sets the will in motion; the sensitive appetite disposes the person to the object, the will moves itself to achieve the object, but it does so inside of being moved by the goodness of the object, all of which is caused by God, who is goodness itself.

16. "Hence it is evident that the will is moved by one and the same movement—to the end, as the reason for willing the means; and to the means themselves" (*Summa theologica* 1-2.8.3).

17. Jonathan Hecht, "Freedom of the Will in Plato and Augustine," *British Journal for the History of Philosophy* 22, no. 2 (2014): 197.

18. There are further qualifications to make: a distinction, for example, between the universal good, which is the last end, and the particular ends individuals adopt as good for them, whether these are in fact good or not, and so forth. The point is that to aim at something as an end is necessarily to take it to be good in some respect.

19. *Not* in the sense of factual data, but in the sense of *donum*. On the difference between these, see Kenneth Schmitz, *The Gift: Creation* (Milwaukee, WI: Marquette University Press, 1982), 34–63.

20. As Plato put it, *when* I do a certain thing for the sake of an end, the object of my will (βούλησις) is not (first of all) the thing I am doing, but the *end* itself, which is to say that the very willing of the action is directed to the end (*Gorgias* 467d), or in other words that the willing of the action transcends the specific act that is willed. We will discuss in more detail the meaning of "will" in Plato in chapter 7.

21. *Gorgias* 468b.

22. Ibid., 466e. It is crucial to recall that this is a specifically "noninstrumentalist" sense of intelligence, which means not just awareness of what one is

doing along with implications but an understanding of what is truly good. We contrasted this in chapter 1 with Locke's sense of reason.

23. It is not uncommon to encounter this strategy of neutralizing a reality by making it one of many possibilities: instead of speaking of "the" tradition, for example, one speaks of tradition*s*, and the plural means that the values and convictions that we have are values and commitments we *happen* to have. This internal detachment from one's convictions is an example of Péguy's definition of what it means to be modern: *ne pas croire ce que l'on croit*, "not believing what one believes."

24. See, e.g., *Physics*, bk. 3, 201a10 f.: ἐντελεχεία τοῦ δυνάμει ἡ τοῦ δυνάμει.

25. Barry Schwartz, *The Paradox of Choice: Why More Is Less* (New York: HarperCollins Perennial, 2005).

26. See, e.g., Karol Wojtyła, "The Personal Structure of Self-Determination" and "The Problem of the Constitutions of Culture through Human Praxis," in *Person and Community: Selected Essays* (New York: Peter Lang, 1993), 187–95; 265–69.

27. For an account of this point from a Hegelian perspective, see D. C. Schindler, "'The Free Will Which Wills the Free Will': On Marriage as a Paradigm of Freedom in Hegel's *Philosophy of Right*," *The Owl of Minerva* 44, no. 1–2 (2013): 577–615.

28. This does not of course mean that positive law is able simply to be deduced from natural law, but only that the natural law abides as a foundation.

29. To say this is not to exclude outright the possibility of a *Stellvertretung*, a vicarious representation that enables internal participation, but simply excludes a merely "forensic" interpretation of such a representation. It also does not exclude in principle political representation, but is arguably the basis for such representation.

30. Here we see what is lacking in Kant's notion (see *Critique of Practical Reason*, pt. 1, bk. 1, chap. 1, §8 [theorem IV]): though autonomy for him, as distinct from Rousseau, from whom he appears to have derived it, is not in the least arbitrary—indeed, it can be said to be the exact opposite of arbitrary, since it becomes identical with reason in its most formal purity—it is nevertheless understood as being *opposed* to heteronomy, which requires what is ultimately a self-contradictory subjectivizing of the form of reason, as Hegel rightly saw.

31. For an in-depth argument, both speculative and historical, regarding the metaphysical and political implications of subordinating relationality in a one-sided way to individual substance, see Adrian Pabst, *Metaphysics: The Creation of Hierarchy* (Grand Rapids, MI: Eerdmans, 2012).

32. The classic texts that make this argument are Michel Villey, *La formation de la pensée juridique moderne*, 4th ed. (Paris, 1975); Macpherson, *The*

Political Theory of Possessive Individualism; Strauss, *Natural Right and History*; Alasdair MacIntyre, *After Virtue*, 2nd ed. (Notre Dame, IN: University of Notre Dame Press, 1984). Cf. Ernest Fortin, "On the Presumed Medieval Origin of Individual Rights," in *Classical Christianity and the Political Order: Reflections on the Theologico-Political Problem*, ed. Brian Benestad (Lanham, MD: Rowman and Littlefield, 1991), 43–64; Simone Weil, *Selected Essays: 1934–1943*, trans. Richard Rees (Oxford: Oxford University Press, 1962); David L. Schindler, "An Interpretation of *Dignitatis Humanae*," in *Freedom, Truth, and Human Dignity*, ed. David L. Schindler and Nicholas J. Healy (Grand Rapids, MI: Eerdmans, 2015), 155–61; Mark Shiffman, "The Eclipse of the Good in the Modern Rights Tradition," *Communio* 40, no. 4 (2013); John Milbank, "The Gift of Ruling." Much of the argument against the modern conception of rights we make in the following pages is anticipated in Milbank's seminal essay.

33. Brian Tierney, "The Idea of Natural Rights—Origins and Persistence," *Northwestern Journal of International Human Rights* 2, no. 1 (2004): 2–12; cf. Tierney, *The Idea of Natural Rights: Studies on Natural Rights, Natural Law, and Church Law 1150–1625* (Grand Rapids, MI: Eerdmans, 1997).

34. Tierney, *Idea of Natural Rights*, 9: "In his polemical writings Ockham did not refer to his nominalist philosophy but he relied on frequent citations of earlier canonistic texts." It is obvious, though, that his "nominalist philosophy" is going to have a profound influence on his interpretation of "earlier canonistic texts."

35. It is important to recognize, moreover, that these powers are already naturally inclined, as it were, to extend in this way. On the premodern sense of nature as self-transcending, see, once again, Spaemann, "Nature," in *Spaemann Reader*.

36. Tierney describes Ockham as defending "a natural right to use external things that was common to all men and that was derived from nature, not from any human statute" (*Idea of Natural Rights*, 9). Ockham was asserting this natural right primarily over against Church law, but at the time Church law was inseparable from the political order.

37. For an outstanding account of the meaning of nature in the premodern context and the changes it undergoes in the rise of modernity, see Spaemann, "Nature," in *Spaemann Reader*, 22–36. According to Spaemann, nature is essentially analogical and so inherently related to orders that transcend it, for example, the order of human culture, or the order of grace.

38. This is not in the least to deny a radical metaphysical difference between the self in itself and the other(s) to which the self is related, but only to insist that this difference is a metaphysical one, and it cannot be established merely empirically. In other words, there is no reality that one can point to and

say it concerns *exclusively* the self and *not* what is other than it—even the very selfhood of the self.

39. Benjamin Constant, "The Liberty of the Ancients Compared with That of the Moderns," in *Political Writings* (Cambridge: Cambridge University Press, 1988), 310–11.

40. See Arendt, *The Human Condition*, 58: strictly private individuals "are all imprisoned in the subjectivity of their own singular experience, which does not cease to be singular if the same experience is multiplied innumerable times. . . . It is with respect to this multiple significance of the public realm that the term 'private,' in its original privative sense, has meaning. To live an entirely private life means above all to be deprived of things essential to a truly human life: to be deprived of the reality that comes from being seen and heard by others, to be deprived of an 'objective' relationship with them that comes from being related to and separated from them through the intermediary of a common world of things, to be deprived of the possibility of achieving something more permanent than life itself. The privation of privacy lies in the absence of others; as far as they are concerned private man does not appear, and therefore it is as though he did not exist. Whatever he does remains without significance and consequence to others, and what matters to him is without interest to other people."

41. To say that it is private is *not* to deny that such doctrines have a social dimension, as Rawls himself clearly affirms; see Rawls, *Political Liberalism* (New York: Columbia University Press, 1996), 14. It is rather to point out that the social, in this case, is interpreted as a collection of individuals (civil society), as opposed to an actual whole, which is *necessarily* political. For Rawls, the culture of a comprehensive doctrine "is the culture of the social, not of the political" (ibid.).

42. In contrast to the interpretation of Augustine as the "inventor" of private interiority—see, for example, Philip Carey, *Augustine's Invention of the Inner Self: The Legacy of a Christian Platonist* (Oxford: Oxford University Press, 2003)—Thomas Prufer sees Augustine as eliminating privacy in the retreat to the interior self, because that interior space is always already filled by an Other: "There is no longer any privacy: man is because he is manifest to another. But this publicity to God is as hidden as God himself"; Prufer, *Recapitulations: Essays in Philosophy* (Washington, DC: Catholic University of America Press, 1993), 28.

43. See D. C. Schindler, "Enriching the Good: Toward the Development of a Relational Anthropology," *Communio* 37, no. 4 (2010): 643–59.

44. See Martin Rhonheimer, *The Common Good of Constitutional Democracy* (Washington, DC: Catholic University of America Press, 2013). Rhonheimer draws a distinction between the integral common good and the strictly political common good.

45. To spell it out: whereas goods include interests, i.e., individual advantage, individual interest defined explicitly *as such* does not include goodness per se. One can (and indeed ultimately *will* by necessity) get from goods to interests, but one cannot get from interests to goods. What is absolute (goodness in itself) does not exclude, but includes, what is relative (good for me), while what is relative excludes what is absolute. This is the difference between the symbolical and the diabolical.

46. To say that the person has no right to do this does not imply that the state therefore has the right to use coercive force to prevent it. The very point of our argument is to reject these alternatives insofar as they both rest on a diabolical notion of freedom.

47. This is not to say that there is no tension at all in the modern view, though we would argue that this tension lies *inside* of the modern view itself, as we will be explaining below.

48. Alexis de Tocqueville, *Democracy in America*, trans. George Lawrence (Garden City, NY: Doubleday, 1969), 504.

49. Ibid.

50. For example, he observes that equality seems easier to achieve, and more permanent, than the good of political liberty, as Tocqueville understands it (ibid., 504–6).

51. According to Plato, "there are two kinds of equality which, though identical in name, are often almost opposites in their practical results" (*Laws* 757b; cf. 744c; 745d). Aristotle distinguishes an *analogical equality* (τὸ κατ' ἀναλογίαν ἴσον), which recognizes equality as rooted in the ontological reality of the persons and so differentiated accordingly, without ceasing to be in a proper respect equal. He contrasts this with absolute and arithmetic equality, which he criticizes (*Politics* 1301a27). See Mogens Herman Hansen, "Democratic Freedom and the Concept of Freedom in Plato and Aristotle," *Greek, Roman, and Byzantine Studies* 50 (2010): 14.

52. Consider Kierkegaard's critique of the drive to *level* all things, which characterizes modernity: "The present age tends toward a mathematical equality"; Søren Kierkegaard, *The Present Age* (New York: Harper Torchbooks, 1962), 48–52. Consider, too, Nietzsche's critique of *ressentiment*, which he takes to represent the essence of the modern soul. *Ressentiment* is the negative expression—and to this extent the more proper, insofar as more adequately potentializing expression—of what is put positively as a love of equality. The proper object of desire is not what I am or own, but rather that no one be better or have more. But what role *in fact* does equality have in love, we have to ask? To be sure, Aristotle affirmed equality (though of course not "arithmetic" or "mathematical" equality) as essential to friendship (*Nichomachean Ethics* 8.6–7). But, interestingly, Aquinas qualifies this perspective when he affirms the

presence of inequality in the original state of innocence (see *Summa theologica* 1.96.4ad2), and he thus integrates a more Platonic note into the meaning of love.

53. Pierre Manent has described modern democracy as, of its essence, an organization of separations, which thus tends to isolate the "parts" from each other at every level. Because the modern notion of freedom is so basically associated with the division of power, otherwise undecided voters tend to support the *form* of the separation of powers in principle, above the *content* represented by any particular party, and this tends to give rise to a mathematical polarization in political office; see Manent, *Cours familier de philosophie politique* (Paris: Gallimard, 2001), 23–37.

54. We can compare this to Athenian democracy: according to Hansen, *Was Athens a Democracy?*, 22–25, the Greeks did not have an arithmetic concept of equality.

55. Again, on this point see Adrian Pabst, *Metaphysics*.

56. This is not to deny that there is some genuinely creative dimension in choice, which would require further discussion in relation to postclassical figures. We will begin this discussion with our interpretation of Plato and Aristotle in part 3.

57. See Locke, *Second Treatise* (2.4): The state of nature is a "State . . . of Equality, wherein all the Power and Jurisdiction is reciprocal, no one having more than another." Cf. Aquinas, *Summa theologica* 1.96.3: "Inequality might also arise [in the original condition of paradise] on the part of nature . . . without any defect of nature" (ad3). Aquinas acknowledges equality in a *relatively abstract* respect, for example, in the sense that all are equally innocent, which allows him to affirm the text he quotes from Gregory ("Where there is no sin, there is no inequality"), but this relative abstraction can coincide with a thoroughgoing real differentiation and hierarchy. As for the movement toward the absolutizing of equality, Hobbes is an interesting transitional figure. He acknowledges natural inequalities as undeniably given, but he levels the state of nature by virtue of the power individuals have to kill one another, regardless of strength, because of the (actual) ability to use devices or make alliances (see *Leviathan*, chap. 13).

58. Aquinas, *Summa theologica* 1.96.3ad3.

59. Tocqueville, *Democracy in America*, 51–54.

60. We might also note here the tendency for the name of noble families to be drawn from *the place*, i.e., from the estate itself: Tocqueville himself represents an example of this.

61. Tocqueville, *Democracy in America*, 506–7.

62. See David S. Crawford, "Is Religious Liberty Possible in a Liberal Culture?" in *Communio* 40, no. 2–3 (2013): 422–37. See again Milbank's description in "The Gift of Ruling."

63. See *Democracy in America*, chap. 3, pt. 4, vol. 2, which bears the title: "How both the feelings and the thoughts of democratic nations are in accord in concentrating political power" (671–74). Note, however, that he also indicates the tendency to dissolve into small communities based on private pleasures, which reflect natural inequalities (604).

64. Ibid., 668.

65. Robert Nisbet, *The Quest for Community: A Study in the Ethics of Order and Freedom* (Wilmington, DE: ISI Books, 2010), 19–38.

66. The notion of subsidiarity seems to have had its origin in Catholic Social Teaching, beginning with Pope Pius XI's encyclical *Quadragesimo anno*, sec. 80.

67. Tocqueville, *Democracy in America*, 247.

68. For a longer presentation of this point, through an interpretation of Plato's *Republic*, see D. C. Schindler, *Plato's Critique of Impure Reason* (Washington, DC: Catholic University of America Press, 2008), esp. chap. 1, "A Logic of Violence," 41–84.

69. Tocqueville, *Democracy in America*, 252.

70. Ibid., 254–55.

71. For a more ample discussion of this idea, see D. C. Schindler, *Catholicity of Reason*, 3–32.

72. Gianni Vattimo argues that the precondition for peace in the postmodern "pluralistic" world is our saying "farewell" to definitive truth claims and learning to achieve a capacity for ironic detachment from all of our own convictions; Vattimo, *Nihilism and Emancipation: Ethics, Politics, and Law* (New York: Columbia University Press, 2004), xxv–xxx, 49–59.

73. This statement does not exclude the use of coercion with respect to external activity in extreme cases: preventing one who rejects all reasoning from doing violence to others, etc. But this too is a kind of abandoning of the claim of truth qua truth and a resorting to the enforcement of its practical implications according to necessity. Plato of course makes a sharp distinction between persuasion, rooted in reason, and (blind) necessity (see, e.g., *Timaeus* 47e). On the distinction between rational persuasion and irrational persuasion in Plato, see Christopher Bobonich, "Compulsion and Freedom in Plato's *Laws*," *Classical Quarterly* 41, no. 2 (1991): 365–88.

74. Tocqueville, *Democracy in America*, 517.

75. One can insist on "accuracy" with respect to abstract details without recognizing a basic responsibility to reality as such, in its wholeness and depth. Heidegger had something similar in mind when he famously contrasted the notion of truth as correctness, which ultimately belongs to a technological conception of reality, and truth as a revelation of being.

76. Tocqueville, *Democracy in America*, 517.

77. As is well known, Heraclitus observed: "Those who are awake share a common world, while those who sleep turn away, each into his own private world" (DK B89). The Greek word for "private" here is ἴδιος, the root of the adjective "idiotic." On the common world as shared, see Spaemann, "In Defense of Anthropomorphism," in *Spaemann Reader*, 77–96.

78. Rousseau quite interestingly saw this point, though he took the opposite position on its implications: for him, the key condition of possibility for generating the "general will," which served to unite in itself the pure subjectivity of the individual with the absoluteness of the collectivity, was that individuals be kept isolated from one another in their voting (see *Social Contract*, bk. 1, chap. 24, sec. 3).

79. See Heidegger, *What Is Called Thinking?* (New York: Harper and Row, 1968), pt. 2, lecture 3, 138–47. Cf. Ulrich, *Homo Abyssus*, 116–17.

80. As we saw above in the *Gorgias*, Plato observes that a desire for the good operates in each act of the will. In Aquinas's formulation of essentially the same point, "because God is the last end, he is sought in every end" (*De veritate* 22.2). This is another way of stating the point made at the beginning of this chapter regarding the symbolical order in relation to the will and human action.

81. We might consider Kierkegaard's estimation of journalism: "The daily press is the evil principle of the modern world, and time will only serve to disclose this fact with greater and greater clearness. The capacity of the newspaper for degeneration is sophistically without limit, since it can always sink lower and lower in its choice of readers. At last, it will stir up all those dregs of humanity which no state or government can control. Only a very few people will ever understand the fundamental falsity of the daily press. And of these few only a very small number will have the courage to speak out, since it will involve a species of martyrdom to break with the majority, and with the power of the press and its enormous circulation. The press will always mistreat and persecute such a man"; cited in David Swenson, *Something about Kierkegaard* (Macon, GA: Mercer University Press, 1983), 198. Nietzsche is even more direct: modern citizens "vomit up their bile and call it a newspaper, they swallow each other up and can't even digest themselves"; from *Also sprach Zarathustra*, vol. 4 of the *Kritischen Ausgabe*, ed. Colli and Montinari (Munich: De Gruyter, 1999), 63.

82. In his discussion of the political implications of television, and the infantilizing of adults it causes, Neil Postman presents a list of the random juxtaposition of items in a given "news" program and concludes that the medium implies the following inference: "There is no sense of proportion to be discerned in the world. Events are entirely idiosyncratic; history is irrelevant; there is no rational basis for valuing one thing over another. The news, in a

phrase, is not an adult world-view"; Postman, *The Disappearance of Childhood* (New York: Vintage, 1994), 106. Postman describes a talk show that was hosted by the famous hairdresser Vidal Sassoon: "As he came to the end of one segment of one of his programs, the theme music came up and Sassoon just had enough time to say, "Don't go away. We'll be back with a marvelous new diet and, then, a quick look at incest!" (81).

83. Thornton Wilder, *The Skin of Our Teeth: A Play in Three Acts* (New York: Samuel French, 1972), 7: "*A project screen in the middle of a drop. The first lantern slide: (#1 slide: 'News Events of the World.' An Announcer's voice is heard.)* Announcer: The management takes pleasure in bringing to you—the news of the world: (*#2 Slide—The sun appearing above the horizon.*) Freeport, Rhode Island. The sun rose this morning at 6:32 am. This gratifying event was first reported by (*#3 Slide*) Mrs. Dorothy Staten, of Freeport, Rhode Island, who promptly telephoned the mayor."

84. Why do we call this a *vicious* circle? Circles are not, of course, inherently vicious. We designate this logical form thus when it seals its meaning up in itself, the end producing the beginning and the beginning generating the end: in this case, it grows and strengthens without ever drawing on what lies beyond it. In other words, it is vicious because it is diabolical.

85. Tocqueville, *Democracy in America*, 520.

86. See Aristotle, *Poetics* 3.4.1449a15.

87. Tocqueville, *Democracy in America*, 255–56.

88. This phrase is hard to hear without reducing it to the very terms we are criticizing: to say one voice could have political significance, in the context of modern liberalism, is taken to mean that "a single voice could be persuasive enough to generate a lot of votes." And if it does not generate votes, it is taken to mean it has no political significance. But the point we are making is that something can have political significance irrespective of any obvious voting patterns, insofar as it serves to bring to light something about the common good.

89. It is well known that reporting on voting trends based on exit interviews while polls are still open in other parts of the country can have a significant prejudicial effect on the remaining voters, thus skewing the outcome of the election.

90. See Tocqueville, *Democracy in America*, 252n4.

91. It is perhaps worth pointing out explicitly that, by criticizing the power to vote as diabolical, we do not mean to argue that this power should be taken away from certain people, reserved only for others, and so forth. The problems we are identifying cannot be resolved by a redistribution of the very same terms, but rather a rethinking of the whole from the ground up (though this is decidedly *not* a call to revolution: revolution would represent only a di-

abolical co-opting of such a rethinking). Any alternative to universal suffrage in the abstract sense we are criticizing is virtually beyond the capacity of the liberal imagination.

92. Ernst Benz, *Evolution and Christian Hope: Man's Concept of the Future from the Early Fathers to Teilhard de Chardin* (Garden City, NY: Doubleday, 1966), 137; cited in Herbert Applebaum, *The Concept of Work: Ancient, Medieval, and Modern* (Albany: SUNY Press, 1992), 197.

93. Heidegger, "The Question Concerning Technology," in *Basic Writings* (New York: Harper and Row, 1972), 283–317, esp. 294–96. For an illuminating inquiry into the specific character of technology, see Albert Borgmann, *Technology and the Character of Contemporary Life* (Chicago: University of Chicago Press, 1984), esp. 33–78.

94. See Heidegger, "The Origin of the Work of Art," in *Basic Writings*, 163 et passim.

95. Heidegger, "Question Concerning Technology," 296–97; Romano Guardini, *Letters from Lake Como: Explorations in Technology and the Human Race* (Grand Rapids, MI: Eerdmans, 1994), 11–14.

96. It is not clear that Heidegger would allow this point, which seems to imply a kind of transcendence of nature to which Heidegger is averse. To affirm this point arguably depends on affirming the difference between the ancient Greek view on which Heidegger principally draws, which lacks a radical notion of creation ex nihilo, and the Judeo-Christian view.

97. See Spaemann, "Nature," in *Spaemann Reader*, 35–36.

98. Consider Socrates's famous argument with Thrasymachus, in which he claims that the art of the shepherd is *ordered to the good of the sheep*, even if that art is, in turn, placed at the service of further purposes (see *Republic* 345c–d). The point, in general, depends on the acknowledgment of a hierarchy of being.

99. Heidegger, "Question Concerning Technology," 296–97.

100. Guardini, *Letters from Lake Como*, 11–14.

101. To be sure, the form of the elements that had been part of the stones but now compose the concrete is essential to the proper functioning of the wall, even if the form of the stone qua stone is not. There is inevitably *some* nature at the basis of any artifice.

102. On the basis of the insight into the metaphysical presuppositions and implications of architecture and city planning, Christopher Alexander makes many observations that bear fruitfully on our present discussion; see Alexander, *The Nature of Order*, esp., vol. 1, *The Phenomenon of Life* (Berkeley: Center for Environmental Structure, 1980).

103. Drawing deeply from Heidegger, Albert Borgmann attempts to discover an analogous expression of some of Heidegger's principles that are not as

strictly bound to the rural peasant setting, and so have some continued relevance in the contemporary world, and he does so by meditating on "focal things and practices" that are still available to us (the word "focus," he explains at length, derives from the Latin word for hearth or fireplace, which was the center of a household—and which Borgmann contrasts with the central heating system, a technological device); see Borgmann, *Technology and the Character of Contemporary Life: A Philosophical Inquiry* (Chicago: University of Chicago Press, 1984), esp. 196–210.

104. We might on this score see the rejection, for example in Ockham, of the essential form of natural things—the *forma totius* as distinct from the sum of the forms of each part individually—as a basic intellectual root of the technological revolution. On this, see Armand Maurer, *The Philosophy of William of Ockham in the Light of Its Principles* (Toronto: Pontifical Institute of Medieval Studies, 1999), 393.

105. For a vivid illustration of this point, see Mary Taylor's discussion of different approaches to navigation, in which she contrasts the use of tools and technological devices to the extraordinary phenomenon of "wayfinding," a "primitive" (!) practice of navigation through the knowledge, accumulated over a lifetime, of local current, wind, and weather patterns, and so forth; Taylor, "A Deeper Ecology: A Catholic Vision of the Person in Nature," *Communio* 38 (Winter 2011): 583–620.

106. Borgmann, *Technology*, 47.

107. Matthew Crawford describes the old process of fabricating a section of a wheel's rim out of wood, which required knowledge extending far beyond the carpenter's workshop: the skills needed went "all the way to the selection of trees to fell for timber, the proper time for felling them, how to season them, and so forth." He then quotes the owner of such a shop, at the turn of the twentieth century, who recorded the sort of challenges the worker faced: "He had no bandsaw (as now [1923]) to drive, with ruthless unintelligence, through every resistance. The timber was far from being prey, a helpless victim, to a machine. Rather it would lend its own special virtues to the man who knew how to humor it"; George Sturt, *The Wheelwright's Shop*, quoted in Matthew Crawford, *Shop Class as Soulcraft: An Inquiry into the Value of Work* (New York: Penguin, 2009), 41. Cf. the discussion of Sturt in Borgmann, *Technology*, 44–47. Such work can only be learned through apprenticeship.

108. See Aristotle, *Physics* 2.1.

109. The classical Neoplatonic triad, being–life–thought, saw each level as a higher recapitulation, and so intensification, of the previous level.

110. Crawford, *Shop Class*, 1–10.

111. See Aquinas, *Summa theologica* 1.76.5ad4.

112. Crawford, *Shop Class*, 57.

113. Ibid., 207–8.

114. See D. C. Schindler, "Why Socrates Didn't Charge: Plato and the Metaphysics of Money," *Communio* 36 (Fall 2009): 394–426.

115. It is worth pointing out that the traditional expression one finds on tombstones in the old churchyard, *Requiescat in pace*, did not, as is generally thought today, first refer to a psychological state, an inner calm, but rather entrusted one to the objective state of being in communion with the Church: rest in the *peace*, that is, in the *communion*, of the Church.

116. Plato, *Phaedrus* 274a et seq.

117. There was recently a proposal to use hot-air balloons and drones to bring Internet access to the remotest villages in Africa. Facebook intended to donate an extraordinary amount of money to this "social justice" project, justifying the expenditure to its board *as an investment*: such an expansion of the market would almost certainly have great long-term financial benefits.

118. See, for example, Anne Mangen, Bente R. Walgermo, and Kolgørn Brønnick, "Reading Linear Texts on Paper versus Computer Screen: Effects on Reading Comprehension," in *International Journal of Educational Research* 58 (2013): 61–68; David Glenn, "Divided Attention," *Chronicle of Higher Education*, February 28, 2010. I would like to thank Edward Trudeau for pointing me to these articles. Cf. Carrie B. Fried, "In-class Laptop Use and Its Effect on Student Learning," in *Computers and Education* 50 (2008): 906–14, which provides an extensive bibliography of studies done already by 2008. For a general discussion of the effect the Internet has on one's capacity to think, see Nicholas Carr, *The Shallows: What the Internet Is Doing to Our Brains* (New York: Norton, 2011).

119. Karl Polanyi, *The Great Transformation* (Boston: Beacon, 1957).

120. The image comes from William Blake's short poem, "And Did Those Feet in Ancient Time," which prefaced his "Milton, a Poem." The notion of the satanic mill is a governing image of Karl Polanyi's book: it forms the title of the first section of part 1, in which Polanyi lays out the terms of the problem.

121. K. Polanyi, *Great Transformation*, 43.

122. See Wendell Berry, *Home Economics* (Berkeley, CA: North Point Press, 1987); Mark Shiffman, "An Ethic of Attentiveness: The Rediscovery of Oikonomia," *Communio* 36 (Fall 2009): 487–509.

123. Aristotle, *Politics* 1.8.1256a.

124. Ibid., 1.10.

125. K. Polanyi, *Great Transformation*, 72.

126. Ibid., 74.

127. Ibid., 163.

128. Ibid., 178, 179.

129. Ibid., 140.

130. Ibid., 74.

131. See Karol Wojtyła, "The Problem of the Constitutions of Culture Through Human Praxis," in *Person and Community: Selected Essays* (New York: Peter Lang, 1993), 263–75. As Pope John Paul II, he took up these themes as the "personalist" meaning of work (*Laborem exercens*, 15), the priority of labor over capital (12), and man as the *subject* of work (6). We will discuss the significance of *praxis* in its original sense at great length in chapter 8.

132. K. Polanyi, *Great Transformation*, 230–31.

133. He singles out *labor* as the crucial one of the three, since it concerns "man himself," but it would seem that each is crucial in a different way: labor effectively concerns man's relation to himself, but Karl Polanyi himself observes that labor gets transformed when man's relation to *land* is dissolved. If land represents the givenness of nature, it clearly has a certain priority, as the condition for all else. Finally, as we will suggest, money can be seen as a *symbol* of the whole.

134. According to Aristotle, "Of all modes of getting wealth, [money's self-reproduction] is the most unnatural" (*Politics* 1.10.1258a7). Aristotle worries about money-making acquiring too much importance for individuals in their management of their households (*oikonomia*), but it does not occur to him that money's self-reproduction could be the very principle of an economic system. The classic account of the deep roots of this process is of course Max Weber, *The Protestant Ethic and the Spirit of Capitalism* (New York: Penguin, 2002). Cf. John Ruskin, *Unto This Last* (New York: Penguin, 1986), and Lewis Hyde, *The Gift: Imagination and the Erotic Life of Property* (New York: Vintage, 1983).

135. This is the importance of the "priority of labor over capital" that John Paul II affirmed in *Laborem exercens* (1981). See section 12 of that encyclical: http://w2.vatican.va/content/john-paul-ii/en/encyclicals/documents /hf_jp-ii_enc_14091981_laborem-exercens.html.

136. Aristotle describes philosophy as "the only free science, for it alone exists for its own sake," as opposed to being subordinated to some practical benefit, however noble (*Metaphysics*, bk. 1).

137. See Robert Spaemann, "Education as an Introduction to Reality: A Speech Commemorating the Anniversary of a Children's Home," in *Spaemann Reader*, 111–20; Spaemann, "The Courage to Educate," *Communio* (Spring 2013): 48–63; cf. also Werner Jaeger, "Introduction," in *Paideia* (Oxford: Oxford University Press, 1945), 1:xiii–xxix.

138. We will also forgo here a discussion of how "identity politics"— which is an expression of the radicalized, abstract equality we discussed

earlier—combined with a bourgeois ethos has created an academic environment in which freedom has come under threat to an astonishing degree. Consider, in this regard, a professor's recent article on *Vox*, in which he describes how his experience in the classroom has changed drastically, even since he began in 2009: "The student-teacher dynamic has been reenvisioned along a line that's simultaneously consumerist and hyper-protective, giving each and every student the ability to claim Grievous Harm in nearly any circumstance, after any affront, and a teacher's formal ability to respond to these claims limited at best. . . . The simplicity and absolutism of this conception [of social justice, egregiously oversimplified in popular sociology] has combined with the precarity of academic jobs to create higher ed's current climate of fear, a heavily policed discourse of semantic sensitivity, in which safety and comfort have become the ends *and* the means of the college experience"; see Edward Schlosser, "I'm a Liberal Professor, and My Liberal Students Terrify Me," http://www.vox.com/2015/6/3/8706323/college-professor-afraid. At the root of the ethos Schlosser describes is, not an attitude first of all, but a loss of a sense of the objectivity and ontological density of truth.

139. It is not an accident that the origins of information theory occurred in the response to the problem Bell Telephone faced in determining how to charge customers. See James Gleick, *The Information: A History, a Theory, a Flood* (New York: Vintage, 2012), 3–12.

140. Ibid., 4.

141. The word "information" is at least distantly related to the classical notion of "form." But the emphasis in "information" lies on the aspect of *transmission* and thus on what can be transmitted. It is revealing that the (modern and ancient) Greek word for information is πληροφορία, which has no reference to form (either εἶδος or μορφή). Instead, the word consists wholly in the reference to transmission: φορία, comes from φέρω, which means "to carry" or "to convey," and πλήρες means "fully." On information as transferrable, see Albert Borgmann, *Holding onto Reality: The Nature of Information at the Turn of the Millennium* (Chicago: University of Chicago Press, 1999), 9.

142. It is interesting to consider the distortions of meaning inevitably entailed by such a packaging; for an example, see Edward Tufte, *The Cognitive Style of PowerPoint*, 2nd ed. (Cheshire, CT: Graphic Press, 2006).

143. To have "inside information" is not so much to enjoy *intimacy* but to have a certain *leverage*, which of course indicates precisely that one stands outside.

144. To be sure, in the general Thomistic philosophy we have in mind, form *as* known is not simply identical with the form that constitutes the nature of a thing, but, in the cognitional act, is abstracted as the intelligible species; it must also be pointed out, however, that it is *not* this species that is the object

known; instead, formulated as a concept, it is that *through which* one knows (see *Summa theologica* 1.85.2). The proper object is the quiddity *of* the material thing. There is an inherent movement in knowledge into the *actual reality* of the thing known.

145. See Aquinas, *Summa theologica* 2-2.8.1; *Summa contra Gentiles* 3.112.5; cf. Aristotle, *De anima* 3.8.431b21, and Plato, *Republic* 490a–b.

146. See Balthasar's discussion of the relationship between truth and (genuine) freedom, in Hans Urs von Balthasar, *Theo-Logic*, Vol. 1, *The Truth of the World*, trans. Adrian Walker (San Francisco: Ignatius, 2000), 79–130.

147. Luciano Floridi, "The Informational Nature of Personal Identity," *Minds and Machines* 21, no. 4 (2011): 549–66.

148. See Sherry Turkle, *Alone Together: Why We Expect More from Technology and Less from Ourselves* (New York: Basic Books, 2012).

149. *Gorgias* 456a. Gorgias had earlier in the discussion referred to this ability to manipulate through words "the greatest good. . . . It is the source of freedom for humankind itself and at the same time it is for each person the source of rule [power!] over others in one's own city" (452d).

150. This is why Plato often repeats the proverb that "the beautiful is difficult" (see, e.g., *Hippias Major* 304e). Beauty is not a matter of surfaces, but of patiently working toward the depth, which is a genuine labor.

151. Augusto Del Noce, *The Crisis of Modernity*, trans. Carlo Lancelotti (Montreal: McGill-Queen's University Press, 2015), 189–90: "*auctoritas* derives from *augere*, 'to make grow.' A shared etymological origin ties it to the words *Augustus* (he who makes grow), *auxilium* (help provided by a higher power), *augurium* (also a word of religious origin: a vow made to obtain divine cooperation in growth). If other languages are considered, one finds a common ideal structure. Thus, the German *auch* (also) is the imperative of the Gothic *aukan* (to make grow). Therefore, the etymology of authority includes the idea that *humanitas* is fulfilled in man when a principle of non-empirical nature frees him from a state of subjection and leads him to his proper end, as a rational and moral being. Man's freedom, as power of *attention* and not of *creation*, consists in his capacity to subordinate himself to this higher principle of liberation and be freed from the pressures from below." Del Noce goes on to explain that in contemporary culture, authority has come to be understood as the very opposite of allowing to grow, namely, repression. It has thus been replaced by the notion of power, which represents a real crisis, since this replacement means the loss of the very condition of freedom. As he puts it, "authority differs from power because its essence is to set in order" (203).

152. See D. C. Schindler, "On Reason's Authority," *Communio* 41, no. 1 (2014): 40–60.

153. See Plato, *Republic* 341d. Cf. Aristotle, *Metaphysics* 1.1.981a24–26.

154. Plato, *Gorgias* 462b–c; Aristotle, *Metaphysics* 1.1.980b26–981b7. In the *Phaedrus*, Plato calls sophistry an ἄτεχνος τριβή, "artless practice," and goes on to observe: "There is no genuine art of speaking without a grasp of truth, and there never will be" (260e). He repeats just this description in *Laws* 938a.

155. On the connection between all of these, see *Gorgias* 505e–508a.

156. Gorgias argues that rhetoric is a neutral skill, which the sophists who teach it mean to be used justly and so have no responsibility for its misuse (*Gorgias* 456b–457c).

157. For a longer argument defending this point, see D. C. Schindler, *Plato's Critique*, 453–58.

158. John Dewey, *Reconstruction in Philosophy* (New York: Henry Holt and Company, 1920), 66–67. I am grateful to Michael Hanby for introducing me to this text.

159. Goethe is no doubt alluding here to God's setting of limits to the sea as a metaphor for his act of creation, which is a determining of order: "Who shut in the sea with doors, when it burst forth from the womb; when I made clouds its garment, and thick darkness its swaddling band; and prescribed bounds for it, and set bars and doors, and said, 'Thus far shall you come, and no farther, and here shall your proud waves be stayed'?" (Job 38:8–11). In this respect, Faust's assertion of power is, at its root, a (fruitless) attempt to undo creation.

160. It is essentially "unhinged" because it has no mooring in reality and its natural limits.

161. A fairly recent example is the outcry over limitations on embryonic stem cell research, when *in actual fact* most of the promising results in stem cell therapies have used the less morally objectionable *adult* stem cells; see David A. Prentice, "The Present and Future of Stem Cell Research: Scientific, Ethical, and Public Policy Perspective," in *Stem Cell Research: New Frontiers in Science and Ethics*, ed. Nancy E. Snow (Notre Dame, IN: University of Notre Dame Press, 2004), 18–19: "Eighty Nobel laureates sent a letter in the spring of 2001 to President Bush encouraging federal funding of human embryonic stem cell research and citing numerous advances in stem cell science. However, most of the advances cited were using adult stem cells, and the vast majority of those signing the letter had no background related to the science discussed." Clearly, the objection is to the very idea of a limit on research, much more than the concrete substance of what is at issue. I am grateful to Fr. Marcin Kryčki for this reference.

162. *Gorgias* 507e.

163. This is a basic background assumption of his "theology of the body": see John Paul II, *Man and Woman He Created Them: A Theology of the Body*

(Boston: Pauline Books, 2006). See also José Granados, "Taste and See: The Body and the Experience of God," *Communio* 37, no. 2 (2010): 292–308.

164. Heidegger's characterization of metaphysics as essentially "ontotheological" represents a recognition of this fact, though of course he meant this characterization as a fundamental critique. It is crucial that one not respond to this critique by conceding the terms, else one end up—as we will argue here—absolutizing the diabolical. See D. C. Schindler, "The Problem of the Problem of Ontotheology," in *Catholicity of Reason* (Grand Rapids, MI: Eerdmans, 2013), 231–61. See also David Bentley Hart, "The Offering of Names: Metaphysics, Nihilism, and Analogy," in *Reason and the Reasons of Faith*, ed. Paul Griffiths and Reinhard Hütter (New York: T&T Clark, 2005), 255–94.

165. Hence the permanent necessity of philosophy; see Benedict XVI, *Faith, Reason, and the University: Memories and Reflections*, address delivered September 12, 2006, http://w2.vatican.va/content/benedict-xvi/en/speeches/2006 /september/documents/hf_ben-xvi_spe_20060912_university-regensburg.html. Cf. Spaemann, "The Traditionalist Error," in *Spaemann Reader*, 37–44.

166. This represents the perfect opposite of what Nietzsche described as the essence of the "will to power": "To impose upon becoming the character of being"; see *The Will to Power*, ed. Walter Kaufmann (New York: Vintage, 1968), 330 (#617).

167. On the relation between reason and tradition, compare Alasdair MacIntyre, *Whose Justice, Which Rationality?* (Notre Dame, IN: University of Notre Dame Press, 1988), who roots reason in tradition, and Augusto Del Noce (*The Crisis of Modernity*), who roots tradition in reason, or at least in eternal truths, which he takes to be the sine qua non of tradition. An adequate account—which we cannot attempt to provide here—would show why both of these affirmations are necessary, even though they are irreducibly distinct from one another. On the importance of the continuity of tradition, see Brad Gregory, *The Unintended Reformation* (Cambridge, MA: Belknap, 2012).

168. The reality is unsurprisingly much more complicated; see William T. Cavanaugh, *The Myth of Religious Violence: Secular Ideology and the Roots of Modern Conflict* (Oxford: Oxford University Press, 2009).

169. There is a difference between recognizing that there are rival interpretations of the nature and reality of God, with concrete histories and theological/ metaphysical commitments, and affirming "religious pluralism" as a set of options, all instances of an abstract essence, "religion," which is differentiated simply in terms of historical and cultural contingences.

170. The key to the question of violence would be to draw on the resources *within* one's actual tradition that enable a welcoming of the other precisely *as other*. This is different from the liberal strategy, which speaks of openness to the other, but in fact means denying the significance of anything that would ac-

tually differentiate. This putative openness to the other hides a contempt for otherness.

171. This is a position associated in the Catholic tradition with John Courtney Murray; See Murray, "The Problem of Religious Freedom," *Woodstock Papers*, 7 (Westminster, MD: Newman Press, 1965). For a fundamental critique of this position, specifically in relation to the interpretation of *Dignitatis humanae*, see David L. Schindler and Nicholas J. Healy, eds., *Freedom, Truth, and Human Dignity: The Second Vatican Council's Declaration on Religious Freedom* (Grand Rapids, MI: Eerdmans, 2015).

172. For a more ample argument on this point, see D. C. Schindler, "Liberalism, Religious Freedom, and the Common Good: The Totalitarian Logic of Self-Limitation," *Communio* 40, no. 2–3 (2013): 577–615.

173. See Michael Hanby, "Absolute Pluralism: How the Dictatorship of Relativism Dictates," *Communio* 40, no. 2–3 (2013): 542–76.

174. David L. Schindler, "'The Religious Sense' and American Culture," *Communio* 25 (1998): 679–99; David L. Schindler, "Beauty, Transcendence, and the Face of the Other: Religion and Culture in America," *Communio* 26 (1999): 916–21; David L. Schindler, "Liberalism and the Meaning of God: The Religious Sense in America," *Communio* 34 (2007): 482–87.

175. See David S. Crawford, *Beyond Heterosexuality: Public Reason, Common Good, and the Concept of Orientation* (Grand Rapids, MI: Eerdmans, forthcoming).

176. See, for example, Ted Chu, *Human Purpose and Transhuman Potential: A Cosmic Vision for our Future Evolution* (San Rafael, CA: Origin Press, 2014). As Chu explains, "The human being is not an 'inexplicable miracle': Despite its limitations, a machine is an excellent metaphor for our understanding of humanity" (164).

177. For a striking formulation of the same point, see Hans Jonas, "The Practical Uses of Theory," in *The Phenomenon of Life* (Evanston, IL: Northwestern University Press, 2001), 196.

CHAPTER 6. STARTING OVER AND STARTING AFTER

1. "*Der Spiegel* Interview with Martin Heidegger," in *The Heidegger Reader*, ed. Günther Figal (Bloomington: Indiana University Press, 2009), 326.

2. Ibid.

3. This criticism ought not to be made with a facile dismissal: Heidegger represents a profound response to the sort of *activism* that we describe as diabolical, and he presents the significance, in this regard, of a genuine act of thinking—as thanking.

4. Heidegger comments on this passage from Hölderlin's poem "Patmos" in "Question Concerning Technology," 333. In another essay, "On the Question of Being," he affirms the need to "ponder the essential possibilities of nihilism"; in *Pathmarks*, ed. William McNeil (Cambridge: Cambridge University Press, 1998), 297. The importance of the negative or the nothing in Heidegger is well known, and it appears not only as an explicit topic but also implicitly in many of the other dominant themes in his thought: for example, the "errancy" and "withdrawal" in truth, the importance given to *polemos* in his interpretation of early Greek thought, the affirmation of *Gelassenheit* as man's highest act, and so forth.

5. Gabriel Marcel, "Sketch of a Phenomenology and a Metaphysics of Hope," in *Homo Viator* (New York: Harper Torchbooks, 1962), 62–63.

6. *Gorgias* 473e: "Don't you think you've been refuted already, Socrates, when you're saying things the likes of which no human being would maintain? Just ask any of these people."

7. Ibid., 472b.

8. See, e.g., *Hippias Major* 304d–e. As Julius Stenzel observes, in spite of the tragic-comic irony of Socrates's proposal of free meals at the Prytaneum as a punishment for his "crime," the point Socrates is making in the *Apology* here is profoundly significant: his attempt to remain true to his very individual calling is "the greatest gift" to the city of Athens, and he ought to be awarded the customary prize for public benefactors; see Stenzel, "Das Problem der Willensfreiheit im Platonismus," in *Kleine Schriften zur griechischen Philosophie* (Darmstadt: Hermann Gentner, 1957), 182. In other words, personal fidelity to truth is always a common good. We will discuss the essentially "social" character of freedom in Plato in chapter 7, particularly the section on "Common Law."

9. *Gorgias* 473a.

10. See ibid., 480a–e.

11. Ibid., 482b–c (emphasis added). The oath, "by the Dog," though rare itself, is a common one for Socrates: if he highlights the connection with Egypt here, it is because Egypt represents, for him, the eternal and the unchanging. A few lines above the passage we quoted, Socrates says, "What philosophy says always stays the same."

12. To avoid misunderstanding, it is good to point out that we do not mean here to advocate a new gnosticism, which would reserve salvation to those who are able to grasp an esoteric truth, and who need to detach completely from their embodied condition and the concrete state of the world in history in order to do so. As chapter 5 made clear, the actuality of history and embodiment is a fundamental part of the truth of freedom. We will suggest in our study of Plato and Aristotle in the next two chapters, moreover, that freedom is never a merely private concern.

13. The man Bacon famously identified as the "primus hominum novorum," the first of the moderns, Bernardino Telesio, began his master work, *De rerum natura*, from the very first sentence, with an attack on the ancients. Bacon himself saw the modern project as a rejection of all received knowledge in order "to commence a total reconstruction of the sciences, arts, and all human knowledge"; see preface to *The Great Instauration*, in *Selected Philosophical Works* (Indianapolis: Hackett, 1999), 66. This is the very gesture of modern thought that is repeated by each new founding figure of modernity in succession—almost like the inheritance of a tradition.

14. Or in his words, "to comprehend the *nomos* of contemporary existence, of the consciousness of the age, against a horizon that is not defined by this consciousness. . . . Philosophy cannot avoid taking a position with respect to the project of modernity, whether for or against; this necessity follows from its aspiration to totality. For the modern project wants to be the source of both the categories that will be used to interpret it in the proper sense, and the criteria that justify it. To understand modernity in any other way means to criticize it" ("A Philosophical Autobiography," in *Spaemann Reader*, 13).

15. Plato regularly makes positive references to "the ancients" in his dialogues: see, e.g., the opening pages of the *Hippias Major*, in which he contrasts the ancients and moderns, explaining that in matters of τεχνή, what is modern is always better, while in matters of σοφία, the opposite is the case. For his part, Aristotle generally begins his own thinking only after rehearsing the views of those who have come before him.

16. As Robert Muller has observed, "with Plato, freedom entered properly speaking into philosophy"; R. Muller, *La doctrine platonicienne de la liberté* (Paris: Vrin, 1997), 309.

17. Heidegger represents an illuminating *failure* in this regard. With incomparable depth, he showed us that the thinking of being requires a retrieval of historical origins; his *seynsgeschichtliches Denken* famously includes a return to the "early Greek thinkers" (behind Plato and Aristotle). But he rejected both the tradition *as such*—and, of course, metaphysics. We discover what we might call a tragic tension in Heidegger, insofar as he affirms the importance of tradition, but at the same time interprets the actual tradition of the West (or more specifically Christianity in its traditional—i.e., Catholic—form) as an occlusion of the truth of being: "Everything essential and great has arisen solely out of the fact that humans had a home and were rooted in a tradition" ("*Der Spiegel* Interview," 325). He seeks, as it were, "traditionality" without the actual tradition.

18. This is not meant to be a general statement regarding the order of the transcendentals; if goodness has a certain primacy in relation to freedom, it does not imply necessarily that the good is first *tout court*.

19. For example: Albrecht Dihle, *The Theory of Will in Classical Antiquity* (Berkeley: University of California Press, 1982); Michael Frede, *A Free Will: Origins of the Notion in Ancient Thought* (Berkeley: University of California Press, 2011); Charles H. Kahn, "Discovering Will from Aristotle to Augustine," in *The Question of Eclecticism*, ed. John M. Dillon and A. A. Long (Berkeley: University of California Press, 1988), 234–59; Hannah Arendt, *The Life of the Mind*, Vol. 2, *Willing* (New York: Harcourt Brace Jovanovich, 1971); Thomas Pfau, *Minding the Modern: Human Agency, Intellectual Traditions, and Responsible Knowledge* (Notre Dame, IN: University of Notre Dame Press, 2013); Miklos Vetö, *La naissance de la volonté* (Paris: Harmattan, 2002).

20. See Hans Jonas, *Augustin und das paulinische Freiheitsproblem: Ein philosophischer Beitrag zur Genesis der christlich-abendländischen Freiheitsidee* (Göttingen: Vandenhoeck and Puprecht, 1930). Heidegger identifies Kant as the thinker in whom the problem of freedom emerges in its authentic essence, but says he was anticipated in the theological tradition by Paul, Augustine, and Luther; see Heidegger, *The Essence of Human Freedom: An Introduction to Philosophy* (New York: Continuum, 2002), 16.

21. Frede points especially to the Stoics as the school of thought wherein the notion of will, as "free will," first emerged (in part as a response to Dihle, who insisted on its theological provenance).

22. See Arendt, *Life of the Mind*, and Dihle, *Theory of Will*.

23. Lucretius, who takes up the ancient atomic notion of the "swerve" presumably from Democritus, represents a classical paradigm, identifying free will precisely with the capacity to "break the bonds of fate," to thwart the necessity of the given order, in order to do what one will; see *De rerum natura*, esp. 2.252–94.

24. According to Georg Kohler, "The human will in its created character is free only to the extent that it says 'no' and thus becomes the origin of evil, and is in no way free if it remains related to God and the good"; see Kohler, "Selbstbezug, Selbsttranszendez und die Nichtigkeit der Freiheit: Zur augustinischen Theorie des Bösen in *De civitate dei* XII," *Studia Philosophica* 52 (1993): 78. We saw in chapter 1 that a prominent scholar interprets this as Locke's essential position.

25. This claim will need further qualification, but it is not possible to develop the point further in the present context. It is hoped that the issue can be taken up in a future work.

26. We ought to recognize that the Christian appropriation of the classical Greek tradition does not simply continue on further from this point of departure but reinterprets it in the light of an even more original starting point, which we will argue is part of the very meaning of freedom. We intend to show this in a future study.

27. Again, we hope to follow this book up with a study of the Christian appropriation of the classical view, and then a constructive metaphysics of freedom.

28. Arendt speaks of "Augustine's philosophy of natality" (*Life of the Mind*, 2:110), by which she means his notion of man as an "initium," a spontaneous beginning of a new causal sequence. This is just what was lacking, she says, in classical Greek thought (see ibid., 2:62–63).

29. See Hegel, *The Philosophy of History* (Mineola, NY: Dover, 1956), 18.

30. Plato, *Meno* 80e.

31. "The word 'will' and its equivalents in modern languages as applied to the description and evaluation of human action denotes sheer volition, regardless of its origin in either cognition or emotion" (Dihle, *Theory of Will*, 20). Not incidentally, in just the way we described above, Dihle looks for the *breaking* of order as the precise evidence of the will: "The will as a faculty of man, by which he can give his response to God quite apart from intellectual understanding . . . is much easier to ascertain in cases of conflicting intentions, when obedience and compliance are refused, than in the case of agreement" (ibid., 17–18).

32. See J. J. Mulhern, Review of *A Free Will*, by Michael Frede, in *Bryn Mawr Classical Review* (October 24, 2011).

33. See, for example, H. J. Muller, *Freedom in the Ancient World* (New York: Harper and Row, 1961), XIII: "I am adhering to the relatively neutral, objective definition . . .; the condition of being able to choose and to carry out purposes."

34. On all of this, see R. Muller, *La doctrine platonicienne*, 49 ff.

35. Émile Beneviste, *Le vocabulaire des institutions indo-européennes*, Vol. 1, *Économie, parenté, société* (Paris: Les Éditions de Minuit, 1969), 322. It appears that even the verb ἐλεύθω, from ἔρχομαι, meaning "to go freely," originally meant "to grow"; see August Fick, *Wörterbuch der Indogermanischen Grundsprache in ihrem Bestande vor der Völkertrennung* (Göttingen: Vandenbroeck and Ruprecht, 1868), 122, 298, 534; cited in R. B. Onians, *The Origins of European Thought about the Body, the Mind, the Soul, the World, Time, and Fate* (Cambridge: Cambridge University Press, 1951), 475n2.

36. R. Muller, *La doctrine platonicienne*, 49.

37. See Mogens Herman Hansen, "Democratic Freedom and the Concept of Freedom in Plato and Aristotle," *Greek, Roman, and Byzantine Studies* 50 (2010): 1–27.

38. See Aristotle's brief discussion in *Politics* 3.1.1275a and following.

39. Herbert Applebaum, *The Concept of Work: Ancient, Medieval, and Modern* (Albany: SUNY Press, 1992), 28.

40. Beneviste, *Le vocabulaire des institutions*, 324.

41. R. Muller, *La doctrine platonicienne*, 55.

42. Onians, *Origins of European Thought*, 475n2; see also 473.

43. Ibid., 472–73.

44. For this reason, ψυχή, contained most basically in the head, was not originally the seat of individual consciousness (that would be the φρένες, located in the chest), but was a life principle that transcended the individuals and bound them all together (see ibid., 93–122).

45. Ibid., 473–74. It is interesting to note, in this regard, that the sole appearance in Homer of the word "freedom"—apart from the already metaphorical expression, "day of freedom" (which appears three times, and indicates a status or mode of existence)—occurs in reference to the "great mixing bowl" used to pour out libations and then take a communal ritualized drink (see *Iliad* 6.528). Bound to a modern conception of freedom, which is essentially negative, some take the word here to refer to the "empty space" of the bowl, but the more natural connection is the outpouring of abundant, celebratory liquid.

46. Onians, *Origins of European Thought*, 474–76 (footnote references omitted).

47. Indeed, in the classic poem *Works and Days*, Hesiod presents *greed* as the primary characteristic of nobles (200–64).

48. Aristotle, *Physics* 2.1.

49. A paradigmatic sense of this was recovered in classical German philosophy, which defined itself in part by its "rediscovery" of the Greeks; on the notion of freedom as perfection, see D. C. Schindler, *The Perfection of Freedom: Schiller, Schelling, and Hegel between the Ancients and the Moderns* (Eugene, OR: Cascade, 2012), esp. chap. 2 on Schiller, 49–110.

50. In the *Theaetetus*, Plato contrasts the "small and warped" soul of one who is a slave to practical success to the one properly educated in leisure, who exhibits a "free, straight growth" (173a). Note that Plato here identifies *growth*, *straightness* (or conformity to a proper measure), and *freedom*: the slave lacks "τὴν . . . αὔξην καὶ τὸ εὐθύ τε καὶ τὸ ἐλεύθερον."

51. See, for example, Jonathan Hecht, "Freedom of the Will in Plato and Augustine," *British Journal for the History of Philosophy* 22, no. 2 (2014): 196–216, and Moira M. Walsh, "Aristotle's Conception of Freedom," *Journal of the History of Philosophy* 35, no. 4 (1997): 495–507. One of the best-known arguments for a normative conception of freedom in modern philosophy is Susan Wolf, *Freedom within Reason* (Oxford: Oxford University Press, 1993).

52. According to Aristotle, "There are also some liberal arts quite proper for a freeman to acquire, but only in a certain degree, and if he attend to them too closely, in order to attain perfection in them, the same evil effects will follow. The object also which a man sets before him makes a great difference; if he

does or learns anything for his own sake or for the sake of his friends, or with a view to excellence, the action will not appear illiberal; but if done for the sake of others, the very same action will be thought menial and servile" (*Politics* 8.2.1337b15 ff).

53. It will arise in our discussion of Plato and Aristotle but will be a principal theme in a future study.

54. It is important to note that both Plato and Aristotle give expression to both of the dimensions of the good we present here, even if there is a difference in emphasis; we make the distinction as a matter of convenience.

55. See *Laws* 797d–e. The *only* good change he says is when something bad becomes good.

56. See Aristotle, *Metaphysics* 12.7.1072b1–5. This is Schelling's classic critique; see Friedrich Schelling, *History of Modern Philosophy* (Cambridge: Cambridge University Press, 1994), 132.

CHAPTER 7. PLATO: THE GOLDEN THREAD OF FREEDOM

1. See R. F. Stalley, "Plato's Doctrine of Freedom," *Proceedings of the Aristotelian Society* 98 (1998): 145. R. Muller makes a convincing argument in this regard, pointing out that the word "freedom" and its variants appear surprisingly often in his corpus (226 times) (*La doctrine platonicienne*, 33n1).

2. Dieter Nestle emphasizes that, even in Plato, for example, the word "freedom" is not a philosophical one, but remains essentially political; Nestle, *Eleutheria: Studien zum Wesen der Freiheit bei der Griechen und im Neuen Testament* (Tübingen: J. C. B. Mohr, 1967), 91. This is true, but it is also true, as we will propose, that Plato gives the political a properly philosophical depth.

3. See Hansen, "Democratic Freedom," 2–3.

4. Commentators focus on the potential problems of justifying a "noble lie," but they tend to overlook that it is told principally, not to control the masses, but to persuade the elite to give up all their private possessions in order to be able to devote themselves to the city unburdened by self-interest (i.e., *freely*). In any event, the "noble lie" is clearly meant to imitate the existing method of education at the time, namely, instilling values through myths (which Plato eventually goes on to subordinate to the properly philosophical education he proposes later in the dialogue).

5. *Symposium* 205e.

6. A few pages before the passage quoted, Socrates confounds Agathon, who concedes he cannot challenge the particular point of view Socrates is putting forth in his questioning, and Socrates responds: "Then it is the truth, my

beloved Agathon, that you are unable to challenge. . . . It is not hard at all to challenge Socrates" (*Symposium* 201c). The theme of Socrates's principal speech in the *Phaedrus* is "truth"—and the dialogue begins with Socrates being led out of the city, beyond what is familiar to him (οἰκεῖον), by the attraction of *logos*. Similar figures and expressions are found throughout the corpus.

7. Of course, Plato is not the first to seek an understanding of justice beyond what is merely relative; one finds a similar concern not only in many of the philosophers, but also in the poets. It is, for instance, a principal theme in Aeschylus's *Oresteia* trilogy.

8. Polemarchus, having been "handed down" (*traditio*) the argument regarding justice from his father, Cephalus (or in other words: having inherited the "traditional" notion, with its tensions), attempts to articulate it as "helping friends and harming enemies," and Socrates tries gently to open this formulation up to a more ultimate perspective. When he does so, Thrasymachus crashes in as the unapologetic champion of *pleonexia* (see *Republic* 331d–336d).

9. The notoriously strange passages from book 6 of the *Republic*, in which Socrates argues for "equality" between the sexes and the common possession of wives and children, can be understood as a trumping of natural relations by the universality and unity of the good, but arguably Plato "returns" to the reality of natural relations in a gesture of confirmation, after having transcended them: on the synthesis of the absolute and relative in the *Republic*, see D. C. Schindler, *Plato's Critique*, esp. 208–16 and the final chapter.

10. See Plato, *Laws* 892c.

11. See Eric Perl, "The Presence of the Paradigm: Immanence and Transcendence in Plato's Forms," *Review of Metaphysics* 53 (December 1999): 339–62.

12. For a fuller exposition and argument on this point, see D. C. Schindler, *Plato's Critique*, 151–60.

13. Proclus, *On the Theology of Plato* (London: A. J. Valpy, 1816), vol. 2, bk. 7, chaps. 41–42, pp. 255–57.

14. Plato, *Republic* 509b.

15. Ibid., 506e–508b.

16. Plato, *Letter VIII* 353a.

17. This is a simplified generalization regarding Strauss, who is quite subtle himself on this point, but the generalization clearly has a foundation.

18. See *Timaeus* 37c. Plato enjoins his addressees in *Letter VI* to take a solemn oath (by which he means both playful and earnest) of fidelity "in the name of the lordly father of this governor and cause, whom we shall all some day clearly know, in so far as the blessed are able to know him, if we truly live the life of philosophy" (323d) (apparent typo amended).

19. Plato, *Timaeus* 29e.

20. Plato, *Sophist* 248e–249e.

21. We are, according to the *Phaedo*, θεοῦ κτήματα (62b). The verb κτάομαι is one that describes exclusively "personal" agency. Cf. *Laws* 803c.

22. *Laws* 644d ff.; cf. 803b ff.

23. Perhaps anticipating this reaction, Plato insists, when he introduces the thought, that this dimension is the "best part" (τὸ βέλτιστον) of human existence (*Laws* 803c).

24. *Laws* 645a.

25. Ibid.: the "leading-string, which is golden and holy, is that of our reasoning, and is referred to as the common law of the city." We will return to the "common law" aspect below. In *Alcibiades I*, Plato (if he is indeed the author) writes: "Then this part [of the soul, namely, the knowing and thinking part] resembles the divine, and someone who looked at it and grasped everything divine—vision and intelligence—would have the best grasp of himself as well." "Vision and intelligence" is an amendment of the text; the manuscript reads "God and wisdom" (θεόν τε καὶ φρονήσιν) (133b–c).

26. In *Theaetetus*, Plato connects Homer's image of the "golden thread," by which the god holds the cosmos, to the light of the sun—though he means in this context the principle of cosmological order (153c).

27. According to Wolfgang Maria Zeitler, the key principle that illuminates everything else in Plato's understanding of freedom is that reason has an essentially "participative" structure, though he notes that virtually no one (except for Stenzel) has recognized this; see Zeitler, *Entscheidungsfreiheit bei Platon* (Munich: C. H. Beck'sche Verlag, 1983), 79–80.

28. The good gives power (to know) to knowers: τῷ γιγνώσκοντι τὴν δύναμιν (*Republic* 508e).

29. *Republic* 508a. Plato is speaking of the sunlight that links the eye with its object, but he goes on to use this as an image of knowledge. Heidegger famously criticized Plato precisely for this, in part because it seems to restrict truth to some form of "correctness": see Heidegger, "Plato's Doctrine of Truth," in *Pathmarks*, 155–82. See also Francisco Gonzalez's convincing rebuttal of Heidegger on this interpretation: Gonzalez, *Plato and Heidegger: A Question of Dialogue* (University Park: Penn State University Press, 2009), 152–55.

30. *Republic* 505d–e; *Symposium* 206a.

31. We present these here in a somewhat oversimplified way for the sake of making a general point.

32. *Republic* 477d. Note that Plato says that the powers of the soul both *depend on* and *bring about* the corresponding aspects of reality.

33. In the *Phaedo*, Plato says that intelligence shows itself precisely in its being directed to what is "best," i.e., what is most truly good (97c–d).

34. We recall that Locke *says* we belong to God, but he then characterizes us absolutely as our own property, as we discussed in chapter 2.

35. The classic text that interprets Plato in a "proto-fascist" direction is Karl Popper, *The Open Society and Its Enemies*, Vol. 1, *The Spell of Plato* (Princeton, NJ: Princeton University Press, 2013). Nestle characterizes Plato as a "reactionary" that seeks to stifle the movements of political freedom and replace them with a purely contemplative, philosophical freedom (*Eleutheria*, 89–101). Hansen argues that Plato ultimately identifies freedom with domination ("Democratic Freedom," 24). Stalley concludes that if Plato has a notion of freedom at all, it is unrecognizable from a modern perspective ("Plato's Doctrine of Freedom," 157).

36. Plato, *Protagoras* 357c.

37. "No one sins willingly" (*Gorgias* 81e–87a).

38. Julius Stenzel, "Das Problem der Willensfreiheit im Platonismus," in *Kleine Schriften zur griechischen Philosophie* (Darmstadt: Hermann Gentner, 1957), 171–87.

39. Ibid., 181. At the end of Stenzel's discussion, he quotes a passage from Goethe that sums up beautifully both the insight and ethos of Plato's view of the matter: "Lessing, who unwillingly underwent a great deal of limitation, has one of his characters say: no one needs to have to (*kein Mensch muß müssen*). An intelligent and more happily-minded man said: he who wills, must (*Wer will, der muß*). A third, and indeed a cultured man, added: he who understands also wills (*wer einsieht, der will auch*). In saying this, he felt he closed the entire circle of knowledge, will, and necessity. But as a general principle man's knowledge, whatever its quality, determines his doing and letting be done; and this is why there is nothing more horrifying than seeing a person act without knowledge" (ibid., 187).

40. Ibid., 12. The adjective he uses is "magic-pantheistic."

41. This point receives qualification with the revelation of a personal God, who enters relation precisely by way of subordination (incarnate as a child). It is crucial to see that this transformation of the principle Plato establishes is not a simple denial of it.

42. Stenzel, "Das Problem der Willensfreiheit," 181. Stenzel wants to show, here, that "grace" is not an exclusively theological phenomenon, but must first of all be recognized as "built in" to the nature of things. We note that it is possible to affirm this without denying an ultimately theological cause of even this "purely natural" dimension of grace.

43. Plato, *Laws* 645a.

44. It might be read as a more receptive version of "συμβάλλω": the latter means, literally, "throw together," but "συλαμβάνω" (συν-λαμβάνω, "to take in jointly") means "gather together."

45. R. Muller observes that Plato uses the word "βούλησις," but not in a technical sense as designating a faculty of the soul distinct from reason or desire (*La doctrine platonicienne*, 95–96); cf. Zeitler, *Entscheidungsfreiheit bei Platon*, 43.

46. Precisely when one expects one term, Plato often uses the other: in *Laws*, he replaces φρόνησις as the top cardinal virtue with νοῦς (963a; cf. 631c). In the *Republic*, Plato identifies φρόνησις as the highest theoretical power (see 518e). Muller judges that φρόνησις and νοῦς are "quasiment synonymes" (R. Muller, *La doctrine platonicienne*, 144–45n8). It is especially interesting to note, as others have observed, that when Plato lists the "four cardinal virtues" in the *Phaedo*, in the place of the usual φρόνησις, he puts "truth and freedom" (114c): we see here both the intrinsic connection between truth and freedom and the resolutely "objective" character of his thought: the highest virtue is not a subjective disposition, first of all, but the reality itself.

47. Stenzel, "Das Problem der Willensfreiheit," 181

48. Zeitler, *Entscheidungsfreiheit bei Platon*, 53.

49. Aristotle, who is often thought to do more justice to the problem of *akrasia*, turns out to be in perfect agreement with Plato on this point, which is the decisive one. We will address this in more detail below in chapter 8.

50. The *locus classicus* for this is the story of Leontinus in *Republic* 439e–440a. On θύμος, in its distinction from reason and desire, as the beginning of a notion of the will, see M. Van Straaten, "What Did the Greeks Mean by Liberty," Part II, "Plato and Aristotle," *Theta-Pi* 3 (1974): 12–44.

51. See *Laws* 860d ff.

52. Ibid., 863c.

53. Zeitler, *Entscheidungsfreiheit bei Platon*, 55. Zeitler's book is especially strong in its characterization of Platonic knowledge in this regard.

54. See Plato, *Timaeus* 90d, in which he characterizes knowledge as a conformity of the soul to the order of the cosmos.

55. In its "coupling" with reality, the soul gives birth to truth and knowledge: γεννήσας νοῦν καὶ ἀλήθειαν (*Republic* 490b). Note how the fruit of this union is both objective and subjective.

56. See *Theaetetus* 150b–151d. In the *Apology*, Socrates denies that he has ever played the role of teacher (19d).

57. Stenzel, "Das Problem der Willensfreiheit," 181.

58. Ibid., 186–87.

59. *Republic* 505a.

60. In the *Phaedrus*, Plato compares education to planting seeds, which take a long time to grow. Only an *unserious* farmer—a sophist—expects immediate results (276b ff.). On the great duration required for a serious education, consider the time set for the program laid out in the *Republic* 539e ff.

61. See D. C. Schindler, *Plato's Critique*, 85–138.

62. Hence, Plato's description of the soul as a self-mover (*Laws* 896a; cf. *Phaedrus*, 245c–e), the nature of which takes the form of an *exitus/reditus* from and to the first principle. This is the form of *eros*, which is beautifully described in the *Phaedrus*, a dialogue that begins with five pregnant words, "Friend Phaedrus, whither and whence?"

63. R. Muller, *La doctrine platonicienne*, 96.

64. "*Vollstrecken*" means "to enforce." At the root is "*strecken*," which means "to distend" or "stretch out," and "*voll*" is an intensifier: to do so "fully." Thus, βούλησις enforces reason by "striving after the actual good" (Zeitler, *Entscheidungsfreiheit bei Platon*, 46).

65. Zeitler, *Entscheidungsfreiheit bei Platon*, 87–88. Cf. R. Muller, *La doctrine platonicienne*, 96n2.

66. See *Laws* 688b: love and desire "accompany" reason and wisdom.

67. Ibid., 967a; "διάνοια" is reason in its "discursive" or active sense.

68. Plato, *The Complete Works*, ed. John M. Cooper (Indianapolis: Hackett, 1997), 1614.

69. *Timaeus* 47e ff. Note that this is not a simple rejection of mechanical necessity, but a relentless subordination of such necessity to the *proper* motion relative to goodness, which is truly intelligible motion. Cf. *Phaedo* 97b–99d, in which Plato insists on the primacy of the causality of the good over the operations of the mechanical causes, without denying the existence and even necessity of the latter (cf. *Timaeus* 46c–e). On the metaphysics of motion and the implications of mechanistic physics, see Simon Oliver, *Philosophy, God, and Motion* (New York: Routledge, 2013).

70. See *Laws* 966a.

71. See Perl, "Presence of the Paradigm."

72. *Republic* 518d. We might compare Plato's notion of education as *conversio*, a turning around *toward* what precedes a person, to Locke's notion of education as *revolutio*, a turning *away* from what precedes a person.

73. Just as the eye gets its vision as "an overflow from the sun's treasury" (*Republic* 508b), the mind, as we indicated, receives its power to know as an "overflow" from the good (508d–509a). It is important to note in this context that Plato has an "extra-missive" optical theory: the eyes are not passive but shine a light outward onto the object, so to speak, though this shining power is a *participation* in sunlight, and does not simply originate in the eyes.

74. The notion of repetition we refer to here as "recollecting forward" comes from Kierkegaard: it is an attempt to integrate the "a priori" dimension of intelligible form with the novelty of human action; see Kierkegaard, *Fear and Trembling/Repetition* (Princeton, NJ: Princeton University Press, 1983).

75. The notion of *eros* as an "intermediary" is of course clearly established in the *Symposium* (202d–203a), but it is also more subtly present in the other "erotic dialogue," the *Phaedrus*, in which Socrates recounts the soul's movement from the good and beautiful and return to it. We might say that this *exitus/reditus* schema is the structure of *eros*, as the Neoplatonic tradition recognized.

76. *Laws* 896a.

77. Cf. *Gorgias* 499e–500a.

78. Note that Plato's description of creation as a bestowal of form is different from the Christian notion of creation strictly *ex nihilo*, as the bestowal of existence *tout court*. This difference will have significant implications for the interpretation of freedom, as we hope to show in a future volume.

79. See *Laws* 896a–b, and *Phaedrus* 245c–d.

80. R. Muller, *La doctrine platonicienne*, 188.

81. Muller ultimately wants to reconcile Plato's notion of freedom with a certain strand of liberalism, and it is illuminating to consider his strategy for doing so. He first "immanentizes" the good, so to speak, by simply identifying reason's relation to the good with reason's relation to itself, i.e., with rational autonomy. This, then, allows Muller to separate philosophical freedom from the political order, which in turn enables him to interpret the political order in simply negative terms (in a manner similar to liberalism generally) as the external conditions for the individual pursuit of freedom. For all of the great insight in Muller's work, in the end he makes Kant the measure of Plato, and fails to do justice to a fundamental dimension of Plato's thought, namely, the profound link between philosophy and politics, which we will address at the end of this chapter.

82. See *Laws* 721a. This is not to say that man is *only* his soul. Plato is notoriously ambiguous on this point. Although Plato comes closest perhaps to identifying man with the soul *rather* than the body-soul unity in *Alcibiades I* (130c), there is a preponderance of evidence scattered throughout the dialogues that suggests a more "holistic" vision of man. On this, see the excellent treatment by Cornelia J. de Vogel, *Rethinking Plato and Platonism* (Leiden: Brill, 1986), 159–212. There is some controversy regarding the authenticity of *Alcibiades I*, but resolving this controversy is not decisive, given the body of evidence that de Vogel presents.

83. On Socrates as image of the good, see D. C. Schindler, *Plato's Critique*, 179–87, 167–70.

84. See *Symposium* 204e. It is to be noted that Diotima, in her conversation with Socrates, replaces beauty with the good, as if they were effectively the same. There are certainly distinctions to be made between beauty and the good in Plato's thinking, but they are not relevant to our current discussion.

85. Ibid., 206e.

86. Indeed, given Plato's view of the cosmic movement driven by goodness, we could say that all activity in the cosmos is analogously a birthing in beauty (or at least in goodness), though this would not exclude a radical discontinuity between the animate and inanimate, and between man and all other animals.

87. *Symposium* 205b–d. In the *Laws* (837a), Plato describes *eros* as an intense form of *philia*, and *philia* is the bond that holds together the parts of the cosmos (cf. *Gorgias* 507e–508a).

88. *Laws* 859e–860a. Every just action or passion is a participation in beauty (τοῦ καλοῦ μετέχον ἐστίν).

89. We might contrast Plato on this point with the Stoic tradition, which is quite directly revived on this score in Spinoza. On the one hand, there is little talk in this tradition of the *good* in the metaphysical sense as a fruitful and generous cause, and there is, connected with this, a tendency toward a materialistic immanentism. Freedom can acquire only a *dialectical* reality in such a cosmos.

90. The *Republic* clearly alludes to the *Odyssey* in a number of ways throughout, but we might see an echo of the *Iliad* in its closing pages: a funeral pyre and games. In the Platonic dialogue, the ultimate contest is the choice of "how to live" (see *Republic* 344d–e, 618b–619a, 608b).

91. *Republic* 617d–e. Stenzel brilliantly interprets the story here as the doctrine of recollection in the order of choice ("Das Problem der Willensfreiheit, 184–85). It is an attempt to bring together freedom and necessity (see also van Straaten, "What Did the Greeks Mean by Liberty," 126–30). On the one hand, the life one leads is a *result* of a choice; on the other, however, it is an "eschatological" choice, one that in some sense has always already been made (though not as something lying simply in the past).

92. On Plato's use of myths for a philosophical purpose, see Catalin Partenie, ed., *Plato's Myths* (Cambridge: Cambridge University Press, 2011), esp. introduction, 1–27.

93. The argument Plato makes in the *Protagoras* assumes as one of its basic premises the essential commensurability of goods, at least with respect to the pleasure they produce (see 354b–d).

94. *Republic* 332d–333d.

95. *Charmides* 167b ff.

96. R. Muller, *La doctrine platonicienne*, 148.

97. Ibid., 131.

98. Plato presents Socrates in this dialogue as not only inherently surprising in himself (like a statue of Silenus, which opens up to reveal a boundless number of astonishing figures), but also doing unexpected things (like spending a full night standing still in contemplation, and so forth), and appearing in surprising places: "You always do this to me," Alcibiades says to Socrates, "all of a sudden you'll turn up out of nowhere where I least expect you!" (*Symposium* 213c). Alcibiades concludes that Socrates is unique, incomparable to anyone else past or present (221c–d). We might say that he represents the epitome of the free human being for Plato.

99. There is something problematic about conceiving the soul's embodied condition as an *imprisonment*, even if Plato does not at all mean by this what he is generally taken to mean; see de Vogel, *Rethinking Plato and Platonism*, and D. C. Schindler, *Plato's Critique*, 283–336; cf. D. C. Schindler, *Catholicity of Reason*, 119–36. It should be noted that Socrates is free even *in* the prison, and so does not need to escape; so too he is free *in* the body, and does not need to do violence to it, or even resist it with contempt.

100. There is no need to work out, in the present context, the significance of the differences in these characterizations, though the theme would be interesting in itself to explore.

101. The whole issue surrounding this problem is summed up in Spaemann's brilliantly simple question: When the hedonist asks what will bring him the most pleasure, does he want a *true* answer, or only a pleasant one?; see "In Defense of Anthropomorphism," in *Spaemann Reader*, 89. A classic critique of the idea that man pursues pleasure itself can be found in Max Scheler, *Formalism in Ethics and Non-Formal Ethics of Values* (Evanston, IL: Northwestern University Press, 1973), 241–53.

102. See *Republic* 475b ff.

103. In the *Republic*, Plato calculates, on the basis of the distinction in degrees of reality, that the lover of wisdom will live "729 times" more pleasantly (!) than the tyrant, who pursues pleasure in abstraction from reality (588e). In the *Phaedo*, Plato presents the *free* soul not as outside of the body and sense experience, but as entering into the depth of them: the colors are more vivid, and so forth (see 109a ff.).

104. See *Republic* 497a–b.

105. In the *Phaedrus*, Socrates ranks the philosopher first, but the "lawful king" second and the "statesman" third. It is interesting to note that, in spite of his self-professed political ineptitude, Socrates is portrayed by Plato as the "true statesman," which implies that philosophy is not indifferent to the political

order but has a direct relation to it: "I believe that I'm one of a few Athenians—so as not to say I'm the only one, but the only one among our contemporaries—to take up the true political craft and practice the true politics" (*Gorgias* 521d).

106. This is the deep sense of the *Crito*, in which Socrates interprets his obedience to the good simply to imply obedience to the given laws under which he was raised.

107. *Republic* 592b.

108. *Symposium* 209a–b (emphasis added). Note that Plato characterizes justice and moderation, here, not as a soul's internal order, but as a giving of order to the larger whole.

109. *Laws* 645a. See Heraclitus, DK B114: "Speaking with understanding (ξὺν νόῳ), they must hold fast to what is shared (ξυνῷ) by all, as a city holds to its law, and even more firmly." Note that Heraclitus connects *understanding* with being *joined together*, and he presents an analogy between the bond of a city and the more fundamental interior grasp of a common order. For a more detailed presentation on Heraclitus's understanding of "logos" and its connection to community, see D. C. Schindler, "The Community of the One and the Many: Heraclitus on Reason," *Inquiry* 46, no. 4 (2003): 413–48.

110. *Laws* 678e ff. It is worth quoting Plato at length here because of the extraordinary contrast his imaginative depiction of the "original state of nature" strikes with Locke's. Plato presents the natural state as having arisen after a great flood has washed away civilization and the strife it inevitably entails. When Clinias asks why war disappeared, Plato has the Stranger answer: "In the first place, men's isolation prompted them to cherish and love one another (ἠγάπων καὶ ἐφιλοφρονοῦτο ἀλλήλους). Second, their food supply was nothing they needed to quarrel about. Except perhaps for a few people in the very early stages, there was no shortage of flocks and herds, which is what men mostly lived on in that age. They always had a supply of milk and meat, and could always add to it plenty of good food to be got by hunting. They also had an abundance of clothes, bedding, houses, and equipment for cooking and other purposes. (Molding pottery and weaving, skills that have no need of iron, were a gift from God to men—his way, in fact, of supplying them with all that kind of equipment. His intention was that whenever the human race was reduced to such a desperate condition it could still take root and develop.) Because of all this, they were not intolerably poor, nor driven by poverty to quarrel with each other; but presumably they did not grow rich either, in view of the prevailing lack of gold and silver. Now the community in which neither wealth nor poverty exists will generally produce the finest characters because tendencies to violence and crime, and feelings of jealousy and envy, simply do not arise. So these men were *good*, partly for that very reason, partly because of

what we might call their 'naivete.' When they heard things labeled 'good' or 'bad,' they were so artless as to think it a statement of the literal truth and believe it. This lack of sophistication precluded the cynicism you find today: they accepted as the truth the doctrine they heard about gods and men, and lived their lives in accordance with it" (*Laws* 678e–679c).

111. See, for example, *Laws* 901e–902b, in which Plato presents man as the "most god-fearing of all living creatures," but at the same time as having a tendency toward vice.

112. *Laws* 626b ff.

113. Ibid., 803e.

114. Megillus responds to the Stranger's description of existence as play with a concern that he is making it something trivial. The Stranger interestingly admits this, and says it is only because he is viewing existence in relation to God. Viewed in itself, it is a serious matter (see *Laws* 804b–c).

115. On this theme in general in classical and Christian literature, see Hugo Rahner, *Man at Play* (New York: Herder and Herder, 1972).

116. *Laws* 803c. Cf. *Laws* 716d: the "noblest and truest" rule is "to engage in sacrifice and communion with the gods continually, by prayers and offerings and devotions of every kind."

117. Ibid., 626d. Note, too, that it is not enough to justify peace as being the fundamental aim of war; instead, peace has to be affirmed simply for its own sake, irrespective of its relation to war (see 803d–e).

118. Ibid., 693b; 693d–e; 694b. At 701d, he refers back to this mention specifically as a "threefold." The number three is of course significant. It bears a connection with *salvation*, as Plato makes explicit at the end of the dialogue, with his reference to the "third, saving Muse" (960c). He insists here on a threefold affirmation of the laws, to give the city a kind of absolute foundation: "It is a proper thing to reiterate twice—yea, thrice—the truth" (957a). The association of the number three with salvation is traditional (see, for example, the regular reference in Aeschylus's *Libation Bearers*). Plato points to this tradition repeatedly in his work (see, e.g., *Charmides* 167b). In *Letter VII*, Plato writes: "in the name of Zeus the Savior, to whom this third libation belongs" (334d). Not incidentally, the first word (which in Plato's dialogues often indicates a principal theme) of the *Laws* is "God," "θεὸς," a word that is repeated three times in the first three lines. "Salvation," in this ancient Greek context, means something very different from the Christian notion: essentially, it indicates what is definitive and complete, or perfect safety.

119. *Laws* 693c. Plato mentions here that there would be other possible expressions for the same thing. He is clearly talking about a single reality that has a rich multitude of aspects.

120. Recall that Plato places "freedom and truth" in the place of φρόνησις in his list of cardinal virtues (*Phaedo* 114c).

121. Nestle, *Eleutheria*, 91. Nestle himself refers to Ilse von Löwenclau, *Der platonische Menexenos* (Tübinger Beiträge zur Altertumswissenschaft, 1961), 74 ff.

122. Aristotle identifies the good in a certain sense with order (see *Metaphysics* 12.10.1075a12–24).

123. *Laws* 832c. One of the meanings of στάσις is "party formed for seditious purposes," or simply "discord." The word στασιωτεία is Plato's own combination of στάσις with πολιτεία, i.e., "political community." We might translate Plato's word simply as "society of devils," in the sense we gave that phrase in chapter 6.

124. If this sounds similar to our formulation of the essence of rights, it is because right and law are themselves closely related. The difference is that rights concern the nature of individuals, while law is an expression of nature in a more objective and comprehensive sense.

125. After explaining the natural foundation of law, Plato turns to the order of community and says that the *natural* place to begin is marriage and family (*Laws* 720e–721a). Later in the dialogue, Plato highlights the connection between respect for one's family (and in particular one's parents), and religious piety. He explains that, if we worship the invisible gods through statues (which might be understood as conveying a sacramental presence), an even more direct presence of God can be found in a person's parents, so that the gods receive the veneration directed to one's parents as their own (931a–c).

126. It is worth observing that Plato's sense of law approaches the original Hebrew sense.

127. Plato argues that there was law in the "original state," even if it was not yet codified (*Laws* 680a), insofar as any harmonious whole is governed by a unifying principle. At stake here is whether one acknowledges the good reality of political order as foundational or sees law instead principally as securing the safety of individuals. It is in light of this issue that we see the shortcomings of Muller's interpretation of Plato's notion of freedom, particularly in its political dimension, that we described in note 81, above.

128. R. Muller, *La doctrine platonicienne*, 98–99, and *Laws* 698b; cf. 700a. Plato is speaking, here, of the Athenians, who represent a tendency toward licentiousness, but who learned through the threat of war to obey laws as a condition of survival.

129. *Laws* 807d–e.

130. We see Plato's point reflected also in Aristotle: "For all [in the cosmos] are ordered together to one end, but is as in a house, where the free men

(τοῖς ἐλευθέροις) are least permitted (ἥκιστα ἔξεστιν) to act at random, but all things or most are already ordained for them, while the slaves and the animals do little for the common good, and for the most part live at random" (translation slightly modified; *Metaphysics* 12.10.1075a19–24).

131. See *Laws* 857a ff., 720b ff.

132. *Laws* 857c–d. Cf. *Gorgias* 484c–485e; *Theaetetus* 172c–e.

133. *Nous* commands, Plato says, if it is truly free, which coincides with its conformity to nature, the originating source of action; see *Laws* 875d: ἐάνπερ ἀληθινὸς ἐλευθερός τε ὄντως ᾖ κατὰ φύσιν.

134. *Laws* 859a.

135. Ibid.

136. See *Laws* 875d; *Republic* 473c–d; *Letter VII* 326a–b.

137. In this case, the English translation is even more fitting than the Greek (προοίμιον, a "pre-path," and so "opening"). See Plato's discussion of the importance of a prelude for the law (*Laws* 722d ff.).

138. *Laws* 918d–919e.

139. On this, see D. C. Schindler, "Why Socrates Didn't Charge: Plato and the Metaphysics of Money," *Communio* 36 (Fall 2009): 394–426.

140. *Laws* 919e–920a.

141. Ibid., 741e–742a.

142. This is why he says Egyptians and Phoenicians (who had the reputation of being rather covetous) are "unfree" with respect to property (747c).

143. *Laws* 941b.

144. Ibid., 731e. Note the ambiguity of *philia*, which tends to be directed, as we indicated at the outset of our discussion of Plato, to "one's own." Plato goes on to say that the ideal would be the rooting out of what is considered purely private interest (τὸ λεγόμενον ἴδιον)—which, we must understand, is *not* the individual simply, but only the individual *interpreted* as opposed to the common—and that greatness is attachment not to self or one's own belongings, but to *justice* (732a). We thus return at the end to the theme with which we began.

145. Ibid., 914c.

CHAPTER 8. ARISTOTLE: FREEDOM AS LIBERALITY

1. Aristotle, *De anima* 3.10.433a5. Cf. Arendt, *Life of the Mind*, 2:57. In *Nicomachean Ethics*, Aristotle concludes his theoretical study of virtue with the observation that the point is not just to learn about being good, but actually to become good (*NE* 10.9.1179a36–1179b11; hereafter cited as *NE*).

2. Lloyd Gerson, *Aristotle and Other Platonists* (Ithaca, NY: Cornell University Press, 2005). MacIntyre has famously argued that tradition is not *exclusive* of conflict, but it is partially constituted by it (see, e.g., *After Virtue*, 222). There is no doubt a profound truth in this observation, but one must nevertheless affirm a unity in principle, but as *generous* so that it is productive of a qualitative kind of difference. In any event, this is a theme that requires more reflection than the present context allows.

3. There have been a variety of translations proposed, since it is recognized that the modern sense of "choice" has voluntaristic overtones that are foreign to Aristotle. On the different proposals, see Charles Chamberlain, "The Meaning of *Prohairesis* in Aristotle's *Ethics*," *Transactions of the American Philological Association* 114 (1984): 147–57; cited in Thomas Pfau, *Minding the Modern: Human Agency, Intellectual Traditions, and Responsible Knowledge* (Notre Dame, IN: University of Notre Dame Press, 2013), 88n27. Chamberlain opts for "commitment." We will translate it in this chapter simply as "choice," but, as we will explain, we mean the word in the sense of setting apart what is best from everything else, which is, as Stenzel explains, the original meaning of the term: Stenzel, "Das Problem der Willensfreiheit," 177.

4. See, for example, the distinction he makes in *Metaphysics* 12.7.1072a27. Cf. *Eudemian Ethics* 2.10.1227a27–32.

5. Hegel, *Lectures on the History of Philosophy, Lectures of 1825–26, Greek Philosophy* (Oxford: Oxford University Press, 2006), 234, in which Hegel identifies this as the precise point on which Aristotle takes a step beyond Plato.

6. Aristotle, *De anima* 2.4.415b11–12; 2.4.415b15; 2.1.412a20–21.

7. As Muller observes, the word "freedom" is virtually absent in Aristotle's discussion of human action in the *Ethics*, appearing only in the virtue of "liberality" (which we will show below is not at all insignificant). The word can be found virtually exclusively in the *Politics*. Nevertheless, Aristotle describes action in the *Ethics* in terms that bear directly on the problem of freedom as we have been engaging it; see Robert Muller, "La logique de la liberté dans la *Politique*," in *Aristote Politique: Études sur la Politique d'Aristote*, ed. Pierre Aubenque (Paris: Presses universitaires de France, 1993), 185–87.

8. Aristotle, *Metaphysics* 9.1.1046a10.

9. At play here is Aristotle's important distinction between first and second actuality (see, e.g., *De anima* 2.1.412a21–30). The first actuality, which is the determination of what a thing is, represents potency with respect to the actualizing of the essence, but it is *not* indeterminate in itself (unlike "power" in Locke).

10. Aristotle, *Metaphysics* 9.8.1050b9.

11. Aristotle, *Physics* 5.1.

12. "Since some of these principles are inherent in inanimate things, and others in animate things and in the soul and in the rational part of the soul, it is clear that some of the potencies also will be irrational and some rational" (*Metaphysics* 9.2.1046a36–1046b2).

13. *Metaphysics* 1046b6–7.

14. Ibid., 9.2.1046b20.

15. Ibid., 1046b11–13.

16. Ibid., 1051a2–4.

17. See ibid., 9.9.1051a4–5.

18. Ibid., 1051a31–32.

19. All of this is treated in ibid., 9.8.

20. The terms are a polarity, so basic they cannot be explained in any more fundamental terms; instead, their meaning becomes manifest through induction from examples and analogies, as Aristotle explains in *Metaphysics* 9.6.1048a35–39. A good recent presentation of Aristotle's understanding of potency and act, and the fundamental importance of these concepts to his metaphysics, is Aryeh Kosman, *The Activity of Being: An Essay on Aristotle's Ontology* (Cambridge, MA: Harvard University Press, 2013).

21. *Metaphysics* 9.8.1049b29–30.

22. See Hegel, *Encyclopedia*, §41, Zusatz 1.

23. *Metaphysics* 1050b5.

24. As always in Aristotle, the proper sense also implies a kind of analogical differentiation.

25. For a good discussion of motion in Aristotle, see Joe Sachs, "Aristotle: Motion and Its Place in Nature," *Internet Encyclopedia of Philosophy*, http://www.iep.utm.edu/aris-mot/. Cf. Kosman, *Activity of Being*, 37–68, and Rémi Brague, *Aristote et la question du monde: Essai sur le contexte cosmologique et anthropologique de l'ontologie* (Paris: Presses universitaires de France, 1988), 497–509.

26. One of the best interpreters of Aristotle's *Physics*, Joe Sachs, gives the title "Motions as Wholes" to chapter 5 of his translation (and "Internal Structures of Motions" to chapter 6) (Sachs, "Aristotle").

27. *Physics* 6.5. The argument turns on the continuity of motion and the infinite divisibility of any stretch of both motion and time.

28. It is *essential* to see that an analogy remains, as our previous paragraph makes clear: motion cannot be *absolutely* different from actuality, which is why there always remains something in motion that is irreducible to mere temporal sequence.

29. Aristotle, *Physics* 8.5.257b7–9; cf. 3.2.201b31–32; 3.1.201a9–11; *De anima* 2.2.417a14–17; 3.7.431a6–7.

30. Aristotle, *Metaphysics* 9.6.1048b23–27. The perfect aspect is not as evident in colloquial English (in which it tends to be used to express a past event) as in Greek, but the point is that the perfect aspect indicates an action that is (already) complete with respect to the present moment, while the present tense indicates that the perfectly completed action is *occurring* in the present moment. See Kosman, *Activity of Being*, 41, 260n5.

31. As Kosman puts it, "It is a feature of activities that such past periods of perfecting are not required; an activity is the sort of thing that is perfected or completed in the very moment of its being enacted. This is not to say that activities cannot happen in time. An activity can indeed occupy time, but it is not the sort of thing that must take time. . . . It is because an activity does not need to await any further development to perfect or complete its being that it is complete and perfect at each and every moment of its duration" (Kosman, *Activity of Being*, 41–42).

32. Aristotle, *NE* 10.4.1174b6–9, 31–34.

33. Aristotle, *Metaphysics* 12.8.1073a24–40.

34. See Peter Ansley, *John Locke and Natural Philosophy* (Oxford: Oxford University Press, 2011). Though some call into question the extent of Locke's commitment to mechanism, the issues at stake in that particular question do not bear on the general contrast we wish to highlight here; see Lisa Downing, "The Status of Mechanism in Locke's *Essay*," *Philosophical Review* 107, no. 3 (1998): 381–414.

35. See *De anima* 2.5.417b5. Here, Aristotle is speaking specifically of the transition from potency to act in knowledge.

36. See Locke, *Essay*, 2.27.

37. See *Metaphysics* 8.6.1045a10–11, where Aristotle distinguishes between a mere aggregate of parts and a genuine whole (ὅλον).

38. Aristotle, *De anima* 2.5.417a15.

39. See Aquinas, *Summa theologica* 1.2.3; 1-2.9.1.

40. *De anima* 2.5.417b20.

41. Ibid., 2.7.419a12–21, where Aristotle makes the argument regarding sight, and then goes on to show similar media for the other senses. He initially distinguishes taste from the others, saying that there is no medium in this case, but then points out that, even here, liquid is necessary (*De anima* 2.10.15–20).

42. Aristotle, *De anima* 3.2.425b26–426a1. Jonathan Lear's classic introduction to Aristotle can be read as an extensive, and illuminating, exposition of just this point; see Lear, *Aristotle: The Desire to Understand* (Cambridge: Cambridge University Press, 1988), esp. chap. 4, 96–151.

43. *De anima* 2.5.418a4–6.

44. Ibid., 3.10.433b26–31.

45. Plato famously makes this argument in the *Symposium* (200a–d). Socrates explains in this passage that even the desire for something that already *is* is a desire for its continued existence in the future, which is in that respect at least not yet actual.

46. See Mark Shiffman's discussion of the soul's self-motion in the introduction to Shiffman, trans., *De anima* (Newburyport, MA: Focus, 2011), 20–24.

47. It is no doubt because of the materialistic tendencies of Hellenistic philosophy, and the attempt therefore to give a generally mechanistic account of the operation of the human faculties, that the problem of "free will vs. naturalistic determinism" became such a regular theme in the thinkers of that epoch.

48. *De anima* 3.10.433b15–19. At the ultimate foundation of any motion there has to be an unmoved mover: this is an implication of the principle that potency can be reduced to act only by something in a state of actuality.

49. In fact, it needs to be affirmed, or else the unity of the principles will ultimately get lost.

50. Shiffman refers to the "natural self-orientation of all living things" (*De anima* 21). Although this description is importantly true, it has to be complemented with an affirmation of the *intrinsic* role played by the good that moves the organism's self-motion. Indeed, the fact that the form at the basis of the soul's natural self-motion is (*also*) universal means that the appetite for the proper good will never be merely "private." We will expand this point further below.

51. *Physics* 7.3.247b1–7.

52. It is also insufficient to think that part of it is derived and part underived: this is essentially the escape from the dilemma that Kant takes, and it brings him to even deeper conundrums. Though we cannot explore the matter fully here, we note that the proper understanding would somehow include a total reception simultaneous with a total spontaneity. It is *really in* sense experience that the soul sees more than what the sensible as such offers; or in other words, the soul receives from sense experience more than that experience is able to give of itself alone. All of this is connected with the meaning of freedom as generous excess, as superfluity.

53. *Physics* 7.3.247b6–8. Note that Kant's critical philosophy, and the idealist tradition that grows from it, represents an attempt to recover this point in Plato and Aristotle in a modern, i.e., "nonsymbolical," context, and the result is exceedingly problematic.

54. Aristotle calls the intellect divine in relation to man (θεῖον ὁ νοῦς πρὸς τὸν ἄνθρωπον), and refers to it as the presence of the divine in him (θεῖόν τι ἐν αὐτῷ) (*NE* 10.7.26–31). Cf. *De anima* 3.5.430a20–25.

55. *De anima* 3.8.431b20–21. Cf. also the description of the soul as the "place of the forms" (3.4.429a27–29) or the "form of the forms" (3.8.432a1–2).

56. As Aquinas would eventually point out, the mind's participation in the divine intellect does not at all compromise the individual substantiality of man's intellect or his activity as an individual agent. Man is not a mere "shadow" of God.

57. *De anima* 3.4.429b29–430a2.

58. See *NE* 3.1.1111a21–23.

59. Ibid., 3.1.1110a1–4.

60. Ibid., 3.1.1110b1–3; 3.1.1110b15–17.

61. See Herbert Weir Smyth, *A Greek Grammar for Colleges*, pt. 4, sec. 44, 1728.

62. *NE* 3.1.1111a23–31.

63. Aristotle, *Physics* 2.8.199a10–19.

64. On the dialectical opposition that came to replace the analogical difference in nature and its pairing with reason, culture, and so forth, see Spaemann, "Nature," in *Spaemann Reader*, 22–36. Plato already points to the sophistic tendency to *oppose* reason and nature, rather than seeing reason as a higher instance of nature (see *Laws* 889e–890d).

65. Note here the decisive difference from Locke, whose nominalism precludes any analogous extension of reason, which is why it is simply *absent* in children (and, a fortiori, animals), who thus become something like the property of the parents.

66. *NE* 9.8.1068b35–1069a3.

67. Ibid.

68. Aristotle presents a tripartite division of the soul reminiscent of Plato's own, but substitutes βούλησις for what Plato had called the "reasoning part." As we have argued, these are essentially the same; see, e.g., *Eudemian Ethics* 2.7.1228a27–28.

69. *De anima* 3.10.433a24–26.

70. *NE* 6.2.1039b5–6.

71. *Metaphysics* 1.1.980a15–16.

72. *Eudemian Ethics* 2.10.1227a16–25.

73. For a good account of Aristotle's explanation of how *akrasia* is possible, see Pierre Destrée, "Aristotle on the Causes of *Akrasia*," in *Akrasia in Greek Philosophy*, ed. Pierre Destrée and Christopher Bobonovich (Leiden: Brill, 2007), 139–65.

74. As Aristotle points out, there is one way to be good in every case, and an infinite number of ways to be bad, because "evil belongs to the class of the unlimited" (*NE* 2.6.1106b26–35).

75. *Metaphysics* 9.2.1046b24.

76. *Eudemian Ethics* 2.10.1227a27–32: "By nature, good is the object of wish, but evil is also its object in contravention of nature; by nature one wishes good, against nature and by perversion one even wishes evil." Aristotle goes on to explain that even an evil act is limited to a contrary or intermediate, and so retains a logical connection to the good.

77. "Man . . . is a source and begetter of actions just as much as of children" (*NE* 3.5.1113b17–20). "All essences are by nature first principles of a certain kind, owing to which each is able to generate many things of the same sort as itself, for example a man engenders men, and in general an animal animals, and a plant plants. And in addition to this, obviously man alone among animals is the originating source (ἀρχή) of certain conduct" (*Eudemian Ethics* 2.6.1222b16–21; translation slightly modified).

78. *De anima* 3.10.433a28–30.

79. *NE* 1.8.1098b30–1099a6. The emphasis on activity explains why Aristotle privileges loving over being loved (*NE* 8.8.1159a12–36).

80. See Aristotle's categorizing of types of goods in *Rhetoric* 1.5.

81. *NE* 4.1.1121a10–15.

82. ὁ ἐλευθέριος . . . δώσει τοῦ καλοῦ ἕνεκα (*NE* 4.1.1120a24–25).

83. Prodigality does not indicate *a greater amount of* giving, but, more precisely, indiscriminate giving, without order, so as to waste one's substance. Though it is the trait of the liberal person not to have regard for himself—τὸ γὰρ μὴ βλέπειν ἐφ' ἑαυτὸν ἐλευθερίου (*NE* 4.1.1120b6–7)—because his action is truly good, it cannot fail to magnify rather than waste away his being (οὐσία). Cf. *NE* 4.1.1120a1–3.

84. *Politics* 7.3.1325b16–33.

85. This does not mean, as we recall, that the act represents a piecing together of two separate "things"; rather, the actuality is a complete unity, in relation to which the principles are potencies.

86. See *Politics* 7.3.1325b18–20.

87. We may recall here Aristotle's distinction between two levels of actuality in knowing: the possession of knowledge and its actual exercise (e.g., *De anima* 2.1.412a22–24).

88. This is not at all "altruistic" in the modern sense of the term (which appears to have been coined by Auguste Comte), insofar as altruism presupposes a (diabolical) opposition between self and other. For Aristotle, self-sacrifice is the pursuit of the greatest good (also) for oneself (see *NE* 9.8.11669a11–1169b2).

89. *Metaphysics* 1.2.982b27–28.

90. *NE* 6.12.1144a1–7.

91. αἱ . . . πράξεις ἄλλων ἕνεκα (*NE* 3.3.1112b34).

92. We ought to qualify this by saying that contemplation is *itself* a specifically human action, and indeed the *most* human, though Aristotle also notes that in a certain respect it is divine *rather than* human, and if man achieves contemplation, it is only because there is present in him something essentially divine, namely, *reason* (*NE* 10.7.1177b27–1178a8).

93. See again *NE* 3.3.1112b34.

94. *Metaphysics* 9.8.1050a24–29. See also *NE* 6.5.1140b6–7. This is why, for Aristotle, it is least free, and there is some ambiguity in his discussion whether τέχνη qualifies as a virtue. This is a point that will get transformed in the Christian context, in which work acquires a new significance in the light of a notion of creation *ex nihilo*.

95. Against the general tendency to identify contemplation alone with leisure, and then to contrast it with the *vita activa*, Arendt helpfully reminds us that, in Aristotle, properly human action of any sort is desirable in itself, and not merely for utilitarian purposes; see Arendt, *The Human Condition*, 12–17. According to Aristotle, leisure is the "first principle of all action" (*Politics* 8.2.1337b33).

96. *Politics* 7.3.1325b20.

97. *NE* 9.8.1068b35–1069a3.

98. Though Aristotle identifies the absolute, highest activity as a perfect unity of subject and object (self-thinking thought in which the thought is the thinking), he emphasizes the nonreceptive character of this unity, which seems to imply an ultimate subordination of the other to the self. This subordination gets likewise reflected in his derivation of love of other from love of self, and so forth.

99. See *NE* 9.8.1169a35–36: "In all the actions, therefore, that men are praised for, the good man is seen to assign to himself a greater share in what is noble."

100. *Politics* 7.15.1334a12–13. This sameness should be understood in the strong sense.

101. *NE* 9.9.1170a16–19

102. *De anima* 2.4.415b12.

103. *NE* 9.9.1070a26–1170b14.

104. It is crucial to note the *natural* quality of friendship in Aristotle, which distinguishes him from the modern thinkers, who operate with a notion of freedom as set off against nature. A root of the modern sense of friendship can be seen clearly in Montaigne, who, for example, *opposes* the relationship of friendship to those that arise by nature, because the former is "chosen" while the latter are not. As we observed in chapter 5, by dissociating friendship from nature, Montaigne is thus reduced to removing any *reason* for the profound friendship he had with Étienne de La Boétie, and he explains its occurrence and

substance only with the famous phrase "because it was he, because it was I." See Montaigne, "On Friendship."

105. ἔστι γὰρ ὁ φίλος ἄλλος αὐτός (*NE* 9.4.1066a32).

106. *NE* 9.12.1071b32–1172a1.

107. Aristotle discusses the question whether a supremely happy man needs friends or not in *NE* 9.9. He ultimately answers yes, by virtue of man's social nature, but there is a tension because of his understanding of happiness as *defined* by completeness and therefore self-sufficiency.

108. Muller misses this point in his attempt to separate philosophy from politics in a radical way, which we mentioned in chapter 7. Muller ultimately interprets Aristotle's politics as presenting conditions for (solitary) contemplation: i.e., politics aims to eliminate itself. See Muller, "La logique de liberté." He thus overlooks the link between the *Nichomachean Ethics* and the *Politics*, which clearly prevents such an interpretation.

109. *Politics* 1.2.1253a1–3.

110. Aristotle compares the lawgiver, who constitutes a political community, to a craftsman, which suggests that the *polis* is something like an artifact (*Politics* 7.4.1325b40–1326a5).

111. David Keyt argues that "there is a blunder at the very root of Aristotle's political philosophy" because he affirms in several places the *natural* character of the *polis*, though it turns out that "according to Aristotle's own principles, the political community is an artifact of practical reason, not a product of nature"; see Keyt, "Three Basic Theorems in Aristotle's *Politics*," in *A Companion to Aristotle's Politics*, ed. David Keyt and Fred D. Miller, Jr. (Cambridge, MA: Blackwell, 1991), 118.

112. *Politics* 3.9.1280a31–34.

113. Ibid., 3.9.1281a3–4.

114. Ibid., 3.9.1280b7–11.

115. *Metaphysics* 7.10.1035b24–25.

116. *Politics* 8.1.1337a26–30.

117. Aristotle does give great weight to birth in his identification of what makes a citizen to be such—which of course recalls the original meaning of freedom. The practical definition of the citizen, he explains, is a person who is born to citizens. But if we read more deeply into Aristotle's account, we see that one can be a citizen only if one is a member of a city, and this is defined specifically by the end, namely, human perfection. It may be true that the good citizen, in Aristotle, is not necessarily a good man, but he insists that the *ruler* in a city must be good, which means that every citizen will have a share in this sense in goodness (*Politics* 3.1–4). Aristotle's notion of intrinsic sharing in the quality of the whole, which itself has to be good in a basic sense in order to be

a *polis*, distinguishes his view from the liberalism articulated, for example, by Rawls, or more recently, in a Catholic context, by Rhonheimer.

118. *Politics* 3.9.1280b30–1281a8. Note that presenting noble actions rather than mere companionship as the end of political society is a political translation of the primacy of actuality. Note, too, in this passage that Aristotle sets nobility of virtue above nobility of birth.

119. Ibid., 7.2.1324a28–29.

120. Ibid., 7.3.1325a39–1325b2.

121. Ibid., 7.3.1325a26–28.

Conclusion

1. It is perhaps worthwhile to point out that "premodern" is not meant here in a strictly chronological sense, but rather first of all in a metaphysical sense, which implies also a historical dimension.

2. It is illuminating that, in the *Social Contract*, for example, Rousseau alludes to a deeper meaning of the word "liberty," but he sets it aside as not relevant to the political discussion. After a single sentence of explanation, he writes: "But I have already said too much on this head, and the philosophical meaning of the word liberty does not now concern us"; Rousseau, *Social Contract*, trans. G. D. G. Cole (New York: E. P. Dutton & Co., 1913), bk. 1, chap. 8. We have here a nice illustration of Chesterton's complaint, which we quoted in the introduction: "Let us not ask what liberty is," Rousseau is saying, "but let us discover how best to protect and promote it."

3. George Grant recounts the response Leo Strauss gave when he asked him at what period of history he would most like to have lived. Strauss answered that our own time is the best, and offered this reason: "because the most comprehensive and deepest account of the whole has been given us by Plato, and the most comprehensive criticism of that account has been given by Nietzsche"; George Grant, *Technology and Justice* (Concord, Ontario: House of Anansi Press, 1991), 90.

4. See Nietzsche, "Prologue," *Thus Spoke Zarathustra*, in *The Portable Nietzsche*: "Bless the cup that wants to overflow," Zarathustra says to the sun, "that the water may flow from it golden and carry everywhere the reflection of your delight" (121–22). See his description of one of Zarathustra's most characteristic virtues: "The Gift-Giving Virtue," 186–88. Nietzsche describes art as arising from an overfullness, which he contrasts to the "anti-artistic instinct," which is neediness and greed: "In this state (of artistic frenzy), one enriches everything out of one's own fullness" (*Twilight of the Idols*, in *The Portable*

Nietzsche, 518). For Nietzsche, it is Heraclitus who understood the nature of God best of all, insofar as Heraclitus saw him as an artist at play; see Nietzsche, *Philosophy in the Tragic Age of the Greeks* (Washington, DC: Gateway, 1987), 61–64.

5. Nietzsche famously wrote, in an unpublished note, "truth is ugly"; *Will to Power* (New York: Random House, 1967), 822. In the end, truth and beauty (not to say goodness too) were relativized to the enhancement of (ultimately biological) life.

6. See Heidegger, "Nihilism and the History of Being," in *Nietzsche*, Vol. 4, *Nihilism* (San Francisco: Harper, 1987), 199–250, here esp. 231.

7. See Heidegger's account of the nature of freedom, for example, in *The Essence of Truth*, in *Basic Writings*, 113–41. For Heidegger, freedom ultimately just *is* the openness (the "clearing" or the "truth") of being, and man's freedom is a participation in this openness.

BIBLIOGRAPHY

Aaron, Richard. "Authority and the Rights of Individuals." In *Life, Liberty, and Property*, edited by Gordon Schochet, 162–67. Belmont, CA: Wadsworth, 1971.

Aarsleff, Hans. "The State of Nature and the Nature of Man in Locke." In *John Locke: Problems and Perspectives: A Collection of New Essays*, edited by John W. Yolton, 99–136. Cambridge: Cambridge University Press, 2011.

Adorno, Theodor, and Max Horkheimer. *Dialectic of Enlightenment*. New York: Continuum, 1969.

Aeschylus. *Volume 1: The Oresteia*. 2nd ed. Translated by David Greene. Chicago: University of Chicago Press, 1969.

Alexander, Christopher. *The Nature of Order*. Vol. 1, *The Phenomenon of Life*. Berkeley, CA: Center for Environmental Structure, 1980.

Allison, Henry. *Kant's Theory of Freedom*. Cambridge: Cambridge University Press, 1990.

Anselm of Canterbury. *The Fall of the Devil*. Minneapolis, MN: Arthur J. Banning Press, 2000.

Ansley, Peter. *John Locke and Natural Philosophy*. Oxford: Oxford University Press, 2011.

Applebaum, Herbert. *The Concept of Work: Ancient, Medieval, and Modern*. Albany: SUNY Press, 1992.

Aquinas, Thomas. *On Kingship to the King of Cyprus (De regno)*. Translated by Gerald B. Phelan and I. T. Eschmann. Mediaeval Sources in Translation, 2. Toronto: Pontifical Institute of Mediaeval Studies, 1949.

———. *On the Truth of the Catholic Faith (Summa contra Gentiles)*. 5 vols. Translated by Anton C. Pegis, James F. Anderson, Vernon J. Bourke, and Charles J. O'Neil. New York: Doubleday, 1955–57; reprinted as *Summa contra Gentiles*. Notre Dame, IN: University of Notre Dame Press, 1975.

———. *Summa theologica*. Translated by the Fathers of the English Dominican Province. 2nd ed. 22 vols. London: Burns, Oates & Washbourne, 1912–36; reprinted in 5 vols., Westminster, MD: Christian Classics, 1981.

———. *Truth (De veritate)*. 3 vols. Translated by Robert W. Mulligan, James V. McGlynn, and Robert W. Schmidt. Library of Living Catholic Thought. Chicago: Regnery, 1952–54; reprint, Indianapolis: Hackett, 1994.

Arendt, Hannah. *Eichmann in Jerusalem: A Report on the Banality of Evil*. New York: Penguin Classics, 2006.

———. *The Human Condition*. Chicago: University of Chicago Press, 1998.

———. *The Life of the Mind*. Vol. 2, *Willing*. New York: Harcourt Brace Jovanovich, 1971.

Aristotle. *Basic Works*. Edited by Richard McKeon. New York: Random House, 1941.

———. *De anima*. Translated by Mark Shiffman. Newburyport, MA: Focus, 2009.

———. *Physics*. Translated by Joe Sachs. New Brunswick, NJ: Rutgers University Press, 2004.

———. *Works in Twenty-Three Volumes*. Loeb Classical Library. Cambridge, MA: Harvard University Press, 1926–57.

Arntzen, Sven. "Kant on Duty to Oneself and Resistance to Political Authority." *Journal of the History of Philosophy* 34 (1996): 409–24.

Ashcroft, Richard. "Faith and Knowledge in Locke's Philosophy." In *John Locke: Problems and Perspectives*, edited by John Yolton, 194–223. Cambridge: Cambridge University Press, 1969.

Augustine, *De doctrina christiana*. Translated by R. P. H. Green. Oxford: Clarendon, 1996.

Axinn, Sidney. "Kant, Authority, and the French Revolution." *Journal of the History of Ideas* 32 (1971): 423–32.

Bacon, Francis. *The Great Instauration*. In *Selected Philosophical Works*, edited by Rose-Mary Sargent. Indianapolis: Hackett, 1999.

Balibar, Étienne. *Identity and Difference: John Locke and the Invention of Consciousness*. New York: Verso, 2013.

Balthasar, Hans Urs von. *Theo-Logic*. Vol. 1, *The Truth of the World*. Translated by Adrian Walker. San Francisco: Ignatius, 2000.

Bastide, C. H. *John Locke: Ses théories politiques*. Paris: Leroux, 1907.

Beck, Gunnar. *Fichte and Kant on Freedom, Rights, and Law*. Lanham, MD: Lexington, 2008.

Beck, Lewis White. "Kant and the Right to Revolution." *Journal of the History of Ideas* 32 (1971): 411–22.

Benedict XVI. *Dogma and Preaching: Applying Christian Doctrine to Daily Life*. San Francisco: Ignatius, 2005.

———. *Faith, Reason, and the University: Memories and Reflections*. Address delivered September 12, 2006. Accessed April 14, 2017. http://w2.vatican

.va/content/benedict-xvi/en/speeches/2006/september/documents/hf
_ben-xvi_spe_20060912_university-regensburg.html.

Beneviste, Émile. *Le vocabulaire des institutions indo-européennes.* Vol. 1, *Économie, parenté, société.* Paris: Les Éditions de Minuit, 1969.

Benz, Ernst. *Evolution and Christian Hope: Man's Concept of the Future from the Early Fathers to Teilhard de Chardin.* Garden City, NY: Doubleday, 1966.

Berlin, Isaiah. "Two Concepts of Liberty." In *Four Essays on Liberty.* Oxford: Oxford University Press, 1969.

Bernard of Clairvaux. *On Grace and Free Choice.* Collegeville, MN: Cistercian Publications, 1977.

Berry, Wendell. "Feminism, the Body, and the Machine." In *The Art of the Commonplace*, 65–80. Berkeley, CA: Counterpoint, 2002.

Bobonich, Christopher. "Compulsion and Freedom in Plato's *Laws.*" *Classical Quarterly* 41, no. 2 (1991): 365–88.

Bolingbroke (Henry St. John). "Fragments or Minutes of Essays," Essay XLV. In Vol. 8 of *Works*, 192–96. London, 1809.

Borgmann, Albert. *Holding onto Reality: The Nature of Information at the Turn of the Millennium.* Chicago: University of Chicago Press, 1999.

———. *Technology and the Character of Contemporary Life.* Chicago: University of Chicago Press, 1984.

Bourne, H. R. Fox. *The Life of John Locke.* Vol. 2. London: Henry S. King and Company, 1876.

Boyle, Robert. *The Works of the Honourable Robert Boyle.* 6 vols. London, 1772.

Brague, Rémi. *Aristote et la question du monde: Essai sur le contexte cosmologique et anthropologique de l'ontologie.* Paris: Presses universitaires de France, 1988.

Burtt, Edwin Arthur. *The Metaphysical Foundations of Modern Science.* Mineola, NY: Dover, 2003.

Carey, Philip. *Augustine's Invention of the Inner Self: The Legacy of a Christian Platonist.* Oxford: Oxford University Press, 2003.

Carr, Nicholas. *The Shallows: What the Internet Is Doing to Our Brains.* New York: Norton, 2011.

Cavanaugh, William T. *The Myth of Religious Violence: Secular Ideology and the Roots of Modern Conflict.* Oxford: Oxford University Press, 2009.

Chamberlain, Charles. "The Meaning of *Prohairesis* in Aristotle's *Ethics.*" *Transactions of the American Philological Association* 114 (1984): 147–57.

Chappell, Vere. "Locke and the Suspension of Desire." In *John Locke: "An Essay Concerning Human Understanding" in Focus*, edited by Gary Fuller and Robert Stecker, 236–48. New York: Routledge, 2000.

————. "Locke on Freedom of the Will." In *Locke's Philosophy: Context and Content*, ed. G. A. J. Rogers, 101–21. Oxford: Clarendon, 1994.

————. "On the Intellectual Basis of Sin." *Journal of the History of Philosophy* 32, no. 15 (1994): 197–207.

————. "Power in Locke's *Essay*." In *The Cambridge Companion to Locke's "Essay,"* edited by Lex Newman, 130–56. Cambridge: Cambridge University Press, 2007.

Chesterton, G. K. *Heretics*. Rockville, MD: Serenity, 2009.

Chisholm, Roderick. "Freedom and Action." In *Freedom and Determinism*, edited by Keith Lehrer, 11–44. New York: Humanities Press, 1966.

Chu, Ted. *Human Purpose and Transhuman Potential: A Cosmic Vision for Our Future Evolution*. San Rafael, CA: Origin, 2014.

Clapp, James Gordon. *Locke's Concept of the Mind*. New York, 1937.

Constant, Benjamin. "The Liberty of the Ancients Compared with That of the Moderns." In *Political Writings*, 307–28. Cambridge: Cambridge University Press, 1988.

Cox, Richard. *Locke on War and Peace*. Oxford: Clarendon, 1960.

Cranston, Maurice. *Locke: A Biography*. New York: Macmillan, 1957.

Crawford, David S. *Beyond Heterosexuality: Public Reason, Common Good, and the Concept of Orientation*. Grand Rapids, MI: Eerdmans, forthcoming.

————. "Is Religious Liberty Possible in a Liberal Culture?" *Communio* 40, no. 2–3 (2013): 422–37.

Crawford, Matthew. *Shop Class as Soulcraft: An Inquiry into the Value of Work*. New York: Penguin, 2009.

Curley, Edwin. "Kissinger, Spinoza, and Genghis Khan." In *The Cambridge Companion to Spinoza*, edited by Don Garrett, 315–42. Cambridge: Cambridge University Press, 1996.

de Beer, E. S., ed. *The Correspondence of John Locke*. 9 vols. Oxford: Clarendon, 1978–2009.

Del Noce, Augusto. *The Crisis of Modernity*. Translated by Carlo Lancelotti. Montreal: McGill-Queen's University Press, 2015.

Dennet, Daniel. *Darwin's Dangerous Idea: Evolution and the Meaning of Life*. New York: Simon and Schuster, 1995.

de Rougement, Denis. *L'amour et l'Occident*. Paris: Librairie Plon, 1972.

Descartes, René. *Meditations on First Philosophy*. 4th ed. Indianapolis: Hackett, 1998.

Desmond, William. *Hegel's God: A Counterfeit Double?* Burlington, VT: Ashgate, 2003.

Destrée, Pierre. "Aristotle on the Causes of *Akrasia*." In *Akrasia in Greek Philosophy*, edited by Pierre Destrée and Christopher Bobonovich, 139–65. Leiden: Brill, 2007.

de Vogel, Cornelia J. *Rethinking Plato and Platonism*. Leiden: Brill, 1986.

Dewey, John. *Reconstruction in Philosophy*. New York: Henry Holt and Company, 1920.

Diels, Hermann, and Walther Kranz. *Die Fragmente der Vorsokratiker*. Zurich: Weidmann, 1985.

di Giovanni, George. "Faith without Religion, Religion without Faith: Kant and Hegel on Religion." *Journal of the History of Philosophy* 41, no. 3 (2003): 365–83.

Dihle, Albrecht. *The Theory of Will in Classical Antiquity*. Berkeley: University of California Press, 1982.

Downing, Lisa. "The Status of Mechanism in Locke's *Essay*." *Philosophical Review* 107, no. 3 (1998): 381–414.

Drury, S. B. "John Locke: Natural Law and Innate Ideas." *Dialogue* 14 (1980): 531–45.

Dunn, John. "Consent in the Political Theory of John Locke." In *Life, Liberty, and Property*, edited by Gordon Schochet, 129–61. Belmont, CA: Wadsworth, 1971.

———. "Justice and the Interpretation of Locke's Political Theory." *Political Studies* 16, no. 1 (1968): 68–87.

———. *The Political Thought of John Locke*. Cambridge: Cambridge University Press, 1969.

Ebbinghaus, Julius. "The Law of Humanity and the Limits of State Power." *Philosophical Quarterly* 3 (1953): 14–22.

Edwards, Jonathan. *Inquiry respecting that Freedom of Will which is supposed to be essential to Moral Agency*. London: Hamilton Adams, 1860.

Ferguson, Michaele. "Unsocial Sociability." In *Kant's Political Theory: Interpretations and Applications*, edited by Elisabeth Ellis, 158–69. University Park: Penn State University Press, 2012.

Feser, Edward. *Locke*. Oxford: Oneworld, 2007.

Fick, August. *Wörterbuch der Indogermanischen Grundsprache in ihrem Bestande vor der Völkertrennung*. Göttingen: Vandenbroeck and Ruprecht, 1868.

Flikschuh, Katrin. *Kant and Modern Political Philosophy*. Cambridge: Cambridge University Press, 2000.

———. "Reason, Right, and Revolution: Kant and Locke." *Philosophy and Public Affairs* 36 (2008): 375–404.

Floridi, Luciano. "The Informational Nature of Personal Identity." *Minds and Machines* 21, no. 4 (2011): 549–66.

Fortin, Ernest. "On the Presumed Medieval Origin of Individual Rights." In *Classical Christianity and the Political Order: Reflections on the Theologico-*

Political Problem, edited by Brian Benestad, 43–64. Lanham, MD: Rowman and Littlefield, 1991.

Frede, Michael. *A Free Will: Origins of the Notion in Ancient Thought.* Berkeley: University of California Press, 2011.

Fried, Carrie B. "In-class Laptop Use and Its Effect on Student Learning." *Computers and Education* 50 (2008): 906–14.

Gadamer, Hans-Georg. *The Relevance of the Beautiful.* Cambridge: Cambridge University Press, 1986.

Garrett, Don. "Spinoza's Ethical Theory." In *The Cambridge Companion to Spinoza*, edited by Don Garrett, 267–314. Cambridge: Cambridge University Press, 1996.

Gauthier, David. "Why Ought One Obey God? Reflections on Hobbes and Locke." *Canadian Journal of Philosophy* 7, no. 3 (1977): 425–46.

Gerson, Lloyd. *Aristotle and Other Platonists.* Ithaca, NY: Cornell University Press, 2005.

Gleick, James. *The Information: A History, a Theory, a Flood.* New York: Vintage, 2012.

Glenn, David. "Divided Attention." *Chronicle of Higher Education*, February 28, 2010.

Goethe, J. W. *Faust.* Munich: Deutscher Taschenbuch, 1979.

Goldwin, Robert A. "John Locke." In *History of Political Philosophy*, 3rd ed., edited by Leo Strauss and Joseph Cropsey, 476–512. Chicago: University of Chicago Press, 1987.

Gonzalez, Francisco. *Plato and Heidegger: A Question of Dialogue.* University Park: Penn State University Press, 2009.

———. "Plato's *Lysis*: A Re-enactment of Philosophical Kinship." *Ancient Philosophy* 15, no. 1 (1995): 69–90.

Granados, José. "Taste and See: The Body and the Experience of God." *Communio* 37, no. 2 (2010): 292–308.

Grant, George. *Technology and Justice.* Concord, Ontario: House of Anansi, 1991.

Guardini, Romano. *Letters from Lake Como: Explorations in Technology and the Human Race.* Grand Rapids, MI: Eerdmans, 1994.

Hanby, Michael. "Absolute Pluralism: How the Dictatorship of Relativism Dictates." *Communio* (Summer-Fall 2013): 542–76.

———. *No God, No Science: Theology, Cosmology, Biology.* Malden, MA: Wiley-Blackwell, 2013.

Hansen, Mogens Herman. "Democratic Freedom and the Concept of Freedom in Plato and Aristotle." *Greek, Roman, and Byzantine Studies* 50 (2010): 1–27.

———. *Was Athens a Democracy? Popular Rule, Liberty and Equality in Ancient and Modern Political Thought.* Copenhagen: Royal Danish Academy of Sciences and Letters, 1989.

Harris, James. *Of Liberty and Necessity: The Free Will Debate in Eighteenth Century British Philosophy.* Oxford: Oxford University Press, 2008.

Hart, David Bentley. "The Offering of Names: Metaphysics, Nihilism, and Analogy." In *Reason and the Reasons of Faith*, edited by Paul Griffiths and Reinhard Hütter, 255–94. New York: T&T Clark, 2005.

Healy, Nicholas, and David L. Schindler, eds. *Freedom, Truth, and Human Dignity: The Second Vatican Council's "Declaration on Religious Freedom."* Grand Rapids, MI: Eerdmans, 2015.

Hecht, Jonathan. "Freedom of the Will in Plato and Augustine." *British Journal for the History of Philosophy* 22, no. 2 (2014): 196–216.

Hegel, G. W. F. *Elements of the Philosophy of Right.* Edited by Allen Wood. Cambridge: Cambridge University Press, 1991.

———. *The Encyclopedia Logic.* Indianapolis: Hackett, 1991.

———. *Lectures on the History of Philosophy, Lectures of 1825–26, Greek Philosophy.* Oxford: Oxford University Press, 2006.

———. *The Philosophy of History.* Mineola, NY: Dover, 1956.

———. *The Positivity of the Christian Religion.* In *Early Theological Writings*, edited by T. M. Knox. Philadelphia: University of Pennsylvania Press, 1971.

———. *Science of Logic.* Atlantic Highlands, NJ: Humanities Press International, 1969.

Heidegger, Martin. *Being and Time.* Translated by Joan Stambaugh and Dennis J. Schmidt. Albany: SUNY Press, 2010.

———. *The End of Philosophy.* New York: Harper and Row, 1973.

———. *The Essence of Human Freedom: An Introduction to Philosophy.* New York: Continuum, 2002.

———. *Nietzsche.* Vol. 4, *Nihilism.* San Francisco: Harper, 1987.

———. "On the Essence of Truth." In *Basic Writings*, edited by David Farrell Krell, 111–38. New York: Harper, 2008.

———. "On the Question of Being." In *Pathmarks*, edited by William McNeil, 291–322. Cambridge: Cambridge University Press, 1998.

———. "The Origin of the Work of Art." In *Basic Writings*, edited by David Farrell Krell, 143–87. New York: Harper and Row, 1977.

———. "Plato's Doctrine of Truth." In *Pathmarks*, 155–82.

———. "The Question Concerning Technology." In *Basic Writings* (2008), 311–41.

———. "*Der Spiegel* Interview with Martin Heidegger." In *The Heidegger Reader*, edited by Günther Figal, 313–33. Bloomington: Indiana University Press, 2009.

————. *What Is Called Thinking?* New York: Harper and Row, 1968.

Hesiod. *Theogony and Works and Days*. Translated by M. L. West. Oxford: Oxford University Press, 2009.

Hill, Thomas E. "Questions about Kant's Opposition to Revolution." *Journal of Value Inquiry* 36 (2002): 283–98.

Hobbes, Thomas. *Leviathan*. Edited by C. B. MacPherson. New York: Penguin, 1982.

Hobbes, Thomas, and John Bramhall. *Hobbes and Bramhall on Liberty and Necessity*. Edited by Vere Chappell. Cambridge: Cambridge University Press, 1999.

Holtman, Sarah Williams. "Revolution, Contradiction, and Kantian Citizenship." In *Kant's Metaphysics of Morals*, edited by M. Timmons, 209–33. Oxford: Oxford University Press, 2002.

Horkheimer, Max. *The Eclipse of Reason*. New York: Oxford University Press, 2013.

Horkheimer, Max, and Theodor Adorno. *Dialectic of Enlightenment*. New York: Continuum, 1969.

Hume, David. *Treatise of Human Nature*. Edited by David Norton and Mary Norton. Oxford: Oxford University Press, 2009.

Hyde, Lewis. *The Gift: Imagination and the Erotic Life of Property*. New York: Vintage, 1983.

Jaeger, Werner. *Paideia: The Ideals of Greek Culture*. 3 vols. Oxford: Oxford University Press, 1945.

John Paul II. *Laborem exercens* (1981). Accessed April 14, 2017. http://w2 .vatican.va/content/john-paul-ii/en/encyclicals/documents/hf_jp-ii_enc _14091981_laborem-exercens.html.

————. *Man and Woman He Created Them: A Theology of the Body*. Boston: Pauline Books, 2006.

Jolly, Nicholas. "Locke on Faith and Reason." In *The Cambridge Companion to Locke's "Essay,"* edited by Lex Newman, 436–55. Cambridge: Cambridge University Press, 2007.

Jonas, Hans. *Augustin und das paulinische Freiheitsproblem: Ein philosophischer Beitrag zur Genesis der christlich-abendländischen Freiheitsidee*. Göttingen: Vandenhoeck and Puprecht, 1930.

————. "The Practical Uses of Theory." In *The Phenomenon of Life*, 188–210. Evanston, IL: Northwestern University Press, 2001.

Kahn, Charles H. "Discovering Will from Aristotle to Augustine." In *The Question of Eclecticism*, edited by John M. Dillon and A. A. Long, 234–59. Berkeley: University of California Press, 1988.

Kant, Immanuel. *Anthropology, History, and Education*. Cambridge: Cambridge University Press, 2011.

————. *The Conflict of the Faculties*. In *Religion and Rational Theology*, edited by Allen Wood and George di Giovanni. Cambridge: Cambridge University Press, 1996.

————. *Critique of Judgment*. Translated by Werner Pluhar. Indianapolis: Hackett, 1987.

————. *Critique of Practical Reason*. In *Practical Philosophy*, translated by Mary J. Gregor. Cambridge: Cambridge University Press, 1996.

————. *Critique of Pure Reason*. 2nd rev. ed. Translated by Norman Kemp Smith. New York: Palgrave Macmillan, 2003.

_____. *Gesammelte Schriften*. Edited by the Royal Prussian (later German) Academy of Science. Berlin: George Reimer (later Walter de Gruyter), 1900–.

————. *Groundwork of the Metaphysics of Morals*. In *Practical Philosophy*.

————. *Perpetual Peace and Other Essays*. Edited by Ted Humphry. Indianapolis: Hackett, 1983.

————. *Religion within the Boundaries of Mere Reason*. In *Religion and Rational Theology*, edited by Allen Wood and George di Giovanni. Cambridge: Cambridge University Press, 1996.

————. *What Is Enlightenment?* In *Practical Philosophy*.

Kelly, Patrick. "All Things Richly to Enjoy: Economics and Politics in Locke's *Two Treatises of Government*." *Political Studies* 36 (1988): 273–93.

Kendall, Willmoore. *John Locke and the Doctrine of Majority-Rule*. Urbana: University of Illinois Press, 1941.

————. "The Right of the Majority." In *Life, Liberty, and Property*, edited by Gordon Schochet, 168–77. Belmont, CA: Wadsworth, 1971.

Kersting, Wolfgang. "Kant's Concept of the State." In *Essays on Kant's Political Philosophy*, edited by Howard Lloyd Williams, 143–65. Chicago: University of Chicago Press, 1992.

Keyt, David. "Three Basic Theorems in Aristotle's *Politics*." In *A Companion to Aristotle's Politics*, edited by David Keyt and Fred D. Miller, Jr., 118–41. Cambridge, MA: Blackwell, 1991.

Kierkegaard, Søren. *Fear and Trembling/Repetition*. Princeton, NJ: Princeton University Press, 1983.

————. *Papers and Journals: A Selection*. Translated by Alastair Hannay. New York: Penguin, 1996.

————. *The Present Age*. New York: Harper Torchbooks, 1962.

————. *Sickness Unto Death*. Princeton, NJ: Princeton University Press, 1980.

Kilcullen, John. "Locke on Political Obligation." *Review of Metaphysics* 45 (1985): 323–44.

Kimbriel, Samuel. *Friendship as Sacred Knowing: Overcoming Isolation*. Oxford: Oxford University Press, 2014.

Kisner, Matthew. *Spinoza on Human Freedom: Reason, Autonomy, and the Good Life*. Cambridge: Cambridge University Press, 2011.

Kohler, Georg. "Selbstbezug, Selbsttranszendez und die Nichtigkeit der Freiheit: Zur augustinischen Theorie des Bösen in *De civitate dei* XII." *Studia Philosophica* 52 (1993): 67–79.

Korsgaard, Christine. "Taking the Law into Our Own Hands: Kant on the Right to Revolution." In *Reclaiming the History of Philosophy: Essays for John Rawls*, edited by C. Korsgaard, A. Reath, and B. Herman, 297–329. Cambridge: Cambridge University Press, 1997.

Kosman, Aryeh. *The Activity of Being: An Essay on Aristotle's Ontology*. Cambridge, MA: Harvard University Press, 2013.

Krupp, Anthony. *Reason's Children: Childhood in Early Modern Philosophy*. Lewisburg, PA: Bucknell University Press, 2009.

Laslett, Peter. Introduction to *Two Treatises of Government*, by John Locke. Cambridge: Cambridge University Press, 1988.

Lear, Jonathan. *Aristotle: The Desire to Understand*. Cambridge: Cambridge University Press, 1988.

Levinas, Emmanuel. "Philosophy and the Idea of the Infinite." In Adriaan Peperzak, *To the Other: An Introduction to the Philosophy of Emmanuel Levinas*, 88–119. West Lafayette, IN: Purdue University Press, 2005.

Lewis, C. S. *The Screwtape Letters*. New York: Macmillan, 1982.

———. *Till We Have Faces: A Myth Retold*. New York: Harcourt, 1956.

Locke, John. "Considerations of the Consequences of Lowering the Interest and Raising the Value of Money." In *The Works of John Locke in 9 Volumes*. Vol. 4. London: Longman, et al., 1794.

———. *An Essay Concerning Human Understanding*. 2 vols. Edited by Alexander Campbell Fraser. New York: Dover, 1959.

———. *Fundamental Constitution of Carolina*. avalon.law.yale.edu/17th_century/nc05.asp.

———. *A Letter Concerning Toleration*. Edited by James Tully. Indianapolis: Hackett, 1983.

———. *Locke on Money*. 2 vols. Edited by Patrick Kelly. Oxford: Clarendon Press, 1991.

———. *Reasonableness of Christianity*. Edited by I. T. Ramsey. Stanford, CA: Stanford University Press, 1958.

———. *Some Thoughts Concerning Education and Of the Conduct of the Understanding*. Edited by Ruth Grant and Nathan Tarcov. Indianapolis: Hackett, 1984.

————. *Two Treatises of Government*. Edited by Peter Laslett. Cambridge: Cambridge University Press, 1960.

López, Fr. Antonio. *Gift and the Unity of Being*. Eugene, OR: Cascade, 2014.

Lowe, E. J. *Locke on Human Understanding*. New York: Routledge, 1995.

Löwenclau, Ilse von. *Der platonische Menexenos*. Stuttgart: Tübinger Beiträge zur Altertumswissenschaft, 1961.

Lucretius. *De rerum natura*. Translated by Anthony Esolen. Baltimore: Johns Hopkins University Press, 1995.

MacIntyre, Alasdair. *After Virtue*. 2nd ed. Notre Dame, IN: University of Notre Dame Press, 1984.

————. *Whose Justice, Which Rationality?* Notre Dame, IN: University of Notre Dame Press, 1988.

Macpherson, C. B. "Editor's Introduction." In John Locke, *Second Treatise of Government*. Indianapolis: Hackett, 1980.

————. *The Political Theory of Possessive Individualism: Hobbes to Locke*. Oxford: Oxford University Press, 2011.

————. "The Social Bearing of Locke's Political Theory." In *Life, Liberty, and Property*, edited by Gordon Schochet. Belmont, CA: Wadsworth, 1971.

Magri, Tito. "Locke, Suspension of Desire, and the Remote Good." *British Journal for the History of Philosophy* 8, no. 1 (2000): 55–70.

Maliks, Reidar. "Kant, the State, and Revolution." *Kantian Review* 18, no. 1 (2013): 29–47.

Manent, Pierre. *The City of Man*. Princeton, NJ: Princeton University Press, 2000.

————. *Cours familier de philosophie politique*. Paris: Gallimard, 2001.

————. *An Intellectual History of Liberalism*. Princeton, NJ: Princeton University Press, 1996.

Mangen, Anne, Bente R. Walgermo, and Kolgørn Brønnick. "Reading Linear Texts on Paper versus Computer Screen: Effects on Reading Comprehension." *International Journal of Educational Research* 58 (2013): 61–68.

Marcel, Gabriel. "Sketch of a Phenomenology and a Metaphysics of Hope." In *Homo Viator*, 29–67. New York: Harper Torchbooks, 1962.

Maurer, Armand. *The Philosophy of William of Ockham in the Light of Its Principles*. Toronto: Pontifical Institute of Medieval Studies, 1999.

McClure, Kirstie M. *Judging Rights: Lockean Politics and the Limits of Consent*. Ithaca, NY: Cornell University Press, 1996.

Meek, Esther Lightcap. *Longing to Know: The Philosophy of Knowledge for Ordinary People*. Grand Rapids, MI: Brazos, 2003.

Milbank, John. "The Gift of Ruling." *New Blackfriars* 85 (March 2004): 212–38.

Miller, David. "Justice and Property." *Ratio* (June 1980): 1–14.

Milton, J.R. "Locke's Life and Times." In *The Cambridge Companion to Locke*, edited by Vere Chappell, 5–25. Cambridge: Cambridge University Press, 1994.

Monson, Charles H., Jr. "Locke and His Interpreters." In *Life, Liberty, and Property*, edited by Gordon Schochet, 33–48. Belmont, CA: Wadsworth, 1971.

Montaigne, Michel de. "Of Friendship." In *The Complete Works of Montaigne*, translated and edited by William Hazlitt, 104–10. Philadelphia: William T. Amies, 1879.

Mulhern, J.J. Review of *A Free Will*, by Michael Frede. *Bryn Mawr Classical Review*, October 24, 2011.

Muller, H.J. *Freedom in the Ancient World*. New York: Harper and Row, 1961.

Muller, Robert. *La doctrine platonicienne de la liberté*. Paris: Vrin, 1997.

———. "La logique de la liberté dans la *Politique*." In *Aristote Politique: Études sur la Politique d'Aristote*, edited by Pierre Aubenque, 185–208. Paris: Presses universitaires de France, 1993.

Murdoch, Iris. *The Sovereignty of Good*. London: Routledge and Kegan Paul, 1970.

Murphy, Jeffrie. "A Paradox in Locke's Theory of Natural Rights." *Dialogue: Canadian Philosophical Review* 8 (1969): 256–71.

Murray, John Courtney. "The Problem of Religious Freedom." *Woodstock Papers*, 7. Westminster, MD: Newman Press, 1965.

Nadler, Steven. *A Book Forged in Hell*. Princeton, NJ: Princeton University Press, 2011.

Nestle, Dieter. *Eleutheria: Studien zum Wesen der Freiheit bei der Griechen und im Neuen Testament*. Tübingen: J.C.B. Mohr, 1967.

Newman, Lex. "Locke on Knowledge." In *The Cambridge Companion to Locke's "Essay,"* edited by Lex Newman, 313–51. Cambridge: Cambridge University Press, 2007.

Nicholson, Peter P. "Kant, Revolution, and History." In *Essays in Kant's Political Philosophy*, edited by Howard Lloyd Williams, 249–68. Chicago: University of Chicago Press, 1992.

Nietzsche, Friedrich. *Also sprach Zarathustra*. Vol. 4 of *Kritischen Ausgabe*, edited by Giorgio Colli and Mazzino Montinari. Munich: De Gruyter, 1999.

———. *Beyond Good and Evil*. Cambridge: Cambridge University Press, 2002.

———. *The Gay Science*. Translated by Walter Kaufmann. New York: Vintage, 1974.

———. *Philosophy in the Tragic Age of the Greeks*. Washington, DC: Gateway, 1987.

———. *Twilight of the Idols*. In *The Portable Nietzsche*, translated by Walter Kaufmann. New York: Penguin, 1976.

———. *The Will to Power*. Translated by Walter Kaufmann. New York: Vintage, 1968.

Nisbet, Robert. *The Quest for Community: A Study in the Ethics of Order and Freedom*. Wilmington, DE: ISI Books, 2010.

Oliver, Simon. *Philosophy, God, and Motion*. New York: Routledge, 2013.

O'Neill, Onora. "Kant and the Social Contract Tradition." In *Kant's Political Theory*, edited by Elisabeth Ellis, 25–41. University Park: Penn State University Press, 2012.

Onians, R. B. *The Origins of European Thought about the Body, the Mind, the Soul, the World, Time, and Fate*. Cambridge: Cambridge University Press, 1951.

Pabst, Adrian. *Metaphysics: The Creation of Hierarchy*. Grand Rapids, MI: Eerdmans, 2012.

Partenie, Catalin, ed. *Plato's Myths*. Cambridge: Cambridge University Press, 2011.

Passmore, John. "The Malleability of Man in Eighteenth-Century Thought." In *Aspects of the Eighteenth Century*, edited by E. R. Wasserman, 21–46. Baltimore, MD: Johns Hopkins University Press, 1965.

———. *The Perfectibility of Man*. 3rd ed. New York: Scribner's, 2000.

Perl, Eric. "The Presence of the Paradigm: Immanence and Transcendence in Plato's Theory of Forms." *Review of Metaphysics* 53, no. 2 (1999): 339–62.

Peterson, John. *Aquinas: A New Interpretation*. Washington, DC: Catholic University of America Press, 2008.

Pfau, Thomas. *Minding the Modern: Human Agency, Intellectual Traditions, and Responsible Knowledge*. Notre Dame, IN: University of Notre Dame Press, 2013.

Pieper, Josef. *Leisure: The Basis of Culture*. Translated by Gerard Malsbery. South Bend, IN: Saint Augustine's Press, 1998.

Pinckaers, Servais. *Sources of Christian Ethics*. Washington, DC: Catholic University of America Press, 1995.

Plato. *The Complete Works*. Edited by John M. Cooper. Indianapolis: Hackett, 1997.

———. *Works in Twelve Volumes*. Loeb Classical Library. Cambridge, MA: Harvard University Press, 1914–1927.

Polanyi, Karl. *The Great Transformation*. Boston: Beacon, 1957.

Polanyi, Michael. *Personal Knowledge: Towards a Post-Critical Philosophy*. New York: Harper Torchbooks, 1964.

————. *The Tacit Dimension*. Chicago: University of Chicago Press, 2009.

Polin, Raymond. "John Locke's Conception of Freedom." In *John Locke: Problems and Perspectives*, edited by John Yolton, 1–18. Cambridge: Cambridge University Press, 1969.

Pope Pius XI. *Quadragesimo anno*. 1931.

Popper, Karl. *The Open Society and Its Enemies*. Vol. 1, *The Spell of Plato*. Princeton, NJ: Princeton University Press, 2013.

Postman, Neil. *The Disappearance of Childhood*. New York: Vintage, 1994.

Prentice, David A. "The Present and Future of Stem Cell Research: Scientific, Ethical, and Public Policy Perspective." In *Stem Cell Research: New Frontiers in Science and Ethics*, edited by Nancy E. Snow, 15–22. Notre Dame, IN: University of Notre Dame Press, 2004.

Proclus. *On the Theology of Plato*. London: A. J. Valpy, 1816.

Prufer, Thomas. *Recapitulations: Essays in Philosophy*. Washington, DC: Catholic University of America Press, 1993.

Rahner, Hugo. *Man at Play*. New York: Herder and Herder, 1972.

Rahner, Karl. "The Theology of the Symbol." In *Theological Investigations*, 4:221–52. Baltimore: Helicon, 1966.

Rawls, John. *Political Liberalism*. New York: Columbia University Press, 1996

Rhonheimer, Martin. *The Common Good of Constitutional Democracy*. Washington, DC: Catholic University of America Press, 2013.

Ricoeur, Paul. *The Symbolism of Evil*. New York: Harper and Row, 1967.

Ripstein, Arthur. *Force and Freedom: Kant's Legal and Political Philosophy*. Cambridge, MA: Harvard University Press, 2009.

Rogers, G. A. J. "Boyle, Locke, and Reason." *Journal of the History of Ideas* 27, no. 2 (1966): 205–16.

————. "The Intellectual Setting and Aims of the *Essay*." In *The Cambridge Companion to Locke's "Essay*," edited by Lex Newman, 7–32. Cambridge: Cambridge University Press, 2007.

Rousseau, Jean-Jacques. *Social Contract*. Translated by G. D. H. Cole. New York: E. P. Dutton & Co., 1913.

Ruskin, John. *Unto this Last*. New York: Penguin, 1986.

Ryan, Alan. "Locke and the Dictatorship of the Bourgeoisie." In *Life, Liberty, and Property*, edited by Gordon Schochet, 86–106. Belmont, CA: Wadsworth, 1971.

Sachs, Joe. "Aristotle: Motion and Its Place in Nature." *Internet Encyclopedia of Philosophy*. Accessed December 31, 2016. http://www.iep.utm.edu/aris-mot/.

Scheler, Max. *Formalism in Ethics and Non-Formal Ethics of Values*. Evanston, IL: Northwestern University Press, 1973.

Schelling, Friedrich Wilhelm Joseph von. *Historical-Critical Introduction to the Philosophy of Mythology.* Translated by Mason Richey and Markus Zisselsberger. Albany: SUNY Press, 2007.

———. *History of Modern Philosophy.* Cambridge: Cambridge University Press, 1994.

———. *System der Weltalter: Münchner Vorlesungen 1827/28 in einer Nachschrift von Ernst von Lasaulx.* Edited by Siegbert Peetz. Frankfurt am Main: Klostermann, 1991.

Schindler, D. C. *The Catholicity of Reason.* Grand Rapids, MI: Eerdmans, 2013.

———. "Enriching the Good: Toward the Development of a Relational Anthropology." *Communio* 37, no. 4 (2010): 643–59.

———. "'The Free Will Which Wills the Free Will': On Marriage as a Paradigm of Freedom in Hegel's *Philosophy of Right.*" *The Owl of Minerva* 44, no. 1-2 (2013): 577–615.

———. "Liberalism, Religious Freedom, and the Common Good: The Totalitarian Logic of Self-Limitation." *Communio* (2013): 577–615.

———. "On Reason's Authority." *Communio* 41, no. 1 (2014): 40–60.

———. *The Perfection of Freedom: Schiller, Schelling, and Hegel between the Ancients and the Moderns.* Eugene, OR: Cascade, 2012.

———. *Plato's Critique of Impure Reason: On Goodness and Truth in the "Republic."* Washington, DC: Catholic University of America Press, 2008.

———. "Why Socrates Didn't Charge: Plato and the Metaphysics of Money." *Communio* 36 (Fall 2009): 394–426.

Schindler, David L. "Beauty, Transcendence, and the Face of the Other: Religion and Culture in America." *Communio* 26 (1999): 916–21.

———. "An Interpretation of *Dignitatis Humanae.*" In *Freedom, Truth, and Human Dignity*, edited by David L. Schindler and Nicholas J. Healy, 39–209. Grand Rapids, MI: Eerdmans, 2015.

———. "Liberalism and the Meaning of God: The Religious Sense in America." *Communio* 34 (2007): 482–87.

———. "Norris Clarke on Person, Being, and St. Thomas." *Communio* 20, no. 3 (1993): 580–93.

———. "'The Religious Sense' and American Culture." *Communio* 25 (1998): 679–99.

Schindler, David L., and Nicholas J. Healy, eds. *Freedom, Truth, and Human Dignity: The Second Vatican Council's Declaration on Religious Freedom.* Grand Rapids, MI: Eerdmans, 2015.

Schlosser, Edward. "I'm a Liberal Professor, and My Liberal Students Terrify Me." Accessed November 1, 2015. http://www.vox.com/2015/6/3/8706323 /college-professor-afraid.

Schmitz, Kenneth. *The Gift: Creation*. Milwaukee, WI: Marquette University Press, 1982.

Schochet, Gordon J. "The Family and the Origins of the State in Locke's Political Philosophy." In *Problems and Perspectives*, edited by John Yolton, 81–98. Cambridge: Cambridge University Press, 1969.

———. Introduction to *Life, Liberty, and Property*, edited by Gordon Schochet. Belmont, CA: Wadsworth, 1971.

———, ed. *Life, Liberty, and Property*. Belmont, CA: Wadsworth, 1971.

Schouls, Peter. *Reasoned Freedom: John Locke and Enlightenment*. Ithaca, NY: Cornell University Press, 1992.

Schwartz, Barry. *The Paradox of Choice: Why More Is Less*. New York: HarperCollins, 2005.

Shiffman, Mark. "The Eclipse of the Good in the Modern Rights Tradition." *Communio* 40, no. 4 (2013): 775–98.

———. "An Ethic of Attentiveness: The Rediscovery of Oikonomia." *Communio* 36 (Fall 2009): 487–509.

———. Introduction to *Aristotle: De anima*. Newburyport, MA: Focus, 2011.

Simmons, A. John. *The Lockean Theory of Rights*. Princeton, NJ: Princeton University Press, 1992.

Smyth, Herbert Weir. *A Greek Grammar for Colleges*. New York: American Book Company, 1916.

Snyder, David C. "Locke on Natural Law and Property Rights." *Canadian Journal of Philosophy* 16, no. 4 (1986): 723–50.

Spaemann, Robert. "The Courage to Educate." *Communio* (Spring 2013): 48–63.

———. "Education as an Introduction to Reality: A Speech Commemorating the Anniversary of a Children's Home." In *A Robert Spaemann Reader: Philosophical Essays on Nature, God, and the Human Person*, edited by D. C. Schindler and Jeanne Schindler, 111–20. Oxford: Oxford University Press, 2015.

———. "The End of Modernity?" In *Spaemann Reader*, 211–29.

———. *Happiness and Benevolence*. Edinburgh: T&T Clark, 2000.

———. "In Defense of Anthropomorphism." In *Spaemann Reader*, 77–96.

———. "A Philosophical Autobiography." In *Spaemann Reader*, 11–21.

———. "Nature." In *Spaemann Reader*, 22–36.

———. "The Traditionalist Error." In *Spaemann Reader*, 37–44.

———. "Das unsterbliche Gerücht." In *Das unsterbliche Gerücht*. Stuttgart: Klett-Cotta, 2007.

———. "What Does It Mean to Say, 'Art Imitates Nature'?" In *Spaemann Reader*, 192–210.

Spinoza, Benedict. *Complete Works*. Translated by Samuel Shirley. Indianapolis: Hackett, 2002.

Sreenivasan, Gopal. *The Limits of Lockean Rights in Property*. Oxford: Oxford University Press, 1995.

Stalley, R. F. "Plato's Doctrine of Freedom." *Proceedings of the Aristotelian Society* 98 (1998): 145–58.

Stein, Edith. *Finite and Eternal Being*. Washington, DC: ICS Publications, 2002.

Stenzel, Julius. "Das Problem der Willensfreiheit im Platonismus." In *Kleine Schriften zur griechischen Philosophie*. Darmstadt: Hermann Gentner, 1957.

Straaten, M. van. "What Did the Greeks Mean by Liberty." Part 2, "Plato and Aristotle." *Theta-Pi* 3 (1974): 123–44.

Strauss, Leo. *Natural Right and History*. Chicago: University of Chicago Press, 1965.

Stuart, Matthew. *Locke's Metaphysics*. Oxford: Oxford University Press, 2013.

Swenson, David. *Something about Kierkegaard*. Macon, GA: Mercer University Press, 1983.

Taylor, Mary. "A Deeper Ecology: A Catholic Vision of the Person in Nature." *Communio* 38 (Winter 2011): 583–620.

Telesio, Bernardino. *De rerum natura iuxta propria principia*. Edited by M. Torrini. Naples: Istituto Suor Orsola Benincasa, 1989.

Tierney, Brian. "The Idea of Natural Rights—Origins and Persistence." *Northwestern Journal of International Human Rights* 2, no. 1 (2004): 2–12.

———. *The Idea of Natural Rights: Studies on Natural Rights, Natural Law, and Church Law 1150–1625*. Grand Rapids, MI: Eerdmans, 1997.

Tocqueville, Alexis de. *Democracy in America*. Translated by George Lawrence. Garden City, NY: Doubleday, 1969.

Tufte, Edward. *The Cognitive Style of PowerPoint*. 2nd ed. Cheshire, CT: Graphic Press, 2006.

Tully, James. *A Discourse on Property: John Locke and His Adversaries*. Cambridge: Cambridge University Press, 1983.

Turkle, Sherry. *Alone Together: Why We Expect More from Technology and Less from Ourselves*. New York: Basic Books, 2012.

Ulrich, Ferdinand. *Gegenwart der Freiheit*. Einsiedeln: Johannes Verlag, 1974.

———. *Homo Abyssus*. 2nd ed. Freiburg im Breisgau: Johannes Verlag Einsiedeln, 1998.

———. *Der Mensch als Logo-Tokos*. In *Logo-Tokos*, 1–163. Freiburg im Breisgau: Johannes Verlag Einsiedeln, 2003.

Van Leyden, W. "John Locke and Natural Law." In *Life, Liberty, and Property*, edited by Gordon Schochet, 22–35. Belmont, CA: Wadsworth, 1971.

Vattimo, Giovanni. *Nihilism and Emancipation: Ethics, Politics, and Law*. New York: Columbia, 2004.

Vetö, Miklos. *La naissance de la volonté*. Paris: Harmattan, 2002.

Vienne, Jean Michel. "Malebranche and Locke: The Theory of Moral Choice, a Neglected Theme." In *Nicolas Malebranche: His Philosophical Critics and Successors*, edited by Stuart Brown, 94–108. Assen: Van Gorcum, 1991.

Villey, Michel. *La formation de la pensée juridique moderne*. 4th ed. Paris: Montchrétien, 1975.

Walmsley, Peter. *Locke's Essay and the Rhetoric of Science*. Lewisburg, PA: Bucknell University Press, 2003.

Walsh, Moira M. "Aristotle's Conception of Freedom." *Journal of the History of Philosophy* 35, no. 4 (1997): 495–507.

Ward, Lee. *John Locke and Modern Life*. New York: Cambridge University Press, 2010.

Weber, Max. *The Protestant Ethic and the Spirit of Capitalism*. New York: Charles Scribner's Sons, 1976.

Weil, Simone. *Selected Essays: 1934–1943*. Translated by Richard Rees. Oxford: Oxford University Press, 1962.

Weithman, Paul J. "Augustine and Aquinas on Original Sin and the Function of Political Authority." *Journal of the History of Philosophy* 30, no. 3 (1992): 353–76.

Wilder, Thornton. *The Skin of Our Teeth: A Play in Three Acts*. New York: Samuel French, 1972.

Wojtyła, Karol. "The Personal Structure of Self-Determination." In *Person and Community: Selected Essays*, 187–95. New York: Peter Lang, 1993.

———. "The Problem of the Constitutions of Culture through Human Praxis." In *Person and Community*, 263–75.

Wolf, Susan. *Freedom within Reason*. Oxford: Oxford University Press, 1993.

Wood, Allen. "Kant's Compatibilism." In *Self and Nature in Kant's Philosophy*, edited by Allen Wood, 73–101. Ithaca, NY: Cornell University Press, 1984.

Woolhouse, Roger. *Locke: A Biography*. Cambridge: Cambridge University Press, 2007.

Yaffe, Gideon. *Liberty Worth the Name: Locke on Free Agency*. Princeton, NJ: Princeton University Press, 2000.

———. "Locke on Refraining, Suspending, and the Freedom to Will." *History of Philosophy Quarterly* 18, no. 4 (2001): 373–91.

Yolton, John W., ed. *Problems and Perspectives: A Collection of New Essays*. Cambridge: Cambridge University Press, 1969.

Zeitler, Wolfgang Maria. *Entscheidungsfreiheit bei Platon*. Munich: C. H. Beck'sche Verlag, 1983.

Zinaich, Samuel, Jr. *John Locke's Moral Revolution: From Natural Law to Moral Relativism*. Lanham, MD: University Press of America, 2005.

Zuckert, Michael. *Launching Liberalism: On Lockean Political Philosophy*. Lawrence: University Press of Kansas, 2002.

INDEX

D. C. SCHINDLER

is associate professor of metaphysics and anthropology at the John Paul II Institute, Washington, DC. He is the author of a number of books, including *The Catholicity of Reason*.